ROBERT G. CALDWELL, Ph.D., University of Pennsylvania, LL.B., Jackson School of Law, Millsaps College, is Professor of Criminology at the University of Iowa, where he has taught since 1948. Dr. Caldwell previously taught at the universities of Delaware and Pennsylvania and the College of William and Mary. A member of the Virginia State Bar, his professional affiliations include the National Council on Crime and Delinquency, American Correctional Association, American Sociological Association, The American Society of Criminology, and the International Society of Criminology. Dr. Caldwell also served for many years as a consultant in criminology for the Iowa Board of Control.

CRIMINOLOGY

ROBERT G. CALDWELL

University of Iowa

SECOND EDITION

THE RONALD PRESS COMPANY · NEW YORK

Library of Congress Catalog Card Number: 65–12744

PRINTED IN THE UNITED STATES OF AMERICA

To

LA MERLE

Preface

Few young people in our colleges and universities are well informed about the real nature and causes of crime; they are even less well informed about the economic costs of these problems and the vast social wreckage and exploitation associated with their growth. And yet, the United States is charged with being the most lawless nation in the world: more than two million major crimes are committed annually in this country, and it has been estimated that crime is costing us billions of dollars every year. In these circumstances, it is not too much to urge that every college student should be alerted to the threat of crime and delinquency, provided with the facts to understand their nature, and stimulated to assist in the fight against them.

Because of the complexity of the problems involved, this book presents a many-sided approach to the causation of crime and delinquency and to their repression and prevention. Thus, it emphasizes the individual as well as the group, the biological factors as well as the environmental influences, the crime as well as the criminal, the limitations of the scientific method as well as its contributions, the responsibility of the private citizen as well as that of the professional and the expert. It utilizes the resources of many fields of knowledge, including sociology; and it calls attention to the importance of the law and its administration and to the desirability of a closer relationship between scholars in the field of law and those in the social sciences. For perspective, both the historical and contemporary aspects of crime, law enforcement, punishment, and correctional administration are discussed. In addition, there is a special chapter on prison life and its problems as seen by an inmate. This book will also prove useful to the social scientist, the judge, the law-enforcement officer, the correctional administrator, and the citizen.

In the revision of this text, the basic point of view has been strengthened and more explicitly stated, and its major elements summarized. The material has been reworked in order to introduce and evaluate the newest theories of scholars in the field, the latest findings of their research, and the most recent statistics on crime and delinquency. The text also provides an analysis of the additional developments that have occurred in criminal law and its administration, and in the organization and operation of correctional agencies and institutions. Material on prison labor has been incorporated in the chapter on prison programs.

During the preparation of the first edition and its present revision, I have drawn upon the knowledge and advice of a number of persons and organizations. In general, I have expressed my indebtedness to them in the footnotes, but here I wish to give specific acknowledgment to Mr. Tom Runyon, who, while he was an inmate of the Iowa State Penitentiary, wrote Chapter 26, "Prison Shocks," and provided me with many important insights into prison life, and to Dr. Jeremiah P. Shalloo, Professor of Sociology, University of Pennsylvania, whose penetrating insight and deep understanding of the field of criminology contributed in an important way to the clarity and accuracy of the material. I am especially indebted to my wife for her patience and encouragement and to Mrs. Frank H. McCabe for her inimitable skill in the typing of the manuscript.

ROBERT G. CALDWELL

Iowa City, Iowa
   January, 1965

Contents

Part I

THE PROBLEM

1

Criminology and Its Methods

THE MEANING OF CRIMINOLOGY

You are about to begin the study of a fascinating subject—one that will conduct you along many avenues of knowledge and introduce you to a great variety of problems. That this is true you will soon discover as you read the following pages. For the present, however, we need only point out that in any attempt to analyze the problem of crime in the United States and its impact upon our society, we must turn to an examination of the contributions of criminology. In its broadest sense, criminology is the entire body of knowledge regarding crime, criminals, and the efforts of society to repress and prevent them. Thus, it is composed of knowledge drawn from such fields as law, medicine, religion, science, education, social work, social ethics, and public administration; and it includes within its scope the activities of legislative bodies, law-enforcement agencies, courts, educational and correctional institutions, and private and public social agencies. One branch of criminology, called "penology," deals specifically with the operation of correctional institutions and agencies and the rehabilitation of offenders. (Some writers object to the term "penology" on the grounds that it does not clearly indicate that nonpenal, as well as penal, methods are today being used in the handling of offenders.)

In a narrower sense, however, criminology is the scientific study of crime and criminals.[1] In this sense, criminology has extended its inquiries along three lines. First, it has investigated the nature of criminal law and its administration and the conditions under which it develops; second, it has analyzed the causation of crime and the personalities of criminals; and third, it has studied the control of crime and the rehabilitation of offenders. In this volume, criminology is discussed in both these senses so as to pro-

[1] For the view that the term "criminology" should be used in the scientific sense, see Marvin E. Wolfgang, "Criminology and the Criminologist," *Journal of Criminal Law, Criminology, and Police Science,* LIV (June, 1963), 155–62.

3

vide the student with as comprehensive an understanding of the subject as possible. The sense in which it is discussed will be clear from the context; and the student, therefore, by bearing in mind the meaning of science, will be able to determine whether opinions or ethical considerations are being presented, or whether implications other than those of a scientific nature are intended.

THE NATURE OF SCIENCE

We have said that criminology, in one sense, is the scientific study of crime and criminals. Does this mean that in this sense criminology is a science? Before we try to answer this question, we must recognize the fact that all kinds of people commit crimes. Criminal behavior is not just one segment of human life. It is all of human life expressed in terms of a set of values that are unacceptable to organized society at a certain time and in a given place, and no special theory for it will suffice, because the answer can be found in nothing less than an explanation of all human behavior. Whether criminology is, or can be, a science, therefore, will depend on whether there is, or can be, a science of human behavior.

But what does "science" mean? It is clear that the present discussion must await our efforts to understand this term. Science is a method, a way of acquiring knowledge by means of a series of steps. *First,* a working hypothesis is formulated. This is a tentative supposition, provisionally adopted to explain certain facts and to furnish guidance in the search for others. Whenever man approaches any situation, he already has some ideas about it which he has secured from his previous experience. These form the basis of his action in dealing with the situation and provide him with what we have referred to as a "working hypothesis." *Second,* the working hypothesis is tested by gathering, recording, analyzing, comparing, and classifying the facts. *Third,* generalizations are made regarding the uniformities and regularities found in the facts. The investigator proceeds from the particular to the general in a process known as induction. These generalizations may or may not be in agreement with the working hypothesis and may actually lead to its complete rejection. *Fourth,* certain conclusions are drawn from the generalizations which have been formulated. At this step the investigator proceeds from the general to the particular in a process known as deduction. *Finally,* the conclusions are verified by additional research, and, wherever necessary, the original explanation is revised to fit the new understanding of the facts. Thus, science moves from observation through induction and deduction to verification in a never-ending process designed to eliminate error.

The findings of science that have been tested and appear to be correct are known as scientific truths. They constitute the insights into reality which we have achieved through science, although, as we have indicated, they are subject to continuous re-examination and modification in the light of new evidence. The findings of science that have been put into words may be classified into laws, theories, and hypotheses. A statement of an order or relation of phenomena which, so far as known, is invariable under the given conditions is called a law. When the statement cannot be so definitely formulated, because the evidence upon which it is based is not so conclusive as for a law, it is known as a theory. When the supporting evidence is even less conclusive, the statement may be called a hypothesis. All three of these terms are sometimes included under the heading of "principles." At any given time, therefore, science may be defined in terms of its content as a body of known facts, classified and correlated, with laws and principles, deduced from them, describing the behavior of the subject matter with which the science deals. By means of this system of knowledge, the scientist seeks to provide a basis for prediction, planning, and control, which are the practical goals of all science.

A distinction is usually made between pure science and applied science.[2] This distinction is based upon the objective that the scientist has at the time he is performing his work. If his objective is merely to solve a theoretical problem without any immediate application of his findings to a practical purpose, his work may be classified as pure scientific research. If, however, he is engaged in the application of scientific knowledge to the solution of a practical problem, then his work may be called applied science. However, it must be emphasized here that science is not interested in the protection or advocacy of values. It merely seeks to reveal all the facts, regardless of how values may be affected. This may be easy to understand in the case of pure science, but may be perplexing in the case of applied science, where the scientist works with practical problems. Nevertheless, even here the scientist, as scientist, is neither advocating nor condemning values. He is simply saying, in effect, that if you want certain values, this is what science can do for you; but if, on the other hand, you want some other values, then science can do something else for you. In this respect, the applied scientist is like a cabinetmaker who, if given one kind of material and one set of specifications, will make a certain type of desk, but if furnished with another kind of material and a different set of specifications, will make a different type of desk or table or chair. It is of no importance to him as a cabinetmaker what kind of furniture is made. He is interested only in using the material and specifications at hand to the best of his ability.

But does not the scientist believe that his method will produce results, and does he not, therefore, value his method? And is he not thus inter-

2 Some writers prefer the term "basic science" instead of "pure science."

ested in protecting this value? This may be true, but this value is related to science, the instrument, and not to the purposes for which it can be used; and in any particular culture, the value of this instrument may be rated lower than other values, such as those of beauty and the supernatural. Moreover, although science has been successful in providing us with insights into reality, there is no certainty that it can reveal all of reality, or that it is always the best instrument and the only mode of comprehension.

But in so far as it is successful, is science, the instrument, more productive under certain social conditions which involve certain values? And if this is so, should not the scientist be interested in preserving these values? In considering these questions we must recognize that science has been used in all kinds of societies—monarchies, dictatorships, and republics. And certainly it is debatable whether science is more productive under a certain set of social conditions than under others. In some societies it has been very fruitful along one line; in other societies, along another line. Dictatorships, for example, have clearly demonstrated that science can work wonders when it operates under the sponsorship of centralized political power and has great wealth and influence at its disposal. Therefore, if the scientist becomes an advocate in so controversial a question, he is clearly outside the realm of science. To avoid this, he must distinguish between science, the instrument, and the social conditions under which it is used.

Thus science at all times should be thought of as an instrument, in itself devoid of values, and the scientist as a person who, when he functions as a scientist, assumes a neutral position regarding the values for which his skills are being used.[3] It is only in this way that science can be freed from bias and the scientist can remain aloof from partisanship. This is not to deny, of course, that the scientist is also a citizen, and that as a citizen he is deeply interested in values, or that the scientist may be in the employ of another person who is using the findings of science for the destruction or preservation of certain values.

It must be quite obvious that what we have been describing as science is nothing extraordinary or mysterious. The processes to which we have referred are merely those which characterize the approach of most normal persons when they are bent upon learning the facts about anything. However, the scientist is specially trained to understand the nature of these processes, to be thoroughly familiar with their points of strength and weakness, and to know how they can be most effectively used. He is taught to appreciate the importance of facts, to be unbiased, patient, and

[3] For a different point of view regarding science, see George Simpson, *Man in Society: Preface to Sociology and the Social Sciences* (New York: Random House, 1954), pp. 74–82.

diligent in their accumulation, to be objective and critical in their presentation, and to be creative in their interpretation. Thus with him science becomes a finely made instrument in the hands of an expert craftsman.

OBSTACLES TO A SCIENCE OF HUMAN BEHAVIOR

The application of science to human society and its various phases is known as social science. Although noteworthy advances have been made in its development, many serious obstacles still stand in its way. Let us consider first the obstacles that grow out of the nature of the subject matter with which social science deals. The social scientist is confronted with not only a bewildering multiplicity of data regarding exceedingly complex matters, such as values, wishes, influences, and social relationships, most of which at present are not susceptible of measurement, but also a serious lack of reliable information about even his most fundamental problems. Unlike the physical scientist, he can seldom conduct his work in a laboratory where he can manipulate his variables under controlled conditions and thus observe the results of a carefully prepared and supervised experiment. It is true that some social experimentation is possible, for example, that which is conducted through the passage of legislation and the application of regulations of government bureaus; but it must be admitted that the results of such experimentation are almost always obscured and distorted by intrusive factors over which the experimenter has no control. Usually the social scientist must study the facts as he finds them in society; and often events take place so rapidly and unexpectedly that facts escape observation entirely or at best are only inaccurately and incompletely recorded. Moreover, much of the historical data to which the social scientist might turn as a substitute for experimentation are not only fragmentary, even for the modern period, but also tend to be slanted and twisted by the bias and the prejudice of the recorder.

Other obstacles, which have their roots in the nature of the observer himself, further aggravate the situation for the social scientist. One of these is the fallibility of man's senses. Although these are good enough to cope with the ordinary problems of life, their fallibility constitutes an obstacle in scientific work. This is bad enough in physical science, where instruments and devices are widely used to help the senses of the observer, but they become even more serious in social science where the techniques of measurement are in their infancy and the subtleties of social relationships can easily escape the attention of the investigator. Another such obstacle is man's tendency to automorphic interpretation, by which is meant his tendency to conceive of the lives of others in terms of the experiences of his own. Since no two lives are the same, this may lead one far from the truth. A third is the lack of historical perspective from which many investigators suffer. This causes them to mistake that which they have just recognized for that which has just come into existence and to tend, therefore, to overemphasize its importance. The belief of some endocrinologists that the cause of crime is the malfunctioning of the duct-less glands is a case in point. Man's proneness to rationalize, or to find good reasons to adhere to the beliefs that he already has regardless of the facts, is a fourth obstacle of this kind. A fifth is man's tendency to over-simplify in his interpretation. Crime is attributed to a "bad heredity" or to "wicked parents." This tendency is often expressed in terms of a dichot-omy, as when people are classified as "good and bad," or "criminal and law-abiding"; and thus the two categories involved are made to appear sharply divided when, as a matter of fact, they blend into each other, and the complexity of causation is thereby obscured. The last of these obstacles which we want to mention here is caused by the fact that man is part of the very situation which he is trying to analyze and measure. It is not surprising, therefore, that he tends to be emotionally attached to what he finds in it, to fear what may change it, and to be biased in all his interpre-tations of it. Thus, for example, any observer tends to be handicapped by a sex, racial, national, class, and religious bias; and often what he calls the "prejudice" of another is simply a prejudice which is different from his own.

In comparing social science with physical science, it is easy to exagger-ate the size of the obstacles which we have just discussed to the discredit of social science. Therefore, it is necessary for us to explore this matter a little further. Although, as we have explained, social science, unlike physical science, can seldom conduct an experiment under the controlled conditions of a laboratory, this does not mean that the social scientist can exert no control over the situation when phenomena are being observed under "natural" circumstances. For example, sometimes he can use con-trol groups and various statistical techniques and thereby isolate and analyze the data in which he is interested. The point is that although a laboratory is a great aid to the scientist, science is possible without it. Indeed, some of the physical sciences, for example, astronomy, have achieved considerable development despite the fact that they cannot in-troduce their subject matter into the controlled conditions of a laboratory.

We should also guard against exaggeration of the difference between predictability in physical science and in social science. Although it is true that prediction in physical science can be far more precise than that in social science, it is also true that in many cases the predictions made by the social scientists are approximately correct. In support of this, one can readily cite examples such as the prediction of the social effects of the business cycle, or the prediction of the effects of war on birth and divorce rates. It must also be noted that the physical scientist can make only inexact statements about the behavior of many phenomena, and that he is utterly unable to make any predictions about certain other phenomena. Furthermore, it must be realized that all the laws of science are expressions of probability. Although mathematics can express itself in terms of absolutes, these do not deal with reality, as do the findings of science, but with the necessary relationships between symbols devised by man to enable him to measure relationships in reality.[4] Thus, it can be seen that all of the findings of science are subject to modification. Even the physical sciences have had to modify many of their laws, and at the present stage of our knowledge the area of the unknown is so large that any theory, if pressed far enough, becomes untenable.

Social science, moreover, is not helpless in the face of the obstacles that have their roots in the nature of the observer himself. To offset these, the social scientist can be strictly trained in the maintenance of objectivity during research, in the skillful use of the best techniques of measurement in social science, and in the practice of having his findings verified by other scientists in order that errors caused by the fallibility of his senses and by his bias and prejudices may be detected and eliminated. But even when all these points are taken into consideration in this comparison, one must admit that social science faces formidable obstacles and that its progress has been slower and more limited than that of physical science.

Now that we have examined the nature of science and explored the obstacles that stand in the way of social science, we can again ask the question: Is criminology in one sense, at least, a science? The way in which we answer this question will depend on how we define the term "science." If by the term "science" we mean method, then it is clear that criminology is a science, for it uses the method that we have defined as science. The contention that it has not yet produced an impressive accumulation of findings is irrelevant, since this merely refers to the lack of success with which the method has been used and not to the absence of its use. However, if by the term "science" we mean the content of science, that is, the body of scientific findings, then it is clear that criminology is not a science, for although we have achieved some important insights into human behavior, we have not as yet developed a system of verified laws and principles regarding it.[5]

4 Mathematics and formal logic are classified as formal science to distinguish them from empirical science, which embraces all the sciences called "physical" and "social." Whereas empirical science deals with what can be experientially known and attempts to formulate laws about it, formal science asserts nothing about the facts of experience and interests itself only in the connection of statements or symbols with one another; for example: Does statement A follow logically from statements B, C, and D?

5 For further reading on the nature of science, see Norman Campbell, *What Is Science?* (New York: Dover Publications, Inc., 1952); George H. Mead, *Movements of Thought in the Nineteenth Century* (Chicago: University of Chicago Press, 1936),

THE CASE STUDY AND STATISTICS IN CRIMINOLOGY

The case study and statistics are two important tools used by the criminologist in his application of the method which we have defined as science.[6] The use of the case study involves the application of science to the individual unit, that is, to a particular unit of a certain kind. Thus, the unit in a case study may be a person, a nation, an institution, a community, a historical period, a family, an episode, or a gang; and the analysis which is made may be called, among other things, a biography, an autobiography, a history, or just a case study. The use of statistics, on the other hand, involves the application of science to large groups of individual units. With statistics the investigator deals with quantified facts in mass form and seeks to discover among them the attributes that are typical and recurrent.

Much has been said about the relative merits of these tools, but it is as futile to speak of one of them as superior to the other as it is to speak of the carpenter's saw as superior to his hammer, his screwdriver, or his chisel. Like the carpenter's tools, each is important for its own purpose, and each must be used if science is to be applied completely. Thus, if one is to understand an individual unit as fully as possible, one must not only examine it intensively by means of the case study, but also compare it extensively with other individual units by means of statistics. In many investigations, the case study and statistical analysis complement each other.

The virtue of the case study lies in the fact that it can give us an analysis of the development through which the individual unit has gone to become the kind of person, situation, community, or other unit that it is. Thus the case study can help us to understand the factors that have operated in this development, how they have interacted and when, and under what conditions. By stressing all factors and their interaction in the total situation, the case study enables us to secure a comprehensive,

---

pp. 264–91; H. Poincaré, *Science and Hypothesis* (New York: Dover Publications, Inc., 1952), pp. 1–34, 150–59; Herbert Spencer, *The Study of Sociology* (New York: D. Appleton and Co., 1873), pp. 65–285; J. W. N. Sullivan, *The Limitations of Science* (New York: The Viking Press, Inc., 1933); Max Weber, *The Methodology of the Social Sciences* (Glencoe, Illinois: The Free Press, 1949), pp. 1–63; Alfred N. Whitehead, *Science and the Modern World* (New York: The Macmillan Co., 1926).

[6] Some textbooks list the following as other tools that are used by criminologists: (1) the therapeutic method, by which the investigator studies an individual while he is under treatment; (2) the method of the participant observer, by which the investigator, while actively associated with another person or with a group, studies the other person or the group; and (3) the use of life histories, by which is meant the study of another's account of his own life. The author prefers to consider the first two as descriptive of the circumstances under which the case study and statistics may be used, and the third as a source of material upon which the case study and statistics may draw.

dynamic interpretation of behavior. We can, therefore, readily appreciate why it can be a valuable tool for the criminologist in his efforts to understand the causation of crime and the development and rehabilitation of criminals.

One who uses the case study, however, is confronted with certain difficulties. In order to employ it most effectively, the investigator must be well trained, and both this training and the use of the case study take considerable time and money. The bias and the prejudice of the investigator, furthermore, may permit him to find only what he wants to find; and if he is not careful, he may adjudge that which comes first as the cause of that which follows and thus fall into what is known as the *post hoc, ergo propter hoc* fallacy. Moreover, when the individual unit that is being studied is a person, rapport must be established with him in order to obtain his cooperation in gathering the necessary facts. This in turn may lead to an emotional involvement which makes it difficult for the investigator to retain his objectivity and induces the person who is being studied to say what he thinks the investigator would like him to say. One other difficulty needs to be mentioned. When a person is being studied, he must be intelligent, lucid, and mature enough to cooperate; and this means that the case study is not very helpful in dealing with young children, the mentally deficient, and some cases of mental derangement.[7]

Statistics has the merit of enabling us to reduce a complex mass of data to simple units of measurement.[8] By means of a few statistical concepts, it is possible to indicate how statistics can be utilized to simplify and manipulate a mass of data. After an investigator has gathered his data, which he may have secured by various sampling techniques, he must put them into some sort of order by a process of classification. To do this, he may set up an array in which items are arranged according to their magnitude or distributed according to their incidence. He next obtains a single figure or average (a mean, a median, or a mode) which will measure the central tendency of the whole group of items, and another figure (standard deviation) to measure the dispersion of items around the central tendency. Finally, by means of the statistical device known as a coefficient of correlation, he may compare these figures with those of other groups of items in order to reveal potential relationships. A discussion of the use of statistics on crime and delinquency and some of the

---

[7] In his consideration of these difficulties and those which confront the user of statistics, which we shall take up later, the student should keep in mind the obstacles to social science that we have already discussed.

[8] The word "statistics" has two meanings. It may be used, as it is here, to refer to a tool of science, but it may be used also to refer to numerical facts, such as the number of arrests or the number of persons placed on probation. It will be employed in this second sense later in this chapter when we discuss the use of available statistics on crime and delinquency in the United States.

difficulties that are involved in their use will be presented later in this chapter.

The investigator who uses statistics as a tool of science, also, is faced with certain difficulties. Data with which he can work are often entirely lacking, many of the available records are incomplete or inaccurate, and when statistical material has to be collected, the necessary expenditures in time, money, and effort are sometimes almost prohibitive. Bias can be especially troublesome in the use of statistics, for an investigator can almost always find data that will seem to support a particular, even if one-sided, point of view. Thus, an increase in the number of cases handled by a juvenile court may be cited to support the statement that there has been an increase in juvenile delinquency, when perhaps what has really happened is that the police have become more active in bringing juveniles before the court while the amount of possible delinquency has not changed or has even decreased. It can be seen, therefore, that the investigator must guard against ignoring pertinent information. Failure to do this may cause him to commit such serious errors as the use of nonrepresentative data as a basis for generalizations and the comparison of data that are not comparable. Therefore, generalizations regarding the characteristics of criminals based upon data drawn from the records of American maximum-security prisons, since the populations of these institutions do not constitute a representative sample of the criminal population of the United States, would be fallacious; and efforts to demonstrate the effectiveness of the crime-prevention program of a sparsely populated, rural state by comparing its crime rate with that of a thickly settled, industrial state would be utterly misleading.

The analysis of statistical data for the purpose of revealing the causes of crime is a particularly hazardous undertaking. The presence of a factor does not necessarily mean that it is a cause of crime; two factors may be correlated without being causally related; and the possible effects of unknown elements, within factors that are insufficiently refined, may be overlooked. A delinquent may come from a broken home, but the broken home may not be a cause of his delinquency; and a statistical relationship may exist between delinquency and inadequate recreational facilities, but the mere fact of a positive correlation is no proof of a causal relationship. In these examples another factor, or a group of factors, may be the cause of the delinquency, or unknown elements within the analyzed factors may be influencing the child's behavior; and it may be only a coincidence that the home is broken in the one case and that the recreational facilities are inadequate in the other. The fact is that a statistical analysis does not tell us very much about how factors affect one another in their interaction. Furthermore, this limitation is rendered the more serious by the tendency of the investigator who employs statistics to select for measurement only those factors which are susceptible of measurement and in this way to permit the more subtle and intangible ones, which may be the essence of the problem, to escape from the analysis. It is here that the case study can be utilized to offset the limitations of statistics, for it can reveal not only what factors are present but also how, why, and when they interact.[9]

THE CONCEPT OF CAUSE IN SCIENCE

We have used the concept "cause" a number of times thus far in our discussion, and it is therefore appropriate to ask ourselves what it means in science. By "cause" science means the sufficient antecedent conditions necessary for the evocation of a given phenomenon. When these conditions are sufficient, the phenomenon appears; when they are insufficient, it does not. It refers, therefore, to a functional relationship between the phenomenon studied and the conditions necessary for its appearance. These conditions must be thought of in terms of their interaction in the total situation. Some exert more influence than others, but the functioning of all is necessary to produce the phenomenon, which would be different if there were the least modification in the total situation. If Tom, Dick, and Harry are present in a room, their pattern of behavior is not just the sum of the patterns of behavior that would exist if each were alone, but rather the product of the interaction of these three men in this particular room; and if Tom leaves the room, that part of the interaction which Tom's presence produces is removed, and an entirely new pattern of behavior, caused by the interaction of just Dick and Harry, exists.

It is clear, therefore, that when a condition or factor is abstracted for the purpose of simplification and to permit a more complete study of it apart from the other factors, we must see it not merely in its abstracted form, but also in its interaction with all the other factors in the total situation. If we study the broken home as a factor in delinquency, we must see it in its entire pattern of interaction, for the breaking of a home may relieve tension in the family and thus actually reduce the possibility of delinquency.

Science deals not with the ultimates in reality, although it is constantly striving to enlarge the area in which we have insights into reality, but rather with the functional relationships among the conditions, or factors, which it can isolate and identify in the immediate situation. However, the causes in the immediate situation are actually the effects of preceding

[9] For a further discussion of the study of causation, see John Dollard, *Criteria for the Life History* (New Haven: Yale University Press, 1935); R. M. MacIver, *Social Causation* (New York: Ginn and Co., 1942). See also Don Martindale, "Limits to the Uses of Mathematics in the Study of Sociology," *Mathematics and the Social Sciences* (Philadelphia: The American Academy of Political and Social Science, June, 1963), pp. 95–121.

causes; and since every effect in its turn becomes a cause, science is dealing with a stream of cause and effect which flows from the enigma of the past into the mysteries of the future. Limited as science is in its powers, it can study only the part of this stream which is within its present view, and the explanation that it advances at any given time is only its best description of what it can so far comprehend.

In social science, when we wish to simplify a situation which is too complex for us to understand, we use the principle of abstraction to remove factors from it. We can thus reduce the situation to its fundamentals and study each factor apart from the others and without the confusing interference of their interaction. Sometimes we do this in order to see society as it is at a particular time, in which case we use such terms as "structure," "state," and "static" to describe what we see. At other times, we do it in order to see society in motion, and then we employ terms like "function," "process," and "dynamic" for the purpose of description.

In our discussion of cause in the field of criminology, we shall use the term as science defines it, and, therefore, by it, we shall mean the sufficient antecedent conditions necessary to evoke crime. Thus, our attempts to understand the causation of crime will be a search for these conditions and for the uniformities and regularities existing among them.

USE OF STATISTICS ON CRIME AND DELINQUENCY

The study of statistics has never been a popular pastime. People avoid statistics, sometimes because they do not understand them, sometimes because they do not want to be annoyed with their technical details, and sometimes because they are suspicious of those who employ figures to support their views. Whatever the reasons are, and undoubtedly there are many, statistics are generally neglected.

And yet statistics are important. Certainly they are in criminology, where they can furnish us with much valuable information. In the first place, in criminology they can tell us about the volume and trend of crime and delinquency for different periods of time, both in total and for such categories as types of offenses, segments of population, and geographical areas. This information can provide a basis for the evaluation of the existing preventive and remedial programs and for action by administrative agencies and legislative bodies. Second, they can keep us informed regarding the number of persons who have come into contact with the law in different ways (for example, the number who have been arrested, prosecuted, convicted, acquitted, committed, and placed on probation or parole), how they have been handled, and what has happened to them. In this way, we can be placed in a better position to determine the efficiency of the agencies of law enforcement and the problems that confront them. Third, they can give us a picture of the characteristics of criminals and delinquents and their backgrounds (for example, their sex, age, race, nativity, marital status, social class, residence, occupation, education, and record of previous offenses). This information enables us, through the use of control groups, to compare criminals with noncriminals and thus gain some insight into the possible causes of crime and delinquency. It likewise indicates the kind of preventive and remedial measures that are needed to cope with these problems.[10]

The use of statistics in criminology, however, involves certain difficulties. The first of these is due to the fact that the law changes, and so what is defined as criminal or delinquent also changes from time to time and from place to place. Consequently, increases or decreases in the figures shown in the records or reports may reflect the action of the legislatures in altering the criminal codes by addition, modification, or elimination of offenses and not any changes in the habits or activities of the people. A second difficulty exists because there is no way of securing a complete record of all the acts and omissions that might be adjudged to be crimes or delinquencies by a court, that is, a complete record of the possible criminality and delinquency.[11] Statistics, therefore, can supply us with only a sample of the possible criminality and delinquency, and this sample can be used as an index of possible criminality and delinquency only if we can assume that there is a reasonably constant ratio between it and the sample. Since there are so many interfering factors, such as public opinion, politics, administrative policies, and so on, which continually distort this ratio, it is evident that this assumption is not valid under all circumstances and that the total recorded criminality and delinquency is not a reliable guide for the criminologist in his efforts to understand all aspects of these problems. Thorsten Sellin, in discussing this difficulty, has stated:

Generally speaking, all criminal statistics are in fact statistics of law enforcement, in the broad sense of that term. Our problem is to discover whether or not these statistics can also be employed for measuring criminality. In view of what has been said above, it is obvious that for such purpose we cannot use the *total* recorded criminality. We must extract from that total the data for only those offenses in which the recorded sample is large enough to permit the assumption that a reasonably constant relationship exists between the recorded and the total criminality of these types. We may make that assumption *when*

[10] Thorsten Sellin, "The Uniform Criminal Statistics Act," *Journal of Criminal Law and Criminology*, XL (Mar.–Apr., 1950), 679, 680.

[11] According to law, an act or omission is not a crime or a delinquency until it has been so adjudged by a court. The total of known acts and omissions which might be adjudicated as crimes or delinquencies plus unknown acts and omissions which if known, might be so adjudicated will be referred to here as "possible criminality" and "possible delinquency."

the offense seriously injures a strongly embraced social value, is of a public nature in the sense that it is likely to come to the attention of someone besides the victim, and induces the victim or those who are close to him to cooperate with the authorities in bringing the offender to justice [and] we may suggest as a second principle that *the value of criminal statistics as a basis for the measurement of criminality in geographic areas decreases as the procedure takes us farther away from the offense itself.*[12]

Thus, according to Professor Sellin's second principle, we must consider police statistics a more reliable index of possible criminality and delinquency than court statistics, and court statistics a more reliable index of possible criminality and delinquency than prison statistics. This is true since, as he has explained, various factors, such as the policies and practices of courts and institutions, reduce the validity of the index as the distance between it and the act or omission itself is increased. We shall examine this difficulty further when we discuss the sources on crime and delinquency in the United States.

A third difficulty arises because the recorded criminality and delinquency, in order to be meaningful, must be related to population figures by the computation of rates—that is, the magnitude of crime per unit of population. If this were not done, an increase in the absolute numbers of recorded crimes and delinquencies might be interpreted as an increase in criminality and delinquency when in fact it might merely reflect an increase in population. And at this point we begin to see more clearly the difficulty that is involved; for these rates should be refined so that they will be expressed in terms of such categories as age, sex, race, and geographical area; and much of the information that is necessary for these calculations is available only for the years in which the decennial censuses are taken and, therefore, becomes increasingly inaccurate as the decade passes. Estimates can be made to offset this to some extent, but the difficulty is still a serious one.

A fourth difficulty exists because many times still other information is needed if we are to have a clear picture of what has happened. For example, the detecting and reporting of crimes will be affected by such factors as the attitudes of citizens in a community regarding various crimes and the efficiency of law-enforcement agencies. Anyone engaged in a study of the volume and trend of crime in a certain area, therefore, should have intimate knowledge about the customs, traditions, and public administration of that area. Additional difficulties which are more spe-

---

[12] Thornsten Sellin, "The Significance of Records of Crime," *The Law Quarterly Review*, LXVII (Oct., 1951), 496–98. For a more detailed discussion of this difficulty, see Thorsten Sellin, "The Basis of a Crime Index," *Journal of Criminal Law and Criminology*, XXII (Sept., 1931), 335–56, and *Research Memorandum on Crime in the Depression* (New York: Social Science Research Council Bull. 27, 1937), chap. IV.

cifically related to the particular sources of statistics will be considered as we analyze these sources.

SOURCES OF STATISTICS ON CRIME AND DELINQUENCY IN THE UNITED STATES

In the United States, police departments and other local law-enforcement agencies, courts, and correctional institutions provide the three major sources of statistics on crime and delinquency. In addition, surveys, community studies, and the records and reports of certain public bureaus and private corporations and associations furnish a fourth possible source. Each of these sources will be briefly examined.

1. **Police Statistics on Crime.** OFFENSES KNOWN TO THE POLICE. Statistics on crimes known to the police are contained in the *Uniform Crime Reports,* which have been published by the Federal Bureau of Investigation since 1930 and are based on data received on a voluntary basis from police agencies throughout the United States.[13] The term "offenses known to the police" refers to those crimes which become known to the police through reports of police officers, citizens, prosecuting attorneys, and court officials, or otherwise. It includes the following seven classes of grave offenses, which experience has shown to be those that are most generally and completely reported to the police: criminal homicide (which includes both murder and nonnegligent manslaughter), forcible rape, robbery, aggravated assault, burglary (breaking or entering), larceny—theft (except auto theft) $50 and over in value, and auto theft.[14]

However, since the local law-enforcement agencies are not compelled to furnish the Federal Bureau of Investigation with the information compiled in the *Uniform Crime Reports,* some communities forward no information at all, and a greater percentage of urban communities than of rural areas are cooperating in the compilation of these reports. But these weaknesses are rapidly disappearing. During 1963, crime reports were received from law-enforcement agencies representing 98 per cent of the population living in metropolitan areas, 91 per cent of that in other cities, and 77 per cent of the rural population. In their combined coverage, these

[13] In accordance with the recommendations of a Consultant Committee on Uniform Crime Reporting (see Federal Bureau of Investigation, *Uniform Crime Reports, Special Issue, 1958*) some important changes were made in the reporting system of the Federal Bureau of Investigation. For example, the *Uniform Crime Reports* are now published only once a year instead of twice a year as they were prior to 1958, and negligent manslaughters (mainly traffic deaths) and larcenies under $50 are no longer included in the index of crime tabulation. Furthermore, on its own initiative, the Federal Bureau of Investigation had already excluded statutory (nonforcible) rapes from this index.

[14] Federal Bureau of Investigation, *Uniform Crime Reports, 1963,* pp. 2, 3, 43–45.

reports came from areas containing 92 per cent of the total population of the United States.[15]

It should be noted, also, that some possible criminality does not become known to the police and that the accuracy of the *Uniform Crime Reports* ultimately depends upon the honesty and efficiency of the reporting agencies. On this point, it has been claimed, for example, that the police in some cases may not want to furnish information regarding the number of offenses known to them, since this might indicate that they are not making as many arrests as they should. In reply to this, the Federal Bureau of Investigation, although not vouching for the validity of the reports received, has stated that they believe that the reports are reasonably reliable and that its field workers are attempting in every way to improve them. Nevertheless, marked differences remain in the criminal laws and their administration in the various states, and this must be taken into consideration in the use of the *Uniform Crime Reports.*

Finally, it must be recognized that *offenses known to the police* are only *alleged* offenses known to the police and that further investigation or court action sometimes reveals that no crime was committed or that some crime different from the one that was reported actually occurred. Despite this and the other shortcomings of the *Uniform Crime Reports*, criminologists generally agree that *offenses known to the police* are the best existing index of possible criminality in the United States. Among their virtues is the fact that they are the most extensive national criminal statistics in existence. Besides, they are closer to the total possible criminality than any other criminal statistics, which, as we have explained, tends to eliminate many of the intrusive factors that reduce the validity of an index of possible criminality.[16]

ARRESTS. Almost all municipal police departments compile and publish statistics on arrests, and, in addition, the *Uniform Crime Reports* contain data on arrests by urban and rural police, which the Federal Bureau of Investigation secures from reports sent to it by urban and rural agencies throughout the country.[17] The *Uniform Crime Reports* give information on the age, sex, race, and offense of those who have been arrested for the

15 *Ibid.,* 40. In the *Uniform Crime Reports, metropolitan areas* are generally made up of an entire county or counties having at least one core city of 50,000 or more inhabitants with the whole meeting the requirements of certain metropolitan characteristics. *Other cities* are urban places of 2,500 or more inhabitants outside *standard metropolitan statistical areas. Rural areas* are the unincorporated portion of counties outside of *other cities* and *standard metropolitan statistical areas.*

16 For an analysis of some of the problems involved in the use of these statistics for scientific research, see Marvin E. Wolfgang, "Uniform Crime Reports: A Critical Appraisal," *University of Pennsylvania Law Review,* III (Apr., 1963), 708–38.

17 Information for rural arrests was presented for the first time in the *Uniform Crime Reports* in 1960. Prior to that time the data had been shown for only urban areas (Federal Bureau of Investigation, *Uniform Crime Reports, 1960,* p. 16).

violation of state laws and municipal ordinances, and they represent the most complete tabulation of statistics on arrests that are now available. During 1963, according to these reports, 4,437,786 arrests were made by 3,988 urban, suburban, and rural law-enforcement agencies serving 67 per cent of the total population of the United States.[18]

Statistics on arrest are not a reliable index of possible criminality in the community. In the first place, there is no constant relationship between the possible criminality and the number of arrests. One person, or many persons, may be arrested during the investigation of a single alleged crime, and many alleged crimes may be committed by one person before he is arrested. Then, too, many alleged crimes are committed for which no arrests are made at all, and the number of arrests that are made will vary with the efficiency and the policies of police administration. Thus, the zeal of a mayor who has been elected on a reform ticket may greatly increase the number of arrests for gambling, even though the amount of gambling has not increased in the community. The action of our courts and legislatures also may affect the reliability of statistics of arrests as an index of possible criminality. The leniency and incompetence of a judge may discourage police from making arrests, and the inefficiency of legislators may cause laws to be so poorly worded that their enforcement is exceedingly difficult. Such considerations as these remind us that comparisons between departments and states cooperating in the compilation of the *Uniform Crime Report* should be made with extreme caution.

2. **Court Statistics on Crime.** Statistics on such items as prosecutions, dismissals, acquittals, convictions, prison sentences, fines, and probation are compiled and published by some courts, and some states systematically collect such data from their courts and publish them in regular reports. The Administrative Office of the United States Courts is at present doing this for the federal courts. In 1932, the United States Bureau of the Census began to collect and publish such statistics for state and District of Columbia courts and attempted to increase the usefulness of these statistics, but it discontinued this publication in 1947 when it appeared to be of little value. The available court statistics on crime are fragmentary and lack uniformity, and in only a few states are they of much assistance to the criminologist. Although court statistics are too far removed from the possible criminality to be an index of it, we must have this information if we are to know what our courts are doing and how effectively they are performing their functions.

3. **Institutional Statistics on Crimes.** The United States Bureau of the Census publishes special and decennial censuses of prisoners in local, state, and federal penal institutions. In addition, beginning in 1926, this

[18] Federal Bureau of Investigation, *Uniform Crime Reports, 1963*, pp. 103–105.

bureau prepared annual reports on prisoners committed to federal and state prisons and reformatories, but it discontinued the publication of these reports in 1948. The Federal Bureau of Prisons also publishes institutional statistics. Its annual report contains data on federal prisoners, and its *National Prisoner Statistics,* issued at irregular intervals, contains information about prisoners in state and federal institutions and provides the most extensive sources of statistics on prisoners in state prisons and reformatories. Furthermore, the individual states and some local communities publish reports on their own correctional institutions.

It should be obvious that institutional statistics cannot be used as an index of possible criminality since they are so far removed from this criminality. They are influenced by all kinds of factors which in no way bear a constant relationship to the possible criminality in the community. Thus, they are affected not only by the efficiency, honesty, and justice of police and judges, but also by other factors, such as the character and ability of prison administrators, which further compound the errors that accumulate in statistics on crime from the time that they originate in our police departments. Nevertheless, it should be just as obvious that we need these statistics in order to have a basis for the evaluation and improvement of our correctional institutions.

4. **Other Statistics on Crime.** Statistics on crime will also be found in such crime surveys as the *Cleveland Crime Survey,* the *Missouri Crime Survey, The Report of the Minnesota Crime Commission,* the *Illinois Crime Survey,* and *Crime and the Georgia Courts,* and in such public reports as those issued by coroners and fire departments. Private corporations and associations, too, can furnish us with information about crimes. For example, the American Bankers Association collects data regarding burglaries and robberies of its member banks; insurance companies maintain records of crimes against their clients; and newspapers have a great deal of information in their files about crime and criminals. It can be seen, therefore, that the student of crime can find valuable data regarding special aspects of his problem in reports and records such as these.

5. **Police Statistics on Juvenile Delinquency.** Statistics on arrests of juvenile delinquents are contained in the *Uniform Crime Reports* of the Federal Bureau of Investigation and are based on data received on a voluntary basis from urban and rural police agencies in the United States.[19]

[19] Some local police agencies publish their own reports containing statistics on arrests of juvenile delinquents, but since the meaning of "arrest" as used in these reports may vary from one agency to another, the data on arrests are not always comparable. In the collection of data for the *Uniform Crime Reports,* however, a juvenile is counted as arrested when he or she has committed an alleged crime, and the circumstances are such that if the individual were an adult, an arrest would have been made.

The data secured in this way constitute the only source of national statistics on alleged juvenile delinquents arrested by the police. However, since these statistics are collected on a voluntary basis, they are neither complete for the country as a whole nor a representative sample. Furthermore, not all alleged juvenile delinquents who are detained are handled by the police, but instead are taken care of by other agencies. For this reason alone, the data on arrests of alleged delinquents in the *Uniform Crime Reports* understate the amount of possible delinquency.

6. **Court Statistics on Juvenile Delinquency.** Juvenile court statistics on a national scale are collected annually by the United States Children's Bureau, which has been gathering and publishing such data since 1927. The information so collected is released through the press, special bulletins, and the *Children's Bureau Statistical Series*. There is always a press release each year, giving over-all figures, and the reports on juvenile court statistics in the *Statistical Series* are issued annually, the latest of these, *Juvenile Court Statistics, 1964*, being published in 1965.[20] In addition, local reports on juvenile courts are published by some cities and counties.

The basic unit of count in the juvenile court statistics collected and published by the United States Children's Bureau is the delinquency case that is disposed of either officially or unofficially. This means that a child who appears before a court several times during one year will be counted as a separate case upon each appearance if a new complaint is filed and handled separately each time. Therefore, the number of cases reported for the year is larger than the number of different children involved.[21] On the other hand, many cases which might have been adjudged delinquent are not included in the statistics at all, either because the juveniles are not apprehended or because they are taken care of by other institutions or agencies in the community. These statistics are also affected by differences in the state laws which determine the age group of children and the types of cases over which the courts have jurisdiction, variations in administrative and law-enforcement practices, and the availability of other community resources, such as family societies and welfare agencies.

In commenting on the factors that affect these statistics, Richard Perlman of the Children's Bureau has stated: "These limitations re-emphasize the impracticability of using juvenile court statistics alone to make comparisons of the extent of juvenile delinquency in different communities or regions. However, juvenile court delinquency cases furnish an indica-

[20] See also Edward E. Schwartz, "Statistics on Juvenile Delinquency in the United States," *The Annals of the American Academy of Political and Social Science*, CCLXI (Jan., 1949), 9, 10; I. Richard Perlman, "Reporting Juvenile Delinquency," *National Probation and Parole Association Journal*, III (July, 1957), 242–49.

[21] United States Children's Bureau, *Juvenile Court Statistics, 1962*, Statistical Series, No. 73, p. 9.

tion of the extent of juvenile misbehavior serious enough to need court attention."[22]

In order to obtain more precise information on the total volume of juvenile delinquency, the Children's Bureau in 1955 initiated a plan for collecting data from a representative national sample of 502 juvenile courts, but it also continues to use the older system of collecting data from any courts that wish to send in reports. According to the new plan, the Children's Bureau publishes estimates of delinquency for the entire country, instead of merely giving actual figures reported by a limited and changing group of courts. These estimates provide information on the number of cases, the sex of the juvenile, the urban or rural location of the court, and the official or unofficial handling of the case but give no information on the age of the juvenile, the nature of the alleged offense, or the disposition of the case.[23] The Administrative Office of the United States Courts publishes additional data on juveniles whose cases are handled under federal law and not diverted to state or local authorities.

7. **Institutional Statistics on Juvenile Delinquency.** The United States Bureau of the Census publishes special and decennial censuses on juvenile delinquents in institutions. In addition, the United States Children's Bureau collects statistics on children in institutions, including those in institutions for delinquents, and issues publications based on this information at irregular intervals. It should also be pointed out that the annual reports of the Federal Bureau of Prisons include statistics on federal juvenile offenders committed to correctional institutions and that some states, counties, and municipalities publish reports on their own correctional institutions for juveniles. All these institutional statistics cover too small a portion of the total group of juvenile delinquents to serve as an index of the volume of possible delinquency in the United States.

8. **Other Statistics on Juvenile Delinquency.** A considerable amount of information on juvenile delinquency has been accumulated by state and local agencies throughout the country. Investigating commissions, councils of social agencies, crime-prevention bureaus, universities, and other research and civic agencies have played a leading role in this undertaking. Although much of this information is of limited usefulness, this source of statistics on juvenile delinquency should not be neglected. In fact, for certain purposes it may be more valuable than any other source of such data.

[22] I. Richard Perlman, "The Meaning of Juvenile Delinquency Statistics," *Federal Probation*, XIII (Sept., 1949), 65. For an investigation of the differential selection of juveniles by the police for court appearance, see Nathan Goldman, *The Differential Selection of Juvenile Offenders for Court Appearance* (New York: National Council on Crime and Delinquency, 1963).

[23] United States Children's Bureau, *The Children's Bureau and Juvenile Delinquency* (Washington, D.C.: Government Printing Office, 1960), p. 70.

THE UNIFORM CRIMINAL STATISTICS ACT

Even though they still have serious limitations, statistics on crime and delinquency have been considerably improved within recent years. One of the most significant steps for improving these statistics was taken in 1946, when the National Conference of Commissioners on Uniform State Laws and the American Bar Association approved the Uniform Criminal Statistics Act. As Professor Sellin has explained:

The adoption of this act by a state, the selection of competent persons to administer it, and the appropriation of sufficient funds for their work would ultimately give to such a state a good system of criminal statistics. . . . When this has been achieved in a considerable number of states, the groundwork will be laid for good national criminal statistics, assembled by some federal agency from the various state bureaus. For in spite of the worthwhile attempts made by different federal bureaus to compile national data, the next forward steps of any importance in this direction will be impossible without the improvements of state statistics and the assistance of state bureaus created for their collection.[24]

Thus far, however, only California has adopted the Uniform Criminal Statistics Act,[25] although the essential parts of it have been written into the law of New York, and a few other states have central statistical bureaus which publish statistical information derived from reports received from their political subdivisions.

POINT OF VIEW OF THIS BOOK

Now let us turn to a number of ideas which are basic in the point of view of this book and which will be stressed over and over again. These ideas may be summarized as follows:

1. In the study of criminology, the crime as well as the criminal must be emphasized if the interests of the individual and those of society are to be balanced properly. The criminal and his social relationships must be emphasized if we are to understand why he commits a crime and how his behavior may be modified. And crime as a legal concept must be emphasized if we are to understand how to protect society and its moral

[24] Sellin, "The Uniform Criminal Statistics Act," 681. See also National Conference on Prevention and Control of Juvenile Delinquency, *Report on Statistics* (Washington, D.C.: Government Printing Office, 1947); Ronald H. Beattie, *Manual of Criminal Statistics* (New York: The American Prison Association, 1950); Orin S. Thiel, "Judicial Statistics," *The Annals of the American Academy of Political and Social Science*, CCCXXVIII (Mar., 1960), 94–104; Ronald H. Beattie, "Criminal Statistics in the United States—1960," *Journal of Criminal Law, Criminology, and Police Science*, LI (May–June, 1960), 49–65.

[25] The Council of State Governments, *Record of Passage of Uniform and Model Acts, as of December 1, 1963.*

code against the criminal, on the one hand, and the defendant and his rights against his accusers, the general public, and those who wield authority, on the other.

2. The law is functionally related to the culture of the society in which it operates and must be seen as only one part of the larger system of social control in that society. Some of this system of social control is highly formalized, like that which is exerted through the family, the church, the various economic agencies, and the law, carrying with it the weight of institutionalized authority. Much of it, however, is informal and includes such influences as public opinion, gossip, the praise or condemnation of the community, and the respect or ridicule of friends and acquaintances. In the larger system of social control, it is not the fear of legal penalties that keeps many persons from violating the law, but rather the desire to find love, respect, and security among relatives, friends, and business associates. This is an important form of social control, and it will always function regardless of what methods are used in dealing with criminals.

3. Crime is both a legal and a social problem, and when it is examined from both of these points of view, a better understanding of its nature is achieved. In serving its purpose, the law is necessarily subject to certain limitations, and its point of view must be supplemented by those of other professions, such as psychiatry, psychology, and sociology. Because this many-sided view of the problem of crime is needed, a clear and definite terminology must be decided upon at this time. Every society, if it is to survive, must establish social norms, that is, rules and standards for the guidance and regulation of its members. These norms, varying in degrees of complexity, rationality, and compulsiveness, may be classified into such categories as folkways, mores, and social institutions. In this textbook, one who violates a social norm will be called a social deviant; and his act, a social deviation. If a person is accused of violating the criminal law, one of the social norms, he will be referred to as an alleged criminal; and his act, as an alleged crime. However, not until a person is convicted of a particular crime in a criminal court, will he be termed a criminal; and his act, a crime.

4. The scientific approach to crime is important, but its nature and limitations must be clearly understood. Such an understanding is necessary if the student is to guard against those who thoughtlessly invest certain values with a false attractiveness through the implication that these values are based upon the findings of science, or who deliberately confuse ethics and science in order to peddle nostrums under the guise of science.

By using the scientific method, the sociological study of crime and criminals has made important contributions. It has made us deeply conscious of social relationships, the cultural nature of law, the activities of pressure groups, and the ossification of social institutions; but often in its eagerness to do this, it has minimized the individual and his unique qualities. Yet, the individual has a reality apart from the group, and no personality organization is ever the same as the social organization in which it functions. It is only by recognizing this fact that we can secure a well-rounded picture of the individual, whether he is a law-abiding citizen or a criminal.

5. All kinds of people commit crimes. Criminal behavior is not just one segment of human life. It is all of human life expressed in terms of a set of values that are unacceptable to organized society at a certain time and in a given place, and no special theory for it will suffice, because the answer can be found in nothing less than an explanation of all human behavior. At the present time, the area of the unknown regarding human behavior is so great that any theory becomes untenable if it is pressed very far.

Criminal behavior, therefore, like all human behavior, must be studied through the cooperation of many disciplines, each using its own concepts and specialized techniques. This, unfortunately, seems to have escaped the understanding of some students of the problem who have come to look upon criminology as exclusively within the province of this or that specialty. Instead of adopting so limited a view, we should use all available resources and organize them in a coordinated attack along all approaches to the problems of causation, correction, and prevention. Much could be accomplished by the establishment of institutes of criminology participated in by all types of specialists in the field of human behavior. Such institutes are now conducted in various European countries, where they are usually attached to law schools and offer instructions to officials in the public service, police, prosecutors, judges, prison administrators, and the like.

6. A textbook, unlike a monograph, should not try to present all its material in terms of one theory, and this is especially true in criminology, where the subject matter is so complex. Instead, a textbook should review theories, discuss their strengths and weaknesses, and draw such conclusions as are justified in the light of existing knowledge. In a field like criminology where knowledge is so slight, the frame of reference must of necessity be rather wide; and the conclusions, loosely drawn. This is not to say that a particular theory should not be employed as a guide in a specific research project—indeed, this must be done— but it does mean that the conclusions of such research must be primarily related to the area explored and the level of abstraction used. Thus within a broad frame of reference, a closely reasoned theoretical system can be created on this or that level of abstraction, but the possibility of other theories on the

same or other levels of abstraction should be clearly recognized by such a system.

7. There are no pure criminal types. In some cases of crime or delinquency the deviation factors may be more personal than environmental, whereas in other cases the reverse may be true; but never is a person a criminal only because of personality characteristics or only because of the internalization of values that are unacceptable to organized society. There is always a mixture of these influences in varying proportions. However, the classification of criminals into more homogeneous subgroups or types by means of different criteria, although always more or less arbitrary, does provide deeper insights into criminal behavior and a more systematic basis for further research.

8. Courts and correctional institutions can never be just therapeutic agencies. They must be also moral agencies in the sense that they must express, protect, and strengthen the values of the organized society in which they function. In fact, courts and correctional institutions must act in this way if they are to promote the rehabilitation of the offender. If they did otherwise, they would flout the very values to which he must learn to adjust and for which he must develop a loyalty. This is not to ignore the considerable confusion regarding moral values in the United States, but the point is that courts and correctional institutions have a responsibility to do what they can to lessen this confusion. Indeed, the primary objective of the correctional process is not to reduce personality maladjustments, but to induce law-abiding behavior, even, if necessary, at the expense of causing personality maladjustments.

9. Both punishment, with its emphasis upon society and its values, and treatment, with its emphasis upon the individual and his rehabilitation, must be given a place in modern penology. Indeed, in practice they are inextricably interwoven at almost every stage in the handling of offenders. The important question, then, is: How can we most judiciously balance treatment and punishment in the correctional process so as to give due recogition to the interests of both the individual and society?

10. In the field of criminology, however, we must see beyond the professional and the expert. To give them the complete responsibility of dealing with crime and delinquency is to undermine the foundations of representative government, endanger the rights of the individual, and enfeeble the independence, vigilance, and self-reliance of a republic's citizenry. In the United States, therefore, citizen participation is an essential element in all programs of law enforcement, criminal prosecution, correctional administration, and crime prevention.

2

Crime as a Legal Problem

CRIME IS A LEGAL CONCEPT

An act, or a failure to act, must have a peculiar quality before it can be said to be a crime. It must be so defined by the law, for crime is a creature of the law and attains its identity through the action of our legislative bodies and courts. In the absence of being labeled as a crime by the law, an act or a failure to act is not a crime, even though it may be shocking to the individual conscience.

Some writers, however, would broaden the concept of crime to include certain acts regardless of whether or not they have been designated as criminal by the law.[1] This, they assert, should be done because these acts are the same, or nearly the same, as other acts that are now called criminal and should therefore be similarly labeled and condemned even though the legislatures and the courts fail to do this.

Although one can readily understand the desire of these writers to reduce the injustices of our law and to provide a sounder basis for the study of crimes and criminals, it is undesirable that the concept of crime should be so broadened at the almost certain risk of causing great confusion throughout our society. In the first place, social scientists have not thus far demonstrated any great inclination to agree upon the meanings of some of their most fundamental terms. Certainly there does not appear to be any great assurance that they could, or would, agree upon the extent to which the concept of crime should be so broadened, and so crime might come to mean many things to different persons and groups. Furthermore, the legal profession is already entrusted by society with the responsibility of interpreting and administering the criminal law, and it is deeply aware that the terms "crime" and "criminal" carry serious implications regarding rights, responsibilities, and reputations. To apply

[1] See, for example, the discussion of the white-collar criminal in Chapter 7.

the term "criminal" to a person is not only to lower his status by publicly stigmatizing him, but also to declare that his guilt has been proved, that certain of his rights have been forfeited, and that he should be punished. In order to protect all parties concerned, the legal profession has always insisted upon a strict interpretation of the meaning of the terms "crime" and "criminal" and has carefully constructed around them a technical procedure designed to reduce the possibility of injustice. It is not likely that the legal profession will change the meaning of these terms at the mere suggestion of persons outside the profession. In fact, the expanded meaning of crime and criminal might actually tend to undermine the understanding and confidence between two professional groups whose increased cooperation is so important in the improvement of our laws and their administration.

Moreover, the terms "crime" and "criminal" have political implications. A strict usage of these terms clearly recognizes that, in a republic like ours, an act becomes a crime only by being so defined in the law through legislative and judicial action. Such usage, therefore, emphasizes that acts are to be called "crimes" and persons are to be called "criminals" only when, through their representatives, the people have exercised their right to do this and that this decision is not to be made, by so-called experts, for the alleged "good" of the people, as in totalitarian countries.

All this, of course, does not mean that we should forbid research and discussion regarding what *ought* to be called criminal. On the contrary, we should encourage these activities so that the influence of an informed public opinion, exerted through legislative and judicial channels, can bring the law more closely into line with the needs and desires of our people and more securely establish its just administration.

It is clear from what has been stated thus far that a student of crime and criminals must have some understanding of the criminal law. He may be well trained in the physical and social sciences; he may have a great deal of insight into the adjustment of personalities; he may have considerable skill in the manipulation of statistical data; but if he does not have some legal knowledge, he will be severely handicapped in his attempts to understand the nature of crime. Obviously he need not be a lawyer, nor need he have a detailed knowledge of specific crimes, but it is essential for him to grasp the significance of the principles and doctrines of the criminal law. Until he appreciates the point that crime is a legal concept, until he learns to observe the limitations of that concept as defined by the law, he is likely to confuse problems of morality, ethics, and metaphysics with the problems of crime.[2] It is the purpose of this

2 Arthur Evans Wood and John Barker Waite, *Crime and Its Treatment* (New York: American Book Co., 1941), p. 333.

chapter, therefore, to introduce the reader to some of the major aspects of the criminal law.

CRIME AS DEFINED BY THE LAW

According to the law, a crime may be generally defined as "the commission or omission of an act which the law forbids or commands under pain of a punishment to be imposed by the state by a proceeding in its own name."[3] This definition should be carefully examined, for every part of it is important. It is obvious that not every act or failure to act could, or should, be regulated by law. Crimes are only those acts or failures to act that are considered to be so detrimental to the well-being of a society, as judged by its prevailing standards, that action regarding them cannot be entrusted to private initiative or to haphazard methods but must be taken by organized society in accordance with tested procedures. In fact, even if the victim of a crime takes no action, opposes it, forgives the criminal, or tries to conceal the crime, the state can and may press the charges.

As we all know, a crime is only one of several kinds of human behavior which are usually known as wrongs. In addition to crimes, torts, sins, and vices are also designated as wrongs, but of these, only crimes and torts are defined as wrongs by the law. A tort is a civil or private wrong, other than a breach of contract, for which the court will provide a remedy in the form of an action for damages.[4] In a tort, unlike a crime, contributory negligence on the part of the injured party may be a complete defense. Although a tort is a legal wrong, the harm involved in it is not so serious as that caused by a crime, and, therefore, private initiative in a civil suit is relied upon to redress the wrong. If only a tort has been committed, whether or not the person affected takes action, the state usually has no power to interfere. A sin is a transgression, such as blasphemy, which is in violation of divine authority, while a vice is an immoral act, such as gluttony, which is directed primarily against one's self, or "a wrong in which the offender is also the chief sufferer."[5]

At first glance it seems easy to make these distinctions regarding wrongs, but further thought soon convinces one that there are perplexing difficulties. In the first place, no sharp lines can be drawn between what

[3] Justin Miller, *Handbook of Criminal Law* (St. Paul, Minn.: West Publishing Co., 1934), p. 16. In order to emphasize that the consequences of an act or omission is the essential element of a crime, Perkins has defined a crime as "any social harm defined and made punishable by law." See Rollin M. Perkins, *Criminal Law* (Brooklyn: The Foundation Press, Inc., 1957), p. 5.

[4] William L. Prosser, *Handbook of the Law of Torts* (St. Paul, Minn.: West Publishing Co., 1955), pp. 1–12.

[5] Harry Best, *Crime and the Criminal Law in the United States* (New York: The Macmillan Co., 1930), p. 4.

affects an individual's interest and what affects society's interest.[6] In the law, a crime is known as a public wrong, while a tort is referred to as a private wrong. Obviously, however, any harm done to one individual affects other individuals, and in this sense, at least, all wrongs may be thought of as public. For example, if one person is injured by an automobile carelessly driven by another, a tort has been committed against the injured person that may seriously endanger the welfare of his family by depriving them of his loving care and earning power. They, in turn, as their savings become exhausted, may have to be provided for by some public agency operated by funds raised through taxation. Furthermore, the victim of the accident may die, and his death may be no less overwhelming to his family merely because it was due to the carelessness of another, instead of the premeditation of a murderer. It is clear, therefore, that the use of the terms "private" and "public" is just another way of indicating that the harm caused by a tort is not so serious nor so pervasive as that caused by a crime. In our society, in the case above cited, the harm involved would have been serious enough to raise the act from a tort to a crime if the person had been run over intentionally by the driver of the car.

In the same way, it can be shown that a sin, like the failure to honor one's parents, or a vice, like excessive drinking, neither of which is a legal wrong, definitely affects the lives of others and indirectly may contribute to the most shocking tragedies. What we have in these wrongs, then, is a gradation of harms, the degree of the seriousness of each being measured in terms of the dominant values of our society. Thus, the way in which a wrong is classified depends in general on whether the good of the state is best served by denouncing it as a crime and prescribing a penalty to be imposed in a proceeding by the state; by defining it as a tort and leaving it to the individual to seek redress in damages in a private action for the injury suffered; or by not defining it by law at all and allowing it to be designated as a sin or a vice without any legal provision regarding the injuries received.

Here another difficulty confronts one in any analysis of wrongs, for one soon discovers that wrongs are not mutually exclusive. For example, a wrong may be not only a crime, but also a sin and a tort. The seduction of a woman by a man who is already married is not only criminal and tortious but also, according to religious principles, sinful. Indeed, most legal wrongs are both criminal and tortious, exposing the doer to punishment by the state and rendering him liable to damages in a civil suit.[7] Other illustrations of this are assault and battery and criminal libel.

---

[6] Jerome Hall, *General Principles of Criminal Law* (Indianapolis: The Bobbs-Merrill Co., 1947), pp. 205, 206.

[7] Miller, p. 21.

Thus, even in those cases where the acts involved are serious enough to be called criminal, we also tend to grant the individual an opportunity to secure damages.

A third difficulty further complicates the analysis we have undertaken. Wrongs are relative to time and place, so what is right today may be wrong tomorrow, and what is wrong in one place is right in another. There is no act, except perhaps treason, that we now condemn as criminal that has not at some time or place been considered honorable. In the United States, the content of the criminal law has been changed down through the years and today varies from state to state. In some cases, old laws which are still on our statute books are no longer enforced but linger on as anachronistic reminders of a simpler society.[8]

There is still another difficulty. It has been stated that crimes are those wrongs which are considered the most dangerous in terms of the values of a society, but this statement is clearly an oversimplification, for such questions as "Dangerous to whom or to what?" and "What values or whose values?" immediately come to mind. Any society is composed of a number of groups competing and conflicting with one another in the advancement of their interests. Although many of the acts that are made criminal in a society are considered dangerous in terms of the values of all groups in that society, it is obvious that some acts which are defined as crimes may be judged as unimportant or even as desirable by some of its members or groups, and that still other acts may be criminal simply because some members or groups are powerful enough to make them so regardless of the values of others. Thus, some of the provisions of the criminal law may in this way merely express the demands made by a certain group for the protection of its interests, which may, as a matter of fact, be detrimental to the interests of other groups in the state or country. If the interests of enough people are adversely affected by such provisions, agitation against the law will develop and public opinion may force the repeal or modification of the objectionable provisions. However, if repeal or modification cannot be accomplished in an orderly way, the agitation may break out into violent action and the law may be openly violated. In this way, revolution may be fomented, and its successful denouement may eliminate the hated restrictions through the establishment of a new social order. The leaders of the revolution, formerly condemned as dangerous criminals, now become widely acclaimed heroes; and conduct which was criminal under the old order is praised as honorable in terms of the new standards.

Naturally, what we have said should not be construed to mean that the distinctions that we make about wrongs serve no purpose, or that

[8] Albert Morris, *Criminology* (New York: Longmans, Green and Co., Inc., 1934), pp. 7, 8.

the interests of the individual are the same as those of the group and
that there is therefore no real difference between a tort and a crime. Nor
should it be interpreted to mean that the criminal law is an instrument
of oppression used by the rich and the powerful to protect their special
interests, or that there is no point in our trying to define wrongs as
crimes and that what we should do is merely let a group of experts in
each case decide whether an act has been, shall we say, antisocial. It is
precisely because such hasty generalizations are made that we have
emphasized the difficulties involved in any analysis of wrongs. Indeed,
the problem is surrounded by so many difficulties that any conclusions
regarding it should be carefully scrutinized.

ELEMENTS OF A CRIME

We have been discussing the legal definition of a crime in a general
way. Now we must turn our attention to a detailed examination of the
elements of a crime so that we can have a deeper understanding of its
meaning. A crime may have two elements: the criminal act or omission
and the mental element commonly called the _mens rea_ (literally, "guilty
mind"), which includes criminal intent and criminal negligence. All
common law crimes must have both of these elements, there being no
crime if either is lacking; but in some offenses that do not owe their
origin to the common law, the mere doing of the prohibited act, regardless of the intent involved, may constitute the crime.

It is a general principle of common law that a crime is not committed
if the mind of the person who commits the act is innocent.[9] So if a
person genuinely believes that a book belongs to him, he commits no
crime when he takes the book. It is likewise true that the law does not
punish a person for harboring an evil intent if the intent is not expressed
in any act. Thus a person may bitterly hate a rival, but if he takes no
action to injure him, he is not guilty of a crime. In the ascertainment of
intent, it is necessary to distinguish between it and motive. Intent is the
purpose or resolve to do an act, whereas motive is the desire or inducement which incites or stimulates a person to commit it. Although motive
is closely related to intent, only in a few exceptional instances is it an
essential element in a crime,[10] and proof of motive is never necessary to

[9] Offenses, not of a common law origin, which make the mere doing of the prohibited act a crime are an exception to this principle. An example of such an offense
in some parts of the United States is the sale of adulterated foods where, according to
the law, the intent of the seller has nothing to do with whether or not a crime has
been committed. For a discussion of strict liability, see Perkins, pp. 692-710. For a
discussion of the view that strict liablty should be removed from the criminal law, see
Hall, pp. 279-322.

[10] One of these exceptional instances is in a case of criminal libel in which, if the
defendant seeks to justify his publication, the motive for his act may become an important issue in the case. For further discussion of motive, see Perkins, pp. 719–25.

support a conclusion of guilt which is otherwise sufficiently established. Therefore, one may be guilty of a crime regardless of whether his motive is shown to be good or bad or even if no motive at all is proved. Thus, if a daughter kills her father to save him from the agonies of a dread disease, she is guilty of criminal homicide even if her motive be love for her father. By the same token, the law does not punish a person merely because he has a bad motive if his act is not a crime. A person who takes a car which he believes belongs to another, although it really belongs to himself, is not guilty of the crime of larceny. However, evidence regarding the motive in a crime is usually admissible in order to help establish the identity of the perpetrator of the crime, the intent with which the crime was committed, and the degree of the offense with which he is charged.

In general, according to the law, an adult person who is sane is presumed to intend his voluntary acts and the natural and probable consequences of these acts. Thus, if such a person shoots another and kills him, he is presumed to have intended to kill him, or if he throws a large stone into a crowd and kills several persons, he is presumed to have intended to kill them. In both these cases, the law would take the position that under such circumstances any reasonable man would know that he might kill someone if he acted as the killer did. As we have implied, children[11] and insane persons are held by the law to be incapable of entertaining criminal intent, but voluntary drunkenness does not relieve a person of criminal responsibility except, as we shall see, in cases where the law requires a specific intent to render an act a crime.

The law likewise presumes that persons know what the law is, and consequently they may be held to have criminal intent in cases in which they do not know that what they are doing is wrong, much less criminal. So if a man acting on the basis of his religious principles and in ignorance of the law marries several women within the same state, he may be charged with a crime and his ignorance of the law is no excuse.

A person may be guilty of perpetrating a crime even though it is not the one which he intended to commit, for if he does one wrongful act while actually intending to do another, he may be criminally liable for the former act. Here the criminal intent, concurring with the act committed, may be enough to make him a criminal. Thus, where a person intends to rob another but while engaged in the act kills the person who is being robbed, he is guilty of a criminal homicide.[12]

11 At common law, the rule was that a child under seven was incapable of committing a crime. In cases of children between seven and fourteen, there was a rebuttable presumption of incapacity. Children over fourteen, like adults, had a rebuttable presumption of capacity.

12 Miller, pp. 61–65; Perkins, pp. 33–36, 713, 714.

Sometimes, however, a crime is so defined as to require not merely that an act be committed voluntarily, but that its commission be accompanied by a specific intent. In such cases, the existence of criminal intent is not presumed from the commission of the act, but the specific intent as required by the law must be proved. Thus, according to the common law, burglary is defined as the breaking and entering of the dwelling house of another in the nighttime with intent to commit a felony therein. Therefore, in order to convict a person of the common law crime of burglary, it must be shown that the defendant intended to commit a felony in the dwelling house. If the proof fails to establish this, but shows instead that the defendant intended to commit a lawful act or to commit just a misdemeanor, he is not guilty of burglary.[13]

Moreover, in certain crimes the *mens rea* consists simply in the state of mind which necessarily accompanies a failure to observe proper caution in the performance of an otherwise lawful act or in culpable failure to perform a duty.[14] Here, negligence sufficient to constitute the *mens rea* consists in the reckless doing or failing to do what a reasonable person would do or would not do under the same or similar circumstances. In addition, when negligence is relied upon as the mental element, it is necessary to show a legal duty, and not just a moral duty, to act with due care under the circumstances. When a person sees a baby on the railroad tracks and does not act to save it, the person is not guilty of any crime if he is a stranger to the railway company and the baby. However, if he is the parent of the child or the engineer of the train, he has a legal duty to make an effort to save the child.[15]

When the law declares that there must be an act and a *mens rea* in order for a crime to exist, the act and the *mens rea* must concur in the causation of the crime. If a person should make up his mind to kill another, then abandon the idea but later kill the person in mutual combat or accidentally, there would be no concurrence of the act and the previously abandoned intent. In this way, repentance before an act is committed may prevent the accused from being convicted of a crime.[16]

Since the act varies with each crime, it is difficult to define. In some cases, it is the doing of something; in others, it is the failure to do something, as for example, the failure to move a train from a street cross-

[13] Miller, pp. 59–61; Perkins, pp. 149–72.

[14] In such cases it is sometimes said that criminal intent may be supplied by criminal negligence. In other words, this means that a person who recklessly exposes another to danger is presumed to have intended the natural consequences of his recklessness. For a discussion of the reasons why mere negligence should not make a person criminally liable," see Jerome Hall, "Negligent Behavior Should Be Excluded from Penal Liability," *Columbia Law Review*, LXIII (April, 1963), 632–44.

[15] Miller, pp. 65–68; Perkins, pp. 663–71.

[16] Miller, pp. 73–76; Perkins, pp. 725–28.

ing within a certain period of time. Sometimes it involves passive participation in the act of another, as in the case of sodomy or adultery. Again, it may involve such conduct as "possessing" or "belonging," as in the possession of burglar's tools or membership in a prohibited organization. Furthermore, whether an act is criminal or not may depend upon the existence of some status or relationship such as marriage. For instance, the absence of the relationship of man and wife may make an act the crime of rape, where, had this relationship existed, it would have been no crime at all.[17]

Finally, in this discussion of the elements of a crime, it must be explained that in some cases, in order for a crime to exist, it is not necessary that the act committed should amount to the complete commission of the crime intended. The three crimes of attempt, solicitation, and conspiracy illustrate this fact. So the crime of attempt is committed when an act is done with specific intent to commit a particular crime and moving toward, but falling short of, its commission; the crime of solicitation exists when one person solicits another to commit a felony even though the person solicited refuses to commit it; and two or more persons are guilty of conspiracy if they combine to commit an unlawful act, even though nothing is done to carry out the objectives of the combination. A person who conspires with others to commit a crime, unless he effectively withdraws, is criminally liable for all the consequences that result from efforts to accomplish the purpose of the conspiracy and for the acts of all who participate with him in the commission of the crime.[18] These three crimes show how our society reaches out and punishes those who may merely threaten important values which are protected by our criminal law.

PROXIMATE CAUSE

An act often has consequences that reach far and touch the lives of many persons, but the law does not hold a person responsible for every consequence of his acts. Thus, A fails to wake B at the time agreed upon. B, finding himself late for work, rushes out of the house and bumps into C, who becomes angry and curses B. However, B pays no attention and hurries away. C, while still very angry, gets into his car and vents his wrath by recklessly driving his car down the street and into another car owned by D, who is injured. If A had waked B on time, B would not have rushed out of the house and bumped into C, C would not have become

---

[17] Miller, pp. 77–86; Perkins, pp. 470–75, 513–27. Perkins defines an act as "(1, positive) an occurrence which is an exertion of the will manifested in the external world, or (2, negative) a nonoccurrence which involves a breach of a legal duty to take positive action" (p. 514).

[18] Miller, pp. 95–117; Perkins, pp. 476–512, 527–49.

angry and recklessly driven his car into D's, and D would not have been injured. The law, however, holds C, and not A, responsible for the injury of D.

Possibly all events occurring in the world are dependent upon one another, and no one of them can be explained without reference to all the others. In a philosophical sense, the consequences of an act go forward to eternity and its causes extend back to the beginnings of time. But human responsibility cannot be measured by such standards. To do so would result in infinite liability for all wrongful acts, stir up boundless conflicts, and fill our courts with endless litigation. Liability for the consequences of any act must be limited in terms of some idea of justice or social policy,[19] which tends to be an expression of the dominant values of the group. In the light of what is considered to be justice in any society, a person's act is said to be the proximate or legal cause[20] of the consequences, and if these constitute a crime and the requisite *mens rea* is present, he is held to be criminally responsible.

Under our system of criminal law, the general rule is that no one is held to be the proximate cause of harm unless his act was in fact a cause thereof. In a few instances, however, there may be a proximate cause even when there has been no factual cause. Thus, the act of a person may be imputed by law to another member of a conspiracy, and the failure to perform a legal duty may be regarded by law as the equivalent of a positive act. On the other hand, not all factual causes are proximate causes. Thus, an act may be too trivial to be entitled to notice by the law, or the chain of causation may be broken by a more immediate independent intervening force, as, for example, when a husband who wounded his wife is not held criminally responsible for her death if she later died of scarlet fever contracted in a hospital where she had been taken for treatment of her wound. If, however, an act is a substantial factor and produces the result directly or with the aid of a dependent intervening force other than an extraordinary response of a human being or an animal, the act is the proximate cause of the harm even if the harm was neither foreseeable nor intended. So if the defendant stabbed another who would have recovered except for the negligence of a doctor, the act of the defendant is the proximate cause of death. Even so, as

[19] The idea of justice includes practical considerations such as the expedition of trials.

[20] The term "proximate cause" is an unfortunate one, for it seems to place much emphasis upon nearness in time or space. Actually it was never intended to do this but only to mean the nearest cause that is recognized by the law. To correct the false implication, some writers have suggested that the term "legal cause" should be used instead of "proximate cause." But the term "legal cause" seems to indicate that an unlawful act is a legal cause, and for this reason, perhaps the term "legally recognized cause" is preferable.

Perkins explains, regardless of circumstances, an act which produces an intended or reasonably foreseeable consequence is always a proximate cause.[21]

A person's act, however, may be the proximate cause even though it is only a contributing one, as in the case of concurrent acts of two persons acting with a common design, or in some instances, if the acts are concurrent or successive but independent of each other. Thus, if each of two persons acting with a common design inflicts a fatal wound, each is liable for the criminal homicide. Furthermore, when two persons, each acting independently of the other, concurrently or successively inflict wounds upon a third person, both are guilty of criminal homicide if the two wounds cooperate in producing the harm. But a person cannot be held liable for an injury resulting from an independent intervening act that breaks the chain of causation. Thus, if A strikes B, and while B is being treated in a nearby drugstore, he is killed by a gunman who holds up the store, A is not responsible for the death of B.

This brief discussion shows why factual causation and legal causation are not the same and how in any particular case the law may disregard certain factors that science would include within its analysis. Science, moreover, would be very much interested in motive, which, as we have seen, is a factor seldom considered to be an essential element in legal causation.[22] However, although the law must operate as it does if it is to be an effective instrument of social control, its principles should be continually re-examined so that they may benefit from the latest scientific research whenever this is possible.

PARTIES IN THE COMMISSION OF CRIMES

When several persons participate in the commission of a crime, the degree of criminal liability of each is determined by the nature and extent of his participation in the offense. A person who actually commits the crime either by his own hand or through an innocent agent is a principal in the first degree, but if, although he is present at the time that the crime is committed, he merely aids and abets another in the commission of the deed, he is a principal in the second degree. One who is absent when the act is committed, but who procures, counsels, commands, or abets the principal is an accessory before the fact. One who relieves, comforts, or assists another in the effort to hinder the operation of the law, knowing that the other has committed a crime, is an

21 Perkins, pp. 596–649. It is customary for the law to analyze problems of factual causation in terms of the *sine qua non*, or the so-called "but for" test or "had not" test. In other words the law asks, "Would the result have occurred, had not the defendant committed the act?"

22 For a discussion of the scientific concept of cause, see Chapter 1.

accessory after the fact.[23] It should be noted, however, that this classification of parties to a crime is not applied in cases of treason or misdemeanor. All parties involved in treason are principals, and in misdemeanors, all parties except accessories after the fact, who are not liable
in any way, are principals. The term "accomplice" may be used to refer
to either a principal or an accessory.

According to the common law, principals in the first and second degree are equally guilty and subject to equal punishment, but no accessory
can be convicted or sentenced until after conviction and sentencing of
the principal. In the United States and England, however, the common
law regarding parties concerned in the commission of crime has been
greatly modified, and in many parts of our country the distinctions between principals in the first degree and accessories before the fact have
become obsolete. Even so, the term "accessory after the fact" has been
generally retained in the United States and is often used to refer to a
crime of lesser degree, exposing the convicted person to a lighter penalty
than that meted out to others implicated in the execution of a crime.

A person who acts as an agent in the commission of a crime, and who
is mentally competent and knowingly carries out the commands of
another person, usually, along with the other person, incurs responsibility for the crime. However, an agent is innocent and is therefore
relieved of responsibility if he is sincerely unaware of his act and has
no grounds to suspect any wrongdoing. As a rule, at common law, a person is not criminally liable for the acts of his agent if he has not previously authorized or assented to them, even though they are done in
the course of the agent's employment.[24]

CLASSIFICATION OF CRIMES

According to the common law, crimes are divided into treason, felonies,
and misdemeanors. In American law today, however, crimes are usually
classified into felonies and misdemeanors, treason being considered a
felony, although some writers still use the common law classification and
place treason in a separate category. In some jurisdictions in the United
States, there are also various subdivisions. For example, the more serious
misdemeanors are classified as high, and the less serious ones as low,
misdemeanors.[25]

In the United States, treason is expressly defined by the federal Constitution, which declares: "Treason against the United States, shall consist only in levying war against them, or in adhering to their enemies,

[23] The present trend is to exclude from this type of guilt those who are intimately
related to the principal.
[24] Perkins, pp. 549–95.
[25] Miller, pp. 41–49; Perkins, pp. 8–21.

giving them aid and comfort. No person shall be convicted of treason unless on the testimony of two witnesses to the same overt act, or on confession in open court."[26] Similar provisions have been written into the constitutions or statutory enactments of many states.

The term "felony" in early England was used to refer to that group of offenses for which the punishment consisted of a total forfeiture of lands and goods. In addition, capital or other punishment might be superadded for such crimes. Later, forfeiture was abandoned as a method of punishment, and the other penalties for felonies were gradually mitigated. As a result, relatively few capital crimes now remain in the law. In the United States today the more serious crimes are called felonies and are usually punishable by death or by confinement in a state or federal prison or reformatory, while the less serious ones are called misdemeanors and are usually punishable by confinement in a jail or by a fine. However, in some American jurisdictions violations of municipal ordinances, such as those which regulate traffic in our cities, are not stigmatized as crimes but are called "violations."

The legal distinction between felonies and misdemeanors has not been clearly preserved in American criminal law, and they vary considerably from state to state. An offense that is a felony in one state may be a misdemeanor in another. Furthermore, sometimes a misdemeanor may be a more serious offense in one state than a felony is in another. Thus, although it is still true that in general felonies are more serious crimes than misdemeanors, there is no sharp and clear line separating these two categories of offenses. In spite of this, however, the legal distinction between felonies and misdemeanors is still an important one in American jurisprudence.[27]

Works on criminal law also make a distinction between crimes *mala in se*, or wrongful from their nature, and punishable at common law, such as murder, robbery, and rape, and crimes *mala prohibita*, or wrong merely because they are prohibited by statute, such as violations of ordinances and regulations designed to secure better management of the affairs of the community. This distinction, however, is a questionable one. A more accurate interpretation would be that these two groups of crimes differ only in degree and not in kind of wrongfulness, that they constitute a continuum that ranges from the least to the most serious violations of moral standards, and that the positions of crimes in the continuum will change as social conditions change.[28]

[26] *Constitution of the United States,* Art. III, Sec. 3.
[27] For a discussion of this distinction, see Miller, pp. 46, 47.
[28] For a discussion of the invalidity of this distinction, see Hall, *General Principles of Criminal Law,* pp. 292–98. Even in England some of the more serious offenses, for example, embezzlement and conspiracy entered the law through legislative action. Moreover, one may question whether any act serious enough to be defined as a crime is wrongful merely because of such definition.

Another classification of crimes divides them into those that are infamous and those that are noninfamous. At common law, an infamous crime is one which, because of its nature, renders the person convicted thereof incompetent as a witness. Included in this category in the common law are treason, felony, and any offense founded in fraud, or the *crimen falsi.* Testimonial disqualification because of infamy has tended to disappear as a result of modern legislation, and the term "infamous crime" would be of no more than historical interest now in most jurisdictions if it had not been included in the Fifth Amendment of the federal Constitution and in certain state constitutional and statutory provisions.[29] Today, in the federal courts a crime is infamous, not because of its nature, but because of the nature of the punishment that may be inflicted. Thus, in these courts a crime is infamous if it is punishable by imprisonment in a penitentiary or by any imprisonment at hard labor. Some state courts follow the federal rule in this matter; others, however, adhere to the common law and use the nature of the crime as a basis for determining whether it is infamous.

Standard textbooks on criminal law and compilations of statutes use still another classification of crimes, which is based on the kind of social harm caused, and arrange them under such headings as offenses against the person; offenses against the habitation; offenses against property; offenses against public health, safety, comfort, and morals; offenses against public justice and authority; offenses against public peace; and offenses against the existence of government.[30]

ESSENTIAL CHARACTERISTICS OF SOME CRIMES

Since the student of criminology is constantly dealing with different kinds of crimes, it is obvious that he should know the meaning of at least the most common ones. Unfortunately, in a book of this kind, it is impossible to do more than examine the essential characteristics of such crimes.[31] This should help the student gain some insight into their nature, but for a more adequate understanding he is urged to refer to textbooks

[29] The Fifth Amendment of the federal Constitution states: "No person shall be held to answer for a capital or otherwise infamous crime, unless on a presentment or indictment of a grand jury, except in cases arising in the land or naval forces, or in the militia when in actual service in time of war or public danger. . . ."

[30] More accurately, these headings should read: offenses against the state in the form of harm to the person: offenses against the state in the form of harm to the habitation; and so on. This is true, because crime is a violation of the prevailing standards of organized society, which are protected by the authority of the state, and regardless of the attitude of the victim to the alleged criminal, the state can and may initiate prosecution.

[31] For the definitions of the crimes presented here, see Miller and Perkins.

on criminal law and the statutes and court decisions of the states and the federal government.

Homicide is the killing of one human being by another, and it may be felonious or nonfelonious. However, the death must occur within a year and a day after the act, or failure to act, which is alleged to have caused it; otherwise, the law conclusively presumes that the death resulted from some other cause.[32] Felonious homicide may be either murder or manslaughter. The unlawful killing of one human being by another with malice aforethought is murder. The term "malice aforethought" is a difficult one to define, but it is said to be present when the person has an intent to cause death or grievous bodily harm, or when he willfully acts under such circumstances that there is obviously a plain and strong likelihood that death or grievous bodily harm may result, or when he is engaged in the commission of a dangerous felony or in obstructing an officer who is making a lawful arrest or preventing a riot. At common law there are no degrees of murder, but in a number of states the crime is divided by statute into two or more degrees according to the heinousness of the deed.

Suicide is murder at common law if done deliberately by one who has the mental capacity to commit a crime. It is still a crime in some jurisdictions in the United States, and where it is so considered, one who aids another to commit suicide is guilty of murder. Voluntary manslaughter is an intentional killing without malice. It occurs when the killing is committed in the heat of passion induced by great provocation. If a husband sees his wife in the act of sex relations with another and he kills her lover, he may be guilty of voluntary manslaughter. Involuntary manslaughter is felonious homicide unintentionally caused and without malice. It may result from the commission of an unlawful act not amounting to a felony, or from criminal negligence. Thus, a person who drives his car recklessly and kills another is guilty of involuntary manslaughter.

Rape is unlawful sexual intercourse with a woman without her consent. Statutes in most states fix an age below which a girl cannot legally consent to sexual intercourse and provide that sex relations with a female under that age is rape regardless of whether she consents or not.

An assault is either an attempt to commit a battery or an unlawful act which places another in reasonable apprehension of receiving an immediate battery. Usually, an assault must consist of more than mere words. If a person raises his cane or fist at another in a threatening manner and thus creates an apprehension that he will strike, or if a person spits or strikes at another and misses him, there may be an assault. A battery is the unlawful application of force to the person of another. For example,

---

[32] This rule has been abrogated in some states.

it is a battery to spit on another, or to shove him angrily to one side. Thus, it can be seen that although the words "assault and battery" are usually employed together, they are two separate crimes. An assault may not result in a battery, but a battery of necessity includes an assault.

Arson at common law consists in the malicious burning of the dwelling house of another. Statutes in most states have materially changed this definition of arson by making it arson to burn not only dwelling houses but also other buildings, such as shops and warehouses, and other kinds of property, such as lumber and hay. In some states, if one burns his own house, especially if this is done to secure the insurance, he is guilty of arson.

Burglary at common law is the breaking and entering of the dwelling house of another in the nighttime, with intent to commit a felony. It is not burglary to enter through an opening in the wall or roof, although it is if the entry is through the chimney, for that is as much closed as the nature of things will permit. It is sufficient, however, if there is the slightest breaking of any part of the house. Although breaking without entry is not burglary, any entry, however slight, is sufficient, as, for example, where a head, a hand, or even a finger is thrust into the house. Burglary is usually committed with intent to steal, but as the definition states, it may exist when there is an intent to commit a felony of any kind. The crime of burglary, like that of arson, has been considerably changed in most states by statutory enlargements so as to include such acts as breaking into buildings other than dwelling houses, entering without breaking, and breaking and entering in the daytime as well as at night.

Larceny at common law is the trespassory taking and carrying away of the personal property of another from his possession and with intent to steal the property. This definition, like others taken from the common law, has been modified by statute in the United States, and the crime of larceny varies from state to state. In general, however, it may now involve the theft of real property, such as growing trees, fruits, and vegetables, as well as personal property; and it is usually divided into petty larceny, a misdemeanor, and grand larceny, a felony, on the basis of the value of the property stolen. However, the line between petty and grand larceny is drawn in terms of different values in different states so that what is petty larceny in one state is grand larceny in another.

Embezzlement, which was not a crime at common law, is the fraudulent appropriation of personal property by one to whom it has been entrusted. The gist of the crime is a breach of trust. Thus, if goods are delivered by the owner to another for purposes of transportation and are fraudulently appropriated by the latter to his own use, he may be guilty of embezzlement.

Obtaining property by false pretenses, not amounting to a common law cheat, was not a crime according to the early English common law, but it has been generally made so by statute. It is defined as knowingly and designedly obtaining the property of another by means of untrue representations of fact with intent to defraud. So-called "puffing statements" or exaggerations for the purpose of selling articles are not false pretenses. On the other hand, specific statements regarding the nature of a product may be. Thus, if a person excessively praises an article by saying that "it is the best buy on the market," he has not committed the crime of false pretenses; but if he makes the statement that a chain is "15 carat gold, and you will see it stamped on every link," and this is not true, he may be guilty of this crime.

One who, with intent to steal, takes personal property from the person or presence of another by violence or intimidation and against the will of the other is guilty of robbery. Some violence or intimidation must be present or there is only larceny. Thus, pocket-picking by stealth is not robbery.

Extortion is one form of malfeasance in office and consists in the corrupt taking from any person, under the pretext of discharging one's duties, of any money or valuable thing which is not due at the time when it is taken. For example, a constable who obtains money for discharging a void search warrant is guilty of extortion. In some states the crime has been extended to include the taking of property from another, with his consent, through wrongful use of force or fear, under circumstances which do not amount to robbery.

Bigamy is committed when one, being legally married, marries another during the life of his or her wife or husband. Adultery was not a common law crime in England, but was regarded as an offense against the ecclesiastical law only, and it was therefore punished exclusively in the ecclesiastical courts. The definition of the crime varies from state to state, but all states agree that in order for the crime to exist, one of the parties at least must be lawfully married to another, and in the prosecution such marriage must be proved. Fornication, like adultery, is not a crime at common law, but it has been made a crime by statute in some states. Although the definition varies from state to state, it may be defined as voluntary sexual intercourse under circumstances not constituting adultery or lawful cohabitation between husband and wife. Thus, voluntary sexual intercourse between two unmarried persons is fornication.

The offense of compounding a crime is committed when one who knows that an offense has been committed agrees, for a consideration, not to prosecute the offender. The consideration need not be money, but any advantage accruing from the alleged offender to the person forbearing is sufficient. Where the owner of stolen goods agrees not to prosecute the thief in return for his giving back the property, the owner is guilty of compounding a crime.

Perjury at common law exists when a person who is under oath, or obligated by some legal substitute for an oath, willfully and corruptly gives false testimony, which is considered material to the question under inquiry, during a judicial proceeding or course of justice. A person who induces another to commit perjury is guilty of subornation of perjury.

EXEMPTIONS AND JUSTIFIABLE ACTS

In some situations the law exempts persons from criminal responsibility. These persons may not be entirely blameless, but because of circumstances beyond their control, they are deemed not sufficiently blameworthy to deserve punishment. Reference to a few of these situations will clarify the position of the law on this point.

As a rule, reasonable ignorance or mistake of fact exempts a person from criminal liability if his act would be lawful were the facts as he believes them to be and his belief is an honest one. Thus, a person is not guilty of a crime if, on reasonable grounds, he honestly mistakes another for a burglar and kills him. However, ignorance of the law is no excuse. If the accused in every case were permitted to plead ignorance of the law as a defense, the prosecution would be confronted with an almost insurmountable obstacle. Moreover, the criminal law is based upon social values that have the support of organized society. To recognize ignorance of the law as a defense would contradict these values. Wise public policy, therefore, dictates the exclusion of this defense, and the courts decide each case as if the accused knew the law.[33]

But if a person unintentionally causes harm quite by accident while he is not engaged in any unlawful conduct and is not criminally negligent, he is not guilty of a crime. Furthermore, a person is usually exempt from criminal responsibility if he is forced to do an act against his will, or is prevented from performing his legal duty by a storm, flood, or some other act of God.[34]

[33] There are some exceptions to the maxim *"ignorantia legis neminem excusat"* ("ignorance of the law excuses no man"). For example, the maxim is held not to apply when specific intent is essential to a crime, and ignorance of law negatives the existence of such intent. Hence where a person takes property which, because of his ignorance of the law, he sincerely believes belongs to him, but which belongs to another, he is not guilty of larceny.

[34] If a person commits an act as a result of actual physical compulsion, he is not criminally responsible. Thus, one is not guilty if a knife is forced into his hand and in spite of his resistance, he is made to stab and kill another. And if, on prosecution for any crime except murder, the accused committed the act because he was compelled to do so by serious bodily harm, he is excused.

In some other situations, acts which otherwise would constitute crimes are not criminal because the law, on the ground of public policy, allows them or imposes duties involving their commission. Important among these acts, which are said to be justifiable, are those done in the performance of public justice, such as executing criminals, making arrests, preventing escapes, preserving peace, quelling riots, and preventing crimes.

Justification may also arise by way of self-defense.[35] This requires that the person claiming such justification shall, without fault upon his part, be placed in imminent danger of assault or honestly believe on reasonable grounds that such danger is present and that the only way in which he can avoid the danger is by repelling force by force. In order to justify a killing in self-defense, there must be an honest and reasonable belief of imminent death or grievous bodily harm which can be avoided only by killing the assailant.[36]

MEANING AND SOURCES OF THE CRIMINAL LAW

Thus far in our discussion, we have focused our attention upon the term "crime" and have emphasized that it is anything that is so labeled by the law, but as yet we have not examined the criminal law itself. What does the criminal law mean? How did it originate? What are its sources? Why must we have it? What are its limitations? These and other similar questions now require our consideration.

In general, the criminal law is a body of rules regarding human conduct which are prescribed by governmental authority and enforced by penalties imposed by the state.[37] More specifically, we may say that the criminal law deals with such matters as the definition and classification of crimes, the criminal act, the criminal intent, the capacity to commit crime, exemptions from criminal liability, the parties involved in the commission of a crime, the elements or characteristics of specific crimes, the penalties for crimes, and the rules of procedure by which the criminal law is administered.

No one really knows how the criminal law originated. Its roots, like those of all other social institutions, are lost in the past. Studies of known primitive societies reveal that in these groups behavior is largely regu-

---

[35] The distinction between justifiable and excusable self-defense was once important, but the two terms are now generally employed synonymously.

[36] For further discussion of exemptions and justifiable acts, see Miller, pp. 152–224; and Perkins, pp. 806–926.

[37] The criminal law may be divided into substantive law and procedural law. Substantive law deals with duties and rights, whereas procedural law consists of the rules according to which the substantive law is administered and includes whatever is embraced by the three terms "pleading," "evidence," and "practice."

lated by custom, and in most cases wrongs are redressed by action taken
by the injured party himself. However, even in primitive societies certain kinds of behavior, such as treason and acts which tend to endanger
the food supply or which might, according to the prevailing belief, arouse
the wrath of the gods, are considered so detrimental to the welfare of the
group that it seeks to regulate them by some form of collective action.
Although such collective action certainly lacks some of the features of
our highly systematized criminal law, it functions for those societies in
the same general way as our criminal law does for ours, that is, by pro-
hibiting certain kinds of behavior under threat of penalties imposed by
established authority. Thus, as far back as research goes, we find criminal law, albeit in a crude form, already at work.

Nevertheless, certain theories have been advanced to explain the
origin of criminal law. One theory posits that, originally, all wrongs were
redressed by action taken by the injured individual, but that gradually,
in order to reduce the ensuing disorder, which tended to endanger the
safety of all, the group imposed restrictions on individual action; and out
of this effort developed the regulations of criminal law. According to
this theory, then, all crimes originated in torts. A second theory attributes
the origin of criminal law to the crystallization of the mores as the passage of time wove about them a system of thought and machinery for
their enforcement. Still another theory claims that criminal law grew
out of the conflict of the interests of different groups as one group sought
to impose its values upon another. A fourth theory finds the origin in the
application of man's reason to his problems and their reduction, while a
fifth sees the beginnings of the criminal law in an expression of emotion
as groups were stirred to action by their indignation and endeavored to
prevent the repetition of offensive behavior.

Although each of these theories throws some light upon how some of
the criminal law originated and how it has grown through the years, no
one of them, nor all of them together, can give a complete explanation.
It now seems, on the basis of the available evidence, that this question
will never be satisfactorily answered, and that when man first appeared
as a social being, some of his behavior was even then being regulated
by collective action and that therefore the roots of criminal law were
already present in his relationships.[38]

[38] For additional reading on various points of view regarding the meaning and
origin of criminal law, see Georges Gurvitch, Sociology of Law (New York: Philo-
sophical Library and Alliance Book Corporation, 1942), pp. 1–67; E. Adamson Hoebel,
The Law of Primitive Man (Cambridge: Harvard University Press, 1954), pp. 3–45;
Henry Sumner Maine, Ancient Law (New York: Henry Holt and Co., 1906), pp.
109–65; Bronislaw Malinowski, Crime and Custom in Savage Society (New York:
Harcourt, Brace and Co., Inc., 1926), pp. 9–16, 55–84; Leopold Pospisil, Kapauku
Papuans and Their Law (New Haven: Yale University Publications in Anthropology,

In our society, the criminal law is applied to those accused of crime through the administration of our courts. In effect, this means that some judge must exercise his judgment in a particular case, but in doing so he may not give free rein to his personal opinion and bias, for to permit this might result not only in the abuse of judicial authority but also in glaring inconsistency, if not utter confusion, in the body of our law. This naturally would soon lead to the complete loss of a most fundamental legal principle, highly prized in our culture, which requires that, within the same jurisdiction, certain acts be consistently ruled as criminal and certain others be consistently ruled as noncriminal. The judge therefore must look beyond himself and be guided by well-defined rules which are derived from two sources. One of these sources is the statute law, which is enacted by legislative bodies and which labels certain types of behavior as criminal and prescribes penalties for those convicted of such behavior. In general, courts may not condemn acts as criminal unless they have been so designated by the statute law.[39] A great deal of our criminal law is of this kind, but much of the statute law in turn is rooted in the second source, which is generally known as the law of precedent.

The law of precedent originated during the twelfth century in England, when the local baronial courts were being replaced by tribunals presided over by the King's judges, who, traveling about the country, used the same principles as guides for their deliberations regardless of where the court was held and sought precedents for decisions in the customs that were common throughout the realm, rather than in those that were limited to a particular locality. As court decisions based on such customs accumulated, therefore, they became known as the common law. This judicially compiled law was also called the unwritten law to distinguish it from that which was written into the statute books by legislative bodies, and it continues to develop as judges deal with new problems, interpret new statutes, and weave into their decisions such influences as ethics, expert opinions, and hitherto unrecognized customs. Furthermore, since the body of judicially formulated principles became a guide for judges in the preparation of their decisions, one can understand why it is now referred to as the law of precedent.[40] Indeed, it is a

---

No. 54, 1958), pp. 248–89; Roscoe Pound, *An Introduction to the Philosophy of Law* (New Haven: Yale University Press, 1954), pp. 1–47; William Seagle, *The History of Law* (New York: Tudor Publishing Co., 1946), pp. 3–69; N. S. Timasheff, *An Introduction to the Sociology of Law* (Cambridge: Harvard University Committee on Research in the Social Sciences, 1939), pp. 273–300.

[39] In the United States, however, treason is defined in the federal Constitution, and there are similar definitions in state constitutions. In addition, of course, judges must be guided by whatever other constitutional provisions are controlling in the field of criminal law.

[40] Adherence to precedent in the law is known as the doctrine of *stare decisis*. It rests upon the principle that law should be fixed, definite, and known, and that when

guide not only for judges in their deliberations, but also for legislators in their enactment of statutes. Thus, it can be seen how the sources of criminal law interact to form a well-integrated system of legal principles.[41]

WHY CRIMINAL LAW IS NECESSARY

But why is it necessary to have these complex rules and elaborate procedures? In other words, why should we have any criminal law at all?

A little thought will readily persuade one that not only do we need criminal law but that for several important reasons we need a well-developed and integrated criminal law. In the first place, we need it in order to restrain and facilitate our social relationships. In primitive society, most behavior is regulated by custom, which tends to remain unchanged over long periods of time. Populations are small, the accumulation of wealth is slight, social relations are direct and intimate, and people clearly understand their rights and duties. Only a rudimentary criminal law is necessary in such a society.

We, on the other hand, have learned to exercise great control over nature, have contrived to amass huge stores of wealth, have made it possible to satisfy the physical and mental needs of vast numbers of people, and have created great opportunities for leisure and education. But all this has not been achieved without a price. With this have come complexity and indirectness of social relationships. Specialization has meant not only greater skill and increased production, but also increased ignorance of one another's needs, ambitions, dreams, and wishes. We live in a world of well-organized interest groups furiously competing with one another for wealth, privileges, and power. Migration and mobility throw into contact and commingle many groups which cling tenaciously to diverse and conflicting sets of values. It should be clear, then, that we cannot entrust some major aspects of our lives to the uncertainties of our changing customs and fluctuating public opinion. In many areas of social interaction we need specific rules enforced by political authority if we are to know what is expected of us, if we are to know what we may or

the law is declared by a court of competent jurisdiction authorized to construe it, such declaration, in the absence of palpable mistake or error, is itself evidence of the law until changed by competent authority (*Black's Law Dictionary* [St. Paul, Minn.: West Publishing Co., 1933], pp. 1651, 1652).

[41] Edgar Bodenheimer, *Jurisprudence* (Cambridge: Harvard University Press, 1962), pp. 269–324; John Chipman Gray, *The Nature and Sources of the Law* (New York: The Macmillan Co., 1921), pp. 152–309; Karl N. Llewellyn, *Jurisprudence* (Chicago: The University of Chicago Press, 1962), pp. 77–165; Frederic W. Maitland and Francis C. Montague, *A Sketch of English Legal History* (New York: G. P. Putnam's Sons, 1915), pp. 26–87, 200–18; George W. Paton, *Jurisprudence* (London: Oxford University Press, 1946), pp. 52–55, 158–81; William F. Walsh, *A History of Anglo-American Law* (Indianapolis: The Bobbs-Merrill Co., 1932), pp. 49–72.

may not do in safety and without interference from others. Without them our social relations might rapidly degenerate into ruthless exploitation and destructive conflict.

The law, however, must be seen as only one of a number of sets of social norms, that is, rules and standards for the guidance and regulation of human behavior, which every society must establish and preserve if it is to survive. These norms, varying in rationality, complexity, and compulsiveness, and tending to express the dominant values of the group,[42] are woven into a system of social control, part of which, including the law, is highly formalized and carries with it the weight of institutionalized authority; but much of it is informal, consisting of such influences as public opinion, gossip, the praise and condemnation of the community, and the respect and ridicule of friends and acquaintances. Nevertheless, because of its definition of crimes and prescription of penalties by legislative and judicial action, its general applicability to all members of the group, and its enforcement by political agencies with the full support of the authority of the state, the law has a specificity, universality, and officiality not possessed by other parts of the system of social control.[43]

Although we need the regulations provided in the law, we must also be protected from officials who are placed in positions of authority. This, then, is another function that the criminal law can perform and thus another reason why we need it. Everywhere in our society we have insisted that limitations be imposed upon the exercise of authority by officials through the prescription and application of specific rules. This is known as the principle of legality, and it functions in our culture in four significant ways.[44]

First, it means that no conduct shall be criminal unless it is so described by the law. In this way each person can determine what is considered to be criminal and insist that when he is accused, specific charges must be made against him so that he may be able to prepare an adequate defense. Despite the protection that this guarantee affords, there are some who would eliminate the specific definitions of crimes and bring to court all those who are "socially dangerous." Those who argue for this

[42] See Chapter 3 for a discussion of the functional relationship between law and culture. For an analysis of the functional relationship between the law on theft and culture see Jerome Hall, *Theft, Law and Society* (Indianapolis: The Bobbs-Merrill Co., Inc., 1935).

[43] For additional reading on the subject of social control, see F. J. Davis, H. H. Foster, Jr., C. R. Jeffery, and E. E. Davis, *Society and the Law* (New York: The Free Press of Glencoe, 1962), pp. 7, 14–18, 39–43, 64–90, 266, 267, 300, 301; Richard T. LaPiere, *A Theory of Social Control* (New York: McGraw-Hill Book Co., Inc., 1954); Edward A. Ross, *Social Control* (New York: The Macmillan Co., 1916).

[44] Hall, *General Principles of Criminal Law*, pp. 19–60.

change do not tell us by what standards persons would be so judged, but apparently the decision would be made by specialists who unfortunately at present cannot be equipped with a systematic science of human behavior. Thus we are left in great doubt as to what this would involve; but it is well to remember that, simply by calling the one in authority a criminologist, or a psychologist, or a psychiatrist instead of a judge, we neither miraculously endow him with an omniscience to penetrate the fog of our ignorance regarding human behavior nor suddenly make him less susceptible to the temptation to abuse power. We have but to study the unfortunate results of such experiments in the totalitarian countries of Europe if we would learn what such abuse of power can mean. Therefore, in answer to those who protest that we must stress the criminal and not the crime, it should be explained that the question is not so simple. It is not one or the other, but rather a matter of emphasizing *both* the criminal and the crime, for the criminal can be protected against his accusers only by a specific definition of his crime in the law.

Second, the principle of legality means that no person shall be punished except in pursuance of a statute which provides a penalty for the crime. If anything at all can be done to any convicted person, then any guarantee that he has against the abuse of power vanishes. This does not mean that increased flexibility cannot be introduced into the law—for example, by the passage of indeterminate sentence laws and probation and parole legislation—but it does mean that checks must be included in the law to restrict the exercise of the authority involved.

Third, the principle of legality entails the strict interpretation of both statute law and the law of precedent. This requires the judge to adhere to the authoritatively established and unequivocal meaning of words. He may not, simply because another case is somewhat similar to the one under consideration or because a statute might be stretched to apply to a case, use this as a basis for the application of the statute or the precedent to the case before him. This practice in the law is termed "judicial legislation." Its use might readily lead to the destruction of the legislative branch of our government and the centralization of great power in our judges, for it can readily be seen that all cases are similar in some respects, that some means can always be found for stretching a statute to apply to a case, and that thus all bounds to the authority of a court could soon be broken down.

Fourth, the principle of legality forbids retroactivity in our criminal law. This further protects the accused, for it means that a legislative body may not enact any law which (1) makes an act committed before its passage, and which was innocent when done, criminal and punishes it, (2) aggravates a crime and makes it greater than when committed, (3) changes the punishment and inflicts a greater or different punishment than that which was prescribed at the time of the act, or (4) changes the rules of evidence so that less or different testimony is sufficient to convict than was required when the act was committed.[45] A law which is designed to accomplish any of these purposes is known as an ex post facto law, and the Constitution of the United States forbids Congress or any state to enact this type of legislation.

Thus, the operation of the principle of legality protects the individual from abuse of authority by public officials. It is true that in doing this it permits some criminals to escape punishment, but that is a price that most of us would gladly pay in order to preserve our liberties and guard ourselves from the threat of centralized power.

There remains another aspect of this function of the law to which we should direct our attention. It will be recalled that the criminal law not only restricts but also facilitates social relationships in general. It should now be explained that it performs a similar dual function in regard to the members of the legal profession. As we have seen, it curbs them in the use of their power, but we must also observe that its firmly established rules, doctrines, and principles provide a solid foundation upon which can be erected standards of ethics and proficiency and the security of a career. Through the administration of the law, knowledge of human behavior is deepened, legal research is encouraged, and efficient procedure is achieved. About it are woven splendid traditions of fairness and justice, and its symbols and concepts become fine tools in the skilled hands of its practitioners. Thus the law which evokes and fosters the legal profession is in turn strengthened and enriched by it.

LIMITATIONS OF THE CRIMINAL LAW

We should now be able to understand why the criminal law is important and how it serves a valuable purpose in our society, but we must also learn to appreciate its limitations. As we have seen, the criminal law is a body of rules regarding prohibited forms of behavior for which penalties are prescribed. Those who are entrusted with its administration are, therefore, primarily, but by no means exclusively, concerned with whether or not a person has behaved in some prohibited way. Thus the emphasis is upon the crime rather than upon the criminal, and some very important facts about the criminal do not come within the purview of the law at all, while some others are considered only because they are directly related to the essential elements of the crime in question.

For example, as we have already learned, the law is usually very much interested in the intent, or purpose, of the person who is being charged with a crime; but since, except in a few instances, a bad motive will not

[45] Miller, pp. 35–37.

make an act a crime, nor a good one prevent an act from becoming a crime, the law is not primarily concerned with motive. Nor would the law be primarily concerned with the type of personality of the accused, nor in how he became the kind of person that he is, nor how his personality might be changed. But it is obvious that different kinds of persons, with different kinds of personalities, backgrounds, and motives, and requiring different kinds of treatment, may commit the same kind of crime. Three different men may all be arrested for burglary. One may be a college student who has begun a career of crime in order to secure money for his educational expenses. One may be a professional criminal who specializes in the theft of jewelry. The third may be a sexually maladjusted person who breaks into houses for the purpose of attacking women. How different these three men are! And yet the law is first of all concerned with the fact that they all committed the crime of burglary.

Furthermore, so far as the law does interest itself in facts about criminals, most of its attention is directed toward a particular criminal. Its emphasis is upon a single personality rather than upon how this personality has developed and functioned in interaction with other personalities. Now, although it is not to be denied that one can learn a great deal about an individual just by a study of him as an individual, it is equally obvious that much about him will escape the attention of one who does not see the person in his relationship with others, that is, in his interaction with others in group life. Here, then, is another limitation of the law.

A third limitation appears when we realize that the law stresses the rational elements in human behavior and largely neglects the nonrational. With its emphasis upon will and intent, upon the threat of prescribed penalties as a deterrent of crime, the law counts heavily upon the role of reason in human behavior. But research in the social sciences has taught us that man is greatly influenced by habit and emotion, and so important aspects of his behavior lie beyond the calculation of the law.

The tendency of the law to regard itself as an entity apart from the culture to which it is functionally related constitutes a fourth limitation. This characteristic emerges naturally from the tightly integrated system of principles and doctrines which, being handed down from generation to generation in the legal profession, creates a false impression of independence and self-perpetuation. Members of the legal profession tend to forget that the law came into existence to meet human needs, and for them, therefore, the law tends to become an end in itself. Instead of considering crime as a possible indication that the law may not be serving man's needs and that therefore it should be revised, lawyers are inclined to see in crime an unmistakable sign that the law should be made more severe. And yet social science has demonstrated not only that there are many forms of social control but also that the law is merely one of the less effective forms of such control. We know, too, that unless a law is supported by public opinion there is a tendency for it to be disregarded, and thus it may actually contribute to the increase of disrespect of all law.

We have seen that the law looks to precedent for guidance. This makes for stability in the law and certainty in its interpretation, but it also creates in the law a resistance to change. Social change, consequently, may leave the law hopelessly behind and bring into bold relief this fifth limitation of the law. In this way, legislation that at one time greatly helped man in meeting his problems may become largely nominal or may in itself constitute a serious obstacle to his social adjustment.

From this discussion it can be seen that the law tends to emphasize the crime rather than the criminal, the individual rather than the group, the rational rather than the nonrational, the entity of the law rather than its cultural relationship, and the static rather than the dynamic. This does not mean that the law should necessarily do otherwise or that it should be abandoned in favor of something else. It simply means that in serving its purpose the law necessarily has certain limitations and that, if a deeper and broader understanding of crime is to be achieved, the law must be supported by other professions which see the same problem from different points of view. The sociologist in his efforts to understand the problem of crime has made use of the concept "social problem," and to an examination of this concept we shall devote the next chapter.

3

Crime as a Social Problem

MEANING OF SOCIAL PROBLEMS

The term "social problem" has been defined in various ways by different sociologists,[1] but it seems to be generally agreed among them that a social problem exists when there is a situation which involves a considerable number of persons, which some persons deem to be a threat to certain values, and which can be dealt with only through collective action. According to this definition, then, a situation does not become a social problem until some persons are aware of its existence and have come to the conclusion that it constitutes a threat to certain values cherished by them and that they must work together "to do something about it."

It should now be clear why sociologists call a crime a social problem, for crime involves all of the elements included in the definition presented above. The existence of larceny, for example, means that there is a situation in which some persons act in such a way that certain property values,

[1] For some definitions of the term "social problem," the reader is referred to the following: J. H. S. Bossard, *Social Change and Social Problems* (New York: Harper and Bros., 1938); Lawrence Guy Brown, *Social Pathology* (New York: Appleton-Century-Crofts, Inc., 1942); J. F. Cuber and R. A. Harper, *Problems of American Society: Values in Conflict* (New York: Henry Holt and Co., 1951); M. A. Elliott and F. E. Merrill, *Social Disorganization* (New York: Harper and Bros., 1961); Robert E. L. Faris. *Social Disorganization* (New York: The Ronald Press Co., 1955); J. M. Gillette and J. M. Reinhardt, *Current Social Problems* (New York: American Book Co., 1937); Abbott P. Herman, *An Approach to Social Problems* (New York: Ginn and Co., 1949); Joseph S. Himes, "Value Analysis in the Theory of Social Problems," *Social Forces,* XXXIII (March, 1955), 259–62; P. B. Horton and G. R. Leslie, *The Sociology of Social Problems* (New York: Appleton-Century-Crofts, Inc., 1960); Edwin M. Lemert, *Social Pathology* (New York: McGraw-Hill Book Co., Inc., 1951); Francis E. Merrill, "The Study of Social Problems," Discussion by Albert K. Cohen, Ernest R. Mowrer, and Stuart A. Queen, *American Sociological Review,* XIII (June, 1948), 251–62; R. K. Merton and R. A. Nisbet, *Contemporary Social Problems* (New York: Harcourt, Brace, and World, Inc., 1961); W. Wallace Weaver, *Social Problems* (New York: William Sloane Associates, 1951); Willard Waller "Social Problems and the Mores," *American Sociological Review,* I (Dec., 1936), 922–33.

which are not respected by them but which are held dear by other persons, are endangered and that these other persons have been influential enough to have society so organized that collective action is taken through law-enforcement agencies to combat this threat. Such other crimes as murder, rape, burglary, and bigamy may likewise be used as examples in order to show the applicability of the concept "social problem" to acts which have been defined as crimes by the law.

Sociologists have emphasized that social problems have certain other important characteristics which are not necessarily implied in the definition which has been given here. The first of these is *multiple causation,* which means that an explanation for a social problem cannot be found in the operation of any one factor in society but must be sought in an analysis of the interaction of many factors. Furthermore, all social problems are *interrelated,* and we can neither understand nor attempt to solve them unless we recognize this fact. In addition, every social problem has the characteristic of *relativity,* and we must see it as relative to a particular place and a certain time.

An examination of the problem of crime will reveal that it, too, has these three characteristics. As we shall see, crime is not caused by heredity, poverty, or mental deficiency, but by the interaction of all these and many other factors. Moreover, it is obvious that crime is interrelated with other social problems, for example, unemployment, divorce, drug addiction, and mental disorders. It is equally obvious that any program for dealing with crime will be strengthened by programs designed to reduce other social problems, such as prostitution, illegitimacy, and poverty. Finally, it is apparent that crime is relative to time and place, that what is defined as crime today may not be so defined tomorrow, and that it is one thing in a simple rural society and quite another in a complex industrial community.

SOCIAL PROBLEMS AS AN INDICATOR OF SOCIAL DISORGANIZATION

Social problems have still another characteristic. They are an indicator of social disorganization, which may be defined as the phase of social change that is marked by "a decrease of the influence of existing social rules of behavior upon individual members of the group."[2] The onset of

[2] W. I. Thomas and Florian Znaniecki, *The Polish Peasant* (New York: Alfred A. Knopf, Inc., 1927), II, p. 1128. Merton defines social disorganization in terms of status and role and states that it "refers to inadequacies or failures in a social system of interrelated statuses and roles such that the collective purposes and individual objectives of its members are less fully realized than they could be in an alternative workable system" (Merton and Nisbet, p. 720). For a summary of the literature on the subject, consult: Stuart A. Queen, "Social Disorganization," *Sociology and Social Re-*

this phase of social change, therefore, is indicated by the increase in the number of the situations which we have defined as social problems. Naturally, the greater the amount of social disorganization[3] in a society, the larger the number of social problems it will have; but, on the other hand, a society may have many social problems without necessarily having social disorganization.

It is important to note that social disorganization is a phase of social change. No society, however simple or isolated, is ever without social change, which in a complex industrial society such as ours assumes great proportions. Even in the most stable society, complete conformity to the established rules of behavior is never achieved, and in highly unstable societies, social disorganization may become so widespread that revolution results. As change occurs, attitudes regarding social values vary, sometimes approaching consensus (social reorganization) and sometimes moving away from it (social disorganization), and this variation in turn expresses itself in the decrease and increase of social problems. But—and this is significant—since every society has a certain amount of nonconformity to the established rules of behavior, every society, if for no other reason, always has some social problems.

The amount of social disorganization is the resultant of the interaction between the divisive and cohesive forces at work in society. Some parts of society are always more organized or disorganized than others, and some may be organized while others are disorganized. Regardless of these variations, however, the resultant is measured in terms of the dominant values of society, although the very maintenance of these values, which are always opposed by some individuals and groups, may be a factor in the increase of social problems. Moreover, whereas society as a whole is organized or disorganized in terms of the dominant values, groups within it may be organized or disorganized in terms of their own values, and these subcultures in turn may be contributing to social disorganization.

To describe with any degree of adequacy the forces which have been transforming modern American society would be a monumental task, manifestly beyond the limitations of the present discussion. It is sufficient for our purposes merely to indicate that such interrelated factors as the unprecedented movement of populations, the amazing utilization of natural wealth, the rapid accumulation of inventions and discoveries, the acceleration of transportation and communication, the growth of eco-

---

search, XLII (Jan.–Feb., 1958), 167-75. See also Elliott and Merrill, pp. 5, 23–41, 46, 457; Reece McGee, *Social Disorganization in America* (San Francisco: Chandler Publishing Co., 1962).

[3] Social reorganization and social disorganization may be thought of as states or as processes. Thus, social reorganization is the state or process in which there is an increase of the influence of existing social rules of behavior upon individual members of the group.

nomic specialization and interdependence, the increase in the complexity of economic organization, the rise of metropolitan communities, the decline of rural life, the shifting of occupational patterns—all these and many more, with their far-reaching social implications, have operated to produce great and rapid changes in our society. Our failure to cope with these changes has been a major cause of the increase in the social problems of our country.[4]

Sociologists have used various other concepts to provide us with greater understanding about the way in which social problems arise. Some of the most important of these intellectual tools, as well as the manner in which they have been used for this purpose, will be presented here, although the following discussion is not intended to be a systematic treatment of the subject.

CULTURE AND SOCIAL PROBLEMS

Man adjusts himself to the world of nature, but he also modifies that world and thus creates a man-made environment. All about him he has built up an accumulation of houses, factories, machinery, tools, techniques, customs, and ideas, which have become essential to his life. It is this artificial environment of material objects and ideas that social scientists have in mind when they speak of "culture." *Culture*, therefore, may be defined as all of the transmittable results of living together. It would be a mistake, however, to think of this crystallization of man's experience as something that merely imposes controls and restrictions. Obviously, it does this—and here the criminal law plays an important role—but it also provides channels through which our interests can be developed and our wishes satisfied.

The nonmaterial culture is composed of patterns of behavior, or so norms, which the group develops for the purpose of facilitating ment to situations that have occurred repeatedly in the past. O plest level these patterns appear as folkways, "the spontaneous, unpre-

---

[4] Merton maintains that to confine the study of social problems to those circumstances that are expressly defined as problems by members of a society, which he defines as manifest social problems, is arbitrarily to disregard conditions which are also dysfunctional to values held by people in that society, although not recognized by them as being so. He admits, however, that present limitations of knowledge place serious obstacles in the way of scientific detection and analysis of such conditions, which he defines as latent social problems. The author of this text prefers to apply the term "sociological problems" to the conditions which Merton calls "latent social problems" (Merton and Nisbet, pp. 708-23). The distinction that is thus made between sociological problems and social problems clearly recognizes that although studies and advice by experts are important, in a republic the decision regarding the existence of social problems must be made by the people, who may even decide— and indeed, have the right to decide—that they are willing to pay the price of having certain social problems in order to preserve certain values.

meditated, common ways of acting," the violation of which elicits only mild disapproval. When patterns of behavior are related to group welfare and are vested with definite ideas of right and wrong, they become mores and their infraction provokes moral indignation. Enforced by public opinion, the mores strongly influence our attitudes toward sex, property, and the persons of others, and so it can be seen how important it is for the criminal law to have their support. Still other patterns of behavior are considered of such importance to the group welfare that certain members of the group are given the responsibility of preserving and enforcing them. When in this way the pattern of behavior becomes enforced not merely by public opinion, as the mores are, but by authority, a social institution is created. A social institution, therefore, may be defined as a complex, integrated organization of group behavior, established in the culture, meeting some persistent need or want, and enforced by authority.[5] Although the law depends upon the mores for much of its effectiveness, this does not mean that it cannot initiate changes in them. Indeed, in our rapidly changing society, where many of the folkways and mores have lost some of their meaning and effectiveness, we must rely to an increasing extent upon the law and its influence for the regulation of our complex social relationships. However, there is a point beyond which reliance upon the law as a substitute for the convictions of the people marks the death of a republic and the usurpation of power by an excessively centralized government.

Characteristics of Social Institutions. Since the criminal law is one of the social institutions, it is important to understand their characteristics. Social institutions are interdependent and functionally related to one another and to the folkways and mores, without whose support they tend to lose their meaning and influence. No one institution stands alone, and in no sense does each constitute a distinct entity. Rather, economic, domestic, political, religious, and all other institutions function together, each acting and reacting upon all others and helping to produce the organic whole which we call society. The family, for example, influences the school, the church, and the state and is acted upon by them and reacts to changes in them.

[5] For further reading on the subject of culture, consult: Charles Horton Cooley, Robert Cooley Angell, and Lowell Juilliard Carr, *Introductory Sociology* (New York: Charles Scribner's Sons, 1933), pp. 78–98, 402–15; William Graham Sumner, *Folkways* (Boston: Ginn and Co., 1906); Edward Sapir, *Selected Writings*, edited by David G. Mandelbaum (Berkeley and Los Angeles: University of California Press, 1958), pp. 305–85; Ralph Linton, *The Tree of Culture* (New York: Alfred A. Knopf, 1959), pp. 29–60. For a critical review of the concepts and definitions of culture, see A. L. Kroeber and Clyde Kluckhohn, *Culture* (New York: Random House, Inc., 1963).

For the purpose of illustrating the importance of the interdependence of institutions, suppose we take the case of Jimmy Smith. Jimmy's home was broken by divorce, his mother was an alcoholic and desperate in her poverty, and he ran the streets with a gang of older toughs that "rolled" drunks and plundered empty houses. At length he stole a car, and at the age of fourteen he was brought before the juvenile court.

"Oh," you may say, "it's no wonder, for wasn't Jimmy's home broken by divorce?"

Yes, it was, but then so are many other homes that do not produce delinquents.

"Well," you will probably reply, "then certainly it was his mother. She was no good, was she? An alcoholic and all that . . ."

Yes, undoubtedly his mother's drunkenness was a factor in the delinquency of Jimmy. But perhaps this in turn was the result of her poverty, which was caused in part by her divorce. And where in this case were the church, the school, and the welfare agencies? if they had been alert, might they not have prevented Jimmy's delinquency? And so we come to realize that his case is not so simple after all—that a number of institutions (familial, economic, political, religious, educational, and welfare) have interacted with his hereditary traits to cause his problem; and that stable homes, economic security, good schools, and thriving churches make the task of law-enforcement agencies much easier.

Our age has been marked by the shifting of functions from one institution to another. In this movement of functions the church and the family have lost, while industry and the state have gained. However, the great growth of the state and industry has not come entirely from this source, for inventions, the development of technology, and the increase and mobility of populations have in themselves forced these institutions to expand. So at the very time when the need of new controls is increasing, the family and the church, institutions that in the past have been important agencies of control, have been declining in strength and influence. It is not surprising, therefore, that delinquency and crime have increased and that industry and the state, saddled with a crushing burden of responsibility, have failed to cope successfully with these problems and have in some ways actually contributed to their growth.

Institutions, in fulfilling their functions, operate through physical equipment, such as furniture, offices, and buildings, and various designated persons, such as parents, teachers, directors, and public officials, whose duty it is to carry out the purposes of the institutions. And yet these are not indispensable to institutions, the essential part of which is the group behavior patterns deemed necessary for group welfare. So it is that we may place our courts in fine edifices and staff them with numerous officials, but if the law has lost its vitality and ceased to be meaningful in terms of the needs of the people, buildings and officials will not protect our courts from the rot of formalism and eventual destruction.[6]

Culture and Social Change. We have already explained that no society is ever completely without change. It is now necessary to add that non-material innovations, technological changes, population growth and mobility, vested interests, emotional attachment to the past, and many other factors cause the different parts of culture to change at different rates of speed, and therefore the parts of culture tend to diverge from one another. Since the parts of culture are interrelated and interdependent, the fact that the parts change at different rates of speed is of significance to the student of social problems. If some parts of culture diverge from others in the process of social change, it is evident that a strain must be placed upon a social structure in which all parts are interrelated and interdependent, that existing social institutions will not adequately meet human needs, and that social values will thus collide, as culture conflicts, in situations which we have defined as social problems. In America the rapidity of technological development has placed a great strain upon the home, the church, the state, and the economic institutions themselves as new needs have demanded new patterns of adjustment. The employment of women and children outside of the home, the periodic unemployment of many persons, the congestion of large numbers of workers in our great cities, the uprooting and mobility of our people—all these to a large extent can be traced to this technological development, and all, too, contribute to the increase of our serious problems of crime and delinqency.

It should be clear, then, that as the parts of culture diverge, without the necessary counteracting adjustments, there appears eventually that phase of social change which is marked by "a decrease of the influence of existing social rules of behavior upon individual members of the group." This, as we have explained, is what we mean by social disorganization, the onset of which is indicated by the increase of social problems. We should now be able to understand how sociologists have used the concepts "culture," "culture lag," and "culture conflict" in order to give us greater insight into the rise of crime, unemployment, divorce, and other social problems.[7]

[6] For additional reading on the subject of social institutions, see Kingsley Davis, *Human Society* (New York: The Macmillan Co., 1948), pp. 435–638; James K. Feibleman, *The Institutions of Society* (London: George Allen and Unwin, Ltd., 1956); J. O. Hertzler, *American Social Institutions* (Boston: Allyn and Bacon, Inc., 1961); Constantine Panunzio, *Major Social Institutions* (New York: The Macmillan Co., 1939).

[7] J. B. Bury, *The Idea of Progress* (New York: Dover Publications, Inc., 1955); Joseph Kirk Folsom, *Culture and Social Progress,* (New York: Longmans, Green and Co., 1928); L. T. Hobhouse, *Morals in Evolution* (New York: Henry Holt and Co., 1915); William Fielding Ogburn, *Social Change* (New York: The Viking Press, Inc., 1928).

THE GROUP AND SOCIAL PROBLEMS

The rise of social problems has been explained also in terms of the *group*, which may be defined as "two or more people in a state of social interaction."[8] One form of association that has always been essential and fundamental in every human society is the *primary group*. Some important examples of this type of group are the family, the old-fashioned neighborhood, and the spontaneous playgroup of children. In other words, primary groups are those groups which are "characterized by intimate face-to-face association and cooperation."[9] They are the nursery of human nature, the soil in which the roots of social institutions are nourished. In them, the foundation of the personality is laid down, basic ideals and attitudes are created, and the individual members are fused into a common whole, involving the sort of sympathy and mutual identification for which "we" is the natural expression. This is not to say that there is no friction or disagreement in primary groups. Opportunities for self-expression and the pursuit of individual interests are present, and quarrels and conflicts occur; but these tend to be checked by common loyalties and spontaneous controls that arise out of the "feeling of belonging together."[10] This cohesiveness is time after time dramatically exhibited in the courtroom where discarded wives and neglected children rally about accused men to protect them and their family names from outside dangers.

In Western civilization, especially in the United States, primary groups have been sweepingly undermined by such developments as industrialization, urbanization, and the amazing growth of new methods of transportation and communication. Other forms of association, more attractive and exciting, are tending to crowd out the neighborhood, the spontaneous playgroup, and even the home. The resulting decline of primary groups has meant a corresponding increase in that type of association which sociologists have termed *secondary*. In primary groups, people meet in intimate face-to-face association, unconstrained by artificiality and special purpose; "in secondary groups, on the other hand, they are functioning units in an organization, or mere acquaintances at best. *Secondary association is partial association*. It is association narrowed down by special purpose, by communication at a distance, by rules, by social barriers, or

[8] Kimball Young, *Sociology* (New York: American Book Co., 1949), p. 617. See also Davis, pp. 289–391; George C. Homans, *The Human Group* (New York: Harcourt, Brace and Co., Inc., 1950).

[9] Charles Horton Cooley, *Social Organization* (New York: Charles Scribner's Sons, 1929), p. 23. We are indebted to Cooley for the introduction of the term "primary groups" into sociological literature. He called them primary because they are first both in time and importance.

[10] Cooley, Angell, and Carr, pp. 55, 56.

by the casual nature of contact."[11] Corporations, unions, lodges, political parties, and radio publics are examples of secondary association. Thus, what we are witnessing is the emergence of the individual from the close bonds of primary group life and his circulation on secondary levels of association. In other words, instead of just being in close contact with relatives, neighbors, and friends, all of whom have about the same set of values, the individual to an increasing extent is now interacting in secondary group relationships, where other individuals present only special facets of their personalities, and in this way he is coming into contact with different, and often conflicting, sets of values. Consequently, adjustment in terms of the values that an individual has learned in his home may expose him to ridicule, embarrassment, exploitation, or even criminal prosecution elsewhere.[12]

Subjected to such pressures, many individuals change their behavior as they go from group to group and tend to bring it into conformity with values of the group in which they find themselves. This tendency can be seen in the behavior of youths who conduct themselves in accordance with certain values when in the home but follow different ones at school or with the gang. Since the number of choices for the satisfaction of needs is in this way increased, the compulsiveness of custom and tradition is reduced and the challenge of new situations is met by demands for the adoption of new sets of values.[13]

As the secondary nature of social relationships in America has increased, many persons who have been torn from their cultural roots in primary groups have become oppressed by loneliness and urban impersonality and have sought comfort and security in such special-interest groups as labor unions and business associations. Furthermore, although it is true that increased division of labor and specialization have brought greater interdependence of individuals, this interdependence is unstable, external, and segmental and exposed to the shattering blows of rapid social change. As a result, large groups of people, in their confusion and uncertainty,

[11] *Ibid.*, p. 214.

[12] In the analysis of primary and secondary groups, it must be recognized that intimacy is a quality that varies in degrees from group to group, that there are not just two decidedly different kinds of groups, as far as this quality is concerned, but that there is a gradation of groups all the way from those in which relations are very close to those in which relations are very distant. Nevertheless, since an increasing number of our social relationships are moving along this gradation away from great closeness, which is at one extreme, toward great distance, which is at the other, it is still accurate to say that they are becoming more and more secondary in nature.

[13] Talcott Parsons, *The Social System* (Glencoe, Ill.: The Free Press, 1951), pp. 68–150; Georg Simmel, *Conflict*, translated by Kurt H. Wolff, *The Web of Group-Affiliations*, translated by Reinhard Bendix (Glencoe, Ill.: The Free Press, 1955); Ralph H. Turner, "Value-Conflict in Social Disorganization," *Sociology and Social Research*, XXXVIII (May–June, 1954), pp. 301–8.

have become highly susceptible to propaganda and eagerly listen to demagogues who promise magical cures for all human ills. Often, too, such people turn to materialism as a common measure for the great variety of experiences in which they are engulfed. Thus, a man is measured by the length of his car; a city, by the extent of its area; a business, by the size of its office building; a family, by the gadgets in its home; a state, by the proliferation of its bureaus; and a church, by the height of its spire. Some writers have used the term "mass society" to characterize this vast mass of culturally uprooted individuals, who in our modern world find themselves fastened together by the clamps of an external interdependence which provides man with little nourishment for his emotional needs. It is this "mass society," with its confusion of values, that has helped to create a climate so favorable to the rise of social problems.[14]

Secondary Groups and Social Control. Another profitable way of analyzing the significance of the decline of primary social relationships is in terms of social control. Conflicts that threaten the integrity of primary groups are quickly detected and usually blocked by informal methods, such as scolding, ridicule, reproach, and gossip, which spring from the emotional unity of the group. The primary group, therefore, can provide an excellent agency of social control. In secondary groups, on the other hand, individuals are associated in only an indirect, casual, and specialized way, are not intimately acquainted, and so are not quickly responsive to the wishes, needs, and interests of one another. In short, the decline of primary groups has meant a weakening of an important agency of social control; and laws, rules, and regulations, which are less efficient than the methods of primary groups, have had to be substituted in many areas of social relationships.

What this weakening of primary groups means can be shown by reference to the changes that have taken place in the family and the neighborhood in America. With the passing years, industrialization, urbanization, and mobility have not only transformed the functions of the family, but have freed its members from much of its control. The social cohesion of the American family, which in the early days derived much of its strength from the many common enterprises that were conducted in the home, has been reduced, and the members of the family are finding their work and the satisfaction for many of their wishes outside the home. In essence, this means that for the first time in many centuries mankind is seeking to maintain a family life that is not held together by the coercive bonds of a common economic enterprise.[15]

[14] For one view regarding the changes that have taken place in the character of the people of modern America, see David Riesman, with Nathan Glazer and Reuel Denney, *The Lonely Crowd* (New Haven: Yale University Press, 1950).

[15] Bossard, pp. 595–613.

The neighborhood, too, has been greatly changed by the years. Such factors as the improvement of transportation and communication, the encroachment of expanding industries, the increased mobility of population, the coming of immigrants from distant shores, the growth of population, and the accumulation of wealth have reduced the social cohesion of the neighborhood. Stripped of important common interests and emotional bonds, often filled to the point of congestion with many people from different cultural backgrounds, usually occupied by those who have not lived there long and expect to move again soon, often deprived of the intelligence and stabilizing influence of the better educated, who tend to be constantly on the move in search of greater opportunities, many neighborhoods are now mere camping grounds for modern gypsies who have but a transitory interest in their surroundings and little respect for the interests and property rights of others. Instead of being an agency of control for socially accepted values, they are often a breeding place of vice, crime, and delinquency.

Membership and Reference Groups. Groups have also been classified into membership and reference groups. A *membership group* is one in which a person is recognized by others as belonging. Examples of this type of group are the family, the lodge, the bridge club, the union, and the religious sect. A *reference group* is one the values of which influence a person's attitudes and behavior regardless of whether or not he is recognized by others as a member.[16] Thus, one school boy may try to imitate the daring exploits of a criminal gang, while another may make the "G-men" his idol and prepare himself to be a law-enforcement officer. For these two boys, the gang and the "G-men" are reference groups. The significant thing about a reference group is that its norms provide frames of reference which actually influence the attitudes and the behavior of a person. In modern society, where the primary group does not exert its former influence and where rapid means of communication and transportation widely disseminate different sets of values, many persons have reference groups in which they are not recognized by others as members. It becomes clear, therefore, why such reference groups are important in both the causation and prevention of crime and delinquency.[17]

[16] Theodore M. Newcomb, *Social Psychology* (New York: The Dryden Press, Inc., 1950), pp. 225–32.

[17] Groups have been classified in a number of other ways. For example, they have been divided into the small, extended, territorially defined, and transitory groups. For some of the rapidly increasing literature on small groups, see R. F. Bales, A. P. Hare, and E. F. Borgatta, "Structure and Dynamics of Small Groups: A Review of Four Variables," *Review of Sociology*, ed. Joseph B. Gittler (New York: John Wiley and Sons, Inc., 1957), pp. 391–422; R. F. Bales, "Small-Group Theory and Research," *Sociology Today*, eds. R. K. Merton, L. Broom, and L. S. Cottrell, Jr. (New York: Basic Books, Inc., 1959), pp. 293–305; A. P. Hare, E. F. Borgatta, and R. F. Bales, *Small Groups* (New York: Alfred A. Knopf, 1955).

We are now in a position to understand how sociologists have used the concept of the group to explain the origin and increase of social problems. According to some who emphasize this concept, a solution of these problems is to be found in the creation of new and greater sources of cooperation in and among secondary groups through education and legislation. Just how far they would let the primary groups decline is not clear, but it is a sobering thought that "no attempt to organize society on a non-primary basis has ever been permanently successful."[18]

THE SOCIAL PROCESS AND SOCIAL PROBLEMS

The rise of social problems has been discussed also in terms of the *social processes,* which are the fundamental ways in which men interact.[19] The two basic processes of group life are cooperation and opposition, the latter of which includes competition and conflict.[20] Heredity is a factor in both cooperation and opposition, as well as in other social processes, such as differentiation, stratification, accommodation, and assimilation, but any natural tendencies that man may have to strive for and against his fellow men are greatly influenced by his culture.

Thus, both criminals and noncriminals reared in our society, as they play their roles and strive for status in cooperation and opposition with others, are influenced by America's emphasis upon competition in the accumulation of wealth. Nor is it surprising that many criminals form large organizations, since so many of our law-abiding citizens seek the goods of the world in the same manner. And, as we should expect, the intensity of opposition in America may drive both the criminal and non-criminal organizations into greater and greater units of power and monopolistic combinations. In short, in the very violation of some of our laws criminals want the same things and use the same techniques and instruments to secure them as do law-abiding persons; but they proceed in a way which our society has defined as criminal. Of course, this observation is being made here not as an argument against competition in the amassing of wealth, but simply to call attention to the relationship that exists in every society between culture and the social processes and to the fact that both criminals and noncriminals are affected by this relationship.

In-Group and Out-Group Relationships. The social processes should be seen also in their relationship to the group. For this purpose, the classification of group life in terms of the in-group and the out-group is especially helpful. The *in-group* is "any association towards which we have a

[18] Cooley, Angell, and Carr, p. 56.

[19] William F. Ogburn and Meyer F. Nimkoff, *Sociology* (Boston: Houghton Mifflin Co., 1958), p. 144.

[20] Whereas competition is largely impersonal, conflict is direct, personal, and conscious.

sense of solidarity, of loyalty, friendliness, and cooperation." Members of the in-group are bound together by ties of sympathy, obligation, and affection; and their feeling of belonging together finds expression in such phrases as "we belong," "we believe," "we feel," and "we act." In crises, the members of the in-group, driven together by their common dangers, rally about such distinctive symbols as a banner or an anthem and close their ranks through the use of shibboleths. Seeking nourishment for our most basic emotional needs in the association of our in-groups, such as the family, the school, the church, and the gang, we tend to center our lives around the ones to which we belong.[21]

The *out-group* is "that association of persons toward which we feel a sense of disgust, avoidance, dislike, competition, aggression, fear, or even hatred."[22] It is the group toward which we direct our reproaches, ridicule, condemnation, prejudice, and imprecations. It is the objectionable family next door, the rival labor union, the ruthless enemy, the vicious syndicate, the ubiquitous police.

Although under primitive conditions there is a tendency for an entire society to be bound together as an in-group against all other societies as out-groups, in the modern world improved methods of communication and transportation have reduced this cleavage; but these and other factors have at the same time built up within a single society many special-interest groups which are in a constantly shifting in-group versus out-group relationship. In the modern world, therefore, since special-interest groups often become in-groups, many in-groups are secondary in nature, whereas under primitive conditions all in-groups are primary.

The in-group versus out-group relationship appears whenever two groups come into opposition, either in competition or in conflict. And whether a group is an in-group for a particular individual depends upon his identification with it in the process of cooperation. Thus, a criminal identifies himself with his gang and in cooperation with them opposes the law-enforcement authorities, who in their efforts against the gang strive to keep all other persons in the community in cooperation with them against the gang, in an in-group versus out-group relationship. In this way, ranks are solidified under the symbol of law and order against a common enemy. However, if the members of the gang are apprehended, their rehabilitation depends upon society's success in having them assimilated into the ranks of law-abiding citizens, who function in an in-group versus out-group relationship with those who are still criminals.

Furthermore, what is an in-group for a particular individual on one occasion may be an out-group for him on another. In the morning a youth may find himself aligned with members of his family against his gang, but

[21] Young, p. 26.
[22] *Ibid.*, pp. 26, 27.

later in the day the same youth in cooperation with members of his gang may be engaged in a fight against another gang. In this way, individuals in modern society are constantly shifting from one in-group to another in an ever-changing pattern of cooperation and opposition.

Other Social Processes. The analysis of other social processes provides us with additional insights into the causation of crime, the development of criminal careers, and the rehabilitation of prisoners. *Differentiation* is the process by which roles (or sets of socially expected and approved behavior patterns associated with statuses, or positions in a social structure) are ascribed or achieved in a society. Thus, in every society distinctive roles are played by the man, the woman, the child, the intelligent, the dull, the strong, and the weak, each role carrying with it certain rights, privileges, and responsibilities, and varying from time to time and place to place in terms of the prevailing culture. The role that a man plays as a law-abiding citizen tends to influence his behavior if he turns to crime. Hence a well-educated man, trained in accountancy, tends to commit some crime like embezzlement, whereas a poor laborer tends to perpetrate crimes like larceny or robbery. Furthermore, in a rapidly changing society like ours, many persons play sharply conflicting roles, and frustrated and confused, they may turn to crime as a solution for their troubles. Thus, a bank teller of moderate means, living in a good neighborhood, prominent in community activities, and striving to keep up with his friends and business associates, may misappropriate funds in order to send his children to college.

Stratification is the process by which castes, classes, and other status-giving groups are formed in a society. Since castes and classes differ in their standards of behavior and the opportunities which they give to their members, they are clearly related to criminality. Thus, a member of a low economic class may not have the same kind of sex morals as those in a higher economic class and therefore may not be inclined to abide by laws regarding sex enacted largely through the efforts of those in the higher class. And in an open-class society, where all are encouraged to climb from one class to another, an individual in a socially inferior group tends not to defer to those in socially superior groups, and his failure to obtain the material things that they have may fill him with bitterness and resentment and drive him into crime.

Accommodation is the process by which arrangements are worked out so that opposing individuals and groups can get along together. In dealing with crime, societies have always utilized various forms of accommodation. Sometimes it is a compromise, as, for example, when the prosecuting attorney reduces the severity of the charge in order to enlist the aid of one offender in the conviction of another. Sometimes it is toleration, as, for example, when a community permits prostitution and gambling to exist in certain areas in order to avoid the exhausting and expensive battle of repression. And sometimes it may be compulsory arbitration, as, for example, when a family court intervenes in a family relationship endangered by desertion and nonsupport.

Assimilation is the process by which divergent habits, attitudes, and ideas of two or more groups or individuals are fused into a common set of habits, attitudes, and ideas. In the field of crime, the process of assimilation operates when offenders more and more identify themselves with the world of crime, when later they participate in a prison rehabilitation program, and finally when after abandoning their life of crime, they become law-abiding citizens.[23]

In the study of society, each of the social processes may be considered separately, but it must be emphasized that they all coexist in every society and that they interweave and interact in an endless manner. Every society, therefore, may be visualized as a moving equilibrium in which cooperation and its related processes, which tend to unify and increase the conformity to the established rules of behavior, interact with opposition and its related processes, which tend to divide and reduce the conformity to the established rules of behavior. As sociologists have explained, when the divisive processes predominate, social disorganization develops and social problems increase.

In this chapter, we have undertaken an analysis of the way in which sociologists have used three of their most important concepts to explain the rise of social problems. In our treatment of the concepts "culture," "group," and "social process," each in turn has been stressed, although it should have been clear, as each was being discussed, that the presence of the other two was at all times implicit. In other words, culture, groups, and the social processes coexist and interact in every situation, and an understanding of all three provides us with three different ways of looking at a society. We should, therefore, use all three points of view in our examination of social problems in order to obtain a more adequate picture of their origin and development.

CONTRIBUTIONS OF THE SOCIAL-PROBLEMS APPROACH

The social-problems approach has made some important contributions to our understanding of crime. In the first place, unlike the legal approach, it persistently calls attention to the causation of crime; and by the use of

[23] Young, pp. 59–82; Ogburn and Nimkoff, pp. 121–98; Robert E. Park and Ernest W. Burgess, *Introduction to the Science of Sociology* (Chicago: University of Chicago Press, 1921), pp. 505–784; Kurt B. Mayer, *Class and Society* (New York: Random House, Inc., 1955); W. Lloyd Warner, with Marchia Meeker and Kenneth Eells, *Social Class in America* (New York: Harper and Bros., 1960); S. F. Nadel, *The Theory of Social Structure* (Glencoe, Ill.: The Free Press, 1957); Robert K. Merton, *Social Theory and Social Structure* (Glencoe, Ill.: The Free Press, 1957), pp. 121–94.

such intellectual tools as "culture," "group," and "social process," it seeks to identify some uniformities and regularities that can be used as a basis for generalizations, prediction, and control.

This approach also emphasizes the importance of group life, insists that we can understand the individual only as we see him in his relationships with others, and demonstrates that different kinds of social relationships affect human behavior in different ways and tend to produce and require different forms of control. Thus, it helps to counteract the point of view of the average person, who tends to see society as a series of more or less isolated relatives, friends, and acquaintances, and that of the legalist, who tends to see crime as a series of more or less unconnected acts committed by a procession of defendants in the dock before him.

Furthermore the social-problems approach, by the use of the concept "culture," clearly shows that crime and criminal law are functionally related to the whole system of behavior patterns in which, and through which, all men in society interact. Thus, it demonstrates that all men live by values and that an individual who commits a crime, like his fellows, is expressing himself in terms of values, albeit those that have been defined as criminal by organized society, but which nevertheless are being followed in varying degrees by others in his community. In this way, too, it shows that it is not the fear of legal penalties that keeps many persons from violating the law, but rather the desire to find love, respect, and security in terms of the values that are considered right among relatives, friends, and business associates. The mores thus constitute an important form of control, and this form of control will always exist regardless of what methods are used in dealing with criminals. Such an approach likewise makes clear that the criminal law, like all other social institutions, should have the support of the mores and that without it law enforcement becomes exceedingly difficult, if not impossible. By an analysis of the characteristics of social institutions, it reveals that they come into existence to meet human needs, that an institutional form, even though it persists for a long time, may not be the one that will most adequately meet the needs for which it came into existence, and that, since social institutions are interdependent, they constantly affect one another in their operation. The criminal law is thus shown to be not an entity, aloof and apart from the life of man, but, on the contrary, intimately related to it, being affected by, as well as affecting, man's familial, economic, religious, educational, and recreational activities. Therefore, if it is to remain vital and effective, there must not be too great a divergence between its rules, doctrines, and principles and the values of the society in which it functions.

The social-problems approach, by the use of the concept "social process," also demonstrates that criminality is but one of the many manifestations of the interaction between the processes of opposition and cooperation which coexist in every society. Thus, for example, it helps us to understand how both criminals and noncriminals play their roles, strive for status, and make adjustments in the crosscurrents of our rapidly changing society, and how the criminal law tends to express the values of the dominant groups and why it may favor them in its administration.

The social-problems approach makes four other significant contributions to our understanding of crime, and although they are implied in the ones already discussed, they will now be presented separately. This approach makes us aware of the relativity of crime. With its assistance, we can clearly see that different conditions tend to produce different values and that, therefore, crime is relative to time and place. We are thus enabled to be more objective about the criminal law and to understand why its provisions may have to be changed when a divergence develops between the law and the values of the society in which it is being administered. Unlike the legal approach, which tends to be static, this approach provides us with a dynamic interpretation.

Another contribution that this approach makes is its emphasis on multiple causation. It rejects any explanation of criminality that is expressed in terms of one factor; instead, it pictures crime as being produced by the interaction of many factors. It thus shows that the problem of crime is exceedingly complex; any program for its control or prevention must be many-sided in nature.

This approach also demonstrates the importance of the nonrational in human behavior. We are shown how man acquires many of his ideals, attitudes, and habits in the intense, emotional atmosphere of primary-group life and how these tend to resist later influences and to affect his behavior throughout his life. In this way, it gives considerable weight to habits and emotions in the life of man and helps to offset the emphasis that the legal approach places upon will and intent.

As a final contribution, this approach shows that all social problems are interrelated. It thus teaches us that many of the factors that cause other social problems also cause crime. Therefore we must make our crime-prevention programs broad enough to include efforts for the reduction of all social problems.

An examination of the contributions that the social problems approach has made to our understanding of crime will reveal that it tends to counteract the limitations of the legal approach. Indeed, in the very effectiveness with which it does this lie the roots of its own limitations.

LIMITATIONS OF THE SOCIAL-PROBLEMS APPROACH

When we begin to analyze the limitations of the social-problems approach to crime, we are immediately impressed with the tendency to minimize heredity and the geographical environment. With competent sociologists, this, of course, does not amount to a deliberate attempt to obscure the influence of these factors. Reference to their works will show that they include floods, famines, pestilences, and other disasters, as well as the maladaptation between inherited nature and culture, as causes of social problems; but at its best this amounts to a Parthian glance hurriedly thrown by the writer as he rushes by toward a consideration of the social factors. Naturally, one cannot expect a sociologist to have the time and training that are necessary to furnish us with a full treatment of heredity and the geographical environment, but because of this very fact the student of criminal behavior cannot afford to be satisfied with anything less than the most recent statements by the best-informed authorities in the field of biology and geography.

The social-problems approach likewise tends to minimize the individual. Although sociologists do point out that the individual and the group are but two aspects of the same thing—that is, just two different ways of looking at human life and each but an abstraction of what in its entirety is society[24]—nevertheless, in the development of their theories they are inclined to inflate the importance of the group until, in some cases, the individual is reduced to a mere shadowy thing that haunts the writer only in his rare moments of uncertainty. We are told of group conflicts, mass movements, mass media of communications, and group programs to the point where the individual ceases to have any reality. And yet, despite the fact that the individual must be seen in his relations with others, he does have a reality apart from the group. He is a unique combination of heredity and environment, and no personality organization is ever the same as the social organization in which it functions. Furthermore, although the sociologist speaks of "the group" in contrast to "the individual," it is well to remind ourselves that there is not just "the group" but a number of groups, even in the most homogeneous society, which gives a variety of opportunities for individual expression and a flexibility for individual adjustment that often seems to elude the comprehension of the group-minded sociologists. Again, one must hasten to disclaim any desire to require the sociologist to be an authority on all aspects of life. He, of course, is not; and if he is competent, he does not pretend to be such an authority. But we must remember that the sociologist has selected "the group" as the major unit of his study; and because of his specialization, therefore, he is not qualified to supply us with authoritative information on many phases of the individual's behavior. Instead, we must look to the biologist, the psychologist, and the psychiatrist to supplement the views of the sociologist.

[24] Charles Horton Cooley, *Human Nature and the Social Order* (New York: Charles Scribner's Sons, 1902), pp. 1–13.

As we have already explained, change is present in every society, and sometimes, as in the modern industrial community, it is great and rapid; but even when one appreciates this, one can still say that the social-problems approach tends to overemphasize the importance of change. It is here that the historian has an important contribution to make, because, with his principle of continuity, he can help us to understand that the stream of history is never broken as it flows from the past through the present into the future. When measured by the perspective that he can give, many of the developments that seem so tremendous today become but mere ripples upon the surface of this stream. Certainly, as we read the histories of France and Russia after their great revolutions, we cannot fail to be impressed with this truth. Yet, some sociologists entirely ignore this principle; and even competent ones have, by the use of the term "culture lag" rather than a more neutral term such as "culture divergence," colored our view of change and given the implication that we are always chasing change in a losing race against time. Thus the term "lag" carries a value judgment in favor of change and against those who fail to accept it, even before an objective study can be made to ascertain what it involves and whether it can be redirected. Although it is true that man may have to pay a price in serious problems if he clings to old values instead of adopting new ones,[25] it is also true that he may have to pay an even higher price if he surrenders the old in order to make way for the new. For example, he may have to pay the higher price in oppression and despotism if he gives great powers to a centralized government in order to avoid diversity of legislation, which is the price he may have to pay if he preserves the separate governments of the fifty states of the United States.

The failure to agree upon the meaning of important terms is another limitation of this approach. Indeed, this is a handicap to the entire field of sociology. Such terms as "social problem" and " social disorganization" are differently defined by different sociologists, and it is exceedingly difficult to learn their precise meaning by an analysis of sociological literature. The term "social disorganization," especially, has fallen into disrepute, and eventually it may have to be discarded. This is due in no small measure to the fact that it has sometimes been used to imply that any change is bad and that society must return to old rules of behavior in order to solve its problems. However, such a view is not warranted. Social change is a normal characteristic of human society, and the rules of behavior themselves may have to be changed in order to enable man to adjust to new social conditions. Nor is it true that all parts of society are disorganized at the same time. Although the net result of change

[25] Abbott P. Herman, *An Approach to Social Problems* (Boston: Ginn and Co., 1949), p. 31.

may be disorganization as measured by the dominant values, some parts of society may be more organized or disorganized than others, some may be organized while others are disorganized, and within the larger society, subcultures may be organized or disorganized in terms of their own values. The term "social disorganization," if properly used, will take all this into consideration.[26]

Moreover, the social-problems approach is vague and subjective. We are not given the answers to such questions as: How many persons must be involved before the situation becomes a social problem? How much of a threat is there to the values involved? How many persons do not have the values that are threatened? How can we ascertain what values are endangered? How can we determine precisely when social disorganization begins? It is clear that our techniques for the measurement of attitudes will have to be greatly improved before this approach can become something more than a provocative frame of reference.

Another limitation of this approach appears when we realize that, although it gives us a general statement regarding the nature of a social problem, it does not as yet provide us with an adequate basis for prediction and prevention. And we are not helped in this respect if we use the term "sociological problem" instead of the term "social problem" in order to make certain that "what ought to be," or the ethical question, is not confused with the formulation of generalizations regarding verifiable relationships, which is the scientific question.[27] The term "social problem" can be used in the scientific sense as long as it is not confused with its usage in the ethical sense and the sociologist, in his role of scientist, does not become an advocate. The term "sociological problem" would be helpful here only so far as it might carry with it the data to foresee, and the techniques to measure and prevent, the situations which we have called social problems. This, the term in itself cannot do, although there can be no objection to its use if it is believed that greater objectivity can thereby be achieved. What must be stressed, however, is that man has lived by values, is living by values, and will live by values, and that there will always be clashes of values. Even the mitigation of a problem brings in its wake new values and new clashes. There have always been philos-

---

[26] In order to emphasize the importance of the group factor in the causation of crime and delinquency, some writers prefer the term "differential group organization" instead of "social disorganization," thus indicating organization for criminal activities on one side and organization against criminal activities on the other. See for example, Edwin H. Sutherland, "Development of the Theory," The Sutherland Papers, eds. A. Cohen, A. Lindesmith, and K. Schuessler (Bloomington, Ind.: Indiana University Press, 1956), pp. 20, 21. But even if this is done, groups not organized in terms of the dominant values of the larger society can be designated as disorganized according to these values.

[27] George A. Lundberg, Foundations of Sociology (New York: The Macmillan Co., 1939), pp. 29–31.

ophers who have grasped the significance of this, although apparently some social scientists are just beginning to understand it.

The social-problems approach, because it tends to overemphasize the group and to minimize the individual, lends itself, under the guise of science, to the support of collectivism. Of course, such support is not necessarily given to collectivism simply because this approach is used. A competent sociologist who is fully aware of its limitations will guard against this possibility; and in his hands, it becomes an excellent frame of reference for a scientific study of society. However, some sociologists, intentionally or unintentionally, do employ it in such a way as to give support to a collectivistic, usually a socialistic, philosophy.

In partial explanation of this, it should be pointed out that sociologists are part of the mass society to which they have repeatedly called our attention; and so they, too, have been influenced by it and have found difficulty in securing a common basis for understanding the great variety of experiences that they have observed. Like many other persons who have lost their ability to make fine distinctions in the confusion of the mass society, some sociologists have glossed over the unknown, ignored intricate details, and sought a simple, neat, and final formula for the explanation of the problems of society. It is understandable, therefore, that they have tended to push the individual, with his troublesome uniqueness, into the background and that they have tended to make the group, which, they admit, is but one of the abstractions of human life, the basis of an entire philosophy of human life. At the same time, influenced by the drive for precision in the world of machines, they have tried to apply refined statistical techniques to their data even at the expense of squeezing out that which at present is not susceptible of statistical measurement, but which may be the essence of the problem. When one is dealing with a complex problem about which there is little reliable information, this mere shift in emphasis may be the difference between a valid and an invalid generalization.

Moreover, ethics and science are confounded in many books that use the social-problems approach, and certain values are invested with a false attractiveness through the implication, intentionally or unintentionally given, that they are based on the findings of science. This seems to stem from a failure to distinguish clearly and consistently between the nature of values and the conflict of values. Sociology has demonstrated that crime may emerge from a conflict of values, but science has not succeeded in proving that the acceptance of certain values will provide one with the "good life." When a writer refers to a certain pattern of behavior as exploitation or discrimination, he is disapproving of it in terms of his own set of values. And yet, from a scientific point of view, it might be recommended that those who are being "exploited," as measured by a particular set of values, be so indoctrinated that they not only accept this treatment but feel dishonored if they fail to receive it. Furthermore, this result could be achieved with all the more certainty if it is true, as many sociologists contend, that man has no freedom of will and that human behavior at any stated time is the only possible behavior, given its antecedents. Thus it is immaterial to the scientist, *as a scientist*, which side of a conflict of values is eliminated. The advocacy of either side carries one into the realm of ethics.[28]

This analysis of the limitations of the social-problems approach should not be permitted to obscure the important contributions that it has made to our understanding of crime. As in the case of the legal approach, its limitations, however, do mean that it must be supplemented by other approaches, such as those made by the geographer, the anthropologist, the biologist, the psychologist, and the psychiatrist.

[28] The difficulty of making a scientific analysis of social life has moved Merton to state that "would-be diagnoses of social disorganization are often little more than moral judgments rather than confirmable technical judgments about the workings of a social system" (Merton and Nisbet, p. 720). See also A. H. Hobbs, *Social Problems and Scientism* (Harrisburg, Pa.: The Stackpole Co., 1953); F. A. Hayek, *The Counter-Revolution of Science: Studies on the Abuse of Reason* (Glencoe, Ill.: The Free Press, 1952); William H. Whyte, Jr., *The Organization Man* (New York: Simon and Schuster, Inc., 1956), pp. 22-32.

4

Dimensions of the Problem

Although we cannot ascertain the exact dimensions of the problem of crime and delinquency in the United States, we can obtain some indication of their enormity by an examination of the *Uniform Crime Reports* of the Federal Bureau of Investigation and the publications of the United States Children's Bureau. The information contained in this chapter, therefore, is taken mainly from these two sources. However, it must be emphasized that this information is far from adequate and that the problem is much more serious than the available statistics indicate.[1]

CRIME TRENDS IN 1963

During 1963 an estimated total of 2,259,100 major crimes[2] were committed in the United States. As Table 1 shows, this represents a 10 per cent increase over the total for 1962 and 16 per cent increase over the three-year average for the years 1960 to 1962.[3]

Crimes against property—robbery, burglary, larceny ($50 and over), and auto theft—occurred with the highest frequency, contributing 92 per cent to the total of major crimes for 1963 and registering an 11 per cent

[1] For an evaluation of the sources of statistics on crime and delinquency in the United States, see Chapter 1.

[2] The term "major crimes" refers to the crimes of murder, nonnegligent manslaughter, forcible rape, robbery, aggravated assault, burglary, larceny ($50 and over), and auto theft. These crimes represent the index to criminality in this country and are tabulated by law-enforcement agencies as the offenses become known to them.

[3] The estimates of major crimes committed in the United States during 1963 are based on reports received from law-enforcement agencies serving 98 per cent of the population in metropolitan areas, 91 per cent of that in other urban areas, and 77 per cent of that in rural areas. In their combined coverage, these reports come from areas containing 92 per cent of the total population of the United States. However, since some important crimes, such as arson, sex crimes other than forcible rape, carrying concealed weapons, and embezzlement, are not included in the estimated totals of major crimes, the estimates must be considered an understatement of the problem.

Table 1. Estimated number of major offenses in the United States for 1963, and 3-year average for 1960–62.

Crime index classification	Estimated number of offenses		Change for 1963			
			Over 3-year average		Over 1962	
	1960–62 average	1963	Number	Per cent	Number	Per cent
Total	1,946,500	2,259,100	+312,600	+16	+208,500	+10
Murder and non-negligant man-slaughter	8,660	8,500	—150	—2	+100	+1
Forcible rape	16,100	16,400	+300	+2	+90	+1
Robbery	93,210	100,160	+6,940	+7	+4,900	+5
Aggravated assault .	134,500	147,800	+13,200	+10	+8,100	+6
Burglary	854,600	975,900	+121,200	+14	+83,100	+9
Larceny ($50 and over)	505,000	611,400	+106,400	+21	+71,500	+13
Auto theft	334,400	399,000	+64,600	+19	+40,600	+11

SOURCE: Federal Bureau of Investigation, *Uniform Crime Reports, 1963*, p. 2.

increase over 1962. Crimes against the person—murder, nonnegligent manslaughter, aggravated assault, and forcible rape—on othe other hand, showed a 5 per cent increase during the same period.

The increase in major crimes was general throughout the United States and ranged from 6 per cent in cities with a population of over one million to 14 per cent in cities in the 50,000-to-100,000 population group.[4] The average increase for all cities was 10 per cent, whereas suburban areas had a 13 per cent rise and rural areas, a 7 per cent upward trend. Moreover, there were increases in all geographical divisions of the country, the sharpest upswing occurring in the South Atlantic States. Among the major crimes, larceny ($50 and over) had the greatest increase over the three-year average for 1960 to 1962. It was followed closely by auto theft and burglary, whereas only the total for murder and nonnegligent manslaughter showed a decrease.

Murder and nonnegligent manslaughter took the lives of 8,500 persons during 1963, which was 100 more than during 1962. In addition, during 1963, criminals committed 100,160 robberies, taking more than 27 million dollars from their victims—an average of $276 per robbery; raped 16,400

---

[4] The *Uniform Crime Reports* divide cities into these six groups according to the size of their population: (1) cities over 250,000; (2) cities 100,000 to 250,000; (3) cities 50,000 to 100,000; (4) cities 25,000 to 50,000; (5) cities 10,000 to 25,000; and (6) cities under 10,000. In general, under the uniform crime reporting system, a place is urban (city) if it is incorporated and has 2,500 or more people. This broad definition is the same as that used by the Bureau of the Census.

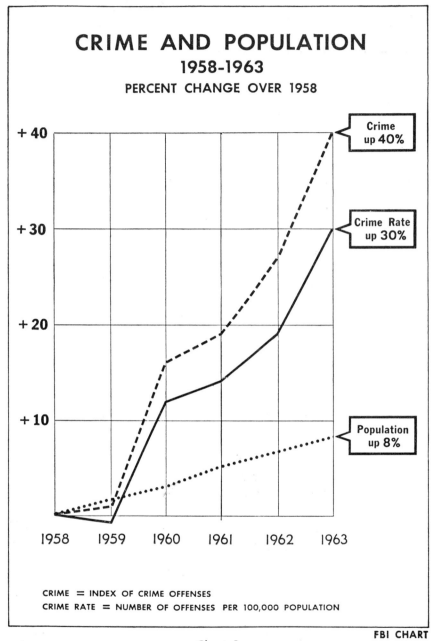

CRIME AND POPULATION
1958-1963
PERCENT CHANGE OVER 1958

Crime up 40%

Crime Rate up 30%

Population up 8%

CRIME = INDEX OF CRIME OFFENSES
CRIME RATE = NUMBER OF OFFENSES PER 100,000 POPULATION

FBI CHART

Chart 1

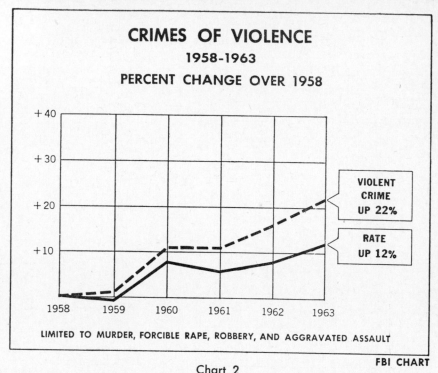

CRIMES OF VIOLENCE
1958-1963
PERCENT CHANGE OVER 1958

VIOLENT CRIME UP 22%

RATE UP 12%

LIMITED TO MURDER, FORCIBLE RAPE, ROBBERY, AND AGGRAVATED ASSAULT

Chart 2

FBI CHART

persons; stabbed, shot, clubbed, or seriously beat 147,800 persons (aggravated assault); committed 975,900 burglaries, obtaining more than $205 million in money and property—an average of $211 per burglary; committed 611,400 thefts, each one involving fifty dollars or more; and stole 399,000 automobiles, the average value of each car being set at $927.

Over the past six years auto theft has increased 39 per cent, and during 1963 this crime constituted 18 per cent of the total of major crimes committed. A total of over 785 million dollars was lost as a result of the robberies, burglaries, larcenies, and auto thefts that occurred during 1963, but this property loss was cut to 46 cents on each dollar by police action. In fact, 91 per cent of the automobiles stolen during 1963 were recovered by law-enforcement agencies, but the remaining 9 per cent of these cars represented a loss of more than $33 million.[5]

Monthly Variations. In the United States, definite seasonal crime patterns have persisted for many years, and they vary so little from year to year that fairly reliable forecasts regarding them can be made. Thus, crimes against the person, which in the *Uniform Crime Reports* include

[5] Federal Bureau of Investigation, *Uniform Crime Reports, 1963,* pp. 1–23.

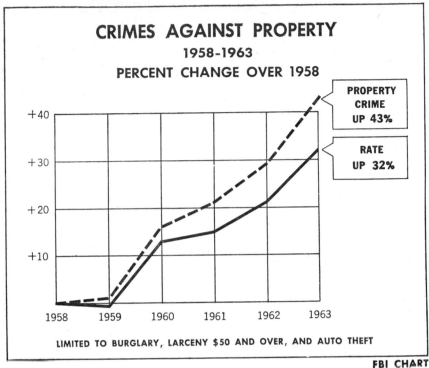

CRIMES AGAINST PROPERTY
1958-1963
PERCENT CHANGE OVER 1958

PROPERTY CRIME UP 43%

RATE UP 32%

LIMITED TO BURGLARY, LARCENY $50 AND OVER, AND AUTO THEFT

FBI CHART

Chart 3

murder, nonnegligent manslaughter, forcible rape, and aggravated assault, tend to be warm weather crimes, occurring most frequently during July, August, and September. Crimes against property, on the other hand, tend to be cold weather crimes. In the *Uniform Crime Reports,* these crimes include robbery, burglary, larceny ($50 and over), and auto theft. Robbery and thievery occur most frequently during the months of October through December—the darker months, which seem more conducive to such activity. However, larceny has the least clearly defined seasonal pattern of all the major crimes included in the *Uniform Crime Reports.* This can be partly explained by the fact that it refers to such a variety of criminal activities, many of which have their high and low points at different periods.[6]

CRIME RATES IN 1963

The amount of crime is increasing faster than the population in the United States. In fact, since 1958 crime has increased five times faster than our population, and, as Table 2 shows, a rate of 1,198 major offenses

[6] *Ibid.,* pp. 6–23.

per 100,000 inhabitants was established in 1963—a 9 per cent rise above the crime rate of 1962.

Table 2. Major crime rates for 1963.

(Offenses per 100,000 inhabitants)

Major crimes	Rate for 1963	Change for 1963 (%)	
		Over 1962	Over 3-year average (1960–62)
Total	1,198.3	+9	+12
Murder and nonnegligent manslaughter ...	4.5	0	−4
Forcible rape	8.7	−1	−1
Robbery	53.1	+4	+4
Aggravated assault	78.4	+4	+7
Burglary	517.6	+8	+11
Larceny ($50 and over)	324.3	+12	+17
Auto theft	211.6	+10	+16

Source: Based on data from the Federal Bureau of Investigation, *Uniform Crime Reports, 1963*, p. 3.

The crime rate for 1963 was 12 per cent higher than the average rate for the period 1960 through 1962, the property offenses of burglary, larceny ($50 and over), and auto theft continuing to grow at a much faster pace than the population. Although the rates for the combination category of murder and nonnegligent manslaughter and for forcible rape remained at about the same level as in 1962, the rates for aggravated assault and robbery increased 4 per cent during the year. In 1963, the rates for all the major crimes were higher in the cities than in the rural areas and tended to vary directly with the size of the city. In general, the states which reported the highest crime rates are those which have the fastest-growing populations.[7]

An examination of Table 3 will reveal that the Pacific States (Alaska, California, Hawaii, Oregon, Washington) had the highest rates for burglary, larceny ($50 and over), auto theft, and forcible rape; the South Atlantic States (Delaware, Florida, Georgia, Maryland, North Carolina, South Carolina, Virginia, West Virginia) had the highest rates for aggravated assault, murder, and nonnegligent manslaughter; and the East North Central States (Illinois, Indiana, Michigan, Ohio, Wisconsin) had the highest rate for robbery.

[7] *Ibid.*, pp. 3, 90, 91.

CRImES

AGAINST THE PERSON

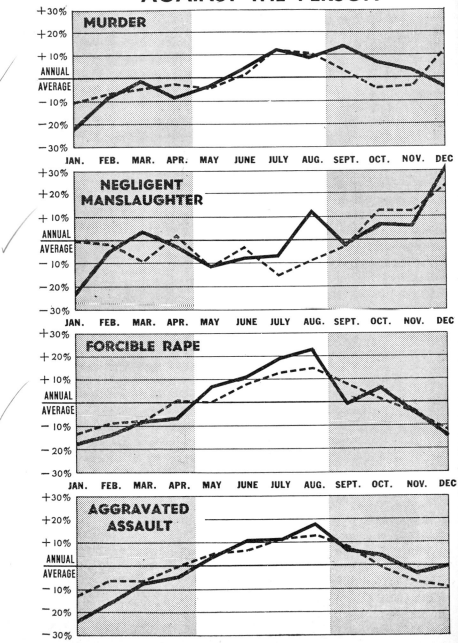

Chart 4

BY MONTH

VARIATIONS FROM 1963 ANNUAL AVERAGE

AGAINST PROPERTY

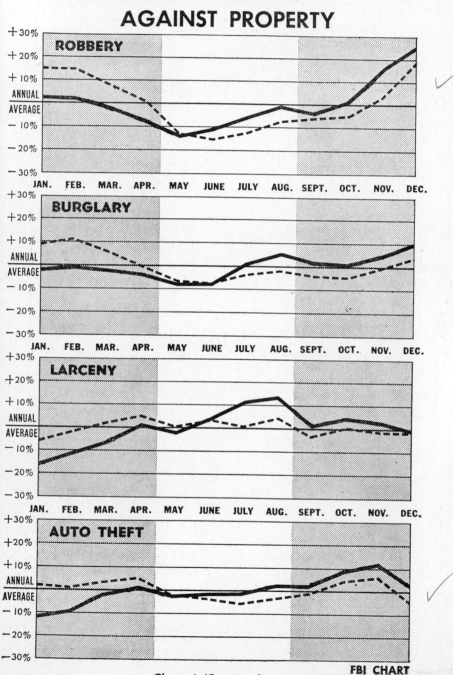

Chart 4 (Continued)

FBI CHART

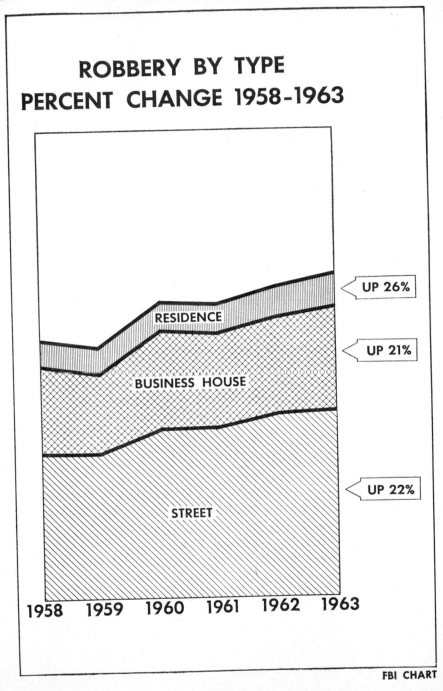

Chart 5

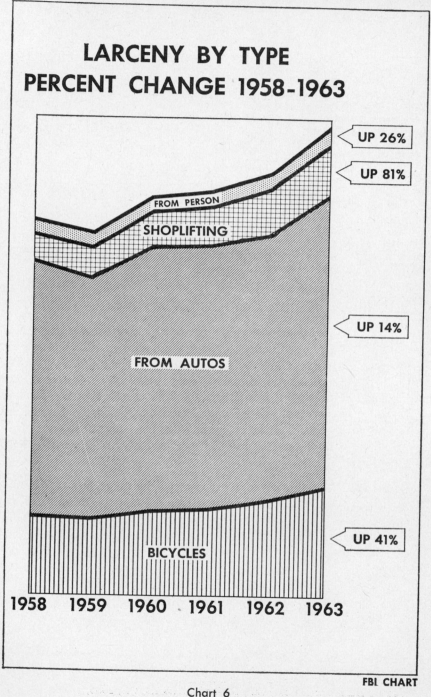

LARCENY BY TYPE
PERCENT CHANGE 1958-1963

UP 26%

UP 81%

FROM PERSON

SHOPLIFTING

UP 14%

FROM AUTOS

UP 41%

BICYCLES

1958 1959 1960 1961 1962 1963

FBI CHART

Chart 6

Table 3. Crime rates for 1963, by geographic divisions.

(Offenses per 100,000 inhabitants)

Division	Murder and nonnegligent man- slaughter	Forcible rape	Robbery	Aggravated assault	Burglary	Larceny ($50 and over	Auto theft
New England	1.9	4.1	19.3	25.7	434.7	254.1	270.3
Middle Atlantic	3.1	7.2	45.4	71.4	422.1	351.2	211.5
East North Central ..	3.5	9.5	87.1	69.4	471.3	301.4	232.2
West North Central .	2.6	7.0	39.8	38.4	415.4	246.0	149.1
South Atlantic	7.7	7.8	43.1	118.4	508.3	284.8	162.5
East South Central ..	7.4	5.7	25.6	72.8	396.2	211.1	114.7
West South Central ..	7.0	8.5	36.1	98.9	520.2	268.9	166.7
Mountain	4.4	11.5	46.8	55.9	627.5	444.9	277.8
Pacific	3.6	14.9	77.2	101.4	882.4	515.5	319.7

SOURCE: Based on data from the Federal Bureau of Investigation, *Uniform Crime Reports, 1963*, pp. 48–51, Table 2.

OFFENSES CLEARED AND PERSONS ARRESTED IN 1963

Offenses Cleared by Arrest.[8] Police cleared by arrest about one out of every four reported major crimes in our cities during 1963.[9] However, the clearance rate for crimes against the person was noticeably higher than that for crimes against property. Thus, while 91.5 per cent of the murders and nonnegligent manslaughters, 72.2 per cent of the forcible rapes, and 74.4 per cent of the aggravated assaults were cleared by arrest, only 41.0 per cent of the robberies, 26.6 per cent of the burglaries, 18.8 per cent of the larcenies, and 26.8 per cent of the auto thefts were similarly cleared.[10]

Persons Found Guilty. Seventy per cent of the persons charged with crimes during 1963 were found guilty as charged and an additional 2 per cent were found guilty of some lesser offense. Of the remainder, 16 per cent were acquitted or otherwise dismissed and 12 per cent were referred to the juvenile court. Almost half of the juvenile offenders taken into custody were handled by the police themselves without any referral to a juvenile court. Of the persons charged with major crimes, the percentages found guilty were: (1) murder and nonnegligent manslaughter,

[8] This information is based on reports from 1,679 cities with a combined estimated population of 52,329,000.

[9] In general, an offense is cleared by arrest when at least one of the alleged perpetrators of the crime is identified with the crime and is arrested and charged, although there are certain technical exceptions.

[10] Federal Bureau of Investigation, *Uniform Crime Reports, 1963*, p. 97.

43.8 per cent, as charged, and 22.9 per cent, of a lesser offense; (2) forcible rape, 31.7 per cent, as charged, and 17.6 per cent, of a lesser offense; (3) aggravated assault, 27.5 per cent, as charged, and 21.7 per cent, of a lesser offense; (4) robbery, 41.0 per cent, as charged, and 10.8 per cent, of a lesser offense; (5) burglary, 31.2 per cent, as charged, and 9.5 per cent, of a lesser offense; (6) larceny, 42.6 per cent, as charged, and 3.5 per cent, of a lesser offense; and (7) auto theft, 23.2 per cent, as charged, and 7.4 per cent, of a lesser offense.[11]

AGE, SEX, AND RACE OF PERSONS ARRESTED IN 1963

Number of Arrests. During 1963, a total of 4,437,786 arrests was reported by 3,988 agencies serving a population of 127,210,000, or 67 per cent of the population of the United States. The arrest rate per 1,000 inhabitants for the country as a whole was 35; for cities, 42; for suburban areas, 19; and for rural areas, 15.[12]

Age of Persons Arrested. Of the persons arrested during 1963, 17.5 per cent were under eighteen years of age; 26.8 per cent, under twenty-one; and 37.0 per cent, under twenty-five. In fact, persons under eighteen years of age comprised about 46 per cent of the arrests for major crimes in the United States. In rural areas this percentage was 34; and in suburban areas, 51.[13]

Sex of Persons Arrested. During 1963, 3,996,984 males and 513,851 females were arrested in the United States. Thus, male arrests outnumbered female arrests about eight to one. The arrests for females was up 3 per cent over 1962, being greatly influenced by a 12 per cent rise in arrests of girls under eighteen.

Female criminals tended more to crimes of murder and nonnegligent manslaughter, aggravated assault, larceny, embezzlement and fraud, and forgery and counterfeiting than did males. Out of 1,000 arrests for each sex, 2 females and 1 male were arrested for murder and nonnegligent manslaughter; 19 females and 15 males, for aggravated assault, 116 females and 64 males, for larceny; 19 females and 11 males, for embezzlement and fraud; and 10 females and 6 males for forgery and counterfeiting.

On the other hand, male criminals were more active in burglary, robbery, and auto theft than female offenders. Out of 1,000 arrests for each sex, 41 males and 11 females were arrested for burglary; 9 males and 4 females, for robbery; and 21 males and 6 females, for auto theft.[14]

11 *Ibid.*, pp. 27, 28, 97.
12 *Ibid.*, pp. 23–27, 104, 105.
13 *Ibid.*, pp. 24–26, 106–108.
14 *Ibid.*, pp. 26, 109.

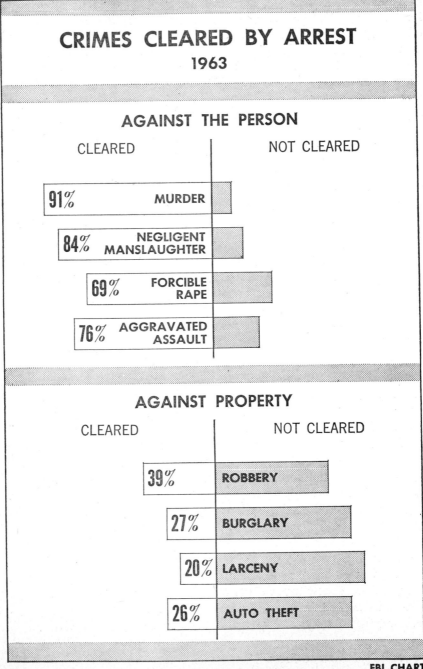

CRIMES CLEARED BY ARREST
1963

AGAINST THE PERSON

CLEARED   NOT CLEARED

91%   MURDER

84%   NEGLIGENT MANSLAUGHTER

69%   FORCIBLE RAPE

76%   AGGRAVATED ASSAULT

AGAINST PROPERTY

CLEARED   NOT CLEARED

39% ROBBERY

27% BURGLARY

20% LARCENY

26% AUTO THEFT

FBI CHART

Chart 7

Race of Persons Arrested. Of the total arrests in the United States during 1963, 69.1 per cent were white and 27.9 per cent were Negro. Thus, about 97 per cent of those arrested were either white or Negro, while the remainder, about 3 per cent, were of Indian, Chinese, Japanese, or other origin.[15]

ADDITIONAL FACTS ABOUT JUVENILE DELINQUENCY

Amount of Juvenile Delinquency. About 555,000 juvenile delinquency cases (excluding traffic offenses) were handled by juvenile courts in the United States during 1962.[16] The estimated number of different children involved in these cases was somewhat lower (478,000), since the same child may have been referred more than once during the year. These children constituted 1.8 per cent of all children aged ten through seventeen in the country. Among the children referred to the juvenile courts, the boys outnumbered the girls more than four to one.[17] In addition, many juveniles were handled by the police without any referral to the court, and a great many others who might have been adjudged delinquent never came to the attention of the law at all. It is not known how many of the latter—sometimes called "hidden delinquents"—there are, but studies indicate that the number is considerable.[18]

Trend of Juvenile Delinquency. In 1960 the United States Children's Bureau, after an analysis of its own statistical compilations and those of the Federal Bureau of Investigation, concluded that both sources showed similar upward trends in juvenile delinquency, that the national rate of reported juvenile court delinquency had doubled in the decade 1948 to 1958, and that the evidence indicated a *real* growth in the size of the problem and not just a "paper increase" resulting from better reporting and more efficient law enforcement.[19]

The number of delinquency cases appearing before the juvenile courts again increased during 1962. Although this was a 10 per cent increase, there was only a 3.5 per cent increase in the number of children in the age group ten to seventeen, inclusive, during the same year. Thus, the upward trend, which began in 1949 and has appeared in every year, except 1961, since then, continued; and, as in most of the years during the past decade, the increase in delinquency cases exceeded the increase

[15] *Ibid.*, p. 111.

[16] For a discussion of the limitations of juvenile court statistics, see Chapter 1.

[17] United States Children's Bureau, *Juvenile Court Statistics, 1962*, Statistical Series, No. 73, pp. 1, 2.

[18] United States Children's Bureau, *Some Facts About Juvenile Delinquency* (Washington, D.C.: Government Printing Office, 1954), pp. 1, 2.

[19] United States Children's Bureau, *Report to the Congress on Juvenile Delinquency* (Washington, D.C.: Government Printing Office, 1960), p. 3.

ARREST RATES BY

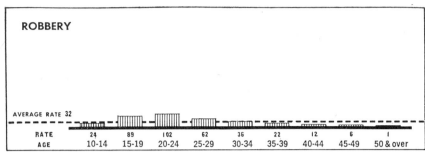

ROBBERY

AVERAGE RATE 32

| RATE | 24 | 89 | 102 | 62 | 36 | 22 | 12 | 6 | 1 |
| AGE | 10-14 | 15-19 | 20-24 | 25-29 | 30-34 | 35-39 | 40-44 | 45-49 | 50 & over |

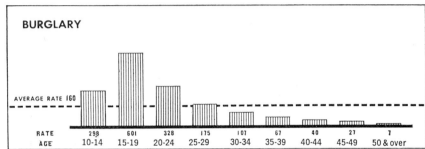

BURGLARY

AVERAGE RATE 160

| RATE | 298 | 601 | 328 | 175 | 107 | 67 | 40 | 27 | 7 |
| AGE | 10-14 | 15-19 | 20-24 | 25-29 | 30-34 | 35-39 | 40-44 | 45-49 | 50 & over |

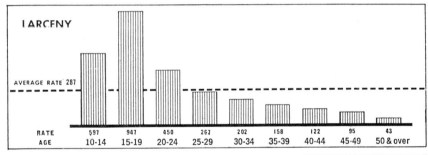

LARCENY

AVERAGE RATE 287

| RATE | 597 | 947 | 450 | 267 | 202 | 158 | 122 | 95 | 43 |
| AGE | 10-14 | 15-19 | 20-24 | 25-29 | 30-34 | 35-39 | 40-44 | 45-49 | 50 & over |

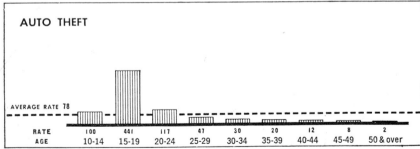

AUTO THEFT

AVERAGE RATE 78

| RATE | 100 | 441 | 117 | 47 | 30 | 20 | 12 | 8 | 2 |
| AGE | 10-14 | 15-19 | 20-24 | 25-29 | 30-34 | 35-39 | 40-44 | 45-49 | 50 & over |

RATES PER 100,000 POPULATION WITHIN EACH AGE GROUP

Chart 8

AGE GROUP -- 1963

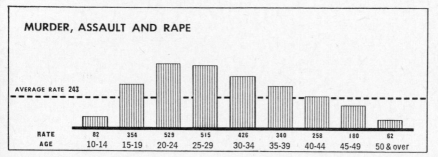

MURDER, ASSAULT AND RAPE

AVERAGE RATE 243

RATE	82	354	529	515	426	340	258	180	62
AGE	10-14	15-19	20-24	25-29	30-34	35-39	40-44	45-49	50 & over

NARCOTICS

AVERAGE RATE 24

RATE	2	31	82	70	50	28	14	7	3
AGE	10-14	15-19	20-24	25-29	30-34	35-39	40-44	45-49	50 & over

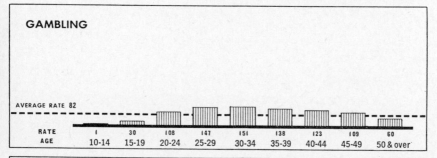

GAMBLING

AVERAGE RATE 82

RATE	1	30	108	147	151	138	123	109	60
AGE	10-14	15-19	20-24	25-29	30-34	35-39	40-44	45-49	50 & over

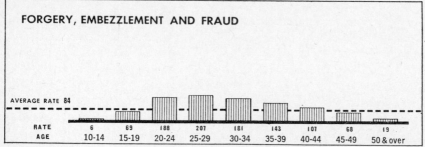

FORGERY, EMBEZZLEMENT AND FRAUD

AVERAGE RATE 84

RATE	6	69	188	207	181	143	107	68	19
AGE	10-14	15-19	20-24	25-29	30-34	35-39	40-44	45-49	50 & over

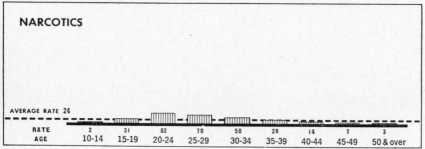

FBI CHART

Chart 8 (Continued)

in the child population. Furthermore, while the total number of juvenile delinquency cases increased 10 per cent during 1962, the number of such cases continued to grow faster in rural courts (16 per cent) than in urban courts (10 per cent). Even so, courts in predominantly urban areas handled more than two-thirds of all the delinquency cases in the country.[20]

Nature of Juvenile Delinquency. The reports received from juvenile courts show that the majority of the boys are brought before these courts for stealing or committing malicious mischief. Most of the girls, however, are referred to the juvenile courts for truancy, running away, being ungovernable, or committing a sexual offense.[21] In 1957 the average (median) age of children referred to all courts was about fifteen and a half years, the average being about the same for both boys and girls.[22]

COST OF CRIME AND DELINQUENCY

No one knows how much crime and delinquency cost the United States each year. In 1931 the National Commission on Law Observance and Enforcement, popularly known as the Wickersham Commission, issued a partial estimate of the cost of crime based upon data collected during its investigations. This partial estimate approached the total of $900 million. More recently, J. Edgar Hoover, director of the Federal Bureau of Investigation, estimated the annual cost of crime in the United States to be $20 billion! In comparison, the cost of public services for helping delinquent children seems small. About ten years ago, the United States Children's Bureau estimated that, conservatively, between $175 and $200 million were being spent each year in this country by the police, courts, detention facilities, and institutions for the care and handling of juvenile delinquents or alleged delinquents.[23]

These estimates—startling as they may be to every citizen and taxpayer —refer only to the economic costs of crime and delinquency. These costs are important, but of far greater significance is the toll of death, disease, insanity, pain, anguish, misery, impoverishment, disruption of families, corruption of government, and disorganization of community life resulting from the growth and persistence of this problem. Who can calculate such intangibles in terms of dollars and cents? Who can hope to reduce them to a definite statement of costs? And yet, they must not be minimized or overlooked, for a recognition of their great import is essential to an understanding of the enormous dimensions of the problem of crime and delinquency.

[20] United States Children's Bureau, *Juvenile Court Statistics, 1962*, pp. 1, 2.
[21] *Ibid.*, pp. 2, 3.
[22] *Ibid.*, 1957, Statistical Series, No. 52, p. 2.
[23] United States Children's Bureau, *Some Facts about Juvenile Delinquency*, p. 12.

5

The Criminal

WHO IS THE CRIMINAL?

The jury slowly returned to the courtroom. It was about to present its verdict. The atmosphere was tense, and the spectators strained forward to listen.

"The defendant will please rise." It was the judge speaking. Then he turned to the jury and said, "Have you reached a verdict?"

"We have, your honor," replied the foreman.

"How do you find the defendant?" asked the judge.

"Guilty, your honor," declared the foreman.

Who is this defendant who has just been declared guilty?

Is he Bill? Bill, a friendly six-footer, is twenty-two. While drunk, he committed larceny. There seemed to be no reason for his crime. He was employed and liked his work, and everything was "all right at home." "When I get drunk, it brings out the larceny in me," he explains.

Born on a farm, he spent most of his childhood in a city, where he completed the twelfth grade in school. He was a good student, popular with his classmates, and well-liked by his teachers. His family life with his parents, brother, and sister was happy and satisfying. A Protestant, he remained religious even after leaving home. He went to work first in a grocery store, but later he became a bartender. His boss said that Bill was a good worker and was liked by the customers. He is the father of one child and was happily married at the time of his arrest on a larceny charge.

Is the defendant Charlie? Charlie is a wealthy physician and surgeon. He had never been in any trouble—"not even arrested for parking in front of a fire plug"—when he was arrested at the age of sixty on a charge of second-degree murder.

His background is one of good family, good education, and hard work. He had retired, but he resumed practice during World War II because of the "doctor shortage." "I could have been running around hitting a golf ball now if I hadn't gone back to work," he explains.

One night, after Charlie had gone to bed, he was aroused by his partner. This man, who was very drunk, pleaded with Charlie to help him dispose of the body of a dead woman. Charlie agreed to help, and they were taking the woman to a friendly coroner when his partner and another man, who also was drunk, "got tired of fooling around and threw the body into the river." Although Charlie insists that the woman died of natural causes and that several persons wanted her body secretly removed from a nursing home so as to avoid a scandal, he now admits that "he should have stayed in bed."

Is Ed the name of this defendant? Ed is twenty-five and not very bright. His was an average boyhood in an average family in the average small mining town. At home they said grace at meals and "took religion rather seriously," but away from home he paid no attention to it. After receiving a sixth-grade education, he went into the mines at thirteen. Away from work he "ran with a sporting crowd" and thinks that was the cause of his getting into trouble. One night he got drunk and shot a man during a tavern brawl over a prostitute. As a result he now faces a sentence for manslaughter.

Is this defendant a Negro boy named Sam? He was fifteen when he committed his first crime by breaking into a place to get some money in order to have a good time. As he puts it, "I just stole so I could have good clothes, go to shows, and flirt with the girls."

His father was dead, and Sam did not get along well with his brothers and sisters. His mother insisted that he go to church and Sunday School every Sunday, but he did not pay much attention to religion. Sam finished the tenth grade and then left school. In explaining this, he says, "I got by, but I was tired of them lessons."

At sixteen he went to work shining shoes and hated it. At eighteen he married, and at twenty he was arrested for breaking and entering. In referring to his crime, he observes: "I think it was mostly showing off and stuff like that that caused it. I wanted to show people I had more than they had." He now threatens to go straight, and with a shake of his head, he says, "It's about time I woke up."

Is Jim the prisoner who has just been convicted? Jim is thirty-three and a few months ago he killed his wife. He returned unexpectedly one day and found her in bed with her lover while his infant son lay sick and neglected in the next room. When he realized what had happened, he found that he had stabbed and killed his wife and badly wounded the man.

As a boy, Jim lived on a farm, the only child of well-to-do parents. He graduated from high school, where he did well in his studies and was liked by his classmates and his teachers. At twenty-one, he married and went to work in a factory. In time, there were three children and Jim had a good job, but the marriage "went to pieces when his wife began to run around." Before that tragic day he had been arrested only once— for running a stop light on his wedding night twelve years before. Now he stands convicted of second-degree murder.

Is Hazel the name of this defendant? Hazel is a pretty twenty-five-year-old bookkeeper who has been indicted for the embezzlement of $50,000. Hazel was born in a small town, where she completed her high school education. She comes from a middle-class home, and she and her two sisters and two brothers had what she describes as "a happy family life."

After being graduated from high school, Hazel went to a large city and attended a university. She majored in economics and accounting and graduated with honors. She then obtained an excellent position with a small, prosperous firm and soon became its head bookkeeper. Her work brought her into close association with the firm's treasurer and soon she was hopelessly in love with him. "I knew he was married," she hastens to explain, "but that didn't matter. I'd have done anything for him."

Hazel began to have dates with this man, and she fell completely under his charm. When he suggested that they "fix" the books and abscond with the firm's funds, she readily agreed, but he took the money and left her to face the charge of embezzlement. Now she's bitter and disillusioned. "I never thought this would happen to me," she laments.

Is Jack the defendant who stands convicted? Jack forged a check when he ran out of money while on a prolonged drunk. He is thirty-six and married, being the father of two children. His thirteen years of married life have been happy except for his drinking, and until about a year ago he was a successful professional man.

His background included life in a large western city, a moderately well-to-do family, and a rather tyrannical father, who was intolerant of others' views. When Jack was very young, his mother died, and he lived with his father, grandmother, and some aunts until his father remarried. Jack's was a strict religious upbringing, and he has remained a devout Catholic.

When he was twenty-three, he married his school-day sweetheart, and they were happy until he began to drink heavily. Jack served as a lieutenant in the Navy during World War II. Gravely wounded, he was honorably discharged after a long period of hospitalization. Well over six feet tall, Jack is a brilliant man with a fine appearance and a winning personality. Despite his present predicament, he confidently declares, "I'm not going to let this lick me."

Is George the convicted defendant in this case? George is a large, muscular man. He was arrested after he had held up and robbed the owner of a tavern. An habitual offender for many years, he has a long police record. Committing his first crime at the age of fourteen when he stole a woman's purse and treated the boys in his gang, George was caught and placed on probation.

George comes from a poor family. His father deserted his mother and her three children when George was only ten. He left school at the age of fifteen and began to drift from one job to another. Soon he became the leader of a tough gang and with them committed many crimes. Larceny, burglary, robbery, and attempted rape are on his record, and today, at the age of forty-five, hard and cynical, he looks back upon a life blackened by fifteen years of imprisonment. "Hell!" he defiantly says, "I can take anything they can throw at me."

Is this prisoner a young man named Paul? He was fifteen when an electric clock in a business establishment caught his eye. "As a prank," he broke in and helped himself to it, but the judge could not see it that way. He gave Paul ten years, suspended the sentence, and placed him on probation.

Paul shivered for a long time over his narrow escape.

A Syrian, Paul comes from a poor home, but he was happy there with his parents, one brother, and three sisters. The family attended church services regularly, and Paul was the only black sheep in the fold.

In referring to his education, Paul says, "I left school when I was sixteen. I was in the ninth grade and I wasn't doing very well in my studies, but I had lots of friends and was on the baseball team." A swarthy, heavy-set fellow, Paul is friendly in an awkward sort of way—prone to cry on any sympathetic shoulder and giving a deceptive appearance of stupidity. Now at thirty he must go to prison for grand larceny.

Is Max the prisoner in this case? When he was sixteen, he was the leader of a group of boys that "hung around pool halls and started drinking." They held up, robbed, and kidnapped a man—"just for the hell of it." As Max says, "We were just running around, and there was nothing to do—so we started stealing." This episode ended in a jail break followed by a one-year-to-life reformatory sentence.

Max was born in a small town. His divorced mother remarried when he was seven, but he did not like his stepfather, who gave him many beatings. As Max looks back on those days, he feels that maybe his unhappy home life had something to do with his trouble. When he entered the reformatory, he had a tough reputation, and he tried to live up to it. He has apparently succeeded, because since then he has served about eleven years in four different prisons, and now at thirty-five, he must serve another sentence for forgery.

Bill, Charlie, Ed, Sam, Jim, Hazel, Jack, George, Paul, or Max—any one of these might have been the convicted defendant in this case. The fact is that all kinds of people commit crimes. The young, the old, the sick, the well, the strong, the weak, the bright, the dull, the rich, the poor, the male, the female, the white, the Negro, the foreign-born, the native-born—all of these can be found in our courts and prisons. The only thing that they all have in common is that they have violated the criminal law. It appears, then, that a criminal is one who violates the criminal law. But this definition is inadequate. We do not know a person as a criminal until he has been properly adjudicated as such in a criminal court, and he may not be subjected to punishment by the state until this is done. A criminal, therefore, is one who has been convicted of a particular offense in a criminal court.

CLASSIFICATION OF CRIMINALS

How would you classify each of the criminals referred to in the earlier pages of this chapter? A little reflection will indicate how difficult such an undertaking can be. Criminologists have made many attempts to classify criminals and have used various criteria for this purpose. An obvious method of classification is in terms of the crimes that persons commit. Thus, criminals may be felons or misdemeanants, or murderers, rapists, burglars, arsonists, robbers, embezzlers, or forgers. However, this classification is not very helpful, since different kinds of persons may commit the same kind of crime. A professional criminal, for example, may kill during a robbery, while an enraged husband, who has lived an exemplary life, may murder his wife's paramour; and a devoted father may steal in order to pay for the medical care of his daughter, while a ne'er-do-well may commit the same offense to obtain money for gambling.

For this reason, many writers have looked beyond the crime and centered their attention upon the qualities of the criminal. Garofalo, a member of the Lombrosian school,[1] divided criminals into murderers, violent criminals, criminals deficient in probity, and lascivious criminals.[2] Ferri, another member of the same school, classified criminals into the insane, the born, the habitual, the occasional, and the passionate.[3]

More recently, Alexander and Staub divided criminals into the acute and the chronic, and subdivided the chronic into the normal, the neurotic, and the pathological. The acute criminal is one who commits a

[1] A school of criminology which was founded by the Italian anthropologist Cesare Lombroso (1835–1909). It is often called the "positive school" of criminology. For a discussion of its principles, see Chapter 9.

[2] Raffaele Garofalo, *Criminology*, trans. Robert W. Miller (Boston: Little, Brown and Co., 1914), pp. 111–32.

[3] Enrico Ferri, *Criminal Sociology*, trans. J. Kelly and J. Lisle (Boston: Little, Brown and Co., 1917), pp. 138, 139.

single crime, or only a few crimes, because of unusual or extreme circumstances. The normal criminal is a product of his environment. As a result of his association with criminals, he has become a criminal. His is a sociological etiology. The neurotic criminal is one who violates the law because of his anxieties, guilt feelings, and personality conflicts. He is a product of a psychological etiology. The pathological criminal is one who engages in criminal behavior because of an organic condition. This category includes the mentally deficient and the organically psychotic. The pathological criminal is a product of a biological etiology.[4]

In 1941 Lindesmith and Dunham suggested that criminals constitute a continuum, with the "social criminal" at one extreme and the "individualized criminal" at the other. The "social criminal" is one whose criminal behavior is supported and prescribed by his cultural milieu; he "achieves status and recognition within a certain minority group by skillfully and daringly carrying out the criminal activity which, in that group, is customary and definitely designated." He has learned to be a criminal as a result of his association with criminals; he is well adjusted in his way of life; and he acts in close collaboration with others whose cooperation he needs in the development of his career. Seeking ends which are socially accepted in the broader cultural milieu, he uses means which are generally regarded as illegitimate. The clearest example of this type of offender is the professional criminal "who pursues crime, deliberately and voluntarily, as an occupation which he shares with other persons."

The "individualized criminal" commits criminal acts which are not supported and prescribed by his cultural milieu, nor does he gain prestige or recognition by committing them. For him crime is not an occupation. He seeks ends which are private and personal rather than socially accepted, commits his crimes alone, and is a stranger to others who commit similar crimes. This type of offender is represented by the person who commits a crime of passion (the husband who kills his wife's lover), steals under the stress of dire economic need, or violates the law while suffering from a mental derangement. Between the "social criminal" and the "individualized criminal" are a number of other types leaning in the direction of one extreme or the other.[5] In commenting on their classification, Lindesmith and Dunham state:

In the literature on crime, sociologists have traditionally concerned themselves mainly with the "social criminal" and psychiatrists with the "individualized criminal," but neither group of specialists has been altogether clear about this fact and each has attempted to appropriate to himself the entire

---

[4] Franz Alexander and Hugo Staub, *The Criminal, the Judge, and the Public* (Glencoe, Ill.: The Free Press, 1956), pp. 42–46.

[5] Alfred R. Lindesmith and H. Warren Dunham, "Some Principles of Criminal Typology," *Social Forces*, XIX (Mar., 1941), 307–14.

field and to extend to all types the theories evolved with respect to one. Such procedure ignores the possibility, which seems very strong, that the term "criminal" refers to many different kinds of individuals whose behavior may have developed in totally different ways.[6]

A few years ago Tappan, after stating that little research had as yet supported any analysis of criminal types, offered a simple typology of property offenders. He divided these offenders into the simple and the professional, and then subdivided the simple into the circumstantial and the amateur, and the professional into the solitary and the organized. The circumstantial offender commits a single or rare crime as the result of the pressure of unusual circumstances, and being a conformist, he tends not to repeat his crime. The amateur criminal, who may be a habitual or an occasional offender, displays little skill or intelligence in the commission of his crime. He is nonconforming and antisocial but lacks the talent or training to make his crimes pay. The solitary professional criminal usually has considerable ability, tends to be egocentric, ambitious, and self-taught in his specialty, resorts to elaborate rationalizations to justify his antisocial attitudes and criminal activities, persists in his crimes, and resists efforts to reform him. The organized professional offender represents the peak of criminal development. Proficient, organized into outfits with strong codes designed for self-preservation, and protected by arrangements for fixing cases, he tends to evade arrest, prosecution, and conviction, and deeply steeped in crime and caught in the web of criminal relationships, he, perhaps more than any other offender, resists attempts at rehabilitation. In suggesting this classification, Tappan emphasized that it did not seek to establish a series of simple causal hypotheses, that it did not include all offenders, that it did not create entirely distinct classes, and that it did not deny the frequent transition from one class to another.[7]

Clinard and Cavan, however, have not confined themselves to such a limited classification of offenders but instead have presented detailed typologies. Theorizing that offenders can be classified according to the degree to which they make a long-term career out of crime, Clinard divides them into the following types: (1) criminally insane, (2) extreme sex deviates, (3) occasional offenders, (4) prostitutes and homosexuals, (5) habitual petty criminals, (6) white-collar criminals, (7) offenders with ordinary criminal careers, (8) organized criminals, and (9) professional criminals. According to Clinard, from the first to the last of these types as they are listed here, there is an increase in the degree of the development of criminal social roles, the identification with crime,

<hr>

[6] *Ibid.*, 313, 314.
[7] Paul W. Tappan, *Crime, Justice, and Correction* (New York: McGraw-Hill Book Co., Inc., 1960), 215–34.

the conception of self as a criminal, the association with criminal activities, and the progression in crime. Progression in crime means "the acquisition of more complex techniques, more frequent offenses, and, ultimately, dependence on crime as a frequent or sole means of livelihood."[8]

Cavan classifies offenders into the following categories, although she emphasizes that they represent a continuum, and that criminal behavior does not differ sharply from noncriminal behavior:

1. Offenders whose behavior is condemned by the public but supported by another culture (criminal contraculture).[9]
   a. Professional criminals, who are the "career men" of crime. They learn definite techniques, depend upon crime for a livelihood, move in the world of other criminals, and develop a philosophy in support of their activities.
   b. Organized criminals, who are professional criminals whose activities are organized like those of a legitimate business. Offenders active in gangs, rackets, and syndicates are organized criminals.
   c. Disorganized habitual criminals, who are the skid row bums, the drug addicts, the chronic alcoholics, the vagrants, the prostitutes, the petty thieves, and other similar offenders.
2. Offenders whose behavior is unapproved or disapproved by the public.
   a. Irresponsible criminals, who are similar to casual offenders except that they threaten the rights of others instead of merely creating inconveniences. They commit such offenses as speeding in heavy-traffic streets, parking in an area reserved for a doctor, driving while somewhat intoxicated, and the stealing of objects for which they could pay if they so desired.
   b. Occasional criminals, who commit one or a few crimes, usually of a minor and opportunistic nature, but who are otherwise law-abiding.
   c. Criminals who systematically commit such offenses as embezzlement and theft from their places of employment over a period of time.
3. Offenders whose behavior is tolerated with approval by the public.
   a. Casual criminals who violate only minor laws and local ordinances, chiefly for their own convenience.
   b. White-collar criminals, who, while engaged in legitimate business, commit acts in violation of the laws regulating business.
   c. Criminals who cooperate with professional and organized criminals, for example, in the patronage of such illegal services as gambling, sale of narcotic drugs, and prostitution.
4. Offenders whose behavior is strongly disapproved by the public but supported by an ideological culture (ideological contraculture). In-

[8] Marshall B. Clinard, *Sociology of Deviant Behavior* (New York: Holt, Rinehart and Winston, Inc., 1963), pp. 210–16.

[9] A "contraculture" is not only different from but opposed to the conventional culture followed by the majority of people (see J. Milton Yinger, "Contraculture and Subculture," *American Sociological Review*, XXV [Oct., 1960], 625–35).

cluded in this category are members of religious groups who, because of their beliefs, practice polygyny, refuse to register for the draft, and the like, and political subversives who give allegiance to other nations.[10]

Only a few of the attempts that have been made to classify criminals have been presented here, but they are sufficient to illustrate clearly the difficulties involved in this hazardous undertaking. Little is known regarding the causes of human behavior, and few empirical studies have been made to determine the differences between offender types.[11] As a result, the categories in the classifications of offenders are not stable and mutually exclusive, and different criteria must be combined in various ways to construct the typologies. Thus, in both Cavan's and Clinard's classifications at least three criteria are used: "the number of crimes committed" (implicit in the professional criminal, the organized criminal, the occasional criminal, and the habitual criminal); "the kind of crime committed" (implicit in the white-collar criminal); and "the kind of person committing the crime" (implicit in the white-collar criminal, the professional criminal, and the organized criminal).[12] These criteria are loosely fitted together in various combinations by the use of such terms as "chiefly," "usually," "as a rule," "frequently," "ordinarily," "for the most part," "to some extent," and "in general." The more refined the typology strives to be, the more it must resort to qualifying terms of this kind, thus clearly revealing the complexity of the problem and the paucity of the knowledge regarding it.

Despite these difficulties involved in classifying criminals, criminologists now tend to propound separate theories and explanations of various types of crimes or criminal behavior instead of general theories of crime or criminal behavior considered in the aggregate. In view of the great complexity of the problem, this tendency appears to have much merit even though as yet no satisfactory system of classification has been devised.[13]

[10] Ruth Shonle Cavan, *Criminology* (New York: Thomas Y. Crowell Co., 1962), pp. 44–67.

[11] For several examples of such studies, see John L. Gillin, *The Wisconsin Prisoner* (Madison, Wis.: The University of Wisconsin Press, 1946); Julian Roebuck and Ronald Johnson, "The Negro Drinker and Assaulter as a Criminal Type," *Crime and Delinquency*, VIII (Jan., 1962), 21–33; *ibid.*, "The Jack-of-All-Trades Offender," *Crime and Delinquency*, VIII (April, 1962), 172–81.

[12] Only the categories common to both Clinard's and Cavan's classifications are listed here. Obviously, more categories could be in the analysis if each typology were considered separately.

[13] For a brief summary of typological developments in criminology, suggested criteria for typologies, and a proposed classification of criminals, see Don C. Gibbons and Donald L. Garrity, "Some Suggestions for the Development of Etiological and Treatment Theory in Criminology," *Social Forces*, XXXVIII (Oct. 7, 1959), 51–58. See also their article, "Definition and Analysis of Certain Criminal Types," *Journal of Criminal Law, Criminology, and Police Science,* LIII (Mar., 1962), 27–35.

The fact is that the term "criminal" refers to such a heterogeneous group of persons, including all kinds of people everywhere, that it is impossible to construct a detailed classification of criminals which has firm and mutually exclusive categories. To do this successfully would amount to nothing less than a successful classification of all human beings. At present, the inadequacy of human knowledge precludes this possibility. However, the classification of criminals into more homogeneous subgroups by means of different criteria, although always more or less arbitrary, does provide deeper insights into criminal behavior and a more systematic basis for further research.

6

The Problem of Vice

THE DRUNKARD[1]

The cell door closed and Pete was again in jail. Drunk, ragged, and dirty, he would lie there until consciousness returned to his sodden brain as it had on so many other occasions.

"Let's see," he speculated when he became sober, "how many times have I been in this jail? I'm sure it must be fifty or sixty times."

And Pete was almost right. The records showed that he had been lodged in the county jail on forty-eight different occasions over a period of seven years, and always the charge was the same, "drunk and disorderly conduct."

Pete was a great hulk of a man—still strong despite a life of reckless dissipation. For years he worked in a steel mill, and each weekend he "celebrated" in the taverns of the town. Gradually, however, these celebrations became prolonged drinking bouts, sometimes lasting for a week and punctuated with brawls and the violent destruction of property.

As his fortunes declined, Pete lost his job, his savings, his home, and finally his wife, who could endure his debauches and abuse no longer. Now he was alone—sick, friendless, and a slave to his habit.

"I'm beginning to see things," he confided. "I guess Old Man Rum has got me."

Pete is not alone in his plight. He is but one in a great mass of tortured human beings who are wracked by their cravings for alcohol. W. Wallace Weaver, in discussing alcoholism, has written:

At mid-century approximately one-half of the 110,000,000 adults in the United States use alcohol as a beverage. Something more than 4,000,000 of

[1] The criminal types included in Chapters 6 and 7 are not intended to constitute a classification. They have been chosen for special treatment, because, in the opinion of the author, they clearly illustrate the complexity of crime and its far-reaching social implications. Naturally, it is not suggested that these are the only types that could be used for this purpose, but limitations of space make it necessary to restrict the number included to a minimum.

them drink to excess, and possibly 750,000 are so addicted as to present serious problems of mental and physical health. Consumers spend eight or nine billion dollars a year for intoxicating drinks, and government taxing bodies collect more than three billion dollars in revenue, over and above the usual taxes on industry. These salient facts establish alcohol as a substantial factor in national life, but scarcely suggest the complications and difficulties of its use.[2]

Today, the estimates regarding the number of alcoholics in the United States continue to be about the same as that quoted by Weaver in the foregoing statement. Writing in 1962, Keller placed the total number of alcoholics at about 4 million, adding that even in a population of 180 million, this was a "titanic number of people, mostly in the prime of life, to be suffering from a single disabling disease."[3]

Drunkenness as a Crime. Everywhere man has sought to control the antisocial effects of drunkenness. According to the first great English statute on the subject, enacted in 1606, the offender had to pay a fine of five shillings or suffer confinement in the stocks for six hours.[4] It is important to note, however, that mere drunkenness is not a crime. One may drink to excess in the privacy of his own home or in the gaiety of a party and commit no crime. It is only when the drunken person exhibits his condition publicly, or disturbs, endangers, or injures others that he becomes an offender and subject to arrest and punishment.

Most states have laws making such drunkenness a criminal offense. In 1941, Jerome Hall found that forty states had this type of legislation, while in the other eight states, the various municipalities regulated the offense.[5] Usually, the statutes specify public drunkenness and forbid boisterous or indecent conduct, or loud or profane discourse by the drunkard in any public place or near another person's private residence. Often the laws also prescribe special penalties for intoxication (usually habitual) by certain professional people, such as doctors, lawyers, and nurses, and every state has at least one statute dealing with drunken drivers.

[2] W. Wallace Weaver, *Social Problems*, p. 298. (Copyright 1951 by W. Wallace Weaver. Reprinted by permission of The Dryden Press, Inc., New York.) In 1947, according to the estimate of the Research Council on Problems of Alcohol, there were 50,000,000 users of alcoholic beverages, 3,000,000 excessive drinkers, 750,000 chronic alcoholics, and 13,500 persons suffering from an alcoholic psychosis (*The Scientific Approach to the Problem of Chronic Alcoholism* [New York: The Research Council on Problems of Alcohol, 1947], pp. 5, 6).

[3] Mark Keller, "The Definition of Alcoholism and the Estimation of Its Prevalence," *Society, Culture, and Drinking Patterns*, eds. David J. Pittman and Charles R. Snyder (New York: John Wiley and Sons, Inc., 1962), p. 326.

[4] Jerome Hall, "Drunkenness as a Criminal Offense," *Journal of Criminal Law and Criminology*, XXXII (Sept.–Oct., 1941), 297.

[5] *Ibid.*, 299.

Drunkenness is also connected with a wide variety of other forms of criminal behavior, usually characterized by violence or negligence. Such behavior ranges all the way from the destruction of property to homicide. Since the chronic alcoholic has difficulty in thinking clearly and acting deliberately, his crimes are likely to be petty or unplanned. Among his typical offenses are breach of peace, assault and battery, petty larceny, forgery, indecent exposure, and nonsupport of his family.[6] When a person who is voluntarily under the influence of alcohol commits a crime, his drunkenness is no defense (although sometimes it may result in a mitigation of his punishment) unless a specific intent,[7] or some other special mental element, is essential to constitute the crime and the state of his intoxication is such as to preclude the possibility of his having this intent or mental element. If an intoxicated person alleges that he was insane at the time that he committed the crime, his defense should be insanity, not drunkenness.[8]

In the United States, more persons are charged with drunkenness than with any other offense except violation of traffic and motor vehicle laws. The *Uniform Crime Reports* show that in 1962 the number of persons arrested for drunkenness totaled 1,593,076; for disorderly conduct, 515,435; and for driving while intoxicated, 216,745.[9] Disorderly conduct in many states is virtually synonymous with drunkenness. However, there is no way of ascertaining how many chronic alcoholics and drunken persons commit felonies and the more serious misdemeanors because in such cases the offenders are charged with their more serious crimes, and often no record is kept of their alcoholic condition. Therefore, the fact that the person used alcohol habitually or was intoxicated at the time he committed the crime is not reflected in statistical compilations.

Even so, studies made of alcoholic prisoners throw some light on this aspect of the problem. For example, Ralph S. Banay, a psychiatrist, studied all men admitted to Sing Sing Prison in New York during a two-year period (from 1938 to 1940). According to him, the significant find-

[6] For a recent analysis of the crimes of the chronic drunkard, see Selden D. Bacon, "Alcohol, Alcoholism, and Crime," *Crime and Delinquency*, IX (Jan., 1963), 1–14. This issue of *Crime and Delinquency* is entirely devoted to alcoholism and crime. See also David J. Pittman and C. Wayne Gordon, "Criminal Careers of the Chronic Drunkenness Offender," *Society, Culture, and Drinking Patterns*, eds. David J. Pittman and Charles R. Snyder (New York: John Wiley and Sons, Inc., 1962), pp. 535–46.

[7] See Chapter 2.

[8] For a discussion of the provisions of the criminal law regarding drunkenness, see Rollin M. Perkins, *Criminal Law* (Brooklyn: The Foundation Press, Inc., 1957), pp. 777–95.

[9] Federal Bureau of Investigation, *Uniform Crime Reports, 1962*, Table 19. The figures quoted here are based on reports received from agencies serving a total population of 123,571,000.

ing of this study was that "in 25 per cent of the total offenders, alcoholism was closely related to the commission of the crime or was directly responsible for it."[10] Several years ago, in another study which analyzed the records of 2,325 newly committed male felons in California, 29 per cent of those who used alcohol (98 per cent of the 2,325 men did) claimed that they were intoxicated at the time when they committed the offense for which they were sent to prison. Furthermore, 29 per cent of the total of 2,325 prisoners stated that the use of alcohol had been a problem prior to their incarceration.[11] A study recently completed at the Florida State Prison at Raiford, Florida, states that according to the official version of the crime, less than one-third (29.9 per cent) of the inmates were drinking, drunk, or intoxicated at the time that they committed the crimes for which they were sent to prison.[12]

Causes of Drinking. No single theory can explain addiction to alcohol, although historians, sociologists, psychologists, psychiatrists, biologists, and chemists have contributed to our understanding of it. One basic fact to be remembered is that alcohol is not a stimulant, as generally supposed (although with the first few drinks it may seem to have stimulating effects), but a depressant in the sense that it retards assimilation, reduces circulation, and decreases respiration. It is for these effects that it is prescribed as a drug and used as a beverage.[13]

Since alcohol acts in this way, its use has been explained as an escape from the unpleasant realities of life. By drinking, one deadens the pain of failures, inferiorities, frustrations, and anxieties and bolsters a battered ego. It seems reasonable to assume that many people, hurt and confused by the complexities of modern society, resort to alcohol for this reason.[14] Strecker believes that the chief difference between the normal drinker and the abnormal one is that the former drinks in moderation

[10] Ralph S. Banay, "Alcoholism and Crime," *Quarterly Journal of Studies on Alcohol,* II (Mar., 1942), 686–716.

[11] Austin H. MacCormick, "Correctional Views on Alcohol, Alcoholism, and Crime," *Crime and Delinquency,* IX (Jan., 1963), 24–27.

[12] Shaw Earl Grigsby, "The Raiford Study: Alcohol and Crime," *Journal of Criminal Law, Criminology, and Police Science,* LIV (Sept., 1963), 296–306.

[13] Haven Emerson, *Alcohol and Man* (New York: The Macmillan Co., 1932), pp. 1–22, 266–70; E. M. Jellinek, "Phases in the Drinking History of Alcoholics," *Quarterly Journal of Studies on Alcohol,* VII (June, 1946), 1–88.

[14] Selden D. Bacon, "Alcohol and Complex Society," *Society, Culture, and Drinking Patterns,* eds. David J. Pittman and Charles R. Synder (New York: John Wiley and Sons, Inc., 1962), pp. 78–93; Morris E. Chafetz and Harold W. Demone, Jr., *Alcoholism and Society* (New York: Oxford University Press, 1962), pp. 39–56; John J. Conger, "Perception, Learning, and Emotion: The Role of Alcohol," *The Annals of the American Academy of Political and Social Science,* CCCXV (Jan., 1958), 31–39 (this issue of *The Annals* contains a series of articles on alcoholism); John D. Armstrong, "The Search for the Alcoholic Personality," *ibid.,* 40–47.

socially to make reality more pleasurable, while the latter drinks to escape from reality.[15]

Certain psychiatrists, however, seek to explain alcoholism as a release of repressed homosexuality.[16] Although this may account for some drinking, for example, that done by men with other men, or by women with other women, it does not provide the answer for heterosexual drinking or for the heightened sexual suggestibility of men and women who are together while under the influence of alcohol.[17]

Some physiologists have turned to endocrinology for an explanation of drinking. They advance the theory that alcoholism results from the excess or deficiency of certain endocrine secretions. A few years ago, James J. Smith, Director of Research on Alcoholism at the New York University–Bellevue Medical Center, reported on a study of 2,000 alcoholics. In his report, he stated that these alcoholics suffered from improper stimulation or deficiency of the adrenal and sex glands and that hormone treatment of acute alcoholism had been successful, although the chronic alcoholics had been less responsive to such treatment.[18] Studies of this type are suggestive but they are still in the exploratory stage of development.[19]

The idea of nutritional disturbances has been important in the work of animal experimenters in the etiology of alcoholism. For example, Williams and his associates found that they could control the appetite for alcohol in mice and rats; and on the basis of this, they concluded that alcoholism develops as a result of nutritional deficiencies, and that abundant satisfaction of nutritional needs eliminates the appetite for alcohol. Chafetz and Demone, however, state that "in terms of evaluation of supporting data, statistical analysis, and methodological approach, Williams's work leaves much to be desired."[20] And Jellinek, while recognizing that Williams and his associates and other workers in the nutritional field have made contributions to our understanding of alcoholism, insists that "neither Williams nor anybody else has ever shown that a craving or need for alcohol exists in the pre-alcoholic state of alcoholics."[21]

[15] Edward A. Strecker and Francis T. Chambers, Jr., *Alcohol, One Man's Meat* (New York: The Macmillan Co., 1938), p. 38.

[16] Carney Landis, "Theories of the Alcoholic Personality," *Alcohol, Science and Society* (New Haven: Journal of Studies on Alcohol, Inc., 1945), p. 134; A. J. Rosanoff, *Manual of Psychiatry* (7th ed.; New York: John Wiley and Sons, Inc., 1938), pp. 377–80; Chafetz and Demone, pp. 40, 41.

[17] Weaver, p. 304.

[18] Waldemar Kaempffert, "Science in Review," *The New York Times*, May 14, 1950, Sec. 4, p. 9. See also E. M. Abrahamson and A. W. Pezet, *Body, Mind, and Sugar* (New York: Henry Holt and Co., Inc., 1951), pp. 148–56.

[19] For a critical analysis of the endocrinological etiologies, see E. M. Jellinek, *The Disease Concept of Alcoholism* (New Haven: Hillhouse Press, 1960), pp. 99–110.

[20] Chafetz and Demone, p. 59.

[21] Jellinek, *The Disease Concept of Alcoholism*, p. 95. For a critical analysis of the nutritional etiologies of alcoholism, see pp. 91–99 of this work.

Sociologists look beyond personal experiences and find the causes of drinking in culture, group relationships, and social processes. In our complex society the use of alcohol is not only widely accepted, but in some circles even glamorized as a symbol of success and superiority. At the same time, rapid social change has sharpened competition, intensified conflict, and undermined the family and other agencies of social control, filling many people with anxiety, tension, and guilt. Thus, while social forces in our society have been enhancing the value of alcohol and driving man to its use, they have also reduced the influences that might have effectively held him in check. Within this frame of reference, sociologists, in seeking to explain the excessive use of alcohol, emphasize the learning process, during which, they claim, such factors as companions, social class, religion, occupation, and ethnic status play an important part in determining whether an individual will become an abnormal drinker.[22]

The Chronic Alcoholic. The chronic alcoholic is one "who from the prolonged and excessive use of alcoholic beverages—usually over many years —finally develops definite physical or psychological changes."[23] He is a pathological individual, probably past thirty years of age, and not merely one who habitually consumes large quantities of alcohol. Although most chronic alcoholics begin as normal drinkers, there is little agreement as to the process by which the normal drinker becomes a chronic alcoholic. At present, it appears that chronic alcoholism results from the interaction of a number of factors, which vary from case to case,[24] and which can be understood, if at all, only by an intensive study of the individual patient.

According to Selinger, "An alcoholic is being made when one consciously or unconsciously begins to *depend* on alcohol's narcotic effects for a 'pick-up,' to sleep at night, to feel 'good,' to cope with business or

[22] For a discussion of some of the social and cultural factors in the causation of drinking, see Selden D. Bacon, "Alcohol and Complex Society," *Society, Culture, and Drinking Patterns,* eds. David J. Pittman and Charles R. Snyder (New York: John Wiley and Sons, Inc., 1962), pp. 78–93; Gregory P. Stone, "Drinking Styles and Status Arrangements," *ibid.,* pp. 121–140; Joseph J. Lawrence and Milton A. Maxwell, "Drinking and Socio-Economic Status," *ibid.,* pp. 141–45; Robert F. Bales, "Attitudes toward Drinking in the Irish Culture," *ibid.,* pp. 157–87; E. M. Jellinek, *The Disease Concept of Alcoholism,* pp. 13–32; Harold A. Mulford and Donald E. Miller, "Drinking in Iowa," I, *Quarterly Journal of Studies on Alcohol,* XX (Dec., 1959), 704–26; II, *ibid.,* XXI (Mar., 1960), 26–39; III, *ibid.,* XXI (June, 1960), 267–78; IV, *ibid.,* 279–91; V, *ibid.,* XXI (Sept., 1960), 483–99; Albert D. Ullman, "Sociocultural Backgrounds of Alcoholism," *The Annals of the American Academy of Political and Social Science,* CCCXV (Jan., 1958), 48–54.

[23] H. W. Haggard and E. M. Jellinek, *Alcohol Explored* (New York: Doubleday, Doran and Co., 1942), p. 15.

[24] Robert V. Seliger, "What Makes an Alcoholic?" *Proceedings of the American Prison Association, 1949,* pp. 79–81. See also Seliger, "Practical Aspects of Alcoholism," *Federal Probation,* XIII (June, 1949), 38–45.

domestic problems, to enjoy social gatherings, to get away from oneself, to repress inner urges of rebellion, or resentment, or of a psychosexual nature, to relieve vague but very distressing motor restlessness, and so on."[25] As the person becomes more and more dependent upon alcohol,[26] his personal efficiency and morale decline. Loss of job, physical deterioration, disruption of family relationships, physical disturbances, and difficulties with the law usually follow. Finally, he is unable to discontinue the use of alcohol without the help of others and is greatly distressed if he cannot get it. The process of his habituation, however, is a subtle one and tends to be obscured by much rationalization. To be considered a social drinker is apparently the alcoholic's last line of defense. Almost always he struggles against the obvious fact that he has stepped over the line of social drinking and has become an abnormal drinker.[27]

There is a growing tendency to refer to the chronic alcoholic as a sick person and to his condition as a disease.[28] Although this may foster more tolerance and understanding and promote greater public assistance, it should not be permitted to conceal other important aspects of the problem. Even if chronic alcoholism is classified as a disease, persons who drink alcoholic beverages, regardless of the degree of their indulgence, have moral and legal responsibilities to themselves, to their relatives, friends, and business associates, and to the community—as is true of all persons, both well and sick, except those who are found to be mentally incompetent by the law—and the rights of alcoholics must be protected during the course of any necessary treatment.[29]

Treatment of Alcoholism. In the treatment of alcoholism, the attitude of the patient is very important. He must want to be cured and must believe that he can be, or the treatment will fail. Usually, he is subjected to a "drying out" process during which he is deprived of alcohol, given plenty of rest, and provided with adequate exercise and a proper diet. The administration of vitamins has proved effective in the physical re-

[25] Seliger, "What Makes an Alcoholic?" p. 78.

[26] Emerson, pp. 224–70.

[27] Strecker and Chambers, p. 89. See also Harriet R. Mowrer, "A Psychocultural Analysis of the Alcoholic," *American Sociological Review*, V (Aug., 1940), 546–57.

[28] For a discussion of some of the implications of the disease concept of alcoholism, see John R. Seeley, "Alcoholism Is a Disease: Implications for Social Police," *Society, Culture, and Drinking Patterns*, eds. David J. Pittman and Charles R. Snyder (New York: John Wiley and Sons, Inc., 1962), pp. 586–93; Paul R. Brown, "The Problem Drinker and the Jail," *Quarterly Journal of Studies on Alcohol*, XVI (Sept., 1955), 474–83.

[29] For a discussion of rights and responsibilities, see Chapters 14, 15, 16, 17. See also Harold A. Mulford and Donald E. Miller, "Measuring Public Acceptance of the Alcoholic as a Sick Person," *Quarterly Journal of Studies on Alcohol*, XXV (June, 1964), 314–23.

habilitation of the patient, since frequently he has suffered from a deficiency of these vitamins in his inadequate consumption of food.

Several methods of therapy have attracted considerable attention. These are the Antabuse treatment,[30] the conditioned-reflex or aversion treatment, psychotherapy, and the program of Alcoholics Anonymous. Antabuse is a drug which will cause violent nausea at any time during a period of several days if any form or amount of alcohol is ingested. In fact, the physiological reaction is so extreme that it may be dangerous, and for this reason the greatest caution must be exercised in the usage of this drug.[31] The conditioned-reflex treatment seeks to create an aversion to alcohol by the administration of a nauseating drug followed by a drink of liquor. Vomiting results, the patient associates his sickness with the liquor, and thus develops a dislike of alcohol.[32] Advocates of the conditioned-reflex method claim that more than half of their patients are cured by it. Neither of these methods, however, attacks the underlying psychological problems, but when combined with counseling or psychotherapy, they may prove helpful in getting the patient through a transitional period leading to complete cure.

The method of psychotherapy aims to eliminate the emotional tensions that drive the patient to drink. Through therapeutic interviews, it undertakes to make him aware of why he drinks and to provide him with the perspective and strength necessary to combat his problem.[33] The program of Alcoholics Anonymous[34] is based on conversion and fellowship. It emphasizes that alcoholics understand alcoholism better than anyone else, that man is dependent upon God and must turn to Him for help, that the alcoholic must sincerely desire to stop drinking, and that he must admit that he is an alcoholic and cannot drink in moderation. The alcoholic is encouraged to attend the meetings of ex-alcoholics, to participate in their fellowship, and to make himself available for service to others who are suffering from alcoholism. Alcoholics Anonymous utilizes the intimacy of the primary group as a therapeutic tool to effect a funda-

[30] Antabuse is the trade name of the purified chemical compound tetraethylthiuram disulfide. It is known also as disulfiram.

[31] For an attempt to evaluate four different therapies in the treatment of 178 alcoholic patients, see Robert S. Wallerstein and Associates, *Hospital Treatment of Alcoholism* (New York: Basic Books, Inc., 1957). In this study, 25 of 47 patients improved under Antabuse therapy; 12 of 50, under conditioned-reflex; 14 of 39, under group hypnotherapy; and 11 of 42, under milieu therapy. The research project extended over two and a half years of treatment and two years of follow-up.

[32] E. A. Strecker, F. G. Ebough, and J. R. Ewalt, *Practical Clinical Psychiatry* (7th ed.; Philadelphia: The Blakiston Co., 1951), pp. 172, 173; Wallerstein and Associates, pp. 7, 53–76, 160–64, 175–81.

[33] Sidney Vogel, "Psychiatric Treatment of Alcoholism," *The Annals of the American Academy of Political and Social Science*, CCCXV (Jan., 1958), 99–107.

[34] Alcoholics Anonymous was founded in 1935. In 1957, it was estimated that there were 200,000 members in 7,000 groups, some of which were in prisons and hospitals.

mental change in the personality of the alcoholic. However, its service is supportive rather than aggressive, and the individual must learn to assume responsibility for his own cure.[35] Although it is impossible to determine the effectiveness of Alcoholics Anonymous, there is considerable evidence that there has been a high rate of recovery among its members, one estimate claiming that 75 per cent of those who sincerely participate in its program are rehabilitated.[36]

A diversified attack on alcoholism is being made by the Yale Plan Clinics, the first of which was established in New Haven in 1944. These are public clinics, open to all classes of people, and are staffed by psychiatrists, psychologists, physicians, and psychiatric social workers. By a cooperative approach, the members of the staff undertake to discover and eliminate the causes of the patient's alcoholism.

Since each case of alcoholism differs from others in terms of environmental factors and the reaction of the personality to them, no one type of therapy can be effective in all cases. The advantage of the approach used by the Yale Plan Clinics, therefore, is obvious. By coordinating the activities of a number of specialists and by employing the services of hospital and laboratory facilities, it can meet the problem of alcoholism with a range of diagnostic and remedial skills capable of dealing with the considerable spread of individual differences existing among inebriates.[37]

Fines and jail sentences have not proved effective in handling chronic alcoholics. The average jail or workhouse, in which many of them are lodged, does not have the facilities for their treatment and can do little more than provide them with a safe place in which to sober up. Since incarceration alone is futile, prisoners suffering from chronic alcoholism should be committed to institutions where special programs have been set up to effect their rehabilitation.[38]

[35] Harrison M. Trice, "Alcoholics Anonymous," *The Annals of the American Academy of Political and Social Science*, CCCXV (Jan., 1958), 108–16; Chafetz and Demone, pp. 146–65; Robert F. Bales, "The Therapeutic Role of Alcoholics Anonymous as Seen by a Sociologist," *Society, Culture, and Drinking Patterns*, eds. David J. Pittman and Charles R. Snyder (New York: John Wiley and Sons, Inc., 1962), pp. 572–76; Milton A. Maxwell, "Alcoholics Anonymous: An Interpretation," *ibid.*, pp. 577–85.

[36] *Alcoholics Anonymous: The Story of How Many Thousands of Men and Women Have Recovered from Alcoholism* (New York: Works Publishing Co., Inc., 1946); Oscar W. Ritchie, "A Sociohistorical Survey of Alcoholics Anonymous," *Quarterly Journal of Studies on Alcohol*, IX (June, 1948), 119–56; Charles H. Upton, "Alcoholics Anonymous," *Federal Probation* VIII (July–Sept., 1944), 29–32.

[37] Raymond G. McCarthy, "A Public Clinic Approach to Certain Aspects of Alcoholism," *Quarterly Journal on Studies of Alcohol*, VI (Mar., 1946), 500–14; Joseph Hirsh, *The Problem Drinker* (New York: Duell, Sloan and Pearce, Inc., 1949), pp. 150–64; Chafetz and Demone, 135–39.

[38] For a suggested comprehensive program, see Thomas P. Weil and Charles P. Price, "Alcoholism in a Metropolis," *Crime and Delinquency*, IX (Jan., 1963), 60–70.

Within recent years, a new approach to the problem of chronic public drunkenness has developed through the establishment of "half-way houses," which are so called because they serve as a middle ground between both therapeutic and punitive agencies and organized, respectable society. A half-way house provides a clean, safe place where chronic public drunkards can live voluntarily together according to certain simple rules, which require them to stay sober, get a job, pay for room and board, and help in the maintenance of their living quarters. A man can thus find security and comfort in the companionship and understanding of others who have had similar experiences, and the influences of the group, as well as pressures from the staff, help to keep him sober and prepare him for a more stable way of life. The half-way house is still in the experimental stage, and no empirical studies of its effectiveness have as yet been published.[39]

THE DRUG ADDICT

As he dragged on his cigarette, the young dope addict confessed his sordid tale of addiction and revealed how drugs had made him oblivious to family, friends, and all sense of decency.

"I got started with marihuana when I was sixteen," he said. "I got it for free. Come on, they told me, it'll give you a thrill—show you what livin' really is.

"I did get a thrill but I couldn't stop. Once they had me on the hook, I had to pay for the marihuana. For a Prince Albert can packed tight, they charged me $20. You can make two hundred cigarettes from a can.

"Well, from marihuana, it was easy to drift into something with a bigger kick to it like heroin. I spent thousands of dollars on heroin during the two and a half years I was on the stuff. One number five capsule costs from $1.25 to $1.50, and you can get a number four capsule for two bucks. A small square cellophane pack costs from $10 to $15. You cap this stuff yourself, buying a number four or five empty capsule from the druggist. You pay $25 to $30 for one-eighth of an ounce and $65 for a half ounce.

"When a person takes a shot, first he feels nauseated, on a full stomach. He feels a warm sensation, is drowsy, and his eyelids are heavy. You itch around your chest and upper lip, and your reactions are slow. You think you're thinking and operating fast, and you're more conscious of your thinking. You first lay back and relax, and you can't work when you're feeling drowsy and lazy like that.

[39] Earl Rubington, "The Chronic Drunkenness Offender," *The Annals of the American Academy of Political and Social Science*, CCCXV (Jan., 1958), 70–72; Weil and Price, p. 66.

"The big peddlers don't use the stuff themselves. They gather a bunch of young women from eighteen years up and younger men around them, who are tied to the peddler. He'll let them get as big a habit as they want. Then he gets them to do his dirty work for him and get other customers for him.

"Most addicts can't make enough money working to pay for the stuff, and they drift into the underworld as boosters, shoplifters, and pick-pockets. The dealers are smooth operators. They've got so many dodges to get you hooked. It might be a pretty girl acting as a lure or almost anything. Once they have got you hooked, they don't care about you."

"All I can say," concluded the youth, "is if you want to stop the dope racket, stop the source. Young people must stay away from all narcotics. Educate them in high school. Educate the young kids, the thousands of young high school kids that are just starting to find out about life."[40]

How many people in the United States, like this young man, are addicted to drugs? No one really knows, and the estimates range from less than one hundred thousand to more than a million.[41] According to what was considered a conservative estimate, there were 500,000 narcotic addicts in the United States in 1938.[42] The Bureau of Narcotics estimated that there were 46,798 active narcotic addicts in this country in 1961;[43] but many informed persons believe that this figure greatly understates the real extent of the problem and that drug addiction has increased, especially among young people.[44] The *Uniform Crime Reports* show that 32,956 persons were arrested for the violation of narcotic drug laws

[40] Adapted from "Confessions of a Narcotics Addict," *The Dope Peril* (Chicago: Reprinted and distributed by the Crime Prevention Bureau, 1952), pp. 13–16.

[41] For estimates, see Bingham Dai, *Opium Addiction in Chicago* (Shanghai, China: The Commercial Press, 1937), p. 6; Lawrence Kolb and A. G. DuMez, "The Prevalence and Trend of Drug Addiction in the United States and Factors Influencing It," *Public Health Reports*, XXXIX (May 23, 1924); W. L. Treadway, "Drug Addiction and Measures for Its Prevention in the United States," *Journal of the American Medical Association*, XCIX (July, 1932), 372–79; M. L. Harney, "The Drug Menace in the United States," *Proceedings of the American Prison Association, 1952*, pp. 101, 102.

[42] H. S. Williams, *Drug Addicts Are Human Beings* (Washington, D.C.: Shaw Publishing Co., 1938), p. 4.

[43] *Traffic in Opium and Other Dangerous Drugs,* Report of the Bureau of Narcotics, for the year ended December 31, 1961, U.S. Treasury Department (Washington, D.C.: Government Printing Office, 1962), pp. 52–54. This estimate is about 13,000 less than that which was made by U.S. Commissioner of Narcotics Harry J. Anslinger during Congressional hearings in 1955.

[44] See, for example, David W. Maurer and Victor H. Vogel, *Narcotics and Narcotic Addiction* (Springfield, Ill.: Charles C. Thomas, 1962), p. 9; Edwin M. Schur, *Narcotic Addiction in Britain and America* (Bloomington: Indiana University Press, 1962), pp. 43, 44; Subcommittee to Investigate Juvenile Delinquency of the Committee on the Judiciary, U.S. Senate, *Hearings* (May 9, 17, 20, Sept. 20, 21, 1962) (Washington, D.C.: Government Printing Office, 1963), Parts 11, 13, "Illegal Narcotics Traffic and Its Effects on Juvenile and Young Adult Criminality."

(federal laws excluded) in the United States during 1962.[45] However, since so many drug addicts are not reported or arrested, this figure cannot be regarded as a reliable indication of the total number of such persons in the country.

Nature of Drug Addiction. In a broad sense it may be said that "any drug that is regularly taken to produce unusual mental reactions rather than for a specific medical need is an addicting drug."[46] Many such drugs exist—some are stimulants and some are depressants. All, however, can be harmful when used for nonmedical purposes, although the unusual reactions that they produce are in the main pleasurable. The stimulants, by increasing physical and mental perception, "bring the addict into more intimate contact with the environment and give him an increased sense of power." The depressants, on the other hand, by decreasing physical perception or the acuity of certain mental processes, "enable the addict to escape innate difficulties and disagreeable features or situations of the environment."[47]

The continued use of an addicting drug will lead to drug addiction, which may be defined as "a state in which a person has lost the power of self-control with reference to a drug and abuses the drug to such an extent that the person or society is harmed."[48] In drug addiction there is compulsive and repetitious use of the drug, and the harm that the user suffers varies with the degree of his personality disorder. Furthermore, one or more of the following related but distinct conditions are always present:

1. *Tolerance,* which means that there is a gradual decrease in the effect produced by the repeated administration of the drug, and the user

[45] Federal Bureau of Investigation, *Uniform Crime Reports, 1962,* Table 19. The figure quoted here is based on reports received from agencies serving a total population of 123,571,000. The use of the Nalline test has been helpful in some cities in the detection of drug addiction. Nalline is antagonistic to opium and its derivatives, and when it is administered to an addict, it produces withdrawal symptoms and other diagnostic indications.

[46] Lawrence Kolb, "Drug Addiction as a Public Health Problem," The Scientific Monthly, XLVIII (May, 1939), 391.

[47] *Ibid.*

[48] V. H. Vogel, H. Isbell, and K. W. Chapman, "Present Status of Narcotic Addiction, with Particular Reference to Medical Indications and Comparative Addiction Liability of the Newer and Older Analgesic Drugs," *Journal of the American Medical Association,* CXXXVIII (Dec. 4, 1948), 1019.

According to the United Nations World Health Organization, "drug addiction is a state of periodic or chronic intoxication, detrimental to the individual and to society, produced by the repeated consumption of a drug (natural or synthetic). Its characteristics include: (1) an overpowering desire or need (compulsion) to continue taking the drug and to obtain it by any means; (2) a tendency to increase the dose; (3) a psychic (psychological) and sometimes a physical dependence on the effects of the drug" ("Expert Committee on Drugs Liable to Produce Addiction," *World Health Organization Technical Report Series,* No. 21 [March, 1950], pp. 6, 7).

must take progressively larger amounts to secure the initial euphoric or analgesic effect.

2. *Physical dependence,* with resulting abstinence illness when the drug is withheld.

3. *Habituation* or *psychological dependence.*[49]

According to this definition, a person might become addicted to alcohol, tobacco, or even coffee, but in criminology, the term "drug addiction" usually has reference to opium, cocaine, marihuana, and peyote, and their various derivatives, compounds, and preparations,[50] although there is some uncertainty as to whether peyote is an addicting drug.[51] Of these, cocaine and peyote are stimulants, while opium and marihuana are depressants.[52]

Opium is obtained from the opium poppy, and in its many forms it is widely used for medical purposes. Morphine, codeine, and heroin, derivatives of opium, have been used by many drug addicts in the United States. Heroin, because it is easy to adulterate and transport, has become the favorite drug of addiction in the Western world. When a person takes opium or any of its derivatives, his skin becomes slightly

[49] Maurer and Vogel, p. 32.

[50] Federal legislation is directed primarily against these four drugs and their synthetic equivalents, such as the synthetic opiates demerol, methadone, numorphan, and prinadol. However, congressional action is not necessary to put a drug under federal control. At present, this can be done quickly and easily by presidential proclamation upon the recommendation of the commissioner of narcotics after tests made under the auspices of the U.S. Public Health Service show that a new drug is addicting. Although peyote is not controlled, peyote users are eligible for treatment in federal narcotics hospitals. Apparently, however, thus far no peyote users have been treated in these hospitals (Maurer and Vogel, p. 34). According to the federal law, an addict is a person who habitually uses any drug which it defines as habit-forming so as to endanger public morals, health, safety, or welfare, or who has become so addicted that he has lost the power of self-control with reference to his addiction. See U.S. Code, Title 42, Section 201; Title 26, Section 4731; Title 21, Sections 502, 504.

In addition to the drugs covered by the federal law, some other drugs, such as the barbiturates, bromides, and certain synthetic stimulants are potentially dangerous, although they are not addicting if taken as prescribed or in accordance with the directions shown on the labels of the bottles.

[51] See, for example, Maurer and Vogel, pp. 126–28; Schur, p. 34.

[52] M. J. Pescor, "The Problem of Narcotic Drug Addiction," *Journal of Criminal Law, Criminology, and Police Science,* XLIII (Nov.–Dec., 1952), 471–73; Maurer and Vogel, pp. 54–68, 102–13, 115–18, 123–26.

The term "narcotic drugs" is sometimes used to refer to both depressants and stimulants, but in the strict sense of the word, narcotics are only those drugs which, like opium, are sleep-inducing. In the federal law, the controls on so-called "narcotic drugs" do not cover all true narcotics and include some drugs which are not really narcotic in nature.

There is also some question as to whether marihuana is a stimulant or a depressant. Probably, this difference of opinion exists because initially the user of marihuana experiences an apparent stimulation and exhilaration, which, however, is followed by depression, drowsiness, and sleep. Thus the net effect is a depressant one.

flushed, warm, and moist, the pupils of his eyes constrict, and his mouth feels dry. Usually, he has a feeling of warmth and well-being and experiences a dreamy state during which the imagination is given free play and drowsiness shades off into sleep. This is the effect that the addict seeks to create.

Cocaine, which comes from the leaves of the coca plant, brings on a feeling of calmness, increases endurance to fatigue and hunger, and stimulates both mental and physical activity. However, its pleasant effects are usually followed by disagreeable sensations, which cocaine addicts learn to counteract with morphine or heroin. A user of cocaine will be more efficient for a short period, and then will become suspicious and fearful and in general will manifest paranoid symptoms. Some addicts use a combination of cocaine and morphine or heroin, which is known as a "speed ball."

Marihuana, a drug derived from Indian hemp, tends to cause hallucinations, a peculiar distortion of the sense of time, and a releasing of inhibitions.[53] Many investigators in the United States are inclined to minimize its effects and tend to regard it as a relatively innocuous vice, whereas many students of the problem abroad are convinced that the use of marihuana is dangerous to the individual and society. However, everyone is agreed that the use of marihuana should not be condoned if for no other reason than it tends to lead its victims into more serious forms of addiction.

Peyote or mescal is secured from a species of cactus plant. Its use is almost entirely confined to Indians in the southwestern part of this country, who take peyote during certain religious ceremonies. Its effects are very much like those produced by cocaine, but there is a greater tendency to visual hallucinations.[54]

Various methods may be used to introduce drugs into the body. Opium and marihuana may be smoked;[55] powdered cocaine and heroine may be snuffed; and virtually all drugs can be taken through the mouth. However, the veteran morphine or heroin addict prefers to use a hypodermic needle to inject the drug either under his skin or directly into his veins because this method gives him quick action with a minimum of wastage. Most addicts who use hypodermic needles become careless about sterilizing them and consequently tend to develop infections and abscesses which cause unsightly scars. These scars and fresh needle marks are

[53] Hashish is a powdered and sifted form of the resin derived from the Indian hemp plant.
[54] Pescor, 472–76; Erich Hesse, *Narcotics and Drug Addiction* (New York: The Philosophical Library, 1946), pp. 76–81.
[55] Marihuana cigarettes are popularly known as "reefers."

regarded by law-enforcement authorities as presumptive signs of drug addiction.

Users of opium or any of its derivatives develop a tolerance, and perhaps those who use cocaine or marihuana also develop some tolerances;[56] but apparently those who use peyote build up little or none. All forms of opium, cocaine, marihuana, and perhaps peyote cause habituation or psychological dependence, but of these four drugs, only opium and its derivatives produce a physical dependence in the user. When a person becomes physically dependent upon a drug, it becomes as necessary as food in maintaining the physiological balance of his body, and abrupt withdrawal of it results in distressing symptoms. The first of these symptoms are yawning, watering of the eyes, running nose, sneezing, and sweating. These are followed by loss of appetite, dilation of the pupils, tremor, restlessness, and the appearance of goose flesh, and about the third day after the withdrawal of the drug, by rapid breathing, fever, marked restlessness, insomnia, increased blood pressure, nausea and vomiting, diarrhea, marked loss of weight, and generalized aches and pains. In some cases, even death may occur. But the suffering of the addict may be relieved by resuming the use of the drug. The use of opium or any of its derivatives, therefore, involves not only the securing of psychic satisfactions, but also the prevention of serious distress.[57]

Drug Addiction and Crime. Any person who illegally imports, manufactures, purchases, or sells drugs commits a crime.[58] The federal regulation of drugs is administered by the Bureau of Narcotics, which was established in 1930 in the Treasury Department, in accordance with the provisions of the Harrison Narcotic Law of 1914, the Marihuana Tax Act of 1937, the Opium Poppy Control Act of 1942, the Narcotic Control Act of 1956, and other such acts and their amendments. The federal statutes are supplemented by state and municipal laws and regulations. Within recent years, the entire program of control has been given greater strength and coherence through the operation of the Uniform Narcotic Drug Act. This act, which was drafted by the National Conference of Commissioners on Uniform State Laws in 1932, has been passed (some-

[56] A question exists as to whether cocaine and marihuana users develop a tolerance. See Maurer and Vogel, pp. 111, 116, 126; Schur, pp. 32, 33.

[57] Maurer and Vogel, pp. 53–128; National Research Council, Committee on Drug Addiction, "Studies on Drug Addiction," *Public Health Reports,* Supp. No. 138 (Washington, D.C., 1938), pp. 115, 116; Abraham Wikler, *Opiate Addiction* (Springfield, Ill.: Charles C Thomas, Publisher, 1953).

[58] In June, 1962, by a six to two decision, the United States Supreme Court ruled that it is unconstitutional for a state to make narcotic addiction a criminal offense on the grounds that such a law inflicts a cruel and unusual punishment in violation of the 14th Amendment. The broad power of a state to regulate the traffic of narcotic drugs within its borders was not an issue in this case. (*Lawrence Robinson v. State of California,* 370 U.S. 660.)

times in an amended form) by forty-eight states, the District of Columbia, and Puerto Rico.[59]

Like drunkenness, drug addiction is related to the commission of other crimes although there is considerable disagreement regarding this relationship.[60] It is certain, however, that occasionally an addict, while under the influence of a drug, commits a violent crime and that many others resort to crimes against property in order to secure money for the purchase of drugs. Nevertheless, when an addict commits a crime, it does not necessarily mean that his addiction caused him to become a criminal. Other more basic factors may have produced his criminality, just as, perhaps, they have caused his addiction.

Kolb even goes so far as to say that criminal addicts are criminals in the vast majority of cases before they begin to use drugs and that opiates never cause their users to commit violent crimes.[61] He does admit, however, that a person under the influence of cocaine might commit a crime in a frenzy of fear, following the initial period of stimulation, but insists that such a person, after passing the point of maximum stimulation, would not be able to plan and commit a deliberate crime.[62] More recently, Kolb has written that "a critical review of all the evidence strongly suggests that the impact of drug addiction on major crimes is so slight that it is imperceptible in statistics."[63] Bromberg states that only 67 of the more than 16,000 felons convicted in New York City during the period 1932–1937 were users of marihuana;[64] and later Bromberg and Rodgers discovered "no positive relationship between aggressive crime and marihuana usage in the Naval Service."[65] Pescor is of the opinion that "the average opium, heroin, or morphine addict is not inherently a criminal," although he may resort to begging, borrowing, or stealing in

[59] California and Pennsylvania have not passed the Uniform Narcotic Drug Act. However, California and Pennsylvania have adopted a different law which is considered to be equally effective. See the Council of State Governments, *Record of Passage of Uniform and Model Acts, as of December 1, 1963.*

[60] See, for example, Alfred R. Lindesmith, " 'Dope Fiend' Mythology," *Journal of Criminal Law and Criminology,* XXXI (July–Aug., 1940), 199–208; Twain Michelsen, "Lindesmith's Mythology," *ibid.,* XXXI (Nov.–Dec., 1940), 375–400; Alfred R. Lindesmith, "The Drug Addict: Patient or Criminal?" *ibid.,* XXXI (Jan.–Feb., 1941), 531–35. See also Paul B. Weston (ed.), *Narcotics, U. S. A.* (New York: Greenberg, Publisher, 1952), pp 143–53; Harold Finestone, "Narcotics and Criminality," *Law and Contemporary Problems,* XXII (Winter 1957), 69–85.

[61] Lawrence Kolb, "Drug Addiction and Its Relation to Crime," *Mental Hygiene,* IX (Jan., 1925), 74–83.

[62] *Ibid.,* 76.

[63] Lawrence Kolb, *Drug Addiction* (Springfield, Ill.: Charles C. Thomas, Publisher, 1962), p. 34.

[64] Walter Bromberg, "Marihuana, A Psychiatric Study," *Journal of the American Medical Association,* CXIII (July, 1939), 10.

[65] Walter Bromberg and Terry C. Rodgers, "Marihuana and Aggressive Crime," *American Journal of Psychiatry,* CII (May, 1946), 826.

order to purchase drugs. He further states that since marihuana, cocaine, and peyote do not produce physical dependence, the user of them, unlike the person addicted to opium or any of its derivatives, does not have the extreme drive to get them at any cost. According to him, these three drugs, like alcohol, release inhibitions, thereby revealing the true character of the person, and if the user is base, vicious, or criminally inclined, he will exhibit these traits more readily when under the influence of the drugs than when he is not.[66] In a study of 1,036 patients at the United States Public Health Hospital for Narcotic Addicts at Lexington, Kentucky, Pescor found that three-fourths of them had no official record of delinquency prior to addiction and that most of those who had such a record after addiction had violated only the drug laws, while the majority of the remaining offenders had been guilty of only petty crimes in addition to their drug law violations.[67] Ausubel reports that most studies of the criminal records of opiate addicts show that about three-fourths of all investigated cases had no history of criminal violations before addiction.[68] Maurer and Vogel, after examining the results of a number of studies, conclude that "addicting drugs do not appear to be the direct cause of crime, with the possible exception of cocaine and hemp, which is not as yet consumed in its concentrated form in the United States," but that the demands of the drug habit will, unless the addict has almost unlimited funds, "force him to become a liar, a forger, a thief, and, eventually, a total social parasite."[69]

The most serious offenders in the activities connected with drug addiction, however, are the smugglers, the distributors, and the peddlers. They often introduce the addict to the drug, heartlessly keep him supplied with it, even to the point of guiding him into crime so as to get money to maintain the habit, and contribute to the corruption of public officials and the support of organized crime.

Causes and Treatment. As in the case of alcoholism, no one theory can explain drug addiction. It is produced by the interaction of many factors, which vary from patient to patient and which can be analyzed only by an intensive study of the individual case.[70] On the basis of our present

[66] M. J. Pescor, "Drug Addiction," *Encyclopedia of Criminology* (New York: The Philosophical Library, 1949), p. 132.

[67] M. J. Pescor, "A Statistical Analysis of the Clinical Records of Hospitalized Drug Addicts," *Public Health Reports,* Supp. No. 143 (Washington, D.C., 1938), pp. 25, 26.

[68] David P. Ausubel, *Drug Addiction: Physiological, Psychological, and Sociological Aspects* (New York: Random House, Inc., 1958), p. 68.

[69] Maurer and Vogel, pp. 256, 257.

[70] Arnold Z. Pfeffer, "Narcotic Addiction," *Journal of Criminal Law, Criminology, and Police Science,* XLIII (Sept.–Oct., 1952), 328. See also Kenneth W. Chapman, "What Makes a Drug Addict?" *Proceedings of the American Prison Association, 1949,* pp. 67–74.

knowledge, this appears to be the best statement that can be made. In fact, our knowledge of the causes of drug addiction seems to be even more incomplete and fragmentary than that of the causes of alcoholism, but among the causative factors that have been emphasized by various studies are pain, illness, fatigue, mental abnormalities, escapism, medical habituation, association with drug addicts, curiosity about the effects of drugs, and "proselytizing" by confirmed addicts.[71]

However, several interesting theories regarding drug addiction have been advanced by sociologists. Lindesmith states that a person becomes addicted to opiates when he realizes that they can relieve the symptoms of distress which he perceives to be caused by the withdrawal of drugs. In the process of addiction, the individual, finding that he cannot free himself from dependence on drugs, changes his conception of himself and more and more begins to play the role of the addict. Thus, according to Lindesmith, opiate addiction is learned just as other behavior is learned, primarily from association with others who are addicts, and it is not caused by certain personality traits or by the desire to escape from the harsh realities of life.[72] Critics of this theory, however, point out that it applies only to those cases of addiction in which there is a physiological dependence, that it does not explain the reason for the positive satisfaction enjoyed by users, and that it fails to account for the selective incidence of addiction. It thus leaves unanswered such questions as: Why does only a small minority of persons with access to drugs begin to use them habitually? and Why do certain persons find drugs more pleasurable than others and continue to use them for adjustive purposes?[73]

Becker has proposed a similar theory to explain the genesis of marihuana addiction. Dispensing with personality predispositions, he seeks to explain the use of marihuana entirely in terms of the learning process, during which the user comes to recognize the effects, to connect them with the smoking of the drug, and to enjoy the sensations he perceives.[74] As in the case of the parallel theory advanced by Lindesmith, Becker's

[71] For some of these studies, see Lawrence Kolb, "Drug Addictions: A Study of Some Medical Cases," *Archives of Neurology and Psychiatry*, XX (July, 1928), 171–83; M. J. Pescor, "The Kolb Classification of Drug Addicts," *Public Health Reports*, Supp. No. 155 (Washington, D.C., 1939); Alfred R. Lindesmith, "A Sociological Theory of Drug Addiction," *American Journal of Sociology*, XLIII (Jan. 1938), 593–609; and J. D. Reichard, "Narcotic Drug Addiction, a Symptom of Human Maladjustment," *Diseases of the Nervous System*, IV (Sept., 1943), 275–81.

[72] Alfred R. Lindesmith, "A Sociological Theory of Drug Addiction," *American Journal of Sociology*, XLIII (Jan., 1938), 593–613. See also Alfred R. Lindesmith, *Opiate Addiction* (Bloomington, Ind.: Principia Press, Inc., 1947).

[73] For a critical analysis of Lindesmith's theory, see Ausubel, pp. 34–36, 67.

[74] Howard S. Becker, "Becoming a Marihuana User," *American Journal of Sociology*, LIX (Nov., 1953), 235–42.

views have been criticized for failing to explain why only certain individuals find the use of a drug pleasurable in the first place, and why only a minority of those who do enjoy it continue its usage.[75]

Educational programs regarding the nature and ill effects of drugs, conducted through churches, schools, clubs, the press, the radio, and television, undoubtedly can contribute in an important way to the prevention of drug addiction.[76] What can be accomplished along this line was demonstrated a few years ago by a Boston University television series, during which high school students were brought into talk about the dangers of drugs. Calling drug addiction a disease also has increased public understanding of its ravages, but drug addiction, like alcoholism, can never be just a disease. To consider it so may actually permit, or even encourage, the addict to shift his moral and legal responsibilities to others and to employ further rationalization in support of his addiction, and, moreover, increase the number of addicts by removing the stigma from drug addiction.

During the years immediately after World War I, forty-four or more narcotic clinics or dispensaries were opened by municipal or state health officials in large cities throughout the United States in an effort to reduce the problem of drug addiction. Persons suffering from the habit were permitted to make daily visits to these clinics in order to receive a course of treatment, during which they were given restricted doses of drugs at a low cost. Abuses arose, however, and it soon became clear that this experiment had failed. Addicts were unable or unwilling to complete the course of treatment, and the drugs that were dispensed found their way into a thriving illicit traffic, thus contributing to the number of drug addicts and largely nullifying the constructive efforts of the clinics. Many medical authorities and law-enforcement officials condemned the clinical program, urged that it be abolished, and insisted that institutional isolation could provide the only effective treatment for drug addiction. By the end of 1925, all of these clinics had been closed and the experiment was abandoned,[77] and today most leading authorities in the field are strongly opposed to suggestions that it be revived.

According to these authorities, any person who has become physically dependent on drugs cannot be treated at home or in a general hospital. He must be placed in a special hospital or institution which has custodial precautions to insure a drug-free environment. The first step in his treat-

[75] Ausubel, pp. 100, 101.

[76] Ibid., pp. 111–19; Maurer and Vogel, pp. 164–66.

[77] Narcotic Clinics in the United States (Washington, D.C.: Government Printing Office, 1953); U.S. Senate Special Committee to Investigate Organized Crime in Interstate Commerce, Hearings (May 29, June 7, 12, 26, and 27, 1951) (Washington, D.C.: Government Printing Office, 1951), Part 14, "Narcotics," pp. 129–38, 226–29, 237–52.

ment is the withdrawal of the drug, which usually takes about ten days. This involves a gradual reduction in dosage so as to minimize the severity of the withdrawal symptoms.[78] Next, an effort is made to remove his psychological dependence on the drug. This is more difficult than the removal of the physical dependence and includes the correction of physical defects, psychotherapy, recreational therapy, occupational therapy, vocational training, education, religious instruction, and the like. It appears that the optimum period for this stage of the treatment is about four to six months.

When a person is not physically dependent on a drug, he may be treated extramurally. The emphasis in his treatment is upon the removal of his psychological dependence on the drug. However, he must be kept away from drugs and carefully supervised by someone who can coordinate all available services in behalf of the patient.[79]

Some authorities, however, are not satisfied with the way the problem of drug addiction is being handled in the United States and they advocate the establishment of a system of noncoercive, ambulatory treatment in free out-patient clinics or in the offices of physicians. In support of this advocacy, they contend that the public-clinic plan was not given a fair trial after World War I, that it would allow addicts, some of whom are incurable, to lead productive lives and abandon criminal activity, that it would abolish the illicit traffic in drugs by removal of the profit motive, and that the nonpunitive, medical method used in Britain has been more successful than our legalistic, punitive one, which, they claim, has been able to effect cures in only a small percentage of drug-addiction cases.[80]

[78] When opiates are withdrawn abruptly, the patient's skin tends to take on an appearance similar to that of a plucked bird. For this reason, the abrupt withdrawal method is often referred to as the "cold turkey" treatment. This procedure is sometimes used in jails because it is cheap and quick, but care must be exercised to prevent the death of the patient.

[79] M. J. Pescor, "Problem of Narcotic Drug Addiction," *Journal of Criminal Law, Criminology, and Police Science*, XLIII (Nov.–Dec., 1952), 476–78; Victor H. Vogel, "Treatment of the Narcotic Addict by the U.S. Public Health Service," *Federal Probation*, XII (June, 1948), 45–60; Stephen J. Corey, "A Chaplain Looks at Drug Addiction," *Federal Probation*, XV (Sept., 1951), 17–24; Maurer and Vogel, pp. 162–91.

[80] For a presentation of the case for the nonpunitive, medical method of dealing with drug addiction, see Edwin M. Schur, *Narcotic Addiction in Britain and America* (Bloomington: Indiana University Press, 1962). See also William Butler Eldridge, *Narcotics and the Law: A Critique of the American Experiment in Narcotic Drug Control* (New York: New York University Press, 1962); Rufus King, "An Appraisal of International, British and Selected European Narcotic Drug Laws, Regulations and Policies," *Drug Addiction: Crime or Disease?* Interim and Final Reports of the Joint Committee of the American Bar Association and the American Medical Association on Narcotic Drugs, Appendix B (Bloomington: Indiana University Press, 1961), pp. 121–55.

In 1955, the New York Academy of Medicine proposed a program in which the addict would be treated as a sick person rather than a criminal, the profit motive

In reply, the opponents of the public-clinic plan have argued: that there is no reason to believe that the typical drug-satiated addict would lead a socially productive life in the community and complete his course of treatment; that the profit motive would not be entirely eliminated from the illicit drug traffic since there would still be a market for drugs among new converts; that, as was the case in attempts to legalize prostitution, public officials would be corrupted and become involved with organized criminals in illicit activities; that some registered addicts, by theft, deceit, or connivance, would obtain more drugs from the clinic than they required and sell the surplus at high prices to nonregistered addicts; that comparatively few addicts need to be maintained indefinitely on drugs; that British success in the problem of drug addiction is due largely to aversion in their culture to the use of drugs rather than to the effectiveness of their methods;[81] and that legalization, even for confirmed addicts, would give drug addiction a social sanction and thus tend to encourage it and undermine the moral structure of society.[82] Many authorities in the fields of law and medicine hope that out of this controversy will develop a more fruitful combination of legal and medical controls for dealing with the problem of drug addiction.

Although progress has been made in the treatment of drug addiction, the prognosis is still unfavorable. Investigations indicate that most addicts,

---

would be taken out of the illicit traffic by furnishing drugs at low cost through a national system of federally controlled dispensary clinics, and the current enforcement machinery would be maintained to suppress the illicit market in drugs (*Drug Addiction: Crime or Disease?* pp. 93–95).

In 1956, the Joint Committee of the American Bar Association and the American Medical Association on Narcotic Drugs issued a report which, although not recommending the establishment of public clinics, did urge that research be conducted in an out-patient experimental clinic for the treatment of drug addicts (*Drug Addiction: Crime or Disease?* p. 161).

In 1956, the Council on Mental Health of the American Medical Association, in a report on narcotic addiction, stated, "In view of all of the available evidence at the present time it does not seem feasible to recommend the establishment of clinics for the supply of drugs to addicts" (*Drug Addiction: Crime or Disease?* p. 173).

[81] In 1960, a team of medical men from the New York Department of Health visited England to investigate the so-called "British System" and reported that the controls there were effective because the problem was very much smaller and not because of any unique system, that there were no "clinics" for the dissemination of drugs to addicts, who were hospitalized for treatment much as they are in the United States, and that the chief difference between the States and England seemed to be a marked difference in the susceptibility of the population to the use of drugs and to addiction (Maurer and Vogel, pp. 225, 226). Schur has called this report "a misleading account" and attacked its validity (Schur, pp. 182–85).

[82] Maurer and Vogel, pp. 166–70, 225, 226; Ausubel, pp. 75–79; Kolb, *Drug Addiction*, pp. 147–50; Harry J. Anslinger and Will Oursler, *The Murderers: The Story of the Narcotic Gangs* (New York: Farrar, Straus and Cudahy, 1961), 234–43; Harry J. Anslinger and William F. Tompkins, *The Traffic in Narcotics* (New York: Funk and Wagnalls Co., 1953).

after receiving treatment, return to the use of drugs. One estimate states that as many as 96.7 per cent suffer such a relapse within five years.[83] However, the figures reported in 1948 by the United States Public Health Service Hospital at Lexington, Kentucky, are more encouraging. A study made there of patients discharged during the years 1942 through 1946 indicated that 22.3 per cent of the men and 29.8 per cent of the women, excluding voluntary patients who left against advice, were reliably believed not to have relapsed to the use of drugs; that 35.1 per cent of the men and 36.6 per cent of the women were reliably believed to have relapsed to the use of drugs; and that the status of 42.6 per cent of the men and 33.6 per cent of the women was unknown. It was believed that a fair proportion of those whose status was unknown had not again taken up the use of drugs.[84]

THE PROSTITUTE

Sue was only twenty-two but she had seen a lot of life. The police picked her up in the vicinity of a large army camp and charged her with prostitution. She readily admitted intimacy with many servicemen and was found to be infected with gonorrhea. Sue had good features, and she might have been an attractive woman; but she suffered from tuberculosis, and her face was badly scarred as the result of a tavern brawl. Hard and cynical, she appeared to be satisfied with her mode of life.

"I've been making it alone since I was fourteen and I guess I don't need help from nobody now," was the way she sized up her situation.

Life stretched out behind Sue in a series of hardening experiences. Her father died when she was five. After that she and her mother traveled about the country for several years with a carnival, but finally the mother abandoned Sue and passed entirely out of the child's life. Sue was taken care of by the owner of the carnival until she was fourteen, when she ran off with a married man who deserted her a year or so later. She then began living with another man who taught her the ways of prostitution and solicited customers for her. However, this relationship, too, was short lived, and Sue went to work in a tavern where she served as waitress and part-time prostitute. It was while she was working there that her face was cut by a broken beer bottle thrown by a customer.

"After I got patched up," Sue explained, "I went to work in a regular house of prostitution, and soon I was going around the country from house to house. I was making real money and everything was going fine for about two years when—just my luck—I got sick and had to quit."

[83] Alfred R. Lindesmith, *Opiate Addiction* (Bloomington, Ind.: Principia Press, Inc., 1947), p. 49.

[84] Vogel, "Treatment of the Narcotic Addict by the U.S. Public Health Service," 48, 49.

In need of money, Sue drifted to the army camps and shortly thereafter was arrested.

Prostitution, the crime with which Sue was charged, is "the act or practice of a woman who permits any man who will pay her price to have sexual intercourse with her."[85] It may be said to have three essential elements: hire, promiscuity, and emotional indifference.[86]

It is not known how many prostitutes there are in the United States, and estimates vary widely. One estimate, made about the end of World War II, stated that America had about 600,000 public prostitutes and about the same number of women who had engaged in prostitution but also had other means of livelihood.[87] The *Uniform Crime Reports* show that 27,580 persons were arrested for prostitution and commercialized vice during 1962,[88] but because of the difficulty of detecting such crimes and because police often pick up prostitutes on some other charge, such as vagrancy, this figure probably represents only a small fraction of the total possible violations. As a result of a vigorous program of suppression,[89] open prostitution sharply declined during World War II, but for a few years after the war, it apparently increased, especially in those cities where the population was about 100,000. Between 1948 and 1956, however, the size of the problem definitely decreased.[90]

Personnel of Prostitution. There are various types of prostitutes. Egen, using the method of operation as the basis of his classification, distinguishes four principal types: (1) the call girl, (2) the hustler, (3) the doorknocker, and (4) the factory girl.[91] The call girl receives telephone calls from a selected group of customers and makes arrangements to meet them at designated places. She may work alone or in partnership with an intermediary with whom she shares her earnings. The hustler may be a bar

[85] *Black's Law Dictionary* (3d ed.; St. Paul, Minn.: West Publishing Co., 1933), p. 1451.

[86] See Kingsley Davis, "The Sociology of Prostitution," *American Sociological Review*, II (Oct., 1937), 749.

[87] "Vice, Regulation of," *Encyclopedia Americana* (New York, 1945), Vol. XXVIII, p. 58.

[88] Federal Bureau of Investigation, *Uniform Crime Reports, 1962*, Table 19. The figure quoted here is based on reports received from agencies serving a total population of 123,571,000.

[89] See *Federal Probation*, VII (Apr.–June, 1943). This entire issue is devoted to the problem of prostitution and the program formulated to control it during World War II.

[90] Paul M. Kinsie, "Law Enforcement Progress During 1947," *Journal of Social Hygiene*, XXXIII (Dec., 1947), 446; *ibid.*, "Prostitution—Then and Now," *ibid.*, XXXIX (June, 1953), 241–48; Robert Y. Thornton, "Organized Crime in the Field of Prostitution," *Journal of Criminal Law, Criminology, and Police Science*, XLVI (Mar.–Apr., 1956), 775–79.

[91] Frederick W. Egen, *Plainclothesman* (New York: Greenberg, Publisher, 1952), pp. 100–104.

or tavern "pickup" or a streetwalker. The bar or tavern "pickup" frequents places where liquor is sold, sometimes operating with the knowledge of the management. The streetwalker is the oldest and probably the most common type of prostitute. She finds her customers in various places and makes the contact herself, but she may work with taxicab drivers and commit the act of prostitution in a taxicab. The door-knocker is a newcomer in the field of prostitution. She frequents small hotels and furnished room houses occupied by Chinese, Puerto Rican, and Filipino men, and roaming the hallways of these places, she knocks on doors and calls out, "Girlie, girlie, cheap." The factory girl works in a regular house of prostitution. She is so called because her work can be likened to employment in a factory. She accepts all comers, has nothing to do with selecting or soliciting the customers, works regular hours, and is under the direct supervision of the madam.[92]

Various auxiliary personnel may be associated with the prostitute in her work. The madam is the general manager of a house of prostitution. She supervises the girls, meets the customers, handles the cash, and transacts all business for the house. Today there are three types of houses: the disorderly house, the furnished-room house, and the call house. The disorderly house, which employs from about four to eight girls, is becoming scarce in the United States because it is an easy target for the organized program against prostitution. The furnished-room house is usually operated by an experienced madam who has left an organized ring and gone into business for herself. She has two or three girls and also rents rooms to legitimate roomers in order to maintain an appearance of respectability. A call house is merely a place where a telephone is maintained by a madam. When a customer calls, the madam sends the girl out to meet him. Thus, this type of house differs from the other houses of prostitution in that the unlawful sex acts do not usually take place in it.

The procurer functions as a member of an organized mob concerned with prostitution and is charged with the responsibility of getting girls to work as prostitutes. Years ago, the procurer used to team up with an older woman and with her intimidate and coerce girls into prostitution. Today, however, this is unnecessary. Girls are available, and many of them are willing and even eager to get into the business.[93] The transporter is a man or woman who takes prostitutes from one town to another. He is a highly trusted person, usually operating with an automobile and is held responsible for the safe arrival of the girls. The pimp, who may be a

---

[92] *Ibid.*, p. 104.

[93] In the United States, the obtaining of girls to serve as prostitutes in brothels has been given the name of "white slave traffic." The term is intended to emphasize the idea that procuring may force white girls into prostitution, as the Negroes were forced into slavery, and then keep them like slaves in brothels.

bellboy, taxicab driver, newsboy, bartender, or even the girl's own husband, gets the customers. For a salary or for a percentage of the earnings, he solicits customers for a house, for several girls, or for one girl.[94]

Prostitution and Crime. Prostitution has been defined as the indiscriminate sexual intercourse of a woman for hire, and in the absence of statutes to the contrary this definition is usually followed by the courts.[95] In most states in the United States, prostitution and all activities associated with it, such as procuring, pimping, and keeping or patronizing a house of prostitution, are crimes (usually misdemeanors) and punishable by fines, imprisonment, or both. In fact, prostitution is a crime in every state except Nevada (where, however, it may be made such in a town or city by local ordinance); and even in Nevada it is against the law to engage in procuring or to live off the earnings of a prostitute.[96]

Furthermore, prostitution is inextricably interwoven with many other criminal activities. Sometimes the house of prostitution is only part of the organized criminal activities of a syndicate; often it is a haven for fugitives from justice and a "hang-out" for gunmen, gangsters, dope peddlers, drug addicts, bootleggers, hijackers, and a general assortment of criminals and underworld characters. The prostitute herself often commits other crimes, supplementing her earnings by stealing from her customers, shoplifting, and peddling dope, and finding relief from the conflicts of her life in the use of drugs and alcohol.[97]

Personal Causes and Effects of Prostitution. The causes of a woman's entrance into prostitution vary from case to case, but Reckless, while admitting this, is of the opinion that (1) poor social background and personality handicaps constitute the basis for drift into prostitution; (2) previous sexual experience, mostly unfortunate, in or out of wedlock, is a factor which adds to a girl's vulnerability for drift into prostitution; and (3) contact with persons in or on the fringe of prostitution is necessary to lead the vulnerable girl to enter prostitution.[98] Although Reckless, in

[94] Egen, *Plainclothesman*, pp. 94–100.

[95] George Gould, *Laws Against Prostitution and Their Use* (New York: The American Social Hygiene Association, Publication No. A–458x, 1944), p. 4.

[96] *Ibid.*, pp. 4, 7. Also letters dated December 18, 1953, from the attorneys general of Arizona and Nevada. The Supreme Court of Nevada has held that prostitution is a nuisance per se, and where it is discovered, the district attorney is obligated to call it to the attention of the county commissioners with a request that the nuisance be abated (letter dated November 4, 1963, from the attorney general of Nevada).

[97] See Courtney Ryley Cooper, *Designs in Scarlet* (Boston: Little, Brown and Co., 1939), for a vivid account of prostitution and crime prior to World War II. For a recent statement on vice conditions in Chicago, see Virgil W. Peterson, *A Report on Chicago Crime for 1962* (Chicago: Chicago Crime Commission, June 28, 1963), pp. 69–79.

[98] Walter C. Reckless, *The Crime Problem* (New York: Appleton-Century-Crofts, Inc., 1950), pp. 229, 230.

general, may be correct in his appraisal of the situation, investigations of commercialized vice reveal that many women enter prostitution principally because they want to make money, and not because they are forced into it by poverty, loneliness, desertion, or broken promises.[99]

Unusual women may be able to avoid the occupational hazards of prostitution, but the average prostitute tends to succumb to a process of demoralization and physical deterioration. Arrests, imprisonments, venereal infection, social ostracism, poor personal hygiene, the excessive use of alcohol, and irregular habits of eating and sleeping take their toll and force her downward to the status of a derelict.[100]

The Control of Prostitution. The two major methods of controlling prostitution are regulation and suppression. The method of regulation, perhaps best typified by the French system established under the direction of Napoleon Bonaparte in 1808, involves (1) the segregation of brothels and soliciting to restricted districts, (2) the licensing of houses of prostitution, (3) the registration of prostitutes, and (4) their periodic medical examination. This method of control, however, suffers from serious, if not fatal, defects.[101] Important among these are the following:

1. *Segregation does not segregate.* It has proved impossible to keep even most of the prostitutes within the restricted district.

2. *Many prostitutes fail to register, either through negligence or desire to avoid the stigma which registration imposes.* The young prostitute especially seeks to evade regulation so that her record will not interfere with future employment and marriage, and yet she is the very one who serves the most customers and is most likely to contract venereal disease.

3. *The medical inspection does not protect.* Reputable and competent doctors avoid the work; reliable blood tests and examinations are expensive and time-consuming; and the prostitute in order to avoid unemployment tries to conceal her infection. As a result, the inspection tends to be perfunctory, detecting only the most obvious cases. Even if the examination is thorough, an infection may not be discovered, or the infected girl

---

[99] See, for example, Michael Stern, *The White Ticket* (New York: National Library Press, 1936). For additional insights into the causes of prostitution, see Anonymous, *Streetwalker,* (New York: The Viking Press, 1960); Harold Greenwald, *Call Girl* (New York: Ballantine Books, 1958); John M. Murtagh and Sara Harris, *Cast the First Stone* (New York: McGraw-Hill Book Co., 1957); Norman R. Jackman and Richard O'Toole, "The Self-Image of the Prostitute," *The Sociological Quarterly,* IV (Spring, 1963), 150–61.

[100] Reckless, p. 234; Social Protection Division, Federal Security Agency, *Challenge to Community Action* (Washington, D.C., 1945), pp. 2–6; Miriam Van Waters, "Study and Treatment of Persons Charged with Prostitution," *Federal Probation,* VII (Apr.–June, 1943), 27–30; Helen Hironimus, "Survey of 100 May Act Violators Committed to the Federal Reformatory for Women," *ibid.,* 31–34.

[101] See Abraham Flexner, *Prostitution in Europe* (New York: Appleton-Century-Crofts, Inc., 1920). France abolished the system of regulation shortly after World War II, but through subsequent legislation virtually restored it.

may not be isolated and given effective treatment. Moreover, if the prostitute is free of disease at the time of examination, she may be infected shortly thereafter and communicate disease to many customers before her next examination. And furthermore, an uninfected woman may be at any time a mechanical conveyor of infection from one customer to succeeding ones. During World War II, "controlled" prostitution in the city of Honolulu was a dismal failure. Sex crimes did not decline, and venereal disease flourished despite the fact that the Navy established prophylactic stations at or nearby the entrances of most of the houses, and the prostitutes had contact with a selected group of customers—most of them were military personnel—rather than with riffraff that usually frequents the houses of prostitution in our big cities.

4. *Regulation creates a false sense of security.* The ignorant or reckless individual who visits a licensed brothel contracts syphilis or gonorrhea all the more surely because, in his overconfidence, he takes no precautions and does not look for symptoms or consult a doctor if they develop. Since regulation makes possible the processing of a large number of patrons, and since it does not protect them from infection, it actually spreads disease while lulling the community into a false sense of security.

5. *Regulation promotes prostitution, fosters immorality, corrupts officials, and increases crime.* By advertising prostitution, by presenting an ever-present and protected opportunity for its use, by providing a show place for special obscene and depraved exhibits, regulation stimulates the demand for prostitution and thus increases its supply. Prostitution is a business, and when it is legalized, its profits are employed to make its wares more attractive and to expand its market. Free rein is given to the exploitation of prostitutes; new ones must be recruited; and sexual perversions and abnormalities are featured to attract jaded patrons. Regulation increases graft by tempting dishonest public officials and law-enforcement officers to exact illegal revenue and to confer illegal privileges. It incites crimes against women by fostering sexual promiscuity, brutalization, and degeneracy. It gives aid and comfort to the criminal, idle, and vicious elements in society by furnishing them with licensed meeting places and by pandering to their depravity and lasciviousness. It complicates law enforcement by providing a business enterprise which lends itself to domination by syndicates engaged in organized criminal activities such as illegal drug and liquor traffic.[102]

102 Thomas B. Turner, "The Suppression of Prostitution in Relation to Venereal Disease Control in the Army," *Federal Probation,* VII (Apr.–June, 1943), 8–11; Eliot Ness, "Federal Government's Program in Attacking the Problem of Prostitution," *ibid.,* 17–19; Philip S. Broughton, *Prostitution and the War* (New York: Public Affairs Committee, Inc., Pamphlet No. 65, 1943); The American Social Hygiene Association, Inc., *Why Let It Burn?* Publication No. A–304, 1941; The American Social Hygiene Association, Inc., *The Case Against Prostitution,* Publication No. A–303, 1940.

The method of suppression, sometimes called the "American plan" because it has received its greatest support in this country, where it is consistent with the mores, recognizes that prostitution cannot be entirely eliminated, but claims that it can be greatly reduced by unrelenting, organized opposition. This method includes the following major elements:

1. *Strict enforcement of legislation against prostitution and all activities connected with it.*[103] This involves the inspection and supervision of potential trouble spots, the revocation of the licenses of offending business establishments, and the vigorous prosecution of all offenders. The argument that such repression spreads prostitution is not borne out by the facts when there is efficient law enforcement. As one veteran police officer put it, "Prostitution will not spread unless the police force is too stupid to prevent it.[104] The federal government, all states, and many cities have some kind of laws to control prostitution. The Mann Act of 1910, which prohibits the transportation of women across state lines for immoral purposes, and the May Act of 1941, which makes prostitution a federal offense in areas within a reasonable distance of army or navy establishments when this is deemed necessary to protect the health of servicemen, provide a legal basis for action by federal law-enforcement officers. State legislation varies considerably, and although many states have adequate laws, some gaps still exist. For example, in 1945, it was not a crime to live off the earnings of a prostitute in seven states or to own a house of prostitution in four states.[105] However, many states have adopted the Standard Vice-Repressive Law which was drafted by the federal government in 1919. This law provides for the punishment of prostitutes, pimps, customers, and keepers of houses of prostitution.[106]

2. *Education of the public regarding sex, prostitution, and venereal disease.* The American Social Hygiene Association has played a leading part in this educational program. It has used newspapers, posters, pamphlets, books, films, and the radio to inform people regarding the nature of venereal disease and its dangers and to urge them to report for treatment.

3. *Adoption of medical measures and establishment of medical facilities for the diagnosis and treatment of venereal disease.* In 1938, Congress

[103] For manuals for the use of law-enforcement officers in dealing with the problem of prostitution, see: National Advisory Police Committee on Social Protection of the Federal Security Agency, *Techniques of Law Enforcement Against Prostitution* (Washington, D.C.: Government Printing Office, 1943), and *Techniques of Law Enforcement in the Use of Policewomen with Special Reference to Social Protection* (Washington, D.C.: Government Printing Office, 1945).

[104] Broughton, p. 20.

[105] Social Protection Division, Federal Security Agency, *Challenge to Community Action* (Washington, D.C., 1945), p. 21.

[106] Gould, p. 5. In 1944, nineteen states had the Vice-Repressive Law in its entirety on their statute books while ten other states had adopted major parts of it.

passed the National Venereal Disease Control Act. It supplied funds for the first nation-wide attack on venereal disease by providing grants-in-aid to the states and money for research and education. All states and most large cities have divisions of venereal disease control, although many counties still have no full-time health department. The United States Public Health Service, in cooperation with state and local authorities, operates clinics and hospitals for the treatment of venereal disease.[107]

4. *Rehabilitation of prostitutes.* This involves medical examinations, treatment, detention for at least the period of venereal infection, case studies, counseling, material aid, vocational education, job placement, and post-release guidance. As yet, few jails and workhouses in the United States can do more than detain prostitutes for medical treatment, but state correctional institutions, to which chronic offenders are committed, provide various types and grades of rehabilitation services.[108]

5. *Adoption of codes of self-regulation and organization of community cooperation.* Operators and owners of taxicabs, taverns, bars, juke joints, eating places, bowling alleys, dance halls, motion picture theaters, hotels, tourist camps, motels, and other such public places, with the assistance of their associations, law-enforcement officers, health officials, and welfare workers, are encouraged to adopt codes of self-regulation and to enforce their provisions. Citizens' committees are organized to assist in the education of the public and to give support to law-enforcement, medical, and welfare officials. The method of repression is thus given a depth and vitality that it would not otherwise have.[109]

[107] The evidence indicates that venereal disease, especially among teenagers, is increasing in the United States. See, for example, U.S. Department of Health, Education, and Welfare, Public Health Service, *The Eradiction of Syphilis*, Publication No. 918 (Washington, D.C.: Government Printing Office, 1962).

[108] *Challenge to Community Action*, pp. 13–44; Walter C. Reckless, "A Sociologist Looks at Prostitution," *Federal Probation*, VII (Apr.–June, 1943), 12–16; Raymond F. Clapp, "Social Treatment of Prostitutes and Promiscuous Women," *ibid.*, 23–27; Bascom Johnson, "When Brothels Close, V. D. Rates Go Down," *Journal of Social Hygiene*, XXVIII (Dec., 1942), 525–35; Richard A. Koch and Ray Lyman Wilbur, "Promiscuity as a Factor in the Spread of Venereal Disease," *Journal of Social Hygiene*, XXX (Dec., 1944), 517–29.

[109] *Challenge to Community Action*, pp. 60, 61.

7

Professional and White-Collar Criminals

THE PROFESSIONAL CRIMINAL

Jack's parents were killed in an automobile accident when he was a baby, and he lived with his grandmother. She was employed during the day, and after school Jack spent most of his time with a neighborhood gang. It was to impress them that he committed his first crime at fifteen, when he broke into a store and stole candy and cigarettes.

In explaining this act, he now says: "I wanted to show them that I had guts. I got away with it, and I suppose that made me want more of that kind of excitement. Anyway, soon after that some of the other guys and I began to break into other stores in the neighborhood. We got caught and they sent us to the industrial school. While I was there, I learned a lot about crime and met some fellows with whom I pulled some stick-up jobs later."

But the "stick-up business" was not a very successful one for Jack, and within a year or so he found himself in the state reformatory. This convinced him that he would have to have more education if he was going to make crime pay, and during his term of imprisonment he studied English, typing, shorthand, psychology, and salesmanship.

After his release, he and his cousin carefully planned to burglarize apartment houses in the better residential areas. Posing as commercial representatives of various corporations, sometimes as sales engineers, sometimes as public relations experts, with forged credentials and stolen brochures, they called at apartment houses during the day in order to study the layout and learn the habits of the occupants. Then, equipped with this knowledge, they committed their burglaries at night. In this way, during the next three years, they traveled about the country, spending their winters in Florida and their summers in the best northern resorts. They committed over sixty burglaries, lived well, and were regarded as two of the best in the business. "What is more," Jack insists, "we'd still be living on the fat of the land if we hadn't become careless." And after listening to this soft-spoken, well-poised, handsome man, one is inclined to agree with him.

The professional criminal, of which Jack is an example, has certain characteristics which distinguish him from other types of criminals. The most important of these characteristics may be summarized as follows:

1. The professional criminal makes crime a business. It is his livelihood, and to it he devotes his working time and energy and constantly seeks to improve himself in its pursuit. Like other American businessmen, he tends to specialize, committing a certain type of crime and obeying the law except when it interferes with his criminal specialty.

2. The professional criminal operates with proficiency, taking pride in the smoothness with which he commits his crimes and having contempt for those who bungle and fail. He carefully plans his work, taking calculated risks but using his technical knowledge and experience to avoid unnecessary ones, and then performs his acts with skill, polish, and finesse. It is in this proficiency that the professional criminal differs from the habitual criminal who commits crimes regularly but without specialized skills.

3. The professional criminal is a graduate of a process of development during which he acquires his specialized attitudes, knowledge, experience, and skills. Usually this development takes place under the tutelage of someone who has already achieved proficiency and status in his criminal specialty, although rarely as part of a formal program of recruitment and apprenticeship. Some professional criminals begin their careers as juvenile delinquents and then graduate into more serious crimes, but others take the first steps as adults and move into crime from allied legitimate occupations and professions. Thus, a physician may step over into the drug traffic; a bond salesman, into the sale of bogus stock; and a store employee, into shoplifting. But even these do not become professional criminals immediately.

4. The professional criminal makes crime a way of life and develops a philosophy regarding it. He organizes his life around his criminal pursuit and adjusts his other activities to its requirements.

5. The professional criminal identifies himself with the world of crime and criminals, commonly referred to as the underworld, and is accepted as a member of it. In it he finds understanding, congeniality, friends, sympathy, affection, security, recognition, and respect. He orders much of his life in terms of its values, reacting to its approval and disapproval and looking to it for status. However, this does not mean that he is completely

isolated from conventional society, for he continues to have friends in it and responds to many of its demands.[1]

Types of Professional Criminals. The following are some of the major types of professional criminals:[2]

1. *Receivers of stolen property,* commonly called "fences." These criminals provide places for the disposal of loot, and without them a thief would find most of his crimes unprofitable.

2. *Burglars.* These are thieves who break into residences, stores, lofts, and other buildings and take money, merchandise, or other property. They may be classified on the basis of their techniques into house, apartment, store or loft, and safe burglars.

3. *Merchandise thieves.* Usually operating as members of a highly organized group, these criminals specialize in merchandise in transit and steal from piers, railroad cars, truck loading platforms, and trucks.

4. *Sneaks.* These thieves may be *shoplifters,* who steal merchandise from stores, *office sneaks,* who walks into an office, tell some plausible story, and while attention is diverted from them, steal whatever is available, and *auto sneaks,* who steal from parked automobiles.

5. *Purse-snatchers,* who take handbags from women.

6. *Pickpockets,* who usually work in teams. Protected by his assistants, known as stalls, the wire, hook, or tool, as he is variously called, takes the pocketbook, the movements of his hand, or duke, being covered by the dukeman, and passes it to a stall, who may then hand it on to another member of the team. The stalls also help to locate the victim's pocketbook by feeling his pockets, distract his attention by stepping on his feet or pushing against him, move him into a position where he can be worked on by the hook, and keep a lookout for police. Most pickpockets operate with a stiff, which is a folded newspaper or some article of clothing, such

---

[1] Chic Conwell, *The Professional Thief,* annotated and interpreted by Edwin H. Sutherland (Chicago: University of Chicago Press, 1937); Jack Black, "A Burglar Looks at Laws and Codes," *Harpers Magazine,* CLX (Feb., 1930), 306–13; Victor F. Nelson, *Prison Days and Nights* (Boston: Little, Brown and Co., 1933); Charles L. Clark and Earle E. Eubank, *Lockstep and Corridor* (Cincinnati, Ohio: University of Cincinnati Press, 1927); John Landesco, "The Criminal Underworld of Chicago in the '80's and '90's," *Journal of Criminal Law and Criminology,* XXV (Sept.–Oct., 1934), 341–57.

[2] All professional criminals have many similar characteristics, but the various types differ somewhat among themselves. See, for example, Edwin M. Schur, "Sociological Analysis of Confidence Swindling," *Journal of Criminal Law, Criminology, and Police Science,* XLVIII (Sept.–Oct., 1957), 296–304; Edwin M. Lemert, "An Isolation and Closure Theory of Naive Check Forgery," *Journal of Criminal Law, Criminology, and Police Science,* XLIV (Sept.–Oct., 1953), 296–307; Irwin A. Berg, "A Comparative Study of Forgery," *Journal of Applied Psychology,* XXVIII (June, 1944), 232–38; Erving Goffman, "On Cooling the Mark Out: Some Aspects of Adaptation to Failure," *Psychiatry,* XV (Nov., 1952), 451–63; James T. Barbash, "Compensation and the Crime of Pigeon Dropping," *Journal of Clinical Psychology,* VIII (Jan., 1952), 92–94.

as a coat. This is used to screen the removal of the pocketbook, wallet, or loose cash, and to conceal the loot after it is taken. Pickpockets may be classified on the basis of their specialties into (1) bag-openers; (2) patch-pocket workers; (3) pit-workers, the pit being the inside coat pocket; (4) pants-pocket workers; (5) fob-workers, who steal from fob or change pockets; (6) lush-workers, who pick the pockets of drunks; and (7) seat-tippers, who tip theater seats from behind and take the pocketbooks placed thereon.

7. *Auto thieves,* who specialize in the theft and disposal of stolen automobiles.

8. *Robbers,* who use force or threats to take possession of the victim's property. They may be armed or unarmed and may specialize in various types of robbery, such as home, store, bank, highway, or payroll robbery.

9. *Forgers and passers of illegal checks.*

10. *Confidence men,* who work in well-organized groups. A con game usually begins with the contact, which is the initial approach to the sucker, then moves to the buildup and the business, and concludes with the breakaway. The buildup is the story designed to gain the confidence of the victim, while the business is the method of getting his money. The breakaway is the departure of the con men with the victim's money.

The major con games require a rather large personnel, including a fixer, an inside man, a dozen or so shills, a manager, a roper, and other assistants. The roper or steerer makes the contact and flatters, entertains, and lures the victim to a phony gambling establishment, stock exchange, or brokerage office. The shills aid in the buildup by appearing to win large sums, while the inside man completes the swindle and obtains the sucker's money. Con men also engage in many lesser forms of swindling. These include coin matching, the money machine (which is supposed to manufacture paper money), crooked dice and card games, charity rackets, three-card monte, the Spanish prisoner bunco, and many others.

The Spanish prisoner bunco is one of the oldest con games. The victim is shown a letter from a prisoner in Spain, Mexico, or Cuba, who claims that he is being held on an unjust charge. This prisoner can secure his freedom if someone will send him money, and in return he will share a fortune, which he has hidden away, with his benefactor. Sometimes a beautiful girl is introduced into the story, her picture being enclosed in the prisoner's letter. Thus, the victim is lured into the trap by the prospect of a beautiful friendship as well as the ownership of a fortune.[3]

[3] Maurice J. Fitzgerald, *Handbook of Criminal Investigation* (New York: Greenberg, Publisher, 1951), pp. 126–50, 173–89; Alfred R. Lindesmith, "Organized Crime," *The Annals of the American Academy of Political and Social Science,* CCXVII (Sept., 1941), 124, 125. The latent dishonesty of many persons materially contributes to the success of confidence men. See Hans von Hentig, *The Criminal and His Victim* (New Haven: Yale University Press, 1948), pp. 383–89.

Development of the Professional Criminal. The development of the professional criminal is an educational process involving habituation to a life of crime. In this process he learns about crime, develops favorable attitudes toward it, and acquires a proficiency in it. More and more he participates in criminal activities and progressively shifts his loyalty from the world of law and law-abiding citizens to the world of crime and criminals.

This development is most clearly shown in the delinquent who grows into a professional criminal. His education takes place in unsupervised, progressively delinquent groups, but it is also present, although much less evident, in the adult who moves from an allied legitimate occupation or profession into crime. It is true that he already has the skill to commit his crimes, but usually he must learn how to apply his skill effectively in his criminal pursuit. Furthermore, it requires more than skill and its use in crime to make a professional criminal. He must consider himself a criminal, and the world of crime must accept him as one. Even he must undergo a hardening process during which he not only makes money by committing crime, but comes to consider crime a livelihood and a way of life and achieves status in the world of crime.

Philosophy of the Professional Criminal. The professional criminal, like all human beings, has a philosophy—a criminal philosophy, that is true, but a philosophy none the less. And in him, this criminal philosophy is more explicit than in other criminals, for he is the mature product of all the processes that operate in the formation of a criminal. Like any other philosophy, it is a body of beliefs that are acquired in a process of adjustment over a period of time, organized into a system of principles, hardened and crystalized in terms of experience, and used to explain the world and its ways.[4]

It gives meaning to his life and to the lives of others, making them seem reasonable, rational, logical. It provides him with attitudes toward life, his fellows, his work, his play, his joy, his sorrow. It furnishes a basis for right and wrong, colors his views, gives him insights, pushes him toward bias, binds him to prejudice. It is his shield and his sword. By it he lives and by it dies. But although possession of a philosophy identifies him as a normal human being, its content sets him apart from law-abiding men and women, for much of it is expressed in terms of a set of values unacceptable to organized society.

Thus, his philosophy brings the professional criminal into conflict with organized society. He preys upon society but at the same time hopes that it will prosper, for its prosperity means a richer field in which to work.

[4] Frank Tannenbaum, *Crime and the Community* (Boston: Ginn and Co., 1938), p. 177.

And since it is so powerful, he fears it, distrusts its representatives, and is suspicious of most of the people around him.

But even a criminal does not live by bread alone. He, too, seeks security, recognition, and love, and he finds them in the world of crime. It nourishes him, protects him, cares for him, entertains him, and when he excels in his work, welcomes him as a hero. Small wonder, then, that he feels that he is a part of the world of crime and tends to be loyal to it. But just as it has its heroes, so also it has its cowards, and the most craven are its betrayers. Upon these it showers such insults as "rat," "squealer," and "stool pigeon." The professional criminal may not like certain types of criminals, just as the businessman may not like certain types of business, but in the face of danger from the common enemy, the law, all criminals tend to unite. As Tannenbaum says, "With loyalty on one side and danger on the other, the professional criminal plays the game of a soldier at war with society.[5]

However, the professional criminal is never completely segregated from the conventional world. He has friends in it, must find his victims in it, and when apprehended, he must get help from those who have influence in it. Furthermore, he respects many of its values and often violates only those laws which interfere with his professional pursuits.

The professional criminal sees life through the eyes of his specialty. He thinks in terms of crime. Houses are made to be burglarized; pockets, to be picked; suckers, to be fleeced; purses, to be snatched, depending upon the specialty of the observer. Always, however, the goal is the same: Make a big haul and retire. But few ever retire even when they strike it rich, for their habits are deeply engrained and their records hang heavily over their heads.

In support of his way of life, the professional criminal contemptuously declares that law-abiding citizens really envy him. They, too, would live as he does if they had the courage and the intelligence to do so. And the victims get only what they deserve, since they are so stupid, or naive, or eager to make an "easy, dishonest buck." Furthermore, everybody has his racket. Every politician has his price. And what businessman will not cheat and defraud if he has the chance?

And if the professional criminal is caught, he suffers not remorse but chagrin—chagrin because his skill was not good enough to cope with the law. He must be more careful next time. Everybody runs into "tough luck" once in a while, but he will get his chance some day. In the meantime, he must "beat the rap." He knows that he can "fix" the case if he can reach the "right" person, but failing in this, he will "cop a plea" (plead guilty to a lesser charge). It is not easy to penetrate his system

[5] Tannenbaum, p. 186.

of attitudes, and during imprisonment he usually obeys the rules to get time off for good behavior but resists efforts to effect his rehabilitation.

The philosophy of the professional criminal finds expression through what is called the code of the underworld. According to it, the criminal should be honest with members of his gang and should divide the loot with them. He should also stick to his specialty and avoid unnecessary crime and cruelty. If he is arrested, he should be loyal to the underworld. He should not double-cross; he should not turn "stool pigeon." He should take his medicine like a man, without fear and whining. Of course, this code is often violated, but it does constitute an ideal toward which the underworld strives. Many criminals observe its principles,[6] and within its terms "they choose to fight their own battles and bury their own dead."[7]

The World of Crime and Criminals. Habitual and professional criminals, their criminal activities, and such social relationships as they have beyond the bounds of conventional society may be said to constitute the world of crime and criminals, commonly called the underworld. However, in describing this underworld, one can easily oversimplify its nature by making it seem more tangible, rational, formal, and organized than it really is. This is especially true in any description of the underworld in the complex society of America, where mobility tends to break down compact groups and rapid and efficient means of communication spread the ideas and knowledge of all groups to all people.

The underworld is not necessarily located in any particular geographical area. It does not have to have any specific building or equipment, nor need it have any official meetings, representatives, or paid membership. Indeed, a professional criminal may know few other criminals intimately, may live among law-abiding persons, and may not be fully aware of the social implications of his way of life. Furthermore, the criminal everywhere governs some of his life in terms of the values of the conventional world. It is clear, then, that the essence of the underworld is to be found in the system of attitudes that habitual and professional criminals have toward themselves, toward one another, and toward conventional society.

[6] See Black; Conwell; Clarke and Eubank; Nelson; Clifford R. Shaw, *The Jack Roller: a Delinquent Boy's Own Story* (Chicago: University of Chicago Press, 1930); Clifford R. Shaw and M. E. Moore, *The Natural History of a Delinquent Career* (Chicago: University of Chicago Press, 1931); Clifford R. Shaw, Henry D. McKay, and Harold B. Hanson, *Brothers in Crime* (Chicago: University of Chicago Press, 1938); Frank Tannenbaum, "The Professional Criminal," *The Century Magazine*, CX (Sept., 1925), 577–88.

[7] John Landesco, "Organized Crime in Chicago," *The Illinois Crime Survey*, Part III (Chicago: Illinois Association for Criminal Justice, 1929), p. 1051; quoted by Tannenbaum, p. 193.

Nevertheless, the underworld has developed its own customs, traditions, institutions, social classes, occupations, techniques, language, and, as we have already seen, its own philosophy and code. Many criminals live together in certain urban and suburban districts, especially in socially disorganized areas such as slums, where social control is not effective. Cheap hotels, rooming houses, and trailer camps are favorite lodging places for criminals, many of whom are constantly on the move and are unencumbered by any family life or dependents. Sexual life tends to be loose, temporary relationships often being formed with prostitutes or mistresses. Taverns, restaurants, and poolrooms afford safe meeting places where criminals gather, exchange gossip, discuss their plans, seek assistance, and make contact with politicians who can "fix" charges or secure political favors. Fences, who often pose as law-abiding merchants, provide places for the disposal of stolen goods. Relaxation and recreation are found in taverns, night clubs, gambling joints, houses of prostitution, athletic clubs, movies, and burlesque shows. Techniques and patterns of crime are handed down from generation to generation, and criminals form small groups, called mobs, troupes, and outfits, and large groups, called organized gangs, in order to commit their crimes. Skill and financial success bring recognition and respect, and the professional criminals and the organized gangs compose the elite of the underworld. Out of this way of life has emerged a language, and its picturesque terms, such as bookie, hijacker, punk, and shill, constitute for the criminal not only a medium of communication, but also a means of identification.[8]

THE WHITE-COLLAR CRIMINAL

For many years, Frank was the senior member of a prosperous law firm in the Middle West. A father of five children, a deacon in his church, a trustee of the local college, a member of many lodges and fraternal organizations, an energetic worker in civic affairs, he was a highly respected member of the community. Now looking back on his crime, he is not sure how it all happened.

"I suppose I just wanted to get all those things that I had always dreamed about," he says, as if half to himself. "I began by misappropriating small amounts, and then, as we moved up the social ladder, the amounts grew larger. It was easy to manipulate the accounts of the large estates that we were handling, and I could always cover up. Anyway, I fully expected to return the money."

[8] For the terminology and slang of criminals, see Conwell, pp. 235–43; Fitzgerald, pp. 198–218; Frederick W. Egen, *Plainclothesman* (New York: Greenberg, Publisher, 1952), pp. 203–23.

But one day the unforeseen happened. While on a hunting trip, Frank's two law partners and two of the firm's richest clients, whose estates the firm had been handling, were killed in an automobile accident. Dissolution of the firm, an audit of its books, exposure of Frank's misappropriation of funds, and his conviction followed in quick succession.

"How much was it?" he asks. "Over seventy thousand, you say? Yes, that's about right."

It will be many months before he has recovered from the shock of his disgrace and can think of rebuilding his life for the future. But in a way Frank is lucky. His family is standing by him.

Frank was guilty of what has been called a white-collar crime, a term which was coined by E. H. Sutherland. According to his original definition, white-collar crime is "a violation of the criminal law by a person of the upper socioeconomic class in the course of his occupational activities." He added that "the upper socioeconomic class is defined not only by its wealth but also by its respectability and prestige in the general society." Thus, a fraud by a wealthy confidence man of the underworld or a murder by a businessman in a love triangle would not be a white-collar crime, but a fraud by a realtor in the sale of a house or a murder by a manufacturer in strike-breaking activities would be.

Most white-collar crimes involve a breach of trust which is usually accompanied and consummated by misrepresentation. This misrepresentation occurs, for example, in the financial statements of corporations, in advertising and other sales methods, in manipulations on the stock exchange, in short weights and measures, in embezzlement and misappropriation of funds, in the bribery of public officials, in tax frauds, and in the misapplication of funds in receiverships and bankruptcies.[9]

Extent and Effects of White-Collar Crimes. Sutherland, Clinard, Hartung, and other sociologists assert that white-collar crimes are very serious, persistent, and prevalent in American society.[10] In order to support

[9] Edwin H. Sutherland, "Crime and Business," *The Annals of the American Academy of Political and Social Science,* CCXVII (Sept., 1941), 112.

[10] Sutherland studied the careers of seventy large corporations, against which courts and commissions had rendered 980 decisions for the violations of laws governing such matters as restraint of trade, misrepresentation, fraud, unfair labor practices, and war regulations. Although only 158, or 16 per cent, of these decisions were made by criminal courts, he maintained that actually 779, or 79 per cent, could be interpreted as decisions that crimes had been committed (Edwin H. Sutherland, *White Collar Crime* [New York: The Dryden Press, Inc., 1949], pp. 17–55). See also his "White-Collar Criminality," *American Sociological Review,* V (Feb., 1940), 3, 4.

Clinard estimates that there were about 810,000 serious violations of price regulations during the five-year period 1942 to 1947, and he classifies nearly all such violations as white-collar crimes even though criminal proceedings constituted less than 6 per cent of all cases in which sanction actions were initiated (Marshall B. Clinard, *The Black Market* [New York: Rinehart and Co., Inc., 1952], pp. 28–50, 226–62).

their views, they point to the conditions revealed by numerous governmental investigations and to their own independent research into various aspects of our economic system. They insist not only that the financial losses resulting from white-collar crimes reach staggering proportions, but also that these losses are the least important of the consequences of such crimes.[11] Ordinary crimes cause some inconvenience to the victims and, occasionally, if they involve serious bodily attacks, or are repeated in quick succession, they cause a general community disturbance. White-collar crimes, on the other hand, according to Sutherland and other sociologists, spread feelings of distrust, lower public morale, and produce social disorganization.[12]

Prosecution of White-Collar Criminals. The white-collar criminologists further contend that although white-collar crimes are very prevalent and very costly, few of the perpetrators are prosecuted or convicted in criminal courts. This, they claim, is true because (1) the criminal courts are very lenient toward persons accused of white-collar crimes, (2) no effective method of dealing with offending corporations under the criminal law has as yet been devised, (3) efforts to make the criminal law more effective in cases involving corporations have been blocked by business interests, and (4) action in the civil courts and regulations by boards and commissions are widely relied upon to protect society against white-collar crimes.[13]

On the basis of this analysis, Sutherland and those who are in agreement with him conclude that those who commit white-collar crimes are relatively immune because of the class bias of the courts and the power of the upper classes to influence the implementation and administration of the law, and that therefore the difference in criminality between the lower and upper classes is made to appear greater in the record than it really is. This, in turn, in their opinion, has contributed to a distortion of the criminological theories of causation, since criminologists to a great extent have restricted their data to cases dealt with in criminal and juvenile courts, agencies which are used principally for offenders from the lower economic strata. In other words, they believe that the theory of causation which attributes criminal behavior in general either to

---

See also Frank E. Hartung, "White-Collar Offenses in the Wholesale Meat Industry in Detroit," *American Journal of Sociology*, LVI (July, 1950), 25–34; James S. Wallerstein and Clement J. Wyle, "Our Law-abiding Law-breakers," *Probation*, XXV (Apr., 1947), 107–12, 118.

11 Much of the material in this chapter has been adapted from the author's article, "A Reexamination of the Concept of White-Collar Crime," *Federal Probation*, XXII (Mar., 1958), 30–36, and is quoted by permission.

12 Sutherland, "Crime and Business," 113; also, "White-Collar Criminality," 5.

13 See, for example, Sutherland, "Crime and Business," 114, 115.

poverty or to the psychopathic and sociopathic conditions associated with poverty is "based on a biased sample which omits almost entirely the behavior of white-collar criminals."[14] Thus there are two major issues involved in the controversy over the concept of white-collar crime, namely, (1) the moral issue and (2) the scientific issue.

The Moral Issue. The moral issue has arisen from the contention that our criminal laws and their administration are biased and unfair, and that they tend to favor the rich and the influential and to discriminate against the poor and the friendless. Those that assume this point of view argue that many acts are the same, or nearly the same, as other acts that are now called criminal and should be similarly labeled and condemned, even though the legislatures and the courts fail to do this. This is justified by some writers on the grounds that an act should be called criminal regardless of whether the provisions concerning it are in the criminal law, the civil law, or governmental agency regulations, as long as it can meet these two requirements: (1) Is it proscribed or prescribed by a duly constituted legislative body? and (2) Has the legislative body declared it to be punishable and specified the sanctions to be imposed?[15] Furthermore, it is urged by those who favor the concept of white-collar crime that we should stigmatize as white-collar criminals both those who are convicted in the criminal court and those who might have been so convicted but, instead, through pressure or influence, were able to avoid conviction or for various reasons were taken into a civil court or before an administrative board, bureau, or commission.[16] To a large extent, this point of view on the moral issue is a result of the strong influence exerted in American criminology by the Positive School, which focuses attention upon the criminal while ignoring the legal definition of crime.[17]

How Do We Know a Person Has Committed a Crime? These arguments are seductive in their simplicity, but their limitations become apparent when a careful examination is made of the terms "crime" and "criminal." Crime is a legal term and has a legal meaning. Basically, it is an act, or a failure to act, which is in violation of the criminal law and made punishable by the state.[18] You might say, then, that anyone who commits a crime is a criminal, but this definition immediately suggests an important

[14] Sutherland, "White-Collar Criminality," 9.
[15] Hartung, 25.
[16] Sutherland, "White-Collar Criminality," 5–9.
[17] Jerome Hall, *General Principles of Criminal Law* (Indianapolis: The Bobbs-Merrill Co., 1960), pp. 600–21; Clarence R. Jeffery, "The Structure of American Criminological Thinking," *Journal of Criminal Law, Criminology, and Police Science,* XLVI (Jan.–Feb., 1956), 658–72; *ibid.*, "Crime, Law and Social Structure," *Ibid.*, 47 (Nov.–Dec., 1956), 423–35.
[18] For the legal definition of crime, see Chapter 2.

question: How do we know that a person has committed a crime? Thus, in any particular case, it becomes clear that the definition of a criminal as one who violates the criminal law is not adequate. We must supplement it by establishing definite, exact, stable criteria to determine whether the accused actually committed a crime.

But why is it so important to have such criteria to determine the guilt of the accused? The answer to this question can be found in the fact that a person's rights and reputation are involved. To apply the term "criminal" to a person is not only to lower his social status by publicly stigmatizing him, but also to declare that his guilt has been proved, that certain of his rights have been forfeited, and that he should be punished. The law, which defines the term "crime," is deeply aware of the serious implications of the term "criminal." Down through the years, it has carefully, and at times painfully, built up a definite procedure to determine the guilt of the accused and at the same time to protect his rights. By clearly defining terms, by precisely formulating methods, and by judiciously introducing changes, the law has promoted stability, dependability, and security of justice in its criminal procedure.[19]

In this procedure, one of the important rules of evidence is that which requires proof of the corpus delicti. This term defined literally means "the body of the offense" or "the substance of crime." Although in popular language it is used to describe the visible evidence of the crime, such as the dead body of a murdered person, it is properly applicable to any crime and relates particularly to the act element of criminality. This means that it must be proved that a certain prohibited act has been committed and that it was committed by a criminal human agency. Furthermore, in addition to establishing the corpus delicti in a particular case, the state must also prove beyond a reasonable doubt that the accused was the human agent who committed the act or caused it to be committed.[20]

When this has been accomplished according to the exacting regularities of legal procedure and due process,[21] the "accused" becomes the "convicted." Then, and not until then, does the "alleged crime" become the "crime," and the "alleged criminal," the "criminal." Anything short of this will often be inaccurate and unjust. Certainly, charges of crime by the press, the public, and the police do not meet the standard of rigorous precision that is required. Decisions by civil courts and administrative agencies, based as they may be upon a slight preponderance

[19] Paul W. Tappan, "Who Is the Criminal?" *American Sociological Review*, XII (Feb., 1947), 100.

[20] Justin Miller, *Handbook of Criminal Law* (St. Paul, Minn.: West Publishing Co., 1934), pp. 93, 94.

[21] See Chapter 15 for a discussion of due process.

of evidence, and not upon proof beyond a reasonable doubt, as convictions must be in the criminal court, can mean nothing more than that a civil wrong has been committed.[22]

Crime Must Be Defined by the Criminal Law. Consequently, it must be insisted that no person is a white-collar criminal or any kind of criminal until he has been properly adjudicated as such in the criminal court. This is as true in the case of a corporation charged with some type of criminal behavior as it is in the case of a person accused of murder. This is not to deny that there are imperfections in the criminal law and its procedure. But the remedy for this is not to disregard the preventive devices that the law has created to shield the innocent. The correct approach to this problem lies in the improvement of the criminal law, in the stricter enforcement of its provisions, and in the vigorous, but unbiased and impartial, prosecution of the accused.

Sutherland's original definition of white-collar crime, quoted above, had some merit, inasmuch as it did not depart entirely from the principles of criminal law.[23] Clinard, in discussing the black market, defines white-collar crime as "a violation of the law committed primarily by groups such as businessmen, professional men, and politicians in connection with their occupations."[24] Hartung, using what he terms a narrower definition of the concept, defines white-collar crime as "a violation of law regulating business, which is committed for a firm by the firm or its agents in the conduct of its business."[25] Clinard, then, would make any businessman, professional man, or politician who engages in *any* illegal activity in connection with his occupation a white-collar criminal, while Hartung would confine the term to a firm or its agents that violate a law regulating business in the conduct of the firm's business. Like Sutherland, both Clinard and Hartung do not consider conviction in a criminal court an essential element in white-collar crime. Furthermore, it is quite clear that the criminal law is in no way concerned with much

[22] Paul W. Tappan, "Crime and the Criminal," *"Federal Probation,* XI (July–Sept., 1947), 41–44. See also Tappan, "Who Is the Criminal?" 100, 101.

[23] In discussing his definition, Sutherland states: "White-collar crime is real crime. If it is not a violation of the criminal law, it is not white-collar crime or any other kind of crime" (Sutherland, "Crime and Business," 115).

[24] Marshall B. Clinard, *The Black Market* (New York: Rinehart and Co., Inc., 1952), p. 127. In presenting this definition, Clinard says, "Contrary to popular thinking, however, the use of a criminal sanction is not essential for a black market violation of law to be considered sociologically as a 'crime'" (p. 127).

[25] Frank E. Hartung, "White-Collar Crime: Its Significance for Theory and Practice," *Federal Probation,* XVII (June, 1953), 31. See also his "White-Collar Offenses in the Wholesale Meat Industry in Detroit," *American Journal of Sociology,* LVI (July, 1950), 25–34.

of the activity to which Clinard and Hartung refer, since many illegal acts and violations of business regulations are not defined as crimes by the criminal law.

Even Sutherland abandoned his earlier position and later defined crime as any act which the law describes as socially injurious and for which it provides a penalty.[26] Thus, he made the violation of any law, civil or criminal, a crime when it is "socially injurious" and carries a penalty. But he did not stop with this. Later still, in writing of the dangers of white-collar criminality, he said, "Some of the offenses are not even a violation of the spirit of the law, for the parties concerned have been able by bribery and other means to prevent the enactment of laws to prohibit wrongful and injurious practices."[27] Here, then, the term "white-collar criminal" has deteriorated to the point where it can be used to refer to anyone who engages in what the observer considers to be unethical or immoral behavior. Now, at last, the shrewd businessman, the inefficient workman, the immoral politician, the unethical doctor or lawyer—all can be condemned as criminals by a stroke of the pen.[28] The result, states Tappan, may be "fine indoctrination or catharsis achieved through blustering broadsides against the 'existing system' [but] it is not criminology and it is not social science."[29]

However, what has been said here should not be regarded as an attempt to minimize the immoral and unethical practices of many American businessmen, which have been exposed and justly condemned by a series of shocking investigations.[30] The point is that morality and ethics

[26] Edwin H. Sutherland, "Is 'White-Collar Crime' Crime?" *American Sociological Review*, X (Apr., 1945), 132. See also his *White Collar Crime*, pp. 29–55.

[27] Edwin H. Sutherland, *Principles of Criminology* (4th ed.; Philadelphia: J. B. Lippincott Co., 1947), p. 37.

[28] In introducing his chapter on white-collar crime, Vold writes, "There has been no official or legal definition anywhere, and the term remains ambiguous, uncertain, and controversial." (George B. Vold, *Theoretical Criminology* [New York: Oxford University Press, 1958], p. 243). Geis, after saying that the concept "white-collar crime" can fairly be said "to stand convicted of Vold's charge," suggests that the term "be restricted to corporate violations of a reasonably homogeneous nature and to cognate criminal acts," and that it "be tied to the legal codes which state and define such offenses" (Gilbert Geis, "Toward a Delineation of White-Collar Offenses," *Sociological Inquiry*, XXXII [Spring, 1962], 169–71).

[29] Tappan, "Who Is the Criminal?" *American Sociological Review*, XII (Feb., 1947), p. 99.

[30] See, for example, Richard Austin Smith, "The Incredible Electrical Conspiracy," *Fortune* (April, 1961), 132–80 (May, 1961), 161–224; abridged with editorial adaptations in *The Sociology of Crime and Delinquency*, eds. M. E. Wolfgang, L. Savitz, and N. Johnston (New York: John Wiley and Sons, Inc., 1962), pp. 357–72. See also Edwin H. Sutherland, "Crime of Corporations," *The Sutherland Papers*, eds. A. Cohen, A. Lindesmith and K. Schuessler (Bloomington: Indiana University Press, 1956), pp. 78–96.

are not the same as the law, and an immoral or unethical person is not necessarily a criminal.[31] But should criminologists not study what they consider to be antisocial behavior with the view to having it defined as crime by the law? Yes, by all means, but until it has been so defined some terms other than "crime" and "criminal" should be used in describing it. Failure to do this can result only in the corruption of the terms "crime" and "criminal," the integrity of which the law has sought so vigilantly to preserve, and to open the door to endless confusion. That the danger of this is real is eloquently attested to above by the fact that the white-collar criminologists cannot agree among themselves as to the meaning of the terms "white-collar crime" and "white-collar criminal." Unless they can come to some agreement regarding these terms and define them according to the principles of criminal law,[32] they should discard the concept of white-collar crime entirely, because "vague omnibus concepts defining crime are a blight upon either a legal system or a system of sociology that strives to be objective."[33]

As a result of the way in which the term "white-collar crime" is variously defined by different sociologists, there are major difficulties involved in any attempt to estimate the amount of this type of crime in the United States. For example, if we use Sutherland's original definition, we find these obstacles: (1) white-collar crime is a nonlegal term which refers to certain criminal acts, such as embezzlement and bribery, but does not specifically name the criminal acts to which it has reference; (2) it refers to a certain type of person, namely, a member of the upper socioeconomic class, but does not provide us with specific criteria by which to determine the social class of the person involved; and (3) the criminal law in defining acts that are usually referred to by the term "white-collar crime," with few exceptions, does not make any distinction regarding the social class of the offenders. Other definitions of white-collar crime present similar difficulties. It should be clear, therefore, why there are no official sources of criminal statistics by which to estimate the amount of white-collar crime.

If sociologists were to use the term "white-collar crime" to refer to acts that are defined as crimes by the law, official compilations of white-collar offenses known to the police might then be included in the *Uniform Crime Reports*. Although this arrangement would not provide a

31 In considering the views of those who argue in favor of the term "white-collar crime," Vold states, "The real plea is for a change in the mores basic to attitudes about what is to be considered right or wrong in business practice" (Vold, p. 259).

32 Tappan uses the term "white-collar crime" to refer to "real violations of the criminal law, systematically or repeatedly committed by business, professional, and clerical workers incidental to their occupations." Paul W. Tappan, *Crime, Justice and Correction* (New York: McGraw-Hill Book Co., Inc., 1960), p. 217.

33 Tappan, "Who Is the Criminal?" 99.

complete coverage of white-collar crimes, however defined, nor satisfy all the requirements set up by the white-collar criminologists, it would furnish official and highly reliable data that could be employed in a systematic and continuing revelation of the enormity of these crimes and in agitation for any necessary reforms in the criminal law and its administration.

The Scientific Issue. The scientific issue springs from the contention that those who commit white-collar crimes are relatively immune because of the class bias of the criminal law and its administration, and that this in turn has led to a distortion of the criminological theories of causation, since these theories have been based to a great extent on the official records of the criminal and juvenile courts and law-enforcement agencies. While this contention has merit, the remedy is to be found in the further development of an independent science of human behavior and not in the mere tinkering with legal concepts and statistics as suggested by the white-collar criminologists.

The criminal law and the data about crimes and criminals accumulated during the law-enforcement process are useful in scientific research, but if the investigator in the field of criminology is to contribute to the science of human behavior, he must free himself from the concepts and terminology created by the criminal law. He must define his own terms and base them on the intrinsic character of his material so that they will designate properties in that material which are assumed to be universal. The legislator and the administrator speak one language; the scientist, another. These languages are fundamentally irreconcilable, and this is as it should be, for they are being used for essentially different purposes.[34]

The irreconcilable difference between the language of the criminal law and that of science can be no more sharply delineated than by a comparison of the meanings given the concept "cause" in these two fields. By "cause" science means the sufficient antecedent conditions necessary for the evocation of a given phenomenon.[35] The law, on the other hand, gives the concept "cause" a narrower meaning, limiting the liability for the consequences of any act by means of some idea of justice or social policy, which tends to be an expression of the dominant values of the group. In the light of what is considered to be justice in any society, a person's act is said to be the proximate or legal cause of the consequences, and if these constitute a crime and the requisite mental element is present, he is held to be criminally responsible.[36] But it is obvious that, in any particular case, this procedure may disregard certain factors that

[34] Thorsten Sellin, *Culture Conflict and Crime* (New York: Social Science Research Council, Bull. 41, 1938), pp. 23, 24.
[35] For a discussion of the concept "cause" in science, see Chapter 1.
[36] For a discussion of the concept "cause" in law, see Chapter 2.

would be included by the application of the scientific concept of cause. The law, therefore, by its very nature and without necessarily being subject to any class bias or any unethical or immoral pressures or practices, may produce official data which do not meet scientific standards. Thus, the psychiatrist in certain cases may find himself in conflict with the legal concept of insanity, which may serve socially defined ends as agreed upon by most of the members of all socioeconomic classes but which does not square with the scientific concept of mental disease.

But why not strip the terms "crime" and "criminal" of their legal meanings in scientific research and give them a content which is acceptable to scientists? In answer to this question, it must be insisted that such a redefinition of terms, as in the case of the moral issue, would lead only to misunderstanding and confusion, and that everything that could be accomplished by it could be secured much more easily and effectively by the use of an independent scientific terminology. This is the course that has been followed by the psychiatrist who avoids the legal term "insanity" in his scientific research, even though he may agree that certain persons who have been declared insane by the law are mentally diseased and employs data regarding them which are taken from official legal sources.

Sellin, while suggesting that criminologists study the violation of conduct norms in order to put criminology on a scientific basis, calls attention to the dangers involved in the loose usage of the term "crime." In his opinion, it is wiser to retain this term for the violations of the norms that are embodied in the criminal law and to use the term "abnormal conduct" for violations of all norms, whether legal or not.[37] Thus, he would study all deviations from conduct norms[38] as measured by concepts created by sociologists.[39] To the extent that these deviations are already defined as crimes by the law, he would refer to them as such in his scientific investigation but, in his examination of the nature and causes of conduct deviations, he would in no way be restricted by the concepts of criminal law nor would he seek to alter its terminology. The results achieved by such scientific research might then be utilized by the law in the modification of its own concepts and principles. In this way, science and the law could work hand in hand while at the same time directing their efforts toward the attainment of their own goals.

[37] Sellin, p. 32.

[38] Other writers have used the term "deviant behavior" to refer to departures from the norms of a society. In this text, as explained in Chapter 1, one who violates a social norm is called a social deviant; and his act, a social deviation.

[39] The study of social deviations involves not only the identification of social norms (both legal and nonlegal), but also the analysis of the sociohistorical setting in which these norms develop. See, for example, Clarence R. Jeffery, "The Development of Crime in Early English Society," *Journal of Criminal Law, Criminology, and Police Science*, XLVII (Mar.–Apr., 1957), 647–66.

8

Organized Crime

"Once you get organized, you don't have to worry about money. Everything will roll in in a nice quiet manner, in a business-like way. You don't have to worry about it personally. Everybody will be happy, I'm sure.

"One thing I'm against, always was against. I don't like, like I was telling you last night, five or six joints in the radius of six blocks, a joint every block. That's one thing I've always talked against. I like one big spot and that's all. Out in the country, out of the city entirely.

"I don't run any of those places up there, gambling or anything like that. I got my own territory. I got certain business that I take care of for the last sixteen or seventeen years. I do very well, living comfortably, worry about nothing. As far as the set-up, these places like dice rooms or horse rooms and things like that, that's like another department I would call it. If I had a fellow sitting here with me that runs a certain game, he could give it to you in a minute. He could tell you what to expect and all that sort of stuff you see. But I have my own little concession, and that's the end. Well, that's my business, policy. Policy is my business. That I could run. I've been at it for seventeen years."[1]

This was the voice of organized crime emphasizing some of its important methods—organization, specialization, planning, and protection. The speaker was Pat Manno, who was called the "No. 5 man" in the Capone syndicate. As the representative of that syndicate, he had arrived at Dallas, Texas, on November 6, 1946, in order to assist in the organization of gambling and other criminal activities there for the benefit of the Chicago underworld. Manno's words, quoted above were secretly recorded while he was attempting to effect a "working arrangement" with

[1] U.S. Senate Special Committee to Investigate Organized Crime in Interstate Commerce, *Third Interim Report* (Washington, D.C.: Government Printing Office, 1951), p. 57.

Steve Guthrie,[2] Sheriff of Dallas County, who was cooperating in the plan to secure evidence against Manno. This recording was later introduced as evidence at the Chicago hearings of the Kefauver Committee.[3]

NATURE OF ORGANIZED CRIME

Criminal activity is usually a cooperative effort. However, organized crime, as the term is used here, has certain characteristics that distinguish it from other types of crime which involve the cooperation of different persons or groups.[4] For example, it is more than the mere association of a few criminals for the purpose of working as a team (which may be called a mob, troupe, or outfit) in the commission of such crimes as confidence games, picking pockets, robbery, and burglary.[5] It is, in fact, a complicated and extensive form of criminal behavior that involves the following:

1. Association of a group of criminals for the purpose of committing crimes for profit. In some cases, this association is relatively permanent, lasting over a period of several decades.

2. Centralization of authority in the hands of one or a few members of this group.

3. Creation of a fund of money to serve as capital for the group's criminal enterprises.

4. Organization of the group, involving division of labor, delegation of duties and responsibilities, and specialization of functions. Some groups specialize in one type, or a few types of crime, but others, especially the more powerful ones, are multipurpose in character, engaging in any activity in which a "fast buck" can be made.

[2] A representative of the Capone syndicate said that a "working arrangement" with Guthrie would be worth $150,000 a year to him (Virgil W. Peterson, *Barbarians in Our Midst* [Boston: Little, Brown and Co., 1952], p. 293).

[3] Peterson, pp. 293–97.

[4] For a general survey of the nature of organized crime in the United States, see, among others, U.S. Senate Special Committee to Investigate Organized Crime in Interstate Commerce, *Second and Third Interim and Final Reports* (Washington, D.C.: Government Printing Office, 1951); Virgil W. Peterson, *Barbarians in Our Midst* (Boston: Little, Brown and Co., 1952); Burton B. Turkus and Sid Feder, *Murder, Inc.: The Story of "the Syndicate"* (New York: Farrar, Straus, and Young, 1951); Gus Tyler, *Organized Crime in America* (Ann Arbor: The University of Michigan Press, 1962); Frank Tannenbaum, *Crime and the Community* (Boston: Ginn and Co., 1938); American Bar Association Commission on Organized Crime, *Organized Crime and Law Enforcement* (2 vols.; New York: The Grosby Press, Inc., 1952, 1953).

[5] Lindesmith would classify these activities as organized crime. He defines this term as "crime that involves the cooperation of several different persons or groups for its successful execution" (Alfred R. Lindesmith, "Organized Crime," *The Annals of the American Academy of Political and Social Science*, CCXVII [Sept., 1941], 119). For a similar definition, see Philip S. Van Cise, *Fighting the Underworld* (New York: Houghton Mifflin Co., 1936), p. 3.

5. Expansive and monopolistic tendencies. Criminal gangs seek to expand their activities beyond the borders of the area in which they have their headquarters and to secure a monopoly in their criminal enterprises throughout the area in which they operate. They do not hesitate to use murder, bombing, or any other form of violence to eliminate competition, silence informers, persuade potential victims, or enforce their edicts. Often the larger gangs import gunmen from other areas to do this work for them and to make detection of their crimes more difficult.

6. Adoption of measures to protect the group and to guard against the interruption of its activities. These include the maintenance of arrangements with doctors, lawyers, politicians, judges, policemen, and other influential persons, and the use of bribery and other forms of corruption to secure political favors and to avoid arrest and punishment.

7. Establishment of policies of administration, rules of conduct, and methods of operation. The elaborate operations of organized crime require discipline, efficiency, obedience, loyalty, and mutual confidence. Rules, therefore, are strictly enforced and severe penalties are imposed upon their violators.

8. Careful planning to minimize risks and to insure the greatest possible success in the group's criminal enterprises.[6]

It will be observed that organized crime has many characteristics in common with modern business. Organization, division of labor, specialization of methods, careful planning, insurance against risks—all these have been successfully utilized and developed by both. But, then, this is not surprising, for both are products of the same society and so both should be expected to bear marks of the same culture.

TYPES OF ORGANIZED CRIME

Three major types of organized crime have appeared in America. These are (1) organized gang criminality, (2) racketeering, and (3) syndicated crime. Of these, the first is the most simple and possesses the characteristics listed above to the least degree, while the third is the most complex, having the characteristics of organized crime in their most fully developed form. It is, therefore, also the most dangerous to our society.

Organized Gang Criminality. Organized gang criminality includes such crimes as bank robbery, kidnapping, murder, hijacking, automobile theft, truck and warehouse robbery, and jewel theft, committed by gangs or-

[6] U.S. Senate Special Committee to Investigate Organized Crime in Interstate Commerce, *Second Interim Report* (Washington, D.C.: Government Printing Office, 1951), p. 7; American Bar Association Commission on Organized Crime, *Organized Crime and Law Enforcement* (2 vols.; New York: The Grosby Press, Inc., 1952, 1953), I, 7–21.

ganized to engage in such activities on a large scale. Tough, hardened criminals compose these gangs, and they do not hesitate to use violence in order to accomplish their purpose. Equipped with machine guns, tear gas, bullet-proof vests, and high-powered cars for quick "getaways," they are well-disciplined, efficient, and dangerous. As Barnes and Teeters point out, "they live violently and expect violence."[7] They often extend their activities across the country, moving quickly by automobile from crime to crime and sometimes dispersing and re-uniting in prearranged "hideouts." These are the ruthless criminals whose sensational exploits are splashed across our newspapers and whose daring crimes the public follows with such avidity.

The years between the two World Wars saw the spectacular rise of organized gang criminality in the United States. Kidnapping, murder, bank robbery, and other crimes of violence became daily occurrences. Desperate criminals surrounded themselves with thieves, hoodlums, and ex-convicts to form powerful gangs. Hired professional gunmen killed law-enforcement officers, prominent citizens, and members of rival out-fits.[8]

One of the most notorious gangs of the period was the "Cowboy" Tessler gang of New York City, which in the twenties was called "the most highly organized and commercialized group of bandits in history." It is said that "this gang, most of whose members were apprehended in October, 1925, used silencers on its guns, employed a jeweler to remount its stolen gems, maintained two garages where stolen cars could be re-numbered and disguised, established a warehouse and a business office where miscellaneous loot was sold, and maintained a sinking-fund to provide bail and legal fees."[9]

In the early thirties, several spectacular kidnappings shocked the nation. On July 1, 1933, John "Jake the Barber" Factor, the international swindler, was kidnapped near Chicago by the notorious Touhy gang as he was returning home from a gambling casino. A few weeks later, Charles F. Urschel, a wealthy oil man of Oklahoma City, was kidnapped by a gang, one of the leaders of which was George "Machine-Gun" Kelly. On January 17, 1934, Edward George Bremer was kidnapped in St. Paul, Minnesota, by the Barker-Karpis gang and taken to a "hideout" a few miles from Chicago. Peterson states that one of the instigators and the alleged "brains" of the Bremer kidnapping, as well as the earlier abduction of the St. Paul brewer, William Hamm, Jr., which had oc-

[7] Harry Elmer Barnes and Negley K. Teeters, *New Horizons in Criminology* (New York: Prentice-Hall, Inc., 1951), p. 36.

[8] U.S. Department of Justice, *The Story of the Federal Bureau of Investigation* (Washington, D.C., n.d.), p. 2. See also J. Edgar Hoover, *Persons in Hiding* (Boston: Little, Brown and Co., 1938).

[9] Frederic M. Thrasher, *The Gang* (Chicago: University of Chicago Press, 1927), pp. 420, 421.

curred on June 5, 1933, was Fred Goetz (alias Shotgun George Zeigler), who was affiliated with the Capone syndicate.[10]

Arizona Clark Barker was one of the most vicious, dangerous, and resourceful criminals in the annals of American crime. To her followers, she was known as "Mother Barker," leader of the Barker-Karpis gang of hoodlums, highwaymen, and kidnappers. One of her sons became a mail robber, another a holdup man, while the other two were highwaymen, kidnappers, and wanton murderers. Associated with her at various times were some of the most desperate outlaws of the Midwest. Among them were: George Zeigler, known as "Shotgun George" (as previously noted); Charles Harmon, Frank Nash, Francis Keating, and Thomas Holden, ex-convicts, escaped murderers, and high-powered bank robbers; Verne Miller, professional gangster machine-gunner; Harvey Bailey, later convicted of the Charles F. Urschel kidnapping; and Earl Christman—all of whom have been linked to innumerable crimes.

Members of the Barker-Karpis gang operated throughout the North and Midwest, robbing, kidnapping, and killing. For all of them, Ma Barker held open house, taking a cut of the loot, and furnishing the brains by which the gang became even more dangerous. To Ma's gang floated more than a score of satellites, including a politician, cafe owners, hotelkeepers, underworld messengers, women, and hangers-on. Thus, she was not just a pathetically defiant leader of a small group of criminals. "She was queen of a little empire, which consisted of departments, specialists, and hangers-on."[11] But her star was already on the decline. As we shall see, her gang was destroyed, and she was hunted down and killed.

The United States slowly awoke to the threat of organized gang criminality, and law-enforcement agencies, with the FBI playing the leading role, moved into action to crush it. In September, 1933, local law-enforcement officers and FBI agents captured "Machine-Gun" Kelly in Memphis, Tennessee. It was during this arrest that the FBI agents received the name "G-men,"[12] an abbreviation of the term "Government men." By 1934, the gangs had discovered that the "golden era" of the underworld empire was on the wane. One after another, powerful gangland bosses were captured, and "public enemies" were killed or sent to prison.

In recounting the events of this period, the Federal Bureau of Investigation reports:

On July 22, 1934, John Dillinger[13] was killed on a Chicago street while resisting arrest. On October 22, 1934, "Pretty Boy" Floyd met death on

[10] Peterson, pp. 170, 171.
[11] Hoover, pp. 9–40.
[12] See Chapter 13.
[13] John Dillinger was one of the most notorious bank robbers of the period. All of the other criminals mentioned by the FBI were prominent in gangland's activities.

an Ohio farm while resisting federal arrest. On November 27, 1934, "Baby Face" Nelson, murderer of three FBI agents, was mortally wounded in a gun battle on an Illinois highway while resisting arrest. On January 8, 1935, Russell Gibson, member of the powerful Barker-Karpis gang, fell under a hail of lead in a Chicago alley after he had fired at a Special Agent who demanded his surrender. On January 16, 1935, Ma and Fred Barker, leaders of the Barker-Karpis gang, who were hiding out in a Florida cottage, answered the agents' demand for surrender with bursts from Thompson submachine guns. The Barkers were killed in the gun battle.

On October 12, 1937, G-men were fired upon by members of the Brady gang at Bangor, Maine. An FBI agent was wounded but Alfred Brady and Clarence Shaffer were killed and the gang smashed. On October 7, 1938, Adam Richetti was executed in connection with the slaying of four law-enforcement officers, including an FBI agent, in the "Kansas City Massacre." Vernon Miller, also wanted for the same crime, was clubbed and shot to death by underworld "pals," who by that time considered a federal fugitive of his type too dangerous to have around.

In the desperate war with the gang trigger men, several FBI Agents lost their lives. But the fearlessness of the Agents in gun battles and their straight shooting soon caused the word to be passed in underworld circles that it didn't pay to "shoot it out" with G-men.

Within three years after the FBI received general investigative jurisdiction over federal crimes, 11,153 persons had been arrested and convicted. Among these were 4,897 car thieves, 330 kidnappers and extortionists, and 152 bank robbers. Bank robberies dropped 75 per cent, and six years later had gone down 95 per cent. The day and night work of determined investigators was driving the gangsters to cover. Their contacts were broken, communications disrupted. It became dangerous to "deal" with a wanted criminal.[14]

By the beginning of World War II, the power of organized gang criminality in the United States had been shattered, but the other types of organized crime were growing and sending their poisonous tentacles into every channel of American life. Organized gang criminality kills, cripples, ravages, plunders, and destroys. It is dangerous—make no mistake about that. But it does not constitute the threat to America that is to be found in racketeering and syndicated crime. It strikes in the open and can be attacked and brought under control by courageous, alert, and vigorous police action. Racketeering and syndicated crime, on the other hand, are insidious, subterranean, and undermining. They must be patiently and persistently searched for and rooted out.

[14] U.S. Department of Justice, *The Story of the Federal Bureau of Investigation,* pp. 1–5.

Racketeering. Racketeering is extortion from legitimate or illegitimate business through intimidation or force by an organized criminal gang.[15] Unlike organized gang criminality, it does not take and carry away. It stays, attaches itself to the business, and lets the owner continue his operations. But like a parasite, it lives on the blood of its host, collecting tribute, profiting by the industry of others, giving nothing in return, and maintaining its hold by intimidation, force, and terrorism.[16] Fear provides the basis of the racket, and through it the racketeer extracts his regular payments. Beatings and destruction of property often accompany the initial organization of the racket, and later they effectively "persuade" the victim "to stay in line."

The racketeering gang is divided into the "brains" and the "muscle." The "brains" do the thinking, issue orders, solicit new business, and arrange for protection. The "muscle-men" do the "rough stuff," beating, disfiguring, maiming, killing, plundering, and destroying. However, the top men, also, may do a few of these "jobs" from time to time, just to "keep in practice, maintain their reputations, or demonstrate the proper techniques."[17]

Illegitimate businesses, such as prostitution, gambling, drug peddling, liquor traffic, and illegal money lending, fall easy prey to the racketeer.[18] Unable to turn to the law for protection, they must often submit to him and accept his "help." In the battle between employers and labor unions, both sides have at times hired the services of gangsters. In some cases, these thugs have refused to leave and have continued to extort "fees" from their former employers. Sometimes fierce competition in certain fields has opened the door to the racketeer. Businessmen, driven to the wall and unable to make profits, have brought him in to "organize" the field. This he accomplishes by forming an association, which may have full "legal window dressing," and ruthlessly eliminating competition and price cutting. But then he remains as one of the "expenses" of operating

[15] The underworld and some writers have used the term "racket" to refer to all types of organized crime, but criminologists are tending to use the narrower definition given here. See, for example, Barnes and Teeters, p. 37; Ruth Shonle Cavan, Criminology (New York: Thomas Y. Crowell Co., 1962), p. 137; Walter C. Reckless, *The Crime Problem* (New York: Appleton-Century-Crofts, Inc., 1961), pp. 188, 189; Arthur E. Wood and John B. Waite, *Crime and Its Treatment* (New York: American Book Co., 1941), pp. 110, 111.

[16] Gordon L. Hostetter and Thomas Q. Beesley, *It's a Racket* (Chicago: Les Quin Books, Inc., 1929), p. 4; Craig Thompson and Allen Raymond, *Gang Rule in New York* (New York: The Dial Press, Inc., 1940), p. 219.

[17] Maurice J. Fitzgerald, *Handbook of Criminal Investigation* (New York: Greenberg, Publisher, 1951), 163, 164.

[18] For a discussion of the invasion of the field of finance by organized crime in Chicago, see Virgil W. Peterson, *A Report on Chicago Crime for 1961* (Chicago: Chicago Crime Commission, May 14, 1962), pp. 37, 38.

the business, overcoming resistance by the usual methods of physical violence and destruction.

However, circumstances such as these, although favorable, are not essential to the growth of rackets. Racketeers have forced themselves into all kinds of business. A favorite approach is to suggest to the businessman that he needs protection and that it can be furnished at a stipulated monthly fee. If he protests that he needs no protection, he may be bluntly told that he will need it in the future. If this fails to convince him, the breaking of his windows. the destruction of his merchandise, and the beating of his employees usually force him to capitulate. From then on he pays and pays.

The distribution processes of the American economy have proved especially attractive to the racketeer. In New York, distributors of such food products as bread, milk, fish, and poultry have felt the weight of his hand and paid him heavy tribute. Writing of this in 1940, Thompson and Raymond said, "The racket added $1,500,000 a year to the cost of trucking the flour alone, and imposed an additional tariff upon its manufacture into finished foods."[19]

In Chicago, drug stores, restaurants, hotels, taverns, jukebox record distributors, and other places of business have been "muscled into line" by racketeers.[20] In 1958, during the hearings before the McClellan Senate Committee, the proprietor of one of the city's largest eating establishments testified that every restaurant owner in Chicago lived in fear of the underworld.[21] Later, in 1959, before the same committee, the proprietor of a jukebox record service stated that after the Lormar Distributing Company, which was operated by Accardo's associate, Charles "Chuck" English, had been organized, his customers told him that they would have to switch all of their business to that company, or their machines would be thrown into the street by the electrical workers' union.[22] The Lormar Company also engaged in the counterfeiting of record labels, and in 1958, one of its officials had been found guilty of this charge.[23]

---

[19] Thompson and Raymond, p. 245.

[20] Virgil W. Peterson, *A Report on Chicago Crime for 1958* (Chicago: Chicago Crime Commission, July 10, 1959), pp. 26–31; *ibid.*, "Rackets in America," *Journal of Criminal Law, Criminology, and Police Science,* XLIX (Mar.–Apr., 1959), 583–89; *ibid.*, "Chicago: Shades of Capone," *The Annals of the American Academy of Political and Social Science,* CCCXLVII (May, 1963), 30–39. (This entire issue of the *Annals* is devoted to articles on organized crime.)

[21] U.S. Senate Select Committee on Improper Activities in the Labor or Management Field, *Hearings* (July 15, 16, 17, 18 and 31, 1958) (Washington, D.C.: Government Printing Office, 1958), Part 34, p. 12916.

[22] *Ibid., Hearings* (Feb. 26, 1958, Feb. 19, 20, 24, 25, and Mar. 10, 1959) (Washington, D.C.: Government Printing Office, 1959), Part 47, pp. 17021–40.

[23] Peterson, "Chicago: Shades of Capone," 39.

The racketeer has found another fertile field in labor unions. Securing control of the union membership, he can threaten employees with strikes and thus force them to pay tribute. Some trade associations, also, have fallen under his domination. When this happens the association becomes a private club, and failure to belong brings disaster to the offending tradesman.[24] Sometimes racketeers get control of both the labor union and the trade association in the same field. They are then in a position to extort tribute from the workers for the opportunity of working and from the employers for the privilege of having workers on the job. This is what happened some years ago in the restaurant business in New York City[25] and in the cleaning and dyeing industry in Chicago.[26] The great growth in the health and welfare funds of labor unions during recent years has given new opportunities for wealth to organized criminals. A few years ago, after hearing a parade of witnesses relate how they had been forced to make payments to hoodlum union officials, Senator McClellan, chairman of the committee of the United States Senate which was investigating improper activities in labor and management, remarked: "These people are not running a union. They are running a racket."[27]

In the early thirties, the Capone gang became affiliated with powerful New York criminals in highly profitable and large-scale racketeering. In 1934, Frank Nitti, Louis "Little New York" Campagna, Paul Ricca, and Frank Rio formulated a plan to take over control of the International Alliance of Theatrical, Stage Employees, and Motion Picture Operators.

In Chicago [according to Peterson] Willie Bioff, a pander, labor racketeer, and an employee in a Capone gambling house, had been working with George E. Browne, the business agent of Local Number 2 of the Union, in extorting money from theater owners. Their profits were sufficiently high to attract the attention of Nitti, Campagna, Ricca and other Capone gangsters, who promptly declared themselves partners of Bioff and Browne and launched a program that would yield profits amounting to millions of dollars. In the development of the conspiracy, the first move was to elect their representative president of the International Union. A convention of the International Union was scheduled for Louisville in June, 1934. Through the assistance of Lucky Luciano and Lepke Buchalter, the New York union delegates to the convention were instructed to vote for George E. Browne for president. Lepke also promised to see Louis Kaufman, business agent of the big Newark local union, and assure his support for the Capone gang's candidate. The convention in Louisville was a mere formality. George E. Browne became the president of the powerful International Union and 125,000 union members were reduced to the status

[24] Fitzgerald, pp. 165, 166. See also Malcolm Johnson, *Crime on the Labor Front* (New York: McGraw-Hill Book Co., Inc., 1950).
[25] Morris Ploscowe, "Crime in a Competitive Society," *The Annals of the American Academy of Political and Social Science*, CCXVII (Sept., 1941), 109, 110.
[26] Hostetter and Beesley, pp. 29–44.
[27] Peterson, "Rackets in America," 586.

of serfs of the Capone syndicate and its allies. In Chicago, Thomas E. Maloy
had been at the head of the local motion picture operators union since 1920.
On February 4, 1935, two men ambushed Maloy on the Outer Drive and a
.45 caliber pistol and a sawed-off shotgun were emptied into his head. He
was killed instantly. A week later George Browne assumed control of Maloy's
union. In 1935, the Capone syndicate extorted over $100,000 from Chicago
theater owners.[28]

The Capone gang now had a system of rackets extending from New
York City on the East Coast to Hollywood on the West, but these extortion activities led to the prosecution and conviction of some of the
gang's leading figures. Paul Ricca, also known as Paul the Waiter, Louis
"Little New York" Campagna, and Charlie "Cherry Nose" Gioe were
found guilty and sent to prison. The successful prosecution of these
extortion cases marked a milestone in governmental ability to cope with
union infiltration by gangsters and their use of unions to shake down
business enterprises.[29]

Syndicated Crime. Syndicated crime is the furnishing of illegal goods,
such as drugs and liquor, or illegal services, such as gambling and prostitution, by an organized criminal gang. It is big business in the field of
crime and supplies something which large segments of the public demand
and eagerly buy. It creates its own regular business procedures, usually
operates from an established headquarters, and seeks to achieve its objectives without violence. The leaders in syndicated crime often pass as
respectable citizens, living in the finest residential sections of our cities,
associating with prominent businessmen and professional people, belonging to the best clubs, and contributing services and money to many
civic affairs and community projects. Thus, syndicated crime differs in
important respects from organized gang criminality, which intermittently
strikes and carries away its booty and sometimes its victims, often by
violence, and then finds refuge in some "hideout," and from racketeering,
which fastens itself upon the business of another, continually extracts
payments through intimidation or force, and gives nothing in return.

When the Kefauver Committee was investigating organized crime in
1950 and 1951, it found that the two major crime syndicates in this
country were the Accardo-Guzik-Fischetti syndicate, with headquarters
in Chicago, and the Costello-Lansky-Adonis group of New York City.
The Accardo-Guzik-Fischetti group, heirs of the Al Capone gang of prohibition days, was conducting operations in such places as Chicago,
Kansas City, Dallas, Miami, Las Vegas, and the West Coast. The other
group, headed by Frank Costello, was active in New York City, Saratoga

[28] Peterson, *Barbarians in Our Midst*, pp. 174, 175.
[29] U.S. Senate Special Committee to Investigate Organized Crime in Interstate Commerce, *Third Interim Report*, p. 51.

(New York), Bergen County (New Jersey), New Orleans, Miami, Havana, Las Vegas and the West Coast.[30]

Chicago, because of its size and its location as a center of communication, transportation, and distribution of goods, has been and remains a focal point of organized crime in the United States. The roots of organized crime in Chicago extend back to the operations of the Torrio-Capone gang which terrorized that city during the twenties. In the late twenties Torrio abdicated, and Al Capone became the leader.[31] At that time, the activities of the Capone gang consisted largely of illegal liquor rackets, prostitution, gambling, and the control of horse-racing and dog-racing tracks. In 1931, Al Capone was brought to trial and sentenced for federal income-tax evasion, and his place was taken by Frank Nitti, who was an old-time member of the Torrio-Capone gang. Later Nitti committed suicide in 1943, while under indictment with a number of other Capone henchmen, all of whom were tried and convicted for a conspiracy to extort millions of dollars from the motion picture industry. The gang then came under the leadership of Accardo, Guzik, and Fischetti.[32]

After the repeal of prohibition in 1933, the Capone syndicate concentrated its attention on illegal gambling, racketeering, and the infiltration of such legitimate enterprises as hotels, restaurants, laundry services, dry-cleaning establishments, breweries, and wholesale and retail liquor businesses, where its "contacts" gave it a substantial advantage. By acquiring control of the Continental Press Service and its nation-wide network of telephone and telegraph wires, which formed the backbone of illegal gambling on horse racing in the United States, the Capone syndicate was able to participate in the profits of bookmaking operations throughout the country.[33]

This was an important achievement, for the profits from gambling provide the principal support for organized crime in America. The Kefauver Committee found that gambling was big business in every one of the fourteen areas of the country which it visited. A Miami booking syndicate of five local men grossed upwards of $26,000,000 a year. A grand jury in Kansas City estimated the annual gambling take to be in excess of $34,000,000, chiefly through the bookmaking and gambling operations of the Binaggio gang. In Philadelphia and Tampa, lotteries, called "numbers" in the former and "bolita" in the latter, were the most lucrative forms of gambling. In

[30] American Bar Association Commission on Organized Crime, I, 11.

[31] For a fascinating account of the incredible history of crime in Chicago, see Peterson, Barbarians in Our Midst.

[32] U.S. Senate Special Committee to Investigate Organized Crime in Interstate Commerce, Third Interim Report, p. 50.

[33] Ibid., pp. 51, 52; U.S. Senate Special Committee to Investigate Organized Crime in Interstate Commerce, Second Interim Report, pp. 17–26.

Chicago, which is a distribution center for gambling equipment and services, and in surrounding towns and cities in Illinois and adjoining states, an enormous business was being done in slot machines, policy wheels, punchboards,[34] and bookmaking. In Bergen County, New Jersey, and Saratoga, New York, every known game of chance was being played in the gambling casinos. In the industrial plants of Detroit, organized gambling, chiefly the numbers game, was being conducted on a large scale. In the New Orleans area, lush gambling profits were being made by Costello's slot machines, elaborate gambling casinos, and bookmaking operations. At the time of the Kefauver Committee's hearings, a grand jury in New York was investigating bookmaking enterprises estimated to be doing a business of at least $300,000,000, a year.[35]

In 1960, after months of investigation, the McClellan Committee was convinced that the underworld infiltration of business and labor was a national problem and urged Congress to do whatever it could to cope with this menace. With respect to the coin-operated machine industry, the McClellan Committee stated in its conclusions: that this industry, particularly in the music, amusement, and cigarette-vending segments, had been victimized by an astounding number of racketeers; that the operations of criminals had been extended into nongambling amusement games, automatic phonographs, and vending machines; that for many years employers had been acting in collusion with subservient union locals to enforce trade restraints to benefit favored employers and to corrupt labor officials; that captive labor union locals had been used as weapons by criminals to dominate various parts of this industry; that union officials had been guilty of the most gross conflicts of interests, having had proprietary holdings in the very business and area with the employees they purported to represent; that criminals had been knowingly used by management to increase its sales; and that the public had been prevented from enjoying the benefits of competition, and honest men who refused to pay tribute to hoodlums had been driven out of business.[36]

EXPANSIVE AND MONOPOLISTIC TENDENCIES

Modern criminal gangs tend to extend their power over any geographical area or activity where they can operate profitably and without interfer-

[34] The Kefauver Committee stated that it was not possible to estimate with any great degree of exactitude the annual sum played on punchboards, but believed that one hundred million dollars would be a conservative estimate (*Third Interim Report*, p. 60).

[35] American Bar Association Commission on Organized Crime, I, 13, 14.

[36] U.S. Senate Select Committee on Improper Activties in the Labor or Management Field, *Final Report* (Washington, D.C.: Government Printing Office, 1960), pp. 509, 855–58. See also John L. McClellan, *Crime Without Punishment* (New York: Duell, Sloan, and Pearce, 1962).

ence. They accomplish this either by adding new areas and "lines" to those they already have or by taking over the operations and territories of smaller outfits. In the latter case, they may either eliminate the smaller outfits or permit them to operate as separate units and participate in their profits. Thus, a single gang may engage directly or indirectly in all types of organized crime in many areas throughout the country. The Capone gang achieved such a position of power, and its operations probably constitute the best example of the expansive and monopolistic tendencies of organized crime.

However, the operations of another nation-wide organization known as the "Combination" to its members but called "Murder, Inc." by the press provide one of the most amazing stories ever to come out of the underworld. This story, related in 1940, by a sadistic gangster named Abe ("Kid Twist") Reles, describes the "Combination" as an organization that engaged in major criminal activities from coast to coast, trained its personnel, formulated its own code of conduct, and killed on contract. Reles confessed that he himself had committed something like eighteen murders, but that he had killed his victims in an entirely impersonal way for business reasons.

The scores of killings attributed to the "Combination" were said to be mere by-products of business operations involving millions of dollars. These included gambling, prostitution, illicit drug traffic, policy game, bootlegging, and the loan shark racket. It was also alleged that the "Combination" dominated certain trade-union locals, had a financial stake in various night clubs and cabarets, operated certain legitimate enterprises, and played an important, sinister role in urban politics.

In November, 1941, Reles, the informer, was killed under suspicious circumstances when he tried to escape from a hotel room where he had been held under police guard. However, the "Combination" was prosecuted in New York, and several of its members, including its leader Louis "Lepke" Buchalter, were convicted of murder and executed.[37]

ORGANIZED CRIME AND POLITICS

Organized crime cannot long persist without the cooperation and connivance of both police and politicians. As the Kefauver Committee pointed out, no stock can be placed in the professed inability of law-enforcement officials to detect violations of the law which are apparent to any informed citizen. Local officials know perfectly well what is going on in their com-

[37] Lindesmith, pp. 122, 123; Joseph Freeman, "Murder Monopoly: The Inside Story of a Crime Trust," *The Nation*, CL (May 25, 1940), 645 ff; Turkus and Feder, *op. cit.*; U.S. Senate Special Committee to Investigate Organized Crime in Interstate Commerce, *Third Interim Report*, pp. 125–30.

munities, and by vigorous, honest law enforcement, they can, if they so desire, put an end to wide-open conditions in a very short time.[38]

It is clear, therefore, that in order to accomplish their purpose, the leaders of organized criminal groups must circumvent the law, corrupt politicians and police, and penetrate the soft parts of American society. In this task they have benefited by the apathy and ignorance of the public and the wide-spread popular demand for illegal goods and services. When citizens neglect their duties and shift responsibilities to professional politicians, a political party tends to harden into a machine dealing in votes and patronage to the detriment of the public. Conditions are then ripe for an alliance between the machine and the underworld. Each is seeking power and security. The underworld can give votes and money; the machine, protection, public office, and political favors. Candidates for office, the honest as well as the dishonest, usually find it expedient to accept support from the machine even though they know that it contains strong underworld elements. And the public, apathetic and ignorant, stands by—content with the opportunity of having the goods and services which the law forbids. But once the alliance is formed, the "fixing" of cases does not stop with gambling, prostitution, drugs, and liquor. It becomes a creeping paralysis that affects law enforcement in all fields of crime. The underworld knows full well that once a public official allows a case to be "fixed," thereafter he becomes its slave.[39]

One of the most shocking revelations of the Kefauver Committee was "the extent of official corruption in facilitating and promoting organized crime." This corruption was found in state and local government agencies in four different forms:

1. *Direct bribes or protection payments.* Examples of this were the $1,000,000 a year protection money paid by the Gross bookmaking empire in New York City; the $152,000 a month paid to police officials in Philadelphia to avoid interference with gambling; the $7,000 to $11,000 at a time turned over by a deputy sheriff of Dade County, Florida, to the wife of the sheriff; and the $108,000 "juice" entry on the books of the Guarantee Finance Company, a bookmaking operation in Los Angeles.

2. *The unusual and unexplained wealth of law-enforcement officials.* Sheriffs, police chiefs, police commissioners, and investigators of the district attorney have grown rich and powerful as a result of their association with underworld elements engaged in organized criminal activities. One example of this was the chief of police of Fairmont City, Illinois, who had previously been a coal miner. He began to "sport" a Cadillac car and a $1,200 diamond ring after he entered office. His attitude toward

---

[38] *Third Interim Report,* p. 181.
[39] *Ibid.,* p. 182.

bookmaking perhaps explains his sudden wealth. When asked why he permitted a bookmaking establishment to operate within a block of his police station, he answered, "I just never had no complaint about it."[40]

3. *The use of political influence and pressure to protect criminal activities or to further the interests of criminal groups.* Typical examples of this were the sinister influence of gangsters like Frank Costello and Joe Adonis in the Democratic organizations of Manhattan and Brooklyn, respectively; the attempt by the gangster politician Binaggio to acquire control of the police board of Kansas City; and the large contributions made to Governor Fuller Warren's campaign in Florida by a known associate of the Capone gang.

4. *The participation of law-enforcement officials directly in the business of organized crime.* For example, in Hillsborough and Broward counties in Florida, in some of the parishes in the New Orleans area, in Brooklyn, New York, and in Jackson County, Missouri, "there was evidence that certain law-enforcement officials not only took protection money from gamblers and racketeers but actually participated in the criminal operations themselves."[41]

All this points to one conclusion. The ultimate responsibility for the success of any attack upon organized crime rests squarely in the hands of the American people. They themselves can decide the issue. But to win they must learn what the facts are, make known their inexorable determination to fight crime and criminals everywhere by every method, elect honest, courageous, and efficient men and women to public offices, and steadily support them by assuming the responsibilities of good citizenship.

THE KEFAUVER COMMITTEE

During 1950 and 1951, the Kefauver Committee (the Senate Special Committee to Investigate Organized Crime in Interstate Commerce) conducted the most extensive inquiry into organized crime that had ever been undertaken in the United States.[42] This committee drew the following general conclusions from the evidence produced before it:

1. Organized criminal gangs are firmly entrenched in our large cities and are engaged in many kinds of criminal activities.

2. The most dangerous gangs are those which supply goods and services such as narcotics, illegal liquor, and gambling and prostitution, for which there is a widespread popular demand.

[40] *Ibid.*, p. 63.

[41] American Bar Association Commission on Organized Crime, I, 16–18.

[42] Notable among the investigations made before that of the Kefauver Committee were the Missouri Crime Survey of 1926, the Illinois Crime Survery of 1929, and the Wickersham Commission studies of 1931.

3. The individual gangs in particular cities may be merely local representatives of national crime syndicates. The two major crime syndicates in the United States are the Accardo-Guzik-Fischetti group in Chicago and the Costello-Lansky-Adonis group in New York City.

4. A criminal organization, known as the Mafia,[43] binds the two major criminal syndicates and other criminal groups throughout the country into one loose national crime federation.

5. Criminal gangs secure monopolies in the particular criminal enterprises in which they are engaged.

6. The leading criminals remain largely immune from prosecution and punishment despite their records and well-documented reputations. This quasi-immunity can be ascribed to what is popularly known as the "fix."

7. The profits derived from gambling are the principal support of big-time racketeering and gangsterism.

8. Large-scale gambling is vitally dependent upon the use of interstate communication and transportation facilities. The gambling information is provided by a monopoly operated by the Continental Press Service, which in turn is controlled by the Capone syndicate.

9. A breakdown has occurred in law-enforcement machinery in communities which have permitted wide-open gambling and vice conditions.

10. This breakdown is aided by overlapping law-enforcement jurisdictions, ill-defined law-enforcement responsibilities, and lack of centralized direction and control of law enforcement.

[43] The Mafia, also known as the Black Hand in the United States, was originally one of the many secret societies organized in Sicily to free that island of foreign domination. Its methods were later adopted by a criminal group that became the Mafia after the Bourbons were driven from Sicily. Various drives against the Mafia in Sicily had the effect of causing large numbers of its members to migrate to the United States where they continued the activities of the society. However, the Kefauver Committee found it difficult to obtain reliable data concerning the extent of the Mafia and the nature of its organization and methods (U.S. Senate Special Committee to Investigate Organized Crime in Interstate Commerce, *Third Interim Report*, pp. 147–50). There is a difference of opinion as to whether such an organization as the Mafia exists in the United States. For various points of view on the subject, see Frederic Sondern, Jr., *Brotherhood of Evil: The Mafia* (New York: Farrar, Straus, and Cudahy, 1959); Estes Kefauver, *Crime in America* (Garden City, N.Y.: Doubleday and Co., Inc., 1951); Edward J. Allen, *Merchants of Menace: The Mafia* (Springfield, Ill.: Charles C. Thomas, Publisher, 1962); Burton B. Turkus and Sid Feder, *Murder, Inc., The Story of "the Syndicate,"* (New York: Farrar, Straus, and Young, 1951); Daniel Bell, *The End of Ideology* (Glencoe, Ill.: The Free Press, 1960); Giovanni Schiavo, *The Truth About the Mafia* (New York: Vigo Press, 1962).

Although there may be a difference of opinion regarding the existence of the Mafia in the United States, there can be no doubt that leading gangsters in different parts of the country do cooperate from time to time when this is to their mutual interest. This was clearly evidenced by the gangland meeting on November 14, 1957, at Apalachin, New York, which was attended by at least fifty-eight known hoodlums. Additional facts regarding the extent of the control exercised by organized crime in the United States were obtained during 1963 through the congressional investigation into the activities of *La Cosa Nostra*.

11. The largest single factor in the breakdown of law-enforcement agencies in their dealing with organized crime is the corruption and connivance of many public officials.

12. The Treasury of the United States has been defrauded of large sums of money by criminals engaged in organized crime.

13. Some lawyers and accountants who are in close contact with criminal gangs or individual gangsters have been violating canons of ethics and may even be an integral part of the criminal conspiracies of their clients.

14. Legitimate businessmen have aided the interests of the underworld by making their facilities available to criminal enterprises or by awarding valuable franchises and contracts to notorious criminals. In addition, organized criminals have infiltrated various areas of legitimate business to a considerable extent, and in some cases are using the same methods of intimidation and violence that they have used to secure monopolies in criminal enterprise.[44]

On the basis of these conclusions, the Kefauver Committee made twenty-two separate recommendations calling upon the federal government to take action against organized interstate crime. The committee, however, emphasized that the basic responsibility for the conditions which were fostering organized crime rested upon the individual states and local communities and that they, therefore, should strengthen their laws and agencies so as to deal more effectively with it.[45] Since the Kefauver Committee issued its report, local, state, and federal governments have taken important steps to combat the gambling enterprises that produce substantial revenues for organized crime in the United States.[46] However, the effectiveness of this attack has not as yet been determined.

[44] American Bar Association Commission on Organized Crime, I, 9–21; U.S. Senate Special Committee to Investigate Organized Crime in Interstate Commerce, *Third Interim Report*, pp. 1–5.

[45] American Bar Association Commission on Organized Crime, I, 21–24; U.S. Senate Special Committee to Investigate Organized Crime in Interstate Commerce, *Third Interim Report*, pp. 5–20, 26–30.

[46] See Morris Ploscowe, "New Approaches to the Control of Organized Crime," *The Annals of the American Academy of Political and Social Science*, CCCXLVII (May, 1963), 74–81; Eliot H. Lumbard, "Local and State Action against Organized Crime," *ibid.*, 82–92; Herbert J. Miller, Jr., "A Federal Viewpoint on Combating Organized Crime," *ibid.*, 93–103; Edwyn Silberling, "The Federal Attack on Organized Crime," *Crime and Delinquency*, VIII (Oct., 1962), 365–70 (this entire issue of *Crime and Delinquency* is devoted to articles on organized crime). For a discussion of the legal problems involved in the suppression of organized crime, see "Legal Methods for the Suppression of Organized Crime," *Journal of Criminal Law, Criminology, and Police Science*, XLVIII (Nov.–Dec., 1957), 414–30; *ibid.*, (Jan.–Feb., 1958), 526–41; Edward S. Silver, "Organized Gambling and Law Enforcement," *ibid.*, L (Nov.–Dec., 1959), 397–403; Earl Johnson, Jr., "Organized Crime: Challenge to the American Legal System," *ibid.*, LIII (Dec., 1962), 399–425; *ibid.*, LIV (Mar., 1963), 1–29; *ibid.*, LIV (June, 1963), 127–45.

SHOULD GAMBLING BE LEGALIZED?

The Kefauver Committee's disclosure that illegal gambling exists on a large scale in the United States has led to the suggestion that the business of gambling should be legalized and licensed. Those in favor of this suggestion argue that:

1. It would provide an additional source of revenue for state and local governments.

2. It would remove gambling from the control of organized criminal gangs and thus eliminate a major cause of lawlessness and corruption.

3. It would regulate the strong human impulse to gamble rather than undertake the impossible task of suppression.[47]

However, the following cogent arguments can be advanced against legalized gambling:

1. Much of the revenue that might be derived from the legalization of gambling operations would be absorbed by the expense of running the machinery of regulation. At present, Nevada is the only state that permits all types of gambling under a licensing system. It is a state with a small population where gambling operations can be easily policed; yet even it has had to increase police surveillance substantially as a result of the influx of hoodlums, racketeers, and other parasites who are always attracted to the gaming tables. Furthermore, it has had to stand by and watch its legalized gambling strengthen some of America's most dangerous criminal gangs by pouring thousands of dollars into their coffers.

2. The legalization of gambling would not take it out of the hands of the criminal elements. Past experience demonstrates that legalization has never succeeded in doing this. The underworld is interested in gambling not because it is illegal, but because it is a highly lucrative business and offers opportunities for getting easy money through the exploitation of human weakness. There is no reason to believe that the underworld would be less successful in gaining control of the licensing system than it has been in securing protection. If gambling were legalized, the same politicians that now give protection would grant licenses to the organized criminal gangs. This contention is borne out by the investigations of the Kefauver Committee, which found that criminal elements were in firm control of Nevada's legalized gambling.

3. History shows that legalization advertises gambling, makes it more attractive and convenient, and thus leads to an increase in it, especially among small-wage earners—the very people who are least able to bear the inevitable losses. And if the raising of revenue is made the principal goal

---

[47] For further explanation of this point of view, see Robert K. Woetzel, "An Overview of Organized Crime: Mores versus Morality," *The Annals of the American Academy of Political and Social Science*, CCCXLVII (May, 1963), 1–11.

in legalization, the increase in gambling is even greater. The combined pressure of politics and desire for revenue results in the removal of any semblance of adequate control.

4. Wherever large-scale gambling has been carried on, violence and crime have increased. Gambling houses inevitably become breeding places of crime and the headquarters of the most dangerous criminals. Whether legalized or not, gambling drives its operators to intimidation and corruption in order to achieve and maintain a monopoly, and its victims to embezzlement, robbery, and other crimes in order to recoup their losses.

5. The difficulty of enforcing the laws against gambling is not an adequate reason for its legalization. Society has had to regulate desires that are far more powerful than the desire to gamble. For example, legislation cannot eliminate the sex drive; yet society has had to pass laws designed to prevent the evils of promiscuity. On this point, it must be remembered that the great majority of those who oppose the legalization of gambling do not want to regulate private morals or to interfere with private or casual gambling. What they want to do is to prohibit the business of gambling.[48]

On the basis of its investigation, the Kefauver Committee opposed the legalization of gambling. It noted that a number of states considered it desirable to permit "on-track" betting under conditions that are most easily subject to policing and control. However, in its opinion, this did "not furnish any basis for the legalization of other forms of gambling which are far more likely to be dominated by underworld elements and most apt to lead to violent competition and criminal activity."[49] In support of the Kefauver Committee, the American Bar Association Commission on Organized Crime also went on record against the legalization of gambling and formulated a comprehensive model antigambling act for adoption by the various states.[50]

After the Kefauver Committee had completed its work, there was an apparent decline in such forms of organized criminal activities as lotteries, slot machine operations, bookmaking, and the system of wire services, which were the main instruments of syndicated crime and which had been funneling great wealth into the underworld. Nevertheless, public officials

[48] Virgil W. Peterson, "Gambling—Should It Be Legalized?" *Journal of Criminal Law and Criminology,* XL (Sept.–Oct., 1949), 257–329; U.S. Senate Special Committee to Investigate Organized Crime in Interstate Commerce, *Third Interim Report,* pp. 192–95; American Bar Association Commission on Organized Crime, II, 19–26; Frederick W. Egen, *Plainclothesman* (New York: Greenberg, Publisher, 1952), pp. 10–14. See also Virgil W. Peterson, *Gambling: Should it Be Legalized?* (Springfield, Ill.: Charles C. Thomas, Publisher, 1951).

[49] U.S. Senate Special Committee to Investigate Organized Crime in Interstate Commerce, *Third Interim Report,* pp. 194–195.

[50] American Bar Association Commission on Organized Crime, II, 18, 19.

and law-enforcement officers throughout the country warned that this might be just a lull before another outburst of organized crime.[51] That they had reason to be wary has been demonstrated by subsequent events. The leaders of the underworld have not been crushed. Not only have they moved into new illegitimate areas of income, but they have also seriously infiltrated legitimate business, thus creating another threat to the American economy,[52] for when organized crime invades a legitimate business, it usually takes with it all the techniques of violence, intimidation, and corruption which it has used in its illegal activities. It forces competitors into subservient positions or out of business entirely and induces customers to buy from suppliers that it controls or sponsors. Thus, it undermines free economy and regiments the market to serve its purposes rather than those of the consuming public.[53]

Organized crime has greatly increased its power by its investments in legitimate business. Its political allies are biding their time, testing the temper of public opinion, and hoping that the storm of protests caused by the Kefauver and McClellan investigations will blow over. The alliance between the underworld and the political machine cannot be destroyed without a vigorous, sustained campaign, whole-heartedly supported by an aroused and enlightened public opinion. Americans cannot continue to enjoy the illicit goods and services provided by organized crime and at the same time expect their public officials to remain honest and their economy, uncorrupted. They must make a choice and abide by the consequences.[54] Thus far only the initial battles of the campaign against organized crime have been fought. All signs, therefore, clearly indicate that effective measures to suppress it should be adopted now while public opinion still affords a favorable climate for such action.

[51] American Bar Association Commission on Organized Crime, II, 6–18, 207–59.

[52] See Dwight S. Strong, "New England: The Refined Yankee in Organized Crime," *The Annals of the American Academy of Political and Social Science*, CCCXLVII (May, 1963), 40–50; Louis J. Lefkowitz, "New York: Criminal Infiltration of the Securities Industry," *ibid.*, 51–57; Alvin J. T. Zumbrun, "Maryland: A Law-Enforcement Dilemma," *ibid.*, 58–66; Virgil W. Peterson, "Chicago: Shades of Capone," *ibid.*, 30–39.

[53] Earl Johnson, Jr., 406, 407.

[54] Robert K. Woetzel, 6–11; Gus Tyler, "The Roots of Organized Crime," *Crime and Delinquency*, VIII (Oct., 1962), 325–38; Herbert A. Block, "The Gambling Business: An American Paradox," *ibid.*, 355–64. For the distinction between the manifest and the latent functions of the social order, see Robert K. Merton, *Social Theory and Social Structure* (Glencoe, Ill.: The Free Press, 1957), pp. 60–82.

Part II

CAUSATION

9

Causation in General

Obviously, the prevention of crime is dependent upon a knowledge of its causes. Thus far, however, despite years of study and research and the publication of tons of literature, efforts to increase this knowledge have not been very fruitful. It is true that techniques have been refined and some helpful insights have been acquired, but on the whole the gains are not great. Although these gains represent the work of centuries, this discussion will deal primarily with about 150 years, the most recent and productive period of men's efforts to understand the causes of crime.

THE CHRISTIAN INFLUENCE

The introduction of Christianity produced far-reaching changes in the moral fabric of European civilization. Largely as a result of its influence, the notion of a deliberate transgression for which the individual is responsible eventually spread throughout Europe and formed the basis of the Christian conception of sin. It was through the ecclesiastical law that the idea of responsibility began to prevail in the domain of criminal law, and with it came emphasis upon the individual criminal, who had to be purified and regenerated through expiation and punishment.[1]

The way was also prepared, however, for the arbitrary and unequal imposition of penalties. Since the responsibility of the offender was held to vary from crime to crime, the judge was permitted to exercise considerable discretion in adjusting the punishment to fit the individual case. But this in turn made it possible for him to indulge his prejudices, to wreak personal vengeance upon the criminal, and to impose severe sentences for minor offenses.[2] It is not surprising, then, that Europe was

[1] Raymond Saleilles, *The Individualization of Punishment* (Boston: Little, Brown and Co., 1911), pp. 35–39.

[2] Those who today would weaken the principle of legality might well learn a lesson from this abuse of judicial authority. For a discussion of the principle of legality, see Chapter 2.

the scene of strange contrasts during the eighteenth century. Eminent statesmen and distinguished writers emphasized justice and human rights. Yet, torture was applied daily, secret accusations were encouraged, capital penalties were indiscriminately increased, and innumerable abuses were perpetrated.[3]

At the same time, new ideas of liberty and toleration had emerged, and the old foundations of society had been shaken. It was inevitable, therefore, that the general intellectual movement[4] of the eighteenth century should include a consideration of the criminal law and the arbitrary and cruel practices that characterized its administration.[5] It was to the reform of the criminal law and its administration that the classical school directed its efforts, although in doing so it also contributed to the establishment of a point of view regarding the causation of criminal behavior.

THE CLASSICAL SCHOOL

The principles of Montesquieu, Voltaire, Rousseau, and other eighteenth-century philosophers with regard to crime were collected and presented by the Italian Cesare Beccaria (1738–94) in his small volume *Essay on Crimes and Punishments*.[6] This famous book, which was published in 1764, became the theoretical basis for the great reforms in the field of criminal law which soon followed, and its principles still underlie, to a considerable extent, most of the existing systems of procedure. It also provided the starting point for the classical school of criminal law and criminology.

In this book, Beccaria declared that the object of law should be the greatest happiness of the greatest number and adopted Rousseau's doctrine of the social contract as the basis of society.[7] Each individual has a tendency to go beyond the bounds of the social contract and to commit acts which destroy it. These acts are crimes, and the right of punishment is derived from the necessity of suppressing crime in order to preserve the social contract. The duty of judges is only to decide whether the laws

[3] Coleman Phillipson, *Three Criminal Law Reformers* (New York: E. P. Dutton and Co., Inc., 1923), p. 27.

[4] See Chapter 20 for a discussion of the influence of rationalism upon the treatment of criminals.

[5] Saleilles, p. 52.

[6] Cesare Beccaria, *On Crimes and Punishments,* trans. Henry Paolucci (Indianapolis: The Bobbs-Merrill Co., Inc., 1963). See also Elio Monachesi, "Pioneers in Criminology: Cesare Beccaria (1738–1794)," *Journal of Criminal Law, Criminology, and Police Science,* XLVI (Nov.–Dec., 1955), 439–49.

[7] According to this doctrine, men were absolutely free and independent in a state of nature but surrendered a small part of their freedom through a social contract in order to secure the benefits of union. The doctrine of the social contract has no foundation in history, and Rousseau himself probably knew that it was a fiction, but it gave him a basis upon which to plead the cause of liberty and to protest against tyranny.

have been broken. They have no right to interpret the laws according to their own ideas of justice, but must apply them exactly in accordance with the provisions of the legislative authority. Although the measure of punishment should be the injury done to the public welfare by a crime, the object of punishment should be to restrain the criminal from doing further injury to society and to keep others from committing similar crimes. Torture should be abolished, more use should be made of imprisonment instead of corporal punishment, and a fair trial should be insured. Punishment should be "public, prompt, necessary, the least possible in the given circumstances, proportionate to the crimes, dictated by the laws."[8]

The classical school of criminal law and criminology, which grew out of the thought and writings of the eighteenth-century philosophers, had three important principles. *First,* the rights and liberties of the individual must be conserved. Since all persons are equal, those who commit the same crime should be treated alike. *Second,* crime is a juridical abstraction, and, therefore, a definite penalty should be attached to each crime and invariably inflicted. *Third,* punishment should be limited by the social need. Its social utility consists in its deterrent influence, and as much of it should be inflicted as is necessary to prevent others from committing the same crime.

Back of these principles, but not so clearly formulated, was a belief in the existence of a free will and the moral responsibility of the criminal. It was also assumed that man exercised his will in terms of a balancing of pleasure and pain and directed his behavior toward securing the greatest net total of pleasure. It followed from this that a definite penalty should be attached to each crime and invariably inflicted so that every would-be offender might take the penalty into consideration in the calculation of pains and pleasures that would result from his violation of the law.

Through the application of the principles of the classical school an orderly procedure and rational rules of evidence were introduced into the criminal courts, the severity of punishment was reduced, and a check was imposed upon the arbitrary use of judicial authority. These principles were first exemplified in the French penal code of 1791. However, the work of the school tended to direct attention from the criminal to the crime and thus away from an inquiry into the causes of crime. Its principles, furthermore, exaggerated the role of reason in human affairs and underestimated the importance of habit, emotions, and the social factors in criminal behavior.

[8] Beccaria, p. 99. See also Maurice Parmelee, *The Principles of Anthropology and Sociology in Their Relations to Criminal Procedure* (New York: The Macmillan Co., 1908), pp. 9–14; Phillipson, pp. 56–82.

Gradually modifications crept into the practices of the classical school as it became clear that exceptions had to be made in the application of its principles. For example, children and lunatics were exempted from punishment on the ground that they were unable to calculate pleasures and pains intelligently. This modified approach is sometimes called the neoclassical school of criminology.[9]

MODERN THEORIES

Modern theories regarding the causes of crime may be divided into three periods: (1) the period of particularistic theories, (2) the period of first-hand research and segmented studies, and (3) the period of reformulation.[10]

The first period contains theories which were usually based on speculation and inadequate data. They attributed most, if not all, crimes to some single cause or to a few simple factors. This period, which begins with the early years of the nineteenth century, was brought to a close by William Healy, whose study of individual case histories, published in 1915, forced him to conclude that the facts were too much for general theories. He affirmed the principle of *multiple causation* in individual cases in contrast to a single-factor explanation of all crime and criminals.[11]

The emphasis in the second period was upon the importance of securing first-hand data, but in the drive for these, studies became "segmented and disjointed." They did, however, serve "to liquidate many of the earlier pronouncements regarding the causes of crime and to discount many current claims." In general, progress was more negative than positive, the studies indicating more of what had to be rejected than what was tenable.

The third period is just beginning. While most of the research is still of the segmented type, the time seems opportune to use the insights secured during the second period as a basis for a reformulation of ideas about criminal behavior. In fact, some research is already emanating from reformulated theories of criminal behavior and is endeavoring to become more systematic.[12]

Modern theories of crime may be classified also in terms of their approach to the problem of causation. In this respect they may be divided into the biological, geographical, psychiatric, psychological, sociological,

[9] Parmelee, pp. 15, 16; Saleilles, pp. 63–98.

[10] Walter C. Reckless, *The Etiology of Delinquent and Criminal Behavior* (New York: Social Science Research Council, Bull. 50, 1943), pp. 1–3.

[11] William Healy, *The Individual Delinquent* (Boston: Little, Brown and Co., 1915), pp. 16, 33–125, 130–38.

[12] Reckless, pp. 2, 3. For an attempt to provide a systematic theory of criminality, see Anthony J. Cacioppo, "A Reformulated Theory of Criminality: An Empirical Test" (unpublished Ph.D. dissertation, State University of Iowa, June, 1954).

and social-psychological. These approaches, however, are not mutually exclusive, and each theory referred to here is classified according to the approach which it emphasizes.

Biological Approach. The latter part of the nineteenth century saw a great advance in the biological sciences. Darwin's writings on evolution, especially, stimulated the imaginations of scholars everywhere. It was natural, therefore, for some to speculate on the possible atavistic tendencies of men and to reason that criminals and others who endanger the public welfare might be throwbacks to an earlier evolutionary stage of the human race.

Positive School of Criminology. The classical school of criminal law and criminology was founded before the great modern development of the biological sciences and was very slightly influenced by them. It was therefore left to a more recent school of criminology to utilize their methods and the results of their investigations. This school, usually called the "positive school," was inaugurated in 1872 by the Italian anthropologist Cesare Lombroso (1835–1909).[13] His fundamental ideas were developed gradually over a period of years, from the time when he was a doctor in the Italian army to 1876, when he published the first edition of his book on criminal man.[14]

This was soon supplemented by Ferri's *Criminal Sociology*[15] in 1881, and by Garofalo's *Criminology*[16] in 1885. Because these three men and others who have contributed to the development of the positive school were Italians, it has been called the Italian school of criminology. This, however, is not an accurate title since the school has had adherents in all European countries.[17]

Lombroso's theory in its earlier and more sharply defined form contained the following important elements:

1. There is a distinct, born criminal type.

[13] The word "positive" as used here has the same meaning that it has in the phrase "positive science." Modern science has been called "positive" because it uses a method which brings positive and definite results.

[14] Gina Lombroso Ferrero, *Criminal Man, According to the Classification of Cesare Lombroso* (New York: G. P. Putnam's Sons, 1911), pp. XI–XX.

[15] See Enrico Ferri, *Criminal Sociology,* trans. Joseph I. Kelly and John Lisle (Boston: Little, Brown and Co., 1917); Thorsten Sellin, "Pioneers in Criminology: Enrico Ferri (1856–1929)," *Journal of Criminal Law, Criminology, and Police Science,* XLVIII (Jan.–Feb., 1958), 481–92.

[16] See Raffaele Garofalo, *Criminology,* trans. Robert W. Millar (Boston: Little, Brown and Co., 1914); Francis A. Allen, "Pioneers in Criminology: Raffaele Garofalo (1852–1934)," *Journal of Criminal Law, Criminology, and Police Science,* XLV (Nov.–Dec., 1954), 373–90.

[17] Parmelee, pp. 17–19. See also Marvin E. Wolfgang, "Cesare Lombroso," *Pioneers in Criminology,* ed. Hermann Mannheim (Chicago: Quadrangle Books, Inc., 1960), pp. 168–227.

2. This type can be identified by certain stigmata or anomalies, such as protruding jaws, asymmetrical skull, retreating forehead, large outstanding ears, low sensitivity to pain, etc.

3. The stigmata are not the causes of crime but rather the symptoms of atavism (reversion to a more primitive type) or degeneracy, especially that characterized by epileptic tendencies. Thus, according to Lombroso, atavism and degeneracy are the causes of crime.

4. The person who is a born criminal type cannot refrain from committing crime unless he lives under exceptionally favorable circumstances.

Lombroso never claimed that all criminals belonged to the born criminal type; and as he continued his studies, he modified his theory, eventually admitting that most criminals should not be so classified.[18]

Garofalo, Ferri, and others made additional modifications and presented various classifications of criminals,[19] and the school gradually lost its earlier, clearly defined characteristics. Finally, Charles Goring, an Englishman, in order to check the claims of the positive school, made a comparative study of several thousand criminals and noncriminals, the interpretations and conclusions of which were published in 1913. On the basis of his study, Goring concluded that there is no anthropological criminal type, that there are no physical stigmata of crime, and that criminals are not differentiated either from the noncriminal population or among themselves by particular physical characteristics.[20] This study proved to the satisfaction of most scholars that criminals do not constitute a distinct born type that can be identified by certain stigmata.

Lombroso's theory of crime was a biological theory in which he attempted to introduce social and psychological factors during the later years of his career. Living at a time when the biological sciences were rapidly developing, he exaggerated the importance of the biological factors in human life and greatly underestimated the role of the social factors, and being a determinist, he found all the causes of crime in heredity and environment and relieved the individual of moral responsibility. However, even though Lombroso and his followers failed in their attempt to explain crime, they clearly called attention to the fact that we must look beyond it and study the criminal if we are to learn more about the causes of criminal behavior. Thus the positive school helped to counteract the influence of the classical school, which in its efforts to reform the criminal law, tended to center attention on the crime.

[18] See Cesare Lombroso, *Crime, Its Causes and Remedies* (Boston: Little, Brown and Co., 1911); George B. Vold, *Theoretical Criminology* (New York: Oxford University Press, 1958), pp. 27–32.

[19] For the classifications of criminals made by Garofalo and Ferri, see Chapter 5.

[20] Charles Goring, *The English Convict* (abridged ed.; London: His Majesty's Stationery Office, 1919), pp. iii–xvi, 9–33, 269–75. See also Edwin D. Driver, "Pioneers in Criminology: Charles Buckman Goring (1870–1919)," *Journal of Criminal Law, Criminology, and Police Science,* XLVII (Jan.–Feb., 1957), 515–25.

Other Biological Theories. It must be emphasized that the scientific investigation of crime and criminals began prior to the birth of Lombroso. Furthermore, long before his time the belief that criminals have distinct physical characteristics had already made its appearance.[21] However, the ideas of the positive school proved so challenging that they gave us an unprecedented impetus to the study of the offender and for this reason, at least, the school is deserving of a special place in the study of criminology.[22]

The work of Franz Joseph Gall (1758–1828) marks the first appearance of anything worthy of the name "scientific" in the study of abnormal behavior. According to his theory, the roots of which go back to the days of Aristotle, the external formation of the skull indicates the conformation of the brain and the development of its various parts or "faculties." These faculties, Gall argued, are in turn related to the various qualities of character, such as acquisitiveness, combativeness, amorousness, etc.; and since development of the faculties is reflected in the shape of the corresponding parts of the skull, it is possible to determine a person's character by "reading the bumps" on his head. Gall believed, therefore, that the shape of the criminal's head differs from that of the noncriminal person. Gall called his theory "craniology," and his disciple, Johann Christoph Spurzheim (1776–1832), popularized it and gave it status in the intellectual circles of Europe. However, it remained for Thomas Ignatius Forster, the English naturalist, in 1815, to call it "phrenology," the name which it now bears, and under the name it was introduced into America, where the outstanding phrenologist of the period was Charles Caldwell, whose book, *Elements of Phrenology*, was published in 1824.[23] There is a direct line of descent from Gall to Lombroso and the positive school, and like the positive school, "faculty" psychology and phrenology collapsed under the attack of modern scientific investigation.[24] As we now know, the brain is not divided into compartments each of which can be related exclusively to a certain aspect of a person's character. Human behavior is entirely too complex to be explained by any such simple, mechanical principle.

Other theories, closely allied with that of atavism, explained crime in terms of arrested development, degeneracy, and the pathological nature of the criminal. Today these theories have little more than academic value. Their real importance lies in the fact that they emphasized the

[21] Alfred Lindesmith and Yale Levin, "The Lombrosian Myth in Criminology," *American Journal of Sociology*, XLII (Mar., 1937), 653–71.

[22] Thorsten Sellin, "The Lombrosian Myth in Criminology," *American Journal of Sociology*, XLII (May, 1937), 897–99. This is a letter to the editor in which Sellin makes an appraisal of the article by Lindesmith and Levin cited in footnote 21.

[23] Arthur Fink, *Causes of Crime* (Philadelphia: University of Pennsylvania Press, 1938), pp. 1–19.

[24] Harry Elmer Barnes and J. P. Shalloo, "Modern Theories of Criminology and Penology," *Contemporary Social Theory* (New York: Appleton-Century-Crofts, Inc., 1940), pp. 688, 689.

study of the individual criminal and thus helped to point the way to modern scientific research.[25]

An effort to revive the biological interpretation of crime has appeared with the rise of the science of endocrinology, which devotes itself to the study of the glands of internal secretion. In such works as M. G. Schlapp and E. H. Smith's *The New Criminology* (1928), the tendency is "to reduce crime to the product of endocrine deficiencies, excesses, and disturbances." Although endocrinology undoubtedly can make some contribution to our understanding of crime, it is highly unlikely that any theory about glands can ever completely explain the existence of crime. Glands do affect personality, but personality is something more than glands, and many persons with disordered glands never become criminals.[26]

Shortly before World War II, Earnest A. Hooton, an anthropologist of Harvard University, made a most ambitious attempt to correlate crime with the biological factors. In 1939, after more than a decade of intensive research, he published his book *Crime and the Man,* which appeared to lend support to the contentions of the positive school. In this book, he presented the findings of a comparative study of 13,873 male convicts in ten states and 3,203 noncriminals, including patrons of a Massachusetts bathing beach, firemen in Nashville, members of a military company, and a few outpatients of a hospital. On the basis of this study, Hooton concluded that all races and nationalities represented in his survey were biologically inferior to the corresponding classes of law-abiding citizens. He did not claim that this inferiority directly causes crime, nor did he contend that a criminal can be recognized by certain physical stigmata, but he did assert that crime is the resultant of a complex process of biological and social forces by which mentally and physically inferior individuals of every race and nationality are selected for criminality. He also believed that biological inferiority is the primary cause of crime and that, therefore, the increase in criminality can be checked only by the extirpation of the physically, mentally, and morally unfit or by their complete segregation in a socially aseptic environment.[27]

Hooton's study has been subjected to severe criticism. His samples of criminals and noncriminals are not representative. Convicts, who constitute his sample of criminals, are only those criminals who have been sent to prison; and firemen and militiamen, who are in his sample of noncriminals, are groups that are probably above the average in physical

[25] *Ibid.,* pp. 700–3.

[26] *Ibid.,* pp. 716, 717; Max G. Schlapp and Edward H. Smith, *The New Criminology* (New York: Boni and Liveright, 1928).

[27] See Earnest A. Hooton, *Crime and the Man* (Cambridge: Harvard University Press, 1939). In this popular edition, a thorough treatment is presented of Hooton's larger work, *The American Criminal: An Anthropological Study,* which was published in 1939 by the Harvard University Press.

development. Besides, he does not explain how he translates physical deviations into inferiority. Failing to present independent evidence of inferiority, he appears to use criminality to appraise inferiority and inferiority to explain criminality. This is mere circular reasoning and proves nothing. Furthermore, Hooton argues that biological inferiority is inherited, but he provides little evidence of this. Without doubt, some of it is inherited, but much is caused by such environmental factors as accidents and poor nutrition. Despite his great efforts, it does not appear that Hooton has made any significant contribution to our understanding of the causes of crime.[28] In fact, many other recent studies indicate that the physical traits of criminals are not significantly different from those of noncriminals.[29]

The year after Hooton made known the results of his research, Professor William H. Sheldon and his associates at Harvard University published their volume *Varieties of Human Physique*. This attempts to correlate certain physical types of body build with certain types of personality. Thus, it follows and perhaps parallels the earlier work of the German Ernst Kretschmer. In a later book, *Varieties of Delinquent Youth,* Sheldon seeks to establish the thesis that behavior is a function of structure and can be predicted on the basis of careful physical measurements.[30] It may be that there is a direct causal relationship between body build and personality, but it does not appear that Sheldon and his associates have incontrovertibly proved their thesis. Moreover, at present it seems very improbable that an answer to the complex riddle of human behavior can be found in so simple an explanation as the one that they advance.[31]

[28] For appraisals of Hooton's work, see the following: T. C. McCormick in *American Sociological Review*, V (Apr., 1940), 252–54; F. A. Ross in *American Journal of Sociology*, XLV (Nov., 1939), 477–80; E. H. Sutherland in *Journal of Criminal Law and Criminology*, XXIX (Mar.–Apr., 1939), 911–14; and Robert K. Merton and M. F. Ashley Montagu, "Crime and the Anthropologist," *American Anthropologist*, XLII (July–Sept., 1940), 384–408.

[29] For a summarization of the recent studies on the physical traits of criminals, see W. Norwood East, "Physical Factors and Criminal Behavior," *Journal of Clinical Psychopathology*, VIII (July, 1946), 7–36.

[30] See William H. Sheldon, S. S. Stevens, and W. B. Tucker, *Varieties of Human Physique* (New York: Harper and Bros., 1940); William H. Sheldon and S. S. Stevens, *Varieties of Temperament* (New York: Harper and Bros., 1942); and William H. Sheldon, Emil M. Hartl, and Eugene McDermott, *Varieties of Delinquent Youth* (New York: Harper and Bros., 1949); Ernst Kretschmer, *Physique and Character,* trans. W. J. H. Sprott (New York: Harcourt, Brace and Co., Inc., 1925).

[31] For a review of *Varieties of Delinquent Youth*, see E. H. Sutherland in *American Sociological Review*, XVI (Feb., 1951), 10–13. For a summary and appraisal of the general morphological theories of human behavior, see William A. Lessa, "An Appraisal of Constitutional Typologies," No. 62 of the Titles in the Memoirs Series of the American Anthropological Association, *American Anthropologist*, XLV, No. 4, Part 2 (Oct., 1943), 5–96. See also George B. Vold, *Theoretical Criminology* (New York: Oxford University Press, 1958), pp. 50–74.

Nevertheless, Sheldon deserves credit for having reminded psychologists that the behaving human has a physique; and according to Hall and Lindzey, "this physique provides valuable cues to an underlying set of determinants, which in the end may prove quite as coercive and pervasive as environmental factors."[32] The work of Sheldon and his associates has also received some support from the Gluecks, who, in several of their latest books, have intimated that body-build is a more important factor in the causation of delinquency than most of us have believed it to be.[33] In their studies they found that the delinquent boys were significantly more mesomorphic, that is, more solid and muscular, than the nondelinquent boys in the control group, and the Gluecks therefore recognize mesomorphy as a factor in the causation of delinquency. Although they do not state that body-build causes delinquency, or even that it exerts a major influence in its causation, their findings indicate a clear relation between physique and delinquency and a differential response of body types to the forces of the environment. A definitive assessment of these findings, however, must await further consideration by competent specialists in biology, psychology, psychiatry, statistics, and sociology.[34]

The biological approach has not been able to show that the biological factors are the cause of crime, or even that they are the most important cause of it, but this does not mean that they are unimportant or can be disregarded by the criminologist. Nevertheless, it is clear that more research is needed if we are to understand the relationship between the biological factors and crime.

Geographical Approach. Since early times, various writers have held that climate, rainfall, soil, and other geographical factors exert an important influence on human behavior. The French philosopher Montesquieu (1689–1755), in his *Spirit of Laws* (1748), while presenting this view, also laid down the law that criminality increases in proportion as one approaches the equator, and drunkenness increases in proportion as one approaches the poles. About a century later, Quetelet, the "father of statistics," formulated his famous "thermic law" of delinquency, in which he claimed that crimes against the person predominate in the south and

[32] Calvin S. Hall and Gardner Lindzey, *Theories of Personality* (New York: John Wiley and Sons, Inc., 1957), pp. 370–75.

[33] Sheldon and Eleanor T. Glueck, *Unraveling Juvenile Delinquency* (New York: The Commonwealth Fund, 1950); *ibid., Physique and Delinquency* (New York: Harper and Bros., 1956).

[34] For an analysis of the Gluecks' *Physique and Delinquency*, see the critique by Albert Morris in the *Harvard Law Review*, LXX (Feb., 1957), 753–58. Two major criticisms have been directed against the conclusions of the Gluecks regarding body build and delinquency: (1) stronger bodies and more aggressive temperaments may be the result of delinquent activities instead of the cause of them; and (2) the low level of statistical significance in the Gluecks' study does not warrant their generalizations.

during the warm seasons, while crimes against property predominate in the north and during the winter time.

During the nineteenth century various other scholars arrived at about the same conclusion as Quetelet. Among these were de Champneuf, whose conclusions were based on a study made in France during the years 1825 to 1830, Lombroso, Ferri, and Aschaffenburg, whose studies were for later periods in Italy, France, and Germany, and the scholarly American statistician, Mayo-Smith, who, in his *Statistics and Sociology* (1895), maintained that later investigations had tended to confirm Quetelet's law.

In 1904, Dexter, in his book *Weather Influences*, presented a challenging statement regarding the direct influence of meteorological conditions such as barometric pressure, heat, humidity, and air currents upon the commission of crime.[35] This statement was based upon a statistical analysis of certain criminal cases in New York City and Denver. He found that crimes of violence were most numerous during the warm months of the year, and during periods of low humidity and low barometric pressure.[36]

Although all of these geographical theories oversimplify the problem of crime and exaggerate the geographical factors, they do mark out a fertile field for further research. And yet, since Dexter's study, no investigator has attempted systematically to relate crime to the geographical factors. Apparently the geographers are not sufficiently interested in crime to study the relationship, and the criminologists are not inclined to regard the geographical influences as important enough to warrant investigation. This is surprising "in view of the definitely seasonal and regional character of many crimes, as indicated by such sources as the *Uniform Crime Reports*."[37] Furthermore, the statement that the influence of the geographical environment, where it is present in the causation of crime and delinquency, is indirect and operates through other factors, such as social and cultural conditions, is not sufficiently explanatory. Even if it is granted that the geographical environment acts in this way, there remains the important question as to how and to what extent it interacts with other factors in producing such behavior.

Psychiatric Approach. Psychiatry, that branch of medicine which deals with mental disorders, is primarily a product of the nineteenth and twen-

35 Edwin Grant Dexter, *Weather Influences* (New York: The Macmillan Co., 1904).

36 Joseph Cohen, "The Geography of Crime," *The Annals of the American Academy of Political and Social Science*, CCXVII (Sept., 1941), 31, 32; Barnes and Shalloo, pp. 706, 707; Maurice Parmelee, *Criminology* (New York: The Macmillan Co., 1924), pp. 48–51.

37 Cohen, 32. See also Sidney J. Kaplan, "The Geography of Crime," *Sociology of Crime*, ed. Joseph S. Roucek (New York: Philosophical Library, Inc., 1961), pp. 160–92.

tieth centuries. Its origin, however, can be traced back to the sixteenth century work of Johann Weyer, "whom Zilboorg calls the 'father of psychiatry' and Bromberg designates as the founder of individualized treatment."[38] The first great work in the field, a book entitled *A Medical and Philosophical Treatise on Mental Alienation*, was produced by Pinel, a Frenchman, in 1801. More than a half century later in 1857, Morel published his *Physical, Intellectual, and Moral Degeneration of the Human Species*, which contained "the first important theory underlying modern criminology."[39]

In its modern form psychiatry was established chiefly through the efforts of Charcot and Bernheim in France during the latter part of the nineteenth century. But it remained for Sigmund Freud (1856–1939), a student of Charcot, to originate psychoanalysis, the most popular branch of modern psychiatry. Introduced into the field of criminology, it has been applied by such investigators as Bernard Glueck, William Healy, William A. White, Ben Karpman, Bromberg, Selling, Larson, Thompson, and others. Compared with the application of the psychoanalytic technique, the pioneer work of Pinel, Maudsley, and others has been relatively unimportant for modern criminology.[40]

In America, William Healy, director of the Juvenile Psychopathic Institute, organized in Chicago in 1909,[41] used the psychiatric method in studying all of the factors in the individual case rather than searching for some trait that might be used to identify persons as delinquents or criminals. Through his efforts, he has "made it clear for all time that we must cease dogmatizing about the criminal as a unified type or a collection of arbitrary classes," and that instead we must study the criminal as an individual if we hope to modify his behavior.[42]

In his pioneer volume, *The Individual Delinquent*, published in 1915, Healy presented an analysis of the cases of 1,000 juvenile delinquents who had been treated at his institute. Here, as in his succeeding publications, he consistently maintained that delinquency is an expression of the mental content of the individual. As a result of his analysis of mental content, Healy came to the conclusion that personality conflict is the central element in the causation of conduct problems. His explanation runs like this: Frustration of the individual causes emotional discomfort; personality equilibrium demands removal of such pain; the pain is eliminated by substitute behavior, that is, delinquency. In order to understand these

[38] Barnes and Shalloo, p. 692.

[39] *Ibid.*, pp. 692, 693.

[40] *Ibid.*, p. 693. The psychoanalytic theory will be critically analyzed later in Chapter 10.

[41] At the end of five years, the county took over this institute, made it part of the juvenile court, and administered it with public funds.

[42] Barnes and Shalloo, pp. 714, 715.

difficulties and to treat the individual, we must subject him to a thorough examination, utilizing physical, mental, sociological, and psychiatric analyses for this purpose. This, as Barnes and Shalloo point out, "constitutes case study of the individual in its most highly developed form."[43]

In a later volume entitled *New Light on Delinquency and Its Treatment* (1936), Healy attempted to explain how wish satisfaction is related to delinquent behavior.[44] By comparing the cases of a group of delinquent children with those of their nondelinquent siblings, he indicated that the nondelinquents were better able to find substitute satisfactions in acceptable channels than were delinquents. The delinquents were less able to maintain satisfying relationships under adverse conditions of family life and more lacking in restraining social ties and ideals. While only 13 per cent of the nondelinquents were found to have profound emotional disturbances, 91 per cent of the delinquents were so affected. The delinquents, therefore, being more distressed and disturbed than the nondelinquents, tended to seek substitute satisfaction of wishes in ways that lead to delinquency.[45] Thus Healy strives to integrate the personal and environmental factors in his explanation of the causation of delinquency. The community provides patterns of delinquency, but the motivating force that drives the juvenile into delinquency is his failure to find socially approved satisfactions for his impelling desires. However, grave doubt may be cast upon Healy's findings, since it is relatively easy for the case analyst to fall prey to his bias and to find in his studies what his theory of criminality prepares him to find, and Healy may have thus been misled into finding emotional disturbances and other related shortcomings much more prevalent in delinquency than in nondelinquency cases.[46]

Aichhorn, one of the leading exponents of the Freudian theory,[47] finds the causes of delinquency in the faulty development of the child during the first few years of his life. The child, says Aichhorn, seeks direct instinctual gratification, and if his upbringing does not teach him to control his pleasure impulses, he will come into conflict with the demands of society. The delinquent, failing to make the transition from the uncon-

---

[43] *Ibid.*, p. 715.

[44] In 1923, William I. Thomas in his *The Unadjusted Girl* (Boston: Little, Brown and Co., 1923) had presented his theory of the "four wishes" (security, new experience, recognition, and response). This theory found its clearest expression in Healy's doctrine of frustration. See also John Dollard, Leonard Doob, *et al., Frustration and Aggression* (New Haven: Yale University Press, 1939). These investigators found that the urge to aggression varies directly with the amount of frustration, provided that the anticipation or threat of punishment remains contant (p. 38).

[45] Reckless, pp. 19, 20; William Healy and Augusta F. Bronner, *New Light on Delinquency and Its Treatment* (New Haven: Yale University Press, 1936), pp. 1–13, 48–50, 121, 122.

[46] Reckless, p. 20.

[47] For a general critical analysis of the Freudian theory, see Chapter 10.

scious pleasure world of the small child to that of reality, suffers from a disturbed or faulty ego development.[48] Friedlander[49] and Redl,[50] two disciples of Aichhorn, elaborate on his theory of delinquency, the former stating that the faulty development of the ego produces a character structure which cannot handle strains and frustrations, the latter, that it results in a control system which cannot manage impulses.

Not all of those who have used the psychiatric approach, however, have adhered so closely to the Freudian theory. For example, Hewitt and Jenkins, taking into consideration both personality maladjustments and environmental situations, have presented this classification of three syndromes (groups of symptoms) of delinquent behavior: (1) unsocialized aggressive behavior; (2) socialized delinquent behavior; and (3) over-inhibited behavior.[51] And Abrahamsen, recognizing the importance of both personal and environmental factors, has attempted to explain the causation of criminal behavior in terms of a formula, in which the criminal act equals the criminalistic tendencies or inclinations plus the crime-inducing situation (both environmental and psychological) divided by the person's mental and emotional resistance to temptation.[52] Although this formula describes what probably happens when a person commits a crime, it is not sufficiently definitive or incisive to help us very much in understanding the causation of criminal behavior.

The psychiatric approach has helped to turn our attention to the individual criminal, has contributed to our understanding of the importance of childhood in the formation of personality, has increased our knowledge of the nonrational in human behavior, and has provided us with new and deeper insights into the functioning of the personality. However, considerable research, discussion, and interpretation are needed to correct and clarify the findings of the psychiatric approach, stabilize its concepts, and standardize its terminology.

---

[48] August Aichhorn, *Wayward Youth* (New York: The Viking Press, Inc., 1936). See also Ivy Bennett, *Delinquent and Neurotic Children: A Comparative Study* (New York: Basic Books, Inc., 1960), pp. 201–29.

[49] Kate Friedlander, *The Psycho-Analytical Approach to Juvenile Delinquency* (New York: International Universities Press, Inc., 1947); *ibid.*, "Latent Delinquency and Ego Development," *Searchlights on Delinquency*, ed. Kurt R. Eissler (New York: International Universities Press, Inc., 1949), pp. 205–15.

[50] Fritz Redl and David Wineman, *Children Who Hate* (Glencoe, Ill.: The Free Press, 1951).

[51] Lester E. Hewitt and Richard L. Jenkins, *Fundamental Patterns of Maladjustment: The Dynamics of Their Origin* (Springfield, Ill.: State Printer, 1956). See also R. L. Jenkins and Lester Hewitt, "Types of Personality Structure Encountered in Child Guidance Clinics," *The American Journal of Ortho-psychiatry*, XIV (Jan., 1944), 84–94.

[52] David Abrahamsen, *The Psychology of Crime* (New York: Columbia University Press, 1960), pp. 29–41. See also his *Crime and the Human Mind* (New York: Columbia University Press, 1944).

Psychological Approach. Until recent years, the psychological approach to the problem of causation has been concerned largely with an exploration of the relationship between mental deficiency and crime. Goring, on the basis of his study of English convicts, claimed that there was more weakmindedness in the prison population than in the general population.[53] This led many to assume that mental deficiency was an important cause of crime. When intelligence tests became available through the work of Binet and Simon in France, enthusiastic investigators put them to use in measuring the intelligence of prison inmates. Tests were often inexpertly given and loosely interpreted, but the results were hailed as proof that a high percentage of criminals were feeble-minded. The search was still on to find a single cause of all crime. Physical characteristics had failed to give the answer, but here at last appeared to be a definite, simple way of identifying criminals.

Henry H. Goddard, director of the research laboratory of the New Jersey Training School for the Feeble Minded at Vineland, was an especially enthusiastic supporter of the theory that mental defects were the most important cause of criminality. In 1920, he stated that it was no longer to be denied that the greatest single cause of delinquency and crime was "low-grade mentality, much of it within the limits of feeble-mindedness,"[54] and his books did much to popularize this view throughout the United States. Later, however, Goddard revised his point of view and eventually admitted that everyone is a potential delinquent.[55]

Challenged by such statements as the early ones of Goddard, American psychologists set out to prove or disprove the alleged relationship between mental deficiency and crime. Among the early attempts to do this was that of Murchison, who compared prisoners' ratings on intelligence tests with those of American draftees of World War I.[56] This study and others that followed, including those by such investigators as Zeleny[57] and Tulchin,[58] failed to support the claim that offenders are mentally inferior to law-abiding persons. In fact their cumulative effect has been to prove that feeble-mindedness is no more prevalent among the inmates of correctional institutions than among the free citizens of the United

[53] Goring, pp. 269–75.

[54] Henry H. Goddard, *Human Efficiency and Levels of Intelligence* (Princeton, N.J.: Princeton University Press, 1920), p. 73.

[55] Mabel A. Elliott, *Crime in Modern Society* (New York: Harper and Bros., 1952), p. 327.

[56] Carl Murchison, *Criminal Intelligence* (Worcester, Mass.: Clark University, 1926).

[57] L. D. Zeleny, "Feeblemindedness and Criminal Conduct," *American Journal of Sociology*, XXXVIII (Jan., 1933), 564–76.

[58] Simon H. Tulchin, *Intelligence and Crime: A Study of Penitentiary and Reformatory Offenders* (Chicago: University of Chicago Press, 1939).

States.[59] Furthermore, since convicts as a group are probably more stupid than the criminals who are not in prison, it may be true, as some have claimed, that "the criminal class as a whole is more intelligent than the mass of our citizenry.[60]

During the past few decades, an increasing number of psychologists has been examining the personalities, and especially the attitudes, of delinquents and criminals. Tests and measurements have been developed, refined, and used to probe more deeply into human motivation.[61] Even so, questions have been raised regarding the extent to which these efforts have actually proved that certain personality elements are associated with criminality. For example, in 1950, Schuessler and Cressey, after a survey of 113 studies in which personality tests had been used, concluded that "as often as not the evidence favored the view that personality traits are distributed in the criminal population in about the same way as in the general population."[62] This conclusion, however, would have been more impressive if the survey had not thrown together indiscriminatively "a jumble of well, badly, and indifferently controlled studies, so that percentages computed on the total are of quite uncertain meaning."[63] Furthermore, it appears that criminals differ from noncriminals more in the interrelatedness of characteristics in their personalities than in the presence or absence of characteristics. This seems to be the principal conclusion that may be drawn from the comparisons made by the Gluecks in their study of 500 delinquent boys and 500 nondelinquent boys and reported in *Unraveling Juvenile Delinquency*.[64]

In 1958, after a review of the carefully controlled comparisons of the Gluecks and the results obtained by Hathaway and Monachesi[65] in their

[59] Reckless, pp. 7, 8; Barnes and Shalloo, pp. 716, 717.

[60] See Barnes and Shalloo, p. 716.

[61] For an evaluation of these tests and measurements, see Chapter 24. For one of these tests devised by a European scholar (the Szondi test), see Hans Walder, *Drive Structure and Criminality,* trans. Marvin W. Webb (Springfield, Ill.: Charles C. Thomas, Publisher, 1959).

[62] Karl F. Schuessler and Donald R. Cressey, "Personality Characteristics of Criminals," *American Journal of Sociology,* LV (Mar., 1950), 476–84. In this article, the authors suggest that the Guttman technique may help to determine whether criminals possess attitudes that distinguish them from noncriminals (p. 484). It should be suggested here, however, that the mere shifting of attention from personality traits to attitudes, which are even more elusive, is not going to simplify the problem for the sociologist.

[63] Vold, p. 127.

[64] *Ibid.;* Sheldon Glueck and Eleanor Glueck, *Unraveling Juvenile Delinquency* (New York: The Commonwealth Fund, 1950).

[65] See Starke R. Hathaway and Elio D. Monachesi, *Analyzing and Predicting Juvenile Delinquency with the M M P I* (Minneapolis: University of Minnesota Press, 1953); E. D. Monachesi, "Some Personality Characteristics of Delinquents and Non-Delinquents," *Journal of Criminal Law and Criminology,* XXXVIII (Jan.–Feb., 1948), 487–500; *ibid.,* "Personality Characteristics of Male Delinquents," *Journal of Criminal*

use of the Minnesota Multiphasic Personality Inventory (MMPI),[66] Vold stated that tests and scales had not yet provided us with a basis for "significant theoretical formulations about personality deviation and delinquency."[67] Nevertheless, new insights are being acquired and more and more data are being accumulated. In the future, these may well provide us with a much more fruitful psychological approach to the problems of delinquency and crime.[68]

Sociological Approach. The sociological approach emphasizes the factors which operate in the social environment. The theories using this approach vary all the way from those which represent an attempt to explain the interaction of the biological, psychological, and social factors to those which regard all factors except the social as of little importance.

Some roots of the modern sociological approach to crime can be found in the writings of European scholars during the early decades of the nineteenth century. The Belgian scholar Adolphe Quetelet (1796–1874), the founder of modern statistics, used statistical data in the analysis of the social causes of crime and its geographical distribution. Similar research was conducted by others, such as A. M. Guerry, and maps were used to show crime rates and related social conditions. In England, Germany, and France, studies and articles on the professional criminal appeared. They discussed his origin, traditions, customs, language, philosophy, and skills, thus clearly foreshadowing the modern emphasis upon the study of the social factors in the causation of crime.[69]

Law and Criminology, XLI (July–Aug., 1950), 173–74; Starke R. Hathaway and Elio D. Monachesi, "The Personalities of Pre-delinquent Boys," *Journal of Criminal Law, Criminology, and Police Science,* XLVIII (July–Aug., 1957), 149–63.

[66] The Minnesota Multiphasic Personality Inventory (MMPI) is a lengthy questionnaire scale of 550 items, which was developed to facilitate diagnosis in the psychiatric clinic.

[67] Vold, pp. 127–38. Vold considers the work of the Gluecks and Hathaway and Monachesi two of the best available sources for evaluating the efforts that have been made to relate personality deviation to delinquency by means of tests and scales.

[68] In general, the reaction to the predictive instruments of the Gluecks, Hathaway and Monachesi, and Kvaraceus has been unfavorable. For some recent statements regarding these instruments, see Elizabeth Herzog, *Identifying Potential Delinquents,* U.S. Children's Bureau, Juvenile Delinquency: Facts and Facets, No. 5 (Washington, D.C.: Government Printing Office, 1960); David J. Bordua, *Prediction and Selection of Delinquents,* U.S. Children's Bureau, Juvenile Delinquency: Facts and Facets, No. 17 (Washington, D.C.: Government Printing Office, 1961); Eleanor T. Glueck, "Toward Further Improving the Identification of Delinquents," *Journal of Criminal Law, Criminology, and Police Science,* LIV (June, 1963), 178–85; Maude M. Craig and Selma J. Glick, "Ten Years' Experience with the Glueck Social Prediction Table," *Crime and Delinquency,* IX (July, 1963), 249–61; Charles S. Prigmore, "An Analysis of Rater Reliability on the Glueck Scale for the Prediction of Juvenile Delinquency," *Journal of Criminal Law, Criminology, and Police Science,* LIV (Mar., 1963), 30–41.

[69] Lindesmith and Levin, 653–71.

In France, Gabriel Tarde (1843–1904) advanced the theory that society can be explained in terms of the influence of mind on mind through the force of imitation, and that in this way criminal activities are spread from person to person.[70] The other leader of French psychological sociology, Émile Durkheim (1858–1917), held that crime is a natural and inevitable incident of social evolution. Some individual freedom must exist if progress is to continue. But freedom is always abused by certain groups, and so crime is the price that we must pay for progress.[71]

William A. Bonger (1876–1940), the Dutch criminologist, basing his theory on the writings of Karl Marx, attributed crime to the weaknesses of capitalism.[72] Thus, Bonger belonged to the socialistic school of criminology, which found such strong support in Italy. According to this school, the exploitation of the laboring class leads to poverty and the misery of the masses and these conditions in turn cause crime. The existing system of criminal justice, which merely protects the interests of the usurping and capitalistic class, must be swept away and society must be reorganized along socialistic or communistic lines. Once this is accomplished, the basic causes of crime and delinquency will be removed and then crime and delinquency will naturally tend to disappear.[73] This, of course, is the familiar nostrum of the deluded medicine men of communism.

All these early sociological theories oversimplified the problems of crime and delinquency and arrived at sweeping generalizations without adequate supporting evidence. However, by featuring the social factors, they helped to counteract the great emphasis that was being placed on the biological factors during the latter part of the nineteenth and the early part of the twentieth centuries.

Since the end of World War I, the sociological approach to crime has had its greatest development in the United States. In following this approach, American research scholars have used two methods that have contributed much to the understanding of crime and delinquency. These are (1) the ecological study[74] of the distribution of these problems, and (2) the life-history method.

The ecological method has been used by many investigators, but it has become most widely known through the work of Clifford Shaw and

[70] Gabriel Tarde, *Penal Philosophy* (Boston: Little, Brown and Co., 1912). See also Margaret S. Wilson Vine, "Gabriel Tarde," *Pioneers in Criminology*, pp. 228–40.

[71] Barnes and Shalloo, p. 704. See also Walter A. Lunden, "Émile Durkheim," *Pioneers in Criminology*, pp. 301–15.

[72] William A. Bonger, *Criminality and Economic Conditions* (Boston: Little, Brown and Co., 1916).

[73] Barnes and Shalloo, pp. 705, 706.

[74] Human ecology is that branch of science which treats of the reciprocal relations between man and environment. See the *Dictionary of Sociology* (New York: The Philosophical Library, 1944), p. 101.

Henry McKay and their associates at the Institute for Juvenile Research in Chicago. In his *Delinquency Areas* (1929), Shaw uses this method to demonstrate the influence of the transitional, or interstitial, zone upon delinquent behavior. This zone, which contains the highest rate of delinquency, is immediately adjacent to the center, or business, financial, and political district, of the city. It is characterized by deteriorated property, cheap rents, undesirable influences, gangs, heterogeneous cultural and racial groups, and absence of social controls. Thus it is an area of social disorganization and as such tends to produce disorganized personalities and delinquent careers.[75]

The ecological method has provided us with valuable information regarding the distribution of crime and delinquency, but it has not shown how the causal factors operate in the individual to produce these problems. And it is important to note that crime and certain other conditions, such as poverty, may coexist without being causally related. In fact, many persons living in the transitional zone remain law-abiding citizens throughout their lives.

In order to supplement his areal studies, Shaw has also utilized the life-history method. In his books *The Natural History of a Delinquent Career* (1931) and *The Jack Roller* (1930), the individual tells his own story and thus provides the interviewer with insights that he cannot easily, if ever, secure from formal case-work reports.[76] Often, however, it is difficult to separate truth from fiction in such a story, and the interviewer must guard against reading into the life history what he wants to find there.

Etiological research in the United States has been characterized by a distinct absence of any commitment to a particular school or system of causation. However, there has been a general emphasis upon the process of conflict, both mental and cultural.[77] For example, Edwin H. Sutherland in his *Principles of Criminology*, one of the most widely used texts in the field, has made the process of conflict a basic part of his theory of differential association.[78]

Thorsten Sellin, in his *Culture Conflict and Crime* (1938), has presented a scholarly, critical analysis of the role of culture conflict in crime causation. Sellin contends that studies of the causation of criminal behavior are handicapped by the inadequacy of the data about crimes and criminals which can be derived from legal categories. The nature of the criminal law depends upon the character and interests of those groups

---

[75] See Chapter 12 for a detailed discussion of the ecology of crime and delinquency.
[76] Barnes and Shalloo, p. 712.
[77] *Ibid.*, p. 713.
[78] The theory of differential association will be critically analyzed later in Chapter 10.

in the population which influence legislation, and it changes as the values of the dominant groups change. Such variability does not permit the scientist to formulate universal categories, which must emerge from the intrinsic character of his material.

In order to put criminology on a scientific basis, Sellin suggests that criminologists study the violation of conduct norms, which are the rules that prohibit, and conversely enjoin, specific types of persons, as defined by their status in the normative group, from acting in a certain specified way in certain circumstances.[79] Such norms are not necessarily embodied in the criminal law, and if they are not, their violation should not be termed crime. "This extension of the meaning of the term *crime* is not desirable. It is wiser to retain that term for the offenses made punishable by the criminal law and to use the term 'abnormal conduct' for the violations of norms whether legal or not.[80]

Conduct norms arise as a group reaction to conduct which is assumed to be prejudicial to the interests of the social groups, but the norms acquire validity to the extent that they are incorporated in the personalities of those who are members of the group. According to Sellin, "the fundamental aim of sociological research on norm violators must be the isolation of personality elements which characterize them in contrast with conformists."[81] He defines "personality elements" as the meanings which the person attaches to social or cultural elements, including conduct norms. When the personality elements are isolated, they will probably be found to exist in patterns of a characteristic nature, the identification of which should lead to the discovery of personality types. The goal of the scientist, then, should be the establishment of "generalizations which would state that if a person of type A is placed in a life situation of type B, he will violate the norm governing that life situation."[82]

Sellin concludes that in the study of conduct it is necessary to think of culture conflict as a conflict of conduct norms. Such conflict may arise as a result of a process of differentiation within a cultural system or area, or as a result of contact between norms drawn from different cultural systems or areas. We may study these conflicts either by an investigation of the person in whom the conflict is assumed to be internalized or by a study of violations in groups or areas within which the conflicts are assumed to occur.[83] However, even if the criminologist follows Sellin's advice and turns his attention to conduct norms and their conflicts, he

[79] Thorsten Sellin, *Culture Conflict and Crime* (New York: Social Science Research Council, Bull. 41, 1938), pp. 21–25, 32, 33.
[80] *Ibid.*, pp. 30–32.
[81] *Ibid.*, pp. 39, 40.
[82] *Ibid.*, pp. 40, 41.
[83] *Ibid.*, p. 107.

will still have to face not only the very difficult problems involved in the identification and measurement of such norms, and the various personality elements, but also all the other problems that thus far have interfered with the establishment of a science of human behavior.

Vold, viewing crime as ordinary, learned behavior, focuses attention on the role of the "normal antagonisms and conflicts of human groups to one another as the setting for or condition generally explanatory of large areas of criminal activity." Such criminality is seen in gang warfare, strife generated by reform movements, political turmoil, labor-management disputes, and syndicate activities. However, Vold hastens to add, "it is also clear that group conflict theory is strictly limited to those kinds of situations in which the individual criminal acts flow from the collision of groups whose members are loyally upholding the in-group position."[84] Obviously, many crimes are not caused in this way, and furthermore, the durability and cohesiveness of the gang, or other in-group, and its influence on members can be easily exaggerated.[85] Some persons who associate with delinquent gangs do not participate in their delinquencies, and others who are members violate the law at times when they are not with the gang.

Following the lead of Durkheim,[86] both Parsons [87] and Merton[88] have used the concept "anomie" to refer to a breakdown in the cultural structure, that is, to a condition of relative normlessness in society. Merton states that a source of anomie exists when goals that are deemed appropriate for all are accessible through legitimate means for only a few. This conflict between goals, which are culturally defined as important and open for all, and legitimate opportunities leads to social deviation, one form of which is crime and delinquency, and this in turn, in a process of interaction, contributes to the further spread of anomie. In applying

[84] Vold, pp. 203–19.

[85] Lewis Yablonsky, "The Delinquent Gang as a Near-Group," *Social Problems,* VII (Fall, 1959), 108–17. See also his *The Violent Gang* (New York: The Macmillan Co., 1962), pp. 222–33.

[86] Émile Durkheim, *Division of Labor in Society,* trans. George Simpson (New York: The Macmillan Co., 1933), pp. 297–301; see also his *Suicide: A Study in Sociology,* trans. John A. Spaulding and George Simpson (Glencoe, Ill.: The Free Press, 1951), pp. 241–76.

[87] Talcott Parsons, *The Social System* (Glencoe, Ill.: The Free Press, 1951), pp. 36–45, 141, 302, 303; *ibid.,* *Essays in Sociological Theory* (Glencoe, Ill.: The Free Press, 1954), pp. 118, 119, 125–31, 136–39.

[88] Robert K. Merton, *Social Theory and Social Structure* (Glencoe, Ill.: The Free Press, 1957), pp. 131–94. For the use of the concept "anomie" in empirical research, see Bernard Lander, *Towards an Understanding of Juvenile Delinquency* (New York: Columbia University Press, 1954). For a discussion of the application of the concept "anomie" in research, see U.S. Children's Bureau, *New Perspectives for Research on Juvenile Delinquency,* eds. Helen L. Witmer and Ruth Kotinsky (Washington, D.C.: Government Printing Office, 1956).

this theory to the United States, Merton claims that we tend to measure success in terms of economic affluence, that we expect everyone to strive for such success and to achieve it and yet at the same time make this impossible for many in the lower classes and subcultures, that those who face denial of economic opportunity tend to feel justified in using any means, legitimate or illegitimate, to reach economic success, that the amount and nature of social deviance thus vary with the structural and cultural levels, that the norms lose their power to regulate behavior in this process of demoralization, and that increased anomie ensues.

Although Merton[89] explains that this theory can account for only some kinds of crime and delinquency, and although the conflict between goals and means undoubtedly does cause some frustrated persons to commit crimes or delinquencies, the extent to which it does this is open to question. Despite the increasing rigidity of our class structure, many persons can still work their way up to economic success, and many others—perhaps the great majority—in the lower classes, even though they may feel some frustration, accept their lot and realistically adjust to their limitations. Furthermore, even though the "common man" cannot have everything that the rich enjoy, he can have a good approximation of it, the disparity in "life styles" having diminished under the impact of large-scale industrialization, unionization, and welfare-state regulation.[90] Finally, we must not overlook the unique qualities of the individual and thereby exaggerate the homogeneity and solidity of the social class. Man's choice of goals and means is the creative expression of his entire personality as it interacts with others in terms of his culture. There is a diversity of response here—not just a mechanical function of a class; and Merton's theory does not tell us which persons among those who are denied legitimate means will commit crimes.

During the past decade, a number of sociologists, in line with the earlier studies of Shaw, McKay,[91] and Thrasher,[92] have examined the delinquency subculture, especially the relationship between social class and the delinquent gang. Cohen, drawing some of his ideas from Whyte's *Street Corner Society*,[93] maintains that the delinquent subculture is non-

[89] It must be emphasized that Merton's theory is designed to explain not only crime and delinquency, but all forms of social deviance resulting from *any* extreme conflict (not just economic) between goals and means when a substantial number of persons (not all persons) are oriented toward such goals in the social strata where this conflict exists (Merton, pp. 170–194). Here we see how the theorist, confronted with the complexity of the problem and his paucity of knowledge regarding it, must greatly reduce the specificity of his theory.

[90] Paul W. Tappan, *Crime, Justice, and Correction* (New York: McGraw-Hill Book Co., Inc., 1960), p. 171.

[91] For a discussion of the ecological studies of Shaw and McKay, see Chapter 12.

[92] Frederic M. Thrasher, *The Gang* (Chicago: University of Chicago Press, 1936).

[93] William F. Whyte, *Street Corner Society* (Chicago: University of Chicago Press, 1943).

utilitarian, malicious, and negativistic.[94] Concentrated in the male, working-class sector of the juvenile population, it represents a reaction against a low-class stigma by those who cannot achieve the middle-class standards of the dominant culture and an attempt to enhance status by defiance of those standards. Although Cohen does not claim that the delinquent subculture is the only form of delinquency or that all the boys who function in it do so because of the same problem of adjustment, he does believe that it is the major source of delinquency.[95] Critics of this theory, while agreeing that it does help to explain one form of the delinquency, also contend that it exaggerates the division between classes and the homogeneity of their membership, fails to account for other kinds of delinquent subcultures[96] and the maintenance of the working class variety, and underestimates the extent of individual differences and the diversity of response and choice.[97]

Cloward and Ohlin have combined Merton's theory of social structure and anomie with Sutherland's theory of differential association in an attempt to explain the problem of juvenile delinquency.[98] According to Cloward and Ohlin, the gap between financial success, which American culture emphasizes, and the limited access to it causes frustration and alienation among lower-class youths who aspire to economic advance-

[94] Cohen uses the words "non-utilitarian" and "negativistic" to mean that the delinquent subculture is not directed toward economic gain but toward the negation of middle-class values.

[95] Albert K. Cohen, *Delinquent Boys* (Glencoe, Ill.: The Free Press, 1955), pp. 25, 104, 105, 119, 124, 125, 130, 131, 135, 147–49, 150–57.

[96] In response to this criticism, Cohen, in collaboration with Short, has recognized the existence of other delinquent subcultures. Among these he describes the conflict-oriented, the drug-addict, the semiprofessional-theft, and the middle-class. However, Cohen insists that the working-class subculture, described in *Delinquent Boys,* is the parent subculture, because it is probably the most common variety in this country and because its characteristics seem to constitute a common core shared by other important variants (Albert K. Cohen and James F. Short, Jr., "Research in Delinquent Subcultures," *Journal of Social Issues,* XIV [No. 3, 1958], 20–37). See also Solomon Kobrin, "The Conflict of Values in Delinquency Areas," *American Sociological Review,* XVI (Oct., 1951), 653–62; Ralph W. England, Jr., "A Theory of Middle Class Juvenile Delinquency," *Journal of Criminal Law, Criminology, and Police Science,* L (Mar.–Apr., 1960), 535–40.

[97] For criticism of Cohen's *Delinquent Boys,* see Harold L. Wilensky and Charles N. Lebeaux, *Industrial Society and Social Welfare* (New York: Russell Sage Foundation, 1958); Gresham M. Sykes and David Matza, "Techniques of Neutralization: A Theory of Delinquency," *American Sociological Review,* XXII (Dec., 1957), 664–70; David J. Bordua, "Delinquent Subcultures: Sociological Interpretations of Gang Delinquency," *The Annals of the American Academy of Political and Social Science,* CCCXXXVIII (Nov., 1961), 121–27, 135, 136; John I. Kitsuse and David C. Dietrick, "Delinquent Boys: A Critique," *American Sociological Review,* XXIV (Apr., 1959), 208–15; Albert J. Reiss, Jr., and A. Lewis Rhodes, "Status Deprivation and Delinquent Behavior," *The Sociological Quarterly,* IV (Spring, 1963), 135–49.

[98] Richard A. Cloward and Lloyd E. Ohlin, *Delinquency and Opportunity: A Theory of Delinquent Gangs* (Glencoe, Ill.: The Free Press, 1960). See also Richard A. Cloward, "Illegitimate Means, Anomie, and Deviant Behavior," *American Sociological Review,* XXIV (Apr., 1959), 164–76.

ment. This, in turn, produces three types of subcultures, namely, the criminal, the conflict, which features acts of violence, and the retreatist, or drug-use, among lower-class boys who blame the system rather than themselves for their impending or actual failure. The criminal subculture develops in stable neighborhoods that provide illegitimate opportunities for financial success; the conflict subculture, in very disorganized neighborhoods that do not offer even illegitimate opportunities; and the retreatist, among youths who fail to find either legitimate or illegitimate opportunities for financial success. Although this theory of differential opportunity supplies us with some insights into the relationship between opportunity and delinquency, it has been criticized for exaggerating the importance of social class, for attributing excessive class consciousness to lower-class youth, for underestimating the importance of other factors, such as the family, ethnic background, and race, for failing to appreciate the significance of individual differences and the diversity of response and choice, for minimizing the existing opportunities for financial success, both legitimate and illegitimate, and for confusing justification with causation. It should be added that Cloward and Ohlin, as well as Cohen, view juvenile delinquency as a rather grim business into which strained and frustrated youths are driven by the grinding realities of life. That the excitement and adventure of delinquency can be "just plain fun" has apparently escaped the consideration of these theorists.[99]

Miller has described juvenile delinquency as the adolescent expression of lower-class culture[100] rather than of a delinquent subculture that has developed through conflict with middle-class culture, as depicted by Cohen, Cloward, and Ohlin. According to Miller, the lower-class culture is characterized by a female-based family[101] and certain "focal concerns," including trouble, toughness, smartness, excitement, fate, and autonomy.[102] For boys reared in female-based households, the corner group provides the first real opportunity to learn essential aspects of the male

[99] For criticisms of the Cloward and Ohlin theory, see Bordua, 131–36; *ibid.*, "Some Comments on Theories of Group Delinquency," *Sociological Inquiry*, XXXII (Spring, 1962), 245–60; David Matza, "Book Review," *American Journal of Sociology*, LXVI (May, 1961), 631–33.

[100] Walter B. Miller, "Lower Class Culture as a Generating Milieu of Gang Delinquency," *Journal of Social Issues*, XIV (No. 3, 1958), 5–19; William C. Kvaraceus and Walter B. Miller, *Delinquent Behavior: Culture and the Individual* (Washington, D.C.: National Education Association of the United States, 1959), especially Chapter 9.

[101] The typical female-based family consists of one or more adult females, usually related by blood, and their children, legitimate and illegitimate, and in its struggle to survive, it does not depend upon the presence or steady economic support of a male.

[102] By "trouble," Miller means constant awareness of trouble; by "smartness," ability to outwit others; by "autonomy," freedom from external restraint.

role. In the intensity of their desire to be seen as "adult"[103] and thereby gain recognition in the eyes of their peers, they express the "focal concerns" to a much greater degree than a lower-class male, and so through their heavy drinking, gambling, toughness, smartness, and similar behavior, they tend to commit acts of delinquency. Miller does not claim that his theory explains all delinquency but only that committed by adolescent street-corner groups in lower-class communities. In analyzing this theory, critics have commended Miller for calling attention to the importance of lower-class culture, but have also stated that he underrates the fluidity and variability of American urban life, exaggerates the features of lower-class culture, especially the female-based household, and engages in circular reasoning by failing to support his concept "focal concerns" with sufficient independent data, the result being that "focal concerns" appear to be derived from observing behavior and then used to explain the same behavior.[104]

Still another theory of juvenile delinquency has been propounded by Bloch and Niederhoffer. They theorize that when a society, like our own, "does not make adequate preparation, formal or otherwise, for the induction of its adolescents to the adult status, equivalent forms of behavior arise spontaneously among adolescents themselves, reinforced by their own group structure, which seemingly provides the same psychological content and function as the more formalized rituals found in other societies." Apparently this is what the gang does for youth in American society. Thus originate "the adolescent drinking, sexual escapades, wild automobile rides, immature assertiveness, violent reactions to parental restraints, protests against authority, and the other forms of intransigency," much of which is legally defined as delinquency, but which, at least to the youth, may seem to be the prerogatives of the mature adult.[105] This theory has the merit of being applicable to all classes, instead of just the lower class (as is true, for example, of the theories of Cohen, Cloward, Ohlin, and Miller), and of recognizing the psychological malaise of adolescence, but it suffers, say the critics, from being highly specula-

[103] Here Miller differs from Thrasher, who believes that lower-class boys get into difficulties, not because of their desire to be "real men," but because of the inadequacies of social control.

[104] For a critique of Miller's theory, see Bordua, 127–31, 136. For an attempt to test the theoretical positions of Cohen, Cloward and Ohlin, and Miller regarding values and delinquency, see R. A. Gordon, J. F. Short, Jr., D. S. Cartwright, and F. L. Strodtbeck, "Values and Gang Delinquency: A Study of Street-Corner Groups," *American Journal of Sociology*, LXIX (Sept., 1963), 109–28.

[105] Herbert A. Bloch and Arthur Niederhoffer, *The Gang: A Study in Adolescent Behavior* (New York: Philosophical Library, 1958). See also Herbert A. Bloch, "The Juvenile Gang: A Cultural Reflex," *The Annals of the American Academy of Political and Social Science*, CCCXLVII (May, 1963), 20–29.

tive and from failing to take into account the influence of social class on the growing-up process.[106]

Major Elements in the Sociological Approach. Although in this chapter and in Chapter 3 the major elements contained in the sociological approach have been indicated, it will be helpful now to summarize them more explicitly in the following manner:

1. Men in their adjustment to the geographical environment and to one another have created a man-made environment called *culture,* which not only imposes restrictions and controls upon human behavior, but also provides for the satisfaction of human needs. The nonmaterial culture consists of patterns of behavior, or social norms, which range in an ascending scale of consciousness and compulsiveness from *folkways* through *mores* to *social institutions,* such as the criminal law. All parts of culture are interdependent and interrelated, so that what affects one part tends to affect all the other parts.

2. Every society has social controls which operate continuously to bring human behavior into conformity with rules and standards. These controls are both informal, like scolding, ridicule, and gossip, and formal, like the criminal law, which is enforced by the courts and the police.

3. Human life is group life. In *primary groups,* like the family, the social relationships are intimate and face-to-face, but in *secondary groups,* like unions and corporations, they are indirect and specialized. In the United States, the decline of primary groups has weakened an important agency of social control; and laws, rules, and regulations, which are less efficient than the means of primary groups, have had to be substituted in many areas of human behavior.

4. The fundamental ways in which men interact are called *social processes.* The two basic social processes are *cooperation* and *opposition,* from which arise other social processes such as *differentiation, stratification, accommodation,* and *assimilation.* These processes operate in all forms of human behavior, whether they be criminal or noncriminal.

5. No society or community, however simple or isolated, is ever without *social change.* Inventions, economic disturbances, mobility, urbanization, floods, earthquakes, wars, etc. tend to upset the balance of social relationships and introduce conflicting values. Unless a society or community can cope with such changes, its *social organization* no longer adequately regulates human behavior so that human needs can be satisfied in terms of a generally accepted set of values. If this situation persists, the influence of existing social rules of behavior declines, and there

[106] For a criticism of Bloch and Niederhoffer's theory, see David J. Bordua, *Sociological Theories and Their Implications for Juvenile Delinquency;* U.S. Children's Bureau Juvenile Delinquency: Facts and Facets, No. 2 (Washington, D.C.: Government Printing Office, 1960), pp. 14, 15.

appears that phase of social change called *social disorganization,* whose onset is marked by the increase of *social problems,* including crime and delinquency.

6. The individual, whose *original nature* is so plastic, becomes a member of society by a *process of learning.* Although at first his behavior is dictated largely by innate drives and impulses, during the learning process it is expressed more and more in terms of the values acquired from others, who previously have received them from their life's experiences in various groups. In this way the individual obtains not only the social rules and standards of his society, but also much of the basis of his *attitudes* and *personal controls.*

Receiving his first *social definition* of behavior in the intimate and informal association of the family, the individual gets other and often conflicting social definitions and encounters increasingly rigid and formal social controls as he moves first into the activities of other primary groups, such as the play-group and the gang, and then into the membership of secondary groups in the neighborhood, the church, the school, and the world of business and industry.

7. In every society the individual plays many and often conflicting *roles* and achieves *status* in terms of the values contained in the culture of the group. As this takes place in modern society, the individual is constantly shifting from one *in-group* to another in an ever-changing pattern of cooperation and opposition. This situation is further complicated by the fact that our social relationships are becoming more secondary in nature, and the individual is being subjected to a stream of conflicting values as he moves from group to group. In the *mass society* that has emerged, *reference groups* and mass media of communication, such as newspapers, motion pictures, radio, and television, appear to be exerting an increasing influence on human behavior.

8. No person completely conforms to all the social rules and standards in even the most simple, homogeneous, and stable society or community. Differences in heredity, the unique qualities of the individual, variations in the learning and teaching processes, divergence in social change, and so on militate against this everywhere; and in modern, complex, rapidly changing societies and communities, where persons come into contact with very diverse and conflicting values, the amount of nonconformity, including crime and delinquency, becomes especially large. During periods of social disorganization, persons who have already acquired chronic patterns of nonconformity find increased opportunities for violating the *social norms,* and many others who have usually conformed to the social rules begin to violate them on a large scale for the first time. If social disorganization persists, crime and delinquency tend to become institutionalized in certain areas and neighborhoods, which not only attract

law violaters, but also produce and protect them. It is in these areas and neighborhoods that *subcultures* favorable to law violation develop and the principal roots of *professional* and *organized crime* flourish.

Using this frame of reference, most sociologists seek to explain crime as a product of definitions of situations acquired in life experience. Generally skeptical of "individualistic explanations of criminal behavior in terms of constitutional and abnormal personality patterns," they believe that "the origin of crime must be sought in definitions which are present in the culture in the form of competing value systems or culture conflict," and that "these competing value systems arise out of disorganization in social institutions and community situations."

Although American sociologists generally agree that attitudes derived from social experience are of primary importance in the causation of crime and delinquency, they disagree "as to the extent and nature of this emphasis, particularly as to whether the personality pattern (psychogenic traits) should also enter into the explanation." Some of them, like Sutherland, have taken the extreme position that "differential association" (see Chapter 10) alone is responsible for crime and delinquency. Others have emphasized certain characteristics of culture as the major cause of criminal behavior. Taft, for example, while acknowledging that his explanation is based chiefly on conditions in the United States and admitting that biological and psychological factors must be taken into account, believes that "crime grows out of a materialistically minded society with its constant striving for prestige and wealth."[107] This, however, is a hazardous position to assume since it exposes the sociologist to the charge that he is confusing ethics with science and falsely implying that certain values, because of their very nature, can be shown by science to be superior to other values. The sociologist, as a scientist, can show how to reduce social problems by removing one side or the other of a conflict of values, but he cannot advocate either side and remain a scientist.[108] Still other American sociologists, like Reckless, Sellin, Clinard, Tappan, and Cavan, although attributing primary importance to culture conflict, do not believe that this alone can explain all criminal behavior; they believe that we must also take into account personality elements and the "differential response patterns" of individuals.[109]

The sociological approach to the problem of causation has revealed the importance of the social factors and conclusively demonstrated that

[107] Marshall B. Clinard, "Sociologists and American Criminology," *Journal of Criminal Law and Criminology,* XLI (Jan.–Feb., 1951), 551, 554–56. See also Donald R. Taft, *Criminology* (New York: The Macmillan Co., 1950), chap. 15.

[108] See the sections on the "Limitations of the Social-Problems Approach," in Chapter 3, and "The Nature of Science," in Chapter 1.

[109] Clinard, "Sociologists and American Criminology," 556, 557.

they must be taken into consideration in any attempt to explain crime and delinquency, but it has failed to show that we can disregard the other approaches or assume that the causation of crime and delinquency is exclusively sociological. Criminal behavior is human behavior, and any explanation of the former must be nothing less than an explanation of the latter. Therefore, any theory of criminal behavior must include an examination of the biological and psychological factors that influence man's receptivity to social influences and his adaptation to social situations.[110]

Social-Psychological Approach. Social psychology deals not only with the psychological functioning of the individual but also with the interaction of individuals in their social and cultural environments. It thus strives to bridge the gap between psychology and sociology, and during its development, it has received important contributions from both these fields. Social psychology began to flourish after World War I, and by the early 1950's, it had firmly established itself as a separate discipline, although within its confines, various theories still struggle for dominance.[111] Unfortunately, limitations of space here permit the presentation of just the bare outlines of only three of these, namely, the psychoanalytic theory,[112] the stimulus-response theory, and the self theory,[113] all of which, however, have attracted strong support in the field of criminology.

The stimulus-response theory, also known as the psychological learning theory, has developed through the work of many scholars, such as Pavlov, Watson, Thorndike, Hull, Guthrie, Mowrer, Dollard, and Mil-

---

[110] Reckless, p. 51; Thorsten Sellin, "The Sociological Study of Criminality," *Journal of Criminal Law and Criminology,* XLI (Nov.–Dec., 1950), 406–22; Dennis H. Wrong, "The Oversocialized Conception of Man in Modern Sociology," *American Sociological Review,* XXVI (Apr., 1961), 183–93. For a review of recent literature on the sociological approach, see the articles of Marshall B. Clinard: "The Sociology of Delinquency and Crime," *Review of Sociology: Analysis of a Decade,* ed. Joseph B. Gittler (New York: John Wiley and Sons, Inc., 1957), pp. 465–99; "Criminological Research," *Sociology Today: Problems and Prospects,* eds. R. K. Merton, L. Broom, and L. S. Cottrell, Jr. (New York: Basic Books, Inc., 1959), pp. 509–36.

[111] For a discussion of the meaning and development of social psychology, see Gordon W. Allport, "The Historical Background of Modern Social Psychology," *Handbook of Social Psychology,* ed. Gardner Lindzey (Cambridge, Mass.: Addison-Wesley Publishing Co., Inc., 1954), Vol. I, pp. 3–56; Hall and Lindzey, pp. 1–28, 538–58; M. Brewster Smith, "Recent Developments in the Field of Social Psychology," *The Annals of the American Academy of Political and Social Science,* CCCXXXVIII (Nov., 1961), 137–43; Kimball Young, *Social Psychology* (New York: Appleton-Century-Crofts, Inc., 1944), pp. 1–10; Theodore M. Newcomb, *Social Psychology* (New York: The Dryden Press, Inc., 1950), pp. 2–38; Alfred R. Lindesmith and Anselm L. Strauss, *Social Psychology* (New York: The Dryden Press, Inc., 1956), pp. 3–12.

[112] The psychoanalytic theory will be discussed in Chapter 10.

[113] Self theory has been given other names, such as role theory and self and reference group theory.

ler.[114] In general, this theory attempts to analyze behavior in terms of stimuli and responses and to explain how a person learns to give old responses to new stimuli (conditioning) and new responses to any stimuli (reinforcement). According to Dollard and Miller, who have introduced psychoanalytical and anthropological elements into their theory, learning involves drives (primary or innate and secondary or acquired), cues (stimuli that guide responses), and reinforcements (rewards). They assume that a person has drive stimuli which create tensions and impel to action. Rewards reduce these drives and strengthen the connection between a given response and a particular cue. For example, a child has an appetite for candy (a drive); he hears the next-door neighbor arrive home in his car (a cue); and he responds by running to meet the neighbor who gives him some candy (reinforcement). Thus his drive is reduced, and if this activity is continued, a new pattern of behavior is learned. The stimulus-response theory has been helpful in research with animals and young children, but it has not been fruitful in dealing with complex situations involving adults. Its critics, noting its fragmentary and limited nature and its failure to provide clear definitions for its basic terms, and pointing out that it is based largely on research with animals and the examination of the learning process, assert that its vaunted objectivity, rigor, and formality become highly illusory unless its application is confined to animal behavior or very restricted areas of human behavior.[115]

The self theory also has appeared in various forms,[116] but the one that will receive most of our attention here has become known as the symbolic interaction theory,[117] which has its roots in the writings of such scholars as James, Baldwin, Cooley, Mead, Thomas, Faris, Dewey,

[114] Actually, there is no single stimulus-response theory, but rather a cluster of theories that resemble each other more or less and so can be discussed under a common heading.

[115] John Dollard and Neal E. Miller, *Personality and Psychotherapy: An Analysis in Terms of Learning, Thinking, and Culture* (New York: McGraw-Hill Book Co., Inc., 1950); Hall and Lindzey, 420–66; William W. Lambert, "Stimulus-Response Contiguity and Reinforcement Theory in Social Psychology," *Handbook of Social Psychology*, 57–90; Frederick Elkin, *The Child and Society: The Process of Socialization* (New York: Random House, Inc., 1960), pp. 41–44.

[116] The self theory of Carl Rogers, a psychologist, evolved out of the use of his method of psychotherapy, which is called nondirective or client-centered. See Carl R. Rogers, *Client-Centered Therapy: Its Current Practice, Implications, and Theory* (Boston: Houghton Mifflin Co., 1951). Based on the assumption that what the client does for himself contributes more to a richer, fuller life than what somebody else does for him, nondirective psychotherapy is designed to let the client discover, explore, and understand his own problems. The form of self theory developed by Rogers places more emphasis upon the individual and his psychology than the symbolic interaction theory, which stresses the group and the cultural environment.

[117] The symbolic interaction theory has been so named because of the emphasis that it places upon gestures and language in the development of the self.

Blumer, and Young. According to this theory, the concept "self" means that a person is an object of his own activity, that action is directed toward himself just as it is directed toward others. Through the use of gestures and language, he engages in symbolic interaction, and seeing himself as others see him, he learns what is expected of him in various situations and acts to strengthen and defend his self image. As Mead explains it, the self develops in three continuous stages. In the first, the preparatory stage, the child takes the role of others without understanding what he is doing. In the second, the play stage, the child plays the roles of others and comes to understand their meaning. In the third, the game stage, he must play a number of roles simultaneously and thus comes to view himself from the position of the group, that is, the *generalized other*. As the child develops, the expectations of the group in this way become an internalized model that guides him in his relations with others. Persons who especially affect the individual's development are his *significant others;* groups that influence his attitudes and behavior, his *reference groups*. Thus this theory sees the sharing of common expectations as the basis of human life. The organism does not respond to objects but to their meanings; roles constitute the motives of men; the character of the group largely determines the development of the self; and what a person thinks of himself—his self conception—becomes the important factor in the causation of his behavior, whether it be criminal or law-abiding.

The symbolic interaction theory has found many advocates among sociologists, because it emphasizes the group and cultural factors and gives special prominence to the adaptability, rationality, and purposiveness of man. The sweep of its pretensions does excite the imagination, but discerning critics have attacked it with cogent arguments. These arguments run somewhat as follows. Consciousness is not all there is to personality, and there is abundant evidence to show that the unconscious significantly influences human behavior. Besides, how are we to measure anything so subtle, changing, and elusive as the self? What a person says of himself is highly colored and distorted by defenses of various kinds and the passage of time greatly blurs his powers of memory, perception, and understanding. Self-reports, moreover, are notoriously unreliable, not only because the person may not know the whole truth about himself but also because he may be unwilling or unable to communicate what he does know. In addition, this theory does not tell us very much about the learning process. It must do more than say that man plays roles and internalizes the expectations of the group if it is to command general respect. And here the question of motivation becomes acute. To say that roles are motives without being able to show how and why this is true, is to plunge into the abyss of circular reasoning. It amounts to nothing more than saying that a man acts the way that he does, because he has learned to play certain roles, and that we know that he has done this, because of the way in which he acts. Furthermore, emphasis upon the functioning of the self may divert attention from the importance of the value structure of society, in terms of which the self must function; and yet this structure has distinctive characteristics and requires study independent of any analysis of the self. Besides, does not the individual have a reality apart from the group? The symbolic interaction theory presents an oversocialized conception of man, stripping him of his flesh and blood and reducing him to a mere shadowy reflection of the group's specifications.[118]

The psychoanalytic, stimulus-response, and self theories have generated research and provided some helpful insights into human behavior, but they remain largely speculative and greatly deficient in empirical support. In fact, all the theories in social psychology are weak; little progress has been made in the formulation of a single widely accepted theoretical position; and the entire discipline is still in the early stages of its development.

Conclusions Regarding Approaches. The following are some of the important conclusions that can be drawn from an examination of the various approaches to the problem of causation:

1. Knowledge of crime and delinquency has been increased and some effective techniques have been developed, but on the whole more has

[118] All forms of self theory, striving after clear-cut simplicity, tend toward the error of reductionism, that is, they tend to reduce their explanation to the concept "self," extending this concept too far and neglecting or excluding other important considerations. For further reading on the subject, see Charles Horton Cooley, *Human Nature and the Social Order* (New York: Charles Scribner's Sons, 1902); George H. Mead, *Mind, Self, and Society* (Chicago: University of Chicago Press, 1934); C. Addison Hickman and Manford H. Kuhn, *Individuals, Groups, and Economic Behavior* (New York: The Dryden Press, 1956), pp. 3–48, 80–100; Tamotsu Shibutani, *Society and Personality: An Interactionist Approach to Social Psychology* (Englewood Cliffs, N.J.: Prentice-Hall, Inc., 1961), pp. 247, 248, 532, 533; *Psychology: A Study of a Science,* "Sensory, Perceptual, and Physiological Formulations," ed. Sigmund Koch (New York: McGraw-Hill Book Co., Inc., 1959), Vol. I; Hall and Lindzey, pp. 467–502; Theodore R. Sarbin, "Role Theory," *Handbook of Social Psychology,* pp. 223–58; Dennis H. Wrong, "The Oversocialized Conception of Man in Modern Sociology," *American Sociological Review,* XXVI (Apr., 1961), 183–93.

For the application of self theory in criminology, see Marshall B. Clinard, *Sociology of Deviant Behavior* (New York: Holt, Rinehart, and Winston, Inc., 1963), pp. 45–59; Richard R. Korn and Lloyd W. McCorkle, *Criminology and Penology* (New York: Henry Holt and Co., Inc., 1959), pp. 327–39; Walter C. Reckless, *The Crime Problem* (New York: Appleton-Century-Crofts, Inc., 1961), 346–53; William Nardini, *Criminal Self Conception in the Penal Community: An Empirical Study* (unpublished Ph.D. dissertation, State University of Iowa, August, 1958).

been done to show what is not true than to provide a deeper and more positive understanding of human behavior.

2. There is an increasing awareness of the complexity of the problems of crime and delinquency and of the importance of studying all factors as they interact in the individual case.

3. However, there is still a tendency to overemphasize a particular approach or explanation, and proponents of this or that theory often insist that the truth is to be found only in their own special field of study and that other disciplines can contribute little or nothing.[119]

4. Since so little is known about the intricacies of normal human behavior, we should not be overawed by any branch of science, any school of thought, or any type of methodology and thus neglect other promising leads.[120]

5. Instead, at present, we should use all available resources in every field of human knowledge and organize them into a coordinated attack along all approaches to the problem of causation.[121]

6. Nevertheless, there is still a strong demand for a simple, definite explanation that will give a quick and easy answer to the problem of causation. Two of these explanations that have attracted wide support will be critically analyzed in the next chapter. They are the psychoanalytic theory originated by Sigmund Freud, a psychiatrist, and the differential association theory of Edwin Sutherland, a sociologist.

[119] Sheldon and Eleanor T. Glueck, *Unraveling Juvenile Delinquency* (New York: The Commonwealth Fund, 1950), p. 4.

[120] *Ibid.*, pp. 4, 5.

[121] For the advocacy of the multidiscipline approach to the causation of crime and delinquency by a European scholar, see H. Bianchi, *Position and Subject-Matter of Criminology: Inquiry Concerning Theoretical Criminology* (Amsterdam: North-Holland Publishing Co., 1956), pp. 75–78.

10

Two Theories of Causation

THE PSYCHOANALYTIC THEORY

Psychoanalysis, a branch of psychiatry, was originated by Sigmund Freud,[1] who began his career by studying medicine in Vienna, became interested in mental disorders, and in 1885 went to Paris to study under Charcot, then the outstanding authority on the subject in Europe. Freud developed his psychoanalytic theory over a period of many years as he sought to understand and cure the mental disorders of his patients. During the formative stage of his theory, he developed the following basic elements:

1. *The free association method.* By this method the patient is encouraged to relax, express himself freely, conceal nothing because it seems embarrassing, objectionable, or trivial, and thus bring back to consciousness the repressed painful or disagreeable thoughts or experiences that have caused his difficulties. Regardless of his sufferings, he must face his situation as it actually is, with all its hidden implications. Only by doing this, by gaining insight into the situation, and by reacting to it fully and without equivocation can he overcome his difficulties and find

[1] For a further study of the psychoanalytic theory, see *The Basic Writings of Sigmund Freud,* trans. and ed. A. A. Brill (New York: The Modern Library, 1938); Sigmund Freud, *A General Introduction to Psychoanalysis* (New York: Boni and Liveright, 1920); A. A. Brill, *Freud's Contribution to Psychiatry* (New York: W. W. Norton and Co., 1944); William Healy, A. F. Bronner, and A. M. Bowers, *The Structure and Meaning of Psychoanalysis* (New York: Alfred A. Knopf, Inc., 1930), Ives Hendrick, *Facts and Theories of Psychoanalysis* (New York: Alfred A. Knopf, Inc., 1939); *An Outline of Psychoanalysis,* eds. Clara Thompson, Milton Mazer, and Earl Witenberg (New York: The Modern Library, 1955); *The Complete Psychological Works of Sigmund Freud,* ed. James Strachey (Glencoe, Ill.: The Free Press, 1962); Bartlett H. Stoodley, *The Concepts of Sigmund Freud* (Glencoe, Ill.: The Free Press, 1959); Ruth L. Munroe, *Schools of Psychoanalytic Thought* (New York: The Dryden Press, Inc., 1955); Ernest Jones, *Sigmund Freud: Life and Work* (London: The Hogarth Press, 1955).

release from his pent-up emotions.[2] Freud encountered two major difficulties in the use of this method. He called them "transference," which is the strong emotional attachment for the analyst which the patient develops during treatment, and "resistance," which is the unwillingness or the inability of the patient to proceed with the treatment.

2. *The theory of repression.* This theory holds that a troublesome memory or wish is unconscious, not because it has slipped passively out of consciousness, but because it has been pushed out and held out by force. But it is charged with emotion and desire and so lives on in the unconscious, covertly exerting its influence and twisting conduct into unusual forms.

3. *The theory of dreams.* According to this theory, the dream is a disguised satisfaction for desires that have been repressed during waking life. Every dream has a manifest content, which is the story one tells in recounting his dream, and the latent content, which holds the dream's real meaning, for even in sleep, direct expression of wishes is censored. The analyst, in interpreting the dream, must penetrate the manifest content and reach the latent content, which holds clues to the causes of the patient's difficulties.

4. *The theory of infantile sexuality.* This theory states that sexual strivings operate powerfully before the age of sexual maturity, even as far back as infancy.[3]

The psychoanalytic theory may be regarded as an attempt to integrate and explain these basic elements and the subsequent ideas of Freud and his followers. However, the theory has never been rigid and fixed. Freud modified and supplemented his teachings during his entire lifetime and others have contributed important changes. Nevertheless, the main outlines of the theory have remained fairly constant and will be briefly indicated.

The psychic life of man consists of two principal parts, the conscious and the unconscious. Although the conscious is small and relatively insignificant, the unconscious is vast and powerful and contains the great concealed forces that are the driving power behind human actions. Between these two parts is the preconscious,[4] which merges into both, but which resembles the conscious more than the unconscious and is accessible to consciousness without emotional resistance.

[2] The term "catharsis" is used to refer to the mental purging which is induced by bringing disagreeable or painful thoughts and experiences into consciousness.

[3] Edna Heidbreder, *Seven Psychologies* (New York: Appleton-Century-Crofts, Inc., 1933), pp. 376–87; Coleman R. Griffith, *Principles of Systematic Psychology* (Urbana, Ill.: University of Illinois Press, 1943), pp. 399, 400; Calvin S. Hall and Gardner Lindzey, *Theories of Personality* (New York: John Wiley and Sons, Inc., 1957), pp. 29–55.

[4] The preconscious was formerly known as the foreconscious.

Both the conscious and the unconscious are active, and between them there is incessant warfare. The psychic life is thus organized about two centers: the ego or conscious self, which develops "conscience" as an expression of social approval; and the unconscious, which harbors the powerful sexual desires. These desires, although frustrated and held down by the conscious, live on and persistently strive to circumvent its prohibitions.

Freud used the term "libido" to refer to the sexual drive, but he used the word "sex" in such a broad sense that it is not clear whether he meant the specifically sexual desire or desire for pleasure in general. There is no doubt, however, that he considered the specifically sexual desire of overwhelming importance in human conduct. In fact, on this very point, he came to a parting of the ways with Jung and Adler, two of his pupils who founded divergent schools of thought.

Later in his career, Freud presented a new analysis of the psyche in terms of the three concepts, the id, the ego, and the superego. The relation between this set of concepts and that of the conscious and the unconscious has not been clearly worked out, although Freud appears to have regarded them as just two different views of the psyche. The id corresponds rather closely to the old notion of the unconscious. Its largest component is the instinctive sexual urges, but it contains also suppressed habit tendencies and a kind of blind wisdom inherited from the race. Although powerful the id is blind and rash. The ego develops out of the id through the contact of the self with external reality. It sees reality as the id does not and becomes the mediator between the self and the external world, curbing the id but also making possible whatever genuine satisfactions the id receives. The superego corresponds roughly to the conscience, but it is a conscience which is infantile, unenlightened, and partly unconscious. Often at variance with the conscious beliefs and principles of the individual, it even inflicts suffering and demands expiation for deeds of which he unconsciously disapproves. This greatly increases the possibility of conflict in the personality.

The psychic struggle begins in infancy as the unsocial and instinctive impulses of the id come into contact with social pressures and training procedures. The superego originates when the child, in his early contacts with external reality, incorporates into himself the parent ideal—an ideal in which both parents are somehow represented—and adopts as part of himself the prohibitions enforced by the parents during his infancy and childhood. Thus, he gradually develops ideals and moral standards and represses the cruder and unsocial urges of the id or learns acceptable ways of expressing them.

At first the sexual life of the child is autoerotic, his satisfactions being centered in his own body and derived from the stimulation, at first accidental, of the erogenous zones.[5] From infancy the son loves the mother, but the restrictions of society and fear of the father inhibit the son's sexual drive. The result is the Oedipus complex, that is, the son loves his mother and hates his father or develops an ambivalent attitude toward him. The corresponding complex,[6] developed somewhat differently, is present in the girl. She is in love with her father and either hates her mother or develops an ambivalent attitude toward her.

During the first few years of life, which are very important in the formation of personality, the child passes through the oral, anal, and phallic stages of development, each stage being defined in terms of the modes of reaction of a particular zone of the body. At about six the child enters a latency period, during which the sex drives find expression in socially approved forms of affection, and he spends much of his time with companions of his own age and sex. When puberty arrives, however, the sex instinct again becomes prominent and is definitely directed toward persons of the opposite sex. Each new step in the child's life entails a certain amount of frustration and anxiety, and if these become too great, normal growth may temporarily or permanently halt, the child becoming fixated on one of the early stages of development.

The normal development of the person regularly follows these successive stages, but even the normal person cannot escape the conflict between desire and repression, since everyone is doomed to have some of his impulses thwarted. Consequently, even the conduct of normal persons gives evidence of clashes and tensions and is characterized by mechanisms,[7] such as rationalization and projection, by which the intensity of the conflict is reduced. Furthermore, the same forces operate in both normal and abnormal behavior, although in abnormal behavior these forces are exaggerated and their effects are more conspicuous.[8]

When the id, ego, and superego are not well balanced, the unsocial and instinctive impulses break through and abnormal behavior results. In some cases, this abnormal behavior takes the form of delinquency or criminality as the individual seeks relief from his inner conflict. According to Alexander and Staub, this happens when the suffering of the ego, caused by submission to the person's inhibitions, becomes greater than the expected punishment. The ego then throws off the inhibitions and

[5] Freud assumed that every person is inherently bisexual, i.e., attracted to members of both sexes. This is the constitutional basis for homosexuality, although in most people the homosexual impulses remain latent.

[6] For a time, this was called the "Electra complex," but at present, since the underlying principle is the same in both sexes, the term Oedipus complex is applied to both the girl and the boy.

[7] For a discussion of these mechanisms, see Chapter 11.

[8] Adapted from Heidbreder, pp. 387–400; Griffith, pp. 400–6; and Hall and Lindzey, pp. 36–55.

takes the side of the id tendencies.[9] Thus, from the psychoanalytic point of view, crime and delinquency are at once symptoms of internal maladjustment and alternate forms of adjustment. They give expression to basic needs and appetites, provide "an avenue for the release of accumulated tensions and frustrations," and are "designed to restore the integrity of the person when his security is in some manner threatened."[10]

However, many proponents of the psychoanalytic theory concede that it cannot explain all criminality. Alexander and Staub, for example, in their classification of criminals,[11] include the normal criminal, whose criminality is not due to an inner conflict. His superego is properly developed, but it is criminal. It operates in terms of values unacceptable to organized society. He is a criminal because of the influence of a criminal environment.[12]

The following are some of the major criticisms that may be directed against the psychoanalytic theory:

1. The psychoanalytic theory cannot be proved or disproved on the basis of scientific evidence. Science, through observation and experimentation, must learn whether something is or is not true. But the psychoanalytic theory makes negative cases impossible, not because they do not exist, but because the possibility of such cases is eliminated by the very nature of the theory. Thus, if the analyst finds a sex complex, the theory is confirmed. If he does not, his failure is due to the fact that he has encountered a stubborn resistance,[13] which itself is evidence of a serious sex conflict; and again the theory is confirmed. And here a curious difficulty confronts anyone who objects to the psychoanalytic theory. His objections may be interpreted as resistance and, therefore, evidence that he is concealing his own feelings of guilt. Thus his very objections may be cited as proof of the validity of the theory.

2. Most of the concepts of the psychoanalytic theory are derived from a study of the abnormal. In fact, they are steeped in the abnormal, and their validity has not been adequately tested by a study of the normal. Undoubtedly, they provide us with an insight into pathological behavior,

[9] Franz Alexander and Hugo Staub, *the Criminal, the Judge, and the Public,* original edition translated by Gregory Zilboorg (Glencoe, Ill.: The Free Press, 1956), pp. 83–85. See also Franz Alexander and William Healy, *Roots of Crime* (New York: Alfred A. Knopf, Inc., 1935), pp. 273–91.

[10] Robert M. Lindner, *Stone Walls and Men* (New York: Odyssey Press, 1946), pp. 38, 39.

[11] For Alexander and Staub's classification of criminals, see Chapter 5.

[12] Alexander and Staub, pp. 45, 121.

[13] Resistance means that the patient is protecting himself from pain, and the presence of pain means that the analysis is probing a real wound. The treatment, therefore, is going in the right direction and should be continued. A complex is a system of emotionally toned ideas that have been repressed and give rise to morbid behavior.

but this is no reason why they should be used as the basis of a complete explanation of all behavior.

3. The psychoanalytic theory enormously overemphasizes the role of sex. Although it is true that Freud does not reduce everything to sex,[14] he does assign to sex the major role in human conduct. But at the same time, he uses the word "sex" in such a broad sense as to include virtually the whole life-force of man. This comes perilously close to making the explanation coincide with the phenomenon it seeks to explain by mere definition. Such practice leads to large, loose speculations that discourage the investigation of particulars.

4. The theory of infantile sexuality is based on questionable evidence. The theory was formulated by Freud because he had to push his analyses back into early childhood and infancy, where they commonly terminated in the discovery of an imagined seduction. But does this necessarily indicate infantile sexuality? May it not indicate that Freud's method had failed to uncover the real cause as it reached back to infancy? And should we call the evidence of sex that we find in the child "sexuality" and thus endow it with all the implications that this word carries? Is it anything so specific as this? Certainly, the theory of infantile sexuality cannot be accepted until it is supported by evidence demonstrable to others.

5. The psychoanalytic theory is largely a speculative construct whose meaning is obscured by a vague terminology. Abstractions, without adequate supporting data, are endowed with powers sufficient to explain behavior. Man thus becomes the kind of man that he is because the analyst fills him with the powers designed to make him that kind of man. Here, then, we are caught in the vortex of circular reasoning. Man behaves the way he does because he has in him certain powers, and we know he has in him these powers, because he behaves the way he does. Furthermore, the fictions of psychoanalysis "assume almost the proportions of actors who struggle with one another, push one another into or out of the unconscious, adopt disguises, and otherwise disport themselves as though they were nothing more than the *demons* of medieval folklore."[15] And to make matters worse, such basic terms as id, ego, superego, conscious, unconscious, and libido have never been satisfactorily defined. Consequently, the content of these terms can be changed to fit the occasion, and thus they can be used to provide plausible explanations for all kinds of problems.

6. The psychoanalytic theory overemphasizes the biological factors and fails to recognize the importance of culture. Although research by

---

[14] A. A. Brill, *Freud's Contribution to Psychiatry* (New York: W. W. Norton and Co., Inc., 1944), pp. 204, 205.

[15] Griffith, p. 407.

sociologists and anthropologists has clearly revealed the plasticity of man's original nature and the meaning of culture and its influence, the proponents of the psychoanalytic theory apparently have not fully grasped the significance of this. The neo-Freudians[16] have sought to adjust to this research, but they have not been able to free themselves from the fundamental fallacies of Freud.[17] And yet the marks of Freud's own culture are clearly discernible upon his theory. It is not a mere coincidence that Freud, a Jew, deeply conscious of the oppression of his people and reared in a culture having absolutistic tendencies and a strong patriarchal family system, should find in repression the key to his understanding of human behavior, and should lay so much stress on the son's attachment to the mother and rivalry with the father (Oedipus complex), while paying little attention to the daughter's attachment to the father and rivalry with the mother (Electra complex).

7. The psychoanalytic theory substituted a dogma for what it alleged to be a dogma. Claiming to be completely deterministic, the theory rejects free will but replaces it with the libido, which, however defined, is, like the concept of will, a free and unpredictable agent. It causes man to act as he does, but "when inquiries are made as to why the libido acts as it does, the only answer must be some variation of the theme, *it is that kind of force*."[18]

8. Serious questions have been raised regarding the techniques of psychoanalysis. Is free association really "free"? No matter how carefully the analyst effaces himself, do not his presence and his instructions influence the course of the patient's reflections? Does not the understanding that must be established between analyst and patient constitute a set toward a definite trend of thought? Are not the answers of the patient so interpreted that they support the bias of the analyst? And does free association really reduce the inner conflict? May it not intensify the conflict, deepen the hurt, and create feelings of resentment and revenge? Can the "cures" attributed to psychoanalysis be cited as proof of the psychoanalytic theory? It is well known that a neurotic person will readily believe anything, no matter how absurd, if an air of authority is used in telling him about it. And he may actually benefit by it if it seems to explain his difficulty. Indeed, fortune-telling and astrology can, and have accomplished the same thing.[19]

[16] Horney and Fromm are usually considered revisionists or neo-Freudians. Sullivan, greatly influenced by anthropology and social psychology, is much more of an innovator.

[17] Social scientists and biologists long ago abandoned the idea that human behavior is just a derivative of instincts.

[18] Griffith, p. 411.

[19] For criticisms of the psychoanalytic theory, see Griffith, pp. 406–18; Heidbreder, pp. 400–11; Hall and Lindzey, 64–72; Munroe, 131–42, 168–73; Lewis R. Wolberg,

Despite its many defects, the psychoanalytic theory has made some important contributions to our understanding of human behavior. Among these are: (1) it has helped to call attention to the importance of seeing the personality as a dynamic whole; (2) it has demonstrated the importance of the nonrational in human behavior; (3) it has helped science to appreciate the influence of infancy and childhood in the life of the person; (4) it has emphasized the much-neglected problems of sex; and (5) it has provided psychology with some fruitful hypotheses, enriched social science with such concepts as repression, regression, etc., and stimulated considerable research to test the validity of its postulates.[20]

THE DIFFERENTIAL-ASSOCIATION THEORY

Sutherland's differential-association theory was presented in its original form in the 1939 edition of his textbook *Principles of Criminology*.[21] In this edition, as an introduction to his theory, Sutherland stated that the existing knowledge was not sufficient to explain why a particular person committed a certain crime and that therefore "attention should be concentrated on systematic criminal behavior, either in the form of criminal careers or organized criminal practices." In this way he claimed that it might be possible to discover the processes which are general and uniform and thus facilitate the explanation of specific acts.[22]

In its original form, Sutherland's theory of differential association was presented in the following seven propositions:

1. *The processes which result in systematic criminal behavior are fundamentally the same in form as the processes which result in systematic lawful behavior.* The essential difference lies in the standards by which the two types of behavior are judged.

2. *Systematic criminal behavior is determined in a process of association with those who commit crimes, just as systematic lawful behavior is determined in a process of association with those who are law-abiding.*

3. *Differential association is the specific causal process in the development of systematic criminal behavior.* The principles of the process of

---

The Technique of Psychotherapy (New York: Grune and Stratton, Inc., 1954), pp. 63, 75–79, 109, 110; F. V. Smith, *Explanation of Human Behavior* (New York: Dover Publications, Inc., 1960), pp. 347–57; Joseph Jastrow, *The House That Freud Built* (New York: Greenberg, Publisher, 1932). See also *The American Journal of Sociology*, XLV (Nov., 1939), which is entirely devoted to a discussion of Freudian concepts.

[20] Heidbreder, pp. 411, 412.

[21] Edwin H. Sutherland, *Principles of Criminology* (Philadelphia: J. B. Lippincott Co., 1939), pp. 4–9. Although this was the first formal statement of the theory, the idea of differential association had been indicated in an earlier edition of the text. See *The Sutherland Papers*, eds. Albert Cohen, Alfred Lindesmith, Karl Schuessler (Bloomington, Indiana University Press, 1956), pp. 15-17.

[22] *Ibid.*, pp. 3, 4.

association are the same in the development of criminal and lawful behavior, but the contents of the patterns presented in the two processes of association differ. This is the reason why Sutherland called it differential association.

4. *The chance that a person will participate in systematic criminal behavior is determined roughly by the frequency and consistency of his contacts with the patterns of criminal behavior.*

5. *Individual differences among people in respect to personal characteristics or social situations cause crime only as they affect differential association or frequency and consistency of contacts with criminal patterns.*

6. *Cultural conflict is the underlying cause of differential association and therefore of systematic criminal behavior.* Differential association is possible because society is composed of various groups with varied cultures.

7. *Social disorganization is the basic cause of systematic criminal behavior.* The origin and persistence of culture conflicts are due to social disorganization.

The last statement of Sutherland's differential-association theory appeared in the 1947 edition of his text *Principles of Criminology.*[23] The essential elements contained in the nine propositions of this version of the theory may be summarized as follows: (1) criminal behavior is learned (2) in interaction with other persons in a process of communication, (3) especially in the intimacy of personal association; (4) the learning includes the techniques of committing crimes as well as the motives, drives, rationalizations, and attitudes; (5) the favorable or unfavorable direction of motives and drives is learned from the way surrounding persons define the legal codes either as rules to be obeyed or as rules to be violated; (6) a person becomes delinquent because in his association with others he learns an excess of definitions favorable to violation of law over definitions unfavorable to violation of law, and thus differential association is the cause of criminal behavior; (7) differential associations may vary in frequency, duration, priority, and intensity; (8) the process of learning criminal behavior involves all the mechanisms that are involved in any other learning; and (9) criminal behavior cannot be explained in terms of general needs and values, such as happiness and social status, since noncriminal behavior is an expression of the same needs and values.

The major criticisms of the differential-association theory may be summarized in the following manner:

1. *The scope of the theory has been variously defined.* In its original form, the differential-association theory did not attempt to explain all

[23] Edwin H. Sutherland, *Principles of Criminology* (Philadelphia: J. B. Lippincott Co., 1947), pp. 5–9.

criminal behavior but only "systematic criminal behavior," by which Sutherland apparently meant—although this is not at all clear—criminal behavior that has become a way of life for the individual and is supported by a philosophy in terms of which it is justified. Failure to give a clear definition of this basic term casts a shadow of uncertainty over the entire theory and exposed it to considerable criticism. Moreover, the theory in its original form set up a dichotomy of systematic criminal behavior and systematic lawful behavior and thus tended to oversimplify the problem of crime, for human behavior cannot be so sharply divided. All human behavior, including criminal behavior, consists of gradations that blend into one another.

In the last statement of his theory, Sutherland omitted the word "systematic" and referred only to criminal behavior, although he did not say why this omission was made or how the new scope of his theory was to be construed. However, in an address in 1942, after intimating that all but "the very trivial criminal acts" were systematic, Sutherland stated that he had abandoned the term "systematic" and that his theory applied to every crime "regardless of its systematic quality."[24] These are surprising words from a man who only three years before had written that it was not possible to explain why a particular person commits a crime and for this reason "attention should be concentrated on systematic criminal behavior, either in the form of criminal careers or organized criminal practices," and that if an adequate theory could be developed for systematic criminal behavior, it would be easier to explain specific acts in relation to this framework.[25] Does this seem to be the statement of one who was confident that the term "systematic" covered all but "the very trivial criminal acts"?[26]

In 1939, Sutherland felt qualified to advance only a tentative theory of systematic criminal behavior—whatever that may be—but a few years later, in 1947, when the last statement of his theory appeared, he did not hesitate to offer an explanation of all criminal behavior. However this change in the scope of Sutherland's theory may be interpreted, the theory deals with human behavior and so cannot rise higher than our under-

[24] Edwin H. Sutherland, "Development of the Theory," *The Sutherland Papers*, pp. 21, 22. In referring to the abandonment of his distinction between systematic and other crimes, Sutherland also said, "Some of my friends, especially Lindesmith, have insisted that I shall need to re-adopt this distinction or something much like it" (*ibid.*, p. 22).

[25] Sutherland, *Principles of Criminology* (1939 ed.), p. 4.

[26] On this point Cressey has written, "For reasons which never have been clear, the statement of the theory [in 1939] was qualified so that it pertained only to 'systematic criminal behavior,' rather than to the more general category, 'criminal behavior.'" See Donald R. Cressey, "The Theory of Differential Association: An Introduction," *Social Problems*, VIII (Summer, 1960), 2–6. This issue of *Social Problems* contains three other articles on differential association, to which Cressey's is an introduction.

standing of human behavior. Since so much of human behavior remains a mystery, an attempted explanation of any particular type of human behavior, such as criminal behavior, cannot free itself entirely from the limitations of our knowledge about human behavior.

2. *But the differential-association theory is a completely deterministic and closed system of thought.* It finds the complete answer to the problem of criminal behavior in differential association. In doing so, it fails to recognize that there may be an element of free will in human behavior (science as yet has not eliminated this possibility) and leaves little, if any, room for the introduction of new knowledge. Every scientific theory of human behavior must frankly recognize the element of "the unknown," which intrudes into every aspect of life, since nowhere do scientific truth and reality coincide.

3. *The differential-association theory does not attach sufficient importance to the biological and psychological factors.* To the extent that such factors are recognized, they are relegated to an entirely subordinate position. In the original formulation of his theory, Sutherland stated in the fifth proposition that individual differences "cause crime only as they affect differential association." But the individual, as a unique combination of heredity and environment, has a reality apart from the group, and no personality organization is ever the same as the social organization in which it functions. Not to appreciate this fully is to fail to grasp, for example, the significance of the creativity and ingenuity of man. Therefore, in opposition to Sutherland's contention, one may argue that differential association causes crime only as it gives expression to individual differences. In the last statement of his theory, Sutherland omitted the fifth proposition of the original statement. Apparently he attempted to justify this omission partly by saying that "it is not necessary, at this level of explanation, to explain why a person has the associations which he has."[27] In effect, however, this is an admission that other levels of explanation, also, must be used if the entire picture is to be seen and that his theory cannot explain an important part of the problem. To eliminate this part, then, is to offer only a partial explanation, for it does not take into account that the biological and psychological factors affect a person's receptivity to social influences. As Reckless points out, "Differential association and differential response are more likely to occur together than either one singly and separately."[28]

Sutherland attempted to answer this criticism by stating that a person's susceptibility is "largely, if not wholly, a product of his previous associations with criminal and anti-criminal patterns."[29] But this is really no

[27] Sutherland, *Principles of Criminology* (1947 ed.), p. 8.
[28] Walter C. Reckless, *The Etiology of Delinquent and Criminal Behavior* (New York: Social Science Research Council, Bull. 50, 1943), p. 62.
[29] Sutherland, "Development of the Theory," *The Sutherland Papers*, p. 25.

answer at all, for it merely says that at any particular time a person's response contains the effects of environmental influences, but it does not rule out the operation of biological and psychological factors, whose presence must ultimately be faced regardless of how far back into a person's life the analysis may be pushed. It is exactly this complexity of the problem that the differential-association theory fails to take into consideration. Indeed, Sutherland's answer is tautological, for it consists in nothing more than a reiteration that a person commits a crime because of differential association, which is precisely what must be proved. Sutherland also sought to defend his position regarding the biological and psychological factors by insisting that there was no satisfactory definition of the psychogenic traits and no way of differentiating them from the sociogenic traits. But pointing to the weaknesses in the views of others hardly constitutes an adequate defense for the weaknesses in one's own views. The fact is that there is no way of extricating oneself from the predicament in which Sutherland was caught except by a frank and explicit recognition of the biological and psychological factors in human behavior—factors about which many sociologists often make assumptions but do not specifically mention.

4. *The differential-association theory oversimplifies the process of learning.* In the original formulation of his theory, in which the fourth proposition emphasized the factors of frequency and consistency, Sutherland clearly failed to recognize the complexity of the process of learning, which is the subject of so much controversy in scientific circles.[30] Later, in the revision of his theory presented in 1947, he tried to correct this weakness by stating that the process of learning criminal behavior involves all the mechanisms that are involved in any other learning and that differential associations may vary in frequency, duration, priority, and intensity.[31] But this still does not tell us very much about how and why some persons internalize criminal patterns of behavior and others do not; and yet, Sutherland is here presenting an essential part of his theory. Indeed, it is at this very point that criminology must acquire more precise knowledge if it is to make much progress in understanding the etiology of crime and delinquency. Even so, the fact that learning theories in general also are weak in this respect cannot be interpreted as a recommendation for the Sutherland theory.

5. *The differential-association theory is not susceptible to empirical testing and cannot be proved.* Part of the difficulty here stems from the confusion caused by Sutherland's failure to be clear and consistent in the usage of his basic term "differential association." As the theory now

[30] See, for example, Ernest R. Hilgard, *Theories of Learning* (New York: Appleton-Century-Crofts, Inc., 1956).

[31] Sutherland, *Principles of Criminology* (1947 ed.), p. 7.

stands, this term appears to mean association with patterns of behavior—not with criminals—regardless of the character of the person presenting them. Thus, according to this interpretation of the theory, a person becomes delinquent because of an excess of definitions favorable to violation of law over those unfavorable to such violation, even if he has never met a criminal or has never been aware of coming into contact with criminal patterns of behavior. But suppose we do accept this interpretation, does it help us very much in determining why a person commits a crime? Just imagine trying to identify all the ideas that flow in an endless stream through a person's mind, then, estimating the net result of the complex interaction of all kinds of ideas, and finally, determining whether this result is favorable or unfavorable to law violation! The stupendous proportions of this task have impelled Glueck to inquire, "In the first place, has anybody actually counted the number of definitions favorable to violation of law and definitions unfavorable to violation of law, and demonstrated that in the predelinquency experience of the vast majority of delinquents and criminals, the former exceed the latter?"[32] Short[33] and Glaser,[34] among others,[35] also have called attention to the great difficulty

[32] Sheldon Glueck, "Theory and Fact in Criminology," *British Journal of Delinquency*, VII (Oct., 1956), 92–109.

[33] Short states that the Sutherland theory is not testable because such terms as "favorable to" and "unfavorable to" the violation of law cannot be specified in such a way as to be measurable (James F. Short, Jr., "Differential Association and Delinquency," *Social Problems*, IV [Jan., 1957], 233–39). Short, however, claims that he has found support for the part of the Sutherland theory that states differential associations may vary in frequency, duration, priority, and intensity. See his "Differential Association with Delinquent Friends and Delinquent Behavior," *Pacific Sociological Review*, I (Spring, 1958), 20–25. But Reckless has raised questions about the validity of these findings and urges further study under more rigorous conditions. See Walter C. Reckless, *The Crime Problem* (New York: Appleton-Century-Crofts, Inc., 1961), pp. 306–10. Regardless of the outcome of this type of examination, the crux of the Sutherland theory, i.e., proposition six of the 1947 formulation, will remain untested.

[34] Glaser has contended that "the phrase 'excess of definitions' itself lacks clear denotation in human experience," and in view of the weaknesses of the theory, he has proposed that it be restated in terms of differential identification, by which he means that "a person pursues criminal behavior to the extent that he identifies himself with real or imaginary persons from whose perspective his criminal behavior seems acceptable." He admits, however, that even this restatement cannot be used to explain all crimes. See Daniel Glaser, "Criminality Theories and Behavioral Images," *American Journal of Sociology*, LXI (Mar., 1956), 433–44. Elsewhere Glaser has concluded that differential association is superior to alternative theories from the standpoint of efficiency in codifying observations and utility as a source of valid predictive hypotheses. But this time he thinks that "a differential anticipation theory would meet these standards even more adequately than differential association." See his article, "Differential Association and Criminological Prediction," *Social Problems*, VIII (Summer, 1960), 6–14.

[35] See for example, Albert J. Reiss, Jr., and A. Lewis Rhodes, "An Empirical Test of Differential Association Theory," *The Journal of Research in Crime and Delinquency*, I (Jan., 1964), 5–18.

of subjecting Sutherland's theory to empirical testing, but one of the most damaging statements regarding it has come from Donald R. Cressey. After a study of over one hundred prisoners who had been convicted of crimes involving trust violation, he concluded, "It is doubtful that it can be shown empirically that the differential association theory applies or does not apply to crimes of financial trust violation or even to other kinds of criminal behavior."[36] Nevertheless, when Cressey revised the Sutherland text in 1955, he did not make any modification of Sutherland's final statement of his differential-association theory. This is especially surprising, since Cressey in the same text, while criticizing Dollard's theory of displacement of emotion, states, "The difficulty in the theory is that it cannot be proved or disproved, and an hypothesis which cannot be tested for validity is useless in the development of science."[37] However, apparently wishing to emphasize that the Sutherland theory represented only the tentative point of view of a sociologist, he did change its title from "A Theory of Criminology," to "A Sociological Theory of Criminal Behavior."[38]

In 1960, as the core of the Sutherland theory (proposition six of the 1947 formulation) began to crumble under persistent attacks, Cressey, its chief exponent, retreated and found refuge in the defense that differential association is not really a theory but "an organizing principle" which helps to make understandable both the statistical distribution of criminal behavior in time and space and the process by which individuals become criminals. He also admits, however, that as a principle—he calls it the "principle of normative conflict"—differential association "does not make good sense out of all the facts" in the spatial and temporal distribution of crime, that it is not a precise statement of the process by which one becomes a criminal, that, in fact, it is not precise enough to stimulate rigorous empirical research and so has not been proved or disproved, and that it tends to be tautological and might not be testable.[39]

Despite this retreat, when Cressey again revised the Sutherland text in 1960, no changes were made in the statement of differential association and it was again entitled "A Sociological Theory of Criminal Behavior."[40] If the claim is now made that this theory explains all criminal

[36] Donald R. Cressey, "Application and Verification of the Differential Association Theory," *Journal of Criminal Law, Criminology, and Police Science*, XLIII (May–June, 1952), 51, 52.

[37] Edwin H. Sutherland and Donald R. Cressey, *Principles of Criminology* (Philadelphia: J. B. Lippincott Co., 1955), p. 143.

[38] *Ibid.*, pp. 77–80.

[39] Donald R. Cressey, "Epidemiology and Individual Conduct: A Case from Criminology," *Pacific Sociological Review*, III (Fall, 1960), 47–58.

[40] Sutherland and Cressey, *Principles of Criminology* (1960 ed.), pp. 74–80. No reason is given for the fact that the wording of the statement of differential association has not been changed, but the words "an hypothesis which cannot be tested for

behavior, then the claim is made with Cressey's admission that it is doubtful whether the theory can be proved. But if the theory merely means that many persons learn to be criminals because most of the environmental influences in their lives do not produce a proper respect for the law, then it has been reduced to a polysyllabic elaboration of the obvious—a fate that has befallen many other oversimplifications of human behavior.[41]

Although the differential-association theory has serious weaknesses, it does have much merit. It calls attention to the importance of the social factors, to the similarity between the process of learning criminal behavior and that of learning lawful behavior, and to the fact that criminality cannot be explained entirely in terms of personality maladjustments. Undoubtedly, many, perhaps most, criminals are as well adjusted as the great mass of the population and violate the law chiefly because the values which they have learned, and by which they live, are not acceptable to organized society.

SOME CONCLUDING REMARKS

As the foregoing analysis shows, the theories of Freud and Sutherland are in direct opposition, the former taking an extreme position on the personal factors, and the latter, an extreme position on the environmental factors, but even so, they do have the following characteristics in common:

1. Neither can be proved nor disproved on the basis of scientific evidence.

---

validity is useless in the development of science" is omitted from the criticism of Dollard's theory of displacement of emotion, to which reference has been made above (*ibid.*, p. 143). However, Cressey has written that he did not revise the statement of differential association in the 1955 edition of the Sutherland text, because differential association has value as an organizing principle which helps to explain the data on crime rates, and that as such it can have validity even if it cannot be tested or is even incorrect as an explanation of why individuals become criminals. See his article, "Epidemiology and Individual Conduct: A Case from Criminology," 53. But this still does not tell us why differential association continues to be advanced as a theory which is supposed to explain all criminal behavior.

[41] For further discussion of some of the weaknesses of the differential-association theory, see Harry Elmer Barnes and Negley K. Teeters, *New Horizons in Criminology* (Englewood Cliffs, N.J.: Prentice-Hall, Inc., 1959), p. 159; Herbert A. Bloch and Gilbert Geis, *Man, Crime, and Society* (New York: Random House, 1962), pp. 109–20; Ruth Shonle Cavan, *Criminology* (New York: Thomas Y. Crowell, 1962), pp. 710–12; Howard B. Gill, "An Operational View of Criminology: A Critical Survey and a Review," *Archives of Criminal Psychodynamics* (Oct., 1957), 285–87; Clarence Ray Jeffery, "An Integrated Theory of Crime and Criminal Behavior," *Journal of Criminal Law, Criminology, and Police Science*, XLIX (Mar.–Apr., 1959), 533–52; Richard R. Korn and Lloyd W. McCorkle, *Criminology and Penology* (New York: Henry Holt and Co., Inc., 1959), pp. 297–301; Walter C. Reckless, *The Crime Problem* (New York: Appleton-Century-Crofts, Inc., 1961), pp. 304–11; Goerge B. Vold, *Theoretical Criminology* (New York: Oxford University Press, 1958), pp. 192–98. See also Edwin H. Sutherland, "Critique of the Theory," *The Sutherland Papers,* pp. 30–41, in which Sutherland examines some of the criticisms that until then (1944), had been directed against his theory.

2. Each falls into the error of reductionism. By failing to recognize all aspects of the very complex problem of human behavior, each extends itself too far and falls of its own weight.

3. Each is largely a speculative construct whose meaning is obscured by a vague terminology. Utilizing abstractions without adequate supporting data, each endows man with characteristics sufficient to explain his behavior. A person commits a crime because he has a certain characteristic—for Freud, this means an imbalance of the id, ego, and superego; for Sutherland, an excess of definitions favorable to violation of law—and we know that the person has this characteristic, because he commits a crime. But this is mere circular reasoning, and the theories are thus tautological.

4. Each has produced a cult, the members of which interpret and reinterpret the theories of Freud and Sutherland to fend off the attacks of critics. What is important is not what Freud and Sutherland said but what they intended to say. We are urged to be patient, understanding, and tolerant with respect to these theories, but little consideration of this kind is extended to other theories. And the cultists insist that critics substantiate their views with empirical data, even though the psychoanalytic and differential-association theories remain untested and unproved.

5. Each reflects the influence of the culture to which it is functionally related. Freud's theory, with its emphasis upon repression and the Oedipus complex, bears the marks of having been created by a Jew, deeply conscious of the oppression of his people and reared in a culture having absolutistic tendencies, a strong patriarchal family system, and rapidly growing physical sciences. Sutherland's theory, on the other hand, shows the effects of having originated in a culture where great social changes were tearing large segments of the population from their traditional moorings, piling men and women up in congested cities, submerging the individual in the depths of large organizations and then battering him with the tremendous blows of the most serious depression in the history of the United States, and increasing the wealth and power of large corporations. All this seemed to reveal the relative helplessness and insignificance of the individual before the force of environmental influences, and while stimulating the already expanding social sciences, it also left a definite impression on the thinking of those who, like Sutherland, were working in these fields. Thus, his studies of white-collar crime were essentially a protest against the alleged abuse of power by large corporations, and his convictions regarding the overwhelming importance of environmental influences are clearly expressed in his theory of differential association.

11

Personal Factors[1]

HEREDITY

Heredity is the original nature of man—the total of characteristics transmitted from one generation to another through the germ plasm. It thus provides the marvelous stuff out of which is made the entire human body, including such important features as the nervous system, the ductless glands, the organic drives, and the general and specific mental capacities.

This does not mean, however, that heredity completely determines man's destiny, for the raw material carried by the germ plasm is molded and greatly modified by social experience. It does mean that heredity endows man with potentialities and imposes limits upon his development. To the extent that heredity varies among men, it contributes to individual differences, and when this variation is pronounced, heredity tends to stand out, seriously handicapping in some cases and remarkably facilitating in others. Out of the interaction of heredity with all the other factors in man's life, both personal and environmental, emerges the human personality—a composite of sentiments, attitudes, ideas, habits, abilities, and skills.

But each generation must begin anew, for it receives from heredity only what was given to its predecessor. The acquired characteristics, the effects of man's struggle with life, do not change the germ plasm and are not inherited. This, in one sense, is a blessing, for the accumulated burden of man's pains and diseases, mistakes and failures, compounded over the span of many centuries, would be too much to bear. On the other hand, the splendid accomplishments of each generation—the discoveries of science and the achievements of the arts—would be lost if they were not embedded in the culture and transmitted to the offspring through the

[1] The presentation of the personal factors in this chapter and the environmental ones in the next is not intended to imply any systematic conception of their nature or interaction but is used only to provide a teaching device for the discussion of pertinent information.

process of education and learning. It is because of the great plasticity of man's original nature that he has the capacity to benefit by this process. And to his capacity for learning he owes most of the qualities which are implied in the term "human being."

How much of the human being is produced by heredity and how much by the environment? The answer to this question cannot be fully disclosed in the individual even by an intensive case study. Before his birth, man's heredity is already inextricably interwoven with the influences of his pre-natal environment. Besides, many of his hereditary qualities remain latent in recessive genes, and science has devised no method by which these can be identified. Often, too, recessive genes are defective, and so a normal person may carry undetectable hereditary defects, which, if not counteracted by normal genes in the offspring, may become manifest. It should be clear, therefore, that even if we could identify all the hereditary defects that are manifest and prevent those who have them from reproducing, a whole new crop of hereditary defects would still appear in the next generation. Furthermore, a defect of a certain kind, such as feeble-mindedness, that may be hereditary in one individual may be environmental in another. And the situation is further complicated by the fact that heredity does not completely reveal itself at birth, some of its characteristics appearing only gradually through the process of maturation, during which their nature is obscured by environmental influences. In view of these facts and of our present inability to define the precise roles of heredity and environment, we must conclude that all the other personal factors except race, which is hereditary, have in them some of both heredity and environment, and that in the individual both are present in indeterminable proportions.

Among the approaches that have been used to explore the relationship between heredity and crime, two especially are deserving of our attention. One of these involves the study of family trees, and the other, the study of twins. From the first we have received the stories of the Jukes, the Kallikaks, the Nams, the Hickories, the Pineys, the Ishmaelites, and the Zeros—names that are now well known in the literature of criminology. Studies made by Dugdale, Estabrook, Goddard, Goring, and others, if we grant their accuracy (although this has been questioned), show that there is a strong tendency for criminality to run in the families investigated and thus suggested that criminality is inherited.[2] However, despite claims to

2 See, for example, Arthur H. Estabrook, *The Jukes in 1915* (Washington, D.C.: The Carnegie Institution of Washington, Publication No. 240, 1916); Henry H. Goddard, *The Kallikak Family* (New York: The Macmillan Co., 1912); Charles Goring, *The English Convict* (London: His Majesty's Stationery Office, 1919). In general, the studies of family trees have been criticized on the grounds that they have used neither precise measurements nor comparative statistical analyses of other families, which might have been considered "normal," as controls.

the contrary, they have failed to disentangle heredity from environmental influences and so have not proved that heredity apart from other factors can cause crime. Obviously, violations of the law may persist among members of a family not because they share a common heredity, but because they all live in an environment conducive to crime. Healy and Bronner, in their extensive studies of juvenile delinquency, found no proof of the contention that heredity alone can produce crime.[3]

The second approach to the relationship between crime and heredity, the study of twins, has produced more significant evidence. Twins are of two kinds: identical, or those derived from one egg and hence of identical heredities; and fraternal, or those derived from two different eggs and hence of heredities no more alike than that of ordinary brothers or sisters. These studies clearly show that, when one of a set of identical twins violated the law, the other twin was more likely to do so than was true in the case of fraternal twins. Proponents of these studies contend that the greater similarity of identical twins in respect to criminal behavior demonstrates the influence of heredity. Critics, however, argue that: (1) the number of cases studied is too small to be conclusive, since it would require only a slight change in the observed behavior to produce an entirely different picture; (2) the classification of twins as identical or fraternal must be questioned in many cases, since so often evidence regarding the nature of the birth is lacking; (3) identical twins are more likely to have similar environments than fraternal twins, since the former, whose appearance is similar, are more likely to be treated in the same way than the latter, whose appearance may be quite dissimilar; (4) the failure of both members of a set of identical twins to behave in the same way in all cases proves that environment, and not heredity, is the indispensable condition in the causation of criminal behavior; and (5) the factor of environment has been largely neglected in the studies, which have failed to show that both members of a set of identical twins behave in the same way even when they are reared in entirely different environments.[4] Like the study of family trees, the study of twins has not suc-

---

[3] See William Healy and Augusta F. Bronner, *Delinquents and Criminals, Their Making and Unmaking* (New York: The Macmillan Co., 1926), pp. 97–102; and *New Light on Delinquency and Its Treatment* (New Haven: Yale University Press, 1936), pp. 25–35; Stephan Hurwitz, *Criminology* (London: George Allen and Unwin, Ltd., 1952), pp. 58–63.

[4] Horatio Hackett Newman, *Multiple Human Births* (New York: Doubleday, Doran and Co., 1940); Robert S. Woodworth, *Heredity and Environment: A Critical Survey of Recently Published Material on Twins and Foster Children* (New York: Social Science Research Council, Bull. 47, 1941); M. F. Ashley Montagu, "The Biologist Looks at Crime," *The Annals of the American Academy of Political and Social Science,* CCXVII (Sept., 1941), 53–55; Walter C. Reckless, *The Etiology of Delinquent and Criminal Behavior* (New York: Social Science Research Council, Bull. 50, 1943), pp. 5, 6; Hurwitz, pp. 104–8; Ernest R. Mowrer, "Some Factors in the

ceeded in proving that criminality is inherited. However, in the future, studies such as these, when given the support of improved scientific techniques, may throw valuable light on the role of heredity in human behavior.

Crime and delinquency are not inherited, and no one is foredoomed to a career of law violation because of his germ plasm. But this should not be construed to mean that heredity is not in any way related to crime and delinquency and that its influence can be ignored by the criminologist. Hereditary determinism is unacceptable, but the alternative is not the equally untenable position of social determinism.

Heredity is a factor in criminal behavior—and an important one—just as it is a factor in all human behavior. In its interaction with other factors, both personal and environmental, its influence may be the major one in a criminal career, just as it may be in a successful business or professional career. Thus, in one case an inherited mental deficiency may be the chief factor in an act of delinquency or a crime, whereas in another heredity may be the deciding factor in a successful musical career. In fact, a person's heredity may make his social adjustment exceedingly difficult, perhaps impossible, but this is quite different from saying that as a result of his heredity, and regardless of other factors, he will engage in criminal behavior. The problem is far too complex for so simple an answer. Crime is what the law defines it to be, and the law varies with the time and the place during a person's life, while his heredity remains constant. A law which defines a particular type of behavior as criminal may greatly increase the possibility that a person with certain hereditary traits will become a criminal, but whether he does so will still depend upon the interaction of these traits with many other factors, such as family life, medical care, education, economic opportunity, programs of law enforcement and crime prevention, and so on.

RACE

Heredity varies not only among individuals, but also among groups of individuals called races. A race, therefore, may be defined as a group of individuals who have in common certain hereditary characteristics. Races apparently originated as a result of mutations, natural selection, and inbreeding; and on the basis of certain physical characteristics, they have been classified into three main divisions: (1) the Caucasoid, (2) the Mongoloid, and (3) the Negroid. While the physical differences among races are observable, it is debatable whether they indicate corresponding

Affectional Adjustment of Twins," *American Sociological Review*, XIX (Aug., 1954), 468–71; George B. Vold, *Theoretical Criminology* (New York: Oxford University Press, 1958), pp. 96-98.

differences in racial abilities. There may be inherited mental differences among races, but this has not been conclusively proved or disproved, while many individuals of all races have manifested an ability to participate in the building of the most complex cultures. That individuals are unequal in their heredity is beyond question. That there may be more superior individuals in one race than in another may likewise be true. But this, also, remains a controversial question. And since race mixture has blurred the picture, the question of innate racial differences may never be answered.

All three of the main racial divisions are represented in the United States; but the whites and the Negroes are by far the most numerous. It is not surprising, then, that in 1963 about 97 per cent of the 4,259,463 persons arrested by 3,951 law-enforcement agencies throughout the country were members of the white and Negro races. Whites comprised 69.1 per cent of this total; Negroes, 27.9 per cent; and Indians, Chinese, Japanese, and persons of other racial extractions, only 3.0 per cent. However, since Negroes represent about one-tenth of the population, the Negro arrest rate was disproportionately high, being over twice as high as it should have been. As compared with the arrests of whites, Negro arrests for 1963 were especially disproportionate for murder and nonnegligent manslaughter, forcible rape, robbery, aggravated assault, other assaults, prostitution and commercialized vice, violations of narcotic drug laws, carrying and possessing weapons, violations of liquor laws, and gambling. In fact, during 1963, there were actually more Negroes than whites arrested for murder and nonnegligent manslaughter, robbery, aggravated assault, prosititution and commercialized vice, carrying and possessing weapons, and gambling.[5]

However, statistics on arrest are not a reliable index of possible criminality in the community.[6] In general, criminologists have felt that this is especially true in the case of the Negro, who, they believe, is more likely to be suspected of crime than the white, and more likely to be arrested, prosecuted, convicted, and imprisoned. Thus Professor Sutherland has stated that criminal statistics "probably reflect a bias against all of the minority races but especially against the Negro."[7] Several recent studies, however, have not supported this generalization. Green, in his study of the factors underlying the sentencing practice of the criminal court of Philadelphia, not only failed to find any judicial prejudice against

[5] Federal Bureau of Investigation, *Uniform Crime Reports, 1963,* p. 111. The 3,951 agencies that made the 4,259,463 arrests during 1963 were serving an estimated population of 116,952,000.

[6] For a discussion of statistics on arrests, see Chapter 1.

[7] Edwin H. Sutherland, *Principles of Criminology* (Philadelphia: J. B. Lippincott Co., 1947), p. 121.

the Negro in that court, but after a review of other studies on sentencing, also concluded that they do not provide a sound factual basis for the charge that judges discriminate against minority groups in imposing sentences.[8] Kephart, in a study of racial problems confronting the Philadelphia police department, contends that that city's high Negro crime rate "in general, is not attributable to differential treatment, either by the police or by the courts," but rather to the failure of the Negro community to assume responsibility for its own moral and legal behavior.[9] Whatever the causes of the high Negro crime rate may be, and even when allowances are made for any possible unfair treatment by the police and the courts, all the evidence indicates that the criminality of the Negro is clearly out of proportion to his numbers in the population.[10]

If there are inherited mental differences among races, or if there are more superior individuals in one race than in another, this may account in part for the excessive Negro crime rate in the United States. But at present there is no conclusive proof either for or against such an assumption. There are, however, social, economic, and psychological factors that can explain much of the disproportionately high Negro crime rate. In all of his social relationships, the Negro is disproportionately exposed to the causes of crime. In general, his medical care, education, and training are less; his poverty, greater; his housing, less adequate. He is discriminated against socially and industrially, while to an increasing extent he is expected to strive for higher goals and to meet the white man's standards of competition and law observance. And all of the Negro's ensuing problems are intensified by his traditions of slavery, his growing urbanization, and his migration northward.[11]

[8] Edward Green, *Judicial Attitudes in Sentencing* (New York: St. Martin's Press, 1961), pp. 8–11, 20, 56–63, 97–103.

[9] William M. Kephart, *Racial Factors and Urban Law Enforcement* (Philadelphia: University of Pennsylvania Press, 1957), pp. 174–76.

[10] In a study of criminal homicides in Philadelphia, Wolfgang found that Negroes had over four times their "share" of offenders. See Marvin E. Wolfgang, *Patterns in Criminal Homicide* (Philadelphia: University of Pennsylvania Press, 1958), pp. 31, 32.

[11] Gunnar Myrdal, *An American Dilemma* (New York: Harper and Bros., 1944), pp. 966–79; Carleton Putnam, *Race and Reason: A Yankee View* (Washington, D.C.: Public Affairs Press, 1961); Edward B. Reuter, *The American Race Problem* (New York: Thomas Y. Crowell Co., 1938), pp. 334–59; Carleton S. Coon, *The Story of Man* (New York: Alfred A. Knopf, 1962); Carleton S. Coon, *The Origin of Races* (New York: Alfred A. Knopf, 1962); Audrey M. Shuey, *The Testing of Negro Intelligence* (Lynchburg, Va.: J. P. Bell Co., Inc., 1958); E. Franklin Frazier, *The Negro Family in the United States* (Chicago: University of Chicago Press, 1939), pp. 358–75; Thorsten Sellin, "Race Prejudice in the Administration of Justice," *American Journal of Sociology*, XLI (Sept., 1935), 212–17; E. Franklin Frazier, *The Negro in the United States* (New York: The Macmillan Co., 1949), pp. 638–53; John Dollard, *Caste and Class in a Southern Town* (New Haven: Yale University Press, 1937); Guy B. Johnson, "The Negro and Crime," *The Annals of the American*

Even though it cannot be demonstrated that the factor of race is a direct cause of crime, this does not mean that race can be disregarded in the study of criminology. Entirely apart from the question of innate racial differences, the physical characteristics of a race, as measured by cultural values, help to determine its status in a society, the role that it will play in all of its social relationships, and the concept that its members have of themselves. Thus they affect its opportunities, its handicaps, its rewards, and its conflicts, and so indirectly the nature and extent of its crimes.[12]

PHYSICAL CHARACTERISTICS

Sex. During 1963 about eight times as many males as females were arrested,[13] and during 1962 more than nineteen times as many males as females were received from the courts by state and federal correctional institutions for adults.[14] In the delinquency cases handled by the juvenile courts in the United States during 1962, the boys outnumbered the girls by more than four to one.[15] About half of the boys were referred to the juvenile court for offenses against property, whereas most of the girls were brought in for being ungovernable, for running away, for truancy, and for sex offenses. Women are arrested for a great variety of crimes, but during 1963 over 70 per cent of those coming into conflict with the law were arrested for larceny (11.6 per cent), assaults (5.6 per cent), prostitution, commercialized vice, and other sex offenses (5.9 per cent), liquor-law violations (3.4 per cent), driving while intoxicated (2.7 per cent) dis-

Academy of Political and Social Science, CCXVII (Sept., 1941), 93–104; Hugh P. Brinton, "Negroes Who Run Afoul the Law," *Social Forces,* XI (Oct., 1932), 96–101; Earl R. Moses, "Differentials in Crime Rates between Negroes and Whites," *American Sociological Review,* XII (Aug., 1947), 411–20; Robert L. Cooper, "Racial Antagonism as a Factor in Delinquency," *Yearbook, 1946* (New York: National Probation Association, 1947), pp. 77–85.

[12] Limitations of space prevent a discussion of the crimes and delinquencies of other racial groups whose numbers are comparatively small in the United States, but for further reading on the subject of race and crime, the student is referred to the following: Norman S. Hayner, "Variability in the Criminal Behavior of American Indians," *American Journal of Sociology,* XLVII (Jan., 1942), 602–13; Hans von Hentig, "The Delinquency of the American Indian," *Journal of Criminal Law and Criminology,* XXXVI (July–Aug., 1945), 75–84; Norman S. Hayner, "Social Factors in Oriental Crime," *American Journal of Sociology,* XLIII (May, 1938), 908–19; Walter G. Beach, "Oriental Crime in California," *Stanford University Publications in History, Economics, and Political Science,* III, No. 3 (1932); James E. McKeown, "Poverty, Race, and Crime," *Journal of Criminal Law and Criminology,* XXXIX (Nov.–Dec., 1948), 480–84; W. A. Bonger, *Race and Crime,* trans. Margaret M. Horduk (New York: Columbia University Press, 1943).

[13] Federal Bureau of Investigation, p. 109.

[14] Federal Bureau of Prisons, *National Prisoner Statistics,* No. 33 (Dec., 1963), p. 15, Table 1.

[15] United States Children's Bureau, *Juvenile Court Statistics, 1962,* Statistical Series, No. 73, pp. 2, 3, 10, 12.

orderly conduct (13.1 per cent), drunkenness (23.8 per cent), vagrancy (2.5 per cent), and suspicion (2.0 per cent).[16]

Thus sex is a very important factor in crime and delinquency, affecting not only the amount of law violation but also its nature. This appears to be true even if, following the suggestion of Otto Pollak, we make allowances for the possibility that the crimes of women are more often undetected or unreported and more leniently dealt with than those of men.[17] However, there is no reason to believe that the female is inherently "better" and, therefore, inherently less criminal than the male. On the contrary, there is abundant evidence to show that in her crimes she can be as ruthless, vicious, and dangerous as the male. The biological factor which gives woman the function of bearing children and, in general, makes her physically weaker, operates not alone, but in interaction with the traditions and customs of our society, to produce the differences between the sexes in crime and delinquency. Despite her increased freedom, the average female in the United States is still more closely supervised and protected than the male, is shielded from much of the harsh conflict and competition of the business world, is concerned primarily with domestic affairs, and is given preferential treatment in many social relationships. As a result, she is placed in fewer situations that are conducive to crime and delinquency, and her peculiar interests are reflected in her law violations.[18]

Age. Age, too, is an important factor in the frequency and nature of crime and delinquency. During 1963, of the 4,510,835 persons arrested[19] by the 3,985 agencies throughout the country (serving an estimated population of 125,760,000), 17.5 per cent were under eighteen years of age, 26.8 per cent were under twenty-one years of age, 37.0 per cent were under twenty-five years of age, 47.5 per cent were in the age group twenty-five to forty-nine, inclusive, and 15.4 per cent were fifty years of age and over. These statistics also showed that persons under twenty-five comprised 61.6 per cent of the arrests for forcible rape, 65.6 per cent of the arrests for robbery, 78.5 per cent for burglary and breaking and entering, 72.8 per cent for larceny, 88.0 per cent for auto theft, 59.2 per cent for buying or receiving stolen property, 50.6 per cent for carrying or possessing weapons, 64.2 per cent for violations of liquor laws, and 59.2

[16] Federal Bureau of Investigation, p. 109.

[17] See Otto Pollak, *The Criminality of Women* (Philadelphia: University of Pennsylvania Press, 1950), pp. 1–7.

[18] Mabel A. Elliott, *Crime in Modern Society* (New York: Harper and Bros., 1952), pp. 201–3.

[19] Although arrests are not a reliable index of criminality, they are the best we have for age groupings on a national scale. For a discussion of the limitations of the statistics on arrest, see Chapter 1. On the one hand, the young and the old are more easily caught, but on the other hand, the sympathy of police, judges, and juries tends to reduce the arrest and conviction rates of children and old people.

per cent for suspicion. However, 54.3 per cent of the arrests for murder and nonnegligent manslaughter, 53.3 per cent of the arrests for aggravated assault, and 69.3 per cent of the arrests for embezzlement and fraud involved persons in the age group twenty-five to forty-nine, inclusive, whereas 28.2 per cent of the arrests for drunkenness and 23.6 per cent of the arrests for vagrancy involved persons fifty years of age or over.[20]

The incidence of criminality is small among children, increases with adolescence and early adulthood, declines during the later years, and almost disappears in old age. Such crimes as robbery, burglary, larceny, auto theft and rape, which usually involve considerable physical activity and recklessness, tend to be crimes of youth. Murder and aggravated assault, which often require considerable physical strength, and embezzlement and fraud, which usually involve some skill, tend to be crimes of later adulthood. Vagrancy and drunkenness, often symptoms of personality disorganization and physical deterioration, occur more frequently during the middle years and old age.

In their book *Later Criminal Careers*, published in 1937, the Gluecks advanced their "maturation theory," which holds that there is a general tendency for offenders to abandon their criminal ways as they get older or mature. This tendency exists, according to the Gluecks, because of the decline in aggressiveness and of other psychophysical changes that occur during the aging process.[21] Although this theory appears to throw some light on the problem, it is suggestive rather than explanatory.

Like sex, the factor of age must be seen as it interacts with the cultural factors in a society. Childhood, adolescence, adulthood, and old age have different meanings in different cultures; and the duties, responsibilities, and rights of each vary from society to society. Obviously, certain acts require the agility and daring of youth, while others need the skill and judgment of maturity. Moreover, physiological changes involve difficulties of adjustment regardless of the culture.[22] Nevertheless, whether the act committed is a crime will depend upon its being so defined by the culture of the society in which the individual seeks adjustment.

Anatomical and Physiological Factors. The original contention that criminals manifest physical degenerative stigmata has been thoroughly discredited. Even Hooton's neo-Lombrosian approach and the attempts

[20] Federal Bureau of Investigation, pp. 106–108. For a summary of much material on old age and crime, see David O. Moberg, "Old Age and Crime," *Journal of Criminal Law, Criminology, and Police Science*, XLIII (Mar.–Apr., 1953), 764–76.

[21] Sheldon and Eleanor T. Glueck, *Later Criminal Careers* (New York: Commonwealth Fund, 1937), pp. 103–6, 198–212.

[22] Hans von Hentig, *Crime, Causes and Conditions* (New York: McGraw-Hill Book Co., Inc., 1947), pp. 129, 130, 140–45.

of Kretschmer, Sheldon, and others[23] to show that body-build is directly related to personality types, and thus to crime, have failed.[24] Personality is a product of many factors, and body-build is given meaning by the culture in which the individual is reared. A culture may so stigmatize a certain body-build that its possessor is relegated to an inferior position, but he may be so trained as to accept this position willingly and to find happiness in it. Even if a short man feels insecure because of his build and indulges in compensatory behavior, his aggressiveness may lead him to success in the business world or in the field of sports, rather than to a career of crime. In other instances, a person sensitive about his appearance may find comfort in solitude, meditation, and scholarship; or embittered, he may strike back and, putting his small stature to use in burglary, prey upon his tormentors. Body-build may be a very important factor in human behavior, but the evidence indicates that it operates indirectly through the reaction of the person to its meaning in his life.

Physical defects and abnormalities, such as blindness, deafness, baldness, obesity, acne, lameness, crossed eyes, a club foot, a disfiguring birthmark, and large protruding ears, also may be important factors in human behavior. However, like body-build, their action is indirect. Culture may make obesity a mark of distinction and attribute divine powers to the epileptic, but often physical defects and abnormalities handicap the afflicted person in his social relationships and cause serious emotional and personality disturbances. Sexual precocity, for example, may overthrow self-control, induce feelings of guilt, and create personality problems, while feelings of inferiority may force the undersexed person into bravado and aggressive behavior. But even when such disturbances appear, the person's reaction may not be delinquent or criminal as defined by his culture. Instead, his drive for security and recognition may carry him to a place of prominence among his fellows. As a result, persons with all kinds of defects and abnormalities are to be found in both the law-abiding and law-violating groups in our society, although at present we do not know the incidence of such conditions in each of these groups.

During recent years, the endocrine or ductless glands have been given much attention in the study of human behavior. These glands, including the thyroid, pituitary, thymus, adrenal, parathyroid, gonadal, and pineal, pour their secretions, called hormones, directly into the blood stream. Research indicates that the endocrine glands do not function separately,

[23] For a survey of American attempts to relate body build and crime, see Richard M. Snodgrasse, "Crime and the Constitution Human: A Survey," *Journal of Criminal Law, Criminology, and Police Science*, XLII (May–June, 1951), 18–52. See also Hurwitz, pp. 115–38.
[24] See Chapter 9.

but rather as a system, in influencing the development and behavior of human beings. Some authors, like Schlapp and Smith, have taken the extreme position that the vast majority of all criminals are produced by the disturbances of the endocrine glands.[25] Modern criminology, however, has repudiated this view. It is a gross oversimplification of the causal process, for it assumes that the hormonal factor is virtually the sole factor in the genesis of delinquent and criminal behavior and thus disregards the generally accepted fact that human behavior, whether criminal or noncriminal, is the product of a multiplicity of factors. Endocrine disorders undoubtedly cause serious personality disorders and contribute to crime and delinquency.[26] However, the great majority of patients with such disorders never come into conflict with the criminal law, and many criminals and delinquents have normal glands. Obviously, therefore, although endocrinology has much to offer, it cannot provide us with a panacea for law violations.[27]

PERSONALITY CONFLICTS

Personality is all that a person is—the distinctive integration of all his qualities. Thus it is a unique combination of heredity and environment brought to a focus in the individual. In the making of this combination, the threads of heredity, social experience, and culture are inextricably interwoven as the needs of the developing personality are satisfied. At birth, the individual's needs are predominantly organic, but during his early care, nourishment, and protection these needs are greatly modified, and he quickly acquires others which are largely derived from the group and which can be satisfied only through his continuing social relationships. Important among the needs of the personality are those which

[25] See Max G. Schlapp and Edward H. Smith, *The New Criminology* (New York: Boni and Liveright, 1928); Louis Berman, *The Glands Regulating Personality* (New York: The Macmillan Co., 1921); I. G. Cobb, *The Glands of Destiny* (London: William Heinemann, Ltd., 1936).

[26] Thus certain deficiencies, like hypoglycemia (produced by a low level of glucose in the blood) and lack of calcium, cause emotional instability and aggressiveness that may involve the person in such crimes as disorderly conduct, assault and battery, and murder.

[27] Hurwitz, pp. 142–45; Reckless, pp. 12–16; Montagu, 55, 56; R. G. Hoskins, *Endocrinology* (New York: W. W. Norton and Co., Inc., 1941), p. 348; Roger J. Williams, *Biochemical Individuality: The Basis for the Geneto-trophic Concept* (New York: John Wiley and Sons, Inc., 1956); *Biological and Biochemical Bases of Behavior,* eds., Harry F. Harlow and Clinton N. Woolsey (Madison: The University of Wisconsin Press, 1958); National Commission on Law Observance and Enforcement, *Report on the Causes of Crime,* Report No. 13 (Washington, D.C.: Government Printing Office, 1931), Vol. I, pp. 19–36; Edward Podolsky, "The Chemical Brew of Criminal Behavior," *Journal of Criminal Law, Criminology, and Police Science,* XLV (Mar.–Apr., 1955), 675–78.

W. I. Thomas has described as the wish for response, the wish for recognition, the wish for new experience, and the wish for security.[28]

The personality functions in terms of the satisfaction of its needs. It is developed, enriched, and organized, or frustrated, torn by conflicts, distorted, and disorganized as its needs are satisfied or not. The obstacles that prevent or delay the satisfaction of the personality's needs, and thus cause personality conflicts and pain, may be classified into: (1) environmental obstacles, such as poverty, legal restrictions, and the like; and (2) personal obstacles, which in turn may be divided into (a) personal deficiencies, such as feeble-mindedness, blindness, and so on, and (b) wish conflicts, such as the conflict between the wish to fight for one's country and the wish to avoid physical injury. Thus, an automobile accident or the opposition of a parent may compel a boy to postpone his college education, or a deformed foot or the intense desire for academic honors may prevent him from satisfying his wish to engage in athletics. If we are wise, we face our conflicts realistically, and through our own resources or with the help of others, we resolve them on a factual basis. Sometimes, however, even when we fail to do this, the situation changes in such a way as to eliminate the conflict. In other words, "things take care of themselves." A new experience changes our minds about getting that college education we have had to postpone, or a new face makes us forget the girl who jilted us, and so on.

However, many of our conflicts persist, and we continue the struggle to resolve them by employing various mechanisms, such as repression, daydreaming, regression, sublimation, rationalization, compensation, and projection. Thus we find relief in daydreaming when we cannot flee from humdrum work, belittle that which we cannot obtain, blame others for our failures, reduce our feelings of guilt by imagining that others, too, are guilty, compensate for our physical inadequacies by achieving academic distinction, sublimate our pugnacity by playing football, indulge in rationalization and find "good" reasons to justify decisions that we have already made, regress to childhood practices and weep, kick, sulk, or use "baby talk" when adult methods fail, and repress desires by refusing to admit their existence. All these mechanisms are normal devices that are used every day by normal people to lessen tension and to control anxiety, although in many cases the person is completely, or partially, unaware of the fact that he is employing them.[29]

---

28 William I. Thomas, *The Unadjusted Girl* (Boston: Little, Brown and Co., 1923), pp. 1–40.

29 P. M. Lichtenstein and S. M. Small, *A Handbook of Psychiatry* (New York: W. W. Norton and Co., Inc., 1943), pp. 9–24; Lewis R. Wolberg, *The Technique of Psychotherapy* (New York: Grune and Stratton, 1954), pp. 216–29.

But if any of these mechanisms is used to excess, it may begin to distort the personality and push the individual into some form of mental disease. Thus, the habit of escaping from conflict through the phantasies of daydreaming may eventually divorce the person from reality and envelop him in the delusions and hallucinations of a psychosis; the constant blaming of others may blend into the delusions of persecution that torture the paranoiac; extreme compensation may excite the morbid fears and obsessions that sicken and unman the neurotic; and persistent repression may introduce a whole procession of neurotic symptoms, such as sleep-walking, amnesia, and functional paralysis. In fact, as we shall see, in many instances the symptoms of mental disease are merely the distortion and exaggeration of what is considered normal behavior.

Usually the mechanisms for dealing with personality conflicts find expression in law-abiding behavior, but sometimes they lead a person into conflict with the law. Thus in one case, a youth may compensate for his feelings of inferiority by becoming a daring bank robber; in another, the tendency to blame others may cause a man to murder his supposed persecutors; while in a third, rationalization may provide a young woman with the excuses to carry on a career of shoplifting. Simply because such mechanisms lead a person into crime or delinquency does not necessarily mean that he has become mentally ill. On the contrary, they may cause him to obey the law or to violate it without affecting his mental health in any way.

Furthermore, it must be emphasized that the mere possession of certain personality traits does not necessarily result in criminal or delinquent behavior. The problem is far too complex to be unlocked by so simple a key. Aggressiveness, shyness, frankness, disagreeableness, and conscientiousness may find expression in all kinds of behavior, both criminal and noncriminal, and so highly emotional an experience as frustration may not even produce aggressiveness but may be dissipated through mirth and jocularity.[30] In fact, emotional disturbances and personality traits may largely result from, rather than cause, criminal or delinquent behavior. And in all cases, personality traits interact in a functional relationship with many other factors in a process of changing behavior patterns.

Schuessler and Cressey, in an examination of this question, summarized the results of 113 studies in which personality-test scores of delinquents and criminals were compared with the scores of control groups. They concluded that "as often as not the evidence favored the view that personality traits are distributed in the criminal population in about the same way as

[30] Ellsworth Faris, "Some Results of Frustration," *Sociology and Social Research,* XXXI (Nov.–Dec., 1946), 87–92.

in the general population."[31] However, this does not carry the presumption, as Cressey believes, that "the explanation of criminal behavior must be sought in something else than personality traits."[32] What it does mean is that personality traits alone are not the cause of crime, but that in the analysis of causation they must be seen in their functional relationship with one another and with many other factors.

As the individual's personality develops, he assimilates the values of the culture in which he functions; and although he inevitably suffers from personality conflicts, he tends to become law-abiding. Sometimes, however, the obstacles confronting an individual turn him into a career of delinquency or crime. The development of such a career involves the satisfactions of personality needs; but unlike lawful behavior, it is expressed in terms of values that are unacceptable to organized society. Even so, the personality, like the society in which it functions, is never completely organized, containing, as it always does, inconsistent and inharmonious elements. Prison officials, noting this, have often observed that there is always some good in even the worst of men. In fact, the great majority of offenders obey most laws and many experience remorse when they commit crimes.

THE SELF

Self theorists object to the term "personality needs," because they believe that it places too much emphasis on the biological factors, that need psychology differs little from the discredited instinct psychology, that most needs originate solely in social interaction, and that since a need cannot be directly perceived, an explanation in terms of it involves circular reasoning, i.e., the need is inferred from the act and then used to explain the act.[33] Instead of personality needs, they prefer the concept "self," which emphasizes the social and cultural factors and the rationality and purposiveness of human behavior. Although complete agreement regarding the meaning of "self" has not been reached, it is often defined as that organization of qualities which the person attributes to himself.[34]

31 Karl F. Schuessler and Donald R. Cressey, "Personality Characteristics of Criminals," *American Journal of Sociology*, LV (Mar., 1950), 476–84. In this article, Schuessler and Cressey suggest that the Guttman technique may help to determine whether criminals possess attitudes that distinguish them from noncriminals (p. 484). It should be suggested here, however, that the mere shifting of attention from personality traits to attitudes, which are even more elusive, is not going to simplify the problem for the sociologist.

32 Edwin H. Sutherland and Donald R. Cressey, *Principles of Criminology* (Philadelphia: J. B. Lippincott Co., 1955), p. 128.

33 See, for example, Alfred R. Lindesmith and Anselm L. Straus, *Social Psychology* (New York: The Dryden Press, 1956), pp. 267–83, 413–36.

34 See Chapter 9 for a critical analysis of self theory.

The self develops in the process of socialization as the individual learns to play roles and fashion his behavior in accordance with the group's expectations, but it never becomes completely organized, and always, like the personality, contains inconsistent and inharmonious elements. Even so, the individual tends to become the kind of person he conceives himself to be, and acting to defend and strengthen his self-image, he utilizes the various mechanisms described in the previous section to handle the conflicts that threaten this image with about the same possible results that have already been indicated. However, the self theorist sees these mechanisms as being more rational and conscious than does the psychiatrist.

MENTAL ABNORMALITIES

Mental Deficiency. Mental deficiency, sometimes called feeble-mindedness or *amentia,* has been defined in various ways.[35] For our purposes, however, it may be defined as a state of mental retardation or incomplete development, existing from birth or early infancy, as a result of which the person is unable to meet the social expectation of his society.[36] There have also been different classifications of mental deficiency, but on the basis of mental age and intelligence quotient,[37] it may be divided into three levels about as follows:

Level of mental deficiency	Mental age	I.Q.
Idiocy	Under 3 years	Under 20
Imbecility	3 to 7	20 to 50
Moronity	8 to 12	50 to 70

Idiots, on the lowest level of human intelligence, are unable to guard themselves against common physical dangers and are almost completely

[35] A. F. Tredgold, the noted English psychologist, has presented a widely cited definition of mental deficiency. According to him, mental deficiency is "a state of restricted potentiality for, or arrest of, cerebral development, in consequence of which the person affected is incapable at maturity of so adapting himself to his environment or to the requirements of the community as to maintain existence independently of external support" (A. F. Tredgold, *Mental Deficiency* [New York: William Wood and Co., 1915], p. 8).

[36] *Dictionary of Sociology* (New York: The Philosophical Library, 1944), p. 191.

[37] Mental age is a person's level of performance as measured by that expected of persons at various chronological ages. Thus, if a man has a mental age of 10, it means that his general intelligence is equivalent to that of a normal child of this chronological age. The intelligence quotient of a person is derived by dividing his mental age by his chronological age and multiplying by 100 (to remove decimal places). However, the maximum chronological age used in obtaining the intelligence quotient is set at about 14 to 16, since the evidence indicates that general intelligence tends to reach maturity at about these ages. The intelligence quotients for the three levels of mental deficiency vary somewhat in different classifications.

dependent upon others. However, there are not very many idiots, and their average life expectancy is less than twenty years. Imbeciles, with mental ages at maturity of from 3 to 7, are incapable of managing themselves or their affairs, although some can be taught to do simple tasks under supervision. Often they are physically strong enough to be dangerous when provoked or frustrated. Morons, with mental ages at maturity of about 8 to 12, often have a normal appearance and blend imperceptibly into the borderline groups. Although there is considerable variation among them, in general they require care, supervision, and control for their own protection or for the protection of others.[38]

The problem of mental deficiency is a complex one, and this needs to be clearly recognized in any discussion regarding its relationship with crime and delinquency. There is no sharp line of demarcation between the levels of mental deficiency or between mental deficiency and normal intelligence, and there are mentally deficient persons who are also suffering from mental diseases or disorders. Furthermore, intelligence tests do not separate hereditary and environmental influences, and intelligence quotients have proved to be modifiable. Besides, the contention that almost all feeble-mindedness is inherited has been generally abandoned, and it is now estimated that only 30 to 50 per cent of the cases are of hereditary origin.

In the field of criminology, interest is chiefly centered on the moron, since idiots and imbeciles, who are easily recognizable, are usually subject to such care and supervision as to render them harmless to society. Even morons, apparently, do not constitute a major law-enforcement problem; the available evidence, although admittedly inadequate, indicates that their conflicts with the law tend to involve such crimes as larceny, vagrancy, drunkenness, and the less serious sexual offenses. Often the moronic offender gets into difficulties because he is confused, emotionally unstable, or easily led and exploited by more intelligent companions. The case of Clara is a typical one. When she was sixteen, Clara, together with her brother and two other boys, was arrested for shoplifting. Although the boys were sent to a training school, she was placed under the care of her aunt. This arrangement, however, proved to be unsatisfactory. Clara was seduced by a neighbor and drifted into prostitution. Her sex experiences were varied and extensive; she became the mother

[38] E. O. Lewis, "Mental Deficiency and Criminal Behavior," in *Mental Abnormality and Crime,* eds. L. Radzinowicz and J. W. C. Turner (English Studies in Criminal Science [London: Macmillan and Co., Ltd., 1949]), Vol. II, pp. 93–104; W. Wallace Weaver, *Social Problems* (New York: William Sloane Associates, 1951), pp. 178–87; Richard L. Masland, Seymour B. Sarason, Thomas Gladwin, *Mental Subnormality* (New York: Basic Books, Inc., 1958).

of three children, whose paternity was unknown. At the time she was committed to a reformatory for women on a charge of larceny, she was found to have both syphilis and gonorrhea. Later she was transferred to a training school for the feeble-minded.

There are no reliable, comprehensive statistics on the extent of delinquency or criminality among the mentally deficient. Although early studies led to the conclusion that feeble-mindedness was the major cause of crime and delinquency, the work of Murchison, Tulchin, Zeleny, and others helped to correct this misconception. The evidence now indicates that only a small proportion of the feeble-minded are delinquent or criminal, and that offenders and the general population have about the same distribution of intelligence levels.[39] In 1928 and 1929, Sutherland analyzed about 350 studies on intelligence and crime and showed that the proportion of delinquents and criminals diagnosed as feeble-minded had decreased from more than 50 per cent in the average study made in the period from 1910 to 1914 to 20 per cent in the period from 1925 to 1928.[40] After an exhaustive analysis of a large number of studies, Chassel concluded that "there is a direct and marked relation between morality and intellect among feeble-minded groups, and a direct and low relation between morality and intellect among delinquent groups, in this country and abroad."[41] More recently, Kennedy compared 256 morons and a control group of 129 nonmorons and found that the morons had higher arrest and recidivism rates. However, the family members of the morons, also, had a higher arrest rate than those of the nonmorons.[42] Consequently, the family associations of the morons may have been more influential than their low-grade intelligence in giving them the higher arrest rate.[43]

Like the physical characteristics, personality conflicts, and personality traits, intelligence[44] is a factor in criminal behavior and may be the major one in a particular case, but it is never the only one. Mental deficiency imposes a serious economic and social handicap upon a person, often exposing him to exploitation and ridicule; but whether the resultant be-

[39] For a survey of some of the studies on intelligence and delinquency, see Harry Manuel Shulman, "Intelligence and Delinquency," *Journal of Criminal Law and Criminology*, XLI (Mar.–Apr., 1951), 763–81.

[40] Edwin H. Sutherland, "Mental Deficiency and Crime," in *Social Attitudes*, ed. Kimball Young (New York: Henry Holt and Co., Inc., 1931), pp. 357–75.

[41] Clara Frances Chassell, *The Relation Between Morality and Intellect* (New York: Teachers College, Columbia University, Bureau of Publications, 1935), p. 134.

[42] Ruby Jo Reeves Kennedy, *The Social Adjustment of Morons in a Connecticut City* (Hartford: Governor's Commission to Study the Human Resources of the State of Connecticut, 1948). See also Austin E. Grigg, "Criminal Behavior of Mentally Retarded Adults," *American Journal of Mental Deficiency*, LII (Apr., 1948), 370–74.

[43] See Sutherland and Cressey, *op. cit.*, p. 119.

[44] The concept of intelligence has been defined in various ways, but there is agreement that general intelligence is the capacity to learn from experience.

havior is crime or delinquency will depend upon the interaction of many factors.[45]

Mental Diseases. Mental disease, or mental disorder, is a state of mental unbalance or derangement which prevents a person from assuming responsibility for his own support or causes him to be a positive menace to the health and safety of the community.[46] Unlike mental deficiency, which implies a lack, retardation, or incompleteness of mental development, mental disease refers to a mind that has developed normally, almost always to maturity, but has become disordered or deranged. However, it is possible for a mentally deficient person to become mentally diseased, and there are mentally diseased persons who have deteriorated from the level of normal intelligence to that of a moron. The concept of mental disease should be distinguished also from insanity, which is a legal term. Insanity refers to any defect or disease of the mind which renders a person incapable of entertaining a criminal intent. However, a person is insane only when he has been declared to be so by the law on the basis of certain legal tests. Therefore a person may be judged to be sane even though he has been diagnosed as mentally diseased by psychiatrists.

The mental diseases may be classified into two major groups: (1) the psychoses and (2) the psychoneuroses or neuroses. The terminology of psychiatry and abnormal psychology, however, is not entirely consistent, and the categories employed are overlapping and indefinite. Moreover, according to many psychiatrists, the distinction between the normal and the abnormal in mental functioning is largely one of degree, most normal persons having some characteristics which might be termed abnormal. In fact, say these psychiatrists, human beings may be thought of as being distributed along a scale of adjustment ranging from the normal through the milder types of mental disorder, called psychoneuroses, to the most serious types, called psychoses.[47]

The Psychoses. The psychoses are the forms of mental disease in which there is the most severe disturbance of the personality. A psychotic person loses contact, completely or partially, with the world of reality and manifests such a divergence from the normal as to require medical or even special institutional care. However, the psychotic may not manifest his

[45] Lloyd N. Yepsen, "The Psychologist Looks at Crime," *The Annals of the American Academy of Political and Social Science*, CCXVII (Sept., 1941), 65, 66; National Commission on Law Observance and Enforcement, 37–52.

[46] *Dictionary of Sociology*, p. 191.

[47] Angus Macniven, "Psychoses and Criminal Responsibility," *Mental Abnormality and Crime*, pp. 8, 9; Kimball Young, *Personality and Problems of Adjustment* (New York: Appleton-Century-Crofts, Inc., 1940), pp. 708–10. See also American Psychiatric Association, *Diagnostic and Statistical Manual, Mental Disorders* (Washington, D.C.: American Psychiatric Association, 1952); Ruth L. Munroe, *Schools of Psychoanalytic Thought* (New York: The Dryden Press, 1955), pp. 82–84.

abnormality continuously. He may at times act quite rationally or become irrational in only certain situations or on certain subjects.

The psychoses may be divided into: (1) the psychoses caused by, or associated with, an impairment of the brain, such as that resulting from injury, infection, degenerative changes of tissue, hereditary weakness, and so on; and (2) the psychoses without clearly defined physical cause of structural change in the brain, which until recent years were generally referred to as "functional" psychoses. Even if no physical cause or impairment of the brain can be discovered in a mental disease, the factor of heredity cannot be entirely ruled out. Since some individuals survive stresses that crush others, the difference may be due in part to inherited differences in ability to withstand the strains of life.

Among the most common psychoses caused by, or associated with, an impairment of the brain are epilepsy, paresis, psychoses with cerebral arteriosclerosis, and toxic psychoses. *Epilepsy,* which remains one of the least understood of the psychoses, is not a specific clinical entity but a group of disorders. The most common feature of these is the recurring convulsion or seizure, which may appear in one of two forms: the major attack, or *grand mal,* and the minor attack, or *petit mal.* A state of automatism may follow the fit, and during this the person performs acts of which he has afterwards no recollection. The epileptic person tends to be sensitive, egocentric, and childish in his emotional attachments, and while in his state of automatism he may engage in indecent behavior or even commit acts of violence, such as murder or rape.

Paresis, or *general paralysis,* results from the infection of the central nervous system by the *Spirochaeta pallida,* the organism causing syphilis. Usually the symptoms include lack of concentration, lapses of memory, enfeeblement of the mental powers, childishness, and gross disorder of conduct out of keeping with the person's character. The offenses committed by the paretic person are usually unpremeditated and manifest a lack of intelligence and judgment. Thus, the crime may be the brazen and unconcealed theft of a very inexpensive article or the reckless forging of checks in an absurd display of imaginary wealth.

In the *psychoses with cerebral arteriosclerosis,* or hardening of the arteries of the brain, there are loss of memory, mental confusion, emotional instability, and marked irritability. Sometimes the person suffers from transient persecutory delusions accompanied by fits of rage, during which he may commit acts of violence against himself or others. In other cases, persons who have occupied positions of trust and prominence may childishly squander the funds of clients and investors.

Toxic psychoses are caused by toxins or poisonous substances in the body. Common among these disorders are the alcoholic psychoses, which are characterized by loss of inhibitions, delusions and hallucinations, hysterical rages, physical or verbal violence, and decline of mental activity and physical strength. However, it should be noted that there are a number of other toxic psychoses caused by such poisonous substances as lead, arsenic, carbon monoxide, narcotic drugs, and toxins produced by the body itself.[48]

Important among the psychoses without clearly defined physical cause or structural change in the brain are schizophrenia, manic-depressive psychosis, paranoia, and involutional melancholia. *Schizophrenia,*[49] often called dementia praecox, because it usually makes its appearance during youth or early adulthood, is characterized chiefly by a gradual withdrawal into a world of fantasy and a growing incoherence of thought and speech, ending in the disintegration of the personality. Four major types of schizophrenia are (1) simple schizophrenia, (2) hebephrenia, (3) catatonia, and (4) paranoid schizophrenia. These types overlap so much that it is often difficult to determine which one is present in a particular case. *Simple schizophrenia* involves a general mental retardation accompanied by shiftlessness, apathy, neglectfulness, and detachment. *Hebephrenia,* which usually begins before the age of twenty, is marked especially by silliness and incongruity of actions. *Catatonia* is characterized by peculiar postures, waxy rigidity, and negativism. *Paranoid schizophrenia,* which usually begins later in life than the other types, has delusional ideas as its most prominent symptom. These delusions may be persecutory or grandiose, and often they are extremely bizarre in character.

Schizophrenia may result in any type of antisocial behavior. It tends to make the person careless of his social obligations and inclined to satisfy his immediate desires without regard for the welfare of others or his own safety. Often he is unable to suggest any reason for his actions and may explain that he acted under some mystical influence or at the command of some hallucinatory voice. Believing that he is God, he may not hesitate to punish or even kill anyone who offends him or attempts to thwart his plans. However, the majority of persons suffering from this disorder are quiet, timid, and apathetic. When the schizophrene commits a crime, his offense is often a minor one which arises from his inability to cope with his problems or to discharge his social obligations. Thus, unable to compete on equal terms with others, he may drift into the ranks of the permanently unemployed and become a vagrant, beggar, peddler, or petty thief.

The *manic-depressive psychosis* is characterized by alternating periods of depression or melancholia and periods of mental exaltation or mania.

[48] Macniven, pp. 40–49; Arthur Burton and Robert E. Harris (eds.), *Case Histories in Clinical and Abnormal Psychology* (New York: Harper and Bros., 1947), pp. 307–80.

[49] The term "schizophrenia" means literally a splitting of the mind. The disorder is so called because it involves the development of two or more "selves."

Unlike schizophrenia, in which the chances of recovery are exceedingly poor, the manic-depressive psychosis often responds to treatment. This mental disorder may find expression in a great variety of crimes, ranging from simple breach of the peace to murder. During the period of mania, violence and destructiveness are common symptoms, but since the person's aberration is so obvious, he is usually restrained before he can do serious harm. On the other hand, during periods of depression, although the person's behavior is usually law-abiding, very serious crimes are not infrequent. Overwhelmed by melancholia, the psychotic may commit suicide or assault and kill others. Thus a man in a state of depression, believing that he is financially ruined, may kill his family in order to save them from misery and disgrace.

Involutional melancholia, which occurs in late middle life or in the presenile period, has certain characteristics which distinguish it from the depressive period of the manic-depressive psychosis and so is regarded by many psychiatrists as a distinct clinical entity. It is characterized by intense anxiety, apprehension, painful agitation and restlessness, delusions of sinfulness and unworthiness, and fear of illness and disease. Suicidal impulses are present in many cases, and sometimes acts of violence may be committed against others.

Paranoia, a rare type of psychosis, is marked by delusions of grandeur and persecution. It develops gradually over a long period, and the delusions are well systematized. However, hallucinations do not occur, and the memory, intellectual processes, and the essential core of the personality are preserved. Persons suffering from this disorder often appear to be shy, timid, and sensitive, but their outward appearance conceals feelings of self-importance and a desire to lead and dominate. The paranoiac is always ready to attribute envy, enmity, and hostility to those with whom he comes into contact and to feel unjustly treated when he does not receive praise and recognition.

The crimes of the paranoiac are usually the direct result of his delusions. Offenses against the person may be caused by an impulse to punish alleged persecutors or to protect the government from supposed tyrants and demagogues. The crime may be premeditated and carefully planned or it may be highly impulsive. Thus, a paranoiac, enraged by his wife's denials of unfaithfulness, may impulsively strike and kill her or he may carefully plan the murder and slowly kill her with small doses of poison. Offenses against property may be motivated by fear or revenge as when the deluded person burns or defaces a neighbors's house in the hope that the imagined persecution will cease. When the nature of paranoia is taken into consideration, it is surprising that the deluded person does not commit more crimes of violence. However, many paranoiacs are essentially law-abiding persons and do not resort to violence until legal means of redress appear to have been exhausted. On the other hand, their persistent efforts to secure "justice" may cause them to be charged with various minor offenses such as disorderly conduct and contempt of court.[50]

The Psychoneuroses. The psychoneuroses, or neuroses, are those forms of mental disease which tend to make the person less efficient socially and personally but usually do not incapacitate him to the point where he must be cared for or institutionalized. They do not constitute a sharply defined clinical entity but, on the contrary, blend into the psychoses on one side and normal behavior on the other. In general, according to many psychiatrists, the psychoneuroses are not incipient psychoses and do not develop into these more serious forms of mental disorder. The neurotic does not lose touch with reality and does not suffer from delusions or hallucinations. Although he may laugh and cry immoderately and indulge in erratic behavior, he does not lose control of his reasoning powers and recognizes his eccentricities for what they are. Like anybody else, the neurotic person is trying to adjust to the situations of life, and the type of person who seeks to do this through a neurosis is not likely to suffer also from a psychosis.

Until recent years, the most widely recognized classification of psychoneuroses consisted of the three categories of neurasthenia, psychasthenia, and hysteria; but today, there is a tendency to break these down into a number of subdivisions. Even so, for our purpose, which is merely to indicate some of the types of psychoneuroses, the threefold classification will suffice. It must be emphasized, however, that the categories are not mutually exclusive and simply signify certain recurrent patterns of symptoms commonly appearing together. All the psychoneuroses are generally believed to be functional, rather than organic, in origin.

Neurasthenia is characterized by exaggerated feelings of fatigue, a diminished capacity for work, and often a pronounced sensitiveness to light, noises, and other external stimuli. The neurasthenic tends to be irritable, depressed, pessimistic, and worried about his health.

Psychasthenia is marked by anxieties, morbid fears, obsessions, doubts, and compulsions. The fears, or phobias, may be so great as to block certain actions which seem quite normal to others. Included among these fears are *acrophobia* (fear of high places), *agoraphobia* (fear of open places), and *claustrophobia* (fear of closed places). The compulsions, or manias, may take such forms as kleptomania (compulsive stealing), dipsomania (compulsive and excessive drinking of alcoholic beverages),

[50] Macniven, pp. 8–39; H. Warren Dunham, "The Schizophrene and Criminal Behavior," *American Sociological Review*, IV (June, 1939), 352–61; Edward A. Strecker, *Fundamentals of Psychiatry* (Philadelphia: J. B. Lippincott Co., 1943), pp. 91–148.

and so on. Since the term "psychasthenia" covers so broad a field, it has been generally abandoned in favor of more specific terms such as "anxiety neurosis," "compulsion neurosis," etc., which refer to abnormalities formerly included under the older term.

Hysteria has a wide variety of symptoms, some of which are often called by their own special names; but all the maladies covered by this term have in common the element of dissociation, which may be defined as a state in which certain activities are no longer integrated with the rest of the personality. The hysterical person may suffer from a partial or total loss of vision or hearing, from paralysis of various muscles, from muscular spasms, or from mild or extensive lapses of memory. However, in its technical sense, the term "hysteria" does not mean excessive or uncontrolled emotion, which is the meaning assigned to it by popular usage.

The psychoneuroses are caused by emotional and mental conflicts, the existence of which may be unknown to the person involved. The neurotic symptom is a compromise of some sort between unexpressed thoughts and the repressive forces of the personality, principally the conscience and self-regard. Since the symptom does not fully satisfy the unexpressed thoughts, the conflict persists, with the symptom appearing over and over again in about the same form.

Examples of conflicts which cause psychoneurotic symptoms are not difficult to find. In some cases, these symptoms provide a means of escape from the conflict. Thus the soldier torn between his sense of duty and his desire for self-preservation may find a respectable refuge in hysterical paralysis, or the child with aggressive impulses against his parent may develop a fear of knives, the means whereby the antisocial impulse may be carried into effect. In other cases, the symptom may provide a substitute for an act which morality forbids. A young woman who feels guilty because she entertains murderous thoughts against her invalid mother may inflict an injury on herself that she would have liked to inflict on her mother. In still other cases the symptom may serve as a form of revenge. A girl who feels neglected by her mother may develop an abdominal pain by which she keeps her mother at home and in this way achieves revenge for the supposed ill-treatment.

Most psychoneurotic persons conduct themselves in a socially acceptable manner, but the conflicts in the personalities of some may find expression in acts of delinquency or crime. When this happens, such acts are symptoms in that they represent compromises between the forces at war in the mentally disordered persons. The compulsive stealing of a young woman may be a defense against a desire for premarital sex relations, which for her is even less permissible behavior than stealing; or the brawling and disorderly conduct of a young man may be a compensation for his feelings of inferiority and timidity, which torture and embarrass him. It is also possible that some delinquent and criminal acts may be the expression of a desire for punishment, the conscience apparently allowing the act for the sake of the satisfaction to be obtained through expiation for the deed at the hands of the law.[51]

Psychopathic Personality. Some mentally diseased persons cannot be classified as either psychotic or psychoneurotic, and to these the term "psychopathic personality" has been attached.[52] The psychopath does not have the obsessions, compulsions, anxieties, and morbid fears produced by the conflicts in the personality of the psychoneurotic; and he differs from the psychotic in that he is not divorced from reality, and so does not have delusions and hallucinations. Since the term "psychopathic personality" has been applied to a wide assortment of individuals, it is not surprising that the psychopath has been described by a great variety of words, including cruel, defiant, suspicious, undisciplined, undependable, unstable, egocentric, vindictive, primitive, and ruthless.[53] Psychiatrists, however, now seem to agree that the core of the concept "psychopathic personality" is a permanent, major abnormality of character as a result of which the affected person is lacking in conscience.[54]

Nevertheless, the psychopathic personality has become a wastebasket category, into which have been thrown all kinds of mental disorders that defy more precise classification, and a convenient tag that can be hung upon criminals whose behavior cannot otherwise be "explained." Indeed, often it is used by psychiatrists and others as a label to stigmatize a person for the values that he holds. Thieves, rapists, embezzlers, murderers, sex perverts, vagrants, prostitutes, swindlers, forgers, counterfeiters, burglars, gamblers—all have been called psychopathic. Under the impact of this loose usage, the concept has fallen into such disrepute

[51] R. D. Gillespie, "Psychoneurosis and Criminal Behavior," *Mental Abnormality and Crime*, pp. 72–92; Young, pp. 708–14; Strecker, pp. 148–65.

[52] The term "constitutional psychopathic inferior" was formerly used to refer to these mentally diseased persons. However, since this term implies that the abnormality is inborn or organic, an implication which psychiatry now tends to reject, it has been largely replaced by the term "psychopathic personality." Even so, some psychiatrists, wishing to emphasize the view that the condition is caused by environmental factors, prefer the term "sociopathic personality."

[53] For a detailed case analysis of the psychopathic offender, see Robert Lindner, *Rebel Without Cause* (New York: Grune and Stratton, 1944); and Benjamin Karpman, *Case Studies in the Psychopathology of Crime* (New York: The Mental Science Publishing Co., 1939).

[54] D. K. Henderson, "Psychopathic Constitution and Criminal Behavior," *Mental Abnormality and Crime*, 105–21; Lichtenstein and Small, pp. 87–94; Burton and Harris, pp. 431–72; Hurwitz, pp. 174–85; Benjamin Karpman, "A Yardstick for Measuring Psychopathy," *Federal Probation*, X (Oct.–Dec., 1946), 26–31; Nathaniel Thornton, "The Relation Between Crime and Psychopathic Personality," *Journal of Criminal Law, Criminology, and Police Science*, XLII (July–Aug., 1951), 199–204.

that some psychiatrists believe that it is meaningless and should be discarded. Others, while admitting that it is too broad, insist that it should be retained and broken down into more specific subtypes. Regardless of its future, as the concept now stands it is of little value to the criminologist.[55]

Incidence of Mental Disease in Criminals. We do not know how many persons are mentally diseased or how many mentally diseased persons are delinquent or criminal. In fact, there is considerable disagreement among psychiatrists regarding the nature of the mental diseases, their causes and classification, and the methods of diagnosis. Furthermore, the mental disorders are not clearly defined entities and much of the content of psychiatry cannot be scientifically substantiated.

However, we do have some evidence derived from studies of prisoners, and this indicates that a very small percentage of prisoners are clearly psychotic and that even the percentages of psychoneurotic and psychopathic prisoners are not very large. It is true that certain psychiatrists have insisted that a very large proportion of criminals are psychopathic, but this extreme view has not been supported by the best studies in the field. Bromberg and Thompson report that, of a total of 9,958 prisoners appearing before the Court of General Sessions of New York City and examined between 1932 and 1935, inclusive, only 1.5 per cent were psychotic, 6.9 per cent were psychoneurotic, 6.9 per cent were psychopathic personalities, and 2.4 per cent were feeble-minded. Thus, 82.3 per cent of these prisoners were classified as normal, although many of them had mild personality defects which had contributed to their criminality.[56] Schilder states that, of the convicted felons examined in the clinic of the same court in 1937, only 1.6 per cent were psychotic, 4.2 per cent were neurotic, 7.3 per cent were psychopathic personalities, 3.1 per cent were feeble-minded, and 83.8 per cent were normal.[57] Sutherland concludes that "psychiatric examinations of criminals on admission

---

[55] For a detailed analysis of the use of the term "psychopath" and its synonyms, see Hulsey Cason, "The Psychopath and the Psychopathic," *Journal of Criminal Psychopathology*, IV (Jan., 1943), 522–27. See also Hulsey Cason, "The Symptoms of the Psychopath," *United States Public Health Reports*, LXI (Dec. 20, 1946), 1833–53; Hulsey Cason and M. J. Pescor, "A Comparative Study of Recidivists and Non-recidivists Among Psychopathic Federal Offenders," *Journal of Criminal Law and Criminology*, XXXVII (Sept.–Oct., 1946), 236–38; Edwin H. Sutherland, "The Sexual Psychopath Laws," *Journal of Criminal Law and Criminology*, XL (Jan.–Feb., 1950), 543–54; Harrison G. Gough, "A Sociological Theory of Psychopathy," *American Journal of Sociology*, LIII (Mar., 1948), 359–66.

[56] W. Bromberg and C. B. Thompson, "The Relation of Psychosis, Mental Defect, and Personality Types to Crime," *Journal of Criminal Law and Criminology*, XXVIII (May–June, 1937), 70–89.

[57] Paul Schilder, "The Cure of Criminals and Prevention of Crime," *Journal of Criminal Psychopathology*, II (Oct., 1940), 152.

to state prisons generally show not more than 5 per cent to be psychotic, and in many institutions, less than 1 per cent." He also adds that the psychotics seldom constitute more than 5 per cent of the offenders admitted to jails and houses of correction and that many studies put the figure at about 2 per cent.[58]

Although the incidence of mental disease in criminals is unknown, several other points have been clearly established. Mental disease does not inevitably cause crime or delinquency. Some mentally disordered persons do come into conflict with the law, but many others do not; the great majority of delinquents and criminals, like the great majority of law-abiding persons, can be classified as normal.[59] Like all the other personal factors, mental disease operates in interaction with other factors to influence a person's behavior. In many cases, the conduct of a mentally diseased person is modified by his prior training, education, and experience. Thus, a person who is aggressive may show this trait in an exaggerated form when he becomes mentally ill, or the early moral training of a mentally diseased person may restrain him from engaging in criminal behavior.

Furthermore, what is considered normal in a society is determined in part by its culture; and divergent behavior that is tolerated or even honored in one place may be considered evidence of a serious mental disease in another. Moreover, some mental disorders are characteristic of certain societies and appear to reflect distinctive cultural influences. For example, a society may put great emphasis on fighting ability, with the result that its most common mental disease is the anxiety neurosis found among youths who realize that they can never become competent warriors. In addition, a society torn by culture conflicts can subject its members to tremendous strains and thus increase the incidence of mental disease.[60] All this indicates that the soundest approach to an understanding of mental disease as a cause of crime and delinquency lies in the recognition that all behavior, normal as well as abnormal, is a product of the interaction of the personal and environmental factors, and that it reflects the individual's efforts to achieve adjustment in terms of his culture.

[58] Sutherland, *Principles of Criminology*, p. 107. See also Sol Levy, R. H. Southcombe, John R. Cranor, and R. A. Freeman, "The Outstanding Personality Factors Among the Population of a State Penitentiary," *Proceedings of the American Prison Association, 1950*, pp. 269–76.

[59] Some psychiatrists hold the thesis that criminality is without exception symptomatic of abnormal mental states and is an expression of them. For a presentation of this point of view, see Benjamin Karpman, "Criminality, Insanity and the Law," *Journal of Criminal Law and Criminology*, XXXIX (Jan.–Feb., 1949), 584–605.

[60] Karen Horney, *The Neurotic Personality of Our Time* (New York: W. W. Norton and Co., Inc., 1937), pp. 281–90.

12

Environmental Factors

THE GEOGRAPHICAL ENVIRONMENT

Since the beginning of time, men have gazed in awe and wonderment at the manifestations of the geographical environment and speculated regarding its influence upon the origin and development of society. Few have denied the importance of such factors as climate, temperature, seasons, sunshine, rainfall, floods, droughts, soil, minerals, topography, altitude, land and water formations, latitude, and longitude; some have even advocated geographical determinism, finding the explanation for human history in the operation of geographical factors.

Today, however, geographical determinism has little support. Obviously, man as an organism adapts himself to the geographical environment and is ultimately dependent upon it. But man's adaptation is a creative rather than a passive one, bringing the world of nature increasingly under his control, and the geographical environment exerts its influence in interaction with the biological, social, and cultural factors. Geography offers its resources, but it does not determine which of these shall be used; and man's ingenuity can work wonders within the limits that it imposes. Thus, although the geography of a region remains constant, its culture may change tremendously, and two or more societies may develop entirely different cultures while existing side by side in the same geographical environment.

This, of course, does not mean that the geographical environment is unimportant or that the criminologist can disregard the role that it plays in human affairs. In fact, the evidence from the best available sources, both in this country and abroad, clearly shows that crime rates vary according to definite seasonal and spatial patterns, which thus appear to reflect the influence of the geographical environment. For example, crimes against the person tend to increase in the summer, while crimes against property tend to reach their peak during the winter months; and in the United States crimes of violence have a definite regional distribution, the highest rates for murder and assault appearing, year after year, in the southern states.[1] On the other hand, although the New England states have low rates of crimes against the person, they also have comparatively low rates of crimes against property, and a number of investigations of non-European countries have found crimes of violence to be fewer in particularly hot, moist climates.[2]

In view of such apparent contradictions, one must conclude that much of the influence of the geographical environment in the causation of crime and delinquency is indirect, that is, it operates through the social, cultural, economic, and other conditions which it helps to create. Thus, in the case of the seasonal fluctuations noted above, during the winter months when crimes against property climb to their maximum, darkness provides a better cloak for illegal activities and coldness aggravates the need of money, while during the summer time, when crimes against the person reach their greatest proportions, pleasant weather invites larger outdoor gatherings, increases social contacts, and thereby enhances the possibility of personal encounters. But considerations such as these cannot explain all the spatial and seasonal fluctuations in crime rates. There is still the possibility that sometimes the geographical environment plays a primary role in the causation of crime and delinquency by operating directly upon the human organism, disturbing its physiological balance, creating irritations, provoking certain moods, and so on. This possibility offers a challenge to scholarship and research, and conclusions regarding it must await further study.[3]

SOCIAL DISORGANIZATION

As we have explained in Chapters 3 and 9, men in their creative adjustment to the geographical environment and to one another develop rules and standards by which they regulate their behavior and facilitate the satisfaction of their needs in terms of a generally accepted set of

[1] See the annual bulletins of the *Uniform Crime Reports*, published by the Federal Bureau of Investigation. For a discussion of the seasonal fluctuations of crime in the United States, see Chapter 4.

[2] Stephan Hurwitz, *Criminology* (London: George Allen and Unwin, Ltd., 1952), pp. 245–47.

[3] Joseph Cohen, "The Geography of Crime," *The Annals of the American Academy of Political and Social Science*, CCXVII (Sept., 1941), 29–37; Hurwitz, pp. 247–52; G. Aschaffenburg, *Crime and Its Repression* (Boston: Little, Brown and Co., 1913), pp. 16–30; Manfred Curry, "The Relationship of Weather Conditions, Facial Characteristics, and Crime," *Journal of Criminal Law and Criminology*, XXXIX (July–Aug., 1948), 253–61; Gerhard J. Falk, "The Influence of the Seasons on the Crime Rate," *Journal of Criminal Law, Criminology, and Police Science*, XLIII (July-Aug., 1952), 199–213; Lyle W. Shannon, "The Spatial Distribution of Criminal Offenses by States," *Journal of Criminal Law, Criminology, and Police Science*, XLV (Sept.–Oct., 1954), 264–73.

values. But social change tends to disrupt social relationships and to inject conflicting values. Unless the community or society makes compensating adjustments, the influence of the social rules declines, social disorganization eventually breaks through, and culture divergence, culture conflict, ineffective group controls, and divisive social processes operate as important factors in the rise of crime, delinquency, and other social problems.

Social disorganization manifests itself in various forms. Thus, it may be temporary and spectacular, as in such a catastrophe as a flood, earthquake, or fire; dramatic and pervasive as in a war,[4] or chronic and enervating as in a slum area or in an economic depression. But regardless of the form that it assumes, it touches all aspects of social life, transmitting its repercussions throughout the entire network of relationships that tend to bind a community or a society into a cohesive unit. In the following discussion, therefore, we must remember that social groups and social institutions interact in a functional relationship and that each not only reflects, but also augments, the social organization or disorganization in which it is immersed.

THE ECOLOGY OF CRIME AND DELINQUENCY

Urban Variations. Crime and delinquency rates vary from nation to nation, region to region, area to area, and neighborhood to neighborhood. In the United States, sociologists, using the ecological method, have been especially concerned with the variations within urban communities. Clifford Shaw and his associates, who have made the most important ecological studies of urban crime and delinquency, intensively analyzed the statistics of juvenile delinquency in Chicago. Their major conclusions may be summarized as follows:

1. The rates of delinquency vary widely from one neighborhood to another.

---

[4] For the effects of war on crime and delinquency in the United States, see Edward E. Schwartz, "Statistics on Juvenile Delinquency in the United States," *The Annals of the American Academy of Political and Social Science*, CCLXI (Jan., 1949), 9–20; I. Richard Perlman, "The Meaning of Juvenile Delinquency Statistics," *Federal Probation*, XIII (Sept., 1949), 63–67; Martin H. Neumeyer, "Delinquency Trends in Wartime," *Sociology and Social Research*, XXIX (Mar.–Apr., 1945), 262–75; Walter C. Reckless, "The Impact of War on Crime, Delinquency, and Prostitution," *American Journal of Sociology*, XLVIII (Nov., 1942), 378–86; Edwin H. Sutherland, "Crime," in *American Society in Wartime*, ed. William F. Ogburn (Chicago: University of Chicago Press, 1943), pp. 185–206; Marshall B. Clinard, *The Black Market* (New York: Rinehart and Co., Inc., 1952); Frank E. Hartung, "White-Collar Offenses in the Wholesale Meat Industry in Detroit," *American Journal of Sociology*, LVI (July, 1950), 25–34; Harry Willbach, "Recent Crimes and the Veterans," *Journal of Criminal Law and Criminology*, XXXVIII (Jan.–Feb., 1948), 501–8. For a discussion of human behavior under stress, see *Man and Society in Disaster*, eds. George W. Baker and Dwight W. Chapman (New York: Basic Books, Inc., 1962).

2. The highest rates tend to be near the central business district and large industrial areas and to decrease from the center of the city outward.

3. The areas of high rates have had high rates for a long time.

4. The racial and nationality composition of the population in areas of high rates changed almost completely over a period of several decades, while the relative rates of delinquents in these areas remained virtually unchanged.

5. Like the delinquency rate for the entire population, those of the various nationality groups tend to decrease from the center of the city outward.[5]

These conclusions regarding juvenile delinquency have been supported by studies of other American cities, and crime rates have been shown to have the same general characteristics.[6] Sociologists, therefore, have arrived at this generalization: Urban crime and delinquency rates in the United States tend to be highest near the central business district and heavily industrialized areas and to decrease from the center of the city outward. The areas having the highest rates of crime and delinquency, which Shaw called "delinquency areas," are characterized by physical deterioration, congested but decreasing population, economic insecurity, poor housing, low standards of living, family disintegration, racial and national heterogeneity, high rates of population movement, truancy, infant mortality, mental disorder and tuberculosis, conflicting cultural standards, little concerted action to solve common problems, and other such conditions which are symptomatic of the decline of the neighborhood as an agency of social control. In short, these are areas of

[5] Clifford R. Shaw and Henry D. McKay, *Social Factors in Juvenile Delinquency,* Report No. 13, Vol. II of the reports of the National Commission on Law Observance and Enforcement (Washington, D.C.: Government Printing Office, 1931), pp. 23–59, 140–88. See also Clifford R. Shaw, *Delinquency Areas* (Chicago: University of Chicago Press, 1929).

[6] Clifford R. Shaw and Henry D. McKay, *Juvenile Delinquency and Urban Areas* (Chicago: University of Chicago Press, 1942); R. C. White, "The Relation of Felonies to Environmental Factors in Indianapolis," *Social Forces,* X (May, 1932), 498–509; Calvin F. Schmid, "Urban Crime Areas: Part I," *American Sociological Review,* XXV (Aug., 1960), 527–42; *ibid.,* "Urban Crime Areas: Part II," *American Sociological Review,* XXV (Oct., 1960), 655–78. Not all studies, however, support the contention that the delinquency rate steadily declines from the center of the urban area to its periphery. See, for example, Bernard Lander, *Towards an Understanding of Juvenile Delinquency* (New York: Columbia University Press, 1954). In his study, Lander found that the delinquency rate in Baltimore decreased irregularly from the center of the city and tended to remain constant near the periphery. A study by Chilton, however, does not convincingly support Lander's conclusion that delinquency is more closely related to anomie than to economic characteristics of an area, but they do suggest that delinquency is related to transiency, poor housing, and certain economic variables (Roland J. Chilton, "Continuity in Delinquency Area Research: A Comparison of Studies for Baltimore, Detroit, and Indianapolis," *American Sociological Review,* XXIX [Feb., 1964], 71–83).

marked social disorganization,[7] and it is in this fact that the sociologist finds the major explanation of their high delinquency and crime rates. In his opinion, the environmental rather than the personal factors predominate in the causation of crime and delinquency in the delinquency area. Individuals come and go, the composition of the population changes, but the high rates persist because they are primarily and functionally related to the environment in which the people live. There the pressures toward crime and delinquency are strong and persistent while the restraining influences are few and weak. In the absence of social solidarity and the neighborhood organization, crime and delinquency "gain a foothold, persist over a period of years, and become more or less traditional aspects of the social life." These traditions of delinquency are transmitted through personal and group contacts; and as a result, there is not only a high percentage of criminals and delinquents, but also a disproportionate percentage of recidivists among these offenders.

The development of delinquency areas is, as might be expected, closely related to the processes of city growth, since social disorganization is but one phase of social change. As the city grows, the invasion by either industry or commerce tends to deteriorate the adjacent residential areas and causes the residents to move out. The houses that they leave are not yet needed for business; their rents are driven down to the point where they attract the lowest economic groups; and uncared for and neglected, they tend to fall into a state of shabbiness and disrepair. This physical deterioration accompanies and interacts with the social disorganization noted above, producing the slum area, which is a characteristic of most American cities.[8]

This explanation of the high rates of crime and delinquency in certain neighborhoods, which has been called the "delinquency-area concept,"[9] has been subjected to considerable criticism. The main points of this criticism are the following:

1. The delinquency-area concept does not give adequate recognition to the effects of selective migration. The delinquency area, with its low rents, reduced social controls, and social obscurity, tends to attract the unsuccessful, the inefficient, the discouraged, the personally disorganized, the handicapped, the defective, and the socially unwanted or inferior. It

---

[7] For a discussion of the relationship between crime and delinquency and social disorganization, see Chapter 3.

[8] Shaw and McKay, *Social Factors in Juvenile Delinquency,* pp. 385–91.

[9] The delinquency area is also known as the "interstitial or transitional area," that is, it lies between two other areas, for example, a better residential district and a business district, partaking of the characteristics of both and occupying a stage of development between them. For a critique of the delinquency-area studies, see Terence Morris, *The Criminal Area: A Study in Social Ecology* (London: Routledge and Kegan Paul, 1958), esp. pp. 85–106.

is a natural gathering place for many persons who have already developed delinquent or criminal tendencies elsewhere. Taft, for example, found statistical evidence of such selective forces operating in Danville, Illinois.[10] Although Sutherland states that this may merely mean that persons who move into a delinquency area have come from similar areas elsewhere,[11] as Taft replies, "this is not necessarily so."[12] Furthermore, those who become successful while living in a delinquency area tend to move out, which favors the antisocial influences existing there.

2. It is based upon an unreliable statistical comparison. Because of their poverty and social position, law violators in the delinquency area are more likely to be detected, arrested, prosecuted, and convicted than those in other areas who have wealth, influence, and sympathy on their side. Criminal statistics, therefore, are biased in favor of the latter, and the difference between the crime and delinquency rates of the delinquency area and those of other urban areas is inflated beyond its real proportions. Furthermore, the term "delinquency" is so variously defined and interpreted that its value as a unit of measurement is seriously impaired, and many factors, such as the differences in laws, police and court policies, and local customs and traditions, may affect the statistics on crime and delinquency without necessarily changing the actual amount of behavior that might be adjudged to be in violation of the law.[13] These are difficulties which we have already noted in our discussion of statistics in Chapter 1. However, even when allowances are made for these discrepancies, a significant difference in rates remains.[14]

3. The claim that the racial and national composition of the population in the neighborhood has no appreciable effect upon its crime and delinquency rates[15] is open to question. As Taft explains, some nationalities have cultures which make adjustment difficult, and racial minorities are handicapped in their social relationships.[16] Therefore, the introduction of certain racial and national elements into an area may increase the number of its residents who are likely to come into conflict with law, add to its social disorganization, and thus contribute to its rates of crime and delinquency.

10 Donald R. Taft, "Testing the Selective Influences of Areas of Delinquency," *American Journal of Sociology*, XXXVIII (Mar., 1933), 699-712.

11 Edwin H. Sutherland, *Principles of Criminology* (4th ed.; Philadelphia: J. B. Lippincott Co., 1947), p. 141.

12 Donald R. Taft, *Criminology* (New York: The Macmillan Co., 1950), p. 165.

13 Sophia M. Robison, *Can Delinquency Be Measured?* (New York: Columbia University Press, 1936), pp. 4, 210; Christen T. Jonassen, "A Re-Evaluation and Critique of the Logic and Some Methods of Shaw and McKay," *American Sociological Review*, XIV (Oct., 1949), 608–17.

14 Sutherland, p. 139.

15 Shaw and McKay, *Social Factors in Juvenile Delinquency*, p. 388.

16 Taft, *Criminology*, p. 166.

4. In some cities, especially the smaller ones, the delinquency area is in an isolated part of the town or on the outskirts, along the railroad tracks or near the "dumps."[17] This, however, is not a fundamental objection. It merely states that the delinquency area in certain cases is not located near the central business district or a large industrial area. It does not raise any questions regarding the existence or nature of the delinquency area.

5. The delinquency-area concept does not satisfactorily explain the presence of negative cases. Although the delinquency area has the highest rates of crime and delinquency, even in this area, many of the people are not delinquents or criminals—a fact which should have a sobering effect upon the extreme environmentalists, who are too prone to assume a simple cause-and-effect relationship between slum conditions and law violations. Sutherland attributes some of the negative cases to the effects of counteracting environmental influences. A delinquency area is almost never solidly delinquent. Some streets are comparatively free of criminals and delinquents; some racial, national, and religious groups protect their members from degrading environmental influences; some families carefully supervise and shield their children and instill in them a respect for law and order; some clergymen and teachers become models after which others fashion their behavior. And so it goes—in each instance cited here there are pressures operating toward law-abiding behavior.[18] But this is still largely the environmentalist's argument and does not give sufficient weight to the personal factors, to the uniqueness and creative ability of the individual. This, then, brings us to the next point.

6. The delinquency-area concept tends to neglect the psychological and biological factors. Shaw's use of the concept leaves some room for the operation of these factors, but in the hands of many of his followers it has become excessively sociologistic.[19] Although the concept establishes a relationship between environmental factors and law violations, it does not explain how these factors operate in the personality of the individual, sometimes pushing him into crime or delinquency, but often failing to dislodge him from his law-abiding behavior. As the Gluecks point out, "The ecologic sociologists are compelled to resort to psychologic insights when they come to grapple realistically with causal influences in the individual case."[20]

[17] *Ibid.*, pp. 166, 167; Sutherland, pp. 139, 140.

[18] Sutherland, pp. 142–44.

[19] Paul W. Tappan, *Juvenile Delinquency* (New York: McGraw-Hill Book Co., Inc., 1949), pp. 77–79.

[20] Sheldon and Eleanor T. Glueck, *Unraveling Juvenile Delinquency* (New York: The Commonwealth Fund, 1950), p. 6. For a symposium of reviews of this book, see *Journal of Criminal Law and Criminology*, XLI (Mar.–Apr., 1951), 732–62. See also Frank R. Scarpitti, Ellen Murray, Simon Dinitz, and Walter C. Reckless, "The

Despite the weaknesses of the delinquency-area concept, sociologists have adequately demonstrated the existence of delinquency areas in American cities. Whether crime and delinquency tend to be concentrated in the same way in the cities of other countries is not certain, although an early study by Burt revealed that London's rates of delinquency tended to be highest near the center of the city and lowest in the residential suburbs, and Lind's study of Honolulu in 1930 showed the same tendency for that city.[21] It is when the sociologist attempts to explain the processes by which the delinquency area fosters crime and delinquency that he exposes himself to criticism. The fact that certain environmental conditions and high rates of crime and delinquency exist together does not necessarily mean that these conditions cause the high rates, and the sociologist has not demonstrated conclusively that they do. But even so, the conclusion that in delinquency areas the opportunities for contact with socially demoralizing conduct increases the possibilities of a person's becoming criminal or delinquent is certainly justified.[22] Moreover, the delinquency-area concept has helped to focus attention on undesirable social conditions and has provided a better administrative basis for welfare, education, recreation, slum-clearance, city-planning, and law-enforcement programs. But as Barnes and Teeters conclude, "there is the danger that it will continue to be used, as it has all too frequently in the past, as an oversimplification of the problem."[23]

Urban-Rural Differences. In general, in the United States crime and delinquency rates are higher in urban communities than in rural areas, and there is a tendency for these rates to vary directly with the size of the city.[24] The *Uniform Crime Reports* for 1963, published by the Federal

'Good' Boy in a High Delinquency Area: Four Years Later," *American Sociological Review*, XXV (Aug., 1960), 255–58; Simon Dinitz, Frank R. Scarpitti, and Walter C. Reckless, "Delinquency Vulnerability: A Cross Group and Longitudinal Analysis," *American Sociological Review*, XXVII (Aug., 1962), 515–17.

[21] Cyril Burt, *The Young Delinquent* (New York: Appleton-Century-Crofts, Inc., 1925), p. 67–76; Andrew W. Lind, "Some Ecological Patterns of Community Disorganization in Honolulu," *American Journal of Sociology*, XXXVI (Sept., 1930), 206–20.

[22] National Commission on Law Observance and Enforcement, *Report on the Causes of Crime*, Report No. 13 (Washington, D.C.: Government Printing Office, 1931), Vol. I, p. 95.

[23] Harry Elmer Barnes and Negley K. Teeters, *New Horizons in Criminology*, (Englewood Cliffs, N.J.: Prentcie-Hall, Inc., 1959), pp. 157–59.

[24] For a summary of some of the comparative studies of urban and rural rates of crime and delinquency, see Walter C. Reckless, *Criminal Behavior* (New York: McGraw-Hill Book Co., Inc., 1940), pp. 81–88. See also S. Lottier, "Distribution of Criminal Offenses in Metropolitan Regions," *Journal of Criminal Law and Criminology*, XXIX (May–June, 1938), 37–50; M. G. Caldwell, "The Extent of Juvenile Delinquency in Wisconsin," *Journal of Criminal Law and Criminology*, XXXII (July–Aug., 1941), 148–57; H. L. Yoke, "Crime in West Virginia," *Sociology and*

Bureau of Investigation, tend to support this generalization[25] that has appeared in the works of many sociologists.

Sociologists generally have sought to explain the differences between urban and rural crime and delinquency in terms of social disorganization.[26] According to this view, rural areas have low rates of crime and delinquency because there social disorganization occurs less frequently and to a lesser degree than elsewhere. These areas tend to have a homogeneous and stable population, a minimum of social conflicts, intimate and highly personalized social relationships, and effective social control exercised by primary groups, such as the family and the neighborhood. As Vold explains, "The value and respectability of work, of family stability and continuity, of land as insurance against want and as an indicator of status, and a general scorn for pleasure-seeking and the 'soft' life are all part of the traditional rural culture pattern." The effect of this is to provide the individual with a pattern of conformity and to induce him to accept the regulations and controls of the settled community.[27]

On the other hand, cities have high rates of crime and delinquency because in them social disorganization occurs more frequently and to a greater degree than elsewhere. The cities tend to have a heterogeneous and mobile population, a maximum of culture conflicts, impersonal social relationships, weak and uncertain social control by primary groups, greater opportunities for gainful crime and escape from detection, and a lucrative market for organized vice and gambling. "In contrast to rural people, with their homogeneous and strong moral convictions and habits, the urbanite comes into contact with widely differing, opposite, and mutually critical theories, opinions, beliefs, and ideologies." As a result, it is difficult for him "to feel that any rule, any value, or any doctrine of an institution or party is sacred, for they cannot be viewed as absolute truths."[28]

Social Research, XVI (Jan.–Feb., 1932), 267–73; P. Wiers, "Juvenile Delinquency in Rural Michigan," *Journal of Criminal Law and Criminology*, XXX (July–Aug., 1939), 211–22; P. Wiers, "Can Rural and Urban Delinquency Be Compared?" *Journal of Criminal Law and Criminology*, XXX (Nov.–Dec., 1939), 522–33.

[25] Federal Bureau of Investigation, *Uniform Crime Reports, 1963*, pp. 47, 90, 91. The term "major crimes" here refers to murder, manslaughter, forcible rape, robbery, aggravated assault, burglary, larceny, and auto theft.

[26] Sutherland, in attempting to be more specific, uses his concept of differential association to explain the differences between urban and rural crime and delinquency, but he also states that social disorganization is the basic cause of differential association (Edwin H. Sutherland, *Principles of Criminology* [Philadelphia: J. B. Lippincott Co., 1939], pp. 7–9).

[27] George B. Vold, "Crime in City and Country Areas," *The Annals of the American Academy of Political and Social Science*, CCXVII (Sept., 1941), 45.

[28] Pitirim A. Sorokin, Carle C. Zimmerman, and Charles J. Galpin, *A Systematic Source Book in Rural Sociology* (Minneapolis: University of Minnesota Press, 1931), Vol. II, p. 292.

Since acts of crime and delinquency are symptoms of social disorganization, those who commit them carry the marks of social disorganization, and so the rural offender tends to manifest some of the characteristics of the city dweller. Studies indicate that the rural offender makes more contacts outside his home community, participates less frequently in community organizations and groups, and is more emancipated from home ties than the rural nonoffender. He considers himself a reckless and mobile person, values the possession of things more highly than the opinions of others, and measures status in terms of urban standards. However, he does not regard himself as a criminal or his acts as crimes, does not look upon crime as a way of life but as a mere incident in life, does not usually associate with delinquent gangs or criminals, and, with a few possible exceptions like the "moonshiner" in the southern mountains of the United States, does not consider crime a means of livelihood. In other words, although the rural offender has developed some of the attitudes of the city dweller, he is not a criminal social type. Clinard suggests that the effects of gossip and other informal controls on offenders may be a probable explanation for the slight continuity of crime in rural areas.[29] Reckless, taking note of the fact that the rates of crimes against the person are high in rural areas, seeks to explain this by saying that under conditions of relatively isolated living, where primary group relationships predominate, the spirit of independence burns fiercely, and the reactions to interference and friction are strong and violent. Grudges are nursed, revenge is strenuously demanded, passions and fanaticism are easily stirred, methods of redress are simple and direct.[30] And the absence of effective police control and established courts may very well induce a kind of "law of self-help," such as that which developed in the early West, where a quick, cheap, and satisfying "justice" was demanded.

This explanation of the differences between urban and rural crime and delinquency is open to essentially the same criticisms that have been directed against the delinquency-area concept, which likewise is ex-

[29] Marshall B. Clinard, "The Process of Urbanization and Criminal Behavior," *American Journal of Sociology*, XLVIII (Sept., 1942), 202–13; Marshall B. Clinard, "Rural Criminal Offenders," *American Journal of Sociology*, L (July, 1944), 38–45; Arthur L. Wood, "Social Organization and Crime in Small Wisconsin Communities," *American Sociological Review*, VII (Feb., 1942), 40–46; S. Winston and M. Butler, "Negro Bootleggers in Eastern North Carolina," *American Sociological Review*, VIII (Dec., 1943), 692–97. See also Harold D. Eastman, *The Process of Urbanization and Criminal Behavior: A Restudy of Culture Conflict* (unpublished Ph.D. dissertation, State University of Iowa, August, 1954). This is a replication of Clinard's study of rural crime in Iowa and tends to substantiate his findings. For a replication of Clinard's study in another culture, see Marshall B. Clinard, "A Cross-Cultural Replication of the Relation of Urbanism to Criminal Behavior," *American Sociological Review*, XXV (Apr., 1960), 253–57. This replication supports most of the findings of the original study.

[30] Reckless, pp. 87, 88.

pressed in terms of social disorganization. Selective migration carries delinquents, criminals, and others who have antisocial attitudes and habits from the rural areas to the cities, where the field is richer and where the opportunities for association with kindred souls and for the expression of restlessness and resentment are greater.[31] Some of the differences in the rates reflect variations in definition, referral, and reporting rather than variations in the forces that produce crime and delinquency.[32] The great majority of persons living in cities are not criminals or delinquents, and, on the other hand, criminal behavior has become traditional in some rural areas where the social organization is stable. Evidence showing that certain environmental conditions appear with high rates of law violation does not necessarily prove that the first causes the second, although it may suggest some form of causal relationship; nor does it demonstrate how the environmental factors interact with the personal factors in the personality of the individual to produce the observed criminal and delinquent behavior. However, despite criticisms such as these, the explanation outlined above, while not providing a complete answer, has thrown considerable light on why crime and delinquency rates in rural areas differ from those in urban communities.

Modern means of communication and transportation are reducing the differences between rural and urban dwellers and carrying urban culture into the most remote sections of the country. Motels, taverns, and roadhouses are scattered along our highways and around the borders of our cities. Criminals find security in "hideouts" in villages and on farms. Organized crime has set up gambling establishments beyond the reach of city police departments. Social disorganization has broken through in isolated rural areas and in the ugly fringes of our urban communities. Reckless automobile drivers from the city, by their acts against others along the country's highways, are contributing to the rural rates of crimes against the person. Rural boys are finding themselves defined as juvenile delinquents for behavior in which their fathers took pride or for which they gained status.

Thus far we have referred generally to environmental influences that contribute to crime and delinquency. We shall now examine more specifically the relationship between these problems and the most important social institutions and groups.[33]

[31] Hurwitz, p. 257.

[32] Walter C. Reckless, *The Etiology of Delinquent and Criminal Behavior* (New York: Social Science Research Council, Bull. 50, 1943), pp. 37, 38.

[33] The political factors are not discussed in this chapter for two reasons: (1) the more specific political problems are considered as they arise in connection with such subjects as "crime as a legal problem," "organized crime," "police," "criminal prosecution," "prison administration," and "prevention"; and (2) an examination of such general political questions as "forms of government" and "international relations," about which we have little specific evidence in the field of criminology, would lead us far beyond the restricted enquiry we have undertaken.

THE HOME AND THE FAMILY

The family exerts a deep and persistent influence in the life of the individual. In it he has his first and most intimate experiences with others; receives care, protection, moral instruction, and basic physical and emotional satisfactions during his most impressionable years; first learns about himself and his physical, social, and cultural surroundings; and acquires habits, attitudes, character traits, and a sense of right and wrong that tend to endure throughout his life. Thus, as Shulman says, the family performs at least three major functions: "(1) it provides organic sustenance and habit-training in survival patterns; (2) it affords primary group association for the experiencing of socializing interpersonal relationships; and (3) it is a major source for the transmission of the values and knowledge of the culture."[34] It is, therefore, not only the cradle of personality, but also the nursery of all other social institutions; and being functionally related to them, it tends to reflect and augment their organization or disorganization. Obviously, then, the family is a powerful force for good or evil in the community.

Various writers have sought to classify the family situations and relationships that contribute most directly to crime and delinquency. Carr, in attempting to do this, has stated that "every culture produces certain norms for home life," and that in the United States the so-called normal home appears to have the following characteristics:

1. Structural completeness, which means "the presence of both natural parents in the home."

2. Racial homogeneity, or "identity of race (color) on the part of husband, wife, and children."

3. Economic security, which is "the reasonable stability of income adequate to maintain health, working efficiency, and morale."

4. Cultural conformity, which means that "the parents speak the same language, eat the same foods, observe the same customs, have about the same number of children, and hold substantially the same attitudes as the social world to which their children are exposed."

5. Moral conformity, which is "conformity to the mores *of the child's social world immediately about the home,*" that is, conformity to the mores of the neighborhood.

[34] Harry Manuel Shulman, "The Family and Juvenile Delinquency," *The Annals of the American Academy of Political and Social Science,* CCLXI (Jan., 1949), 21. See also Thomas P. Monahan, "Family Status and the Delinquent Child: A Reappraisal and Some New Findings," *Social Forces,* XXXV (Mar., 1957), 250–58. After a study of 44,448 delinquents appearing in the municipal court in Philadelphia during the period 1949–54, Monahan concluded that the stability and continuity of family life stands out as a most important factor in the development of the child.

6. Physical and psychological normality, which means that the home does not contain a chronic invalid or a mentally deficient or deranged person.

7. Functional adequacy, which means that members of the family "carry on the process of interaction among themselves with a minimum of friction and a minimum of emotional frustration," and that "there is a minimum of parental rejection, a minimum of sibling rivalry, a minimum of inculcation of inferiority, escape from reality, self-pity, or any of the other attitudes that cripple and thwart the growing personality."

To the extent that a home departs from any of these characteristics, it is a deviant home and a center of definite deviation pressures and so may contribute to crime and delinquency. The fact that the great majority of the children from deviant homes do not become delinquent or criminal does not alter the fact that such homes are a handicap to normal adjustment and law observance. A study of forty-six families in Ann Arbor, Michigan, which were analyzed from this point of view, revealed that while the group as a whole had 8.2 deviations per family and 3.7 different kinds of deviations per family, twelve homes that had produced *delinquents* averaged 12.1 deviations per family, or 46.5 per cent *more* than the group average; twenty homes of *maladjusted nondelinquents* averaged 8.5 deviations per family, or 3.5 per cent *more* than the group average; and fourteen homes of *well-adjusted* boys, who happened to be included in the study for other reasons, averaged only 3.8 deviations per home, or 53.6 per cent *less* than the average; and that the delinquents had 40.5 per cent more different kinds of deviations per family than did the group as a whole, whereas the well-adjusted cases had 35.1 per cent fewer.[35]

However, any such attempt as this to measure the "normalcy" or "goodness" of a family or home is open to the criticism that it is highly subjective, since value judgments are involved in the use of such words as "reasonable," "conformity," "normality," "adequacy," and "minimum." Nevertheless, this does not entirely destroy its effectiveness as a tool for estimating and comparing the delinquency potentials of a selected group of homes.

Homes that contribute to crime and delinquency may be classified into these six major types: (1) the broken home; (2) the functionally inadequate home; (3) the home with a physically or psychologically abnormal parent; (4) the socially, morally, or culturally abnormal home; (5) the criminal home; and (6) the economically insecure home.[36]

[35] Lowell Juilliard Carr, *Delinquency Control* (New York: Harper and Bros., 1950), pp. 166–68.

[36] The categories in this classification are not mutually exclusive and numbers five and six might be included as subtypes of number four. They are shown separately

The Broken Home. The broken home is one from which one parent is absent because of death, divorce, separation, desertion, or commitment to an institution. Such homes are thought to produce a disproportionate number of delinquents and criminals because it is assumed that the presence of both parents are essential to the development of well-balanced and socially adjusted children. Many reports and studies, by showing that a high percentage of delinquent children come from broken homes, appear to bear out this assumption. Juvenile court reports and investigations based on them show that from 30 to 60 per cent of delinquents come from broken homes.[37] In 1939, the United States Children's Bureau reported that 36 per cent of the boys' cases and 50 per cent of the girls' cases disposed of by 64 juvenile courts during 1936 had come from broken homes.[38] A study of the Municipal Court of Philadelphia showed that 47 per cent of its cases were from broken homes.[39] The Catholic Charities Probation Bureau in the Court of General Sessions in New York County found that over 47 per cent of the cases studied came from broken homes, and another study of the cases coming to the probation department of the New York City Children's Courts revealed that 56 per cent of them were from such homes.[40] A four-year study by the California Youth Authority showed that 62 per cent of that state's juvenile delinquents were "the result of broken homes."[41] After a study of 4,000 cases in Chicago and Boston, Healy and Bronner found that almost 50 per cent of them had a background of broken homes.[42] Sheldon and Eleanor Glueck, in their study of 966 juvenile delinquency cases, state that 48 per cent of them came from broken homes.[43] In an earlier study, the same authors had discovered that 60 per cent of a group of 500 youths committed to the Massachusetts Reformatory for serious offenses had broken homes.[44] Lumpkin found that 63.5 per cent of the girls committed to correctional schools in Wisconsin were from

for the sake of emphasis. Although these homes do not make crime and delinquency inevitable, they do increase the possibility of such behavior.

[37] Sutherland (1947 ed.), p. 158.

[38] United States Children's Bureau, *Juvenile Court Statistics*, Publication No. 245 (1939), p. 49, Table 6.

[39] Thirty-fifth Annual Report of the Municipal Court of Philadelphia, 1948. Cited by Barnes and Teeters, p. 210.

[40] Nathaniel F. Cantor, *Crime and Society* (New York: Henry Holt and Co., Inc., 1939), p. 50; Edwin J. Cooley, *Probation and Delinquency* (New York: Thomas Nelson & Sons, 1927), pp. 87, 88.

[41] Quoted in *Federal Probation*, XII (Dec., 1948), 59.

[42] William Healy and Augusta F. Bronner, *Delinquents and Criminals, Their Making and Unmaking* (New York: The Macmillan Co., 1926), pp. 121, 122.

[43] Sheldon and Eleanor T. Glueck, *One Thousand Juvenile Delinquents* (Cambridge: Harvard University Press, 1934), pp. 75–77.

[44] Sheldon and Eleanor T. Glueck, *500 Criminal Careers* (New York: Alfred A. Knopf, Inc., 1930), pp. 116–18.

broken homes.[45] Such studies[46] as these could be multiplied many times, all of them indicating that a high percentage of delinquents are from broken homes.

Such statistics have little meaning, however, unless it can be shown that a greater percentage of delinquents than nondelinquents come from broken homes. In 1918, Shideler estimated that about 25 per cent of all American children were from broken homes and concluded that about twice as many delinquents as nondelinquents come from such homes.[47] Burt, after a study of English juvenile delinquents in London, came to about the same conclusion.[48] Merrill found that half of the delinquent children in her study came from broken homes whereas about a quarter of the nondelinquents in the control group were from such homes.[49] On the other hand, Shaw and McKay, in a study which compared delinquent boys with schoolboys of the same age and national extraction, found that 42.5 per cent of the delinquents and 36.1 of the schoolboys were from broken homes, which indicated that this type of home of itself is a relatively unimportant factor in the causation of delinquency.[50] Studies by Silverman, Hirsch, Campbell, and others pointed to the same conclusion.[51] Nevertheless, Shulman, after an examination of the diverse findings on the subject, concluded that the majority of research studies are in agreement with the official court reports in showing that the incidence of broken homes is higher for delinquents than for nondelinquents, "even when such factors as age and ethnic background are taken into account," and that although this does not necessarily prove a causal relation, it strongly suggests one.[52] But, as Sutherland explains, the evidence

[45] Katharine Du Pre Lumpkin, "Factors in the Commitment of Correctional School Girls in Wisconsin," *American Journal of Sociology*, XXXVII (Sept., 1931), 222–30.

[46] A study by Weeks, while finding a positive relationship between delinquency and the broken home, showed that the incidence of such homes varied by sex and offense. Broken homes were more frequent among girls and cases involving ungovernability, running away, and truancy than among boys and cases involving property offenses, traffic violations, and misdemeanors (H. Ashley Weeks, "Male and Female Broken Home Rates by Type of Delinquency," *American Sociological Review*, V [Aug., 1940], 601–9). See also Monahan, 250–58; Jackson Toby, "The Differential Impact of Family Disorganization," *American Sociological Review*, XXII (Oct., 1957), 505–12.

[47] E. H. Shideler, "Family Disintegration and the Delinquent Boy in the United States," *Journal of Criminal Law and Criminology*, VIII (Jan., 1918), 709–32.

[48] Burt, pp. 60–98.

[49] Maud A. Merrill, *Problems of Child Delinquency* (New York: Houghton Mifflin Co., 1947), pp. 66, 67.

[50] Shaw and McKay, *Social Factors in Juvenile Delinquency*, pp. 261–84.

[51] Baruch Silverman, "The Behavior of Children from Broken Homes," *American Journal of Orthopsychiatry*, V (Jan., 1935), 11–18; N. D. M. Hirsch, *Dynamic Causes of Juvenile Crime* (Cambridge, Mass.: Sci-art Publishers, 1937); Marian Campbell, "The Effect of the Broken Home Upon the Child in School," *Journal of Educational Sociology*, V (Jan., 1932), 274–81.

[52] Shulman, p. 26.

in general indicates that the break in the home is less important than it was formerly believed to be.[53] What appears to be far more important as a cause of delinquency, regardless of whether the home is broken or not, is the relationship existing among the members of the family—the meaning of the home to them and their reactions to what the community thinks of it, to what happens in it, and to the behavior of one another.[54] In other words, here as elsewhere, causation must be seen as a functional relationship in which many factors interact in a changing situation. The concept "broken home" is too broad to enable us to do this. The way that the home is broken and the reaction of the members of the family to the break must be considered. The death of a father may consolidate the remaining members of a family as nothing else could, while a divorce might have shattered their relationship forever; and a separation of parents may eliminate tensions that are contributing to crime and delinquency.

The Functionally Inadequate Home. The functionally inadequate home is one in which there is a great deal of friction and frustration in the interaction of its members. It is characterized by a high degree of parental rejection, sibling rivalry, emotional insecurity, self-pity, domination, favoritism, jealousy, pampering, neglect, or any of the other conditions which tend to thwart, cripple, or twist the personalities of its members. In short, it is an emotionally unhealthy home.[55]

Numerous studies and clinical experience have demonstrated that this type of home contributes to crime and delinquency.[56] When the home

[53] Sutherland (1947 ed.), p. 159.

[54] Charles W. Coulter, "Family Disorganization as a Causal Factor in Delinquency and Crime," *Federal Probation,* XII (Sept., 1948), 14, 15; Glueck, *Unraveling Juvenile Delinquency,* pp. 272–83; Monahan, 250–59; Sheldon and Eleanor Glueck, *Family Environment and Delinquency* (Boston: Houghton Mifflin Co., 1962), pp. 122–29; Harrison E. Salisbury, *The Shook-Up Generation* (New York: Harper and Bros., 1958), pp. 118-31. Nye found less delinquent behavior in broken than in unhappy unbroken homes (F. Ivan Nye, *Family Relationships and Delinquent Behavior* [New York: John Wiley and Sons, Inc., 1958], p. 51).

[55] Carr, pp. 167, 168; Coulter, pp. 15, 16.

[56] See, for example, Carl R. Rogers, *The Clinical Treatment of the Problem Child* (Boston: Houghton Mifflin Co., 1939), pp. 179–81; Helen Witmer and students, "The Outcome of Treatment in a Child Guidance Clinic," *Smith College Studies in Social Work,* III (June, 1933), 365–71; William Healy and Augusta F. Bronner, *New Light on Delinquency and Its Treatment* (New Haven: Yale University Press, 1936), pp. 47–52, 128–30; E. M. Bushong, "Family Estrangement and Juvenile Delinquency," *Social Forces,* V (Sept., 1926), 79–83; Austin L. Porterfield, "Delinquency and Its Outcome in Court and College," *American Journal of Sociology,* XLIX (Nov., 1943), 199-208; Burt pp. 92–98, 518–24; Glueck, *One Thousand Juvenile Delinquents,* p. 75; Sheldon and Eleanor T. Glueck, *Five Hundred Delinquent Women* (New York: Alfred A. Knopf, Inc., 1934), p. 454; August Aichhorn, *Wayward Youth* (New York: The Viking Press, Inc., 1951); Raymond A. Mulligan, "Family Relationships and Juvenile Delinquency," *Pacific Sociological Review,* I (Spring, 1958), 40.

blocks the fundamental wishes of its members, it contributes to their personality conflicts, which, as we have seen,[57] may lead to crime or delinquency; or it may drive them into corrupting or demoralizing association elsewhere, which also may bring them into conflict with the law. The child, suffering from neglect, overprotection, excessively severe or inconsistent discipline, and filled with feelings of frustration, rejection, or insecurity, may find recognition or new experience in truancy or obtain the security, admiration, and respect that he craves in directing the delinquent activities of a gang. Although extremes in discipline should be avoided, inconsistency of discipline is even more undesirable, for it leaves the child bewildered and insecure, with no uniform standards to guide his behavior. In any event, the absence of a well-balanced system of discipline greatly increases the possibility of the child's becoming a maladjusted adult, unprepared to assume his life's responsibilities. On the other hand, clinical experience has indicated that a delinquent seldom comes from a home in which the members have love and affection for one another.

The parent, too, may become involved in crime because of the influences of the functionally inadequate home. The husband, harried by the whining and incompetence of an unstable wife, may find comfort in the "bottle" and the association of brawling companions, or he may steal to supplement the family income. And the wife who feels neglected, unwanted, and "left out of things" may turn to prostitution for excitement and money, or through shoplifting, get the fine clothes that she has always wanted. Viewing the effects of the functionally inadequate home, Wood and Waite remark that the subtler influences of personality conflicts in families are probably more destructive of the social adjustment of children than the broken home,[58] and Healy is inclined to believe that an exploration of the deeper sources of criminal behavior would reveal that the lack of satisfying family relationships in delinquency areas is a great factor in the causation of such behavior, "greater than any other feature of the environmental situation."[59]

Many studies have indicated that the same family usually produces both delinquents and nondelinquents. This fact has forced students to inquire into the reasons why a family will affect some children in one way and others in another way. One approach to this problem has led to an examination of the relation of the only child, the order of birth, the foster child, and the size of the family to delinquency and crime. Studies regarding these items, although numerous, are conflicting and inconclu-

[57] See Chapter 11.

[58] Arthur Evans Wood and John Barker Waite, *Crime and Its Treatment* (New York: American Book Co., 1941), p. 183.

[59] William Healy, "The Psychiatrist Looks at Delinquency and Crime," *The Annals of the American Academy of Political and Social Science*, CCXVII (Sept., 1941), 70.

sive,[60] but it appears that, merely because an individual is an only child, the youngest, the oldest, or an "in-between" child, a foster child, or a child in a large or small family, does not mean that he will necessarily become a delinquent child. The outcome depends on the type of home in which he is reared and his treatment in it.

Here again, we must recognize the complexity of causation—and some sociologists are keenly aware of this. For example, Shulman states that we must take the social class of the child into consideration in judging the possible effects of frustration on his behavior. In his opinion, "Tensions are endured by the middle-class child more consistently because they lead to a goal acceptable in our culture, but are less consistently endured by children of the poor as leading to an unacceptable goal."[61] And Reckless, while suspecting that "the family of the delinquent child may be found to be a much more strife-ridden family than that of the nondelinquent child," asserts that "delinquent children more than nondelinquents may find ordinary tensions of family life unbearable."[62] Obviously, then, a home has a different meaning for each of its members, affects each of them in a different way, and no two members have the same experience in it.

The Home with a Physically or Psychologically Abnormal Parent. This is the type of home in which one of the parents is suffering from some serious physical or mental disability, like blindness, deafness, paralysis, mental deficiency, or psychosis. Although it may have the appearance of being well-organized, it lacks a well-balanced system of discipline and supervision. Often the parent is unaware, or only vaguely aware, of his inadequacy, and a pretense is maintained to save his feelings. As a result, frankness, honesty, and understanding, so essential to a normal home, are undermined and destroyed. Love and affection may be present, but the children may feel ashamed, apologetic, and secretly resentful because they must carry what they consider to be an unfair burden. Thus, they may think of their home as a "necessary convenience" and find relief from their tensions, feelings of guilt, frustrations, and conflicts

[60] For a summary of the findings of some of these studies, see Sutherland (1947 ed.), pp. 166–70; Hurwitz, pp. 324–27; Emanuel Miller, "The Problem of Birth-Order and Delinquency," in *Mental Abnormality and Crime,* ed. L. Radzinowicz and J. W. C. Turner (English Studies in Criminal Science [London: Macmillan and Co., Ltd., 1949]), Vol. II, pp. 227–37. The article by Dr. Miller contains an instructive survey of English-American findings on the relation of birth-order to crime and delinquency. See also J. A. Shield and A. E. Grigg, "Extreme Ordinal Position and Criminal Behavior," *Journal of Criminal Law and Criminology,* XXXV (Sept.–Oct., 1944), 169–73; William W. Wattenberg, "Delinquency and Only Children: Study of a 'Category,' " *Journal of Abnormal and Social Psychology,* XLIV (July, 1949), 356–66; Nye, p. 37.

[61] Shulman, p. 30.

[62] Reckless, *The Etiology of Delinquent and Criminal Behavior,* p. 27.

in demoralizing associations elsewhere, which often lead them into delinquency or crime.[63] But, as we have seen, one must be cautious in generalizing about the home, for many subtle influences are at work in it, and a tragedy may solidify its ranks, binding it into a unit which will overcome the greatest adversities.

The Socially, Morally, or Culturally Abnormal Home. This is the type of home which, because of racial differences, immorality, or diverse cultural standards, does not transmit to its children the system of values generally accepted in the community and so does not prepare them for a well-adjusted life. The task of child training is not easy even under the most favorable conditions in modern society, where rapid social changes bewilder parents and often leave them in conflict with friends, relatives, school teachers, and community leaders.[64] In the United States, marriages between members of the white and Negro races make the task exceedingly difficult and usually do not produce happy children. They are marginal persons, comfortable in neither the race of their mother nor that of their father. Often bitter, resentful of their lot, and ridden by conflict, they face many obstacles in their struggle for adjustment.

Lewdness, drunkenness, brutality, immorality, and vice in the home tend to harden the child and debase his tastes. When he is accustomed from his earliest days to low ideals, indecency, obscene language, and degradation of every kind, he readily finds his way into the ranks of those who violate the law.[65] In fact, a number of studies, such as those by Healy and Bronner, Lumpkin, Elliott, and the Gluecks, have shown that the immoral home contributes to crime and delinquency.[66] Nevertheless, as Tappan warns, vice in the home may be more than offset by other influences there, and it may be better to let the child remain in a somewhat defective family where he is loved and secure than to place him in an institution or a foster home where his emotional and affectional needs might not be adequately satisfied.[67]

Homes of immigrants often become the scene of serious culture conflicts. The parents, who have a well-integrated set of attitudes and customs which they acquired in the old country, tend to resist the upsetting

[63] Coulter, p. 16.

[64] See, for example, William H. Sewell, Paul H. Mussen, and Chester W. Harris, "Relationships Among Child Training Practices," *American Sociological Review*, XX (April, 1955), 137–48.

[65] John Lewis Gillin, *Criminology and Penology* (New York: Appleton-Century-Crofts, Inc., 1945), p. 173.

[66] Healy and Bronner, *Delinquents and Criminals, Their Making and Unmaking*, pp. 126–29; Lumpkin, pp. 222–30; Mabel A. Elliott, *Correctional Education and the Delinquent Girl* (Harrisburg, Pa., 1928), pp. 26–28; Glueck, *Unraveling Juvenile Delinquency*, pp. 278–81.

[67] Paul W. Tappan, *Juvenile Delinquency* (New York: McGraw-Hill Book Co., Inc., 1949), p. 141.

influences of their strange surroundings. But their children, subject to constant pressure from playmates, neighbors, schools, motion pictures, and radio and television programs, tend to be assimilated into the new culture and so come into conflict with their parents. Torn between loyalty to their family and desire to be accepted by their friends and companions, having an attitude of superiority toward their parents and an unwillingness to take any guidance from them, confused, reckless and rebellious, many of these children break away from parental control and drift into crime or delinquency.[68] This situation seems to be reflected in the findings of many studies and investigations, which in general show that the American-born children of immigrants have higher recorded crime rates than the foreign-born.[69] But these findings must be interpreted with caution, for the delinquency and crime rates of the American-born children of immigrants are affected not only by culture conflicts, but also by the fact that many foreign-born families are poor and live in delinquency areas.[70]

The Criminal Home. The criminal home is one in which one or both parents are engaged in criminal activities. This situation may affect the child either because the parents deliberately teach him to commit crimes or because he acquires the criminal values of the parents through the subtle conditioning of family life and imitates his parents' behavior. Obviously, this is the most direct way in which the home can contribute to crime and delinquency, and many studies indicate its importance. For example, Burt, in his classical study of vice and crime in England, concluded that these conditions existed five times as often in the homes from which delinquents came as in the homes of nondelinquents; and the Gluecks, in a series of three studies, found that over four-fifths of the juvenile delinquents, women delinquents, and male felons came from homes in which there were other offenders.[71]

[68] National Commission on Law Observance and Enforcement, Report No. 13, Vol. I, pp. 73–76.

[69] For a general summary of the criminal record of immigrants, see Taft, *Criminology*, pp. 110–12.

[70] Limitations of space preclude a discussion of the subject of immigration and crime, but the student is referred to the following: National Commission on Law Observance and Enforcement, *Report on Crime and the Foreign Born*, Report No. 10 (Washington, D.C.: Government Printing Office, 1931); C. C. Van Vechten, "The Criminality of the Foreign Born," *Journal of Criminal Law and Criminology*, XXXII (July–Aug., 1941), 139–47; Hans von Hentig, "The First Generation and a Half: Notes on the Delinquency of the Native White of Mixed Parentage," *American Sociological Review*, X (Dec., 1945), 792–98. For a summary of the studies on the crime rates of various immigrant groups, see Arthur Lewis Wood, "Minority-Group Criminality and Cultural Integration," *Journal of Criminal Law and Criminology*, XXXVII (Mar.–Apr., 1947), 398–510.

[71] Burt, pp. 60–98. See also Glueck: *One Thousand Juvenile Delinquents*, pp. 79, 80; *Five Hundred Delinquent Women*, pp. 72, 73; *500 Criminal Careers*, pp. 111–13.

The Economically Insecure Home. The economically insecure home is one in which there is not "the reasonable stability of income adequate to maintain health, working efficiency, and morale."[72] The relation between this type of home and crime and delinquency is a very complex one. Sometimes poverty operates directly to produce law violations, as when a father steals to supply his children with clothing or children pilfer food so that they will not go hungry, but far more often it operates indirectly through other factors. Thus, it may mean the absence from home of working parents, the lack of medical treatment, the early employment of children, the association of children with delinquent gangs in slum areas, the running away of children from the home to escape its unpleasant surroundings, the worry, irritability, desperation, and discord of parents, the feelings of insecurity, shame, and resentment attendant upon the low status of the home in the community. It may mean the overcrowding of the home, with sacrifice of privacy and failure to provide children of different sexes with separate sleeping rooms. Any one of these may in turn lead to crime or delinquency. Yet poverty frequently does not produce crime or delinquency at all—many law-abiding adults and children come from poor homes—and the rich as well as the poor become violators of the law.

Nevertheless, it seems possible to summarize the situation, as Hurwitz has done, in this way:

1. The great majority of criminals and delinquents come from homes of "humble or downright poor economic conditions."

2. The incidence of such conditions in the parental home of offenders far exceeds that of the general population.

3. Economic conditions of the same or similar nature, however, exist in many homes without producing crime or delinquency.

The essential point is this: Although the economically insecure home usually operates indirectly to produce law violations, or often fails entirely to do this, it still constitutes a very high criminal or delinquency risk.[73]

Marital Status. The statistical information regarding the relation of marital status to crime remains incomplete, unreliable, and problematic in spite of all the efforts to subject it to a refined methodology. At present it cannot be maintained that marriage, of itself, increases or decreases

---

[72] Carr, p. 166.

[73] Hurwitz, pp. 319–24. See also Ernest W. Burgess, "The Economic Factor in Juvenile Delinquency," *Journal of Criminal Law, Criminology, and Police Science,* XLIII (May–June, 1952), 29–42; A. J. Reiss, Jr., "Delinquency as the Failure of Personal and Social Controls," *American Sociological Review,* XVI (Apr., 1951), 196–208; Lee N. Robins, Harry Gyman, and Patricia O'Neal, "The Interaction of Social Class and Deviant Behavior," *American Sociological Review,* XXVII (Aug., 1962), 480–92.

the possibility of criminal behavior. Whether a marriage will exert a strengthening and stabilizing or a disintegrating and demoralizing influence in the life of an individual will depend entirely on the circumstances of the particular case and especially on the personalities of the marriage partners.[74]

THE NEIGHBORHOOD

The neighborhood, like the family, has declined as an agency of social control, but despite this, it still exerts an important influence in our society, especially in the development of the child.[75] Indeed, the neighborhood is "the world of the child exclusive of his family on the one hand, and of the radio, newspapers and other symbols of the larger community on the other." For him, it is essentially the area known through participation—"it is the area in which he works and plays." It is a stage upon which much of the drama of socialization and education is played.[76]

The neighborhood can contribute to crime and delinquency by blocking basic personality needs, engendering culture conflicts, and fostering antisocial values; or it can supplement and fortify the influences of the home, the church, and the school in the maintenance of law and order. Congested neighborhoods with inadequate recreation facilities deny the natural play impulses of children and encourage the formation of delinquent gangs and the development of criminal careers. Neighborhood mores may clash with the values of immigrant families to the detriment of parental control, or as in the case of some religious groups, they may conflict with the values of organized society and thus with the enforcement of law. A neighborhood like the one "across the tracks" may stigmatize its residents, affect their self-attitudes, handicap them in their social adjustment, and thus increase the possibility of their conflict with the law. Influences in the neighborhood can undermine and even destroy the moral precepts of the home; and the informal, intimate, and continuous process of education provided by neighborhood groups can easily nullify the effects of the more impersonal teaching of the school and the church.

Taverns, dance halls, cheap hotels, gambling "joints," bowling alleys, poolrooms, houses of prostitution, and burlesque theaters tend to focalize the antisocial forces of a neighborhood and send them in a corrosive and

[74] For a review of some of the statistical findings on marital status as a factor in crime, see Hurwitz, pp. 347–56. Statistics of penal institutions, Simon Tulchin's study, *Intelligence and Crime,* and the Gluecks' study, *Criminal Careers in Retrospect,* suggest that marriage may be a deterrent to crime.

[75] For a discussion of the neighborhood as a primary group, see Chapter 3.

[76] Henry D. McKay, "The Neighborhood and Child Conduct," *The Annals of the American Academy of Political and Social Science,* CCLXI (Jan., 1949), 32; Salisbury, pp. 73–117.

destructive stream against the individual. Such places often become breeding places of vice and crime and "hang-outs" for members of organized criminal gangs; and owners of fences, operators of junk yards, and petty politicians gravitate into the role of leaders in local criminal activities.[77] As a factor in the causation of crime and delinquency, the neighborhood is at its worst in the delinquency area. In such an area, as we have seen, delinquency and crime persist not only because of the absence of constructive neighborhood influences, but also because various forms of lawlessness have become traditional and are transmitted through neighborhood groups and institutions.[78] In the examination of the neighborhood, however, we must remember that it is functionally related to the organized society of which it is a part; and so although it generates antisocial forces of its own, it also communicates others which originate elsewhere.

THE PLAYGROUP AND THE GANG

All children everywhere participate in spontaneous playgroups, and this intimate face-to-face form of association exerts an amazing influence on them. It affects their speech, their manners, their methods of play, their attitudes toward themselves and others, and their morals and ideals. In fact, the playgroup may surpass the home as an educational agency; and through its unsupervised activities it often preserves and transmits traditions and techniques of delinquency.

The gang has a more permanent membership and a more definite organization than the spontaneous playgroup, from which, however, it frequently emerges. It develops to meet the needs of children and young people where other outlets for their interests and energies fail to do so; and it supplies its members with excitement and adventure, recognition for skills, prowess, and daring, and security and protection from the interference of parents, teachers, and the police. Even so, most gangs are rather loosely organized groups with changing memberships, some of the members moving in and out of the gang's activities as they see fit to do so.[79]

[77] McKay, pp. 32,–41; National Commission on Law Observance and Enforcement, Report No. 13, Vol. I, pp. 76–82; Solomon Kobrin, "The Conflict of Values in Delinquency Areas," *American Sociological Review*, XVI (Oct., 1951), 653–62.

[78] For a discussion of the influence of the neighborhood in the development of delinquent careers, see Clifford R. Shaw and Associates, *Brothers in Crime* (Chicago: University of Chicago Press, 1938).

[79] For a discussion of the theories of gang delinquency, see Chapter 9. See also Bernard C. Rosen, "Conflicting Group Membership: A Study of Parent-Peer Group Cross-Pressures," *American Sociological Review*, XX (Apr., 1955), 155–61; David Lowson, "Delinquency in Industrial Areas," *British Journal of Criminology*, I (July, 1960), 50–55; Clay V. Brittain, "Adolescent Choices and Parent-Peer Cross-Pressures,"

Although most gangs are composed of boys and young men, some include girls and a few contain only girls. Gangs are not necessarily a cause of crime, nor are all gangs criminal, for they have in them the potentialities of both good and evil. Properly directed, they may become assets to the community, developing into clubs, fraternities, lodges, and other such organizations; but neglected or unwisely handled, they come into increasing conflict with the community, acquiring an antisocial solidarity and engaging in demoralizing activities, which range from truancy, rowdiness, and vandalism to the most serious crimes. As a conflict group, the gang develops traditions of crime and delinquency, trains its members in the patterns and techniques of law violation, supports them with an *esprit de corps,* and shields and protects them from detection and apprehension.

The gang appears more frequently in delinquency areas, where it absorbs a disproportionate amount of its members' interests and energies and operates as a most effective agency of demoralization. Indeed, in the slum environment the boy is almost predestined to the life of the gang, for almost nowhere else can he find the interests, activities, and satisfactions which he so urgently needs. Everywhere, the gang reflects the adult life and customs of the neighborhood in which it functions; hence its activities must be studied with reference to the moral codes and conduct of the adult world. On this point, it should be observed that adults cannot persistently violate the moral standards which they advocate for their children and at the same time expect young people to remain unaffected by such bad examples. And yet this is the situation that exists in many neighborhoods.

Studies by Breckinridge and Abbott, Burt, Healy, Shaw, the Gluecks,[80] and others show that delinquents and criminals generally have had less contact with constructive youth organizations and have usually acted under the influence of bad companions and in concert with them. In one of their recent studies the Gluecks found that almost all the delinquents,

---

American Sociological Review, XXVIII (June, 1963), 385–91; James F. Short, Jr., Ray A. Tennyson, and Kenneth I. Howard, "Behavior Dimensions of Gang Delinquency," *American Sociological Review,* XXVIII (June, 1963), 411–28; James H. S. Bossard and Eleanor Stoker Boll, *The Sociology of Child Development* (New York: Harper and Bros., 1960), pp. 498–539. In his classic study, Thrasher defined the gang as "an interstitial group originally formed spontaneously, and then integrated through conflict" (Frederic M. Thrasher, *The Gang* [Chicago: University of Chicago Press, 1936], p. 57).

80 S. P. Breckinridge and Edith Abbott, *The Delinquent Child and the Home* (New York: Russell Sage Foundation, 1912), p. 35; Burt, p. 125; Shaw and McKay, *Social Factors in Juvenile Delinquency,* pp. 191–99; William Healy, *The Individual Delinquent* (Boston: Little, Brown & Co., 1915), p. 130. By Sheldon and Eleanor T. Glueck, see: *Later Criminal Careers* (New York: The Commonwealth Fund, 1937), p. 75; *Five Hundred Delinquent Women,* pp. 85, 109, 214; and by Healy and Bronner, *New Light on Delinquency and Its Treatment,* pp. 63, 64.

in contrast to very few of the nondelinquents, preferred to chum with delinquents and that more than half of the delinquents, compared with less than 1 per cent of the nondelinquents, were members of gangs.[81] Reckless, observing that lone-wolf offenders have been shown to be in the great minority, states that "the companionship factor in delinquency and crime has been found to operate in three interrelated ways: causation of initial delinquency, continuation in a criminal career, and association in the delinquent act or on the criminal job."[82] However, both Hurwitz and Sutherland believe that the influence of bad companions probably has been given undue weight, the latter pointing out that a large number of gangs exist without criminal records and that "to be left out of groups may be just as productive of delinquency as to be included in them."[83]

Furthermore, Reckless states that before we can assay the true weight of the companionship factor in the causation of initial delinquency, we must determine what kinds of children succumb and do not succumb to the corrupting influence of associates.[84] Studies, including those of the Gluecks, suggest that the delinquents are more active, restless, gregarious, and less solitary in their interests than the nondelinquents and thus indicate that the former, because of a differential response, are exposed more than the latter to the risks of getting into trouble.[85] Nevertheless, it is certainly true that where a child is born into an unsatisfactory family situation, where he is reared in a delinquency area, and where his play-group is a delinquent gang, the possibilities are great that he will come into conflict with the law.[86]

EDUCATION AND RECREATION

All observers agree that the school can exert a powerful influence in the life of the child and that it can do much to prepare him for a happy

[81] Glueck, *Unraveling Juvenile Delinquency*, p. 278. The Gluecks, however, contend that gang membership and presumably delinquent companionship appear too late in the lives of delinquent boys to be judged a cause of their delinquency. See their *Physique and Delinquency* (New York: Harper and Bros., 1956), pp. 40–43.

[82] Reckless, *The Etiology of Delinquent and Criminal Behavior*, p. 28. See also Thomas G. Eynon and Walter C. Reckless, "Companionship at Delinquency Onset," *British Journal of Criminology*, II (Oct., 1961), 162–70. In this study, Eynon and Reckless found that the onset of delinquent behavior is associated with companionship.

[83] Hurwitz, p. 338; Sutherland (1947 ed.), p. 147.

[84] Reckless, p. 30.

[85] *Ibid.*, pp. 30, 31; Glueck, *Unraveling Juvenile Delinquency*, p. 278.

[86] National Commission on Law Observance and Enforcement, Report No. 13, Vol. I, pp. 82–86; Frederic M. Thrasher, *The Gang* (Chicago: University of Chicago Press, 1927), pp. 45–57, 369–408; William F. Whyte, *Street Corner Society* (Chicago: University of Chicago Press, 1943), pp. 255–76; T. Earl Sullenger, *Social Determinants in Juvenile Delinquency* (New York: John Wiley and Sons, Inc., 1936), pp. 43–73; "Symposium on Vandalism," *Federal Probation*, XVIII (Mar., 1954).

and successful career.[87] Furthermore, many investigations have shown that offenders include a comparatively large number of persons who have had school behavior difficulties, truancy problems, and an inadequate amount of education. For example, the Gluecks, in one of their recent studies, state that the school accomplishments and behavior records of the delinquents were definitely inferior to those of the nondelinquents covered in the investigation.[88] On the surface, then, it appears that formal education, of itself, bears an important causal relationship to delinquency and crime; but, as a matter of fact, this is not necessarily true and cannot be shown to be true in general, although it may be so in the particular case. However, such a conclusion in turn does not mean that formal education is unimportant, but rather that it must be seen in its interaction with other factors, like the home, the child's personality, the playgroup, the neighborhood, and so on. And even if we attribute importance to formal education, it does not follow that its most essential element is the mere imparting of knowledge. Far more essential is the way in which it directly or indirectly molds the character of the child.[89]

What has been said about formal education applies equally well to supervised recreation. Unguided play is not necessarily delinquent in character, and many persons who never become offenders prefer and need such recreation. Besides, there is strong evidence that delinquents are not attracted by "guided play," and often, when they participate in it, their behavior remains unchanged.[90] On the other hand, this is no argument against supervised recreation, but rather a reminder of the complexity of the situation. Needless to say, every child should have access to wholesome leisure-time activity; and supervised recreation, when properly planned and administered, can be a very important element in a program for the prevention of crime and delinquency.[91]

Newspapers, magazines, cheap literature, comic books, motion pictures, radio, and television have been charged with causing crime and delinquency by peddling lurid tales of immorality, by featuring brutality and lawlessness, by making crime seem attractive, exciting, and profitable, by teaching the techniques of crime and delinquency, by giving publicity and prestige to crooks, gangsters, gamblers, and confidence

[87] For a discussion of the role of the school in the prevention of delinquency and crime, see Chapter 29.

[88] Glueck, pp. 276, 277. See also Arthur C. Johnson, Jr., "Our Schools Make Criminals," Journal of Criminal Law and Criminology, XXXIII (Nov.–Dec., 1942), 310–15; Price Chenault, "Education," in Contemporary Correction, ed. Paul W. Tappan (New York: McGraw-Hill Book Co., Inc., 1951), pp. 224–37.

[89] Hurwitz, pp. 331–37; Salisbury, pp. 132–65; R. J. Havighurst, P. H. Bowman, G. P. Liddle, C. V. Matthews, and J. V. Pierce, Growing Up in River City (New York: John Wiley and Sons, Inc., 1962), pp. 49–88.

[90] Tappan, pp. 148–51.

[91] See Chapter 29.

men, and by ridiculing and interfering with the work of the courts and law-enforcement agencies. Undoubtedly, all these media of communication, especially motion pictures and television programs with their visual imagery, affect the ideas, attitudes, and behavior of children and adults; but our knowledge regarding their relationship to crime and delinquency is so uncertain that generalizations on the subject are extremely hazardous.[92]

It is clear that such media can be used to exert a harmful influence, but it is also true that their effects can be beneficial. They can provide vicarious experience, draining off tensions and converting antisocial tendencies into imaginary adventures; they can keep young people away from mischief, hooliganism, and vice; and they can arouse public opinion against undesirable social conditions, stimulate public demand for civic reform, and provide support for vigorous law enforcement.

Although these media may be important as direct causes of crime and delinquency in some cases, in general it appears that they have almost no direct influence on the person or merely intensify already existent attitudes and personality traits. Blumer and Hauser, in a study which is still our chief source of information regarding the effects of motion pictures on crime and delinquency, concluded that this medium of communication was a factor of importance in the delinquent or criminal careers of about 10 per cent of the male and 25 per cent of the female offenders studied. However, according to these investigators, a child from a high-rate delinquency area is more likely to be influenced toward crime by motion pictures than a child from an area of low delinquency rates.[93]

In their study of the effects of television in the lives of children, Schramm, Lyle, and Parker state that very little delinquency can be traced directly to television. In their opinion, delinquency is complex

[92] For some views on the subject, see Frank Harris, *The Presentation of Crime in the Newspapers* (Hanover, N.H.: The Sociological Press, 1932); Paul G. Cressey, "The Motion Picture Experience as Modified by Social Background and Personality," *American Sociological Review*, III (Aug., 1938), 516–25; F. Perry Olds, "The Place of the Press in Crime Control," *Yearbook, 1947* (New York: National Probation and Parole Association, 1948), pp. 245–59; Paul S. Deland, "Crime News Encourages Delinquency and Crime," *Federal Probation*, XI (Apr.–June, 1947), 3–6; Marjorie Bell, "The N. P. P. A. at the Congress of Correction," *Focus*, XXVII (Nov., 1948), 175–79; Bernard Berelson, "Communications and Public Opinion," in *Communications in Modern Society*, ed. Wilbur Schramm (Urbana: University of Illinois Press, 1948), pp. 167–85; John R. Cavanagh, "The Comics War," *Journal of Criminal Law and Criminology*, XL (May–June, 1949), 28–35; Thomas Ford Hoult, "Comic Books and Juvenile Delinquency," *Sociology and Social Research*, XXXIII (Mar.–Apr., 1949), 279–84; Frederic Wertham, *Seduction of the Innocent* (New York: Rinehart & Co., Inc., 1954); James Jackson Kilpatrick, *The Smut Peddlers* (Garden City, N.Y.: Doubleday and Co., Inc., 1960).

[93] Herbert Blumer and Philip M. Hauser, *Movies, Delinquency, and Crime* (New York: The Macmillan Co., 1933), pp. 35, 38–72, 81, 198, 199, 201, 202.

behavior that usually has a number of roots—"often a broken home, or a feeling of rejection by parents or peer group." They conclude that "television is at best a contributory cause."[94]

As Clinard explains, "Present evidence seems to indicate that the process of acquiring conduct norms, both deviant and conventional, is primarily through intimate association with others and personal experiences of a face-to-face nature."[95] Persons who have already acquired delinquent or criminal tendencies or who have abnormal psychogenic traits may have these tendencies or traits aggravated by a bad motion picture, comic book, or radio or television program; but it is doubtful whether many persons without such tendencies or traits become criminals or delinquents solely because of the effects of such media. It must be added that children are more susceptible to the influence of these media than adults, that there are many highly suggestible, restless, and unstable persons with criminal or delinquent tendencies, and that the agencies of mass communication are exerting an increasing influence in our complex society.

RELIGION

Statistical investigations have attempted to reveal the effects of religion on crime and delinquency, but they have not succeeded in disentangling the factor of religion from other closely related factors, such as the home, the neighborhood, nativity, education, economic status, and race. Nor do these investigations penetrate beyond such externals as church membership, attendance, and avowals of faith, and so reveal nothing regarding the actual influence of religion in the lives of those studied.

European investigations have shown that in Germany, Holland, and Hungary the crime rate is generally highest among Catholics, lower among Protestants, and lowest among Jews; but these differences in rates seem to be more closely related to economic, social, and cultural living conditions than to religion.[96] In the United States, Baptists and Catholics have the highest rates of commitment to prisons, but this appears to be due to the fact that most Negroes are Baptists and most recent immigrants are Catholics, which means that many in these two denominations are in an unfavorable social and economic position and so subject to special criminal risks.

[94] Wilbur Schramm, Jack Lyle, Edwin B. Parker, *Television in the Lives of Our Children* (Stanford, Calif.: Stanford University Press, 1961), pp. 163–66, 173–75.

[95] Marshall B. Clinard, "Secondary Community Influences and Juvenile Delinquency", *The Annals of the American Academy of Political and Social Science*, CCLXI (Jan., 1949), 48.

[96] Hurwitz, pp. 233, 234, 283–85.

Since all kinds of people from all kinds of social and economic backgrounds belong to the various religious denominations, religious doctrines and teachings exert varying influences in the lives of people regardless of their religious affiliations. Furthermore, moral precepts and ethical considerations of a nonreligious nature are so interwoven with religious principles that they cannot be separated for the purpose of evaluation even in the individual case. Nevertheless, as Hurwitz concludes, "it is a fact that the *ethical norms* regularly inculcated by a religious upbringing and typically associated with genuine religious convictions create particularly strong impulses to resist criminal urges."[97]

ECONOMIC FACTORS

There is no adequate empirical basis for comparing the relationship of different economic and political systems to crime and delinquency. The economic determinists, however, argue that the causes of crime and all other social ills are to be found in the operation of the economic factors. Marxian Communists, especially, advance this thesis and contend that crime and delinquency can be dealt with only through the elimination of the capitalist system, that is, the system which is based on private ownership and private profit.[98] According to this view, the capitalist system makes men selfish, leads to the exploitation of the masses, and creates poverty, unwholesome living conditions, and widespread misery, which in turn cause crime and delinquency. Reorganize society along communist or socialist lines and you eliminate class struggle, give labor its just reward, stimulate men to advance the welfare of the group, and solve the problems of crime and delinquency. But why is it, then, that criminality still exists in the Soviet Union? This, the Russians try to explain by saying that the influences of the former capitalist system

[97] *Ibid.*, p. 236. See also John R. Miner, "Church Membership and Commitments of Prisoners," *Human Biology*, III (Sept., 1931), 429–36; A. J. Jaffe and Saul D. Alinsky, "A Comparison of Jewish and Non-Jewish Convicts," *Jewish Social Studies*, I (July, 1939), 359–66; Warren C. Middleton and Paul J. Fay, "Attitudes of Delinquent and Non-Delinquent Girls Toward Sunday Observance, the Bible, and War," *Journal of Educational Psychology*, XXXII (Oct., 1941), 555–58; William C. Kvaraceus, "Delinquent Behavior and Church Attendance," *Sociology and Social Research*, XXVIII (Mar.–Apr., 1944), 284–89; A. M. Carr-Saunders, H. Mannheim, and E. C. Rhodes, *Young Offenders: An Inquiry into Juvenile Delinquency* (New York: The Macmillan Co., 1944); Phillip M. Smith, "Organized Religion and Criminal Behavior," *Sociology and Research*, XXXIII (May–June, 1949), 362–67; William W. Wattenberg, "Church Attendance and Juvenile Misconduct," *Sociology and Social Research*, XXXIV (Jan.–Feb., 1950), 195–202.

[98] The most significant attempt to interpret criminality as the product of the capitalist system is to be found in W. A. Bonger's work, *Criminality and Economic Condition* (Boston: Little, Brown and Co., 1916).

linger on and that they are still involved in the fight to eliminate these influences.[99]

The theory of the economic determinism of crime is open to the same objections that can be raised against any other particularistic explanation of human behavior. The economic factors are functionally related to many other factors, such as the biological, geographical, psychological, domestic, religious, political, and educational factors, and all these factors must be thought of in terms of their interaction in the total situation. To expand the meaning of the economic factors until they appear to explain all social problems is mere tautology. It makes social problems synonymous with economic problems but fails to provide an explanation for either. Pushed to its ultimate implications, it becomes nothing less than this absurd generalization: the whole social life is the cause of the whole social life. On the other hand, to make the economic factors merely the principal factors, and not the only factors, amounts to an abandonment of the Marxian theory and leaves us with no criteria by which to judge what is meant by the term "principal." Naturally, the capitalist system is related to crime and delinquency in the United States, but all kinds of societies have had these problems, and no one can say whether they would increase or decrease if we had a different kind of economic system.

Furthermore, criminologists do not have the facts to compare the relationship between the economic conditions and crime in one country with that of another country. American scholars, therefore, seeking an appraisal of the economic factors, have turned to an examination of the conditions within the United States. In this examination, they have used two major approaches: (1) a comparative analysis of the economic status of offenders and nonoffenders; and (2) a study of the relation between crime rates and the business cycle.

Studies of the economic status of offenders and nonoffenders have indicated that the lower economic class has much higher rates of crime and delinquency than the upper economic class in the United States.[100] How-

[99] For a discussion of crime and its control in the Soviet Union, see, for example, Sidney and Beatrice Webb, *Soviet Communism: A New Civilization?* (New York: Charles Scribner's Sons, 1936), Vol. II; Hermann Mannheim, *Criminal Justice and Social Reconstruction* (London: Kegan Paul, Trench, Trubner and Co., Ltd., 1946), pp. 109 ff., 137 ff., and index of literature, p. 275; N. Berman, "Juvenile Delinquency under the Soviets," *Journal of Criminal Law and Criminology*, XXX (May–June, 1939), 68–76.

[100] See, for example, M. G. Caldwell, "The Economic Status of Families of Delinquent Boys in Wisconsin," *American Journal of Sociology*, XXXVII (Sept., 1931), 231–39; Gillin, pp. 140, 141; William F. Ogburn, "Factors in the Variation of Crime Among Cities," *Journal of the American Statistical Association*, XXX (Mar., 1935), 12–34; Shaw and McKay, *Juvenile Delinquency and Urban Areas*, pp. 141–46; Glueck, *Unraveling Juvenile Delinquency*, p. 280.

ever, these studies are not conclusive. Since they have involved the use
of official criminal statistics, they are subject in general to the criticism
that they are incomplete, inaccurate, and nonrepresentative.[101] In particular they are open to the criticism that they are unfair to the poor,
who, it is claimed, are more likely to be detected, arrested, prosecuted,
and convicted than the rich. In fact, some students of the problem believe that the homes and the neighborhoods of the upper economic class
in the United States are producing far more possible crime and delinquency than the official records seem to indicate.

Many studies have been made of the relation between crime and delinquency rates and the business cycle. These studies, however, have
brought conflicting results. For example, Ogburn and Thomas, using
American data, found some evidence that crime increased slightly with
decreases in business activity and decreased slightly with increases in
such activity; and Winslow showed that in Massauchusetts crime increased in years of low employment and decreased in years of high
employment; but Thomas, employing English data, concluded that there
was no close connection between the fluctuations of crime and business;
and Reinemann, after a study of the situation in Philadelphia, stated that
delinquency is high during a depression period, low in a period of fairly
normal economic development which can be classified as neither prosperity nor depression, but highest during a period of extreme prosperity.[102] In 1937, Sellin reviewed such studies and concluded that they
could not be used as a basis for any definite generalization regarding the
relation between crime and the business cycle; and in 1943, Reckless, in
referring to these studies, said that "the relation of the ebb and flow of
economic activity, of depression and prosperity, to the volume of crime
had been severely discounted by elaborate statistical studies."[103] The
volume of crime may be related in an important way to the business
cycle, but as yet this has not been conclusively demonstrated.

In fact, neither of these approaches has cast very much light on the
significance of the economic factors. The evidence on hand, however,

[101] See Chapter I for an evaluation of criminal statistics.

[102] William F. Ogburn and Dorothy Swaine Thomas, "The Influence of the Business
Cycle on Certain Social Conditions," *Journal of the American Statistical Association*,
XVIII, New Series (Sept., 1922), 339, 340; Emma A. Winslow, "Relationships be-
tween Employment and Crime Fluctuations as Shown by Massachusetts Statistics,"
Report on the Causes of Crime, Report No. 13 (Washington, D.C.: National Commis-
sion on Law Observance and Enforcement, 1931), Vol. I, pp. 310–12; Dorothy Swaine
Thomas, *Social Aspects of the Business Cycle* (New York: Alfred A. Knopf, Inc.,
1927), pp. 135–44; John Otto Reinemann, "Juvenile Delinquency in Philadelphia and
Economic Trends," *Temple Law Quarterly*, XX (Apr., 1947), 576–83.

[103] Thorsten Sellin, *Research Memorandum on Crime in the Depression* (New
York: Social Science Research Council, Bull. 27, 1937); Reckless, *The Etiology of
Delinquent and Criminal Behavior*, pp. 47, 48. See also George B. Vold, *Theoretical
Criminology* (New York: Oxford University Press, 1958), pp. 159–82.

does indicate that these factors do not bear a simple, direct relationship to crime and delinquency, but instead interact with many other factors in a very complex functional relationship with law violations. Thus, poverty is related to crime and delinquency chiefly through such conditions as domestic discord, bad housing, inadequate education and recreation, poor health, early employment of children, and the lack of training and opportunity necessary for the commission of certain offenses. But the complexity of this relationship is evidenced by the fact that many poor persons never become criminals or delinquents, that rich persons violate the law, and that both offenders and nonoffenders come from the same poor family and from the same delinquency area.

INTERACTION OF PERSONAL AND ENVIRONMENTAL FACTORS

This brief examination of the personal and environmental factors has shown that there is no simple explanation of crime and delinquency. The nature of these factors and their varying combinations differ greatly from one case to another. Indeed, the complexity of the problem has led Reckless to suggest that we may have to abandon the search for causes and be content with a study of the factors which, "while not explaining why individuals become criminal, will indicate the risk or liability for becoming criminal."[104] The formulation of new and apparently all-inclusive theories of criminal behavior is a stimulating intellectual adventure that often provides valuable insights into reality, but a recognition of the complexity of causation firmly warns against the complete or uncritical acceptance of such theories.

The personal factors contribute to crime and delinquency by decreasing the adjustment potentialities of the individual; the environmental factors, by blocking the satisfaction of the personality needs of the individual, or by instilling values that bring him into conflict with the values of organized society, or both. However, human behavior, whether law-abiding or law-violating, is the resultant of the interaction of personal and environmental factors; and we must understand that in science the term "cause" refers to a functional relationship between the phenomenon studied and the conditions necessary for its appearance. In any given case, some of these conditions exert more influence than others, but the functioning of all in their interaction is necessary to produce the observed phenomenon, which would be different if there were the least modification in the total situation. In other words, as Carr points out, crime or delinquency is "the end term of an equation in which deviation factors exceed conformity factors."[105] In some cases of crime or delinquency the

104 Reckless, *Criminal Behavior,* p. 181.
105 Carr, p. 161.

deviation factors may be more personal than environmental, while in other cases, the reverse may be true; but never is a person a criminal only because of personality characteristics or only because of the internalization of values that are unacceptable to organized society. There is always a mixture of these influences in varying proportions.

After a review of the various approaches to the intricate problem of causation, Barnes and Tetters conclude that thus far no unitary cause of crime has been discovered and that the eclectic or "multiple-causation" thesis is the most fruitful position that can be taken.[106] Sheldon Glueck has expressed a similar view, declaring that a wise eclecticism is still the only promising and sensible credo for the modern criminologist.[107] Vold, while stating that no single theory can explain all the varieties of criminal behavior, calls for the systematic delineation of types of criminality and the development of a consistent theory for each type. This, in his opinion, would be less confusing than attempts to explain all kinds of offenses by one theory and at the same time would correct the absurdities of "a too facile eclecticism."[108] Reckless thinks that the search for a general theory of causation is probably unrealistic and suggests that containment theory be substituted for causal theory. In support of his position, he explains that a containing external social structure (principally the family and other supportive groups) and a containing internal buffer ("self" components) hold individuals in line and protect them against deviation from the social and legal norms. Thus if there are "causes" which produce deviant behavior, they are neutralized or parried by the two containing buffers.[109]

As all these writers have emphasized, criminology deals with very complex problems about which our knowledge is quite meager. The frame of reference in this field, therefore, must of necessity be rather wide; and the conclusions, loosely drawn. This is not to say that a certain theory should not be employed as a guide in a specific research project—indeed, this must be done—but it does mean that the conclusions of such a research must be primarily related to the area explored and the level of abstraction used. Thus within a broad frame of reference,

---

[106] Barnes and Teeters, pp. 206–10. The multiple-factor approach has been criticized as being too vague, unsystematic, and subjective to provide us with any real assistance in our efforts to understand causation. See for example, Albert K. Cohen, "Multiple Factor Approaches," *The Sociology of Crime and Delinquency,* eds. Marvin E. Wolfgang, Leonard Savitz, and Norman Johnston (New York: John Wiley and Sons, Inc., 1962), pp. 77–80.

[107] Sheldon Glueck, "Theory and Fact in Criminology," *British Journal of Delinquency,* VII (Oct., 1956), 108.

[108] Vold, *Theoretical Criminology,* pp. 313–15.

[109] Walter C. Reckless, *The Crime Problem,* (New York: Appleton-Century-Crofts, Inc., 1961), pp. 335–59. See also his "A Non-Causal Explanation: Containment Theory," *Excerpta Criminologica,* II (Mar.–Apr., 1962), 131–34.

a closely reasoned theoretical system can be created on this or that level of abstraction, but the possibility of other theories on the same or other levels of abstraction should be clearly recognized by such a system.

The most important environmental factor is the family, which is still society's first bulwark against the formation of antisocial tendencies. This should not be construed to mean, however, that the family exerts its influence independently of other social institutions, for it is functionally related to them and is affected by, and contributes to, their organization or disorganization.

The influence of the environment in the instilling of deviant values is most clearly seen when a career of delinquency and crime develops largely as a result of this influence. The adjustment of the person during the development of such a career is an educational process—a habituation to a way of life.[110] It depends on instruction, approval, companionship, and discussion, in which companions, friends, and, sometimes, relatives participate, encourage, stimulate, praise, and blame; and like much education, it usually begins in a small, trifling, playful way in group activity and becomes more and more serious as attitudes harden and skills develop. Through delinquency, and later, crime, the person seeks to satisfy the desires that every person has, that is, his desires for recognition, security, affection, and adventure; but unlike the nonoffender, the offender expresses these desires in terms of a set of values which society has stigmatized as unacceptable. And while he is doing this, unwise policies and inept practices of law-enforcement agencies and correctional institutions may drive him more deeply into crime or delinquency and make his rehabilitation more difficult. It follows logically from the preceding points that a fruitful approach to the prevention of crime and delinquency is through the various groups in which children are introduced to the customs and morals of this country. Of these, the family is by far the most important. Given a wholesome and enriching family experience, a child becomes well fortified against the perplexing problems that will confront him later when he reaches adolescence and adulthood.

During our discussion of the personal and environmental factors we have stressed the complexity of the process of causation and our ignorance regarding it. This, however, should not be permitted to obscure the fact that studies have consistently revealed the presence of certain personal and environmental factors, such as serious personality maladjustments, inadequate families, delinquent gangs, and disorganized com-

---

[110] For a detailed analysis of the development of such a career, see the life histories by Clifford R. Shaw in *The Jack Roller* (Chicago: University of Chicago Press, 1930); *Brothers in Crime* (Chicago: University of Chicago Press, 1938); and *The Natural History of a Delinquent Career* (Chicago: University of Chicago Press, 1931).

munities, during the childhood and early adolescence of criminals. That many persons do not succumb to the influence of these factors, but despite them, become law-abiding, should not deter us from modifying or eliminating these factors so that they will *not* influence those who *do* succumb and thus become criminals.[111]

[111] Walter C. Reckless, "The Sociologist Looks at Crime," *The Annals of the American Academy of Political and Social Science,* CCXVII (Sept., 1941), 81–83; Hurwitz, p. 342; Albert Morris, "Crime Causation," *Federal Probation,* VII (July–Sept., 1943), 17–20.

Part III

CRIME AND JUSTICE

13

Police

IMPORTANCE OF THE POLICE

In general, the police are charged with the regulation and protection of the community, especially with respect to matters affecting public health, comfort, morals, safety, or prosperity. Their primary duty, however, is to maintain order and enforce the law.[1]

No public agency is of greater importance to the community than the police. Usually, the police officer is the first point of contact between the citizen and the law. Indeed, for many the police are the law. How the police conduct themselves and what they accomplish do much to destroy or create respect for the law. And the increasing complexity of our society, with its urbanization, industrialization, technological improvement, and mobility, has brought greater need of law and efficient police protection. The police, moreover, are in a strategic position to detect the causes of crime and delinquency and to prevent such acts. They are on the "front line," and their vigor and efficiency largely determine society's reaction to violations of the law. Without the police, the criminal courts would have few defendants; probation officers, few probationers; penal institutions, few inmates; and parole officers, few parolees.

Then, too, the way in which the police handle the offender may influence his future behavior. Clumsy apprehension and brutal treatment by the police may dramatize the offender's break with the law, stigmatize him as a criminal, embitter him, and intensify his criminal tendencies. Skillful and intelligent police work, on the other hand, may reduce the offender's hostility to society and contribute to his rehabilitation. Finally, if for no other reason, the police are important because they are so numerous and cost so much. In 1945 it was estimated that the annual police budget for the United States was $4,000,000,000 and that the number of police per-

[1] Rollin M. Perkins, *Elements of Police Science* (Chicago: The Foundation Press, Inc., 1942), p. vii.

sonnel was in excess of 210,000, of whom about 130,000 were in uniform and about 80,000 were sheriffs, constables, marshals, and other similar peace officers. In 1962 the operation of the police departments in 1,220 cities, which had a total population of 71,157,000, cost over one billion dollars.[2] As a matter of fact, the number of police and their cost would be even greater if all the communities in America were given adequate police service and protection.

COMPOSITION OF THE POLICE

In the United States each political unit may have its own police. Therefore, police agencies of various types, and having general or specialized functions, exist at all levels of government. No attempt will be made here to enumerate all these agencies. Instead, mention will be made of some of the most important ones at the various levels.

At the federal level, several departments have their own investigative units, each of which is charged with the enforcement of the particular laws over which its department has jurisdiction. Among these units are the Federal Bureau of Investigation of the Justice Department, the Immigration Border Patrol of the Justice Department, and the Secret Service Division of the Treasury Department. The Army and Navy also may be used as police forces in emergencies.

A number of states maintain state police units that are authorized to exercise general powers of law enforcement. Other states have statewide organizations that are charged with the patrol of the highways and the enforcement of motor vehicle laws. Some states have established state bureaus of identification which operate at the state level as clearing houses for criminal identification and investigation. These also give assistance to local authorities when requested to do so. In all states, various departments have minor investigative units, each of which operates within a limited scope to enforce the particular laws with which its department deals. The state militias also may perform police functions in emergencies.

On the local level, almost every political unit has some kind of police. The county has a sheriff with as many deputies as he may appoint. Some counties have their own police forces, which either duplicate the sheriff's jurisdiction or virtually displace it. The township has a constable; the village or town, a marshal or a very small police force; and the city, a municipal police department. In the big cities of the country, the police forces, burdened with increasing duties, have grown to impressive propor-

---

[2] J. P. Shalloo, "Modern Police vs. Modern Society," *Prison Journal*, XXV (July, 1945), 70; *The Municipal Year Book, 1963* (Chicago: The International City Managers' Association, 1963), pp. 417, 418. See also V. A. Leonard, *Police Organization and Management* (Brooklyn: The Foundation Press, Inc., 1964), pp. 90–92.

tions. In 1962 New York City had 25,627 employees in its police department, the largest in the nation; Chicago, 11,879; Los Angeles, 6,166; Philadelphia, 6,004; and Detroit, 4,866.[3] As on the state level, various local governmental divisions and departments maintain minor investigative units which have limited police powers.[4]

In addition to the public agencies just discussed, there are the private police. These are privately employed, financed, supervised, and controlled, although they are sometimes commissioned as public agents. Industrial plants, hotels, department stores, railroads, bankers' associations, and insurance companies employ special agents to guard their properties and interests. In many small communities, merchants' associations employ night watchmen to protect their stores and office buildings. Private detective agencies furnish protection for race tracks, conventions, exhibits, entertainments, and various types of public assemblages.

It should now be clear that there is no such thing in the United States as a police system or even a set of police systems within any reasonably accurate sense of the term. What are usually called systems are really only collections of police units which have some similarity of authority, organization, or jurisdiction, but which have no systematic relationship to one another.[5]

BASIC OBJECTIVES OF THE POLICE

The remainder of this chapter will be devoted almost entirely to the regular police units that have broad powers of law enforcement. The basic objectives of these police are the following:

1. The prevention of crime and delinquency by modifying the conditions that produce them, by instilling respect for law and order, and by cooperating with other agencies in the promotion of public welfare.

2. The repression of the criminality and delinquency of those so inclined by patrolling neighborhoods, inspecting premises, and keeping fully informed regarding the affairs of the areas over which they have jurisdiction.

3. The apprehension and identification of offenders and the accumulation of evidence against persons charged with crime.

4. The recovery of stolen property so as to reduce the cost of crime and restrain those who, though not active criminals, might benefit from the gains of crime.

[3] *The Municipal Year Book, 1963*, p. 419.

[4] John D. Holstrom, "Police Administration," *Encyclopedia of Criminology* (New York: The Philosophical Library, 1949), pp. 319–24; Bruce Smith, *Police Systems in the United States* (New York: Harper and Bros., 1960), pp. 20–24. See also Henry S. Dewhurst, *The Railroad Police* (Springfield, Ill.: Charles C. Thomas, Publisher, 1955).

[5] Smith, p. 20.

5. The regulation of people in their noncriminal activities, for example, the direction of traffic and the enforcement of sanitation and licensing laws and ordinances.

Further consideration will be given to these objectives, but this enumeration of what is expected of the police certainly serves to emphasize their importance.[6]

DIFFICULTIES OF POLICE WORK

Police in the United States have been the object of severe criticism. They have been called ignorant, inefficient, brutal, corrupt, and lawless, and many investigations have been cited in support of this indictment. In their defense the police, while admitting that much must be done to improve the law-enforcement agencies of the country, point to the following difficulties which greatly complicate their work:

1. Public apathy often permits corrupt political machines to dominate and hamper police departments.

2. The public does not understand the problems of modern police work, often fails to give adequate cooperation in the apprehension and prosecution of criminals, tends to expect the "impossible" of law-enforcement agencies, and neglects to confer sufficient recognition upon policemen who day after day render efficient and conscientious service.[7]

3. The spirit of "getting something for nothing" is strong in America, and many people do not care how much crime there is as long as they themselves are not hurt or inconvenienced.

4. Modern urban life has imposed an enormous number of duties upon the police, who in the meantime have not been given adequate personnel and authority to cope with their new problems.

5. Political boundaries impede the police and permit many criminals to avoid apprehension.

6. The technicalities of criminal prosecution tend to offset the vigilance of the police and allow thousands of law violators to escape punishment.

7. The laws and court decisions on arrest and the acquisition of evidence are inadequate and obscure, leaving the police uncertain as to how far they may lawfully go in the enforcement of the law.

8. Most policemen are not carefully selected, properly trained, adequately paid, or sufficiently protected against arbitrary dismissals.

[6] O. W. Wilson, *Police Administration* (New York: McGraw-Hill Book Co., Inc., 1963), pp. 3–8, 22; The Institute for Training in Municipal Administration, *Municipal Police Administration* (Ann Arbor, Mich.: Lithoprinted by Cushing-Mallory, Inc., 1961), pp. 7, 8. For a discussion of police work with minority groups, see Joseph D. Lohman, *Principles of Police Work with Minority Groups* (Louisville, Ky.: Division of Police, 1950).

[7] For a discussion of the importance of public support in police work, see William H. Parker, "The Police Challenge in Our Great Cities," *The Annals of the American Academy of Political and Social Science*, CCXCI (Jan., 1954), 5–13.

RURAL AND SUBURBAN POLICE

Much of the rural and suburban law-enforcement machinery of the United States originated in early England. Thus, we find that the offices of sheriff, constable, and town marshal, which are still in existence in the United States, have roots that extend back to the Anglo-Saxon or Norman periods of the mother country.[8]

Every American county has its sheriff, and in all but a few instances he still exercises his ancient police powers.[9] Serious obstacles, however, interfere with the efficient operation of his office. Popular election to the office is the general rule, and the sheriff, therefore, is naturally and inevitably involved in partisan politics. His term of office is usually only four years; sometimes he may not succeed himself; never do the formal qualifications for office extend beyond such elementary matters as age, residence, and citizenship. Once in office, the inefficient sheriff can feel quite secure, since he can be removed only for moral turpitude or malfeasance, and even then only by the operation of complex legal machinery. A "political bird of passage," the sheriff tends to cling to his private occupation, and so he may be also a farmer, a carpenter, a butcher, or a grocer. Rarely has he had any previous police experience, and even if he has, his many other duties seriously limit his use of it. Almost everywhere in the United States the sheriff is responsible for the service of civil process and the management of the county jail. In parts of the South and the Southeast, he is also the tax collector. Furthermore, in some states and counties, the fee system under which the sheriff obtains all or part of his compensation operates to direct his attention to his more lucrative tasks and away from his unpleasant police duties.

Many sheriffs rely heavily upon the fees which they receive for the performance of almost every official act, and in the large populous counties these fees may run into unbelievable figures. In 1949, Bruce Smith reported that the total compensation for the American sheriff ranged all

[8] Bruce Smith, *Rural Crime Control* (New York: Institute of Public Administration, Columbia University, 1933), pp. 36–42, 75–78, 180–86, 218–99; also, see his *Police Systems in the United States*, pp. 66–71.

[9] According to the National Sheriffs' Association, the office of sheriff has not been abolished in any county in the United States. However, the sheriff of Petroleum County, Montana, is appointed under a county management form of government and carries the official title of Director of Law Enforcement. (Correspondence with the National Sheriffs' Association, Washington, D.C., dated March 31, 1955 and April 29, 1955.) The legislature of Connecticut has abolished the county form of government, but the office of sheriff remains, because it is provided for in the state's constitution. Attempts to abolish the office of sheriff in Connecticut by amendment of the state's constitution have been defeated. However, the duties of the sheriff in Connecticut are now primarily those of a deputy jail administrator in charge of what used to be the county jail. (Correspondence with the National Sheriffs' Association, Washington, D.C., dated October 29, 1963.)

the way from $1,200 per year in the smaller rural areas to $100,000 per year in a great metropolitan center.[10] It is not surprising, therefore, that sometimes he is the best-paid public official in the county and that his position is often regarded as the most desirable "political plum" in the state.

In some counties, efforts are being made to overcome the inherent weaknesses of the sheriff's office. Deputies have been employed for regular patrol work, expensive means of transportation and communication have been introduced, and training programs have been inaugurated. These efforts, however, appear foredoomed to failure. In fact, in the great majority of counties the sheriff system has already collapsed. The cumulative effects of untrained officers, short terms, political domination, public distrust, the increasing complexity of rural life, and the encroachment of organized crime have proved too much for machinery that was made to function in a much simpler age; the decline in the effectiveness of the sheriff appears destined to continue. Where the situation has already become serious, the sheriff has had to turn to the urban, state, and federal police for support.

In America the constable is an officer of a town or township. He is selected by popular vote or casual appointment, usually without reference to any standard except residence and citizenship. Almost always he is untrained, and except in a few cases, he derives his sole compensation from fees received for various services, but his office is far less lucrative than the sheriff's. This means that the constable is strictly a part-time officer who must look to private sources for most of his income. It also means that he receives no compensation for doing police work and so tends to devote his time to his other duties, which in addition to serving civil process may include such activities as collecting taxes and issuing notices of local elections. All the evidence indicates that he has outlived his usefulness and that his office might be eliminated without detriment to the administration of justice. In fact, this has already happened in many sections of the country where he has been replaced by regularly organized town police.

The town marshal and the village policeman, still in existence in some parts of the country, are subject to the same criticisms that have been directed against the constable. Like him, they are almost always untrained, dominated by partisan politics, poorly paid, and employed on a part-time basis. It is not surprising, then, that these offices command little respect,

---

[10] A survey conducted by the National Sheriffs' Association revealed that in 1959 the salaries of sheriffs in the United States ranged from $1,500 a year to $25,000 a year (Everett M. King, *Sheriff's Manual* [Washington, D.C.: National Sheriffs' Association, 1960], pp. 45, 46).

often remain vacant for extended periods, and provide little police protection.

The collapse of the sheriff-constable system has led to the establishment of county police forces in some parts of the United States. In some cases these police function as an integral part of the sheriff's office; in others, they serve under other public authorities such as the county board or the county judge.[11]

URBAN POLICE

In England, the first real urban police department was established as the result of an act passed by Parliament in 1829. This act created a police department for the City of London, and its uniformed members were called "Bobbies" in honor of Sir Robert Peel, the sponsor of the act. London policemen have carried this title ever since.[12]

This development came even later in America, where the basis for the modern police department was not laid down until New York passed a statute for this purpose in 1844. Other states followed the example set by New York, and a new period of American police protection was introduced. Nevertheless, regular uniforms were not generally adopted until about 1855, their use being resisted as un-American and undemocratic. Within the next few decades, the unsatisfactory exercise of the police power by local authorities led to the state control of the police forces of nearly all the large cities of the country. This, however, was met with a rising demand for home rule, and in all but a few cities the hand of the state was withdrawn. A reminder of this widespread development is to be found in the present state control of the police forces of Baltimore, St. Louis, Kansas City (Missouri), and a few other smaller cities.[13]

Administrative Controls. There is a great variety of methods by which the public exercises control over the municipal police department. However, these may be classified into five general types of administrative controls. Thus, administrative control may be exercised by (1) the municipal council, (2) a local police board or commission, (3) a state-appointed ad-

---

[11] Smith, *Police Systems in the United States*, pp. 71–103; Edward J. Hickey, "Trends in Rural Police Protection," *The Annals of the American Academy of Political and Social Science*, CCXCI (Jan., 1954), 22–30.

[12] Leon Radzinowicz, *A History of English Criminal Law and Its Administration from 1750* (New York: Macmillan Co., 1957), Vol. II, p. 403; Perkins, pp. 1–9; Leonard, pp. 2–4.

[13] Raymond B. Fosdick, *American Police Systems* (New York: Appleton-Century-Crofts, Inc., 1920), pp. 58–102; Perkins, p. 9; Smith, *Police Systems in the United States*, p. 187. For the history of police in ante bellum South Carolina, see Jack Kenny Williams, *Vogues in Villainy* (Columbia, S.C.: University of South Carolina Press, 1959), pp. 60–74.

ministrator or board, (4) a commissioner of public safety, and (5) the executive official of the city, that is, the mayor or the city manager.

In the first type of administrative control, which is now largely confined to small cities and towns, a committee of the municipal council exercises its control through a police official usually called the chief of police. Its great weakness lies in its tendency to make the police department a pawn in the game of politics.

In the second type of administrative control, which is still in operation in a number of communities, the police board or commission is composed of persons who are not members of the local legislative body. Designed to "take the police out of politics," it has rarely fulfilled the hopes of its sponsors, and in some cases it has generated factional fights to the detriment of the police department.

In a few cities the police force is administered by a state-appointed board or administrator. This type of administrative control, also, was introduced to eliminate politics from the force; but it has succeeded merely in substituting state politics for local politics and in complicating administrative problems by the injection of the thorny issue of home rule.

In cities where the commission form of government has been established, the elected commissioner of public safety exercises not only legislative power as a member of the city commission but also plenary control over a number of city departments, usually including the police, fire, health, and welfare departments. However, his multiple and varied duties and his lack of training and experience have seldom permitted the commissioner of public safety to achieve success in the police field.

The type of administrative control in which the police are an arm of the city's chief executive has assumed various forms. In all, however, the mayor or city manager is the superior police authority, and the chief or police commissioner is in immediate command. In some of the smaller cities, the chief of police is an elected official, but this has little to recommend it, since it immerses the office in the welter of politics and encourages political rivalry between the mayor and the chief to the detriment of the force. Most large cities using this type of administrative control have both a civilian and a professional head of the police department. The civilian head is frequently called the commissioner, while the professional administrator has the title of chief of police. The commissioner, rather than the mayor, handles the general business of the department and interprets its policy to the public, leaving the technical administrative duties to the chief of police. Regardless of what form this type of administrative control may take, it has the important advantage of placing authority over the police in the hands of the public official (that is, the mayor or the city manager) who is held largely responsible by the voters for the effectiveness of law enforcement.

Experience has conclusively shown that no type of administrative control can guarantee an effective and competent police force. However, it has also clearly demonstrated that (1) police work demands a degree of initiative, decisiveness, and vigor which can be displayed only in a single-headed form of administrative control; and that (2) appointment, rather than election, is the best method of choosing the head of the police department.[14]

Principles of Organization. Certain fundamental principles common to all organizations must be observed if efficiency is to be achieved in the operation of the police department. These may be summarized as follows:

1. Basic organization units must be created. Similar activities should be grouped together in divisions and bureaus and each basic unit placed under the control of a single person. Thus, all crime prevention activities should be combined in one unit and all traffic work in another.

2. Lines of demarcation between units must be clearly drawn and precisely defined so that confusion regarding responsibility, duplication of effort, and neglect of duty will be prevented.

3. Channels for the flow of information and the delegation of authority must be established so that the coordination of effort into a unified force can be achieved.

4. The distinction between line and staff activities must be recognized in order to prevent the interruption of the flow of authority and the reduction of the striking power of the force. Line activities are those which carry out directly the purposes for which the department was created. Typical line activities are patrol, investigation, and prevention. Staff activities are not concerned directly with basic objectives, but are designed to be of service to those engaged in line activities. Typical staff activities are records, personnel, communications, and maintenance.

5. Unity of command must be established. Each individual, unit, and situation should be under the immediate control of only one person in order to avoid the friction that results from duplication of direction and supervision. This principle must be observed from the top to the bottom of the organization.

6. The span of control must not be excessive. No more units or persons should be placed under a single executive than he can effectively supervise.

7. Responsibility must be clearly fixed. Each task should be made the unmistakable duty of some particular person.

[14] Bruce Smith, "Municipal Police Administration," *The Annals of the American Academy of Political and Social Science,* CXLVI (Nov., 1929), 1–27; Donal E. J. MacNamara, "American Police Administration at Mid-Century," *Public Administration Review,* X (Summer, 1950), 181–89; Leonard, pp. 17–30; Fosdick, p. 115.

8. Supervision of each person at the level of his work must be provided at all times and places.

9. Responsibility must carry with it commensurate authority.

10. Persons must be held strictly accountable for the authority delegated to them.[15]

Internal Organization. Almost every conceivable arrangement has been used in constructing the internal organization of American municipal police departments. In certain unavoidable respects, however, all are essentially alike. Every department has its head, who is called the chief of police. In large cities he is held responsible to a board of civilians or to a nonprofessional director or commissioner. The major tasks of organization in the large departments may be divided into three administrative branches: staff services, line operations, and inspections. It is the function of inspection to determine whether the quality of performance is at all times in agreement with the standards of the department. Each of these branches is under the command of a deputy or assistant chief. The line operations are performed by such units as the patrol division, the detective division, the traffic division, the crime prevention division, and the vice division. In some communities the head of each of these divisions is called an inspector; in others, he is given the title of assistant chief, major, or supervising captain.

The detective division is essentially a secret service which specializes in criminal investigation. Detectives are nonuniformed or plainclothes men who work out of a central bureau or are attached to the various district police stations. They are most often assigned to cases which cannot be cleared by the patrolmen at the spot and which require a more thorough study for the purpose of gathering evidence and identifying and apprehending offenders. The division of uniformed patrolmen is the backbone of the police department and its largest unit. It is the city's active, open guarantee of orderly government, and its work includes all police functions.

The area served by the patrol division in large cities is divided into districts or precincts for administrative purposes. Each district or precinct has its own station house from which operates a force of patrolmen, sometimes called a company, who are usually under the command of a captain. These patrolmen are divided into shifts or platoons, each of which is on duty for a specified period of the day and is ordinarily commanded by a lieutenant. Shifts or platoons may be composed of squads, each of which may be under the leadership of a sergeant.

Each police district or precinct is divided into routes, beats, or posts. A route is a length of street or streets which is designated for the assign-

[15] Adapted from Wilson, pp. 34–36; and Leonard, pp. 61–90.

ment of traffic patrolmen, although it is sometimes used for foot patrolmen. A beat is an area (in contrast to a length of street) which is almost
always used for the assignment of foot and motorized patrols, but sometimes it is employed instead of a route for motorized traffic officers. A
post is a fixed point to which an officer is assigned for duty. It may be a
desk, an office, or any other place, such as an intersection for traffic duty
or a location for the observation and apprehension of a person who is
wanted for a crime or who is about to commit one.[16]

Further details of the internal organization of the department vary
with the size, character, and special problems of the community involved.
In smaller cities the organization is much simpler, and all patrolmen and
detectives may operate from the police headquarters. In fact, modern
transportation and communication have greatly facilitated police work,
and in the future probably only the largest cities will be able to justify
district stations. However, every police department, regardless of its size,
must perform the following line and staff activities if it is to achieve the
basic police objectives:

Line activities	Staff activities
Patrol	Personnel
Investigation	Records and identification
Prevention	Communications
Traffic and other regulation	Property management
	Public relations[17]

Most departments fail to apply the principles of organization outlined
above and so suffer from a loss of coordination and cohesiveness in their
operation. Each department must determine for itself the number and
kinds of basic organization units that it needs.[18]

Personnel. Good personnel is important in any organization, but in the
police department, where the work consists largely of personal services,
it is a primary requisite. In order to establish and maintain a competent,
well-trained, and loyal police force, it is necessary to create a personnel
policy based upon an adequate classification of positions, the merit system of appointments and promotions, fair compensation, an intensive
program of recruit and in-service training, reasonable promotional opportunities, good working conditions, impartial disciplinary measures, humane
protection against occupational hazards, and an actuarially sound retire-

[16] Wilson, pp. 27–33.
[17] The Institute for Training in Municipal Administration, pp. 45–54; Leonard, pp.
64–66.
[18] Leonard, pp. 63, 64.

ment system. Only in this way is it possible to establish a career service that will attract and hold capable men and women.

Leadership is the most important single factor in the successful operation of a police department. Behind every successful police organization there is the driving force of a dynamic leader. The chief of police, therefore, above all else, must be a leader of men—a man of intelligence, imagination, ingenuity, courage, and tenacity. He must also have a good general knowledge of police work and considerable skill as an administrator and policy maker.

Should the chief of police be selected by an examination under civil service or should the mayor or city manager be given a free hand to appoint him? This is a question that has divided experts in the police field. In favor of selection by an examination under civil service, it is argued that this takes the position out of politics, protects the tenure of the chief, and provides continuity of policy. That the position has been subject to rapid turnover in America is evidenced by the fact that the chief's term in office averages slightly over four years in cities under 300,000 in population and less than two and one-half years in cities over 500,000 in population.

Those opposed to having the chief of police employed under civil service argue that this method of selection may permit an incompetent official to remain in office and prevent the mayor or city manager from putting into effect the policies for which he is being held responsible by the community. However, all experts are agreed that if the position is not placed under civil service, the chief of police should be appointed by the mayor or the city manager, and never by the city council, and that the appointment should be based upon a selective process which is the equivalent of a competitive examination.[19]

An analysis of the duties of the patrolman clearly reveals why he should be carefully selected on the basis of competitive examinations. While on the beat he must be constantly on the alert for everything that may affect the enforcement of the law or the prevention of crime. He must investigate situations that require his attention, question suspicious persons, examine suspicious objects, and give prompt and effective relief in emergencies. He must prepare careful and complete reports regarding what he has observed and investigated. He must recognize what constitutes good evidence and act quickly to preserve it. He must apprehend

[19] *Ibid.*, pp. 44–60; The Institute for Training in Municipal Administration, pp. 152, 153. In 1958 Lunden found that the term of office of chiefs of police in Iowa averaged 4.3 years (Walter A. Lunden, "The Mobility of Chiefs of Police," *Journal of Criminal Law, Criminology, and Police Science*, XLIX [July–Aug., 1958], 178–83). See also A. C. Germann, *Police Executive Development* (Springfield, Ill.: Charles C. Thomas, Publisher, 1962).

offenders, testify in court, respond to all kinds of emergencies, arbitrate disputes, enforce regulations, control public gatherings, quell disturbances, and at all times act in such a way as to increase the prestige of the department and instill respect for law and order.[20]

Many experts in the police field believe that the applicant for employment in the police services should have the following minimum qualifications:

1. Superior intelligence.
2. High school education.
3. Unassailable character and reputation.
4. Unquestionable physical and moral courage.
5. Height of five feet eight or nine inches.
6. Weight of 150 pounds, but weight should be in proportion to height.
7. Robust physical health.
8. Well-balanced personality.
9. Physical strength and agility above average.
10. Age at least 21, but not more than 28, with possible exceptions for certain specialists.[21]

After their appointment, all police officers should be required to go through a probationary period of at least one year, during which time their work should be thoroughly tested, and they should be subject to dismissal for cause without a hearing. It is not yet clear what role civil service will eventually play in the personnel administration of American police departments. In some cities, it has contributed to the improvement of police work. In too many others, it has protected indolence and incompetence and impeded professionalization. It should be emphasized that merit systems are now operating successfully in the police field without the restrictions of civil service. Certainly this much is clear: Civil service restrictions that make it difficult to remove the incompetent and the dishonest should be eliminated. What is needed, regardless of the ultimate fate of civil service, is the establishment of a system of selection and promotion based upon merit examinations.[22]

[20] The Institute for Training in Municipal Administration, pp. 236–39.

[21] Wilson, pp. 135–40; Leonard, pp. 90–102; Richard L. Holcomb, *Selection of Police Officers* (Iowa City, Iowa: Bureau of Public Affairs, State University of Iowa, 1946), pp. 8–15.

[22] Leonard, pp. 102–12; Benjamin Holmes, "Selection of Patrolmen," *Journal of Criminal Law and Criminology*, XXXII (Jan.–Feb., 1942), 575–92; O. W. Wilson, "Problems in Police Personnel Administration," *Journal of Criminal Law, Criminology, and Police Science*, XLIII (Mar.–Apr., 1953), 840–47; The Institute for Training in Municipal Administration, p. 130. In spite of the general feeling in professional circles against the unionization of police forces, the police in about 45 cities of over 10,000 population in the United States were in unions in 1962. However, since the Boston police strike of 1919, no American police force has resorted to the strike as a device

The detective should be selected from the patrol force, and appointment should be made entirely on demonstrated qualifications and merit. The best method of discovering latent investigative talents is to observe the work of patrolmen and give the most promising a trial in detective work. Policewomen, too, should be eligible for such a trial, since their services are sometimes needed in criminal investigations, especially in those involving women and children.[23]

Training. The problems of police work have become so complex that today they can be handled satisfactorily only by officers who are specially trained. To help meet this situation, institutions of higher learning are being urged to introduce pre-employment training programs in police work. Among the colleges and universities offering complete professional police curricula leading to academic degrees are Washington State University, California State Colleges at Fresno and San Jose, University of Southern California, University of California, Michigan State University, University of Houston, and Indiana University. Although college or university training is neither essential nor desirable for all police officers, it will help to provide highly qualified leaders for the future.

In any event, regardless of whether or not a recruit has had pre-employment training, along with all other recruits he should be put through a recruit training program. Such programs are now well established in every metropolitan police department, but in the early days of police work in the United States the recruit received no instruction and was merely told to don a uniform, get a gun, put on a badge, and go to work. Later it became customary to send the recruit out with an experienced policeman. The length of this apprenticeship varied from a few days to several months. At least 85 per cent of America's police officers received their training in this way. Formal recruit training probably began with instruction in the handling of firearms. By 1935, well-organized and well-equipped in-service training schools were being operated by the police departments of Wichita, Indianapolis, Cincinnati, Chicago, Berkeley, Louisville, San Francisco, New York City, and a few other cities.

The training program for the recruit consists of instruction in all aspects of police work and requires at least three months, eight hours a day and

---

to achieve desired goals (Samuel G. Chapman and T. Eric St. Johnston, *The Police Heritage in England and America* [East Lansing, Mich.: Michigan State University, 1962], pp. 40, 41). See also Carl E. Heustis, "Police Unions," *Journal of Criminal Law, Criminology, and Police Science*, XLVIII (Mar.–Apr., 1958), 643–46. Although the police are generally discouraged from joining unions, they are not prevented in any way from affiliating with other organizations for social or professional purposes.

[23] Wilson, pp. 289–97; Leonard, pp. 215–24. See also Felicia Shpritzer, "A Case for the Promotion of Policewomen in the City of New York," *Journal of Criminal Law, Criminology, and Police Science*, L (Nov.–Dec., 1959), 415–19.

six days a week. It covers such subjects as police organization and procedure, criminal law and evidence, traffic control, criminal investigation, scientific crime detection, the use of firearms, psychiatry, and social science. The larger cities provide their own departmental schools for the training of police officers. The Los Angeles Police Academy is one of the most elaborate and complete of these. Small cities that do not have the resources for such a school must make other provisions for the training of their recruits. They may send them to a departmental school in a nearby larger city, enroll them in a state police training school, place them in short courses, such as those run by a number of colleges and universities, utilize regional in-service training schools like those operated in Virginia, Kentucky, New York, California, and Washington, set up part-time schools of their own, or prescribe reading courses based on books purchased by the city for its police library.

Training should not be limited to that for the recruit, but should be continued at intervals for the officer during his entire period of service. Advanced courses in police work are provided by departmental schools and classes, regional in-service training schools, short-course programs offered by colleges and universities (such as that operated by the State University of Iowa), and prescribed reading courses. In addition, regional law-enforcement conferences are conducted by the Federal Bureau of Investigation in all states.

Two nationally prominent schools have been leaders in the movement to provide advanced training for police officers. One of these is the FBI National Academy in Washington, D.C., which was established in July, 1935. Each year police departments in the United States and foreign countries send selected men of superior ability to this school, where they receive twelve weeks of instruction in such subjects as criminal investigation, firearms practice, the maintenance of police records, laboratory methods, criminal law, mathematics, government, applied psychology, and sociology. During the twenty-eight year period from July, 1935, through July, 1963, a total of 4,354 law-enforcement officers were graduated from this academy.

The other outstanding school is the Traffic Institute of Northwestern University, which was officially established in 1936. For a period of nine months each year, selected police officers from the United States and foreign countries are given courses in various aspects of traffic work at this school, and by July, 1963, a total of 1,012 officers had been graduated by it.

Although in-service training is essential, it has as yet reached only a small percentage of America's police officers. On the basis of his personal observation, V. A. Leonard estimates that in 1951 less than 1 per cent of the personnel of American police forces had been exposed to any form of in-service training worthy of the name.[24]

The Patrol. The patrol or uniformed division is the basic element of line power in a police department, and every effort should be directed toward its maximum development. Since the work of the patrol force includes all police functions, the more effective it is the less need there is for other more specialized units. which should always be considered secondary and collateral.

In the chronological distribution of the patrol force, most American police departments divide it into three platoons, each of which works an eight-hour shift. The basis for geographical distribution of the patrol force is the individual patrol area or beat. The size of the beat is determined by the amount of work to be done, and so tends to increase from the center of the city outward toward the suburbs. A number of cities supplement the patrolmen assigned to fixed districts or beats with a small tactical unit or mobile force, which is usually sent where and when police problems are occurring, as determined by research.[25]

The number and kinds of problems existing in a section of the city determines the shape of the beat and the number of rounds which the patrolman should make on his beat while he is on duty. Ordinarily, however, the beat should be so laid out that the patrolman can make at least two rounds during one tour of duty, the second being used to investigate further any unusual conditions that attracted his attention during the first round. Furthermore, he should follow diverse routes in patrolling his beat so that his movements cannot be easily anticipated by the person who is planning to commit a crime. Sometimes duties may be so concentrated along a highway as to justify a "straightaway," that is, an assignment where the patrolman walks to and fro along one street; but usually better protection and service can be given by having the beat cover an area, that is, one or more city blocks, instead of a single street. When the officer is on

[24] Wilson, pp. 161–73; Leonard, pp. 113–33; John Edgar Hoover, "The Basis of Sound Law Enforcement," *The Annals of the American Academy of Political and Social Science*, CCXCI (Jan., 1954), 43, 44; L. J. McEnnis, Jr., "The Background and Development of the Traffic Institute of Northwestern University," *Journal of Criminal Law, Criminology, and Police Science*, XLII (Jan.–Feb., 1952), 663–73; David A. McCandless, "Southern Police Institute," *Journal of Criminal Law, Criminology, and Police Science*, XLII (May–June, 1951), 105–11; The Institute for Training in Municipal Administration, pp. 175–203; John A. Mears, "The Evolution of the Department of Police Administration at Indiana University," *Journal of Criminal Law, Criminology, and Police Science*, LIII (June, 1962), 253–57; A. F. Brandstatter, "The School of Police Administration and Public Safety, Michigan State University," *Journal of Criminal Law, Criminology, and Police Science*, XLVIII (Jan.–Feb., 1958), 564–66; The Traffic Institute, *1962–63 Annual Report* (Chicago: Northwestern University, 1963).
[25] Wilson, pp. 255–80; The Institute for Training in Municipal Administration, pp. 246–53.

his beat, he may be summoned by radio, or by light or sound signals attached to police cars, buildings, or call boxes, and he is required to contact his station by radio or telephone so as to permit a check on his safety and the progress of his work and to receive whatever orders are awaiting him.

Patrolling the beat on foot is still the method used by many officers in America, but the trend today is toward the motorization of the patrol, and a growing number of police administrators believe that most foot patrolmen should be replaced by auto patrols. The motorized patrol, because of its mobility, maneuverability, speed, and facilities for two-way radio communication, tremendously increases the striking power of the force. Nevertheless, the foot patrol is preferred when inspectional duties in a small area occupy the entire time of the officer, or where the officer may be called upon to prevent or dispose of a large number of incidents in a relatively small area, as for example, during the patrolling of an amusement park. In discussing the trend toward the motorization of America's patrol force, Leonard states that in 1950, of the 903 cities reporting the extent to which police work was motorized, 27 did all patrol work with motor vehicles, 875 used both motor and foot patrols, while only one city (with a population of less than 25,000) did not use any motor vehicles for patrolling.[26]

Traffic Control. Traffic control constitutes the greatest of all the regulatory tasks for which the police are responsible. O. W. Wilson, an expert in the police field, has emphasized the magnitude of this task. He points out that more people are injured and killed in automobile accidents than as a result of the combined total of all other acts under police control; that the economic loss from these accidents is greater than all other such losses which the police are charged with preventing; that more people are disgruntled with traffic control than with any other police activity; and that traffic control causes the police more annoyance and subjects them to pressure from more sources than the handling of any other problem. It is well to appreciate these facts in order to understand the amount of time and effort now going into traffic control which otherwise might be devoted to other police responsibilities. Some administrators assign 25 per cent of their personnel to this activity alone.

After the necessary supporting legislation has been enacted, the police have three tools to use in traffic control. These are engineering, education, and law enforcement. The purpose of traffic engineering is to design road-

26 Leonard, pp. 181–213; Wilson, pp. 227–54; Stanley R. Schrotel, "Changing Patrol Methods," *The Annals of the American Academy of Political and Social Science,* CCXCI (Jan., 1954), 46–53; The Institute for Training in Municipal Administration, pp. 261–63; G. Douglas Gourley and Allen P. Bristow, *Patrol Administration* (Springfield, Ill.: Charles C. Thomas, Publisher, 1961), pp. 92–202.

way facilities in such a way as to reduce the number of accidents and the amount of congestion and thus facilitate safe, rapid movement. Education has two major objectives: (1) teaching the public to understand police traffic problems and to support the programs, policies, and methods employed in their solution; and (2) improving the safety habits of drivers, pedestrians, and school children. However, some persons respond only to the pressure of law enforcement, and the police and the courts must take definite action against them to protect the general public.[27]

Records. The records office is the information center of the police department. Through its administration complaint reports, arrest records, identification facilities, property controls, and communications are brought together into an integrated and coordinated system. If this system of records is well administered, it contributes in a significant way to the successful operation and management of the entire police department. But to be effective, it should be centralized under a person who reports directly to the chief or his assistant, and complaint records and reporting procedures should be standardized.[28]

Equipment. The equipment of a police department must be satisfactory if its officers are to provide adequate protection and service for the community. Suitable communication and transportation facilities are especially important in dealing decisively with motorized criminals; but more than this, they permit a more economical and effective use of manpower in all services. In the larger cities the equipment of police departments has been greatly improved and now includes motorcycles, automobiles, armored cars, machine guns, gas equipment, airplanes, laboratory equipment, and telephone, radio, and teletype facilities. All this equipment has tremendously increased the mobility and striking power of these departments and has given them a big advantage over the average criminal.[29] Although some departments have not kept pace with technological changes and improvements, the fact is that "American police have more physical equipment under their control than the combined police strength of all the rest of the world."[30]

STATE POLICE

The earliest form of state police to appear in the United States was that represented by the Texas Rangers, whose history dates back to the days of the Texas Republic. Three companies of Texas Rangers were

[27] Wilson, pp. 353–79; Leonard, pp. 231–44.
[28] Wilson, pp. 383–413; Leonard, pp. 135–80.
[29] Wilson, pp. 445–65.
[30] Bruce Smith, "A Preface to Law Enforcement," *The Annals of the American Academy of Political and Social Science,* CCXCI (Jan., 1954), 2.

Wire photo transmitter for pictures and fingerprints sent over telephone wires. This machine can transmit information as well as receive
it from points in the United States and overseas. (Courtesy of Police
Department, Philadelphia, Pa.)

authorized in 1835 by the provisional government of Texas and were
employed in military service on the Mexican border. However, for many
years the Texas Rangers were used only as a border patrol. In 1865,
Massachusetts appointed a few "state constables" who were granted general police powers to be exercised anywhere in the state. Massachusetts,
therefore, may be said to have been the first state to create a general state
police force. During the first few years of the twentieth century, Connecticut, Arizona, and New Mexico established specialized state police
forces, but it was not until 1905, when Pennsylvania organized its "State
Constabulary," that the nation acquired its first modern state police system authorized to enforce all state laws. New York and Michigan organized their state police in 1917, but the movement did not gain much
momentum until after World War I when, within a few years, West Virginia, New Jersey, and Rhode Island created such agencies. Today every
state has some form of state police, although less than one-third of the

states authorize their state police units to exercise general powers of law enforcement. At the beginning of World War II, about one-third of the state police organizations had the authority to enforce only motor vehicle laws.

State police function under the leadership of an executive who is appointed by the governor (sometimes with the consent of the state legislature or a state board), and who, in most states, serves at the pleasure of the appointing power. Most state police units are not subject to civil service control, and in some the administrative head has complete authority to select, promote, discipline, and control the rank and file. However, the average selective procedure eliminates the unfit, although it does not always secure the exceptionally well-qualified. The best state police organizations require the applicant for an appointment to pass physical and mental examinations, a character investigation, and an oral interview; and most of them emphasize both recruit and in-service training. In general, the state police have been better selected and trained than the local police and, in no small degree, free from the handicap of "politics."

In the fully developed state police departments, like those of Pennsylvania, Massachusetts, New York, New Jersey, and some others, the uniformed trooper patrols highways and roads and has the authority to enforce all state laws. Usually, however, he is prohibited from doing so in municipalities unless local authorities request his assistance, but when in pursuit of a criminal, the state policeman is not limited by city or county boundaries and may go anywhere within the state in order to make the arrest. Equipped with modern means of transportation and communication, state police can now provide protection for great areas that formerly were comparatively isolated. When given full authority, they become the most important law-enforcement agency in rural areas and largely supersede the sheriff-constable system.

But the movement to establish state police has not been without opposition. It has been opposed by organized labor, which has condemned the state police as a tool of the employer and a threat to legitimate activity. It has been opposed by sheriffs, who fear that the state police may eliminate all other law-enforcement officers in rural areas. It has been opposed by some citizens' groups on the ground that the state police may develop into an instrument of oppression comparable to the Ogpu of Soviet Russia or the Gestapo of Nazi Germany. Nevertheless, despite this opposition, the state police have become an important law-enforcement agency throughout the United States, and all evidence points to their continued expansion and development.[31]

[31] Smith, *Police Systems in the United States,* pp. 144–69; August Vollmer and Alfred E. Parker, *Crime and the State Police* (Berkeley, Calif.: University of California Press, 1935), pp. 143–69; David G. Monroe, "Legislative Needs of the State Police,"

FEDERAL POLICE

Under the federal system of government in the United States, general
law enforcement is reserved by the Constitution to the several states,
which in turn have delegated most of it to their political subdivisions—the
counties, cities, towns, villages, and townships. It is also definitely established by court decision that there are no common law offenses against
the federal government, and the powers of the federal police are limited
to the enforcement of federal statutes. The states, therefore, remain the
primary units for crime control. Even so, the responsibilities of the federal government have continued to increase, and over the years, this has
necessitated the creation of a number of law-enforcement agencies of
various kinds. The slow and unsystematic growth of these agencies, however, has produced a fragmentation of police powers, an overlapping of
jurisdiction, and a confusion and rivalry which have interfered with administrative efficiency.

Furthermore, there has been an interlacing of law-enforcement activities with others of a varied nature, and this makes it difficult to determine
which agencies are primarily of a police character. For example, the Coast
Guard, which patrols the ocean and lake shores of the United States, has
general powers of criminal law enforcement and is a police agency with
a broad statutory jurisdiction. Yet, it is not a civil police agency in the
full sense of the term, for its policies, methods, and procedures are closely
related to those of the Army and the Navy, and in the event of war, it is
automatically transferred from the control of the Treasury to that of the
Navy. In fact, in emergencies the Army and the Navy, too, may be used
as police forces. Many other governmental units, like the Public Health
Service and various bureaus of the Departments of Agriculture and Commerce, have certain police characteristics. Before World War II there were
about forty of these units, which under one guise or another performed
some part of the police function.[32]

However, there are eight major federal police agencies of a civil character which enforce penal statutes of general application throughout the
domain of the federal government. These agencies, which perform the
greater part of the law-enforcement activities of the federal government

---

Journal of Criminal Law and Criminology, XXXII (Jan.–Feb., 1942), 498–505; Victor
A. Rapport, "A Unified State-Wide Police Force," *Journal of Criminal Law and Criminology*, XXX (Jan.–Feb., 1940), 706–11.

[32] For a more detailed treatment of the investigative and law-enforcement units of
the federal government, see Arthur C. Millspaugh, *Crime Control by the National
Government* (Washington, D.C.: The Brookings Institution, 1937).

and are located in three major departments—Justice, Treasury, and Post Office—are the following:

1. The Intelligence Unit of the Bureau of Internal Revenue (Treasury Department), which is concerned primarily with major violations of the internal revenue laws, including evasions of the income tax laws.
2. The Enforcement Division of the Alcohol Tax Unit of the Bureau of Internal Revenue (Treasury Department), which is concerned primarily with violations of laws levying taxes upon intoxicants.
3. The Division of Investigations and Patrol of the Bureau of Customs (Treasury Department), which enforces the laws against smuggling and illegal exportation.
4. The Secret Service Division (Treasury Department), which has jurisdiction over counterfeiting and forgery and is charged with the protection of the President, his family, and the President-elect.
5. The Bureau of Narcotics (Treasury Department), which deals with all violations of the federal narcotic laws.
6. The Office of the Chief Inspector of the Post Office Department, which is concerned with mail losses, wrongful use of the mails, and all other violations of the postal laws.
7. The Immigration Border Patrol (Justice Department), which has jurisdiction over the illegal entry of aliens and allied crimes.
8. The Federal Bureau of Investigation (Justice Department), popularly known as the FBI, which exercises full police jurisdiction over all crimes not the immediate and special concern of other federal police agencies.[33]

The work of some of these agencies might well be consolidated under one governmental unit, and greater coordination should be effected throughout the federal law-enforcement service. However, in general, federal police work is of a high quality, and the specialists engaged in it rank among the best in the world.

The Federal Bureau of Investigation. The Federal Bureau of Investigation is the largest and best known of the federal agencies listed above and does more police work than all the others combined. It was founded in 1908 to provide the Department of Justice with a permanent investigative force under its immediate control. In 1924, the Federal Bureau of Investi-

[33] Smith, *Police Systems in the United States*, pp. 171, 172. See also U. E. Baughman with Leonard Wallace Robinson, *Secret Service Chief* (New York: Harper and Bros., 1962); Walter S. Bowen and Harry E. Neal, *The United States Secret Service* (Philadelphia: Chilton Co., 1960); Miriam Ottenberg, *The Federal Investigators* (Englewood Cliffs, N.J.: Prentice-Hall, Inc., 1962); Don Whitehead, *The FBI Story* (New York: Random House, 1956); Norman Ansley, The United States Secret Service," *Journal of Criminal Law, Criminology, and Police Science*, XLVII (May–June, 1956), 93–109; Max D. Phillips, "A Study of the Office of Law Enforcement Coordination U.S. Treasury Department," *Journal of Criminal Law, Criminology, and Police Science*, LIV (Sept., 1963), 369–77.

gation was reorganized and J. Edgar Hoover was appointed director. He accepted the appointment with the understanding that henceforth the FBI was to be a career service in which ability and good character were to be the requirements for appointment, and performance and achievement, the only grounds for promotion. Under his able and vigorous leadership this federal agency has had its greatest development and an outstanding record of achievement. Operating under the direction of the head of the bureau are fifty-five field divisions with field offices strategically located in key cities throughout the United States and Puerto Rico. Each field division, under the direction of a Special Agent in Charge, covers a specified territory, but the work of all is closely coordinated. In addition to directing and coordinating the activities of the field divisions, the admintrative staff at the Washington headquarters of the bureau has under its direct supervision the operation of the Identification Division and the Technical Laboratory, the collection of crime statistics, and the training facilities for special agents and police officers.

1. PERSONNEL. The Federal Bureau of Investigation has built up a large staff of special agents who do the investigative and other police work of the agency. An applicant for the position of special agent must be a male citizen of the United States between the ages of twenty-three and forty-one, in good physical condition, at least five feet seven inches tall, a graduate of a state-accredited resident law school or a graduate of a resident four-year college with a major in accounting and at least three years of practical accounting experience, and a person of unassailable character and reputation. Certain of these qualifications may be suspended from time to time to meet the needs of the bureau, but the general requirements for the position are always maintained at a high level. Each applicant is thoroughly examined and investigated, and if he is accepted, he must take an intensive course of training for a period of fourteen weeks at the FBI facilities located at Quantico and the FBI headquarters. There, attending classes from nine in the morning until six at night, he is given instruction in such subjects as fingerprint identification, photography, toxicology, statistics, the care and use of firearms, first aid, federal criminal law, calisthenics, defense tactics, office management, and organization of field work. Experienced agents are returned to the FBI facilities at Quantico for in-service training approximately every two years so that they may be kept informed regarding the latest methods of scientific crime detection and criminal apprehension.

Through careful selection and thorough training, the FBI has created a well-organized body of courageous and competent agents whose work commands the respect of the criminal and noncriminal alike. The story of this police force is one of which every loyal American can be proud, for the term "G-men" has become a symbol of efficient law enforcement throughout the world. The very way in which the agents of the FBI received the name of "G-men," an abbreviation of the term "Government men," is itself a thrilling episode in this story. It happened during the early hours of September 26, 1933, during the capture of George "Machine-Gun" Kelly, who was wanted by the FBI for kidnapping. When Kelly was about to be arrested, he shouted, "Don't shoot, 'G-men'; don't shoot!" Thus were the FBI agents given their now famous name.

2. THE WORK OF THE FBI. In the field of crime, the work of the FBI is twofold. As a fact-finding agency, it investigates violations of all federal laws, except those specifically placed under the jurisdiction of other agencies, and identifies and arrests the persons involved. As a service agency, it assists law-enforcement officers throughout the country in identification and technical matters. The volume of the bureau's work has steadily increased because of the expansion of its jurisdiction, the increase in certain types of crimes, and the changes in the enforcement policies of the federal government. An important factor in this increase has been the wars in which the United States has engaged in the past few decades and the uncertain state of world affairs. These have thrust a tremendous burden upon the bureau, requiring it to deal with such matters as frauds in the government's war contracts, the location and investigation of deserters, violation of selective service, the illegal export of arms, the investigation of Communists, alleged Communists and subversive groups, espionage, sabotage, and violations of neutrality regulations. A few of the many other matters under the primary jurisdiction of the FBI are violations of the antitrust laws, bankruptcy frauds, crimes on the high seas, crimes on government reservations, violations of the federal kidnapping laws, treason, white slave traffic (which is punishable under the Mann Act), the location of escaped federal prisoners, and the transportation of stolen motor vehicles from one state to another (which is punishable under the Dyer Act).

3. THE IDENTIFICATION DIVISION. In addition to its field investigative officers, the FBI maintains an Identification Division in Washington, D.C., which serves as a clearing house of records pertaining to criminals. In 1963, its files contained over one hundred sixty-seven million sets of fingerprints—the largest collection of its kind in the world. The great majority of these prints, however, do not belong to criminals, but to persons in the armed services, office holders under federal civil service, registered aliens, prisoners of war, and millions of others who for reasons of security and protection have them on record with the FBI.

All peace officers are invited to avail themselves of the data on file in the Identification Division, and the service is given without cost to all

A single-fingerprint expert comparing a latent and ink fingerprint in preparation for testimony in court. (Courtesy of FBI Identification Division, Washington, D.C.)

regularly constituted law-enforcement officers and agencies. This service, however, is essentially a cooperative one. The FBI can accumulate and furnish to law-enforcement agencies only that information which it receives on a voluntary basis from them. Even so, it is now highly effective, and criminals who a few years ago fled from state to state to escape detection now find themselves identified regardless of where they are arrested.

4. THE TECHNICAL LABORATORY. During the latter part of 1932 the FBI established its Technical Laboratory to provide federal facilities for scientific research in the field of criminal investigation. Today, this laboratory has the most modern equipment and a highly trained technical staff. Every known scientific method is here used in the bureau's fight against crime. Documents are examined by handwriting analysts, and bullets, by ballistic experts. Evidence is secured by moulage or other methods of reproduction. Microanalyses of hair and textile fibers are made, and chemical analyses of stains, including blood tests, are performed. In addition to conducting the technical work in cases referred to them, the

Instructor at the FBI Academy using model during discussion of raid planning with new Special Agent. (Courtesy of FBI Academy, Quantico, Va.)

laboratory's technicians engage in research to develop new and improved techniques for the solution of crime. The facilities of the FBI's Technical Laboratory are made available wherever possible and without charge to all law-enforcement agencies throughout the United States.

5. UNIFORM CRIME REPORTING. During 1962, crime reports were received on a voluntary basis from law-enforcement agencies serving 98 per cent of the total population living in metropolitan areas, 94 per cent of the population in other cities, 80 per cent of the rural population, and 94 per cent of the national population. The information contained in these reports, together with the data compiled from the fingerprint files, makes

possible the collection of crime statistics on a nationwide scale. These statistics are issued annually in a bulletin known as "Uniform Crime Reports," which is sent to law-enforcement officials and other interested individuals and agencies.

6. TRAINING PROGRAMS. At its educational facilities in and near Washington, D.C., the FBI offers the following training programs:

1. The Training School for Newly Appointed Special Agents.
2. The Retraining School, which provides a refresher course of instruction for special agents at least once every two years.
3. The School for Special Agents in Charge.
4. The National Police Academy, which provides training for selected police officers from law-enforcement agencies in the United States and foreign countries.[34]

COOPERATION, COORDINATION, AND CONSOLIDATION

In the United States there are about 3,000 counties, 16,000 incorporated municipalities, and 20,000 towns and townships. Thus, since each of these political divisions has its own law-enforcement agency, there are nearly 40,000 separate and independent police units distributed throughout the country. A good example of this multiplicity of law-enforcement agencies is to be found in the area around Chicago, Illinois, where within a fifty-mile radius of that city, there are about 350 municipal, county, and state police forces.

This situation leads to duplication of efforts, overlapping of jurisdiction, lack of coordination in administrative policies, and inadequacies within individual police units. Its effects are dramatically expressed through the burden which it imposes upon sincere, competent police administrators in their battle with the modern motorized criminal. For him, the means of escape are many; and far from being hindered by municipal, county, or state borders, he uses them to serve his own ends. When he strikes in one community and flees to another, the police in the jurisdiction where the crime occurred must rely upon the cooperation of police in other jurisdictions to assist in his arrest. Usually this is given without hesitation, and prearranged road blocks to intercept the offender are often effective. Where statewide telegraph-typewriter (teletype) systems with interstate

[34] U.S. Department of Justice, *The Story of the Federal Bureau of Investigation* (Washington, D.C.: Government Printing Office, n.d.); J. Edgar Hoover, *Persons in Hiding* (Boston: Little, Brown and Co., 1938); *The Federal Bureau of Investigation* (Washington, D.C.: Government Printing Office, Nov. 1, 1941); Federal Bureau of Investigation, *Training Schools: Selection of Personnel* (Washington, D.C.: Government Printing Office, Apr, 20, 1938); John Edgar Hoover, Director, *Report of the Federal Bureau of Investigation*, Fiscal Year, 1963; correspondence with John Edgar Hoover, Director, FBI, dated November 8, 1963.

hook-ups have been established, there is also available a reliable, secret means of sending out a general alarm over a wide area and of securing cooperation in the apprehension of wanted criminals. Statewide and interstate police radio facilities likewise can be used for this purpose.[35]

However, although cooperation is essential, it is not enough. Often, the lack of a coordinated command and standardized procedures causes confusion among the cooperating police units and renders their efforts fruitless. Besides, intensive assistance is likely to be given only in the more spectacular cases, and loopholes often exist through which the alert fugitive can escape.[36] Therefore, several methods have been developed to effect coordination among enforcement facilities.

One of these is the regional police organization, which has been recommended for metropolitan areas. In 1930, such an organization was planned for the region of which the city of Cincinnati, Ohio, is the social and economic center. It was to function in an area which can be said to constitute a single police problem and was designed to cover six counties (four in Ohio and two in Kentucky), 2,045 square miles, a population in excess of 925,000, and 147 separate and independent police agencies. The Cincinnati plan called for (1) the training of the larger police units of the region in the permanent police training school of Cincinnati, (2) the motorized patrol of each of the six countries, (3) communication by means of teletype at strategic points in the area, (4) radio broadcasts to patrol cars operating in the area, and (5) the use of the Cincinnati department as a clearinghouse for the region's criminal identification records. Although this plan did not receive adequate public support and so was never put into effect, some coordination as well as consolidation, has been effected in certain metropolitan areas located entirely within a single state, as, for example, in those of Atlanta, Georgia, and Miami, Florida.[37]

In general, a state may punish only those who violate its own laws, and its laws have no force beyond its own territorial limits. This has led to the development of the interstate compact, another method designed

[35] The International Association of Chiefs of Police, which was organized in 1893, has played a very important role in the establishment of greater cooperation among the police agencies of the country.

[36] Disorganization of Metropolitan Law Enforcement and Some Proposed Solutions," *Journal of Criminal Law, Criminology, and Police Science,* XLIII (May–June, 1952), 63–78.

[37] Personal correspondence with the Police Department of Cincinnati, Ohio, dated July 9, 1954; Virgil W. Peterson, "Issues and Problems in Metropolitan Area Police Services," *Journal of Criminal Law, Criminology, and Police Science,* XLVIII (July–Aug., 1957), 127–48; Gordon E. Misner, "Recent Developments in Metropolitan Law Enforcement," *Journal of Criminal Law, Criminology, and Police Science,* L (Jan.–Feb., 1960), Part I, 497–508; *ibid.,* LI (July–Aug., 1960), Part II, 265–72; *ibid.,* "The Police Service Contract in California," *Journal of Criminal Law, Criminology, and Police Science,* LII (Nov.–Dec., 1961), 445–52.

to promote coordination of police agencies. Article I, Section 10, of the Constitution provides that states may enter into compacts with the consent of the Congress. In 1934 Congress, by the Interstate Compact Bill, gave consent in advance to all states to form pacts in the field of crime prevention and criminal law enforcement. This action laid the basis for the formation of a number of such compacts. Among these are the extradition law, which simplifies the procedure by which a state can secure an offender who has fled to another state (passed by 45 states as of December 1, 1963); the attendance-of-witnesses law, which improves the method for securing out-of-state witnesses (passed by 46 states, the District of Columbia, and Puerto Rico as of December 1, 1963); the fresh pursuit law, which permits an officer in pursuit of a felon, or a suspected felon, soon after the commission of the crime, that is, in fresh pursuit) to cross the state boundary into any state that has passed the law in order to make the arrest (passed by 38 states and the District of Columbia as of December 31, 1954); and the probationer and parolee-supervision law, which makes it possible for probationers and parolees to be transferred from one state to another and at the same time remain under supervision (passed by all states).[38]

In addition to the steps that have been taken to promote cooperation and coordination of existing police units, proposals have been advanced which go beyond this and recommend the consolidation of certain police agencies into larger units. Among these are the following:

1. All county, town, and small municipal forces should be consolidated into a single police agency clothed with county-wide jurisdiction. Some counties have already moved in this direction by the creation of county police forces. It is doubtful, however, whether small-city taxpayers would want to assume the additional financial obligation which such a consolidation would involve, or whether their police departments would want to give up their separate existences. But there can be no denial that the county plan would be feasible in many areas and would improve the police services of the counties adopting it.

2. All county, town, and municipal forces, both large and small, in metropolitan areas should be consolidated into a single metropolitan district police force and vested with district-wide jurisdiction. Thus far this proposal has received only sporadic support, and it faces almost insur-

[38] The Council of State Governments, *Record of Passage of Uniform and Model Acts, as of December 1, 1963; The Handbook on Interstate Crime Control* (Chicago: The Council of State Governments, 1955), p. II. In 1960 it was reported that 26 states had accepted the interstate compact for juvenile probationers and parolees. See E. A. Burkhart, "Interstate Cooperation in Probation and Parole," *Federal Probation*, XXIV (June, 1960), 24–30. See also Brevard E. Crihfield and Mitchell Wendell, "Crime Control and Uniformity of Criminal Laws," *Journal of Criminal Law, Criminology, and Police Science*, XLII (Jan.–Feb., 1952), 571–88.

mountable obstacles in metropolitan areas where two or more states are involved. However, in a few metropolitan areas some steps toward consolidation have been taken in various ways within the borders of a single state, as, for example, in Atlanta, Georgia, and Miami, Florida.

3. The police agencies of a state should be consolidated and placed under the control of a centralized state administration. Where well-developed state police organizations exist, many rural areas are already receiving most of their police protection and services from the state units. In these states, the transition to a consolidated police organization for all rural areas might be feasible. However, many experts in the police field oppose the inclusion of cities and towns in this plan on the ground that it would contribute to an excessive centralization of power on the state level. Besides, although law enforcement may have state and national implications, it deals fundamentally with problems that must be solved on the local level.

4. All the police agencies of the country should be consolidated into a national police force under centralized federal control. This proposal has little support among police authorities. It involves a complete violation of the principles of our form of constitutional government, which seeks to maintain a system of checks and balances in a federal union of states. J. Edgar Hoover, director of the Federal Bureau of Investigation, is opposed to any further centralization of police power in a state or federal agency and believes that a consolidation of police power in the federal government would be a distinct danger to representative government in America.[39]

A variation of this proposal, which attempts to avoid the constitutional issue, would distribute federal grants-in-aid to those states introducing standards laid down by the federal government. This, too, however, would eventually sacrifice local autonomy for national uniformity; for history has demonstrated that he who holds the purse strings with one hand carries the scepter in the other. It also involves the questionable practice of utilizing federal funds for local activities. This, in the long run, can result only in the progressive desiccation of the sources of revenue available for local governments and the shifting of more and more power to the federal government. In the arena of politics, there is always more to be considered than efficiency, which can be bought at too high a price. It is far better to have some criminals escape than to sacrifice the values of local enforcement in the name of efficiency—even if this is called for by the expert. If all the recommendations of the various experts were adopted, we might well have a government for the expert but hardly one for the people; for often the expert is inclined to empha-

[39] John Edgar Hoover, "The Basis of Sound Law Enforcement," pp. 39–42.

size the work of his own field at the expense of the interests of the country as a whole.

In the future development of the police agencies of America, it is unlikely that the impending changes will adhere to any one pattern. In some states, a single police force for all rural areas and under centralized state control may eventually be established. The police departments of the great cities "will probably undergo only slight adaptations, if for no better reason than that they are large enough and strong enough to defend and maintain their separate existences." Elsewhere, however, consolidations can be expected at the county level, especially in metropolitan areas, and hold high promise for improved service at a lowered cost.[40]

THE POLICE AND POLITICS

A police department cannot successfully discharge its responsibilities if it is dominated by politics. When political "pull" and preference are introduced, the welfare of the party, rather than that of the people, is given primary consideration. Yet because the police department is a veritable gold mine for the politician, pressure by the political machine to gain control of it is unrelenting. Once such control is established, votes can be won and campaign contributions can be secured by granting favors to those who come into conflict with the law, seek relief from onerous civic duties, or want to avoid exacting legal regulations. And the possibilities of rendering service to friends, relatives, partisans, and powerful allies are limitless. Traffic violation summonses can be "fixed"; criminal charges can be "adjusted" or nolprossed; police officers can be "persuaded" not to appear as witnesses; evidence can be "lost"; investigations can be "bogged down"; juries can be controlled.

But the stakes are higher than this. Protection can be given to gambling joints, houses of prostitution, burlesque houses, and the bootlegging and hijacking of racketeers; and members of the force and their political superiors may actually be taken in as partners by powerful underworld groups. Here the "take" is large and is distributed up and down the political ladder, from the cop on the beat, who conveniently winks at violations and irregularities, to the judge on the bench, the mayor in the city hall, or even the governor in the state house, who "pulls the strings and makes the wheels go around."

Legitimate business, too, can come in for its "cut." Building contracts and franchises can be awarded, assessments and taxes can be lowered, and regulations such as those governing sanitation, safety, building con-

[40] Smith, *Police Systems in the United States*, pp. 300–28. See also Chapman and St. Johnston, pp. 41–45.

struction, and weights and measures can be avoided without fear of molestation from the district attorney's office or the force—and all this for the benefit of "friends" of the party. Here, too, the graft can be enormous. Illegal establishments that do not "play ball" soon learn what it means "to buck the machine" by being subjected to raids, fines, and arrests.

Even the cop on the beat, in his own little way, can get petty graft by a "shake-down" of merchants, businessmen, and home owners. If they do not give him Christmas presents, tickets to places of amusement, or special prices on his purchases, they may soon find themselves inconvenienced and put to considerable expense by a very "exacting" enforcement of city regulations. Fruit stands may have to be moved; signs, taken down; new garbage containers, purchased; new plumbing, installed; and so on and on until greater "appreciation" is shown for the police. However, in defense of the officer it must be said that many persons invite exploitation by their desire for special favors and exceptional treatment.

Furthermore, when the department is dominated by politicians, jobs on the force are distributed on the basis of party affiliation. Even when jobs are under civil service, ways are devised to circumvent the rules so that the "party's man" gets the job. The situation becomes worse when the jobs on the force are divided among the ward leaders, each of whom gets control of a certain number of them. In this way the unity of command is broken, the force is subject to many masters, the orders of the chief can be countermanded, and for the cop on the beat the ward leader is the "boss." Under such conditions, effective police work is impossible.

In any event, when the affairs of the department are geared to the operation of the political machine, the officer is under increasing obligation to the party. To it he owes his appointment, protection from disciplinary action or discharge, unearned salary increases, undeserved promotions, extra vacations, leaves of absence, and placement in a "soft job." Thus, the "creeping paralysis of political favoritism" spreads through all parts of the force, sapping its vitality, destroying its morale, corrupting its officials, and leaving it helpless under the rule of the bosses. And time is against the policeman. His obligations to the party grow, his family responsibilities increase, the years leave him too old to begin a new career, and finally he becomes completely subservient to the party.

Naturally, politics cannot be blamed for everything that is wrong with American police departments. Public apathy, lack of financial support, technological obsolescence, jurisdictional limitations, and many other factors must be included in the indictment. Nevertheless, any attack upon the problem of police inefficiency in our large cities must begin with an attack upon the problem of corrupt political domination. This is basic, and all else is futile until the citadel of the machine is stormed, taken, and destroyed.[41]

THE POLICE AND THE PUBLIC

The maintenance of good relations between the police and the public greatly facilitates police work. Public support and cooperation mean faster and better reporting of crimes, more efficient criminal investigation, a greater percentage of cases solved, more adequate budgets, more competent personnel, modern equipment, and fewer crimes. Public suspicion and hostility, on the other hand, bring unjust charges, the impeding of sound and progressive programs, the undermining of morale, and a hesitation to initiate constructive action for fear of ridicule and derision.

Good public relations are a product of the interaction of the attitudes of the public and the police. In the development of these relations, the leadership must come from the law-enforcement agencies. Although other influences are involved, the police themselves are the most important factor in the creation of the public's attitudes. When the police put their own house in order, the problem of securing public support and cooperation is greatly simplified. A program for the establishment of good public relations must be directed toward these three important objectives:

1. The avoidance of public resentment by the fair and reasonable enforcement of the law.
2. The development of public good will through the performance of courteous, efficient, and economical services.
3. The education of the public regarding the work and the problems of the police.

In the achievement of these objectives, the individual police officer must understand that he occupies a most strategic position. In fact, for most people, he is the department, and it will be judged largely by his appearance, his attitude, his conversation, and his actions. At all times, he should be neat, clean, alert, efficient, courteous, dignified, and erect in bearing. When called upon to serve, he should listen courteously and attentively to complaints and reports and move quickly to the assistance of those in trouble. When dealing with the offender, the officer should act with firmness and decisiveness but avoid abuse, lecturing, and scolding.

[41] See the Institute for Training in Municipal Administration, pp. 10, 11; Frank Tannenbaum, *Crime and the Community* (Boston: Ginn and Co., 1938), pp. 153–72; National Commission on Law Observance and Enforcement, *Report on Police*, Report No. 14 (Washington, D.C.: Government Printing Office, 1931), pp. 17–52; V. O. Key, Jr., "Police Graft," *American Journal of Sociology*, XL (Mar., 1935), 624–36.

In the formulation of its policies and the establishment of its methods, the police department should not only maintain a high standard of efficiency, but also give the appearance of being efficient. Buildings should be kept clean and everything should be maintained in good order. The patrolman should establish friendly relations with residents on his beat and promote in them a respect for law and a favorable attitude toward its enforcement. The office personnel should always be on the job and ready to serve the public. The enforcement program must be selective, that is, it must be directed at hazardous locations, at the time of greatest violation frequency, and against the persistent offenders. In minor offenses, the violator should be sent a "notice to appear" or a summons instead of being arrested. In the exercise of their discretion, the police should dispose of both adult and juvenile cases without prosecution when the best interests of the individual and society can be served in this way.

In addition to conducting its regular work, every department should initiate a program designed primarily to build public good will. Included in this program should be such matters as the following: (1) the establishment of mutual understanding and harmonious relations with the press, radio, and television; (2) public lectures, talks, and demonstrations by members of the department on various aspects of police work; (3) public awards to officers who render outstanding services; (4) special services for those in distress, underprivileged children, and visitors to the city; (5) traffic surveys to eliminate hazards and to reduce accidents; and (6) consultation with businessmen in order to discover and eliminate any insecurity or unwise practices that might offer an opportunity for criminal activities. Such a program cannot provide a substitute for effective police work, nor can it long conceal an inefficient and corrupt administration, but it can help to create a climate in which a police department can grow to full stature and maturity.[42]

[42] Wilson, pp. 182–224; Ervis W. Lester, "Some Aspects of American Police Problems," *Journal of Criminal Law and Criminology*, XL (Mar.–Apr., 1950), 796–809; G. Douglas Gourley, "Police Public Relations," *The Annals of the American Academy of Political and Social Science*, CCXCI (Jan., 1954), 135–42; Joseph Goldstein, "Police Discretion Not to Invoke the Criminal Process: Low-visibility Decisions in the Administration of Justice," *Yale Law Journal*, LXIX (Mar., 1960), 543–94.

14

Criminal Investigation

THE MEANING OF CRIMINAL INVESTIGATION

Criminal investigation is police activity directed toward the identification and apprehension of alleged criminals and the accumulation, preservation, and presentation of evidence regarding their alleged crimes.[1] Since crime may occur anywhere and at any time, and since action against the criminal must begin as soon as possible, no single unit of the police can be charged with criminal investigation. In urban communities the patrolman is usually the first member of the department at the scene of the crime, and the action taken by him is often of the greatest importance in criminal investigation.

Duties of the Patrolman in Criminal Investigation. The duties of the patrolman in criminal investigation usually consist of care of injured persons, apprehension of the criminal either at the scene of the crime or in flight, protection of the scene of the crime until it can be searched for physical evidence, and recovery of stolen property. In some cases, however, the patrolman may have to go beyond this and conduct what is known as a preliminary investigation. This is that part of the investigative procedure which extends up to the point at which postponement of further action will not endanger the successful completion of the case. It consists of interviewing the victim, searching for and interviewing witnesses and suspects, and taking suspects into custody when there is enough evidence against them or when there is the possibility that delay might permit them to take flight.

O. W. Wilson, an authority on police administration, believes that the patrolman should always conduct a preliminary investigation. He advo-

---

[1] In order to simplify the language of the text, the terms "crime" and "criminal" will be used hereafter instead of "alleged crime" and "alleged criminal," although in the strict sense of the words, an act is not a crime and a person is not a criminal until they have been properly adjudicated as such in the criminal court.

cates this for the following reasons: (1) it enables the department to act while the trail is fresh and may thus provide information which quickly leads to the arrest of the criminal; (2) it permits detectives to concentrate their special skills on the most important aspects of the work and, except in large departments, eliminates the necessity of having them on duty twenty-four hours a day; (3) it gives the patrolman a heightened sense of responsibility by having him participate in the investigation of a crime which he was charged with preventing; and (4) it affords patrolmen an opportunity to acquire investigative skills and their superiors an opportunity to discover investigative talent.[2]

If the case requires further investigation after the patrolman has performed his duties, which may include a preliminary investigation, detectives take over the work and attempt to press it to a successful conclusion. However, this step in the investigation often constitutes a point of friction in the department, since patrolmen, in general, resent doing what they refer to as an "errand boy's job" for the detectives.

Major Phases of an Investigation. The major phases of criminal investigation are (1) gathering and preservation of evidence, (2) identification of offenders, (3) apprehension of offenders, (4) recovery of stolen property when such property is involved, and (5) presentation of evidence.

1. GATHERING AND PRESERVATION OF EVIDENCE. The initial stage in the gathering of evidence consists of interviews[3] with the victim and other witnesses and a visit to the scene of the crime. Sometimes it is advisable to hold the interviews first, sometimes it is better to do this after a visit to the scene of the crime, and sometimes it is possible to combine both of these in one action. The decision regarding this will depend largely on the nature of the case.

If the victim of the crime is alive and conscious and is well enough to be questioned, he should be the first to be interviewed. This should be followed by interviews with other witnesses and persons who may be able to give information regarding the case. These interviews should be conducted as soon as possible after the crime so that the facts can be secured while they are still fresh in everyone's mind. All interviews are directed toward answering the questions: When? Where? Who? What? How? and Why? In interviewing the victim, the investigator must first determine

---

[2] O. W. Wilson, *Police Administration* (New York: McGraw-Hill Book Co., Inc., 1963), pp. 281–97.

[3] The questioning of persons during a criminal investigation may be classified into "interviews" and "interrogations." Interviews are conducted to learn facts from persons who are cooperating with the police. Interrogations are used to secure information from witnesses and suspects who are reluctant to give it to the investigator. Thus interrogations require more persistence and skill than interviews. In this text, however, in order to simplify the writing, the term "interview" will be used to refer to both types of questioning.

whether the evidence indicates that a crime has been committed. If it does, he must then determine what the crime is and secure information regarding the identity of the person who is apparently involved and the circumstances under which he apparently acted. The investigator should never use force, threats, or brutal "third degree" methods in questioning witnesses or suspects. The aim at all times should be to discover the facts and not merely to get a conviction by piling up evidence against a suspect. To insure this, the investigator must maintain as objective an attitude as possible during the handling of the entire case.[4]

Statements should always be verified. The scene of the crime should be photographed or sketched or both,[5] and this should be done before the area is searched so that everything will be pictured as it was upon the arrival of the investigator. The purpose of the search of the scene of the crime is to discover any physical evidence, such as fingerprints, footprints, tire tracks, weapons, and clothing, which will assist the investigator to determine the facts of the crime, identify the criminal, and lead to the arrest and conviction of the criminal or the exoneration of innocent persons. The physical evidence which is uncovered should be preserved, and if it is susceptible to scientific analysis, it should be forwarded to the laboratory for examination. Man's memory is so short that every bit of evidence that might be of use at the trial should be carefully recorded in a notebook. Usually, investigations are not successfully completed without a great deal of hard work in the gathering and preservation of the evidence. Armchair detectives are of the fictional type only.[6]

2. IDENTIFICATION OF OFFENDERS. If the criminal is not apprehended at the scene of the crime, a distinctive description of him should be secured from persons who can give the best account of his distinguishing characteristics. In addition to this information, the investigator should obtain any other evidence, such as fingerprints, tool marks, lint, or buttons, which may help to establish the identity of the person involved.[7]

3. APPREHENSION OF OFFENDERS. In most major crimes, the immediate alarm that is sent out for the apprehension of the offender is solely a

[4] Maurice J. Fitzgerald, *Handbook of Criminal Investigation* (New York: Greenberg, Publisher, 1951), pp. 9–30; Department of the Army, *Criminal Investigation* (Washington, D.C.: Government Printing Office, 1951), 36–56.

[5] Harry Söderman and John J. O'Connell, *Modern Criminal Investigation,* revised by Charles E. O'Hara (New York: Funk and Wagnalls Co., Inc., 1962), pp. 110–27; Floyd N. Heffron, *Evidence for the Patrolman* (Springfield, Ill.: Charles C. Thomas, Publisher, 1958).

[6] Fitzgerald, pp. 37–43; Charles E. O'Hara and James W. Osterburg, *An Introduction to Criminalistics* (New York: The Macmillan Co., 1952), pp. 30–36; Department of the Army, pp. 57–103.

[7] Fitzgerald, pp. 48–61. For a specialized area of criminal investigation, see Le Moyne Snyder, *Homicide Investigation* (Springfield, Ill.: Charles C. Thomas, Publisher, 1959).

preliminary procedure. The additional detailed information regarding the fugitive must be filled in through further investigation. Often this information can be secured by an examination of various records, such as those kept by law-enforcement agencies, government bureaus, newspapers, hotels, schools, churches, lodges, and insurance, telephone, and telegraph companies, and by talks with various persons, such as merchants, physicians, dentists, barbers, cab and bus drivers, hotel employees, and household servants. Persons who give information to an investigator are officially referred to as informants, although in the underworld they are called "stool pigeons." Some informants sincerely desire to assist in the apprehension of offenders. Others, however, motivated by selfish reasons, want revenge, protection for illegal activities, special favors, or money. Of course, the investigator should never grant protection for crime in return for receiving information. This is too high a price to pay, especially, since the investigator, without making undesirable or illegal deals, can usually get the same information from other sources.

In a criminal investigation, it may be necessary to keep a close watch over some place, building, or person. This is called a surveillance. In police terminology, a static or fixed surveillance is known as a "plant," while the surveillance of an individual or motor vehicle which involves movement from place to place is known as "tailing."[8]

The police in their efforts to capture a dangerous person may use a highly organized system of blockade which involves the cooperation of many police departments. For example, the Michigan state police, in cooperation with police chiefs and sheriffs along the Michigan-Ohio, and Michigan-Indiana boundary lines, have organized the tri-state blockade. This enables law-enforcement officers to block quickly all roads leading across Michigan's southern border whenever it is reported that dangerous persons are fleeing from one state to another.

4. RECOVERY OF STOLEN PROPERTY. When it is claimed that property has been stolen, an accurate description of it should be given to the police for broadcast purposes. Included in this should be a statement of all distinguishing marks, defects, scratches, and inscriptions in order to facilitate the identification of the property. The responsibility of recovering stolen property requires the police to keep in close contact with pawnshops and places that may be used as fences.

[8] Fitzgerald, pp. 45–73; William Dienstein, *Techniques for the Crime Investigator* (Springfield, Ill.: Charles C. Thomas, Publisher, 1952), pp. 35–61; Frederick W. Egen, *Plainclothesman* (New York: Greenburg, Publisher, 1952), pp. 131–48; Charles E. O'Hara, *Fundamentals of Criminal Investigation* (Springfield, Ill.: Charles C. Thomas, Publisher, 1956), pp. 5–186. See also Malachi L. Harney and John C. Cross, *The Informer in Law Enforcement* (Springfield, Ill.: Charles C. Thomas, Publisher, 1960).

5. PRESENTATION OF EVIDENCE. The successful prosecution of criminals depends to a great extent upon the skill and efficiency of those who conduct the criminal investigation. They must carefully preserve the evidence and put it into such form that it can be used most effectively by the prosecutor. Moreover, they are key witnesses for the state. Their testimony, the skill with which they give it, their general conduct in court, and their ability to answer questions and supply information may easily make the difference between a conviction and an acquittal.

CRIMINALISTICS

Criminalistics is the science of crime detection. It involves the application of psychology, physics, chemistry, physiology, and other sciences to the investigation of crimes and the apprehension of criminals, and requires the services and collaboration of various specialists. The term "criminalistics" was coined by Hans Gross (1847–1915), an Austrian lawyer who was one of the principal founders of this science.

Some important methods have been developed in the field of criminalistics. Among the most famous of these is the *Bertillon system,* which was devised by Alphonse Bertillon (1853–1914), head of the Criminal Identification Department of Paris, and introduced into France in 1883. This system uses various measurements of the human anatomy, such as height, length of the head, and span of the arms, and is based on the assumption that no two human beings are exactly alike and that the dimensions of certain bony portions of the human frame do not change after maturity has been reached. It also keeps a record of photographs (front and profile), hair and eye color, complexion, scars, tattoo marks, amputations, and other distinguishing characteristics. This system, however, has been largely replaced by the fingerprint system, which is simpler, quicker, and more accurate; today, no American police department maintains an active Bertillon file.[9]

The *portrait parlé,* or spoken picture, another invention of Bertillon, seeks to supplement the investigator's memory by giving an objective description of the criminal. The use of this method requires the recording of such distinguishing characteristics and qualities as the criminal's name, address, nationality, age, sex, height, weight, complexion, eye and hair color, body build and carriage, scars, moles, deformities, manner of dress, language facility, and occupation. When combined with the *picture file* (formerly called the "rogues' gallery"), which is a file containing the photographs of criminals, this method provides the investigator with a

[9] Rollin M. Perkins, *Elements of Police Science* (Chicago: The Foundation Press, Inc., 1942), pp. 147, 148; Nigel Morland, *An Outline of Scientific Criminology* (London: Cassell and Co., Ltd., 1950), pp. 40–43; Raymond B. Fosdick, *European Police Systems* (New York: The Century Co., 1915), pp. 319, 320.

store of information which can help him to arrest the wanted person on sight.

The *fingerprint system,* or dactyloscopy, which is largely the product of Sir William Herschel (1833–1917) and Sir Francis Galton (1822–1911), is the most effective known method for the identification of criminals. Fingerprints are the impressions left by the extremely complex pattern of ridges and depressions on the surface of the finger tips. The ridges contain the openings of sweat glands, or ducts, while the nerves of sensation, which give us the sense of touch, terminate in the depressions, or furrows, between the ridges. The fingertips carry an accumulation of oil and perspiration, and this provides a medium which leaves a print on any suitable surface.

It is believed that there are no two identical fingerprints—at least none have yet been discovered, and there are millions on file throughout the world. This is true even in the case of identical twins. The patterns of ridges and depressions that form fingerprints appear before birth, remain unchanged during life, and disappear after death only with the dissolution of the body. Hard manual labor, illness, wounds, superficial burning, chemical action, and accidental damage are all equally impotent in destroying the basic characteristics of these patterns. It is, then, the distinctiveness, durability, and unchangeableness of fingerprints which give them such great value as a method of identification.

The apparatus that is required for making fingerprints a matter of record is simple and inexpensive. Printer's ink, or ink of a similar type, is usually employed for making the impressions. It is rolled on a metal or glass sheet or block, a rubber-covered roller being used for spreading the ink. Before the fingers are inked, they are thoroughly cleaned in order to remove all traces of greasiness, and the impressions are then made on the fingerprint blank.

Two types of impressions are taken in fingerprinting. One is called the plain impression; and the other, the rolled impression. When the plain impression is made, the fingers of each hand are inked with a thin coat of printer's ink and placed flat on a sheet of white paper or fingerprint blank. In this operation, the thumb of each hand is printed separately, but the other four fingers of each hand are held together and simultaneously inked and then printed. When the rolled impression is made, each of the ten fingers is rolled separately on the inked slab from one side to the other and then in the same manner on the paper or fingerprint blank. The finger should be rolled only once so that the print will not be blurred. The rolled impression is made in order to reveal the whole fingerprint pattern. If the whole pattern is not obtained, it cannot be properly classified. The plain impressions are taken in order to check the rolled impressions and thus to ascertain whether the latter have been recorded in their proper sequence. If the sequence is not correct, the fingerprints cannot be properly classified.

Several classifications are employed to reduce fingerprints to a simple formula for the purpose of identification, but the most widely used today is the Henry or universal system, which was devised by Sir Edward Henry, who became the commissioner of the metropolitan police force of London in 1903. It was introduced into Great Britain in 1901 and is now used throughout the British Empire and the United States.[10] This system, however, is based on the prints of all ten fingers and, therefore, has definite limitations. Since all ten prints are rarely found at the scene of the crime, its principal uses have been to identify repeaters who have been previously fingerprinted and who are again in custody and to compare prints left at the scene of the crime with those of known suspects whose prints are on file. Many of the fingerprints found on various surfaces are called latent fingerprints because they are not clearly visible. These are clarified by the application of special powders, liquids, and other developing agents and are then usually photographed to convert them into a permanent record.

Within the last few decades, it has become possible to use a print found at the scene of a crime as a basis for a search through large fingerprint collections in order to uncover the identity of a previously unknown person. This procedure, which obviously may be of great importance in a criminal investigation, is now feasible because of the development of *single fingerprint* classifications. The most outstanding of these is the Battley system, which was published in 1930. It was invented by Harry Battley when he was in charge of the fingerprint bureau of New Scotland Yard, London. Single-print collections can now be made, and one has been installed at the Federal Bureau of Investigation in Washington.

It must be emphasized that the fingerprint system can be used as a method of identification only when the criminal's fingerprint's are on file. The building up of collections of fingerprints, therefore, is most important. All persons who are arrested should be promptly fingerprinted, and their prints should be cleared through the Federal Bureau of Investigation and the state bureau of identification.

Poroscopy, a method of identification based upon the patterns of pores in the tips of the fingers, is used by the police to supplement the fingerprint system. It is especially helpful when the fingerprint pattern cannot be properly identified. However, since there is no classification system

10 E. R. Henry, *Classification and Uses of Finger Prints* (London: His Majesty's Stationery Office, 1922). For a recent treatment of the subject, see Annita T. Field, *Fingerprint Handbook* (Springfield, Ill.: Charles C. Thomas, Publisher, 1959). See also B. C. Bridges, *Practical Fingerprinting,* revised by Charles E. O'Hara (New York: Funk and Wagnalls Co., 1963).

of pore patterns, a suspect must first be apprehended before a comparison of pore patterns can be made. *Retinoscopy,* another method of identification, is based on the photographic recording of the blood vessel patterns of the eye, which, it is claimed, do not change.

Modus operandi, the Latin phrase meaning method of operation, is a means of identification based on the fact that many criminals tend to use the same methods over and over again in committing their crimes. It is, therefore, often possible to classify criminals in terms of their methods of operation, and to identify the perpetrator of a particular crime by the similarity between the method used in its commission and that employed in other offenses which he is known to have committed. The modus operandi system was used first in England, where it was invented by Sir Llewelyn Atcherley, and was developed in this country by August Vollmer, formerly the chief of police of Berkeley, California. By referring to the modus operandi file, the investigator may be able to reduce the list of suspects to a small number of possibilities.

A *show-up, or line-up,* involves the presentation of a line of suspects for examination and possible identification by witnesses of a crime. In some departments, colored slides of suspects are shown to witnesses for the purpose of identification.

Handwriting, also, is often employed as a means of identification in crimes where ransom notes, forged instruments, or controversial documents are involved. Furthermore, since each typewriter has some peculiarity in its type, experts, by an examination of typewriting, can often determine not only the make of typewriter involved, but also the particular machine used.

Forensic ballistics is that branch of criminalistics which is concerned with the identification of firearms and ammunition for the purpose of securing evidence. Its principal object is to determine whether a given bullet was used in a particular weapon. *Moulage,* a term derived from the French word *mouler,* meaning to cast or to mold, is the art of making casts or molds of the material evidences of a crime. It is employed to provide permanent records of such evidence as footprints, tool impressions, tire marks, and human features and organs.

Medical jurisprudence, also known as forensic medicine, is one of the oldest scientific aids in criminal investigation. It is invaluable in providing evidence regarding such questions as the cause of death, the reason for illness, the time of death, the existence of drug addiction, the presence of a mental disorder, and so on. *Toxicology,* an important branch of medical jurisprudence, is the study of the origin, properties, actions, and detection of poisons, and their appropriate antidotes and treatments. *Forensic chemistry* is concerned with the use of chemical knowledge to provide legal evidence. It may serve to reveal the identity of an unknown substance, the presence of poisons in human organs, the contents of an explosive, the nature of a stain, and similar purposes. Through blood tests, it may also help to determine whether a certain blood stain came from a particular suspect.[11] *Photography* is an important tool of the modern investigator and is now used in such procedures as the preservation of the crime scene, the identification of suspects, and the presentation of accurate copies of records, documents, handwriting specimens, and other types of evidence. When the camera is combined with the microscope, it becomes possible to make photographs of what the naked eye cannot detect and thus secure such evidence as invisible stains, writings, alterations, and fingerprints.

Lie detectors, probably the most spectacular device in the modern police laboratory, have proved to be a great aid in criminal investigation. All of the various types of lie detectors are based on the principle that an emotional disturbance will have a physiological effect, and that when an individual consciously lies, he will be emotionally disturbed because of the fear of detection and the "pangs of conscience."

The most widely known lie detector is the polygraph, which was developed in 1926 by Professor Leonarde Keeler of Northwestern University. It is really a combination of several instruments. When the polygraph is used, several attachments are connected to the suspect. He is then questioned, and the physiological effects of this questioning are mechanically recorded. During the operation, a pneumograph records respiratory movements, a cardiograph records the heart beat, a sphygmograph records the blood pressure, and a galvanograph records a reflex closely following the activity of the sweat pores. Thus, it is a *many-writing* machine and, therefore, is called a polygraph. A compensating device allows for what might be termed normal irregularities of these bodily reactions, but significant changes in them give the interrogator important leads when the suspect is lying.[12] The Reid polygraph, which is a modification of the Keeler polygraph, has an additional unit for recording certain muscular activity.[13]

No one claims that the lie detector is infallible, but those who advocate its use claim that it is accurate in a large percentage of cases. Morland

---

[11] Perkins, pp. 29–35, 53–59, 110–80; Fitzgerald, pp. 119–25; Morland, pp. 43–47, 85–191; Department of the Army, pp. 141–46; O'Hara and Osterburg, pp. 77–99; Fosdick, pp. 344–48.

[12] Perkins, pp. 11–13.

[13] Fred E. Inbau and John E. Reid, *Lie Detection and Criminal Interrogation* (Baltimore: The Williams and Wilkins Co., 1953), pp. 5–8. See also *Academy Lectures on Lie Detection,* ed. V. A. Leonard (Springfield, Ill.: Charles C. Thomas, Publisher, Vol. I, 1957, Vol. II, 1958); Richard O. Arther, "Blood Pressure Rises on Relevant Questions in Lie Detection—Sometimes an Indication of Innocence Not Guilt," *Journal of Criminal Law, Criminology, and Police Science,* LXVI (May–June, 1955), 112–15.

states that in the hands of a competent operator the Keeler polygraph is approximately 86 per cent accurate.[14] Inbau and Reid, on the basis of examinations conducted with the Reid polygraph, estimate that *under the most favorable conditions*, the lie-detector technique can achieve an accuracy of 95 per cent, with a 4 per cent margin of indefinite determinations and a 1 per cent margin of possible error.[15]

However, the lie detector seems to be unreliable in the interrogation of those who have mental disorders, physiological abnormalities (such as excessively high or low blood pressure, heart disease, or respiratory disorders), or strong emotional tensions caused by fear or guilt feelings but not necessarily related to the crime being investigated, or of some who for various reasons can lie without apparent physiological effects. It must be emphasized, furthermore, that the successful use of the polygraph, or of any other lie detector, depends largely upon the skill of the operator in selecting the questions asked and in interpreting the emotional responses. As a matter of fact, lie detectors do not detect lies, but only the symptoms of lying, which can be discovered and interpreted only by an expert. This is the reason why Professor Keeler believed that the results of polygraph tests should not be available for courtroom use until competent operators are selected by examination and licensed by the state.[16]

Certain *drugs* have the power to release a person's inhibitions to the point where he will talk freely about matters which he would otherwise not mention or discuss only in confidence. Some of these drugs, principally scopolamine, sodium amytal, and sodium pentothal, have been administered in order to detect lying and to secure the truth. Therefore, where a drug is used for this purpose, it is sometimes called "truthserum." Favorable results with such drugs have been obtained in experimental cases and in a few actual criminal investigations, but as yet the percentage of accuracy is not large.[17]

THE LEGAL BASIS OF CRIMINAL INVESTIGATION

The efficiency of criminal investigation is vitally affected by the laws upon which it is based. If these laws are adequate, they greatly facilitate

[14] Morland, pp. 244, 245.

[15] Inbau and Reid, pp. 110, 111. The accuracy of these claims, however, has been questioned. See, for example, Elinor Langer, "Lie Detectors: Sleuthing by Polygraph Increasingly Popular; Claims of Accuracy Are Unproved," *Criminologia*, II (May, 1964), 11–13.

[16] Jack Streeter and Melvin M. Bell, "The 'Fourth Degree': The Lie Detector," *Vanderbilt Law Review*, V (Apr., 1952), 551.

[17] Fred E. Inbau, *Self-Incrimination* (Springfield, Ill.: Charles C. Thomas, Publisher, 1950), pp. 68, 69; C. W. Muehlberger, "Interrogation Under Drug Influence," *Journal of Criminal Law, Criminology, and Police Science*, XLII (Nov.–Dec., 1951), 513–28.

police work and contribute to prompt and effective enforcement. On the other hand, if they are unwise or defective, they seriously hamper the police and actually operate as a cause of crime. Therefore, it is necessary to understand the most important provisions of these laws in order to have any real appreciation of the problems of police agencies.

The Law on Arrest. An arrest is the taking of another into custody for the actual or purported purpose of bringing him before a court, body, or official, or of otherwise securing the administration of the law. Although no physical touching is essential, there can be no arrest without either a touching or a submission to the authority of the person making the arrest.[18] It is generally desirable to give prompt notice of the purpose of the arrest, but such information may be properly withheld if the arrester reasonably believes that this is necessary to protect himself or others or to consummate the arrest. Arrests may be made with or without a warrant, by police officers or by private persons, and for either a felony or a misdemeanor, but most arrests are made without a warrant.[19]

1. ARRESTS UNDER WARRANT. A warrant for arrest is a written order issued by some competent authority in the name of the state to some authorized officer or individual, directing him to arrest an alleged offender and to bring the arrestee before some proper person to be dealt with according to the law. Usually, a warrant is obtained on the basis of a written complaint or information which alleges under oath or affirmation certain facts from which the one issuing the warrant can reasonably assume that a particular person is probably guilty of a specific crime. In most states, however, just information and belief, rather than knowledge, are enough to support the complaint. The warrant must name the person to be arrested, or if his name is unknown, it must describe him with a reasonable degree of accuracy. When the name of the person sought is not known, the warrant, in addition to containing a description which is sufficient to identify him with reasonable certainty, may also refer to him as "John Doe." Such a warrant is called a "John Doe warrant." However, a warrant which neither names a particular person to be arrested nor adequately describes him is invalid, and anyone who makes an arrest under it is liable to the person whose rights have been violated. This means, then, that the name "John Doe" may not be inserted in a warrant with the intention of having it refer to some unknown person who is to be selected for arrest at a later time. Such a "John Doe warrant," lacking an adequate description of a particular person, is a legal nullity.

[18] Perkins, pp. 223, 224, 227.

[19] Joseph A. Varon, *Searches, Seizures and Immunities* (Indianapolis: The Bobbs-Merrill Co., Inc., 1961), Vol. I, pp. 70–113; Arthur H. Sherry, *The Law of Arrest, Search and Seizure*, revised by Rex A. Collins, Jr. (Sacramento: Bureau of Industrial Education, California State Department of Education, 1962), pp. 1–44.

A warrant of arrest can be lawfully executed only by the person or the class of persons authorized by its terms to make the arrest. At common law, either a police officer or a private person could be authorized by a warrant to make an arrest. Modern statutes, however, frequently omit any provision for the execution of warrants by private persons; but even under such a statute, an officer may deputize a private citizen to execute a particular warrant. If the warrant appears to be valid, that is, *fair on its face,* it is the duty of the officer to make the arrest even though he has reason to know, or even knows, a fact which makes the warrant invalid, and in making such an arrest, he is protected from any legal action which the wronged arrestee may later initiate. Unless otherwise provided by statute, an arrest under a warrant may be made only in the territory within which the official, court, or body has the authority to order an arrest. A warrant of arrest usually remains valid until executed. When the warrant is executed, ordinarily the arrested person should be told about the warrant for his arrest and informed of the offense or conduct with which he is charged therein.[20]

2. ARRESTS WITHOUT A WARRANT. *a. By an officer in case of a felony.* Both at common law and under the statutes, a police officer may arrest without a warrant for a felony committed in his presence. An offense is committed in the presence of the person making the arrest if it is made known to him at the time by any of his senses. When a felony is not committed in the presence of an officer, the general rule is that he may arrest without a warrant if he has reasonable grounds to believe both that a felony has been committed and that the person to be arrested has committed it. This rule, which is the modern common law rule, has been modified by statute in some states.

b. By an officer in case of a misdemeanor. Under the early common law, the police officer might arrest without a warrant for a misdemeanor committed in his presence if it amounted to a breach of the peace.[21] At the present time, however, in the great majority of the states, he has the authority under the statutes to arrest without a warrant for *any* misdemeanor committed in his presence. On the other hand, in most states an officer may *not* arrest without a warrant for a misdemeanor *not* committed in his presence.[22]

c. By a private person in case of a felony. Like a police officer, a private person both at common law and under the statutes may arrest with-

---

[20] Perkins, pp. 231–48; Hubert E. Dax and Brooke Tibbs, *Arrest, Search and Seizure* (Milwaukee: Hammersmith-Kortmeyer Co., 1950), pp. 41–53.

[21] Here the phrase "breach of the peace" refers to an offense done by violence or to one causing or likely to cause an immediate disturbance of public order.

[22] Perkins, pp. 253–57; Dax and Tibbs, pp. 14–26.

out a warrant for a felony committed in his presence. When a felony is not committed in the presence of a private person, his authority to arrest without a warrant varies from state to state. In some states, such an arrest is not lawful unless a felony was actually committed by the very person arrested. In another group of states, the private person has the same powers of arrest when a felony is not committed in his presence as a police officer, that is, he may lawfully arrest if he has reasonable grounds to believe both that a felony was committed and that the arrestee committed it, even though no felony was in fact committed. In the great majority of states, however, a private person may lawfully arrest without a warrant for a felony not committed in his presence if the felony was actually committed and he has reasonable grounds to believe that the arrestee is the felon even if in fact this is not true.[23]

   d. By a private person in case of a misdemeanor. The authority of a private person to arrest without a warrant for a misdemeanor committed in his presence differs from state to state under the existing statutes. Some states give him no authority to arrest without a warrant for a misdemeanor committed in his presence. On the other hand, in nearly half the states he may lawfully arrest without a warrant for *any* misdemeanor committed in his presence. Still other states permit him to make such an arrest only if the misdemeanor is petit larceny, while a fourth group of states specify that the misdemeanor committed in his presence must amount to a breach of the peace before he may lawfully arrest without a warrant. However, when the misdemeanor is *not* committed in the presence of the private person, there seems to be no exception to the general rule that he may *not* lawfully arrest without a warrant.[24]

   e. "Posse comitatus." Police officers in making an arrest have the right to call upon private citizens for assistance, and such a request does not have to be made in any formal way. It may be merely a despairing cry for help. Since the private person is required to give the requested assistance, or be charged with a misdemeanor, and since he is not entitled to delay while he conducts an inquiry into the officer's authority in the particular case, the private person not only acquires the authority of the officer, but also is protected even if the officer is exceeding his authority in the particular case, provided the private citizen does not know this fact or has no reason to know it.

   Those who act in this capacity do not become officers nor do they remain mere private citizens. Their legal position becomes that of a *posse comitatus.* Although the term "posse" is commonly used to signify a group

---

[23] Perkins, pp. 253, 254.
[24] *Ibid.,* pp. 250–54; Rollin M. Perkins, *Criminal Law* (Brooklyn: The Foundation Press, Inc., 1957), pp. 870, 871.

summoned to aid an officer, it may be used to refer simply to one or more persons. Since the sheriff was the officer particularly charged by the common law with keeping the peace, he was authorized whenever necessary to command all the people of his county to attend him. This group was called the *posse comitatus*, that is, the force or power of the county. The *posse comitatus* must be distinguished from the deputy. If a person is duly appointed a deputy, even if for a special purpose, he serves as an officer, with the authority and responsibility of an officer.[25]

A simple illustration will suffice to show how the law on arrest may hamper police activities. Let us assume that an officer, responding to loud cries for help, discovers the owner of a parked car holding fast to a thief caught in the act of stealing hub caps. Let us further assume that this is a misdemeanor and that it occurs in a state where a private person may not lawfully arrest without a warrant for a misdemeanor committed in his presence, and an officer may not lawfully arrest without a warrant for a misdemeanor not committed in his presence. In this case, then, neither the officer nor the owner of the car may lawfully arrest the thief until they obtain a warrant. This means that they must let the thief go, proceed to a magistrate, secure the warrant, and then go in search of the thief, who in the meantime has probably made good his escape. As a matter of fact, however, the officer would probably make the arrest and take the chance of being held liable for damages and perhaps even criminally prosecuted for false arrest.

Meaning of "Reasonable Grounds." Reference has been made to the fact that an officer or a private citizen may lawfully make an arrest in some situations where he has "reasonable grounds" for doing so. What constitutes "reasonable grounds" cannot be stated in a simple rule since whether or not these grounds exist depends upon the circumstances of each case. "Reasonable grounds" are present if the circumstances of the case are such as to induce a reasonable and prudent man to believe the arrestee guilty of the crime for which the arrest is made, or to cause him to believe that there is a likelihood of such guilt. The person making the arrest, therefore, may arrest two or more persons if he has reasonable grounds to believe that any one or all of them committed a crime. In one case the statement of a witness of a crime might provide "reasonable grounds," while in another, where more time could be taken to investigate without endangering the public safety, such a statement would not be enough.

The right of a person to act upon "reasonable grounds" in making an arrest is based upon the belief that every member of our society must sacrifice some of his freedom of action in the interests of all. Therefore,

---

[25] Perkins, *Elements of Police Science*, pp. 248, 249.

when a lawful arrest is made upon "reasonable grounds," the fact that the arrestee is actually innocent does not give him any right of action against the arrester. However, any unlawful arrest makes the arrester liable to suit for damages and often to criminal prosecution.

A police officer retains his official authority at all times—both off and on duty; but unless otherwise provided by law, he can function as a police officer only within the jurisdiction of the governmental body which appointed him, and elsewhere he has only the authority of a private person. A number of states, however, have enacted laws which give to officers of another state, "in fresh pursuit" of one believed to have committed a felony in such other state, the power to cross their boundaries and to come into them with the same authority to arrest the fugitive and hold him in custody as local officers have in regard to one believed to have committed a local felony.[26]

Use of Force. The general rule is that a police officer or a private person is privileged to use reasonable force in order to make a lawful arrest. Hence, regardless of how much authority a person has to make an arrest, he acts unlawfully if he employs more than reasonable force. What constitutes "reasonable force" depends upon the facts of each case, but it may be said to be what an ordinarily prudent and intelligent person, with the knowledge and in the situation of the arrester, would have deemed reasonable.

If the arrestee resists or flees, the arrester (an officer or a private person) who is making a lawful arrest may use deadly force, that is, means intended or likely to cause death, in order to arrest on a charge of felony, but not on a charge of misdemeanor.[27] Of course, the arrester, regardless of the actions of the arrestee, can never use more force than reasonably appears necessary. The American Law Institute has taken the position that the arrester is privileged to use deadly force in case of resistance or flight only when the arrestee is sought for a "dangerous" felony, that is, a felony such as arson, burglary, kidnapping, manslaughter, mayhem, murder, rape, robbery, and felonious assault. Some jurisdictions in the United States have adopted the same position.

The arrester, however, is always privileged to use deadly force if this is necessary, or reasonably appears necessary, to save himself from death or great bodily harm irrespective of the kind of offense (that is, regard-

---

[26] *Ibid.*, pp. 260–62, 267, 268; Dax and Tibbs, pp. 17–19.

[27] According to the English common law, a private person seeking to arrest without a warrant was never privileged to use deadly force merely to arrest another if that person was in fact innocent. Perkins states that this seems to be equally true in the United States, where the statutes usually require a warrant of arrest to be executed by a peace officer and the authority of a private person to make an arrest without a warrant is seldom exercised, although this authority is very broad. See Perkins, *Criminal Law*, p. 874.

less of whether it is a misdemeanor, a "non-dangerous" felony, or a "dangerous" felony) for which the arrest is being attempted. The arrester must of necessity be the aggressor, and in attempting to make a lawful arrest, he is never required to abandon the attempt where he has the choice between abandonment and the use of deadly force in self-defense.[28]

Disposition of the Prisoner. Since the purpose of lawful arrest is to take the prisoner before a magistrate, court, body, or official, or otherwise secure the administration of the law, such disposition of the prisoner should be made with reasonable promptness.[29] If this is not done, the detention of the prisoner will become unlawful even if his arrest was lawful. However, this does not mean that the officer is deprived of the privilege of locking up the arrestee temporarily for a reasonable time if the circumstances of the case make this necessary. Thus, if a lawful arrest is made at night, at an hour when the normal facilities for obtaining release on bail are not open, the prisoner may be locked up for the night and taken before a magistrate at a reasonable hour in the morning. Furthermore, it would certainly seem to be reasonable to delay taking a man before a magistrate if this is necessary to save lives, preserve important evidence, or insure the arrest of dangerous criminals.[30]

Holding for Questioning or Investigation. No person, without his consent or without authority conferred by special statute, may be locked up in jail or imprisoned elsewhere for questioning or for investigation if the circumstances of the case are not sufficient to arrest him lawfully on a criminal charge. However, a court or magistrate may imprison a material witness in a criminal case if he will not agree to appear and testify in court. Furthermore, when officers arrive at the scene of a serious crime, they may require persons found there to remain for a reasonable time for questioning. This is a technical "confinement" and does not amount to an arrest or imprisonment.

An officer does not have the authority to make wholesale arrests of innocent persons merely because he feels that one of the group is guilty of a crime. Such arrests have led to the serious abuse of the authority of the police in some communities. When officers send out a "dragnet" to bring in a number of persons, they should have reasonable grounds for the arrest of each one.

Sometimes it is necessary to hold a prisoner incommunicado for a short period after his arrest in order (1) to prevent the disappearance of other persons who are wanted by the police, (2) to preserve evidence which

[28] Perkins, *Elements of Police Science*, pp. 334–52; Dax and Tibbs, pp. 54–66.

[29] Rule 5(a) of the Federal Rules of Criminal Procedure requires that an arrested person be taken "without unnecessary delay" before the nearest available commissioner or committing officer.

[30] Perkins, *Elements of Police Science*, pp. 283–93, 300.

has not yet been uncovered, or (3) to protect the lives of important witnesses. Unfortunately, the law needs clarification on this point. In most jurisdictions, the police are not sure how far they can lawfully go in holding prisoners incommunicado. Usually this is done without express authority either in the statutes or in the court decisions, and it is justified as being reasonably necessary under the circumstances of the particular case.[31]

Nevertheless, experience has repeatedly demonstrated that, unless this procedure is kept strictly within proper bounds, it easily develops into a vicious practice of unreasonably depriving persons of their liberty. Thus, although every person should be given reasonable opportunity to consult with counsel, sometimes persons who have not been lawfully arrested have been detained for days and refused permission to communicate with their attorneys, friends, and relatives. This is especially apt to happen when the public is clamoring for the capture of dangerous criminals and the police must "get results" or run the risk of being severely condemned for apparent incompetence. Here, as in many other areas of criminal investigation, the evidence strongly indicates that the law on arrest requires careful re-examination, and appropriate legislation and supporting court decisions are urgently needed to provide a clearer definition of the authority and responsibilities of both officers and private persons in the making of arrests and the disposition of arrestees. Undoubtedly, this would reduce the number of unlawful arrests and detentions and greatly facilitate police work, the complexity of which has greatly increased during recent years.

The Law on the Acquisition of Evidence. SEARCH AND SEIZURE. The Fourth Amendment to the Constitution of the United States declares that "the right of the people to be secure in their persons, houses, papers, and effects, against unreasonable searches and seizures, shall not be violated, and no warrants shall issue, but upon probable cause, supported by oath or affirmation, and particularly describing the place to be searched, and the persons or things to be seized." Although originally this amendment applied only to the federal government, it has become a limitation on the states through incorporation into the due process clause of the Fourteenth Amendment, which specifies that "No state shall . . . deprive any person of life, liberty, or property, without due process of law; nor deny to any person within its jurisdiction the equal protection of the laws." Moreover, all state constitutions have a due process clause and provisions similar to those of the Fourth Amendment.[32]

It should be noted that the protection provided by state and federal constitutions is not from *all* searches and seizures, but only from *unrea-*

[31] *Ibid.*, pp. 294–303.
[32] Richard C. Donnelly, "Police Authority and Practices," *The Annals of the American Academy of Political and Social Science*, CCCXXXIX (January, 1962), 92.

sonable ones. What is "unreasonable" cannot be exactly defined and will depend upon the facts of each case. However, search and seizure is held legally "reasonable": (1) when it is properly incident to a lawful arrest; (2) when it is properly made under a valid search warrant; or (3) when under certain circumstances there are reasonable grounds to believe that evidence of a crime will be revealed by the search. In addition, even when a search or seizure is unreasonable, its impropriety may be waived or consented to if this is freely done. A search and seizure is clearly "unreasonable" when it is merely *exploratory* and made *solely* for the purpose of finding evidence of guilt. In other words, if there are not reasonable grounds for believing that a search will uncover evidence of a crime, it is unlawful to search another's house, office, building, papers, or effects merely in the hope of getting evidence to convict him of some crime. Nevertheless, a search otherwise lawful may include efforts to find stolen goods, articles or weapons used in the commission of the crime, or property, such as gambling devices, that has been forfeited to the government.

When a search is made incident to arrest, the search must be reasonable and based upon the arrest and *not* the arrest upon the search. In other words, it is "unreasonable" to search a person and then arrest him on the basis of what is discovered by the search. Furthermore, if the arrest is unlawful, the search incident to it also is unlawful. As incident to lawful arrest the arrester may search the person of the arrestee, his clothing, luggage, and personal effects, and take from him weapons, stolen property, and anything which might help to establish his guilt or enable him to escape. If it is *reasonably* necessary for the arrester's own protection, it is not unlawful to *frisk* the arrestee, that is, to run one's hand over the arrestee's clothing in order to determine quickly whether or not he carries any deadly weapons. A reasonable search incident to a lawful arrest may extend beyond the person of the arrestee to premises under his immediate control, such as his living quarters, office, or automobile, where the arrester has reasonable grounds to believe that means, instrumentalities, or weapons used in the alleged crime, or property stolen during it, may be concealed.[33] If during this search contraband unrelated

---

[33] Just how far the search incident to a lawful arrest may extend remains a troublesome question. Donnelly, in commenting on this, states that "probably the most extreme case decided by the Supreme Court of the United States was *Harris v. United States,* 331 U.S. 145 (1947), where a majority of five to four held that an incidental search might extend to an entire five-room apartment even though the defendant was arrested in the living room" (Donnelly, 97, 98).

Many courts have ruled that only the area of the dwelling clearly visible from the spot of the arrest can be searched when the search is incident to the arrest. This is known as the "plain view" or "plain sight" rule. Some recent decisions, however, have ruled that such a search may cover the area of the dwelling under the "immediate control" of the arrestee.

to the alleged offense is discovered, this, too, may be seized and used in additional charges against the arrestee.[34]

Lawful search and seizure may be conducted also under a search warrant. This is a written order, in the name of the state, signed by a magistrate or other official having the authority to issue it, directed to an officer, and commanding him to search for certain property and to bring it before the magistrate or other issuing official. To be valid, a search warrant must be based upon a showing of "probable cause," supported by oath or affirmation, and must particularly describe the place to be searched and the things to be seized. Since the warrant must point to a definitely ascertainable place, it is unlawful to issue one for a general search, and an officer may not seize one thing under a warrant describing another.[35] Usually, a search warrant involves the seizure of things, but it may call for the search and seizure of persons, in which case they must be particularly described. "Probable cause" can be established by sworn testimony as to the facts, but it is the magistrate, not the complainant, who determines whether there is "probable cause," that is, reasonable grounds for the issuance of the search warrant.[36] A search warrant must be executed within a reasonable time or within the time specified by statute. After the expiration of this time, the warrant becomes void. In the United States the home is given special protection under the law, and it is well established that a person's home may not lawfully be searched without a search warrant, except as an incident to a lawful arrest therein.[37] When an arrest is not made at the arrestee's residence, officers may not thereafter go to it and there conduct a search without a warrant unless they have his consent to do so.

Although most searches and seizures are incident to arrest or made under a search warrant, some are made upon "probable cause," that is,

[34] Varon, pp. 103–13, 189–201; Sherry, 45–50.

[35] However, items of contraband discovered during a search under a warrant not specifically describing these items may be seized on the basis of what is sometimes called the "naked eye" doctrine. According to this doctrine, these items may be seized if they can be seen by the person making the search from a spot where he has a legal right to be.

[36] The terms "probable cause" and "reasonable cause" are equivalent, since the Supreme Court of the United States has applied the "probable cause" requirement of the Fourth Amendment to arrests as well as to searches. In actual practice, however, the standards used in cases involving arrests or searches without a warrant appear to be less strict than in those involving a warrant (Donnelly, 94).

[37] The Fourth Amendment of the United States Constitution, however, yields to the reasonable exercise of the police powers for the protection of the public health, morals, and welfare. Thus in 1959, the United States Supreme Court ruled in a five-to-four decision that the city code of Baltimore which authorized a health inspector without a warrant to enter any premises where he suspected there was a public nuisance did not violate the due process clause of the Fourteenth Amendment. See *Frank v. State* (Md.), 359 U.S. 360 (1959). Despite this decision the various states differ on the question (Varon, Vol. I, pp. 199–201).

when under certain circumstances there are reasonable grounds to believe that a search will reveal evidence of a crime. The principal situation where such a search and seizure is lawful involves the search of an automobile or other vehicle. For example, an officer without a warrant may search an automobile if he has reasonable grounds for believing that it is being used to transport liquor in violation of the law. This kind of search has been held to be reasonable and therefore legal upon such utilitarian grounds as that an automobile might move away before a warrant could be secured, As in the case of a home, a business office may not be lawfully searched without a warrant, except as an incident to a lawful arrest therein; but there is authority for search and seizure upon "probable cause" in any other building or property. The whole question of "probable cause" needs clarification by the courts, because as matters now stand, it is too difficult for the police to decide whether they have "reasonable grounds" to search without a warrant.

Anyone who engages in unlawful search and seizure is subject to a suit for damages and perhaps to criminal prosecution, but in actual practice this affords little protection, largely because of the ignorance and poverty of most victims and the legal technicalities involved in obtaining redress. Furthermore, under the common law the admissibility of evidence is not affected by the illegality of the means by which it is obtained. The United States Supreme Court, however, by a series of decisions has abolished this common law doctrine. These began in 1914 with the case of *Weeks v. United States*, 232 U.S. 383, in which the court said that the admission of illegally secured evidence was violative of the Fourth Amendment and that therefore such evidence should be excluded from *federal* cases, although this ruling did not affect the police activities of *state* officers. In 1949, in *Wolf v. Colorado*, 338 U.S. 25, the Supreme Court went a step farther and ruled that unreasonable searches and seizures by state law-enforcement officers violated the due process clause of the Fourteenth Amendment but that the states were still not required to adopt the exclusionary rule of evidence. However, in 1961, a divided Supreme Court, in *Mapp v. Ohio*, 367 U.S. 643, overruled the *Wolf* case and, as a result, evidence obtained by an unlawful search and seizure is now inadmissible in *both* federal and state courts.

The question of whether or not to exclude illegally secured evidence has evoked considerable controversy, and prior to the *Mapp* case, a substantial number of states had declined to follow the lead of the federal government in adopting the exclusionary rule. On the one side, it is claimed that the most satisfactory assurance of respect for the law is afforded by denying to the police the right to use evidence which has been illegally obtained, and that it is better that guilty men should go free than that the prosecution should be able to avail itself of the fruits of illegal activities. On the other side, it is contended that the federal rule permits thousands of obviously guilty criminals to go free and forces the police, regardless of this rule, to adopt lawless practices in order to provide the public with the protection it demands and has a right to expect. Furthermore, although some students of the Supreme Court have hailed its recent decisions affecting law enforcement, the criminal courts, and other aspects of our political and social life as a great advance in the fight to protect the innocent, the friendless, and the poor, many jurists, legislators, and law-enforcement officials have condemned them as an unnecessary interference with local self-government and a dangerous encroachment upon the rights of the states. These decisions, the latter argue, are helping to create a centralization of power in the federal government that will be used to destroy the very rights which the court claims it is trying to protect. In fact, they conclude, through a perversion of the Fourteenth Amendment, we already have in Washington a government of *delegating* powers instead of one of *delegated* powers, and so the original purpose of the Constitution has been defeated.[38]

Related to this controversy is another troublesome question. Does the interception of telephone conversation by wire tapping constitute an unreasonable search and seizure within the meaning of the Fourth Amendment? The majority of the United States Supreme Court has never decided

[38] For some critical analyses of recent United States Supreme Court decisions affecting law enforcement and criminal prosecution, see Francis A. Allen, "The Supreme Court, Federalism, and State Systems of Criminal Justice," *De Paul Law Review*, VIII (Spring–Summer, 1959), 213–55; Allen, "Federalism and the Fourth Amendment: A Requiem for Wolf," *The Supreme Court Review*, ed. Philip B. Kurland (Chicago: University of Chicago Press, 1961), pp. 1–48; *Police Power and Individual Freedom*, ed. Claude R. Sowle (Chicago: Aldine Publishing Co., 1962); Edward L. Barrett, Jr., "Police Practices and the Law—From Arrest to Release or Charge," *California Law Review*, L (Mar., 1962), 11–55; Edward Martin Einhorn, "The Exclusionary Rule in Operation—A Comparison of Illinois, California and Federal Law," *Journal of Criminal Law, Criminology, and Police Science*, L (July–Aug., 1959), 144–60; Fred E. Inbau, "Public Safety v. Individual Civil Liberties: The Prosecutor's Stand," *ibid.*, LIII (March, 1962), 85–89; Yale Kamisar, "Public Safety v. Individual Liberties: Some 'Facts' and 'Theories'," *ibid.*, LIII (June, 1962), 171–93; Fred E. Inbau, "More About Public Safety v. Individual Civil Liberties," *ibid.*, LIII (Sept., 1962), 329–32; Yale Kamisar, Some Reflections on Criticizing the Courts and 'Policing the Police'," *ibid.*, LIII (Dec., 1962), 453–62; Frank D. Day, "Criminal Law Enforcement and a Free Society," *ibid.*, LIV (Sept., 1963), 360–65; Virgil W. Peterson, "Law and Police Practice: Restrictions in the Law of Search and Seizure," *Northwestern University Law Review*, LII (Mar.–Apr., 1957), 46–64; Peterson, "Recent Trends of Decisions of the Supreme Court of the United States in the Field of Criminal Law," Presented at Regional Meeting of the American Bar Association, June 13, 1958 (mimeographed); Peterson, *A Report on Chicago Crime for 1962* (Chicago: Chicago Crime Commission, June 28, 1963), pp. 17–21; The Conference of Chief Justices, "Report of the Committee on Federal-State Relationships as Affected by Judicial Decisions," Adopted August, 1958 (Richmond, Va.: Reprinted and Distributed by the Virginia Commission on Constitutional Government, 1959).

that it does.[39] In the federal courts, any protection that Americans have against wire tapping stems from the Supreme Court's interpretation of the Federal Communications Act of 1934.[40] On the basis of this interpretation, the Supreme Court has forbidden the reception in evidence in federal courts of messages intercepted by wire tapping; but the federal government has rarely prosecuted those who engage in wire tapping, and federal officials do not consider wire tapping per se to be illegal.[41]

Furthermore, the ruling of the Supreme Court regarding the admissibility of evidence obtained by wire tapping applies only to cases arising under federal law. Therefore, it is within the power of the individual states to determine whether such evidence may be used in cases prosecuted under state law. Although most states have outlawed wire tapping, some, like New York, permit it under court order and most, regardless of whether or not they have banned wire tapping, permit the admission of evidence secured through its use. In fact, only a few states explicitly forbid the use of such evidence. Moreover, even in states where the law bars wire tapping, police often resort to it in their search for evidence, especially in large cities where they are fighting organized crime.[42]

---

[39] In 1928, in *Olmstead v. United States,* 277 U.S. 438, the United States Supreme Court, in a five to four decision, ruled that wire tapping did not violate the Fourth Amendment. Since then no constitutional limit has been placed on off-the-premises wire tapping.

[40] Section 605 of this act provides that no person shall intercept any communication and divulge the contents. In *Nardone v. United States,* 302 U.S. 379 (1937), 308 U.S. 338 (1939), the Supreme Court held that wiretap evidence or evidence directly derived from it was inadmissible in Federal Courts. In *Weiss v. United States,* 308 U.S. 321 (1939), the Court applied the Federal Communications Act to prohibit the interception and divulgence of intrastate as well as interstate calls. However, in *Schwartz v. Texas,* 344 U.S. 199 (1952), the Court refused to interfere in a case in which a state court accepted wire-tap evidence secured by state officers. On the other hand, in *Benanti v. United States,* 355 U.S. 96 (1957), the Court ruled that wire-tap evidence regardless of its source, that is, whether obtained by federal or state officers, was inadmissible in federal courts. See also *Pugach v. Dollinger,* 81 Sup. Ct. 650 (1961). As a result of recent United States Supreme Court decisions, it is uncertain whether a state conviction based upon wire-tap evidence would be reversed by that Court. See Alan H. Swanson, "Wiretapping: The State Law," *Journal of Criminal Law, Criminology, and Police Science,* LI (Jan.–Feb., 1961), 534–44; Lawrence M. Dubin, "Wiretapping: The Federalism Problem," *ibid.,* LI (Mar.–Apr., 1961), 630–36.

[41] The FBI, for example, maintains that wire tapping by its agents is legal. This is so, the FBI claims, because the Federal Communications Act requires that there be both interception and divulgence, that its agents merely report wire-tap information to superior officials and do not make any public disclosure of it, and that only public disclosure constitutes divulgences under the act. The Supreme Court has never expressly ruled on this question.

[42] Although wire tapping is only one of the forms of eavesdropping, the federal statute and most of the state statutes are limited to it. When other forms, such as microphones, are used, the presence of a search or seizure will depend upon whether there has been a trespass. See, for example, *On Lee v. United States,* 343 U.S. 747 (1952); *Silverman v. United States,* 81 Sup. Ct. 679 (1961).

Competing claims regarding individual privacy and the security of society swirl about wire tapping and create an intense controversy. Opponents call it a "dirty business" and an insidious invasion of individual rights and insist that it is too high a price to pay for evidence which in most cases can be secured by other less dangerous methods. However, many police and public officials argue that wire tapping is essential to effective law enforcement and that when wire tapping is used, care can be exercised to protect the rights of innocent persons.

In view of the great threat to our national security by organized crime and the Communist conspiracy, a realistic appraisal of the situation indicates that it would be unwise to remove entirely so effective a weapon as wire tapping from the arsenal of law enforcement. The real question is not whether wire tapping should be allowed, but rather to what extent and under what conditions it should be permitted. Most state and federal legislators seem inclined to permit wire tapping in treason, espionage, sabotage, sedition, organized illegal gambling, and certain other cases, but they want to keep it under strict controls, such as a court order issued for probable cause, in order to protect the individual against unnecessary invasion of his privacy.[43]

The use of informers and entrapment by the police creates additional problems for the courts. Informers are especially helpful in the investigation of vice and organized crime, and in order to protect them from reprisals and to keep this source of information fruitful, the courts have developed the "informer's privilege," which means that the state does not have to disclose the identity of such a person. However, this privilege is not absolute. For example, the contents of the informer's communication must be disclosed if this will not reveal his identity. Furthermore, when the identity of the informer has become known to those who have reason to resent the communication, the privilege no longer exists; and if his identity or the contents of his communication are important in the establishment of the defense, then the privilege must yield or the case will be dismissed.[44]

[43] Perkins, *Elements of Police Science,* pp. 304–33; Dax and Tibbs, pp. 111–75; Zelman Cowen, "The Admissibility of Evidence Procured through Illegal Searches and Seizures in British Commonwealth Jurisdictions," *Vanderbilt Law Review,* V (Apr., 1952), 524–28; Charles Marshall, "How Far Can Federal Officers Search in Connection with an Arrest?" *Journal of Criminal Law and Criminology,* XLI (Sept.–Oct., 1950), 325–30; Ferdinand J. Zeni, Jr., "Wiretapping—The Right of Privacy Versus the Public Interest," *Journal of Criminal Law and Criminology,* XL (Nov.–Dec., 1949), 476–83; Paul T. Heffron, "Wiretapping and the Law," *The Catholic World,* CLXXIX (May, 1954), 110–15; "The Busy Wiretappers," *Newsweek,* XLV (Mar. 7, 1955), 31–34; "The Debate on Wiretapping," *Time,* LXIII (Jan. 4, 1954), 12, 13.

[44] Donnelly, 99, 100, 103, 104; Charles T. McCormick, *Handbook of the Law of Evidence* (St. Paul, Minn.: West Publishing Co., 1954), 309–11. In *Roviaro v. United States,* 353 U.S. 53 (1957), the United States Supreme Court held that the identity of the informer must be revealed if this is helpful in the defense of the accused.

Entrapment raises the question of how far law-enforcement officials can go in their efforts to ensnare offenders. The mere fact that officers have given the defendant an opportunity to commit a crime is not enough to block his prosecution. Tactics involving misrepresentation, deception, and artifice are indispensable in effective police work. Nevertheless, the defense of illegal entrapment is available if the intent to commit a crime did not originate in the mind of the accused but was planted there by the police and his offense was thus a product of their creative activity.[45]

COMPULSORY SELF-INCRIMINATION. The Fifth Amendment to the Constitution of the United States declares that "no person . . . shall be compelled in any criminal case to be a witness against himself, nor be deprived of life, liberty, or property, without due process of law . . ." The self-incrimination provision of the Fifth Amendment has always applied to the federal government, but not until June, 1964, did the United States Supreme Court—and then in a five-to-four decision—extend its application to the states by way of the Fourteenth Amendment.[46] Even so, as a result of independent action, this privilege in some form has been recognized for a long time in all of the states. Therefore, when evidence against a person is obtained through compulsory self-incrimination, it is inadmissible in a criminal case in either a state or a federal court. However, some difficulties have arisen as to what constitutes "compulsion" and "self-incrimination"; and on these questions the states have differed among themselves and with the federal government.

a. *What constitutes "compulsion"?* "Compulsion" appears in its most dramatic form in the so-called "third degree."[47] This refers to the employment of methods which inflict suffering, physical or mental, upon a person in order to obtain information about a crime. The person subjected to the "third degree" may be suspected of either having committed the crime or having been a possible witness thereof. "Third-degree" methods range all the way from protracted questioning, threats, and deprivation of necessary sleep and food to such physical brutality as kicking and beating with fists and clubs, but regardless of the methods employed, the evidence

---

[45] Varon, pp. 546–73; Perkins, *Criminal Law*, pp. 921–26. See also *Sorrells v. United States*, 287 U.S. 435 (1932); *Sherman v. United States*, 356 U.S. 369 (1958).

[46] See *Malloy v. Hogan*, 84 Sup. Ct. 1489 (1964). The Supreme Court of the United States had previously established the rule that it is a violation of due process of law to base a conviction solely or partly upon confessions secured by physical violence or undue psychological coercion. This type of conviction is unconstitutional in either a state or federal court.

[47] It is believed that the term "third degree" was suggested by the Masonic third degree. In 1910, Major Richard Sylvester, of Washington, then president of the International Association of Chiefs of Police, in explaining the origin of the term, said that the arrest was the "first degree," the transportation of the suspect to a place of confinement, the "second degree," and the interrogation of the suspect, the "third degree."

secured thereby cannot be used directly or indirectly against the victim.[48]
Furthermore, persons who employ the "third degree" are subject to civil
action for damages and criminal prosecution for assault and battery or
other crimes.

Although there is no doubt that some police still resort to the "third
degree," it is now far less frequently used than the public has been led
to believe. Where it persists, it is often defended as being necessary to
convict dangerous criminals, who otherwise would utilize outworn legal
limitations to escape justice, and to protect the police against charges of
inefficiency and corruption when the public and the press are clamoring
for results. Although the questioning of prisoners immediately after their
arrest is justified, since it often produces quick confessions, such questioning must be carefully regulated or it may deteriorate into the "third
degree." This, under no circumstances, can be tolerated; for the "third
degree" not only involves the dangers of false confessions and injuries to
prisoners, but also tends to brutalize the police, harden the prisoner
against society, and lower the public esteem for the administration of
justice.[49]

The constitutional protection against compulsory self-incrimination also
extends into the courtroom, where an accused person cannot be compelled
to take the witness stand and testify. He may do so *voluntarily*, but not
under compulsion. Moreover, in many jurisdictions the prosecuting attorney cannot comment unfavorably upon the failure of the defendant to
testify nor can the jury take this into consideration in arriving at a verdict.
To permit otherwise, it is claimed, would amount to forcing the accused

[48] For a revealing study of third-degree methods, see National Commission on
Law Observance and Enforcement, Report on Lawlessness in Law Enforcement, Report No. 11 (Washington, D.C.: Government Printing Office, 1931). See also William
A. Westley, "Violence and the Police," *American Journal of Sociology,* LIX (July,
1953), 34–41.

[49] According to the McNabb-Mallory rule, a confession must be excluded from a
federal prosecution if it is made during illegal detention due to failure to take a
prisoner promptly before a committing magistrate, regardless of whether or not the
confession is obtained by physical or psychological torture. See *McNabb v. United
States,* 318 U.S. 332 (1943); *Mallory v. United States,* 354 U.S. 449 (1957). However, this rule is based on the Federal Rules of Criminal Procedure, which stipulate
that an arrested person must be taken "without unnecessary delay" before a committing magistrate, and not on any constitutional provision, and therefore the Supreme
Court has refused to impose it upon the state courts. Most law-enforcement officials
oppose this rule, and the states, without exception, have rejected it. In opposition to
the argument that the rule tends to discourage unlawful police activity, the contention has been made that the police should be able to hold suspects long enough to
check available facts and run down leads, that this relatively short period of investigation not only protects the public from unnecessary risks but also prevents innocent
persons from acquiring an arrest record, and that to require the police to delay arrest
until they have sufficient evidence to show probable cause is impractical and would
seriously reduce their effectiveness. See Donnelly, pp. 107, 108.

to testify under the threat that to refuse might be interpreted as an admission of guilt. But since actually juries cannot be prevented from drawing their own conclusions about a defendant who fails to testify in his own defense, many members of the bar are beginning to favor the view that the prosecutor should be permitted to comment upon the failure of the defendant to testify and that the jury should take this fact into consideration in its deliberations. However, if the accused does volunteer to become a witness, he may be cross-examined on matters that are relevant to the charge for which he is being tried, although in some jurisdictions he may reserve the right not to answer certain questions during this examination.

On the other hand, *voluntary* confessions and admissions by a person, regardless of how damaging to him they may be, are not in any way affected by the constitutional prohibition against self-incrimination. Whether a confession or admission is voluntary depends upon all the facts of the particular case. Neither the fact that a person is under arrest nor the length of time that he is held before making an admission or confession is of itself sufficient to render such confession or admission inadmissible. It is true that the suspect is not obligated to talk or answer any questions, but a confession may be voluntary even though the prisoner is not informed of his constitutional rights, is not warned that his statement will be used against him, does not have the benefit of counsel, and is told that it would be advisable to tell the truth. But a confession is not voluntary and, therefore, is not admissible as evidence if officers put a prisoner under oath, or pretend to do so, in securing it, or extract it by a promise of immunity or leniency. Trickery of itself, however, although it may be considered unethical, may not constitute compulsion. If officers, in order to obtain a confession, tell a suspect that his fingerprints have been found at the scene of a crime when in fact they have not, and thereby induce him to confess, his confession is still considered to be voluntary. The rule appears to be that the employment of any artifice, deception, or fraud does not of itself make a confession involuntary if it is *not* calculated to procure an untrue statement.

A confession which is not corroborated in any way will not of itself be sufficient to secure a conviction, but a confession, when taken together with other evidence, may be used to establish the guilt of the defendant.[50] The law gives special sanctity and weight to so-called "dying declarations," and such declarations, unlike other statements which might be excluded as hearsay, may be used in later court proceedings. However, a

---

[50] A confession made in open court during the course of criminal proceedings and before a judicial authority having appropriate jurisdiction and power to fix punishment in the case constitutes a plea of guilty, and the case may then be concluded and disposition made. Even so, in such a case the court must be satisfied that the confession is a free and voluntary act.

statement is admissible as a "dying declaration" only when the person making it has no hope of recovery and feels that death is imminent.[51]

b. *What constitutes self-incrimination?* There has been a great deal of controversy in the courts and elsewhere as to what constitutes self-incrimination. Here we shall confine ourselves to a statement of the majority view on some of the most important questions that have been raised about it. According to the weight of authority, there is *no* self-incrimination when a person is compelled: (1) to surrender his shoes for the purpose of having them compared with tracks at the scene of the crime, or to place his shoes or feet into prints so that a comparison can be made; (2) to submit to an examination of his body for identifying scars, marks, and wounds; (3) to change his wearing apparel for the purpose of assisting witnesses to a crime in identifying the perpetrator; (4) to shave, submit to a haircut, take off spectacles, or remove other disguising effects for the purpose of identification; (5) to stand up in court or place himself within full view of witnesses and jury; (6) to submit to a police "line-up" or "show-up" so that he can be viewed alongside other persons by witnesses to a crime; (7) to submit to fingerprinting so that his prints can be compared with those found at the scene of a crime; (8) to submit to the taking of his photograph; (9) to provide a specimen of his handwriting for purposes of comparison with a questioned document; (10) to speak so that his voice may be compared with that of the perpetrator of a crime; (11) to submit to the removal of foreign objects of evidentiary value either from the surface of the body (as in the removal of scrapings from underneath the fingernails for the purpose of determining the presence of blood) or from within the body (as in the removal of the contents of the stomach for the purpose of determining the presence of marihuana); and (12) to submit to the taking of specimens of his body fluids, such as blood and urine, or his breath for purposes of subjecting them to tests for alcoholic intoxication.[52] In all these instances, therefore, since self-incrimination is not involved, the use of compulsion does not of itself have any effect upon the admissibility of evidence.

However, legal authority is clearly of the opinion that the compulsory submission to the lie-detector or to truth-serum tests falls within the limits

[51] Dax and Tibbs, pp. 98–104; Varon, Vol. II, pp. 773–808.

[52] The United States Supreme Court, however, has ruled that if unreasonable force is used in extracting something from the body of a person, this violates due process of law and the evidence is inadmissible in state and federal courts. See *Rochin v. California,* 342 U.S. 165 (1952). A similar question was raised in *Breithaupt v. Abram,* 352 U.S. 432 (1957), but in this case a majority of the Supreme Court declined to reverse the conviction. In handing down its decision in the *Breithaupt* case, the Court said that there was nothing brutal or offensive in the taking of a sample of blood when this was done, as it was in this case, under the protective eye of a physician. The *Breithaupt* case, therefore, was to be distinguished on this ground from the *Rochin* case.

of the self-incrimination clause of our constitutions and that therefore evidence obtained by such compulsion is inadmissible. But suppose the suspect is willing to take a lie-detector or truth-serum test, does this affect the admissibility of the evidence? The answer to this is that the results of such a test, at the present time, are inadmissible in evidence, except possibly where opposing attorneys agree and stipulate to have the tests made and to permit the results to be received in court. The conservatism of the courts on this point is understandable. The lie detector is not infallible, and the truth-serum test is far from being accurate. But despite this, the public has been led to place a great deal of faith in them, and juries therefore would be inclined to rely excessively upon such evidence.

The ultimate test as to the applicability of the self-incrimination clause of our constitutions is whether the compulsory evidence is of a *testimonial* nature. In other words, has an *incriminating oral* or *written statement* been extracted by compulsion from the accused? The self-incrimination clause was never intended to cover physical evidence like fingerprints, scars, footprints, and handwriting. This view is supported not only by the weight of legal authority, but also by policy considerations, which justify the existence of the privilege. Since the policy behind the privilege is to stimulate the investigating and prosecuting authorities to a diligent search for evidence obtainable by their own efforts, that policy would be obstructed rather than facilitated by the application of the self-incrimination clause to physical evidence obtained through compulsion.[53]

[53] Dax and Tibbs, pp. 104–8; Fred E. Inbau, *Self-Incrimination*, pp. 9–15, 21–51, 70–82; Arthur E. Wood and John B. Waite, *Crime and Its Treatment* (New York: American Book Co., 1941), pp. 394–401; Inbau and Reid, pp. 122–27; Audrey M. Davis, "Police, the Law, and the Individual," *The Annals of the American Academy of Political and Social Science*, CCXCI (Jan., 1954), 143–51; Varon, Vol. I, pp. 451–98; Fred E. Inbau and John E. Reid, *Criminal Interrogation and Confession* (Baltimore: The Williams and Wilkins Co., 1962), pp. 189, 190; John MacArthur Maguire, *Evidence of Guilt* (Boston: Little, Brown and Co., 1959), pp. 10–106.

15

Criminal Prosecution

HISTORICAL BACKGROUND

American criminal prosecution had its origin in the judicial system of England, and the organization and procedure of American and English courts are still remarkably similar.[1] During the early years of the United States, the memory of the conflict between the courts of England and the Crown, the abuse of prosecutions by the Stuart kings, and the use of the criminal law as an instrument of religious persecution and political oppression was still fresh in the minds of the people. It is not surprising, then, that the understanding and fear born of this memory combined with the self-reliance of a pioneering people to become a decisive influence in the development of American criminal law and procedure during their formative period. As a result, the founders of our republic imposed restrictions upon criminal prosecution in order to insure the protection of individual liberty and curtailed the power of the judge to direct the trial and to guide the jury in its deliberations. In their zeal, they undoubtedly went too far in certain respects, but the fundamental principles which they had learned through bitter experience and which they so ardently espoused are sound and enduring. America owes them an eternal debt of gratitude and should vigilantly and courageously guard the legal devices which they so wisely and carefully wrought to protect the rights of the people.

ORGANIZATION OF AMERICAN COURTS

In the United States the administration of justice operates through the federal and state judicial systems, which are entirely independent of each other. Persons charged with the violation of state laws are tried in state courts, whereas the jurisdiction of the federal courts is restricted to mat-

[1] Although the state of Louisiana was of Spanish and French origin, its legal institutions have tended to become more and more like those of other states.

ters arising under the United States Constitution and the federal laws and treaties. Since it is definitely established that there are no common law offenses against the United States, federal crimes can be created only through the enactment of statutes by the Congress.

In the federal judicial system, the principal courts are the United States Supreme Court, the circuit courts of appeal, and the district courts. In 1963 there were eleven circuit courts of appeal and ninety-one district courts. The Supreme Court, composed of a chief justice and eight associate justices, has limited original jurisdiction, that is, it has authority over few cases at their inception. In practice it is essentially an appellate court, receiving most of its cases from the lower federal courts. Each of the circuit courts of appeal normally has three judges (although the number may go as high as nine), who review cases appealed from the district courts. The circuit court of appeal has no original jurisdiction, and like the Supreme Court, it functions without a jury. The district courts, each of which is usually presided over by a single judge, are the courts of original jurisdiction in the federal system. It is in these courts that the great bulk of federal cases are begun, either before a judge or before a judge and a jury. All the judges in the federal judicial system are appointed for life by the President and confirmed by the Senate.

In each federal judicial district is an officer called a United States commissioner. He is appointed for a term of four years by the district court, is supervised by it, and performs duties similar to those of a magistrate in the state judicial system. Another officer known as a United States marshal, who is appointed for a term of four years by the President and confirmed by the Senate, is attached to each district court and functions in a capacity similar to that of a sheriff. Assigned to each federal judicial district is a third officer who has the title of United States district attorney. He is appointed for a term of four years by the President and confirmed by the Senate and serves under the supervision of the Attorney General. His duties include the prosecution of all persons accused of federal crimes and the handling of civil actions to which the United States is a party. At the head of the United States justice department is the Attorney General, who is appointed by the President and is a member of the cabinet. He represents the federal government in cases before the United States Supreme Court and gives legal advice upon questions submitted to him.

The state judicial system for the disposition of criminal cases usually consists of a supreme court, a number of trial courts of general jurisdiction, and a larger number of inferior courts. In some states pressure on the supreme court has been relieved by the creation of intermediate courts of appeal, and some large cities have been forced to create various special courts, such as traffic courts and family courts, to handle the increasing volume of cases.

Like the United States Supreme Court, the state supreme courts are essentially appellate courts with limited original jurisdiction. The number of justices serving on the state supreme court varies from state to state; usually they are selected by popular vote.

The trial courts of general jurisdiction bear different names in different states, having such titles as superior courts, courts of oyer and terminer, courts of quarter sessions, circuit courts, district courts, and criminal courts.[2] In many states these courts handle both civil and criminal cases. They have wide original jurisdiction and are served by both a judge and a jury, although cases may be tried in them without a jury. Most serious litigation originates in the trial courts, and they take care of the great majority of the major cases that are disposed of throughout the country, relatively few cases tried in them being appealed. They also have the power to review cases brought before them on appeals from the inferior courts. Most states select their trial court judges by popular election.

Every state has a large number of inferior courts that handle litigation of a minor character with as little formality as possible. Known by such names as justice of the peace courts, magistrate's courts, police courts, mayor's courts, and municipal courts, these courts try cases without a jury, and appeals may be taken from them to the trial courts. The inferior court performs two functions in the administration of criminal justice: (1) it holds preliminary hearings of cases involving serious offenses, which are later handled by the trial court; and (2) it conducts summary trials of minor offenses, as a result of which it may impose fines or imprison offenders for short terms. Most states provide that the justice of peace, magistrate, or other official who presides in the inferior court should be selected by popular vote.

County or district attorneys prepare the formal charges, marshal the evidence, and conduct the criminal prosecution for the state. The attorney general is the chief law officer of the state and is the head of its legal department. All these law officers are usually chosen by popular election.

STEPS IN CRIMINAL PROSECUTION

Arrest or Summons. The essential steps in criminal prosecution, as shown in the chart on page 348, are the same in the state and federal judicial systems. The criminal case begins with either an arrest or a sum-

---

[2] Each of these names indicates some aspect of the court to which it was originally applied. For example, "oyer and terminer" is an Anglo-French term, the literal meaning of which is to "hear and determine"; the term "circuit" refers to the fact that the judge travels a circuit from one county to another, holding court in each; and the term "quarter sessions" indicates that the court has four sessions each year. The names used may no longer accurately describe the courts to which they are applied. In this text the term "trial court" will be used to refer to all these courts.

Steps in Criminal Prosecution

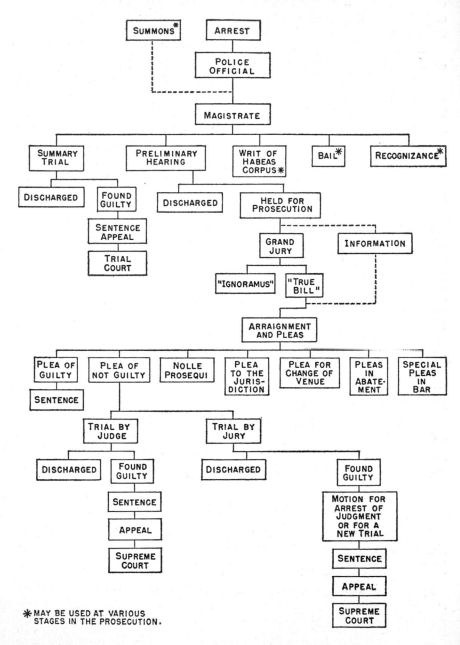

* MAY BE USED AT VARIOUS
  STAGES IN THE PROSECUTION.

mons. The summons is an official notice ordering the person to appear in court at a certain time to answer the complaint made against him. It is often used in cases involving minor offenses such as traffic violations. When an arrest has been made, the prisoner is taken to a police station or jail and confined until a hearing can be held. Sometimes he is given a brief hearing before a police official prior to an appearance in the magistrate's court.[3] In general, a person who has committed a crime but "turns state's evidence," that is, testifies against his confederates, is given exemption from prosecution. Although there seems to be no authority in the common law upholding this practice, numerous federal and state statutes do expressly provide for it. However, promises of immunity from further prosecution, given by law-enforcement officials in order to induce a defendant to plead guilty to one of his offenses, have no sanction in the law and constitute no bar to prosecution.

Rights of the Accused. The accused has many valuable rights.[4] He has the right to be released on bail except in certain cases involving serious crimes, to have free access to counsel, to have a copy of the charges against him, to confront the witnesses for the prosecution and to cross-examine them in person or by counsel, to have the use of the court's process for subpoenaing witnesses, to have protection against prejudicial, irrelevant, and hearsay testimony, to refuse to testify in his own behalf so as to avoid self-incrimination, to have proof of guilt beyond a reasonable doubt, and to have access to a higher court for the purpose of an appeal.

Summary Trial. If the accused is charged with a minor crime, his case will be disposed of by a summary trial before a magistrate and almost always without a jury. Usually a prosecutor is not present, and in most cases the accused is not represented by counsel. The magistrate decides both questions of law and questions of fact, and if he finds the accused guilty, he imposes a fine or commits the prisoner to jail. Most states permit the defendant to appeal from a summary conviction, and sometimes the state, also, has this right.

Preliminary Hearing. When a person is accused of a serious crime, he may be given a preliminary hearing, or examination, before a magis-

[3] For the purpose of simplification, the term "magistrate" will be used throughout this discussion of the steps in criminal prosecution whenever reference is made to the judge of an inferior court.

[4] Most of the rights of the accused are included in what is referred to as due process of law. This may be defined as such exercise of the powers of government as the settled maxims of law permit and under such safeguards for the protection of individual rights as those maxims prescribe for the class of cases to which the one in question belongs (*Black's Law Dictionary* [St. Paul, Minn.: West Publishing Co., 1933], pp. 626, 627).

trate, ordinarily within a few hours after arrest; but usually this hearing is not used if the grand jury is, since both have about the same function. In fact, in most states where both are made available, the preliminary hearing may be waived by the accused. The purpose of this hearing is to determine whether there is sufficient evidence to justify holding the accused for further proceedings by the grand jury or the trial court. If he is discharged, this usually concludes the prosecution in the case, but he may be rearrested on the same charge if for any reason it later appears that he may be more successfully prosecuted. If he is held for trial, he may be released on bail or detained in the local jail.

Bail. Bail is security furnished to the court for the appearance of the defendant whenever his presence is needed. When it is granted, the defendant is released under conditions imposed by the court. In certain cases, usually of a minor nature, the prisoner may secure a release on his own recognizance or promise to return for the hearing. The constitutions of most of the states provide that all persons shall be bailable by sufficient sureties, except for capital crimes where the proof is evident or the presumption of guilt is great. If the prisoner is entitled to bail, it must be granted by the court. The state and federal constitutions stipulate that excessive bail shall not be exacted, and, therefore, it must be set at an amount which is deemed reasonably necessary to guarantee the subsequent appearance of the defendant. Bail may be granted at various stages of the prosecution, usually up to the time of final conviction and sometimes after this if an appeal is taken to a higher court. However, the general constitutional guarantees of bail are applicable only before conviction. The power to admit a defendant to bail after his conviction is usually entrusted to the discretion of the trial court. If bail is defaulted, the accused is subject to arrest and confinement in jail until final disposition is made of his case.

Writ of Habeas Corpus. The right to the writ of habeas corpus is secured by provisions in the constitutions of the states and the federal government. It is so called because it is directed to a person who detains another in custody and commands him to produce or, according to the meaning of the Latin words, "habeas corpus," have the body of that person before the court for a specified purpose. This is the proper remedy for anyone who is being held in custody without a legal right. Application for the writ of habeas corpus is made in the form of a petition to the court by the person detained or by his attorney. The person is then brought before the judge, who investigates the circumstances of the case; if he finds the restraint illegal, he discharges the person, releases him on bail, or makes some other proper disposition of the case. If, however, the judge finds that the detention is lawful, he recommits the prisoner to his custodian.

The Indictment. If as a result of the preliminary hearing the magistrate finds that further action should be taken in the case, or if the case is to be taken directly to the grand jury without a preliminary hearing, the district or county attorney prepares an indictment, which is a formal written statement charging the person named therein with an offense. The indictment is then submitted to the grand jury, whose duty it is to determine whether there is sufficient evidence to continue the prosecution, that is, whether the evidence before it, if not contradicted or rebutted, is enough to convict the accused of a crime. If the grand jury so decides, the accused is held for action by the trial court. In some jurisdictions, if the grand jury supports the indictment, the foreman indorses "true bill" on the indictment and signs it; but if the investigation fails to disclose a case, the jury "ignores the bill" and the foreman marks it "ignoramus" (Latin for "we do not know").

Sometimes during an investigation the grand jury discovers definite evidence of the commission of a crime by someone against whom no indictment has been prepared. When this happens, it has the authority to make a "presentment" against such person. This amounts to an instruction to the district or county attorney to prepare an indictment for submission to the grand jury. After this has been done, the indictment is then approved by the grand jury.

Information by the Prosecuting Officer. An indictment by a grand jury is not the only method by which a person may be brought to trial in the higher criminal courts. The same result can be accomplished by means of an information prepared by the district or county attorney and filed with the court without the intervention of the grand jury. The provisions regarding this vary from state to state. In some states, the information may be used only for misdemeanors, indictment by the grand jury being required for felonies; in others, it may be used for both felonies and misdemeanors. In the federal jurisdiction, indictment by the grand jury is necessary in felony cases and in some serious misdemeanors, but the information is proper in minor cases and is frequently used. The district or county attorney in some states may employ the information to initiate a criminal prosecution when he is advised by the affidavits of witnesses that a certain crime has been committed. Usually, however, the information is based upon the findings of a preliminary hearing by a magistrate.

Arraignment and Pleas. After the formal indictment, or the preparation of an information, the next step in the criminal prosecution consists of bringing the defendant before the court to answer the charges prepared against him. This is called the "arraignment." If the defendant is in custody, he is brought before the court, but if he is out on bail, he and his sureties are notified to be in court at a certain time. If he fails to appear, the court issues a warrant for his arrest; and in the event that he cannot be found, and there is no satisfactory explanation for his absence, the judge directs the surety to pay the amount of the bail to the county.

The arraignment affords the defendant an opportunity to object to the indictment. He may allege, for example, that it does not set forth the offense as defined by law, or that the facts recited in it do not constitute the offense charged. The objection to the indictment may be by demurrer or by a motion to quash or to dismiss. In either case, a petition is prepared which states the reasons for the action and calls upon the court to set aside the indictment and discharge the defendant. If the indictment is found to contain a fundamental defect which cannot be amended by the court, the judge will sustain the demurrer or motion and discharge the defendant. Otherwise, the judge will order the indictment amended or overrule the objection to it, and the defendant must then enter a plea of "guilty" or "not guilty."[5]

The plea of "guilty" admits the correctness of the charge and confers authority on the court to pass sentence at once, but if the defendant pleads "not guilty," the case goes to trial. Usually a plea of "not guilty" is entered for a defendant who stands mute or refuses to plead, and a plea once made may be changed at the discretion of the court.

Under certain circumstances, however, several other pleas may be entered by the accused. In general, these are subject to the discretion of the court, but if the court's decision is adverse, redress may be sought through an appeal. Among these pleas are the following:

1. *A plea to the jurisdiction of the court.* This questions the authority of the court to try the case, either because the offense was not committed within the territorial jurisdiction of the court or because the court has no jurisdiction over the person of the defendant.

2. *A plea for a change of venue.*[6] This asks for a trial in a different county or district, complaining that the defendant cannot get a fair trial in the place where he is being prosecuted.

3. *Pleas in abatement.* By these the defendant raises such questions as the insufficiency of a preliminary hearing or defects in the organization of the grand jury. These pleas are also called "dilatory pleas" because they merely delay the trial until the formal errors have been corrected.

4. *Special pleas in bar of the prosecution.* One of these is the plea of limitations, which declares that so much time has elapsed since the offense was committed that the statute of limitations no longer permits a prosecu-

---

[5] Some jurisdictions permit the defendant to enter the plea of *nolo contendere* (the Latin for "I do not wish to contend"). It is an implied admission of guilt and permits the court to impose sentence, but unlike the plea of "guilty," it has no effect beyond the particular case and so cannot afterward be taken advantage of by any private interested party. Usually, it is accepted only in cases involving minor offenses.

[6] From the Latin meaning "neighborhood."

tion. The period within which a criminal action must be brought depends upon the crime and varies from state to state, but no limitations are imposed on prosecutions for murder.

Another special plea is the plea of "double jeopardy," which declares that the defendant has previously been acquitted or convicted of the offense charged, or that he was at some prior time placed in jeopardy for the same offense. The Constitution of the United States[7] and the constitutions of almost all of the states provide that a person shall not be twice placed in jeopardy of life and liberty for the same offense, but decisions of the various courts are not in agreement as to when a person is in jeopardy. The general rule, however, may be said to be that the accused is in jeopardy when he has been properly indicted, arraigned, and placed on trial before a jury duly impaneled and sworn, or before a court without a jury. But if a mistrial occurs under certain conditions or the jury disagrees, another trial is not thereby barred. Furthermore, if an act is an offense against two states or against both a state and the United States, the offender may be prosecuted and punished by both, and a plea of former jeopardy in one will not bar a prosecution in the other, unless this is specifically provided for by statute.

Sometimes insanity is a special plea, but usually, it is urged as a matter of defense under the plea of "not guilty." If any special plea is sustained by the court, it constitutes a bar to further prosecution.

"Nolle Prosequi." Sometimes, because witnesses are not available or certain evidence is lacking, or because of some similar reason, the prosecuting attorney is not in a position to continue the prosecution. He may then enter on the record a "nolle prosequi" (Latin for "to be unwilling to prosecute") or "nolpros," which means that he does not intend to prosecute the case further on the existing bill of indictment. If this is done before the jury has been sworn, or before a trial by a judge has begun, it is not a bar to a subsequent prosecution and, therefore, the accused may be arrested, indicted, and tried again for the same offense. In a number of states, the prosecuting attorney must secure the approval of the court before he can enter a "nolle prosequi."

The Trial. If the defendant pleads "not guilty" or enters some other plea which necessitates a trial, the next step is the selection of a jury.[8]

---

[7] The guarantee against double jeopardy embodied in the Fifth Amendment to the United States Constitution has not been interpreted by the Supreme Court as binding upon the states.

[8] Attempts to determine the truth or innocence of the accused have taken various forms in legal history. At one time, the fate of the accused was decided by ordeal—ordeal by fire, water, or combat. If he was not burned, drowned, or defeated, he was declared innocent. In combat, both the accused and the state might be represented by champions.

Although most states and the federal government permit the defendant to waive a jury trial and elect trial by the judge alone, some jurisdictions require a jury trial whether the defendant wants one or not. The methods used in selecting jurors differ in various states, but usually choices are made more or less at random from tax lists or lists of voters. In this way the court is provided with a panel of about thirty or forty jurors, from whom the required number of jurors are chosen by lot. This number is almost always twelve, but in certain cases some states permit the use of a smaller number.

During this procedure, both the prosecution and the defense have the right to challenge jurors. This right is based upon the theory that a litigant is entitled to have a properly selected and impartial jury to hear and decide his case. The challenge may be an objection to the entire jury, stating, for example, that the jury was selected in an irregular manner, or an objection to the competency of an individual juror. The challenge regarding the individual juror may be either a "challenge for cause" or a "peremptory challenge." A challenge for cause cites the reason for the objection. For example, it may state that the juror is not a citizen or that he is related to the defendant. A peremptory challenge, on the other hand, cites no reason for the objection. An unlimited number of "challenges for cause" may be used, but the number of "peremptory challenges" is regulated by statute. Usually only a few "peremptory challenges" are permitted in cases involving minor crimes, but as many as twenty or thirty may be allowed to each side in felonies. If a challenge is overruled by the court, the objecting party may use this as the basis for an appeal.

When the selection of the jury has been completed, the jurors are sworn in and the case is ready to proceed.[9] The defendant is entitled to full and free communication with his counsel and to a public trial when this right can be exercised without danger to the order and decorum of the court. If he is unable to employ an attorney, the state may supply one.

The prosecution has the burden of proof, and therefore the county or district attorney makes the opening speech to the jury, stating briefly the charges contained in the bill of indictment and outlining the evidence to be offered in support of it. When the prosecution has finished, the defense has the opportunity to give its opening statement, although it may postpone its remarks until after the state's evidence has been introduced, or it may decide to omit them entirely. The prosecution then calls the witnesses for the state and conducts the direct examinations, and, after the cross-examination by the defendant's counsel, it may conduct a redirect examination. No leading questions, or questions which directly suggest

[9] The first juror to be selected becomes the foreman, which means that he will announce the verdict when the time for this arrives.

the desired answers, may be asked the witness during the direct examination unless he proves hostile to the examiner and can in no other manner be compelled to disclose the truth, but such questions are permissible during the cross-examination. When all the witnesses for the state have been examined and all other evidence has been introduced, the prosecuting attorney advises the court that the prosecution rests its case.

The defense then proceeds to present its evidence unless it can induce the judge to sustain a motion for the dismissal of the case on the ground that the evidence submitted by the state is not sufficient legally to justify a conviction. When the witnesses for the defense are called, the attorney for the defense conducts the direct and redirect examinations and the prosecution cross-examines. The defendant has the constitutional right to refuse to testify, but if he does take the stand, he thereby waives his constitutional immunity and must submit to cross-examination. Each side objects to questions from time to time, and the judge sustains or denies the objections. In some states the attorney for the defense must take exceptions to the rulings of the court so as to lay the basis for an appeal if that becomes necessary.

The introduction of evidence during the trial is regulated by law. Evidence is the means by which alleged facts are proved or disproved. It may be classified as either direct or circumstantial evidence. Direct evidence tends to show the existence of a fact in question without the intervention of the proof of any other fact. Circumstantial evidence provides inferential or indirect proof of the alleged facts. It establishes a condition of surrounding and limiting circumstances which point to the existence of the principal fact. Evidence may be divided also into testimony, which is evidence given by a competent witness under oath or affirmation, and material or real evidence, which consists of weapons, articles of clothing, fingerprints, and so forth.

The law of evidence regulates the presentation of evidence before the court. It consists of rules regarding (1) the manner of presentation of evidence, and (2) the exclusion of evidence. One of the most important rules of evidence is that which excludes hearsay. Hearsay evidence consists of a narration of what other persons have communicated to the witness concerning the relevant facts of the case. There are three reasons for the exclusion of hearsay evidence: (1) the person who is alleged to have made the statement was not under oath, (2) he cannot be cross-examined before the jury, and (3) repeated tales tend to be unreliable.

However, there are numerous exceptions to the hearsay rule. When these exceptions are examined, there will usually be found (1) some special necessity for the hearsay evidence, and (2) some guarantee of its reliability. Thus, a "dying declaration" is an exception when made by the victim of a homicide who believes that he faces imminent death.

The nearness of expected death provides a solemnity equivalent to that produced by the taking of an oath. Declarations made by another against his interests and confessions are two other exceptions to the hearsay rule.

At the conclusion of the defense the case is ready for the arguments to the jury. As a rule the first speech is made by the prosecuting attorney. His speech may be merely a brief statement, or it may be an elaborate argument, which assembles all the points brought out in the testimony and concludes with an eloquent plea for conviction. Whether it is the former or the latter will depend largely on the importance of the case. However, the attorney for the defense usually takes full advantage of the opportunity to address the jury. He is expected to confine his remarks strictly to the evidence in the case, but actually he resorts to every possible device to appeal to the emotions of the jury. The prosecuting attorney is entitled to the last word, and he is allowed another chance to answer arguments raised by the defense.

After the arguments of the prosecution and the defense have been presented, the judge gives his charge to the jury. The function of the charge is to inform the jury of the legal aspects of the case and to indicate to them how they are to analyze the evidence in arriving at a verdict. He tells them that the presumption is that the defendant is innocent and that the burden is on the state to convince them "beyond a reasonable doubt"[10] that the defendant is guilty. In criminal cases, a verdict of guilty should not be based upon a mere preponderance of proof, although this is enough to justify a verdict in civil cases. In most states, the judge is not permitted to comment on the facts in such a way as to indicate his opinion regarding the weight of the evidence. The rule is that the law is for the judge and the facts are for the jury. The judge may also agree to give to the jurors certain specific instructions suggested by the attorneys for the defense and the prosecution.

The jury is now ready to consider the verdict. In minor cases they frequently render it without leaving the jury box, but in more serious cases, they retire to the jury room. When they have reached a conclusion, they return to the court room and the foreman announces the verdict. In certain cases in some states, the jury may make recommendations regarding the sentence. A unanimous verdict is almost universally required, and it is essential that the judge and the accused be present when the verdict is announced. The accused has the right to have the jury polled, in which case each juror must state that he concurs in the verdict. If a unanimous verdict cannot be reached, the judge dismisses the jury without a verdict, but the defendant may be retried.

[10] Proof "beyond a reasonable doubt" is not beyond all possible or imaginary doubt, but such proof as satisfies the judgment and conscience of upright men in an honest investigation after truth.

If the jury finds the defendant "guilty," he may make a motion for an arrest of judgment or for a new trial.[11] The motion for an arrest of judgment is taken to contest matters appearing on the face of the record which would render the judgment erroneous if it were given. It should be granted, for example, if it appears that the court is without jurisdiction to try the case, or if the statute on which the indictment was framed is unconstitutional. If the motion is granted, the defendant is discharged, but he may be prosecuted again for the same offense. A motion for a new trial is based upon some error committed in the course of the trial which deprived the defendant of some substantial right and thereby prevented him from receiving a fair and impartial trial. It may be based upon such grounds as the exclusion of proper evidence, the admission of improper evidence, the improper conduct of jurors, the prejudicial remarks of the prosecuting attorney or the judge, newly discovered evidence, and so on.

If all motions by the defense have been denied, the defendant is called to the bar of the court for sentence. The sentence is the penalty imposed by the court and consists of a fine or imprisonment, or both, or execution. The penalties to be imposed for the various crimes are provided by state and federal statutes. In certain cases it is within the discretion of the court to suspend sentence and place the convicted person on probation. In cases where the convicted person is committed to an institution, he is usually sent to a state or federal prison or reformatory if he is a felon, or to a jail, penal farm, or camp if he is a misdemeanant, and his sentence may be for a definite or indeterminate length of time.[12]

In some cases the defendant may seek to correct the judgment of the court through a writ of error *coram nobis.* It is applied for in the trial court, and if it is issued, it has the effect of reopening the case. Originally this common law writ was limited to matters not on the record and unknown to the court at the time of the judgment but which prevented the petitioner from having a fair trial. In the United States, however, this writ has been expanded in order to provide relief for the prisoner when no other remedy is available, as, for example, in cases where the time limit imposed on a motion for a new trial or the application for an appeal has expired. Thus, it has been granted in cases where the prisoner was convicted on perjured testimony or was denied counsel or jury trial.

[11] In some jurisdictions, after a verdict of guilty but before judgment, the defendant may move for a judgment of acquittal, notwithstanding the verdict, on the grounds that the evidence is not sufficient legally to justify a conviction. Granting of this judgment means that the defendant may not be retried.

[12] See Sections 6.01–7.09 of the *Model Penal Code, Proposed Official Draft* (Philadelphia: The American Law Institute, 1962) for its criteria of sentencing and correctional procedures. Consult also Advisory Council of Judges of the National Probation and Parole Association, *Guides for Sentencing* (New York: National Probation and Parole Association, 1957). For a discussion of the indeterminate sentence, see Chapter 27.

Appeals. The convicted person has still another step that he can take in his defense. He may appeal to a higher court. The federal and state statutes provide for the taking of appeals in criminal cases and prescribe the method of procedure. The application for an appeal must generally be made within a few weeks after the final judgment of the trial court. The state also has a right of appeal under certain circumstances. In some states, for example, the prosecution may appeal from an order discharging the accused before trial or from a judgment quashing an indictment. However, because of the constitutional provisions which give the defendant the right to plead "former jeopardy," it is an almost universal rule that the state may not appeal from a verdict of acquittal.[13] When an appeal is allowed, it generally acts as a stay of the sentence until final disposition is made of the appeal. The higher court may reverse the lower court and order the release of the defendant, reverse the conviction and remand the defendant for a new trial, affirm the conviction but with some modifications, or simply affirm the decision of the lower court. If the higher court grants a new trial, the whole process of criminal prosecution, from the arraignment onward, must be repeated; but if it upholds the judgment of the lower court, the accused must submit to the penalty unless he can take his case to a higher state court or to the United States Supreme Court.[14]

HABITUAL-OFFENDER LAWS

Habitual-offender laws provide increased penalties for offenders who have been previously convicted of one or more felonies. The provision

[13] In some jurisdictions, the state may appeal in cases resulting in an acquittal in order to obtain a clarification of the law, but even if legal error is found, the defendant may not be subjected to a new trial. See Jerry Kronenberg, "Right of a State to Appeal in Criminal Cases," *Journal of Criminal Law, Criminology, and Police Science,* XLIX (Jan.–Feb., 1959), 473–82.

[14] Clarence N. Callender, *American Courts* (New York: McGraw-Hill Book Co., Inc., 1927), pp. 17–20, 22–48b, 79–125, 165–98; James T. Young, *The New American Government and Its Work* (New York: The Macmillan Co., 1941), pp. 202–6, 654–73; John Henry Wigmore, *A Treatise on the Anglo-American System of Evidence in Trial at Common Law* (Boston: Little, Brown and Co., 1940), Vol. III, pp. 283–330; Robert E. Knowlton, "The Trial of Offenders," *The Annals of the American Academy of Political and Social Science,* CCCXXXIX (Jan., 1962), 125–41; Lester Bernhardt Orfield, *Criminal Procedure from Arrest to Appeal* (New York: New York University Press, 1947), pp. 194–592; Ernst W. Puttkammer, *Administration of Criminal Law* (Chicago: University of Chicago Press, 1953), pp. 125–153, 164–238; Roy Moreland, *Modern Criminal Procedure* (Indianapolis: The Bobbs-Merrill Co., Inc., 1959), pp. 152–282; Charles T. McCormick, *Handbook of the Law of Evidence* (St. Paul, Minn.: West Publishing Co., 1954), pp. 455–79, 546–60; Joseph A. Varon, *Searches, Seizures and Immunities* (Indianapolis: The Bobbs-Merrill Co., Inc., 1961), Vol. II, pp. 725–72; John Jay McKelvey, *Handbook of the Law of Evidence* (St. Paul, Minn.: West Publishing Co., 1944), pp. 5–8; Marshall Houts, *The Rules of Evidence* (Springfield, Ill.: Charles C. Thomas, Publisher, 1956). See also the final report of the American Bar Foundation's *Survey of the Administration of Criminal Justice in the United States.*

for the increased penalty may be permissive or mandatory. Laws of this type were enacted at an early date in the United States, but renewed interest in them was aroused by the passage of the Baumes Act in New York in 1926, as a result of the increase of crime after World War I. This act, which had been recommended by a state crime commission under the chairmanship of Caleb H. Baumes, made life sentences mandatory for all persons convicted of a felony for the fourth time. Today the federal government and almost all the states have habitual-offender laws, which have withstood all attacks upon their constitutionality.

The purpose of habitual-offender laws is to protect society against recidivism by increasing the penalty for crime and by depriving judges and parole boards of their discretionary powers in the punishment of criminals. However, all available evidence indicates that these laws have been a failure. This failure may be attributed not only to the inherent limitations of the laws themselves, but also to the attitudes of judges and prosecutors and to counteracting prosecution practices. Law can help reduce crime; but obviously it cannot do the entire job, and an adverse public opinion can largely nullify its influence.[15] Furthermore, judges and prosecutors have often displayed a reluctance to impose sentences as severe as those provided by the habitual-offender laws and have found ways to circumvent them. More important, in effect, has been the desire to secure convictions for the record. This has resulted very commonly, if not universally, in the practice on the part of the prosecutor of using the habitual-offender laws as a tool to squeeze out pleas of guilty to crimes not covered by these laws. Even in New York City during the very year in which the Baumes Act was passed, 78.8 per cent of the guilty pleas in cases where felonies had been charged were accepted for minor crimes. Thus, instead of accomplishing the intended purpose, habitual-offender laws have often produced shorter sentences for the repeater. In fact, organized and professional criminals—the very persons against whom these laws are primarily directed—have used their experience, influence, and power to avoid the increased penalties, whereas lesser offenders have suffered destructive and needlessly prolonged imprisonment.[16]

The Model Penal Code of the American Law Institute, while recognizing the problem of recidivism, approaches it in a different way—one which enables the court to give greater consideration to the needs of the individual offender. Instead of just specifying increased penalties for

15 See Chapter 17.
16 Paul W. Tappan, "Habitual Offender Laws and Sentencing Practices in Relation to Organized Crime," *Organized Crime and Law Enforcement*, Report of the American Bar Association Commission on Organized Crime (2 vols.; New York: The Grosby Press, Inc., 1952, 1953), Vol. I. 113–76; Sol Rubin, with Henry Weihofen, George Edwards, Simon Rosenzweig, *The Law of Criminal Correction* (St. Paul, Minn.: West Publishing Co., 1963), pp. 391–408.

recidivists, this code provides indeterminate prison sentences, graded according to the seriousness of crimes, and then establishes a set of criteria, including recidivism, which the courts would use in fixing the minimum and maximum terms of these stipulated sentences. Thus, it views recidivism as only one of the elements to be considered within the broader process of balancing the interests of both the offender and the community.[17]

THE DEFENSE OF INSANITY

Insanity may become an issue at several points in criminal procedure and for several different purposes. It may arise: (1) upon the arraignment when the defense may urge that the accused is so insane that he is incapable of making a proper defense; (2) during the trial when the defendant may introduce evidence of insanity to disprove his guilt or to postpone the trial until he regains his sanity; (3) after conviction and before judgment when the defendant may claim insanity and challenge the propriety of sentencing an insane person; and (4) after conviction, sentence, and imprisonment, when interested parties may ask that the prisoner be transferred to a hospital for treatment on the ground that he has become insane.[18]

With reference to criminal responsibility, insanity is any defect or disease of the mind which renders a person incapable of entertaining a criminal intent. Therefore, if when the accused committed the act, he did not have the capacity to entertain criminal intent because of mental disease or deficiency, he is not guilty of the crime charged against him. However, every person is presumed to be sane and to possess a sufficient degree of reason to be responsible for his acts unless the contrary can be proved.

Various tests have been devised to determine whether the accused was insane when he committed the forbidden act. Of these, the so-called "right and wrong" test, which was laid down in M'Naghten's Case in England in 1843, has been most generally adopted and is the one used in England and the great majority of the states of the United States. According to this test, in order to establish a defense on the ground of insanity, it must be clearly proved that when the accused committed the act he was laboring under such a defect of reason, from disease of the mind, as not to know the nature and quality of the act he was doing, or, if he did know it, that he did not know he was doing what was wrong. In practice, the one indispensable fact that is needed to establish crimi-

---

[17] *Model Penal Code*, Sections 6.07, 7.03.

[18] Justin Miller, *Handbook of Criminal Law* (St. Paul, Minn.: West Publishing Co., 1934), pp. 122–25.

nal incapacity under the "right and wrong" test is inability to distinguish right from wrong because of mental disease or deficiency.[19]

The "right and wrong" test has been subjected to unremitting criticism by medical men and psychologists, who claim that it represents antiquated and outworn medical, ethical, and metaphysical concepts.[20] Supporters of the test, on the other hand, have retorted that neither psychiatry nor psychology has established itself as a science in any even moderately rigorous sense, that each is rent by conflicts on almost every important question, and that if the critics would recognize the serious limitations of their own disciplines, they might be induced to study the criminal law regarding mental disorder.[21]

Actually, the real difficulty arises not from the law's indifference to science, but from the lack of medical and psychiatric knowledge of mental disease. This is not to claim that the "right and wrong" test should be regarded as the final answer, but the best way to improve the criminal law's position on insanity is to improve psychology and psychiatry. The criminal law can do no more than to utilize the best that these disciplines can provide. Nor does it help matters to attack the terminology of the law. The ambiguity and vagueness of even the most fundamental concepts of psychiatry and psychology are notorious. Legal language should be simplified and modernized, but this must be primarily the work of legal scholars, who are in the best position to understand the requirements of the law.

Critics of the "right and wrong" test have made the theory of "irresistible impulse" the rallying point of their attack. A few courts have incorporated this theory into the so-called "irresistible impulse" test and use it to supplement the "right and wrong" test. According to this test, a person is insane when mental disease has rendered him incapable of restraining himself, although he understands what he is doing and knows that it is wrong and so would be held sane by the "right and wrong" test. Critics of the "irresistible impulse" test contend that an "irresistible impulse" does not and cannot exist concomitantly with unimpaired knowledge of right and wrong. This, these critics argue, is contrary to the theory of the integration of the self, which is supported by modern research in the field of psychology, and which holds that the various functions of the personality are integrated and that voluntary conduct

[19] Rollin M. Perkins, *Criminal Law* (Brooklyn: The Foundation Press, Inc., 1957), pp. 738–56.

[20] See, for example, Gregory Zilboorg, *History of Medical Psychology* (New York: W. W. Norton and Co., Inc., 1941).

[21] Jerome Hall, *General Principles of Criminal Law* (Indianapolis: The Bobbs-Merrill Co., 1960), pp. 472–86. For a critical analysis of the claims of psychiatry, see Michael Hakeem, "A Critique of the Psychiatric Approach to Crime and Correction," *Law and Contemporary Problems,* XXIII (Autumn, 1958), 650–82.

involves participation of the whole "self," including intelligence.[22] Therefore, according to this view, if a person can distinguish right from wrong,
he can control his behavior, and thus no modification of the "right and
wrong" test is needed in order to give protection to defendants who claim
that they had an "irresistible impulse."

Moreover, even if it is assumed that an "irresistible impulse" exists,
how can it be distinguished from a resistible but unresisted impulse? To
point to repeated acts by the accused as evidence of the presence of such
an impulse is unconvincing, for mere repetition tends to prove habit, not
abnormality. Close examination reveals that such evidence is based upon
circular reasoning. Thus the accused is said to have committed a crime
because of an "irresistible impulse," and it is then claimed that he has
an "irresistible impulse" because he committed the crime. Some "expert"
can always be found who will testify that the impulse was irresistible,
and the test can, therefore, become a mere subterfuge for the criminal.

Although expert opinion is divided, it is probable that most psychiatrists reject the "irresistible impulse" theory.[23] Jerome Hall, an eminent
authority on criminal law, believes that the "irresistible impulse" test
should be discarded, but that the "right and wrong" test should be retained[24] and amended through interpretation (as it has been in the past)
to include modern knowledge regarding the emotional and volitional
aspects of human behavior.[25]

In 1954, the Court of Appeals of the District of Columbia adopted the
"product" rule as a test for insanity in reversing the conviction of Monte
Durham, who had been found guilty of housebreaking.[26] According to

[22] For an attempt to overcome this difficulty, see Manfred S. Guttmacher and Henry
Weihofen, *Psychiatry and the Law* (New York: W. W. Norton and Co., Inc., 1952).
See also Henry Weihofen, *Mental Disorder as a Criminal Defense* (Buffalo, N.Y.:
Dennis and Co., Inc., 1954).

[23] Hall, pp. 486–500.

[24] Hall proposes that the "right and wrong" test be changed to read: "A crime is
not committed by anyone who, because of a mental disease, is unable to understand
what he is doing and to control his conduct at the time he commits a harm forbidden
by criminal law." In making this proposal, Hall explains that it joins the rational and
volitional, thus conforming with the theory of the integration of the self, and at the
same time the layman can easily understand its meaning (Hall, 519–28). For a suggested solution by two psychiatrists, see Walter Bromberg and Hervey M. Cleckley,
"The Medico-Legal Dilemma," *Journal of Criminal Law, Criminology, and Police
Science*, XLII (Mar.–Apr., 1952), 729–45.

[25] Jerome Hall, "Psychiatry and the Law" (a dual review by Jerome Hall and Karl
Menninger of *Psychiatry and the Law*, by Manfred S. Guttmacher and Henry Weihofen
[New York: W. W. Norton and Co., Inc., 1952], *Iowa Law Review*, XXXVIII (Summer, 1953), 695–97. See also Rita M. James, "Jurors' Assessment of Criminal Responsibility," *Social Problems*, VII (Summer, 1959), 58–69.

[26] A year after the "product" rule was formulated, Durham returned to the District
Court and entered a plea of guilty to a charge of larceny. This plea, which amounts
to an admission of sanity, was accepted.

this test, which is essentially the same as that adopted by New Hampshire in 1871,[27] the accused is not criminally responsible if his act was the product of mental disease or mental defect. In applying the "product" test, the jury must consider all symptoms of mental disease or defect, and its range of inquiry may include, but is not limited to, whether the accused knew right from wrong or acted under the compulsion of an irresistible impulse. As soon as some evidence of mental abnormality is introduced, the prosecution has the burden of proving beyond a reasonable doubt that the act was not the product of this abnormality.[28]

The so-called "product" test is really no test at all, for it provides the jury with very little guidance in its efforts to understand such vague terms as "mental disease" and "mental defect," the meanings of which have not been agreed upon by psychiatrists themselves. Furthermore, the burden to disprove a causal relation between a mental abnormality and a particular act implies that knowledge of the cause exists. No such knowledge, however, does exist, and this is all that can be shown; but this is not enough to prove that there was no causal relation between the alleged mental abnormality and the act in issue. Thus the "product" rule raises difficult problems for the jury without assisting the jury, places an overwhelming burden upon the prosecution, adds confusion to an already confused situation, and makes it easier for guilty persons to avoid just punishment by pleading insanity.[29]

The decision handed down in the *Durham* case by the Court of Appeals of the District of Columbia is controlling only within Washington, D.C. Moreover, since even the extremists among the psychiatrists agree that the jury should decide the issue in pleas of insanity, and since almost all lawyers and many psychiatrists believe that the jurors should be given some simple standards to guide them in their deliberations, it is not likely that the "product" test, which was used in the *Durham* case, will be adopted in many jurisdictions in the United States. In fact, enough cases involving this test have been handled in the District of Columbia since

[27] *State v. Pike,* 49 N. H. 399 (1870); *State v. Jones,* 50 N. H. 369 (1871). Until the decision in the *Durham* case, the New Hampshire solution had never been adopted elsewhere except perhaps in Montana (Perkins, pp. 763, 764).

[28] *Durham v. United States,* 214 F. 2d 862. For an analysis of some of the difficulties involved in the use of the Durham rule, see Ray Jeffery, "Behavioral Science and the Durham Rule," and "The Durham Rule and the Behavioral Scientist." These manuscripts, which are in the process of being published, were written while their author was participating in a research project, entitled "Law and Psychiatry in the District of Columbia," which was financed by a research grant from the National Institute of Mental Health. For an analysis of some of the arguments against the use of the term "mental disease," see Thomas Szasz, *The Myth of Mental Illness* (New York: Hoeber-Harper, Inc., 1961).

[29] For a symposium on the *Durham* case, see "Insanity and the Criminal Law—A Critique of Durham v. United States," *The University of Chicago Law Review,* XXII (Winter, 1955), 317–404.

1954 to demonstrate conclusively that the law on mental disease and criminal responsibility has been greatly confused by its use. It is no wonder, then, that since 1954 the "product" test has been adopted in only one state (Maine in 1961), while it has been repudiated in a dozen or more jurisdictions, including several federal circuits, where it has been submitted.

The American Law Institute also has rejected the "product" test and has proposed a different solution in its Model Penal Code. According to this code, a person should not be held criminally responsible for his act if as a result of mental disease or defect he lacked substantial capacity either to appreciate the criminality of his conduct or to conform his conduct to the requirements of law.[30] However, this proposal,[31] like the "product" test, has been severely attacked by critics, who have alleged, for example, that it does not give lay jurors a simple, helpful guide in their efforts to decide whether the accused was insane at the time of his act, and that the second alternative in the test, that is, the part that reads: "or to conform his conduct to the requirements of law," permits the defendant to find refuge in what is the equivalent of the "irresistible impulse" test.[32]

The controversy over the test of insanity represents much more than an effort to change the wording of the test. It is, in fact, as LaPiere has said, "the focus of a strenuous and socially significant struggle for power." The underlying issue is whether the courts—the representatives of the people—shall retain their authority to decide questions of criminal responsibility or whether this authority shall, under some guise or other, be transferred to members of the medical profession specializing in psychiatry[33]—an organization not directly responsible to the people.

[30] The *Model Penal Code* also stipulates that the terms "mental disease or defect" do not include an abnormality manifested only by repeated criminal or otherwise anti-social conduct.

[31] For still another proposal, see *U. S. v. Currens* (3d Cir. 1961), 290 F2d 751. In this case, Chief Judge Biggs of the United States Court of Appeals for the Third Circuit proposed the folowing test of insanity: "The jury must be satisfied that at the time of committing the prohibited act the defendant, as a result of mental disease or defect, lacked substantial capacity to conform his conduct to the requirements of the law which he is alleged to have violated." See also *Insanity and Criminal Offenders,* Special Commissions on Insanity and Criminal Offenders, First Report, July 7, 1962 (Sacramento: California State Printing Office, 1962).

[32] Hall, *General Principles of Criminal Law,* pp. 495–518. See also his "Psychiatry and Criminal Responsibility," *Yale Law Journal,* LXV (May, 1956), 761–85; "Mental Disease and Criminal Responsibility—M'Naghten Versus Durham and the American Law Institute's Tentative Draft," *Indiana Law Journal,* XXXIII (Winter, 1958), 212–25; "The M'Naghten Rules and Proposed Alternatives," *American Bar Association Journal,* XLIX (Oct., 1963), 960–64; Perkins, pp. 763–66.

[33] Richard LaPiere, *The Freudian Ethic* (New York: Duell, Sloan, and Pearce, 1959), pp. 176, 177. For further examination of this issue, see Chapter 17.

Another point of conflict between the law and psychiatry is the use of the hypothetical question in the defense of insanity. This involves the statement of a set of assumed facts and the asking of the expert witness for his opinion based on the assumed facts. The jury may then give such weight to expert opinion as they deem proper, applying it to the facts as they understand them, and balancing it with the other evidence presented during the trial. The advantage of the hypothetical question is that it gets before the jury the facts upon which the expert opinion is based while at the same time leaving to the jury the right to determine what facts in the case are proved.[34] Psychiatrists, however, contend that the hypothetical question prevents the expert from giving his honest opinion of the facts as he understands them, and that it permits the opposing attorneys to elicit apparently conflicting testimony from the expert witness and thus creates the impression that his opinion is unreliable.[35]

When hired experts are called by each side, they may be pitted against each other in a degrading "battle of mercenaries." One way to avoid this undesirable situation is to provide for impartial experts. About half the states and the federal government authorize the trial court to appoint such experts. According to the federal rules of criminal procedure, the appointed impartial expert is required to advise the parties of his findings, and he may thereafter be called by the court or by either party to testify.

The Briggs Law, which was enacted by Massachusetts in 1921, is broader in scope and implications than any of the statutes which authorize the courts to appoint expert witnesses. It establishes a program of discovery by providing that whenever a person is indicted for a capital offense, or whenever a person is indicted for any other offense and known to have been previously indicted more than once or previously convicted of a felony, he must be given an examination by the state department of mental diseases to determine his mental condition. The report containing the results of this examination is made accessible to the court, the probation officer, the prosecuting attorney, and the attorney for the defense, and the examiners may be called to testify as to their findings. The purpose of this law is to set up a routine of psychiatric examination before trial and before any decision is made regarding the defense of insanity.[36]

34 McKelvey, pp. 356, 357, 369.

35 Winfred Overholser, "Psychiatric Expert Testimony in Criminal Cases," *Journal of Criminal Law, Criminology, and Police Science*, XLII (Sept.–Oct., 1951), 296.

36 Rubin, Weihofen, Edwards, and Rosenzweig, pp. 504–6; Weihofen, *Mental Disorder as a Criminal Defense*, pp. 329–52; Albert J. Harno, "Some Significant Developments in Criminal Law and Procedure in the Last Century," *Journal of Criminal Law, Criminology, and Police Science*, XLII (Nov.–Dec., 1951), 432–36.

SEXUAL PSYCHOPATH LAWS

The so-called sexual psychopath laws were enacted largely because of the alarm over a few serious, widely publicized sex crimes. The first of these laws, enacted in Michigan in 1935, was held to be unconstitutional, but at present about half of the states have special legislation dealing with the sexually abnormal offender.[37] Many of the early laws provided for a civil procedure to determine whether the accused was a sexual psychopath. If he was so diagnosed, the criminal proceedings were suspended and he was civilly committed to an institution for an indefinite period. The later statutes, however, adhere more closely to regular criminal procedure, authorizing a hearing on the question of sexual abnormality only after conviction. If the offender is found to be sexually abnormal, special provisions for his commitment and release are invoked. This type of legislation, which provides better protection for the legal rights of the accused, is now preferred, and the earlier laws have been revised accordingly.

Prosecutors and judges have been reluctant to use the sexual psychopath laws, which have been severely criticized on the following grounds:

1. The incidence of serious sex crimes is grossly exaggerated, the vast majority of sex deviates being only minor offenders, so there is no great need for special legislation on the subject.

2. Little protection is provided by the laws, since a vicious act is usually not repeated by a sex deviate, and in any event, such an act cannot be predicted.

3. Although the laws are based primarily on the idea that treatment rather than punishment will be provided for the offender, the fact is that even if the best available services are given to him, he is rarely cured, and under existing conditions such services cannot be offered.

4. There is little scientific knowledge regarding sex deviation, and the value of the laws is especially open to question because of the use of the term "psychopath"—a term which is in disrepute even in psychiatry.[38]

[37] For a psychiatric examination of the sex offender, see J. Paul de River, *The Sexual Criminal* (Springfield, Ill.: Charles C. Thomas, Publisher, 1956); Benjamin Karpman, *The Sexual Offender and His Offenses* (New York: The Julian Press, Inc., 1954). For a sociological view of the subject, see Stanton Wheeler, "Sex Offenses: A Sociological Critique," *Law and Contemporary Problems*, XXV (Spring, 1960), 258–78. See also James Melvin Reinhardt, "A Critical Analysis of the Wolfenden Report," *Federal Probation*, XXIII (Sept., 1959), 36–41; Irving Bieber *et al.*, *Homosexuality* (New York: Basic Books, 1962).

[38] Rubin, Weihofen, Edwards, and Rosenzweig, pp. 408–14; Weihofen, *Mental Disorder as a Criminal Defense*, pp. 195–206; Alan H. Swanson, "Sexual Psychopath Statutes: Summary and Analysis," *Journal of Criminal Law, Criminology, and Police Science*, LI (July–Aug., 1960), 215–35; *Report on Study of 102 Sex Offenders at Sing Sing Prison*, as Submitted to Governor Thomas E. Dewey (Utica, N.Y.: State Hospitals Press, 1950).

As a matter of fact, special legislation on the sexually abnormal offender is unnecessary. The purpose of this legislation can be accomplished, with less danger to the legal rights of the accused, through the regular criminal procedure. If the defendant claims that he was insane at the time of his act, the plea of insanity can be made at his arraignment. If he is convicted of a serious crime, a presentence investigation can be used to determine whether additional steps, such as a psychiatric examination, are needed. The findings of this examination can then be taken into consideration in his institutional treatment.

PERSONNEL IN CRIMINAL PROSECUTION

The Minor Judiciary. The officials presiding over the inferior courts of each state are known generally by the title of justices of the peace. In some states they are also called aldermen, justices, trial justices, and police judges, and in the larger cities they have been given the name of magistrates. However, regardless of the names used to designate them, their duties are similar throughout the country, and they are usually referred to as the minor judiciary.

Most of these justices are elected to office, equipped with little or no legal training, subject to political and other improper influences, paid no salary, and compelled to rely on various fees charged in the performance of their duties and on income from other occupations, such as farming. Although many of them are able and conscientious, as a group they are seriously lacking in ability, and in many instances, in courage and integrity. In order to obtain fees they often decide in favor of those who bring in business. Sometimes this leads them to form "business partnerships" with constables and sheriffs, who through the fee system share in the costs and fines imposed upon minor offenders, or to create traffic "fining mills" based on speed traps for unwary motorists.

In many large cities, "politics" has placed its greedy hand on the magistrate's office, and the "organization" has captured and degraded it. When an offender who has the "right connections" is brought before the magistrate, the precinct party leader is called in and a whispered conversation produces a light sentence or a dismissal. Hundreds of thousands of accused persons are thus freed every year in magistrate's courts by the intervention of party workers.

Since so many of the minor judiciary are unqualified for their offices, business in the inferior courts is often conducted in an undignified and inefficient manner. One is apt to get the impression that this is of little significance because these courts are called "inferior courts." But actually, they are very important. Many more criminal cases are handled in them than in any other type of court, and for many people they are the "halls of justice." These courts, therefore, do much to mold our attitudes toward law and order, and they have contributed more than their share to the gangster's credo that "it's easy to get by if you know the right people." Besides, the whole process of criminal prosecution usually begins in the inferior courts, and if the preliminary hearing is not properly conducted, the offender may completely avoid the penalty he deserves. Although the preliminary hearing is designed to protect the rights of the innocent, the large percentage of dismissals in the past indicates that it has often been used to shield the guilty.

Various remedies have been proposed for improving the inferior courts. Important among these are (1) the selection of the minor judiciary by appointment instead of by popular election, (2) the requirement that legal training be a qualification for the office, and (3) the creation of a coordinated system of inferior courts operating under the direction of a chief justice. All of these ideas have been put into effect in various localities. A few states appoint their minor judiciary. New York City requires its magistrates to have legal training before taking office. Chicago has had a coordinated system of municipal judges for many years. Although experience has shown that these remedies will not cure all the ills of the inferior courts, they do indicate the direction in which improvement can be achieved. In the last analysis, however, there is no substitute for men of wisdom, integrity, courage, and diligence in the public service.[39]

The Coroner. Usually the coroner is chosen by popular election and is not required to be a licensed physician. His principal duty consists of holding inquisitions in cases where it appears that persons have come to their deaths in some violent and unlawful manner. He is assisted in the performance of his duties by a coroner's jury, which hears the evidence at the inquest and renders a verdict or opinion as to the cause of death. If the jury concludes that a crime has been committed, their report, which is only advisory and not binding on the prosecuting attorney, may become the basis of an indictment and a warrant for the arrest of the offender.

In many localities, the coroner's office is dominated by the political machine and occupied by a petty politician who exploits the office for his own interests, sometimes to the point of protecting professional killers who have political connections. Many coroners exercise their official power to get business for favored undertakers, often for a percentage of the funeral expenses. Tragic blunders by untrained coroners have per-

[39] Young, pp. 657, 659; Morris Ploscowe, "The Inferior Criminal Courts in Action," *The Annals of the American Academy of Political and Social Science*, CCLXXXVII (May, 1953), 8–12; Raymond Moley, *Our Criminal Courts* (New York: Minton, Balch and Co., 1930); National Commission on Law Observance and Enforcement, *Report on Criminal Procedure*, Report No. 8 (Washington, D.C.: Government Printing Office, 1931), pp. 6–15; Puttkammer, pp. 87–107.

mitted many murders to go undetected. Investigations have repeatedly revealed these conditions. Consequently, there has been a growing agitation for the elimination of the office of coroner and for the division of his duties between the county or district attorney and a medical examiner. Massachusetts abolished the office in 1877 and gave its judicial and investigative functions to magistrates and prosecuting attorneys and its medical functions to medical examiners appointed by the governor. Other states have adopted similar arrangements. Such moves are in the right direction, for the coroner's office has long outlived its usefulness. It should be obvious that the medical function of the coroner's office should be performed by a licensed physician. What is sometimes overlooked, however, is that the physician should also be a skilled pathologist and an expert in police science.[40]

The Bondsman. The person who signs the bail bond of the accused is known as the surety or bondsman. The surety may be a private individual, perhaps the accused himself who pledges his real estate or cash, a surety company, or a professional bondsman. In large cities, professional bondsmen and surety companies that charge a fee for their services are called upon in many cases.[41]

Although the bondsman has no official status, he plays an important role in criminal prosecution. When he renders his services properly, advantages accrue to both the defendant and the state. The defendant can live a normal life, continue at his work, support his dependents, and avoid a confinement which may be detrimental to his physical and mental health. And in this connection it is well to remember that he is innocent until proved guilty. Furthermore, the state is saved the expense of maintaining the accused in jail and perhaps of supporting his dependents on relief.

On the other hand, such serious abuses as these have crept into the bail system: (1) the poor and the friendless are often needlessly confined because they cannot provide security for their release, while dangerous criminals with the "right connections" are set at liberty under bail; (2) the amount of bail is often determined entirely by the charge against the accused and little attention is given to his character, which should be an important item in determining how much he can be trusted; (3) accused persons can "shop around" to find magistrates who will grant them bail, and this operates to the advantage of the person who can employ a shrewd lawyer with political connections and the knowledge

---

[40] Bruce Smith, *Rural Crime Control* (New York: Institute of Public Administration, Columbia University, 1933), pp. 180–217; Puttkammer, pp. 108–14.

[41] Edwin H. Sutherland, *Principles of Criminology* (Philadelphia: J. B. Lippincott Co., 1947), p. 261.

of how to secure favors for his clients; (4) the bail bond is often based on insufficient security; (5) cash bail is often used as a substitute for a fine, which sometimes permits the accused to forfeit his bail and avoid such punishment as the revocation of his driver's license; (6) dishonest professional bondsmen split fees with police and magistrates in order to get the bail-bond business, work out deals with politicians so that professional criminals can be released, and with the assistance of venal officials, "squeeze" the accused for every penny that he has; and (7) in many cases, when bail is forfeited, no action is taken to apprehend the accused or to collect the amount of the bail bond from his sureties.

Suggestions such as these have been advanced to reduce the abuses of the bail system: (1) the summons should be used more frequently in cases involving minor offenses, thus permitting many more persons to remain at liberty until required to appear in court; (2) more persons should be released on their own recognizance, thus making bail unnecessary; (3) the trial of minor offenders should be expedited, thus eliminating the need of bail in many cases; (4) a bureau should be established, or an official appointed, to investigate the reliability of each applicant for bail and the soundness of the security offered in each case; (5) the activities of professional bondsmen should be carefully supervised and their rates strictly regulated; and (6) in every case where bail is forfeited, vigorous action should be taken to apprehend the accused and to collect the amount of the forfeiture from his sureties. All these suggestions have been adopted in different parts of the country with varying degrees of success. There is no doubt that action such as they call for is greatly needed to improve the bail system.[42]

The Prosecuting Attorney. The state's case against the accused is within the exclusive control of the county or district attorney, who is the prosecuting officer of the state. He is responsible for making every possible effort permitted by law to obtain the conviction of the accused if the facts warrant it, but he is also obligated to protect defendants against persecution and the violation of their legal rights.

It is with good reason that he has been called the most important person in the judicial system. In directing the affairs of his office, the prosecuting attorney functions as criminal investigator, magistrate, solicitor, and advocate. As criminal investigator, he inquires into the causes and complaints of crimes and orders arrests, sometimes in cooperation with the sheriff, the police, and the coroner, and sometimes independently with the assistance of his staff. As magistrate, he determines who shall be prosecuted and brought to trial and who shall not. As solicitor, he

---

[42] Puttkammer, pp. 98–107; Moreland, pp. 180–92; Orfield, pp. 101–34; Caleb Foote, "The Bail System and Equal Justice," *Federal Probation*, XXIII (Sept., 1959), 43–48.

prepares cases for trial, marshaling the evidence and organizing it into a systematic presentation. As advocate, he argues the case at the trial and represents the state on appeals.[43]

His discretionary powers are great, and he is in an excellent position to dominate the minor judiciary, who usually know little about the law, and to control the deliberations of the grand jury. He determines with virtually unrestricted discretion whether or not the case shall be compromised and settled, reduced to a misdemeanor, and thus placed within the jurisdiction of the minor judiciary, or presented to the grand jury. Without appearing to do so, he may end prosecution in a case by deliberately presenting inconclusive evidence to the grand jury. He can grant immunity to the accused to induce him to testify against his accomplices in a crime. He can agree to permit a defendant to plead guilty to a lesser offense than that charged in the indictment, or he may agree not to object to a motion for probation. In fact, he makes most of the decisions in criminal prosecution and terminates most of the cases. Acquittals by juries and by direction of the court after trial are wholly insignificant when compared with those by the prosecuting attorney before trial.[44]

A great deal of the exercise of discretion by the prosecutor now takes the form of bargaining for pleas of guilty. That this has become quite common is revealed by the fact that in 1945 (the last year for which judicial criminal statistics on a national scale are available), of the 37,895 convictions for felonies in twenty-four states and the District of Columbia, 30,865, or 81.4 per cent, were based on pleas of guilty.[45] By its critics this practice has been termed "bargain day in the district attorney's office." However, a recent study by Green showed that the "bargain" process of justice was not a common practice in the criminal court of Philadelphia.[46]

In general, prosecuting attorneys defend the practice of receiving pleas of guilty to lesser offenses on the grounds that it quickly clears the docket of many minor cases, saves expense, makes possible greater concentra-

[43] National Commission on Law Observance and Enforcement, *Report on Prosecution*, Report No. 4 (Washington, D.C.: Government Printing Office, 1931), pp. 11, 12.

[44] For a discussion of the administration of the office of the prosecuting attorney, see Newman F. Baker and Earl H. Delong, "The Prosecuting Attorney," *Journal of Criminal Law and Criminology*, XXV (Jan.–Feb., 1935), 695–720; *ibid.*, XXVI (May, 1935), 3–21; *ibid.*, XXVI (July, 1935), 185–201.

[45] Bureau of the Census, *Judicial Criminal Statistics, 1945* (Washington, D.C.: Government Printing Office, 1947), p. 4, Table 3.

[46] For a study of the practice of accepting pleas of guilty to a lesser charge, see Ruth G. Weintraub and Rosalind Tough, "Lesser Pleas Considered," *Journal of Criminal Law and Criminology*, XXXII (Jan.–Feb., 1942), 506–30; but see also Edward Green, *Judicial Attitudes in Sentencing* (London: Macmillan and Co., Ltd., 1961), pp. 96, 99, 100.

tion on more serious cases, and protects juveniles and innocent persons from the shame and injury of a public trial. Undoubtedly, there is much merit in these arguments. However, it is also certain that larger budgets and more and better trained assistants in the prosecutor's office would reduce the need of bargaining for pleas of guilty. Furthermore, either the accused is guilty of the crime charged or he is not. It does not satisfy the requirements of justice to punish him for one crime simply because he cannot be convicted of another. And what is more important, the practice lends itself to unethical maneuverings to get convictions for the record and to the corrupt schemes of a political machine which wants to protect its friends and allies in organized crime and vice. The possibility of corruption is increased because the bargaining in the prosecuting attorney's office is a secret or semisecret process. In fact, its secrecy gives it an air of shady dealing even though it may be—and usually is—entirely legitimate.[47] Nevertheless, it must be emphasized that a considerable discretion must always be vested in the prosecuting attorney if he is to operate effectively in the process of criminal prosecution.

Thus it is important for the office of prosecuting attorney to be occupied by honest and competent persons. However, in many localities, it does not have sufficient dignity or salary to attract able members of the bar. Often it is filled by young, inexperienced lawyers who use it as a steppingstone to a political career or to a lucrative private practice. Since the prosecuting attorney is usually elected for a relatively short term, he is likely to be deep in politics and subject to political pressure. Sometimes when the office is dominated by a powerful political machine, it becomes a slimy bridge across which passes to safety the whole filthy throng of grafters, crooks, gangsters, murderers, racketeers, dope peddlers, pimps, and prostitutes.

So important is the prosecuting attorney and so grave are the abuses arising from partisan control of his functions that his office should be divorced as much as possible from politics. To achieve this, it has been suggested that he be appointed, for the period of his good behavior, by the governor or the attorney general from a list of highly qualified candidates selected by representative judges and members of the bar. If this were done, the prosecuting attorney would be an assistant of the state attorney general and would function as a member of the state law enforcement organization. There is, of course, no simple solution to the problem, but this suggestion has been supported by many lawyers and jurists. Its critics, on the other hand, claim that it will merely transfer "politics" from the local to the state level and result in a dangerous con-

---

[47] Raymond Moley, *Politics and Criminal Prosecution* (New York: Minton, Balch and Co., 1929), pp. 157, 158, 166–92.

centration of power in the office of the governor or that of the attorney general.

The Attorney for the Defense. In America, the accused has the right to be represented by counsel in all federal and state prosecutions. If the accused is too poor to employ his own counsel, the court must provide one for him, regardless of whether he is charged with a capital or non-capital offense, although he may waive this right. However, the extent of this required legal aid remains uncertain.[48] The lawyer is not under any duty to take a case unless assigned by the court as counsel for an indigent prisoner, and then he may ethically seek relief from his duty only if he has important reasons for doing so. Furthermore, it is the right of the lawyer to undertake the defense regardless of his personal opinion as to the guilt of the accused. Otherwise, innocent persons, victims only of suspicious circumstances, might be denied proper defense, or guilty ones might be punished too severely. Having accepted the case, the attorney for the defense is under duty to prosecute his client's case with zeal and is bound by all fair and honorable means to present every defense that the law permits to the end that the accused may not be deprived of life or liberty except by the due process of law.

However, most lawyers of standing dislike and avoid practice in the criminal courts. Such practice is seldom as remunerative as civil practice, and its technical procedure requires considerable specialization. Furthermore, it involves association with an undesirable element, contact with unpleasant and even revolting situations, and the development of a reputation which may keep away other types of clients. As a result, the criminal courts in our large cities are largely without proper assistance from competent and well-educated attorneys for the defense, and urban crimi-

48 In *Gideon v. Wainwright*, 83 Sup. Ct. 792 (1963), the United States Supreme Court overruled *Betts v. Brady*, 316 U.S. 455 (1942), and unanimously held that the right to counsel guaranteed by the Sixth Amendment is applicable to the states through the due process clause of the Fourteenth Amendment, since representation by counsel is fundamental and essential to a fair trial. Noting that any person who is too poor to hire a lawyer cannot be assured a fair trial unless counsel is provided for him, the Court rejected the doctrine laid down in *Betts v. Brady*, which required the states to provide counsel in all capital cases but in only those noncapital cases where failure to do so would amount to fundamental unfairness. However, in a concurring opinion in *Gideon v. Wainwright*, Mr. Justice Harlan stated that the decision did not affect all criminal cases, but only those involving substantial prison sentences; but what is meant by "substantial" is not certain, and apparently this will have to be clarified by future Court decisions. Nor is it clear just when in the prosecution counsel must be provided for the indigent prisoner. At present the right to assigned counsel prior to arraignment is virtually non-existent in both state and federal courts. See also *Palko v. Connecticut*, 302 U.S. 319 (1937); *Bute v. Illinois*, 333 U.S. 640 (1948); *Powell v. Alabama* 287 U.S. 45 (1932); *Griffin v. Illinois*, 351 U.S. 12 (1956). For further exploration of the subject, see Yale Kamisar, "*Betts v. Brady* Twenty Years Later: The Right to Counsel and Due Process Values," *Michigan Law Review*, LXI (Dec., 1962), 219–82.

nal practice is chiefly in the hands of lawyers in the lower stratum of the profession, many of whom are utterly unscrupulous. Some are "politician-lawyers" who specialize in "arrangements" and take advantage of every mitigating device in criminal prosecution to keep their clients from trial. Some are "shysters" or "jail lawyers" who hang around police stations and courts and prey upon the poor and the friendless. Still others, composing a small, ruthless, and highly skilled group, are allied with professional criminals and use "political connections" to protect their clients. Practitioners such as these degrade the criminal law and impair respect for law enforcement.

In cases where the accused is indigent and cannot employ an attorney,[49] three methods are being used to provide him with counsel:

1. The court may assign an attorney to serve in defense of the accused. However, most states make no provision for the assignment of counsel in misdemeanor cases. Furthermore, in general the statutes do not insure adequate time for the giving of legal advice to the defendant and for the preparation of his defense, and nowhere is the fee for the assigned counsel very large. Therefore, the probability is that the defendant will not be adequately represented by a competent trial lawyer.

2. A private organization supported by private contributions may provide a voluntary defender for the accused. The oldest of these organizations was established in New York City in 1917 as the Voluntary Defenders Committee. It later became the criminal branch of the New York Legal Aid Society.[50] Other cities, including New Orleans, Philadelphia, and Pittsburgh, have similar organizations.

3. A public agency or official, authorized by state or local laws, may provide a public defender for the accused. The first public defender was appointed by the board of supervisors of Los Angeles County, California, after the position had been created by charter in 1913. Later California passed a law authorizing any county to have a public defender, and some other states have adopted similar plans. However, by 1952 only twenty-three public-defender offices were operating in the United States, although this number had grown to seventy-eight by 1956. Advocates of this method argue that it insures adequate legal protection for the indigent defender, expedites criminal prosecution, and reduces public expenses. Opponents, on the other hand, claim that many of the existing abuses could be eliminated without the appointment of a public de-

[49] It is estimated that at least 60 per cent and possibly 80 per cent of the defendants arrested on criminal charges in the United States during 1951, were unable to employ attorneys (Emery A. Brownell, "Availability of Low Cost Legal Services," *The Annals of the American Academy of Political and Social Science*, CCLXXXVII [May, 1953], 122).

[50] A legal aid society is an organization which provides the poor with legal advice, usually in civil matters.

fender, that politics would dominate his office, and that the possibility of corruption and the abuse of authority would be increased by exposing both the prosecution and the defense to domination by one political leader or machine.[51]

About ten years ago, after a survey of legal aid in criminal cases in the United States, the committee in charge concluded: "While in all areas the need for counsel is recognized, whether on the basis of principle or efficiency, there are so many instances in the separate states where no provision whatsoever is made for representation in serious criminal cases as to warrant the conclusion that *there is no adequate country-wide legal representation for poor persons accused of crime.*"[52] This committee also made the following recommendations:

1. All possible means should be used to provide adequate representation by competent counsel at all stages of the criminal proceeding to every accused person unable to procure such service.[53]

2. In the larger communities, at least, this kind of defense should be assured by setting up a system of qualified, paid defenders, free from improper interference and provided with adequate staff and facilities.

3. In the smaller communities, provision should be made to pay attorneys adequate compensation in every case where the indigent defendant is represented by assigned counsel.[54]

In 1963, the Attorney General's committee on poverty[55] and the administration of federal criminal justice estimated that about 60 per cent of the accused in state and federal courts were financially unable to ob-

[51] Martin V. Callagy, "Legal Aid in Criminal Cases," *Journal of Criminal Law, Criminology, and Police Science,* XLII (Jan.–Feb., 1952), 589–624; Raymond Moley, *Our Criminal Courts,* pp. 67–71. See also Mayer C. Goldman "Public Defenders in Criminal Cases," *The Annals of the American Academy of Political and Social Science,* CCV (Sept., 1939), 16–23; Charles Mishkin, "The Public Defender," *Journal of Criminal Law and Criminology,* XXII (Nov. 1931), 489–505; Edward N. Bliss, Jr., "Defense Detective," *Journal of Criminal Law, Criminology, and Police Science,* XLVII (July–Aug., 1956), 265; Puttkammer, pp. 186–90; Frank W. Miller and Frank J. Remington, "Procedures Before Trial," *The Annals of the American Academy of Political and Social Science,* CCCXXXIX, (Jan., 1962), 116, 117, 123.

[52] Callagy, pp. 593, 594. Martin V. Callagy, attorney-in-chief of the New York City Legal Aid Society, was chairman of the committee that conducted this survey. It was based on 657 questionnaires distributed to judges, prosecuting attorneys, and other public officials, public and voluntary defenders, legal aid offices, and bar association groups. Of the total questionnaires distributed, approximately 285, or about 45 per cent, were filled in and returned.

[53] The committee did not contend that vagrants, drunks, or minor violators of local ordinances should be provided with counsel; but it did maintain that, subject to the application of the rule of reasonableness, representation should be given to all cases of felonies and misdemeanors.

[54] Callagy, pp. 606, 607.

[55] The committee stated that a problem of poverty exists when at any stage of the criminal proceedings lack of means in the accused substantially inhibits or prevents the proper assertion of a right or a claim of right.

tain counsel, over one-third of the federal defendants being so handicapped. Furthermore, the committee concluded that efforts to supply
financially incapacitated persons with counsel in the federal district
courts were insufficient to achieve this purpose. It therefore recommended
that legislation be enacted to enable the federal district courts to provide
adequate representation for indigent persons by one of the following
options: (1) private attorneys; (2) a full-time or part-time federal public defender; (3) attorneys associated with legal aid associations, voluntary defender programs, bar association groups, or a state public defender organization; or (4) a plan combining elements in two or more
of the other options. The counsel, said the committee, should be appointed not later than the first appearance of the accused before the
commissioner; or if the accused should be taken before a court first, then,
at that time.[56]

The Grand Jury. The grand jury is so called because it was designed
to have a greater number of jurors than the ordinary petit or trial jury.
At common law, a grand jury consisted of not less than twelve nor more
than twenty-three members. This is still the rule in many states, although
in some the number is otherwise prescribed by statute. In all states,
however, a majority vote is required for the finding of a "true bill." Grand
jurors are usually selected more or less at random in about the same way
that petit jurors are chosen.

When the grand jury convenes, it is addressed or "charged" by the
judge, who defines its powers and duties and instructs it to consider
carefully all indictments submitted to it. He may also direct it to investigate certain matters, such as the conditions in the jails or in other public
institutions. One of the jurors is appointed as foreman by the judge, and
it is his duty to preside at all sessions and to sign the indictments. After
the jury has been sworn, it is ready for business.

Although the defendant and his counsel are not allowed to attend the
sessions of the grand jury, the county or district attorney in most states
is given this right and is usually present. All the proceedings are secret,
and the indictments are taken up one at a time. The witnesses are called
and each is examined under oath. When the work of the jury has been
completed, all "true bills" and reports of investigations are submitted to
the court, and the grand jurors are discharged by the judge.[57]

The grand jury has been severely criticized, and there is a strong
tendency to eliminate it. It was abolished in England in 1933[58] and is on
the decline in the United States. A substantial number of states have

[56] *Poverty and the Administration of Federal Criminal Justice,* Report of the Attorney General's Committee on Poverty and the Administration of Criminal Justice, Submitted on February 25, 1963, pp. 7, 8, 14–49.

[57] Callender, pp. 176–79; Orfield, pp. 135–78; Puttkammer, pp. 115–24.

[58] Albert Lieck, "Abolition of the Grand Jury in England," *Journal of Criminal Law
and Criminology,* XXV (Nov.–Dec., 1934), 623–25.

eliminated the grand jury as a requirement and permit prosecution to proceed on the basis of an "information."[59] However, the constitutions of a number of other states require indictment by a grand jury, and the Constitution of the United States stipulates that "no person shall be held to answer for a capital, or otherwise infamous crime, unless on a presentment or indictment of a grand jury."

Those who object to the grand jury claim that it is an unnecessary, expensive, and time-consuming method of examining the evidence against the accused since his case has already been investigated by the minor judiciary and the prosecuting attorney, and that anyway it tends to do what the prosecuting attorney directs it to do. However, there are several reasons why the grand jury should not be completely eliminated: (1) the possibility of an indictment can act as a check upon the actions of a corrupt or incompetent prosecutor, although prosecution on the basis of an information should be made permissive wherever constitutional provisions do not stand in the way of this; and (2) it can perform an important function as an investigating body, especially when strongly entrenched corruption seeks to perpetuate undesirable conditions in state and local governments.[60]

The Trial Judge. The trial judge exercises broad powers in the process of criminal prosecution. He may order a trial discontinued for lack of evidence or refuse to dismiss the prosecution even though the prosecuting attorney requests it. He supervises the selection of the jury, passes upon the fitness of the jurors to serve, determines, within established rules, what evidence is properly admissible and what is not, exercises his discretion in limiting cross-examination, charges the jury with its duties, and explains the legal aspects of the case to it. He has the power to maintain the dignity of the court room, to insist upon order and respect, to protect the right of the accused to a fair trial, and to punish recalcitrant witnesses and others whom he finds in contempt of court. Although he may not direct a verdict of conviction, he may order a verdict of acquittal, and he has the authority to set aside a verdict of conviction and to grant the accused a new trial. When the accused pleads "not guilty" and waives jury trial, the judge hears the evidence from both sides and renders judgment in the case. Finally, in cases where the accused pleads "guilty" or is found "guilty," the judge has the power to impose sentence within the limits fixed by law.[61]

[59] Harno, pp. 451, 452.

[60] Callender, pp. 232, 233; Young, pp. 669, 670; Harno, p. 451. For a discussion of the criticisms of the grand jury, see Jerome Hall, "Analysis of Criticism of the Grand Jury," *Journal of Criminal Law and Criminology*, XXII (Jan., 1932), 692–704; Orfield, pp. 178–93; Moreland, pp. 197–205.

[61] John Barker Waite, *Criminal Law in Action* (New York: Sears Publishing Co., Inc., 1934), pp. 199–201; Justice Bernard Botein, *Trial Judge* (New York: Simon and Schuster, Inc., 1952), pp. 125–35.

Thus the trial judge is an important figure and is naturally the subject of much controversy. In this controversy, three points of criticism have been stressed:

1. The trial judge is in politics. In about three-fourths of the states he is chosen by popular election and is thus drawn into political campaigns and subjected to party pressures, but a candidate who has popular appeal does not necessarily have the qualities of a competent jurist.

In order to secure more competent judges and to reduce the political pressure on them, the American Bar Association since 1937 has advocated a plan by which judges would be appointed by the governor or by some other elected official from a list of highly qualified candidates named by a non-political nominating commission. At the conclusion of his term and periodically thereafter, the appointee would go before the public for re-election on his record, without facing opposing candidates. Different versions of this plan, affecting all or some of the judges within a judicial system, have been adopted in some of the states, including California, Iowa, and Missouri.[62] The plan, however, has been severely criticized. Its opponents argue that it does not remove the judge from "politics" but merely transfers him from local to state "politics," that it subjects him to secret manipulations of the bar association, and that putting him beyond the reach of the people, it converts him into another arrogant bureaucrat. They add that the provision for the judge "to run on his record" does little to reduce the plan's weaknesses, for the people have few opportunities to know and understand this record unless it is revealed to them by an eager adversary in a contest for the judgeship— the very situation that the plan seeks to eliminate.

2. The American judge is a mere umpire during the trial. Unlike European judges, he allows the attorneys on each side to attack, defend, and maneuver under catch-as-catch-can rules in which stratagem, artifice, appeal to prejudice, and even false pretense are freely practiced. According to the American view, the attorneys have the responsibility of developing the strength and weakness of the case and the jury decides which side has won, while the judge acts as a referee to insure that the rules of the game are observed.[63] The late Dean John H. Wigmore of Northwestern University Law School called this the "sporting theory" of justice.[64]

Too often this view of the role of the judge has caused the trial to become a public spectacle in which facts are obscured, the law is twisted,

[62] See Laurance M. Hyde, "The Missouri Plan for Selection and Tenure of Judges," *Journal of Criminal Law and Criminology*, XXXIX (Sept.–Oct., 1948), 277–87.

[63] Young, pp. 670, 671.

[64] Roscoe Pound, *Criminal Justice in America* (New York: Henry Holt and Co., Inc., 1930), p. 163.

and every effort is made to win regardless of the merits of the case.[65]
To prevent this, the judge should assume full responsibility for directing
the trial toward a just conclusion in accord with the spirit of the law. He
should carefully watch over and, if necessary, actually take part in every
step of the trial, keeping within limits the lengthy harangues of counsel,
the efforts to browbeat witnesses and to distort their testimony, and all
the various tricks for delaying procedure or for deceiving the jury. This
change in the role of the judge requires no modification of the law. He
already has the authority; he need only break the bonds of custom.[66]

3. The judge is not in a position to impose sentences upon convicted
persons. Usually, he has at his disposal only the facts that have been
revealed during the trial. Although these may be sufficient to determine
the guilt or innocence of the accused, they provide little basis for deciding
what should be done with him. The judge, therefore, must piece together
what he has learned about the prisoner and then make a guess at what
will prove beneficial.

Since most judges have few facts to guide them, their sentencing policies
may vary considerably even in the same community.[67] In response to the
criticism that this has caused, attempts have been made to provide judges
with additional information secured by a presentence investigation conducted by probation officers, psychologists, psychiatrists, and other specialists. This is being done in the federal courts and in the courts of such
states as California, Massachusetts, Michigan, New Jersey, New York, and
Rhode Island. In fact, California has gone beyond this and empowered
its Adult Authority to make case studies of convicted persons and to fix
their terms of imprisonment within the limits set by the indeterminate
sentence laws of the state. However, moves to take the sentencing process
entirely away from the judge and give it to a group of "experts" have
been defeated everywhere. Opponents of this argue that it will tend to
deprive the people of the control of their courts, that it exaggerates the
knowledge of the "expert" and underestimates the intelligence of the
judge, that any additional information that the judge may need can be
supplied by a presentence investigation, that it fragmentizes the facts
of the case and makes creative handling of them impossible, and that it

[65] See Jerome Frank, *Courts on Trial* (Princeton, N.J.: Princeton University Press,
1949), pp. 5–13.
[66] Young, p. 678. See also John Barker Waite, pp. 216–29, 301–11.
[67] See, for example, Frederick J. Gaudet, "The Sentencing Behavior of the Judge,"
Encyclopedia of Criminology (New York: The Philosophical Library, 1949), pp. 449–
61; but see also Green, *Judicial Attitudes in Sentencing,* a study which found a "sur-
prisingly high degree of consistency among the judges in the length of the penitentiary
sentences they impose" (p. 99). In accordance with legislation enacted in 1958, federal judges meet periodically, discuss their sentencing practices, and thus seek to
reduce the possibility of inconsistencies in the sentences that they impose.

dilutes the sense of responsibility regarding the interests of both the convicted person and the community.[68]

The Trial Jury. The trial jury is usually composed of twelve members. It is their duty to listen to the evidence, analyze it in the light of the instructions given by the judge, and then after due deliberation decide on the basis of the facts whether the accused is "guilty" or "not guilty." Although the trial jury is deeply embedded in American traditions and is cherished as a symbol of the rights of the people, it has come under increasing fire from its critics,[69] some of whom have even urged its abolition.[70]

The major criticisms against the trial jury are the following: (1) the selection of jurors and the requirement that the verdict be unanimous, which may result in a "hung jury" and a new trial, cause excessive delays and expense; (2) exemptions and excuses from jury duty tend to leave only the least competent to serve as jurors and to wrestle with technical rules and verbiage that are confusing even for the most intelligent; (3) jurors are unduly influenced by emotional appeals; (4) jurors do not confine themselves to the facts, in accordance with their prescribed function, but instead judge the law as well and determine the rights and duties of the accused; and (5) juries are tampered with and "packed" in order to secure a "ready-made" verdict.

In reply to these criticisms, the supporters of the trial jury contend: (1) that the delays in the selection and the deliberations of juries are exaggerated far beyond their real importance; (2) that the competence of jurors can be increased by the reduction of exemptions and excuses from jury service; (3) that the trial can, and should, be simplified by the modification of the laws and procedural rules; (4) that the qualities needed by jurors are fair-mindedness, a sense of responsibility, and especially the capacity to appraise and "size up" witnesses and their testimony, and that these qualities are not necessarily connected with education or wealth; (5) that although jurors may be swayed by emotional appeals, judges, too, give expression to their sympathies and prejudices, and that this susceptibility on the part of the jurors could be materially reduced if the judge would do what he is supposed to do and restrict emotional appeals by attorneys during the trial; (6) that the jurors would more often confine themselves to the facts if the law were clarified and the judge assumed a more active role in the direction of the trial; (7) that corrup-

---

[68] Walter A. Gordon, "California Adult Authority," *Proceedings of the American Prison Association, 1947*, pp. 215–20; Moreland, pp. 296–302. See Chapter 28.

[69] See, for example, Frank, pp. 108–45; Waite, pp. 63–79; Curtis Bok, "The Jury System in America," *The Annals of the American Academy of Political and Social Science*, CCLXXXVII (May, 1953), 92–96; Moreland, 233–50.

[70] See, for example, Harry Elmer Barnes and Negley K. Teeters, *New Horizons in Criminology* (New York: Prentice-Hall, Inc., 1959), pp. 269–81.

tion does not constitute a major threat to the jury system and that whatever now exists could be reduced by the selection of competent and honest court personnel; (8) that jury service is the chief remaining governmental function in which lay citizens can take a direct and active part, thus increasing their sense of civic responsibility and placing a check on those in authority; and (9) that trial by jury is the best means of keeping the administration of justice in tune with the community.[71]

On one point, however, critics and supporters of the trial jury are in agreement. Both recognize that there is a growing sentiment against it. This has found expression in a relaxation of the strict requirement regarding jury trial. In many states a jury trial may be waived. Some states provide that juries of less than twelve may be used in certain cases, and some permit a decision by a majority of the jury in certain cases instead of requiring a unanimous verdict. These are signs of the decline of the trial jury—a decline which is reflected in the judicial statistics of 1945. In that year (the last for which we have judicial statistics on a national scale), of the convictions for major offenses in twenty-four states and the District of Columbia, 10.8 per cent were tried before a jury and 7.8 per cent, before a judge; while the remaining 81.4 per cent resulted from the plea of guilty.[72]

Nevertheless, the trial jury, with all its imperfections, is a safeguard against despotic government and the tyranny of the expert; and the weight of opinion, including that of the American Bar Association, is definitely in favor of its retention. Many of those who want to retain the trial jury, however, strongly urge the adoption of the following suggestions for the improvement of the jury system:

1. Waiver of trial by jury should be facilitated.
2. Statutory exemptions from jury duty should be reduced.
3. The judge should be given greater control over the selection of the jury.
4. Unanimous verdicts should not be required except in cases involving capital offenses.
5. A pamphlet of instructions should be given to prospective jurors to acquaint them with the nature of a trial and its procedures so that they can more intelligently perform their duties.[73]

[71] For a discussion of the techniques and tactics used in jury trials, see Irving Goldstein, *Trial Technique* (Chicago: Callaghan and Co., 1935); and A. S. Cutler, *Successful Trial Tactics* (New York: Prentice-Hall, Inc., 1949).

[72] Bureau of the Census, *Judicial Criminal Statistics, 1945* (Washington, D.C.: Government Printing Office, 1947), p. 4, Table 3.

[73] For a set of instructions for prospective jurors, see Julius H. Miller, "The Jury Problem," *Journal of Criminal Law and Criminology*, XXXVII (May–June, 1946), 1–15. See also Jim Thompson, "A Handbook for Jurors in Criminal Cases," *Journal of Criminal Law, Criminology, and Police Science*, L (Sept.–Oct., 1959), 285–89.

Court Employees. In the performance of his duties, the judge is assisted by various court employees. The most important of these is the clerk of the court, who has charge of the clerical part of the court's business, including the maintenance and custody of the court's records, the issuance of writs and other processes necessary to the conduct of litigation, and the recording of judgments. There are also stenographers, who take verbatim records of the testimony given and furnish copies when these are required by either side, court criers, who make the various proclamations in the court room, and the tipstaff and his assistants, who maintain order and attend the judge in various ways. Since the effectiveness of the court is dependent upon their work, and since they are exposed to the influence of politicians and corrupt professional bondsmen, court employees should be carefully appointed from a list of candidates selected on the basis of merit examinations.

CHECKS UPON PROSECUTION

In any appraisal of criminal prosecution, it is necessary to recognize the many checks which operate for the benefit of the accused. Although experience has shown that these are necessary for the protection of the innocent, they may also be interposed as obstacles by the guilty. In addition to the constitutional and statutory guarantees of the rights of the accused, there is also a series of opportunities of escape extending from the activities of the police and the prosecuting attorney, through those of the minor judiciary and the grand jury, to those of the judge and the trial jury.

That these chances of escape are offered to the accused is a fundamental fact from which all consideration of the subject of criminal prosecution must begin, for they help to explain why there is such a difference between the number of offenses known to the police and the number of convictions in our courts. Thus in the United States in 1962, in 1,655 cities,[74] there was an estimated total of 1,359,820 alleged major crimes, of which 347,053, or 25.5 per cent, were cleared by arrest.[75] As a result, 259,462 persons were charged with crime, and of these, 114,860, or 44.3 per cent, were convicted of some crime.[76] This does not mean that opportunities of escape should not exist; but it does mean that they are used by the guilty as well as the innocent, and that, therefore, they must be

[74] These cities have an estimated total population of 54,396,000.

[75] Generally, an offense is cleared by arrest when at least one of the perpetrators of the crime is identified with the crime, arrested, and charged, although there are certain technical exceptions.

[76] Federal Bureau of Investigation, *Uniform Crime Reports, 1962*, p. 87, Table 11.

carefully guarded by honest, courageous, and competent public officials who are supported by wise laws and effective rules and regulations.

PROBLEMS OF ORGANIZATION AND PROCEDURE

The court systems in many states are needlessly complex. This is particularly true in the metropolitan areas. For example, in 1948 there were 145 separate tribunals in the Detroit metropolitan area, of which 104 were township justices, 18 were city justices, and 6 were municipal courts.[77] As a result of this situation there are excessive costs, gaps, duplications, overlappings, and conflicts which reduce the effectiveness of the courts and delay justice. To meet this problem, it is recommended that the courts of each state be integrated in a statewide system with power and responsibility centered in one chief justice. The metropolitan courts and the rural inferior courts within each county or district would operate as separate integrated units within the statewide system.[78]

In 1938, the American Bar Association became a leader in the movement to unify the judicial system in each state. Although progress has been slow, some results have been achieved, the New Jersey court reorganization being saluted as "the inspiration for all groups working for better court structure."[79] New Jersey's new constitution, which was adopted in 1947, provides for a three-level system of supreme court, superior court, and county courts.

Procedural defects, too, have been an obstacle to justice in America. The purpose of procedure is to accomplish the enforcement of substantive legal rights. Under no circumstances should the litigant be permitted to invoke the aid of technical rules merely to embarrass, delay, or subvert justice.

One important reason why procedural defects persist is that the courts have too little control over the rules which regulate the conduct of litigation. In America, the policy has been for the legislatures to impose procedural regulations upon the courts by detailed practice acts. For many years, the American Bar Association has sought to change this policy and to have the power to make procedural rules lodged in the courts. A very important step in this reform movement was taken in 1935, when Con-

[77] Maxine Boord Virtue, "Improving the Structure of Courts," *The Annals of the American Academy of Political and Social Science*, CCLXXXVII (May, 1953), 141.
[78] *Ibid.*, 146.
[79] *Ibid.*, 145. See also Maxine Boord Virtue, "The Two Faces of Janus: Delay in Metropolitan Trial Courts," *The Annals of the American Academy of Political and Social Science*, CCCXXVIII (Mar., 1960), 125–33; William M. Trumbull, "The State Court Systems," *ibid.*, 134–43.

gress enacted a law conferring upon the Supreme Court the power to adopt rules of civil procedure for the federal court. In 1938 the Supreme Court promulgated these rules and shortly thereafter formulated a set of federal rules of criminal procedure. These rules have exerted an influence for practice reform throughout the United States.[80]

[80] Herbert Peterfreund, "The Essentials of Modern Reform in the Litigative Process," *The Annals of the American Academy of Political and Social Science,* CCLXXXVII (May, 1953), 154; Harold J. Gallagher, "The American Bar Association Program," *The Annals of the American Academy of Political and Social Science.* CCLXXXVII (May 1953), 164; Jerome Hall, *Studies in Jurisprudence and Criminal Theory* (New York: Oceana Publications, Inc., 1958), pp. 215–34.

16

The Juvenile Court

ORIGIN AND DEVELOPMENT

Although the origin and development of the juvenile court are largely a product of American ingenuity and enterprise, the court has roots that can be traced back to principles that are deeply embedded in English jurisprudence. These are to be found in the differential treatment which English children received in the courts of their land, where both common law and equity doctrines threw a protective cloak about their innocence and dependency.[1]

One of the roots of the juvenile court is the principle of equity or chancery that came into existence because of the rigidity of the common law and its failure to provide adequate remedies for deserving litigants. Upon the chancellor, who was head of England's judicial system, eventually devolved the responsibility of rendering the law more flexible in such cases and of balancing the interests of the contending parties in a more equitable manner as measured by the merits of the individual case. Since equity was thus dispensed by the Council of Chancery, the terms "equity" and "chancery" came to be used interchangeably in referring to this aspect of the law. It was through this system of equity that the king acted as *parens patriae*, or as "father of his country," in exercising his power of guardianship over the persons and estates of minors, who were considered wards of the state and as such entitled to special protection. Although originally the chancery court acted chiefly to protect dependent or neglected children who had property interests, we see in its action the

[1] Herbert H. Lou, *Juvenile Courts in the United States* (Chapel Hill, N.C.: The University of North Carolina Press, 1927), chap. 1; Helen I. Clarke, *Social Legislation* (New York: Appleton-Century-Crofts, Inc., 1957), pp. 375–77. See also Roscoe Pound, "The Rise of Socialized Criminal Justice," *Yearbook, 1942* (New York: National Probation Association, 1942), pp. 1–22; and "The Juvenile Court and the Law," *Yearbook, 1944* (New York: National Probation Association, 1945), pp. 1–22.

foreshadowing of the protective intervention of the state, through the instrumentality of the juvenile court, in cases of delinquency.

Another important root of the juvenile court is the presumption of innocence granted to children by the common law. According to the common law, a child under the age of seven was conclusively presumed incapable of entertaining criminal intent and, therefore, could not commit a crime. Between the ages of seven and fourteen, a child was presumed to be incapable of committing a crime, but the presumption might be rebutted by the submission of evidence that the offender was of such intelligence as to understand the nature and consequence of his act and to appreciate that it was wrong. After the age of fourteen, children, like adults, were presumed to be responsible for their actions, and in order to overturn this presumption, they had affirmatively to show that they lacked sufficient capacity to commit a crime. Thus the enactment of the juvenile court law involved the extension of the principle that children below a certain age were relieved of criminal responsibility—a principle long established in the common law.

In America, where English jurisprudence was introduced by the early colonists, such tendencies as the increase of the complexity of social relationships, the growth of humanitarianism, and the rise of the social sciences created an atmosphere that was conducive to the expansion of the area in which the child received differential treatment by the law. This manifested itself in the passage of legislation for the protection of the child, in the modification of criminal law and procedure relating to children, in the creation of special agencies and institutions for juveniles, and in the organization of the system of probation. In 1899 the whole development reached a high point with the establishment of the first juvenile court,[2] which began its legal existence in Chicago, Illinois, on July 1 of that year.[3]

The law creating this new court established the status of delinquency as something less than that of crime,[4] and in doing this, it made two

[2] There is some difference of opinion as to whether the first juvenile court was established in the United States. It is said, for example, that children's courts were introduced in South Australia in 1889, and later legalized under a state act in 1895, but it is generally agreed that the United States should be given credit for having the first real juvenile court.

[3] Lou, pp. 19–23; Charles L. Chute, "The Juvenile Court in Retrospect," *Federal Probation*, XIII (Sept., 1949), 3–8; Paul W. Tappan, *Comparative Survey of Juvenile Delinquency*, Part I, North America (New York: United Nations Department of Economics and Social Affairs, 1958), pp. 14–16; Ben B. Lindsey, "Colorado's Contribution to the Juvenile Court," Julia C. Lathrop, "The Background of the Juvenile Court in Illinois," and Timothy D. Hurley, "Origin of the Illinois Juvenile Court Law," *The Child, the Clinic, and the Court*, ed. Jane Addams (New York: New Republic, Inc., 1925), pp. 274–89, 290–97, 320–30.

[4] Tappan, p. 14.

fundamental changes in the handling of juvenile offenders that are especially noteworthy. First, it raised the age below which a child could not be a criminal from seven to sixteen and subjected the alleged delinquent to the jurisdiction of the juvenile court. Secondly, it placed the operation of the court under equity or chancery jurisdiction and thereby extended the application of the principle of guardianship, which had been used to protect neglected and dependent children, to all children, including juvenile delinquents, who were in need of protection by the state. These two changes, in modified form, remain as essential characteristics of all juvenile court legislation.

After Illinois had taken the initiative,[5] other states soon followed her example and established juvenile courts. In fact, within ten years twenty states and the District of Columbia enacted juvenile court laws. By 1920 all except three states had done so, and in 1945, when Wyoming took action, the list of states having juvenile court laws was finally complete. Today all states, the District of Columbia,[6] and Puerto Rico have some kind of juvenile court legislation,[7] and the movement has had considerable success in other countries.[8]

While the juvenile court movement was spreading, the jurisdiction of the court itself was being extended. In general, the definition of juvenile delinquency was broadened, and the types of nondelinquency cases (such as those involving illegitimacy and mental and physical defectives) under the jurisdiction of the court were increased. Furthermore, the tendency was to raise the upper age level of the children subject to the authority of the court from sixteen to seventeen or eighteen, and for some cases in a few states, to twenty-one. In addition, the juvenile court was given

[5] There is some dispute as to whether Chicago, Illinois, or Denver, Colorado, had the first juvenile court in the United States, but preference is generally given to Chicago, since the law approved in Colorado in April 12, 1899, was essentially a truancy law, although it did contain some of the features of a juvenile court law.

[6] There are no federal juvenile courts. Children under eighteen who violate a federal law not punishable by death or life imprisonment may be dealt with as juvenile delinquents in a federal district court or, if a state law also has been broken, the child may be transferred to a state juvenile or criminal court (Frederick B. Sussman, *Law of Juvenile Delinquency* [New York: Oceana Publications, 1959], p. 76).

[7] Sussman, pp. 65–76.

[8] See Anna Kalet Smith, *Juvenile Court Laws in Foreign Countries*, U. S. Children's Bureau Publication No. 328 (Washington, D.C.: Government Printing Office, 1951); Clarke, pp. 377–83; International Committee of the Howard League for Penal Reform, *Lawless Youth: A Challenge to the New Europe* (London: George Allen and Unwin, Ltd., 1947); John A. F. Watson, *British Juvenile Courts* (London: Longmans, Green and Co., 1948); Basil L. Q. Henriques, "Children's Courts in England," *Journal of Criminal Law and Criminology*, XXXVII (Nov.–Dec., 1946), 295–99; Thorsten Sellin, "Sweden's Substitute for the Juvenile Court," *The Annals of the American Academy of Political and Social Science*, CCLXI (Jan., 1949), 137–49; C. Terence Pihlblad, "The Juvenile Offender in Norway," *Journal of Criminal Law, Criminology, and Police Science*, XLVI (Nov.–Dec., 1955), 500–11.

jurisdiction over adults in certain cases involving children—for example, in cases in which an adult had contributed to the delinquency of a juvenile.

CHARACTERISTICS OF THE JUVENILE COURT

Although the juvenile court has had an uneven development and has manifested a great diversity in its methods and procedures, nevertheless, certain characteristics have appeared which are considered essential in its operation. As early as 1920, Evelina Belden of the United States Children's Bureau listed the following as the essential characteristics of the juvenile court:

1. Separate hearings for children's cases (that is, private and apart from the trials of adults).
2. Informal or chancery procedure.
3. Regular probation service.
4. Separate detention of children.
5. Special court and probation records.
6. Provision for mental and physical examinations.[9]

Many so-called juvenile courts have few of these characteristics, and others possess them in varying degrees; but in the opinion of many observers, if a court does not have them, it cannot claim to be a juvenile court.

A few years ago, Katharine Lenroot, then chief of the United States Children's Bureau, presented a summary of juvenile court standards which indicate the characteristics that many now believe the court should have. These standards call for the following:

1. Broad jurisdiction in cases of children under eighteen years of age requiring court action or protection because of their acts or circumstances.

2. A judge chosen because of his special qualifications for juvenile court work, with legal training, acquaintance with social problems, and understanding of child psychology.

3. Informal court procedure and private hearings.

4. Detention kept at a minimum, outside of jails and police stations and as far as possible in private boarding homes.

5. A well-qualified probation staff, with limitation of case loads, and definite plans for constructive work in each case.

6. Availability of resources for individual and specialized treatment such as medical, psychological, and psychiatric services, foster family and institutional care, and recreational services and facilities.

---

[9] Evelina Belden, *Courts in the United States Hearing Children's Cases*, U.S. Children's Bureau Publication No. 65 (Washington, D.C.: Government Printing Office, 1920), pp. 7–10.

7. State supervision of probation work.

8. An adequate record system, providing for both legal and social records and for the safeguarding of these records from indiscriminate public inspection.[10]

These standards form much of the basis of the *Standard Juvenile Court Act,* the latest edition of which was issued by the National Probation and Parole Association in 1959.[11] This act is the product of the efforts of the National Probation and Parole Association and the United States Children's Bureau together with others who want to promote greater uniformity and higher standards in the juvenile courts of America. It is published in the hope that it will be used as a model by legislators, judges, probation officers, and others interested in juvenile delinquency, and it has been extensively used in the preparation and amendment of state laws.

COMPARISON OF THE JUVENILE AND CRIMINAL COURTS

Another way of defining the characteristics of the juvenile court is to compare it with the criminal court.[12] This is a hazardous undertaking, however, because one must guard against the exaggeration of the differences between the two as they exist at present in the United States. As Paul W. Tappan has explained, there has been a tendency to do this by contrasting the most favorable picture that can be presented of the juvenile court with a most dismal and unrealistic one of the criminal court.[13] Actually, juvenile courts vary greatly from place to place, and most of them differ very little from other courts. Nevertheless, a restrained comparison of what are considered to be the fundamental characteristics of the juvenile and criminal courts should provide a deeper insight into the philosophy underlying the juvenile court movement. A comparison of this kind follows.

1. **Purpose of the Action.** In the criminal court, the purpose of the trial is to determine whether there is sufficient evidence to convict the accused of having committed a specific crime as defined by the law. In the juve-

[10] Katharine F. Lenroot, "The Juvenile Court Today," *Federal Probation,* XIII (Sept., 1949), 10.

[11] *Standard Juvenile Court Act* (6th ed.; New York: National Probation and Parole Association, 1959). See also *Standards for Specialized Courts Dealing with Children* (U.S. Children's Bureau Publication No. 346, Washington, D.C.: Government Printing Office, 1954).

[12] See, for example, Pauline V. Young, *Social Treatment in Probation and Delinquency* (New York: McGraw-Hill Book Co., Inc., 1952), pp. 226–29; and Edwin H. Sutherland, *Principles of Criminology* (Philadelphia: J. B. Lippincott Co., 1947), pp. 304, 305.

[13] Paul W. Tappan, *Juvenile Delinquency* (New York: McGraw-Hill Book Co., Inc., 1949), pp. 179, 180.

nile court, the purpose of the hearing is not only to ascertain whether the child is delinquent, as he is alleged to be, but also to learn why he has behaved as he has. The determination of guilt is not considered to be so important as it is in the criminal court, and the principal objective is the welfare of the child and his protection, guidance, and rehabilitation. In order to facilitate the attainment of this objective—it is claimed—the definition of delinquency is broader than the definition of specific crimes in the criminal law.

2. **Procedure.** In the criminal court, the trial is usually a public one, during which the defense and the prosecution debate the issues in accordance with the technical rules of procedure. A jury is used unless it is waived in accordance with the law, and the defendant is represented by counsel, who is either employed by the accused or provided by the court. Witnesses are examined under oath, and the contending parties seek to establish their conflicting claims, often resorting to a play upon the emotions of the jury. Appeals from the decision of the court may be taken to a higher tribunal. In the juvenile court, emphasis is placed upon making the hearing as private as possible in order to protect the juvenile from the harmful effects of publicity. Although some rules of procedure are employed, flexibility is stressed so as to prevent technicalities from becoming an end in themselves and thus keeping the court from acting in the role of guardian. In many states, the alleged delinquent is permitted to have a jury trial, but usually no jury is used. Counsel may be employed by the parents or guardian of the child, but usually this is not done. The probation officer is present, however, and may act as the counsel for the child. Appeals from the decision of the juvenile court are usually permitted.

3. **Evidence.** In the criminal court, rules of evidence generally exclude material unless it can be shown to be relevant to the specific crime with which the defendant is charged, and the trial is primarily concerned with questions of the motive and intent of the defendant and with the facts directly related to the alleged crime. Much information, therefore, regarding the background and personality of the accused and the circumstances surrounding the offense with which he is charged cannot be introduced during the trial. The court, itself, has neither the authority nor the machinery for making a study of the life of the defendant prior to his conviction or acquittal, and definite rules regulate the inclusion of evidence in the record of the court during the trial. In the juvenile court, rules of evidence are less strictly enforced; motive, intent, and the specific act are considered less important; and great emphasis is placed upon a scientific investigation designed to secure all the pertinent facts relating to the personality, the background, and the social situation of the alleged delinquent. To accomplish this, the court has both greater authority and

more elaborate machinery than the criminal court, and its efforts are directed to the discovery of not only why the child behaved as he did but also what can be done to redirect his behavior in the future.

4. **Result.** In the criminal court, if the defendant is convicted, he is sentenced to punishment as prescribed by law in accordance with the seriousness of the crime. The court does not have broad discretionary powers in the exercise of its authority to sentence a prisoner; the emphasis is on the crime that he committed rather than on his needs as a person; and considerable weight is placed on the deterrent influence which his punishment may have on others. If the verdict of acquittal is rendered, the case is dismissed, and unless there are other charges against him, the defendant is released from the authority of the court. If a person is committed to an institution, the court relinquishes its jurisdiction over him, and this can be restored only if there arise certain conditions which are covered by the law. In the juvenile court, if the child is adjudged delinquent, the court has broad discretionary powers as guardian of the child to provide for his protection and rehabilitation. In its decision, the court places emphasis on the child's needs as a person and on the redirection of his behavior rather than on the specific behavior which brought him within the jurisdiction of the court or on the deterrent influence which its decision may have upon others. If the child is not adjudged delinquent, he is not necessarily released from the jurisdiction of the court, because a study of the facts may reveal that for other reasons he needs the state's protection as exercised through the guardianship of the juvenile court.

THE PRESENT STATUS OF THE JUVENILE COURT

In the United States, the juvenile court varies greatly from one jurisdiction to another, manifesting at present all stages of its complex development. Since there is such diversity, no simple description of these courts can be given, but it will be helpful to indicate in general terms their present status with respect to certain important features.

Philosophy of the Court. Although the juvenile court has roots in equity and the common law, its philosophy and methods have been largely influenced by the ideologies and techniques of modern social work and the child-welfare movement. It appears that the following are important elements in the court's philosophy:

1. The Superior Rights of the State. The state is the "higher or ultimate parent," and the rights of the parents must yield to those of the state when in the opinion of the court the best interests of the child so demand. This is an adaptation of the ancient doctrine of *parens patriae,* under which all English children were made wards of the Crown.

2. Individualization of Justice. The court must adapt its actions to the circumstances of the individual case by ascertaining the needs and potentialities of the child and coordinating the knowledge and skills of law, science, and social work for the promotion of his welfare. This means the balancing of interests in an equitable manner by administrative rather than adversary methods within a flexible procedure such as that provided by chancery.

3. The Status of Delinquency. The state should try to protect the child from the harmful brand of criminality. In order to accomplish this, the law created the status of delinquency, which is something less than crime and is variously defined in different states.

4. Noncriminal Procedure. By means of an informal procedure the juvenile court functions in such a way as to give primary consideration to the interests of the child. In general, the courts have held that the procedure of the juvenile court is not criminal in nature since its purpose is not to convict the child of a crime, but to protect, aid, and guide him, and that, therefore, the action of the juvenile court is not unconstitutional if it denies him certain rights which are guaranteed to an adult in a criminal trial.

5. Remedial, Preventive, and Nonpunitive Purpose. The action of the juvenile court is directed toward saving the child, preventing him from becoming a criminal, and providing him with about the same care and protection that he should receive from his parents. Although the first juvenile court law did not stipulate that the child should not be punished, many court decisions and most of the literature on the subject insist that the substitution of treatment for punishment is an essential element in the philosophy of the court.[14]

Geographical Area Served by the Court. The county is the geographical area served by most juvenile courts in the United States, but for some the area is the town, the city, the borough, or the judicial district. Since the county is the conventional unit of the state government and of many private organizations, the advantages of this arrangement in the coordination of the court's work with that of other agencies interested in child welfare are obvious. Most counties cannot afford to maintain courts at modern standards, however, and even if they could, the amount of delinquency in them would not justify such an expenditure.[15] Some states could help to solve this problem by making the area served by the juvenile court

[14] Robert G. Caldwell, "The Juvenile Court: Its Development and Some Major Problems," *Journal of Criminal Law, Criminology, and Police Science*, LI (Jan.–Feb., 1961), 498, 499.
[15] Lowell Juilliard Carr, "Most Courts Have To Be Substandard," *Federal Probation*, XIII (Sept., 1949), 29–33.

the same as the judicial district which is now being served by other courts in the state and thus enable their juvenile courts to operate within two or more counties. A few states, notably Utah, Connecticut, and Rhode Island, have gone beyond this, and setting up state systems of juvenile courts, have created larger jurisdictional districts within their borders.[16]

Types of Juvenile Courts. According to estimates, there are about 3,000 juvenile courts in the United States, although in practice many are only thinly disguised criminal courts for children. In discussing this sub-standard nature of many juvenile courts, Lowell Carr has said, "In well over 2,000 counties in the United States nobody has ever seen a well-staffed, modern juvenile court in action."[17]

Juvenile courts in the United States may be classified into these three types: (1) "designated courts," such as municipal, county, district, and circuit courts which have been selected or designated to hear children's cases and while so functioning are called juvenile courts; (2) independent and separate courts whose administration is entirely divorced from other courts; and (3) coordinated courts, which are coordinated with other special courts such as domestic relations or family courts.[18] Most of the juvenile courts are "designated courts," and even many of the separate and independent ones are presided over by judges from other courts so that their separateness and independence may be more in name than in practice.

Jurisdiction. All juvenile courts have jurisdiction in delinquency cases. However, the definition of delinquency varies from state to state, although in most states the violation of a state law or municipal ordinance (an act which in the case of an adult would be a crime) is the main category of delinquency. Yet, in all states delinquency is more than this; it includes such matters as habitual truancy, incorrigibility, wayward-ness, and association with immoral persons. Almost all juvenile courts have jurisdiction also in cases of dependency and neglect, and some have authority to handle other problems like feeble-mindedness, adoption, il-legitimacy, and guardianship.

Juvenile court laws vary also with respect to the age of the children over whom the court has jurisdiction. The laws of most states do not specify any lower age limit, merely stating that children under a stipu-lated age are subject to the jurisdiction of the court. Most states set eighteen years as the upper age limit; some make it sixteen or seventeen; a few put it as high as twenty-one. Sometimes the upper age limit differs

16 See John Farr Larson, "Utah's State-Wide Juvenile Court Plan," *Federal Proba-tion*, XIII (June, 1949), 15–17.

17 Carr, p. 31.

18 Negley K. Teeters and John Otto Reinemann, *The Challenge of Delinquency* (New York: Prentice-Hall, Inc., 1950), pp. 295–97.

according to the sex of the child. In many states the juvenile court, after having once acquired jurisdiction over the child, may retain it until he has reached his twenty-first birthday.

In the great majority of states, the juvenile court does not have exclusive jurisdiction over all delinquency cases. In these, there exists a concurrent or overlapping jurisdiction with the criminal court, and delinquency cases may be handled by either court. Often, however, this is limited by law to cases of children above a specified age or to cases involving certain offenses or to certain counties. In addition, in many states certain offenses, for example, murder, manslaughter, and rape, are entirely excluded from the jurisdiction of the juvenile court, and in these states, children charged with such offenses are tried in the criminal court.

The jurisdiction of the court is affected in still another way by the provision in most states that the juvenile court may exercise its authority over adults in certain cases in which children are involved. Thus, in many states the juvenile court may require a parent to contribute to the support of his child, or it may try adults for contributing to the delinquency of a minor.[19]

The Judge and the Probation Officer. Although it is generally agreed that the effectiveness of the juvenile court depends to a very large degree upon the efficiency of its personnel, relatively few courts are staffed by persons who are especially qualified for their duties. The judges of most courts are persons who have been appointed or elected on the basis of their general qualifications for judicial work, and they divide their time between handling the cases of juveniles and those of adults. In many juvenile courts a referee is appointed to assist the judge in the performance of his duties. Considerable progress has been made in improving the qualifications of probation officers in some sections of the country,[20] but the great majority of courts are still without the services of a sufficient number of well-qualified and adequately paid workers.[21]

Procedure. Most delinquency cases begin by action on the part of the police, but many originate in a complaint filed by a parent or some other private person, and some result from a referral by a social agency or court. In recent years, about 50 per cent of the delinquency cases have been handled informally or unofficially, that is, without an official record

[19] Paul W. Tappan, "Children and Youth in the Criminal Court," *The Annals of the American Academy of Political and Social Science,* CCLXI (Jan., 1949), 128–33; Teeters and Reinemann, pp. 297–313; Sol Rubin, "The Legal Character of Juvenile Delinquency," *The Annals of the American Academy of Political and Social Science,* CCLXI (Jan., 1949), 1–8; Sussman, pp. 18, 19, 26–28.

[20] See Chapter 19 for a discussion of the importance of the probation officer.

[21] Lenroot, pp. 14, 15; Frederick W. Killian, "The Juvenile Court as an Institution," *The Annals of the American Academy of Political and Social Science,* CCLXI (Jan., 1949), 92–97; Teeters and Reinemann, pp. 313–19.

or hearing, the judge or someone else, such as a probation officer, making the adjustment in the case. The types of cases that are disposed of in this way vary greatly from court to court, but the tendency seems to be to reserve official hearings for older children and those brought before the court on serious charges.[22]

If the case is not handled unofficially, a petition, which is merely a statement containing such important facts of the case as the names and addresses of the child and his parents or guardian and the cause of the action, is filed in the court and the case is scheduled for a hearing. If the child is not being held in detention,[23] a summons ordering him to appear, or in some cases, a warrant for his arrest, is issued when his presence is required. In most jurisdictions a prehearing investigation is made, so that both the hearing and the disposition of the case can be based on the facts so obtained. However, in some jurisdictions the child must be adjudged delinquent before his case can be investigated by the probation officer. Therefore, in these jurisdictions the hearing is held first, and if the court finds the child delinquent, the court is adjourned, the investigation is made, and the information thus secured is used by the judge in his disposition of the case. The court may continue the case from time to time before a final disposition is made, and such a continuance is often used by the judge to test the child and his parents and to help the court to determine whether any further action is necessary.

Although the investigation of cases is usually provided for by statute, in practice excessive case loads and inadequacy of personnel often keep it from being more than a superficial inquiry that is more misleading than helpful. Many state laws also specify that the records of the juvenile court are to be treated as privileged information and are to be shown only to those who have a legitimate reason for inspecting them.

Juvenile court hearings are generally less formal than trials in the criminal court, but the amount of informality varies considerably throughout the country. Privacy, however, is a characteristic of most hearings, and this means that only those who are definitely connected with the case in some way are permitted to attend. Usually neither a prosecuting attorney nor a counsel for the defense is present, and although jury trials are permitted in many jurisdictions, usually juries are not used. However, the right of appeal in one form or another is available in most jurisdictions.[24]

22 Edward E. Schwartz, "Statistics of Juvenile Delinquency in the United States," *The Annals of the American Academy of Political and Social Science*, CCLXI (Jan., 1949), 14–16.

23 For a discussion of the detention of juveniles, see Chapter 22.

24 Teeters and Reinemann, pp. 319–29; National Conference on Prevention and Control of Juvenile Delinquency, *Report on Juvenile Court Laws* (Washington, D.C.: Government Printing Office, 1947), pp. 6, 7; Sussman, pp. 29–37.

Disposition. As a result of the investigation and hearing, the judge may dispose of the case in one of several ways. Among these are: (1) the dismissal of the petition and the decision that the court need take no further action in the case; (2) the issuance of an order that the child be examined and treated by a physician, psychiatrist, or psychologist, or placed in a hospital or some other institution or agency for whatever care may be considered necessary for his best interests; (3) the requirement that the child make restitution or pay damages; (4) the placing of the child on probation; (5) the placing of the child in a foster home; and (6) the commitment of the child to a correctional institution. Of the delinquency cases disposed of during 1962 by the juvenile courts of the United States, 7 per cent were dismissed (as not involved or complaint not substantiated), 37 per cent were dismissed after warning or adjustment, 22 per cent were placed on probation, 10 per cent were placed under informal supervision, 8 per cent were committed to institutions, and 16 per cent were disposed of in other ways.[25]

Cooperation with Other Agencies. It should be obvious that the work of the juvenile court is interwoven with that of other agencies, such as the police, schools, clinics, churches, welfare organizations, and correctional institutions, and therefore it is not only dependent upon them, but is also in an excellent position to contribute to their success. In some communities the court has coordinated its work very closely with that of other agencies, but in many, it has done little to develop this relationship.[26]

CRITICISMS OF THE JUVENILE COURT

Ever since its establishment over sixty years ago, the juvenile court has been severely criticized by both its friends and its enemies. Yet, the court has persisted and developed, and the acceptance of its philosophy has spread until today few would have the temerity to advocate its abolition. Criticism now is almost always in terms of its modification or improvement and rarely directed toward its elimination. It seems, to use the words of Dr. William Healy, that "the juvenile court is here to stay."[27]

[25] United States Children's Bureau, *Juvenile Court Statistics: 1962*, Statistical Series No. 73 (Washington, D.C.: Government Printing Office, 1964), p. 13, Table 6. The data on juvenile court dispositions shown above were taken from monthly reports received from 22 of the 30 courts serving the largest cities in the United States.

[26] Gustav L. Schramm, "Philosophy of the Juvenile Court," *The Annals of the American Academy of Political and Social Science*, CCLXI (Jan., 1949), 104, 105; National Conference on Prevention and Control of Juvenile Delinquency, *Report on Juvenile Court Administration* (Washington, D.C.: Government Printing Office, 1947), pp. 18–20.

[27] William Healy, "Thoughts about Juvenile Courts," *Federal Probation*, XIII (Sept., 1949), 18, 19.

This does not mean, however, that any informed person considers the existing juvenile court a satisfactory one, and undoubtedly much of the criticism against it has validity. It should be helpful, therefore, to examine briefly several of the most important questions that have been raised during the controversy over the court.

1. *Has the juvenile court dealt effectively with juvenile delinquency?* This question, which is so disarmingly simple, unfortunately cannot be given a simple answer. Perhaps much of the response to it must consist of merely raising other questions.

Various statistical studies have been made to evaluate the effectiveness of the juvenile court. Several of these have shown that from about one-fourth to over two-fifths of older juveniles and adult offenders have previously been in the juvenile court.[28] Another, made by the Gluecks, revealed that 88.2 per cent of the juveniles included in their study again became delinquent within five years after the end of their official treatment by the juvenile court of Boston and that 70 per cent of them were actually convicted of serious offenses.[29]

However, studies such as these have been inconclusive. Not only have the results varied considerably, but comparatively few courts have been carefully studied. Since there are all kinds of juvenile courts, many being such in name only, a measurement of one is hardly a fair appraisal of others. Furthermore, often the delinquents included in the study do not constitute a representative sample of those coming before the court, and the recidivism noted is only that of which we have a record. The fact is that no one knows how much undetected possible delinquency and crime there is among those who have had treatment by a juvenile court. Besides, since the court is only one part of a very complex culture, with which it is inextricably and functionally related, no one knows to what extent influences other than (and perhaps even in spite of) that of the court produced the improvement in those who subsequently did not become recidivistic.

But even if it could be shown that juvenile courts have failed, is the answer the return of delinquent children to the criminal court? Certainly no informed person would want to do this. Is the answer, then, "bigger and better" juvenile courts? Here, again, no simple answer can be given. Most counties are too small to justify, others too poor to afford, better juvenile courts. Large segments of our population are already restive under heavy taxation. Should taxpayers be asked to give more in order to strengthen our juvenile courts? Should some of the funds that are now

[28] Edwin H. Sutherland, *Principles of Criminology* (Philadelphia: J. B. Lippincott Co., 1947), pp. 316, 317.
[29] Sheldon and Eleanor T. Glueck, *One Thousand Juvenile Delinquents* (Cambridge: Harvard University Press, 1934), p. 167.

being used for other purposes, for example, for the operation of public schools, be diverted to the development of the juvenile courts?

Moreover, we must not expect too much of even the "biggest" and the "best." Even they can do little to change the conditions that are causing crime and delinquency or to modify the environments to which they must return delinquents. There is no systematic science of human behavior that they can use, and the science that does exist requires the support of public opinion for its effective application. Besides, how much regulation by a court will a community tolerate? If it is to preserve certain rights and privileges, how much regulation should it tolerate? It is obvious that such questions can be considered only as they are related to other values in our culture.

Still other questions must be asked. What do we mean by a "better" or the "best" juvenile court? What criteria should we use in measuring the quality of a court? There is considerable disagreement. Some claim that the criteria should be the provisions of the *Standard Juvenile Court Act,* but others would dissent from this.

Despite the difficulties involved in any attempt to answer this question regarding the effectiveness of the juvenile court, this much is clear. Many communities could and should spend more on their juvenile courts. Many others could use what they are now spending more effectively. Many courts should have judges who are better trained in both the law and the social sciences, larger jurisdictional areas, and a stronger position in their state's judicial system. All courts should closely coordinate their activities with those of welfare and law-enforcement agencies. Everywhere all available means should be used to strengthen public support for the juvenile court program. These steps can be taken now, and they point the way to more effective juvenile courts in the United States.

2. *What types of cases should be handled by the juvenile court?* Obviously, this is too broad a question to be examined thoroughly here, but reference to a few specific situations will indicate why it has been raised.

After the juvenile court was established, it became the one agency in most communities which could provide some kind of social service for the growing number and variety of children who needed care and protection. However, with the development of educational facilities and child welfare services, there has come an increasing demand for the transfer of certain cases from the jurisdiction of the court to that of the schools and welfare agencies. What this would involve is not quite clear, but one of those who favor having welfare agencies do this sees the juvenile court exercising functions primarily judicial and law-enforcement in nature, and the public welfare agency exercising functions primarily administrative.[30] But this statement is not sharply definitive enough to indicate precisely where the line should be drawn. It undoubtedly would mean the transfer of many of the dependency and neglect cases to welfare agencies, but since neglect, dependency, and delinquency are often interrelated, and since there is so much administrative work in delinquency cases, it might mean also that many of the duties involved in such cases would leave the juvenile court. Opponents of this suggested change contend that the handling of any delinquency case—in fact, many neglect and dependency cases too—require not only the performance of administrative duties, but also the exercise of authority supported by the law. Courts alone have the authority needed to enforce decisions and protect the rights of the children and parents involved, and to deprive the juvenile court of its administrative duties would, in their opinion, unnecessarily complicate the handling of every delinquency case.

Similar objections have been raised to the suggestion that certain cases, like those of truancy and incorrigibility, be transferred to the schools. Included among the arguments in favor of this have been: (1) schools are already doing much of this work through the efforts of such groups as visiting teachers, counselors, clinicians, and parent-teachers' association; (2) schools are in a strategic position to do this since they are in close contact with children and their families and have considerable information about them; (3) children should not be exposed to court experience, with its stigmatizing and traumatic implications, except as a last resort; and (4) if schools were not permitted to shift their responsibilities to the court, they would develop more effective programs for the prevention of delinquency.

Arguments like these are met with the contention that: (1) the personnel in our schools are already overworked and underpaid and should be relieved of some of their responsibilities rather than asked to assume more; (2) the schools do not have the authority which is needed in this work to enforce decisions and protect rights; (3) the stigma of a law-enforcement agency would be fastened on the schools, too, if they assumed more responsibilities in dealing with delinquents; and (4) many children are not attending school or are in private and parochial schools and thus, being beyond the authority of public educational agencies, they would present peculiar problems of control under our form of government.

It can be seen from these arguments that there is no "all or nothing" proposition involved in this controversy. Indeed, moderates on both sides

[30] Alice Scott Nutt, "The Responsibility of the Juvenile Court and the Public Welfare Agency in the Child Welfare Program," *Yearbook, 1947* (New York: National Probation and Parole Association, 1948), pp. 206–23.

see merits in the arguments of their opponents, agreeing that although some of the work of the court can be safely transferred to educational and welfare agencies, many administrative duties must remain with it. But the question remains as to where the line should be drawn. This will probably have to be worked out on a local basis and will involve both a judicious balancing of the needs and resources of local and state situations and a greater cooperation among courts, schools, and welfare agencies.[31]

It has also been insisted that older juveniles who commit serious crimes, such as murder, manslaughter, rape, and robbery, should not be handled by the juvenile court but should be tried in the criminal court. Opponents of this view label it as reactionary and in violation of the philosophy of the juvenile court. In accordance with this philosophy, they explain, the court should have exclusive jurisdiction over all children, should guide and protect those that come before it, and should not stigmatize or punish them or hold them up as examples for others.

In reply, those who believe that older juveniles who commit serious crimes should be handled by the criminal court[32] declare: (1) that the calling of names such as "reactionary" is hardly calculated to produce a solution; (2) that the upper age limit of children over whom the court has jurisdiction is a debatable subject; (3) that this is especially true in the case of older juveniles who commit serious crimes; (4) that although the court uses words like "guidance" and "protection," this does not alter the fact that it, too, uses punitive methods in dealing with children (5) that the public, regardless of what the philosophy of the juvenile court may be, looks upon the court as a place in which violators of the law are sentenced and punished; (6) that one measure of the support that the court and the law receive is the intensity of feeling that law-abiding citizens have against law violators; and (7) that failure to punish serious violators not only encourages others to commit crimes but also discourages law-abiding citizens from supporting law-enforcement agencies.

In this controversy, as in the other examined above, there is much to be said on both sides. Certainly, a court cannot exist apart from the community in which it operates, and to try to ignore the deep feelings and strong desires of the people is a highly unrealistic and arbitrary attitude. It is partly in recognition of this fact that the *Standard Juvenile Court*

---

[31] Thomas D. Eliot, "Case Work Functions and Judicial Functions: Their Coordination," *Yearbook, 1937* (New York: National Probation Association, 1937), pp. 252–66; Pound, "The Juvenile Court and the Law," pp. 14, 15; Gustav L. Schramm, "The Juvenile Court Idea," *Federal Probation*, XIII (Sept., 1949), 21–23; *Controlling Juvenile Delinquency*, U. S. Children's Bureau Publication No. 301 (Washington, D.C.: Government Printing Office, 1943), p. 21.

[32] Many states have laws which require such juveniles to be tried in the criminal court.

Act contains a provision that juveniles sixteen years of age or older charged with serious crimes may be tried in a criminal court if the juvenile court deems this to be in the best interests of the children and the public.[33] However, if the youthful felon is handled by the juvenile court, he should be tried under clearly defined rules of procedure and given all the safeguards provided for adult felons in the criminal court.

3. *Are the rights of the child and his parents protected in the juvenile court?* As the juvenile court has developed, it has become more and more dominated by the ideas and methods of child welfare and social work authorities. The resulting departure of the court from some of the most basic concepts of justice in our culture has produced a growing controversy over whether the rights of the child and his parents are being endangered by the increase in the authority and administrative functions[34] of the court. In this controversy, criticism has been directed especially against (1) broad definitions of delinquency, (2) unofficial handling of cases, (3) prehearing investigations, and (4) extreme informality of procedure.[35]

Those in favor of a broad definition of delinquency argue that it enables the court to take action in situations which warrant its intervention without becoming involved in controversies over the technical interpretation of words. The laws of some states have broadened the definition of delinquency by substituting a few general categories of delinquency for a number of specifically described acts. The laws of some other states

[33] *Standard Juvenile Court Act,* Sec. 13.

[34] Administrative functions of the court include such activities as investigation of cases, planning for the care of children, supervision of probationers, and foster-home placement. These are to be contrasted with the court's judicial functions, which include such matters as adoption and guardianship and decisions regarding custody and commitment.

[35] See Tappan, *Juvenile Delinquency,* pp. 195–223; Schramm, "The Juvenile Court Idea," 19–23; Pound, "The Rise of Socialized Criminal Justice," pp. 1–22; Edward F. Waite, "How Far Can Court Procedure Be Socialized Without Inpairing Individual Rights?" *Journal of Criminal Law and Criminology,* XII (Nov., 1921), 339–47; Roscoe Pound, "The Future of Socialized Justice," *Yearbook, 1946* (New York: National Probation Association, 1947), pp. 6–18; Sol Rubin, "Protecting the Child in the Juvenile Court," *Journal of Criminal Law, Criminology, and Police Science,* XLIII (Nov.–Dec., 1952), 425–40; Alfred J. Kahn, *A Court for Children* (New York: Columbia University Press, 1953), pp. 95–135; Henry Nunberg, "Problems in the Structure of the Juvenile Court," *Journal of Criminal Law, Criminology, and Police Science,* XLVIII (Jan.–Feb., 1958), 500–16; Stephen M. Herman, "Scope and Purposes of Juvenile Court Jurisdiction," *Journal of Criminal Law, Criminology, and Police Science,* XLVIII (Mar.–Apr., 1958), 590–607; Lewis Diana, "The Rights of Juvenile Delinquents: An Appraisal of Juvenile Court Procedure," *Journal of Criminal Law, Criminology, and Police Science,* XLVII (Jan.–Feb., 1957), 561–69; Matthew J. Beemsterboer, "The Juvenile Court–Benevolence in the Star Chamber," *Journal of Criminal Law, Criminology, and Police Science,* L (Jan.–Feb., 1960), 464–75; Francis A. Allen, "The Borderland of the Criminal Law: Problems of 'Socializing' Criminal Justice," *The Social Service Review,* XXXII (June, 1958), 107–19.

and the *Standard Juvenile Court Act*[36] have gone beyond this and merely describe certain situations and classifications of children over which the court has jurisdiction, without using the term "delinquency" at all. This avoidance of the "delinquency tag," it is claimed, supports the philosophy that the court should help and protect the child by a noncriminal procedure and not stigmatize him in any way.

The unofficial handling of cases has been justified on the grounds that official court action is unnecessary in many cases, that wherever possible the official tag of delinquency should be avoided, and that it permits the court to place its facilities at the disposal of many children who, although not yet within the jurisdiction of the court, need help to keep them from becoming delinquent. Prehearing investigations should be used, it is argued, because they make important facts available for the hearings and thus permit the hearings themselves to be employed as part of the treatment process. Extreme informality of procedure is recommended by those who believe that only by minimizing all rules is it possible to give full expression to the philosophy of the juvenile court, and that anyway, since the state is playing the role of guardian and not, as in the trial of an adult, bringing action against a defendant, there is no need to be concerned about shielding the child from possible injury.

However, opponents of these ideas remain unconvinced, and here is their case. Broad definitions of delinquency and the unofficial handling of cases, which are usually justified in the name of prevention, bring an increased number of children who do not have serious problems into courts which, by general admission, are already overloaded and under-staffed and not equipped with adequate facilities for preventive work. This not only gives such children the appearance of being delinquent in the eyes of the public but also exposes them to the possibility of being handled as if they were delinquent—sometimes of even being indiscriminately committed to correctional institutions. Furthermore, when the court engages in extensive preventive work, it discourages the development of other agencies that could do such work more effectively.

Besides, what child does not have a problem? Any court can go into the community and round up hundreds of children who have problems. And in this the court may permit itself to be used by parents as a weapon against their children in situations in which the parents themselves should assume the responsibility of applying discipline. The home is thus given a crutch at a time when it should be encouraged to strengthen itself through its own efforts—and other agencies can assist the family to do this far better than the court.

[36] *Standard Juvenile Court Act,* Sec. 8.

Moreover, the prehearing investigation tends to become the hearing itself—a process during which both the facts are gathered and the decision regarding disposition is reached even before it has been determined that the child is delinquent. And in courts where there is an extreme informality of procedure it is virtually impossible for the child to overturn this decision. If, as it is claimed, the prehearing investigation is not used as evidence against the child, then there is no sound reason why it should be made until after the child has been adjudged delinquent. Then, too, the court is in no position to predict that a problem child will become a delinquent child, and it may by its inept treatment convert a problem into delinquency.

What protection does the child have in all this? He has little if his case is handled unofficially, for in such a procedure few legal checks limit the court's discretion, and redress at law becomes difficult, for no official record exists upon which the child can plead his case. The situation is worse if broad definitions of delinquency are used, because these leave the term vague and fuzzy, and under them all children tend to be pooled indiscriminately as wards of the state. Thus, processed through informal hearings from which many, if not most, of the limitations of due process[37] have been removed, these children are largely at the mercy of the court's discretion, which too frequently is the mere expression of the judge's prejudice. And this is done and justified in the name of equity! But the court of equity has never been without its rules and formality, and they are there for a real reason—for the same reason that rules and formality must be present in the juvenile court, namely, to check the abuse of power and to protect the rights of the individual. Without them, hearsay and gossip may become admissible evidence; and delinquency, what the parents define it to be.

In the words of Judge Edward F. Waite, "No judge on any bench has need to be more thoroughly grounded in the principles of evidence and more constantly mindful of them than the judge of a juvenile court."[38] And as Roscoe Pound has explained, "Good intentions and sentimentality are no substitute for proved techniques."[39] Technicalities should be minimized in the juvenile court, but techniques must be developed and used.

Finally, euphemistic terminology such as "hearing" instead of "trial," or "disposition" instead of "sentence," should not conceal from us the fact that the nature of the entire procedure may be little different from that of a criminal court. Indeed, it may be worse, for it may abandon the fundamentals upon which justice is based under the guise of promoting

[37] For the meaning of due process, see Chapter 15.
[38] Waite, p. 343.
[39] Pound, "The Future of Socialized Justice," p. 9.

a superior justice.[40] It is no wonder, then, that Carr has said, "No man is wise enough or good enough to be trusted with arbitrary power—even the arbitrary power to prejudge the case of some delinquent child in the juvenile court."[41]

This, then, is the case of those who oppose broad definitions of delinquency, unofficial handling, prehearing investigations, and extreme informality of procedure. And it is an impressive one, moving many thoughtful students of social problems to stress the importance of protecting the rights of the child in the juvenile court. Donald R. Taft has observed: "All courts with power to order our lives utilize definite laws, prove the commission of specific offenses, and protect the accused against fake, misleading, prejudiced, irrelevant, or immaterial evidence. The child before the juvenile court requires such protection against arbitrary punishment."[42] And Tappan, in dismay over the violation of the rights of the child by the juvenile court has asked, "Who is to save the child from his saviors?"[43]

It is evident that here we are dealing with problems of emphasis and the making of fine distinctions in a process which involves the balancing of the best interests of the individual and society. Since the juvenile court in the United States is a functioning part of an increasingly complex culture, it must share in all the social problems, including delinquency, that this type of society tends to produce. Although most of the problems of the court are beyond its control, there are major ones of a philosophical and legal nature with which it can deal directly and which are contributing materially to its operational difficulties. The proposals advanced below are designed to strengthen its philosophical and legal foundations by casting the court in a more realistic role.

PROPOSALS REGARDING THE COURT'S PHILOSOPHY AND LEGAL BASIS

Philosophy of the Court. The juvenile court was established as a court, albeit a special one, and in structure, function, and procedure it remains essentially a court. Therefore, efforts should be made to strengthen its true, or judicial, nature and to retain and develop only that part of its social service function that is necessary for the administration of individualized justice. No court, not even the juvenile court, can be just a therapeutic agency. It is, and must be, a moral agency as well. Like all courts, it must try to balance the interests of the individual and society

---

[40] Tappan, *Juvenile Delinquency*, p. 170.
[41] Carr, *Delinquency Control* (New York: Harper and Bros., 1950), p. 240.
[42] Donald R. Taft, *Criminology* (New York: The Macmillan Co., 1950), p. 580.
[43] Tappan, *Juvenile Delinquency*, p. 208.

in the adjudication of its cases. And when a child is adjudicated a delinquent by the court, he is, and of necessity must be, stigmatized as a violator of the moral values of his society. In fact, the court must act in this way if it is to promote the rehabilitation of the child. If it did otherwise, it would flout the very values to which the child must learn to adjust and for which he must develop a loyalty. The action of the court involves both public condemnation of antisocial conduct and the imposition of unpleasant consequences by political authority—the two essential elements of punishment. It is, therefore, highly unrealistic to say that the juvenile court treats, but does not punish. What it really does is to emphasize treatment in a correctional process which includes, and of necessity must include, both treatment and punishment.

Jurisdiction of the Court. The jurisdiction of the juvenile court should be limited to (1) delinquency cases, and (2) those dependency and neglect cases in which a decision must be made affecting the legal status of the child, his custody, or the rights of his parents. All other dependency and neglect cases should be handled by administrative agencies without court action, and truancy should be dealt with by the schools. Juvenile delinquency should be defined as a violation of a state law or city or town ordinance by a child whose act if committed by an adult would be a crime. This simple, specific definition eliminates all the references to such vague conditions as "being ungovernable" or "growing up in idleness" which clutter up our statutes on delinquency and invite loose interpretation and abuse of authority, and it also prevents the court from moving into areas where other agencies can render more affective service.

The juvenile court should have original and exclusive jurisdiction over all children between the ages of seven and eighteen who are alleged to be delinquent, except in cases where a child is charged with a minor traffic offense or where a child of sixteen or over is charged with a serious felony, such as murder, armed robbery, or rape. In the cases involving minor traffic offenses, there is no need of special handling. They can be adequately dealt with by a police or traffic court, and thus the burden on the juvenile court can be reduced. In the cases where children sixteen or over are charged with serious felonies, the criminal court should have original jurisdiction but with authority to transfer such cases to the juvenile court if in the opinion of the judge this would be in the best interests of both the child and the community. The criminal court should have the authority to act first in these cases, because it, more than the juvenile court, is held responsible for the security of society and the protection of its moral code and is organized and administered especially for this purpose. This point is particularly important, since a large and increasing percentage of serious crimes are being committed by young people. Thus, the handling of these young offenders in the juvenile court—a court which is not primarily concerned with the public sense of justice and security—will make the criminal law increasingly inoperative and cause additional confusion regarding our code of morality and the importance of rigorous law enforcement.

The case of an adult charged with an offense against a child should be handled not in the juvenile court but in the criminal court. This will place this type of case in a court better designed to assure protection of all fundamental rights in a criminal proceeding and will help the public to understand that the juvenile court is a special court for children and not in any sense of the word a criminal court.

Procedure of the Court. Through its intake procedure,[44] the juvenile court should carefully screen all cases brought to its attention so as to eliminate those that do not require the attention of the court or any other agency and to insure the referral of as many other cases as possible to agencies that are better equipped than the juvenile court to provide curative and preventive treatment. These cases that are accepted by the court should receive official handling. If a case is not in need of official handling, it should not be handled by the court at all, but should be referred to some other agency. Too often unofficial handling is merely the haphazard, ineffective disposition of cases by understaffed, overloaded courts, which is justified under the guise of avoiding the "delinquency tag."

The court should establish the fact of delinquency in a case before an investigation of the case is made. Prehearing investigations are not only an encroachment upon the rights of the child who has not yet been proved delinquent, but are costly in time, energy, and money in the cases of those who are discharged as not delinquent.

The procedure during the hearing should be informal but based upon sufficient rules to insure justice and consistency. The child and his parents should be fully informed regarding their legal rights. These should include the right to be represented by counsel, to have a clear explanation of the allegations against the child, to cross-examine hostile witnesses, to summon witnesses in the child's defense, to have protection against irrelevant and hearsay testimony and compulsory self-incrimination, to

---

[44] The intake process is a screening mechanism and is essentially an office, and not a field, process. It involves a review or evaluation of information which should be supplied by the person or agency seeking to file a petition, and thus it should be distinguished from the investigation of the case, which seeks to discover the causative factors in the child's behavior and to develop a plan of treatment. See William H. Sheridan, "Juvenile Court Intake," *Journal of Family Law*, II (Fall, 1962), 139–56.

have a jury trial and a public hearing if these are desired, to have at least "clear and convincing" proof of delinquency, and to have access to a higher court for the purpose of an appeal.

Disposition of Cases. The disposition of the case should be made by the judge after a study of the investigation report and consultation with the probation officer and other specialists who have worked on the case. However, simply because the judge must turn to specialists for assistance in his disposition of the case does not mean that it might be better to have the disposition made entirely by a panel of "experts." To do this would obstruct the process by which a creative, responsible, and integrated decision in the case is achieved.

The foregoing proposals have sought to strip away those excrescences that have interfered with the expression of the true nature of the juvenile court, but they have left it with all the characteristics which are essential to its functioning and growth.[45]

COURTS FOR ADOLESCENTS

Since the establishment of the juvenile court, it has exerted an increasing influence on the principles and methods that are used in the handling of adolescent and adult offenders. Special courts for adolescents have been established in several of the largest cities in the United States. The first of these was the Chicago Boys' Court, created in 1914 as a part of the municipal court of that city. It has jurisdiction over nonfelony cases involving boys between the ages of seventeen and twenty-one. A similar court was established in Philadelphia in 1915 and given the authority to handle certain minor offenders of both sexes over the juvenile court age but under twenty-one. New York City followed the example of Chicago and Philadelphia and opened its first adolescent court in Brooklyn in 1935. Since then, New York City has created other adolescent courts for

[45] For further discussion of these proposals, see Caldwell, "The Juvenile Court: Its Development and Some Major Problems," 507–11. The material presented here is adapted in part from this article, by special permission of the *Journal of Criminal Law, Criminology, and Police Science* (Northwestern University School of Law). See also *Standard Juvenile Court Act*, Articles II, III, V; *Guides for Juvenile Court Judges* (New York: National Probation and Parole Association, 1957), pp. 7–11, 34–41, 49–88; *Procedure and Evidence in the Juvenile Court* (New York: National Council on Crime and Delinquency, 1962); Orman W. Ketcham, "The Unfulfilled Promise of the Juvenile Court," *Crime and Delinquency*, VII (Apr., 1961), 97–110; Holland M. Gary, "The Juvenile Court's Administrative Responsibilities," *ibid.*, VII (Oct., 1961), 337–42; Thomas C. Hennings, Jr., "Effectiveness of the Juvenile Court System," *Federal Probation*, XXIII (June, 1959), 3–8; *Report of the Governor's Special Study Commission on Juvenile Justice*, Part I, Recommendations for Changes in California's Juvenile Court Law, Part II, A Study of the Administration of Juvenile Justice in California (Sacramento: California State Printing Office, 1960); Frederick J. Ludwig, *Youth and the Law* (Brooklyn: The Foundation Press, Inc., 1955), p. 311.

both male and female offenders.[46] The Baltimore City Youth Court, for persons between sixteen and twenty-one, was established in 1950 as a part of the criminal court of that city by rule of the Supreme Bench of Baltimore.

In general, the adolescent court represents an attempt to combine some of the principles and methods of the juvenile court with certain ones of the criminal court in proceedings against youthful offenders who are above the juvenile court age but below the age of twenty-one and who, because they have the peculiar problems of adolescence, are deemed to be in need of specialized treatment. Since the adolescent court is neither a juvenile court nor a criminal court, it has been subjected to criticism from both sides, some critics condemning it as an agency for pampering tough young criminals, others ridiculing it as a timid, half-hearted gesture toward those who require full juvenile court treatment. A more realistic attitude toward them seems to be: (1) that such courts are needed in our large cities, where many adolescents are being overwhelmed by the complexities of urban culture; (2) that there are neither funds nor justification for these courts in smaller cities and rural areas where improved juvenile courts should be able to handle the problems of most adolescent offenders; and (3) that the rights of the young person would be better protected in the court for adolescents by a more specific definition of its jurisdiction and a stricter application of the principles of criminal law and procedure.[47]

THE YOUTH CORRECTION AUTHORITY

A much more systematic and inclusive program for dealing with the increasing number of adolescent offenders was proposed in 1940 by the American Law Institute, an organization of prominent lawyers and professors of criminal law and criminology. The proposal was presented in the form of a model act, called the *Youth Correction Authority Act*,[48]

---

[46] Both the wayward minor act and the youthful offender procedure in New York permit a noncriminal adjudication. The probation service of the court conducts a prehearing investigation to determine whether an adequate solution can be found without resort to a criminal prosecution. If the charge is a serious one, however, the consent of the district attorney must be secured before this can be done.

[47] Tappan, pp. 224–50; Teeters and Reinemann, pp. 344–54; Sol Rubin, with Henry Weihofen, George Edwards, and Simon Rosenzweig, *The Law of Criminal Correction* (St. Paul, Minn.: West Publishing Co., 1963), pp. 446–57. See also Paul W. Tappan, "The Adolescent in Court," *Journal of Criminal Law and Criminology,* XXXVII (Sept.–Oct., 1946), 216–29; J. M. Braude, "Boys' Court: Individualized Justice for the Youthful Offender," *Federal Probation,* XII (June, 1948), 9–14.

[48] The American Law Institute, *Youth Correction Authority Act* (Philadelphia: The American Law Institute, 1940).

and was recommended to the states for action by their legislatures.[49] It provides for the establishment of a Youth Correction Authority, which is to be a commission consisting of three full-time, well-qualified members to be appointed by the governor for a term of nine years and to be eligible for reappointment. To this commission every court except the juvenile court must commit all offenders up to the age of twenty-one save those who are discharged or sentenced to a fine, a short term of imprisonment for a minor offense, life imprisonment, or the death penalty.

Further, according to the provisions of the act, the Youth Correction Authority is given the power to determine, with the aid of its agents and employees, what should be done with each offender committed to it, to employ all the facilities of the state for his correctional treatment, to keep him under its control until in its judgment he can be released without danger to the public, and to provide for his supervision, if such is needed, after his release. However, if an offender is less than eighteen when committed, he must be released before he is twenty-one years of age; or if he is more than eighteen at the time of commitment, he must be released within a period of three years unless an order to the contrary has been issued by the Youth Correction Authority and approved by the court. Any individual not released by the time he is twenty-five must be discharged then unless an order to hold him has been issued by the Youth Correction Authority and approved by the court.

Every person must be examined and studied upon commitment to the Youth Correction Authority and thereafter periodically at intervals not exceeding two years so that his treatment can be based upon an adequate understanding of his individual needs. If this is not done, the individual has the right to petition the court for his release, and the court is to discharge him unless the Youth Correction Authority can convince the court that this should not be done. The act further provides for the protection of the rights of the offender by permitting him to have counsel and witnesses and to submit evidence during court reviews of orders issued by the Youth Correction Authority and to petition it to review orders issued by its agents and employees.

Thus this act seeks to remove youthful offenders, between the maximum year of juvenile court jurisdiction and their twenty-first birthday, from the regular criminal procedure and to place them under a system co-

[49] See Joseph N. Ulman, "The Youth Correction Authority Act," *Yearbook, 1941* (New York: National Probation Association, 1941), pp. 227–40; John F. Perkins, "Defect in the Youth Correction Authority Act," *Journal of Criminal Law and Criminology*, XXXIII (July–Aug., 1942), 111–18; John Barker Waite, "Judge Perkins's Criticism of the Y. C. A.," *Journal of Criminal Law and Criminology*, XXXIII (Nov.–Dec., 1942), 293–96.

ordinated from arrest to release and designed especially for their care and treatment. However, a number of criticisms have been directed against the youth authority plan, important among which are the following:

1. The organization of facilities proposed by the plan is defective. First, it seeks to unite essentially different functions under an excessively centralized authority, and then it places this authority in the hands of a multiple leadership instead of a single head. The same officials who make rules, regulations, and long-range policies also sit as a tribunal, performing quasi-judicial duties in the disposition of cases for correctional treatment and function as executives and administrators in the management and supervision of preventive and correctional agencies and institutions. This is somewhat analogous to uniting legislative, executive, and judicial functions of our government in one body. In doing so, by overemphasizing unification in order to secure efficiency, the plan violates the time-tested principles of division of labor, specialization, and the balancing and checking of authority. But at the same time that it creates the structure of centralized power, it makes the exercise of this power difficult by dividing it among the members of the commission.

2. The Youth Correction Authority cannot perform the many duties with which it is charged. The various agencies and institutions that are now charged with these duties are overloaded and cannot successfully perform them; yet one commission is expected to take over the entire job and to do it more effectively. Supporters of the plan claim that much waste and inefficiency would thus be eliminated through the coordination of all the steps involved in the correctional program, but opponents of the plan argue that when the Youth Correction Authority attempts to do this, it will find itself in a serious predicament. If it conducts the investigations and hearings of cases at diagnostic centers, it will be necessary to subject witnesses, prosecutors, police, and all other interested parties to time-consuming travel and attendance. If this is not done, then the Youth Correction Authority will have to rely on the investigations and hearings of local subordinates, which is about what is done in many cases today—and at present the state is not saddled with the elaborate organization proposed by this plan.

3. The establishment and operation of a youth authority is expensive. Its organization requires large initial expenditures for the creation of an adequate staff, and the achievement of its objectives will involve greater costs than are now incurred in the existing system. And, insist the critics of the youth authority plan, it does no good to argue that under this plan the cost per prisoner would be less and his treatment more effective. Even if this could be demonstrated—and it cannot—the total expenditure would be greater than at present since we are not trying to accomplish

what the youth authority plan recommends. An attempt to achieve the objectives of the plan would involve either higher taxes or the withdrawing of funds from some other program, such as that of public welfare or the public schools. The public would not be in favor of either of these even if it could be shown that the adoption of the plan would reduce the crime rate.

4. Certain aspects of the youth authority plan may be unconstitutional. For example, it is questionable whether the rights of a prisoner are adequately protected when he is detained beyond the maximum sentence provided by law for his offense, even though this can be done under the plan only after judicial approval has been obtained.

5. All the objectives of the youth authority plan can be achieved with less expense and with less disturbance to the existing facilities by other arrangements. For example, it is pointed out that presentencing investigation, an indeterminate sentence law, classification, institutional assignment and treatment, the diversification of correctional institutions, the prerelease study of offenders, and supervision after release—all important aspects of the youth authority plan—can be employed and coordinated under the administration of a department of corrections and without the aid of an over-all control like the Youth Correction Authority. Indeed, this has already been done in such states as New Jersey and New York.[50]

Since the publication of the *Youth Correction Authority Act*, the federal government and a few states, notably California, Minnesota, Wisconsin, Massachusetts, and Texas, have passed legislation for the creation of youth authorities.[51] In 1941, California, which has developed the youth authority idea more than any other state, became the first state to enact such legislation, although its plan differs in some important respects from that proposed in the model act. Several of these differences should be

[50] Paul W. Tappan, "The Youth Authority Controversy," *Contemporary Correction*, ed. Paul W. Tappan (New York: McGraw-Hill Book Co., Inc., 1951), pp. 135–40; "The Correction of Youthful Offenders (A Symposium)," *Law and Contemporary Problems*, IX (Autumn, 1942); Joseph P. Murphy, "The Y. C. A. Act—Is It Practical and Needed?" *Yearbook, 1941* (New York: National Probation Association, 1941), pp. 247–59; John Barker Waite, *Twenty-Seven Questions and Their Answers about the Plan for a Youth Correction Authority* (Philadelphia: The American Law Institute, n.d.); Rubin, Weihofen, Edwards, Rosenzweig, pp. 439–46; Jerome Hall, "The Youth Correction Authority Act, Progress or Menace?" *American Bar Association Journal*, XXVIII (May, 1942), 317–21; Alfred J. Kahn, *A Court for Children* (New York: Columbia University Press, 1953), p. 277.

[51] Bertram M. Beck, *Five States* (Philadelphia: The American Law Institute, 1951); John R. Ellingston, *Protecting Our Children from Criminal Careers* (New York: Prentice-Hall, Inc., 1948); Karl Holton, "California Youth Authority: Eight Years of Action," *Journal of Criminal Law and Criminology*, XLI (May–June, 1950), 1–23; Orie L. Phillips, "The Federal Youth Corrections Act," *Federal Probation*, XV (Mar., 1951), 3–11; James V. Bennett, "Blueprinting the New Youth Corrections Program," *Federal Probation*, XV (Sept., 1951), 3–7.

noted here. According to the California law (in 1963), its youth authority[52] is authorized to accept boys and girls from the juvenile courts as well as youthful offenders (who were less than twenty-one years of age at the time of apprehension) from the criminal courts, although the model act covers only youths above the juvenile court age; and unlike the model act, it permits the courts to grant probation and makes no provision for the possibility of a completely indeterminate sentence. However, the juvenile courts may use their discretion in committing offenders to the youth authority, and it, in turn, may use its discretion in accepting them.

In California, the youth authority is now composed of six full-time, well-qualified, paid members appointed by the governor and confirmed by the state senate. Operating under the youth authority are thirteen institutions and two diagnostic reception centers, the purpose of which is to study and classify offenders and to assign them to schools, institutions, and camps in accordance with the needs of each individual.

Thus far, there has been no unique or consistent pattern in the youth authority laws that have been passed.[53] These laws really represent a movement for the renovation of the machinery for dealing with juvenile delinquents and youth offenders. They are not the same thing everywhere but reflect an adaptation to the conditions existing in each state. An understanding of what the youth authority plan means, therefore, can be obtained only by a study of its actual operation in each state.

Although the legislation passed by the federal government deals only with youthful offenders, all states that have adopted the authority plan have placed juveniles within its jurisdiction. This, say critics of the latter arrangement,[54] will result in the treatment of juveniles as if they were youthful offenders and in the sacrifice of the specialized techniques that have been so painstakingly created to deal with the problems of children.

Opponents of the youth authority plan also contend that any success achieved by it in California has been due to the very unusual conditions existing there. The state was in great need of new services, agencies, and institutions; little resistance to the plan was offered by the agencies already there; and the youth authority was fortunate to have the services of able and devoted leaders and the generous support of the governor. Under such conditions, success might have been achieved by any one of a number of other reorganization plans. Besides, add the critics, the plan

[52] In 1943, California changed the name of its authority from "Youth Correction Authority" to "Youth Authority."

[53] Sol Rubin, "Changing Youth Correction Authority Concepts," *Focus*, XXIX (May, 1950), 77–82; Will C. Turnbladh, "More about Youth Authority Concepts," *Focus*, XXX (Jan., 1951), 23–25.

[54] See, for example, Roy L. McLaughlin, "Is Youth Authority a Pattern for Children?" *Proceedings of the American Prison Association, 1948,* pp. 19–28.

has not been uniformly successful in California. In fact, the youth authority plan there has been criticized as being weakest in what is considered to be its most important feature, that is, in the development of adequate diagnostic centers where offenders can be studied and programs for their treatment prescribed. Furthermore, the California Youth Authority has had difficulty in performing the many duties with which it is charged. This was emphasized over a decade ago by the Community Service Society of New York, which made a survey of the youth authority and sharply criticized its work.[55]

Within recent years, however, several steps have been taken to increase the effectiveness of the youth authority program in California. The membership of the youth authority board has been changed from three to six in an effort to handle its increasing case load. Case-hearing representatives have been employed to assist the board in the hearing and disposition of cases. The institutional facilities under the youth authority have been expanded and improved. And the operation of the youth authority has been expedited by a reorganization of California's department of correction.[56]

Nevertheless, it is still too early, even in the case of California, to give an adequate appraisal of the youth authority plan. It may eventually be introduced into many states, but even if it is not, experimentation with it in some states will undoubtedly give considerable impetus to moves everywhere for the improvement of law-enforcement and correctional systems.

THE FAMILY COURT

In some cities, the influence of the juvenile court is shown by the establishment of special courts with jurisdiction over cases involving all kinds of family problems, such as delinquency, neglect, dependency, adoption, illegitimacy, nonsupport, and crimes by members of a family against one another. This, then, is a juvenile court with extended jurisdiction; it is usually called a family court or a court of domestic relations.[57] Although

[55] Harry Elmer Barnes and Negley K. Teeters, *New Horizons in Criminology* (New York: Prentice-Hall, Inc., 1951), p. 807. Paul W. Tappan, "Young Adults under the Youth Authority," *Journal of Criminal Law, Criminology, and Police Science*, XLVII (Mar.–Apr., 1957), 629–46.

[56] Department of the Youth Authority of the State of California, *California Laws Relating to Youthful Offenders* (Sacramento: California State Printing Office, 1963); *California Youth Authority*, Biennial Report for 1961–1962 (Sacramento: California State Printing Office, 1962); *The Youth and Adult Corrections Agency* (Sacramento: California State Printing Office, n.d.).

[57] Alice Scott Nutt, "Juvenile and Domestic Relations Courts," *Social Work Year Book, 1949* (New York: Russell Sage Foundation, 1949), pp. 270–76; Atwell Westwick, "Wider Jurisdiction for the Juvenile Court," *Yearbook, 1939* (New York: National Probation Association, 1939), pp. 184–202; Walter H. Beckham, "One Court

this court has not been widely introduced, it has been in operation in such cities as Cincinnati, Philadelphia, and Wilmington, Delaware, and in 1948 the House of Delegates of the American Bar Association went on record as favoring its establishment.

Strong arguments have been advanced in support of the family court. Among these are: (1) it makes the family the unit of study and thus makes possible the re-education of the entire family, not just one of its members; (2) it reduces the overlapping and conflict which now exists among courts dealing with family problems; and (3) it is in an excellent position to strengthen the family and to fortify it against the divisive influences of our complex culture.

Against the family court have been advanced such arguments as: (1) the juvenile court has not been effective, and to increase its jurisdiction by converting it into a family court would only complicate the problems which thus far it has not been able to handle; (2) the family court would interfere with the separate and informal hearings which should be given to juveniles; (3) its establishment involves increased expenditures and perhaps heavier taxation; (4) no single court can effectively handle all the complicated problems over which a family court is given jurisdiction; and (5) the great majority of existing juvenile courts are overloaded, understaffed, and underfinanced and, therefore, in no position to assume the responsibilities attendant upon their expansion into family courts.

It is clear that there are strong feelings on both sides of this controversy, and that a discussion of the family court can produce definite conclusions only when it deals with specific conditions in a particular place and involves an understanding of the true nature of the juvenile court (see the analysis presented above). In any event, it appears that at present the family court can be justified and financed only in the larger urban communities.

FUTURE OF THE JUVENILE COURT

The juvenile court is firmly established in our laws and in the customs and traditions of our people. Unless there is a revolutionary change in our culture, controversies over the juvenile court in the future will revolve about the question of how to increase its effectiveness. To this end we should improve its personnel, make its services available to more

for Family Problems," *Yearbook, 1942* (New York: National Probation Association, 1942), pp. 80–93; Paul W. Alexander, "The Family Court of the Future," *Federal Probation*, XVI (Sept., 1952), 24–31; Harriet L. Goldberg and William H. Sheridan, "Family Courts—An Urgent Need," *Journal of Public Law*, VIII (Fall, 1959), 337–50. See also *Standard Family Court Act* (New York: National Probation and Parole Association, 1959).

children, especially those in rural areas, increase its cooperation and coordination with other agencies interested in welfare and law enforcement, and encourage its judge and staff to participate in movements for the development of welfare programs and the prevention of juvenile delinquency.

Part IV

CORRECTION AND PREVENTION

17

The Philosophy of Punishment

THE MEANING OF PUNISHMENT

In modern society, punishment is the penalty inflicted by the state upon a person adjudged guilty of crime. Its administration always involves the intention to produce some kind of pain, which is justified in terms of its assumed values. The pain intended may be partly physical, as in a whipping, but today most methods of punishment are designed primarily to cause mental suffering, as in imprisonment, where there is loss of freedom, reputation, and perhaps property. The amount of pain actually experienced by the person will vary from case to case, depending upon the circumstances in the situation and the personality of the offender, but that some pain is always felt, except maybe in certain mental cases, regardless of the method used, seems to be indisputable. Thus, punishment may be said to have two essential elements: (1) public condemnation of antisocial behavior; and (2) the imposition of unpleasant consequences by political authority.

There is considerable difference of opinion regarding the origin of punishment. Some authorities point to vengeance as its source. Some attribute it to the fear of offended gods. Others see its genesis in the conflict of the interests of different groups as one group imposed its authority upon another.[1] It seems unlikely now that we shall ever know

[1] For various views on the subject, see Ellsworth Faris, *The Nature of Human Nature* (New York: McGraw-Hill Book Co., Inc., 1937), pp. 84–95; Robert H. Lowie, *Primitive Society* (New York: Boni and Liveright, 1920), pp. 397–426; Bronislaw Malinowski, *Crime and Custom in Savage Society* (New York: Harcourt, Brace and Co., Inc., 1932); George P. Murdock, *Our Primitive Contemporaries* (New York: The Macmillan Co., 1934), pp. 4, 43, 61; W. I. Thomas, *Primitive Behavior* (New York: McGraw-Hill Book Co., Inc., 1937), chap. xv; and L. T. Hobhouse, *Morals in Evolution* (London: Chapman and Hall, Ltd., 1906), Vol. I, pp. 79–133.

how, when, or why punishment originated, but it is probable that its roots were already present when man first appeared as a social being.

It will be helpful to remember that both crime and punishment are functionally related to the culture in which they occur. That crime is so related and that it varies in kind and incidence from society to society is usually recognized; but that punishment likewise has such a relationship and that the efficacy of its methods is affected by what the people in a particular society feel, want, and believe, is sometimes overlooked. We shall, therefore, seek to conduct this analysis with reference to the following important tendencies that exist in various degrees in many countries of Europe and the Western Hemisphere: (1) the spread of humanitarianism with its emphasis on the value of the individual, the protection of human life, and the reduction of human pain and suffering; (2) the increase of the impersonality of social relationships; and (3) the growth of the belief in the powers of science.[2] In this way it is hoped that we can gain deeper insight into the possibilities and limitations of the purposes and the methods of punishment in modern society.[3]

PURPOSES OF PUNISHMENT

The principal purposes of punishment are retribution, reformation (or rehabilitation), and deterrence.[4]

Retribution. Retribution is the pain which, it is said, a criminal deserves to suffer, because he has broken the law and hurt someone else, and which the law proportions to the gravity of the harm done.[5] Having failed in his duties, which every member of the community is expected to perform, the criminal must pay in pain the debt he owes to society. If this is not done, say those who argue in favor of retribution, the angry victim of crime and his relatives and friends who seek revenge may take the

[2] These tendencies are not necessarily harmonious in their operation. Thus impersonality may cause many persons to be ignorant about the needs, desires, and wishes of others and so exert an influence against humanitarianism.

[3] For an analysis of the relationship between culture and punishment see Émile Durkheim, *Division of Labor in Society,* trans. George Simpson (New York: The Macmillan Co., 1933), Book I; Pitirim A. Sorokin, *Social and Cultural Dynamics* (New York: American Book Co., 1937), Vol. II, chap. xv; Georg Rusche and Otto Kirchheimer, *Punishment and the Social Structure* (New York: Columbia University Press, 1939); Svend Ranulf, *The Jealousy of the Gods and Criminal Law at Athens* (London: Williams and Norgate, Ltd., 1933), and *Moral Indignation and Middle Class Psychology: A Sociological Study* (Copenhagen: Levin and Munksgaard, 1938).

[4] Sometimes expiation is included in this list, but it is now used chiefly in a religious sense. It implies the infliction of suffering to make amends for an offense and to appease the Deity.

[5] Opponents of retribution emphasize the difficulty of proportioning the pain to the gravity of the harm done. That this is true, especially in modern society, cannot be denied; but it is equally clear that the difficulty of acquiring knowledge about reformation and deterrence is even greater.

law into their own hands or refuse to cooperate with society in bringing
the offender to justice.

There can be no denial that the desire to "get even" is a natural human
tendency and that it is to be found in almost everyone, but the question
should be raised as to what extent this feeling should be permitted to
influence our actions against the criminal. If the criminal law is to be
written to satisfy the blind demands of outraged feelings, one may well
ask why we should not make punishment as severe as possible. Why not
gouge out eyes, cut out tongues, crop off ears? Why not flay the criminal
alive and boil him in oil? If it is pain that is wanted, why not get as much
as possible?

But it should be obvious that the passion for revenge cannot be allowed
to drive out reason and control the policy of any state in its treatment of
criminals. To do so would be to encourage and strengthen the very
motives that might destroy all collective action. It would array man against
man and place a premium upon violence. Retaliation is a game at which
two can play, and if unrestrained, it would align the criminal against
society in a mutually destructive process. The sensibilities of offenders,
officials, and spectators would become blunted so that if an impression
were to be made, the process would have to be increasingly severe; and
the public, temporarily satisfied, would tend to settle back and disregard
the causes that produce the criminal. No, a program for dealing with
criminals cannot be constructed in this way. The desire for revenge must
be regulated by the law.

Besides, in most modern societies public opinion does not demand, nor
would it tolerate, sanguinary methods of punishment, and even the victims of crime tend to shrink from the idea of subjecting criminals to
physical torture. In fact, in harmony with the humanitarian movement,
the tendency has been to mitigate the severity of the criminal law and to
eliminate all methods of punishment that cause physical suffering. Of
course, the injury to the victim of the crime and the interests and desires
of the public cannot be disregarded, but neither can the causes of criminality nor the rehabilitation of the criminal, both of which have been
emphasized by the growth of belief in the powers of science. Actually,
all such considerations tend to be equated in terms of the culture in
which they exist. And since the abolition of corporal punishment does
not mean that the offender escapes all pain, any desire that the victim
of the crime and his friends and relatives may have for the suffering of
the offender can still be taken into account in modern society.

But there is still another aspect of retribution that needs to be examined, for retribution involves more than getting revenge. Thus it is urged
that the retribution which the criminal is made to suffer supports the
moral code and helps to unify society against crime and criminals. The

reasoning here is that the development of loyalty and respect for law tends to produce fear and hatred of those who violate it, and that public support for law can remain vigorous only as long as it can express its hostility against the criminal by making him suffer for engaging in activities that threaten the established order. Otherwise, the public would feel thwarted, and its obedience to the law would appear futile and meaningless. If those who disobey the law receive the same consideration as those who obey it, much of the reason for abiding by its provisions and having hostility against its violators disappears. But if a society does not have the capacity to feel deeply about its wrongs, then it probably does not have the capacity to right its wrongs.

Retribution, therefore, provides not only a vindication of the criminal law, which is necessary to make criminal law more than a mere request, but also an opportunity for the public to stand together against the enemy of accepted values. And here it does little good to argue that we should hate the crime but not the criminal. Such fine distinctions, although they may point up an ideal, are largely lost upon the great mass of people. The human tendency has always been to embody "good" or "evil" in the form of a person. Thus, punishment of the criminal supplies a symbol around which law-abiding citizens can rally in support of law enforcement, gives them renewed strength and courage in their fight against crime, and helps to maintain the public sense of justice. Looked at in this way, a decline in the demand for retribution may actually reflect the tendency on the part of the people to feel less responsibility in the enforcement of the law. It may be just additional evidence of the tendency to delegate the duties of citizenship to the specialist and the professional—a tendency which can result only in the development of a society where power is lodged in the hands of a few.

Although punishment through retribution does help to unify society against crime and criminals, it should be seen as only one of the many ways in which greater social solidarity is achieved. In fact, all social movements which enjoy widespread support tend to do this. And in a society such as ours that stresses humanitarianism and scientific progress, a social movement which has strong, positive characteristics—for example, one designed to prevent crime—may accomplish this more effectively than retribution, which is largely repressive.

Furthermore, retribution has other limitations in modern society. In the first place, since almost all prisoners return to society, it is obvious that they must not be so stigmatized that they cannot take up lawful pursuits upon their release. As a matter of fact, the trend in modern society to abolish physical torture and to eliminate public punishments undoubtedly has reduced the force of retribution.

There is, too, an increasing impersonality in modern society. When a crime is committed, unless it is spectacular or of a revolting nature, few know about it and even fewer are directly affected or injured by it. Since there is no widespread and vigorous movement for the apprehension of the average criminal, most citizens can hardly be expected to be deeply impressed or excited when he is punished. Moreover, the shock of the crime is often absorbed by insurance which covers the property stolen or destroyed, and even when a person has no insurance, he is inclined to drop the charges if he can secure his property or adequate restitution. Such abstractions as law and order seem very unreal and remote to the average person. By comparison, the return of a stolen car or an overcoat is very important. When this is accomplished, anger cools and compassion is felt.

And here another point may be raised. The humanitarian movement in Western civilization has made many conscious of the suffering of their fellow human beings and filled some with a desire to reduce pain and misery everywhere. Is there not, therefore, among those whose feelings are affected by retribution, a tendency to reduce rather than solidify opinion against the criminal who is severely punished? Will this not enlist in the ranks of those who spring to his defense many who would otherwise be anxious to have him punished? May not retribution in this way actually drive a wedge into the law-abiding group and divide rather than unify it?

However, even after full consideration is given to the limitations of retribution in modern society, we must still conclude that it remains one of the principal purposes of punishment. In practice deterrence and reformation receive more attention, while retribution, often shunned and condemned, is left to shift for itself. Nevertheless, there are cases where neither deterrence nor reformation is possible; yet something must be done to uphold the law. It is here that retribution stands out distinctly as a purpose of punishment.

Reformation. In America increasing emphasis is being placed upon the reformation, or rehabilitation, of the criminal. With reference to this, no one will deny that it is possible to influence human behavior through pain and fear and that punishment has reformative value in many cases. However, one must also understand the limitations of punishment when used for the purpose of reformation.

If the infliction of pain is to have its greatest effect upon the behavior of a person, it must follow soon after the act for which it is given. But punishment always takes place weeks or even months after the offense has been committed, since the offender must first be apprehended, tried, and convicted. Such delay tends to disconnect the punishment from the offense in the mind of the offender, and it may well be considered as merely another painful experience in an unjust world.

Punishment, furthermore, may not only fail to restrain. It may also act in a positive way to produce harmful effects in the prisoners who are punished. It is true that in modern society punishment seldom involves the infliction of physical pain. Nevertheless, there remains the possibility of serious damage to the personality of the prisoner and the intensification of undesirable tendencies that he might already have.

Punishment can mark a man mentally just as surely as it can mark him physically. It may label him as a criminal in his own eyes as well as in the eyes of the community. Thus stigmatized, a man may be psychologically isolated from the law-abiding group and again driven into the association of criminals upon his release from prison. This, of course, is the very thing that society should try to prevent. Moreover, a painful experience like punishment may simply cause a person to develop caution and skill. An offender may remember the punishment, but in remembering, he may thus become an even more dangerous criminal—one who is difficult to apprehend and convict. In still other cases, a dramatic series of experiences like apprehension, conviction, and imprisonment may give the criminal increased status in the law-violating group, which may be the only group whose opinions are important to him.

Some men who feel hated by society may in turn hate society. Resentful and revengeful, deeply hurt by the indignity of their punishment and with bitterness in their hearts, they may seek an opportunity to strike back at society. Further punishment may merely deepen the grudge that they bear. Other men, broken in spirit by their punishment and deprived of self-respect, may no longer care how society regards them. Shiftless and inert, they may not again violate the law after they have been punished, but society has lost the opportunity to help them, together with the contribution that they might have made. Criminologists have repeatedly stressed the importance of preserving the self-respect of the prisoner. Any procedure which might destroy self-respect is, they agree, extremely unwise. If a prisoner has been deprived of this personality asset, society has lost the only basis it has for building in him renewed loyalties for group standards; for self-respect, when expressed in terms of the values of the law-abiding group, becomes simply a reflection of what that group expects of the individual.

It should also be recognized that certain psychopathic individuals may find delight in punishment. No one knows how many such individuals there are, although it appears that their number has been grossly exaggerated by certain writers. Nevertheless, it must be admitted that punishment may actually satisfy and strengthen the sadistic impulses of those who order it, witness it, or inflict it, and may likewise indulge and encourage the masochistic tendencies of those who suffer from it or see it. Punishment, therefore, may intensify certain traits that are judged to be dangerous and unwholesome by the humanitarianism of the present day, and criminal procedure may thus pander to what is considered to be the worst in society.

A program of reformation or rehabilitation must contain *both* negative and positive elements, *both* pleasure and pain, and *both* persuasion and authority; and to be most effective it must be based upon an intensive study of the individual. It should include the treatment of physical defects, the reduction of personality maladjustments, the overthrow of influences detrimental to organized society, and the inculcation of the principles of good citizenship. Such a program inevitably involves some suffering, if for no other reason than that it requires the restriction of liberty. And yet, if suffering is blindly used for the purpose of control, pain and fear may make reformation impossible. In other words, the reformative procedure must not be so pleasant as to encourage further criminal activities, but it must at the same time be so designed as to produce desirable changes in the personalities of offenders. The resolution of this apparent contradiction is one of the major problems confronting prison administrators and requires the greatest skill in the art of handling prisoners. In the beginning the prisoner may resent what is being done for him, but his resentment must be dissolved, and his cooperation and support in the reformative process must ultimately be secured if success in his case is to be achieved. That this can be done is clearly evidenced by the case histories of many prisoners, but the outcome in any particular case can never be completely foreseen. Naturally, there are certain individuals who understand only force and must therefore be controlled by force, but a person should be so classified only after his personality has been carefully studied over a considerable length of time.

Deterrence. Deterrence is considered by many to be the most important purpose of punishment. By "deterrence" is meant the use of punishment to prevent others from committing crimes. In order to accomplish this purpose, the offender is punished so that he will be held up as an example of what happens to those who violate the law, the assumption being that this will curb the criminal activities of others. It is argued that this is worth while even if some are not deterred by what is done to the offender. It is also said that the existence of crime does not mean that punishment is not efficacious as a deterrent, since it is impossible to determine how much crime there would be if criminals were not punished. Moreover, deterrence involves more than the instilling of fear in those who might be tempted to commit a crime. It involves also the positive moral influence that the law exerts in the educational and training processes where by stigmatizing certain acts in terms of prescribed penalties, it helps to engender attitudes of dislike, contempt, disgust, and even horror for these acts and thus contributes to the development of personal forces hostile to crime. Thus some abstain from murder because they fear the penalty, but many others do so because they regard it with horror.[6]

Many of those who believe that deterrence is important consciously or unconsciously base their belief on the doctrine of freedom of the will. According to this doctrine a person is free, at least to some extent, to do as he pleases, and society must in some way prevail upon him to bring his behavior into conformity with generally accepted standards. When one violates the law, it is assumed that he might have acted otherwise if he had so desired. Therefore, he is held not to have disciplined himself sufficiently, and he deserves to be punished. He must be taught a lesson, and others, impressed by his experience, will choose to obey the law. Those who believe in the doctrine of freedom of the will are known as "libertarians."

However, those who reject this doctrine contend that it is vitiated by a fundamental inconsistency.[7] Their argument may be summarized in this way. Will, according to the doctrine of freedom of the will, is considered to be isolated from all psychological and social processes and conditions and to be an entity which may function independently of all experiences and teachings. But if this is so, how can the individual be reached through any program of education? Furthermore, what is meant by the statement that a man is free to do as he pleases? He is free to do what? Choosing is a process and must operate in terms of the values which man derives from his culture. What pleases a Hottentot may be very disagreeable to an Eskimo. What is right for a Bantu may be an unforgivable sin for an Englishman. How could one behave like a Trobriand Islander if he were not reared as a Trobriand Islander? Right and wrong are relative to time and place, and the plasticity of man's nature makes him susceptible to a wide range of educational programs. All education must rest upon the

[6] Johs Andenaes, "General Prevention—Illusion or Reality?" *Journal of Criminal Law, Criminology, and Police Science,* XLIII (July–Aug., 1952), 176–98; Henry M. Hart, Jr., "The Aims of the Criminal Law," *Law and Contemporary Problems,* XXIII (Summer, 1958), 402–11; Morris Raphael Cohen, *Reason and Law* (Glencoe, Ill.: The Free Press, 1950), pp. 46–51.

[7] See, for example, Harry Elmer Barnes and Negley K. Teeters, *New Horizons in Criminology* (New York: Prentice-Hall, Inc., 1951), pp. 124, 125; Nathaniel F. Cantor, *Crime and Society* (New York: Henry Holt and Co., Inc., 1939), pp. 183–87; Edwin H. Sutherland, *Principles of Criminology* (Philadelphia: J. B. Lippincott Co., 1947), pp. 364–67; Arthur Evans Wood and John Barker Waite, *Crime and Its Treatment* (New York: American Book Co., 1941), pp. 480, 484–86; Chapman Cohen, *Determinism or Free-Will?* (London: The Pioneer Press, 1943). For various views on the subject, consult Sidney Morgenbesser and James Walsh, eds., *Free Will* (Englewood Cliffs, N.J.: Prentice-Hall, Inc., 1962).

assumption that one's "choice" is a function of one's antecedent experience and is expressed in terms of the values which one learns in his association with his fellows. To deny this is to place man definitely beyond the influence of education and send him bounding through life like an utterly unpredictable will-o'-the-wisp. Assuredly this is not what is meant by those who express themselves in favor of the doctrine of freedom of the will, because they also speak of the importance of early training and of children as twigs to be bent and wax to be molded. This, indeed, is confusion confounded: Will is either a function of previous experiences or a grotesque entity that defies education and control and dooms the efforts of science and religion to dismal failure. All reason compels one to reject the latter and to conclude that criminal behavior is not an expression of free will, but rather a product of the forces of heredity and environment as they interact in the life of the individual.

Nor, say those who reject the doctrine of freedom of the will, is it possible to maintain that behavior is partly free and partly determined. This view, they claim, is now held by many persons who hesitate to embrace the doctrine of freedom of the will in its logical completeness, but it is exposed to attacks from both sides. Advanced as a compromise, it is "but a hodgepodge, a mélange, a collection of ill-assorted notions which are given coherency by wishful thinking."[8] Freedom of will must be an "all-or-nothing" proposition. To hold less is to sacrifice logical impregnability for the sake of conformity to the facts of modern science, which, in fact, have already disproved the entire doctrine. One must conclude, therefore, that criminal behavior, like all human behavior, is the inevitable result of hereditary and environmental causes. That is, it is determined, and the individual does not have a single choice from the cradle to the grave.

This, then, explains why those who do not accept the doctrine of freedom of the will are sometimes referred to as "determinists." But let us return to an analysis of their argument. It further maintains that it is both futile and unjust to inflict pain upon a criminal on the assumption that he and others, who by means of his punishment are to be made afraid to commit crimes, can be law-abiding citizens or not as they "freely choose" regardless of their heredity or environment. It is just as foolish to do this as it would be to strike a man over the head for having a toothache so that he and others would choose not to have one. Both criminal behavior and physical pain are but symptoms of underlying causes

[8] Willard Waller, "A Deterministic View of Criminal Responsibility," *Journal of Criminal Law and Criminology*, XX (May, 1929), 88–101. This article was in answer to another, "Pseudo-Science and the Problem of Criminal Responsibility," by C. O. Weber, which had appeared in the August, 1928 issue of the same journal (pp. 181–95).

that must be discovered and eliminated. In any particular case it may be impossible to discover the causes, but that does not mean that they do not exist. The individual, therefore, is responsible only in the sense that he is the type of person who would commit the kind of act that he did. In fact, it might be well to discard the term "responsibility" entirely, since it is so burdened with archaic theological and metaphysical implications, and replace it with the term "accountability." The criminal, then, should be held "accountable" because he has in him the forces that cause him to be a criminal, and not because he has "freely chosen" to be a criminal. In this way the law would be given a scientific basis for its procedure, and its purpose would not be the punishment of the offender, but rather the protection of society by the discovery and elimination of the causes of criminality. So runs the argument of those who reject the doctrine of freedom of the will.

But the libertarians are not thrown into confusion and demoralized flight by the force of this attack. Instead, they countercharge with vigor, and here is their argument. The true scientist, they stoutly insist, "does not, and need not, assume that determinism is universal, because a true scientist does not assume answers to his questions." He need only assume that the scientific method is his appropriate method of research, not that it can answer all questions. There is, moreover, "a vast difference between mechanism[9] accepted as a *guide* to research, and mechanism accepted as the *end product* of research, in advance of research."[10] To conclude that the whole of reality is determined because we find that part of it is, not only goes beyond the evidence but also flagrantly violates the very principles of scientific research to which determinists have dedicated themselves. And during this excursion into speculation, they also plunge into the pitfall of pragmatism[11] by assuming that, because mechanical understanding sometimes succeeds, there are no other modes of comprehension.

Furthermore, the libertarians argue, the advocates of freedom of the will are not the only ones who assert that scientific truth and reality do not coincide. The determinists themselves admit this and agree that the human personality, despite the progress of science, remains in no small degree a mystery.[12] In addition, in their more objective moments, they also concede that, because of the limitations of the human mind, they will probably never be able to demonstrate scientifically the soundness of their

[9] The doctrine that natural processes, and especially the processes of life, are mechanically determined and capable of explanation by the laws of physics and chemistry.

[10] C. O. Weber, "Pseudo-Science and the Problem of Criminal Responsibility," *Journal of Criminal Law and Criminology*, XIX, Part I (Aug., 1928), 190.

[11] The doctrine that truth is the practical efficacy of an idea.

[12] For an admission of this by a criminologist who is a determinist, see Donald R. Taft, *Criminology* (New York: The Macmillan Co., 1950), p. 296.

position.[13] Thus, at the same time that they accuse the libertarians of inconsistency, they inadvertently expose their own egregious inconsistency. While they admit that science has not revealed all of reality, they nevertheless insist that determinism can give us a complete explanation of life. So dogma masquerades as science, and materialism[14] is invested with a meretricious attractiveness through the implication that it is based upon the findings of science. Determinism cannot be demonstrated inductively; neither can it be proved deductively. "The attempt to deduce it involves either a begging of the question in the beginning or a *non sequitur* in the end. Psychologically considered, it is the outcome of jealousy for the scientific method."[15] According to the libertarians, the determinists would thus substitute a dogma for what they allege to be a dogma.

Libertarians, however, are not really disturbed by the charge of inconsistency. Few, if any, of them believe that the will operates without limitations or that it is unaffected by previous experience and attendant circumstances. Few, if any, would deny that man is a product, but libertarians do insist that man is not always and everywhere a product only of forces over which he has no control. Conflicting principles, they explain, struggle for dominance in human nature, and neither mechanism nor vitalism[16] can cover all the facts. Human nature is a dual one, and man, part body and part soul, is the focus of two opposed principles of being, which at once telescope and struggle. "In the oppositions of will and habit, desire and reason, truth and error, good and evil, beauty and ugliness, we discern a deep-seated warfare in our natures which perhaps extends out through the entire fabric of reality." To do justice to the facts, therefore, we must use the concepts of both mechanism and vitalism.[17] But more than this, behind the dual nature of man is a supreme unity that transcends and reconciles all. And what is referred to as relativity in morality is but the varying expressions of absolute morality. All this man could clearly see were he possessed of greater powers. So what appears to be inconsistency is actually the limitations of human comprehension.

The libertarians further state that the thirst for consistency is "the besetting sin of the classroom mind," which must have it at all costs, even at the cost of doing violence to reality. We forget that we may crave the simple and consistent, not because nature is simple, but because we are. And so, making a virtue out of a necessity, we imagine nature simple

[13] See, for example, Waller, p. 101.

[14] The doctrine that matter is the only reality.

[15] Douglas C. Macintosh, "Responsibility, Freedom, and Causality; or the Dilemma of Determinism or Indeterminism," *Journal of Philosophy*, XXXVII (Jan., 1940), 50.

[16] The doctrine that the processes of life are not explicable by the laws of physics and chemistry alone, and that life is in some part self-determining instead of mechanistically determined. It is thus opposed to mechanism.

[17] Weber, p. 194.

because our feeble intellects find only simple laws. "We should simplify, not as much as we can, but only as much as we *dare*. Then if our human nature is twofold, let us accept that as our present result."[18]

But, ask the libertarians, are the determinists really concerned about inconsistency? They did not raise their voices in protest when the physicists seriously proposed their theory of ultimate indeterminacy within the atom. If they can accept indeterminacy there, how can they claim that free will is destructive of science in criminology? "Why cannot there be a criminology that observes, weighs, measures, generalizes about the conditions and factors ordinarily only *predisposing* to crime, and under unusual circumstances even causing it? Why cannot criminology be treated as a science of specifically *human* conduct rather than a cousin-german to physics and chemistry?"[19]

Perhaps, say the libertarians, what the determinist is concerned about is his own security. If man stands alone, without God, to whom he can turn in his hour of need, then he must convince himself that he has the power to handle his own problems. Do this he must if he is to still the fears that are called up by the overwhelming uncertainties of life. So science, the creature of man, becomes his god upon which he calls for answers to the riddles of reality. Or perhaps, in the case of the academician, determinism is but a form of compensation for feelings of inadequacy in a highly competitive world. Having fled from the hard realities of life and sought refuge in a cloistered haven, he can now, in the voice of authority, proclaim to all that in science he has found the power "to unscrew the inscrutable."

Whatever the motivation of the determinist may be, the libertarians are certain that even the most confirmed determinist always acts with a conviction of free will. For how else could he act? The practical reason for casting one's lot with indeterminism is that "it releases energies and avoids the tempting rationalizations in which the determinist can indulge, letting himself slip always into the channel of least resistance and regarding this slothful course as the only one possible."[20] Determinism shrinks reality to the size of man's brain and encases his imagination in an iron coffin of his own making. Vitalism, on the other hand, frees his imagination to soar beyond the frontiers of knowledge and fills him with the spirit of adventure and enterprise. Regardless of his past, he is the architect of his future. "Fortunately, men believe in their will, and even if they

[18] *Ibid.*, p. 193.

[19] John Edward Coogan, "Secularism Alien to Our Covenant Nation," *Federal Probation*, XVI (Sept., 1952), 44. See also his articles, "Some Criminologists and Free Will," *Federal Probation*, VII (Oct.–Dec., 1943), 12–15; and "A Rejoinder to the Strictures of the Determinists," *Federal Probation*, VIII (Oct.–Dec., 1944), 40–42.

[20] Gordon W. Allport, "The Productive Paradoxes of William James," *Psychological Review*, L (Jan., 1943), 108.

are philosophically convinced of determinism, they will not make use of it in actual situations."[21] Determinism is opposed and discredited by "a vivid awareness of one's organized self, functioning daily in hundreds of purposeful actions" in the stream of human experience.[22]

The libertarians assert that the prime fallacy in the reasoning of determinists is that first they universalize determinism and then naïvely proceed to tell us what "ought" to be done about it.[23] Denying responsibility for all humanity, the determinists apparently feel free and responsible for at least one thing, the theory of determinism. "Rather obviously," as Jerome Hall has so well said, "it has never occurred to them to 'determine' what determines their determinism, or to consider whether any significance whatever could be attached to their criticism of the criminal law, or, for that matter, to any other problem-solving, if that dogma were consistently maintained."[24] In the words of the determinist, man's choice is the inevitable function of his antecedent experience. How then can he free himself of his predisposition? How can he objectively judge anything? How can he do more than merely assert that he prefers his own belief? So the determinist finds himself pinned to earth with his own skewer. And with this the libertarian concludes his case.

Now, the fact is that science can neither prove nor disprove that there is freedom of will. All that science thus far has been able to show is that the area in which determinism operates is greater than it was formerly believed to be. Any statement beyond this carries one out of the realm of science into the field of speculation. Nevertheless, it seems safe to conclude that the area of the unknown in human behavior is still so great that, as far as we now know, there may well be an element of free will in every human act. One may, moreover, reject the doctrine of freedom of the will and still favor the punishment of criminals as a means of controlling the behavior of others through the development of law-abiding attitudes and the establishment of fear as causes of behavior. Even the determinist, therefore, agrees that the criminal is responsible in the sense, at least, that he has in him the causes that produce criminality.

But even if we assume that punishment prevents others from committing crime, we must also grant that certain human traits reduce its effectiveness as a deterrent. Man tends to be a creature of habit and emotions; and handicapped as criminals often are, by poverty, ignorance, and malnutrition, he becomes notoriously shortsighted. The possibility of detection

21 Max Wertheimer, "A Story of Three Days," *Freedom: Its Meaning,* ed. Ruth N. Anshen (New York: Harcourt, Brace and Co., Inc., 1940), p. 562.

22 Jerome Hall, *General Principles of Criminal Law* (Indianapolis: The Bobbs-Merrill Co., 1947), p. 377. See also William P. Montague, "Free Will and Fate," *The Personalist,* XXIV (Apr., 1943), 175–80.

23 Weber, p. 193.

24 Hall, p. 529.

and apprehension is given little thought by many violators of the law, and often the penalty is not even considered, even if it is known; in many cases it is not. Indeed, it appears that most normal persons do not so order their lives as to balance the pleasure and pain attendant upon their acts, and obviously the mentally deranged, the mentally deficient, and those who commit crimes in the heat of passion are not in any significant way influenced by thoughts of the future.

Moreover, human nature is exceedingly complex. A criminal may fear punishment, but he may fear the scorn of his companions or his family more, and the fear of economic insecurity may drive him to commit the most daring crimes. Often man fears exclusion from the group in which he has status far more than he does the penalties prescribed by law. Furthermore, man does not live by fear alone. Love, loyalty to the gang, craving for excitement, ambition, greed, lust, anger, and resentment may steel him to face the greatest dangers in violating the law and stimulate his inventive powers to create skills and techniques that defy our most modern police methods. Everywhere, human beings have shown a willingness, even an eagerness, to suffer and die to achieve their goals. Is it too much to assume, then, that many will defy the law and risk detection, apprehension, and conviction in order to satisfy their desires?

However, if punishment were surely, quickly, uniformly, publicly, and severely inflicted, it undoubtedly would prevent many crimes. But this is precisely the point. Certainly the way in which punishment is being administered in modern society, especially in the United States, is not fitted to produce this result.

In the first place, in addition to the uncertainty of detection and apprehension, long delays frequently occur in court procedures, and many offenders avoid conviction. For example, it is estimated that in the cities of the United States during the year 1962, only 26 out of every 100 alleged major crimes were cleared by the arrest of offenders.[25] The significance of this can be grasped when it is realized that the deterrent effect of punishment is greatly weakened if it lacks certainty. Besides, as we have already pointed out, the tendency is to conceal the punishment of criminals from the public and to abolish penalties that cause physical suffering.

And yet, if we know how to make punishment more effective as a deterrent, why do we not take the necessary steps to do this? Indeed, if this is all that is needed, why do we not make the penalties of crimes more severe and institute a stricter enforcement of law? Why do we not increase the number of capital offenses and reintroduce all forms of corporal punishment, not only for men, but for women and children as well? The reasons why we do not take such action are to be found in the rapid

---

[25] Federal Bureau of Investigation, *Uniform Crime Reports, 1962*, pp. 15–17.

change and complexity of our society, which makes quick, certain, and uniform action in the detection, apprehension, and conviction of criminals impossible, and in the fact that modern society is not inclined to support a program of severe punishment. Our impersonal relationships do not demand such a program. Our humanitarianism will not tolerate it.

CONCLUSION

Punishment is an art which involves the balancing of retribution, reformation, and deterrence in terms of the dominant values of the culture in which it is imposed; and in the balancing of these purposes of punishment, first one and then another receives emphasis as the accompanying conditions change. Furthermore, retribution, reformation, and deterrence must be seen in their interrelationship, for each affects and strengthens the others. Reformation must be conducted and deterrence exerted in terms of values—the values of organized society, whatever they may be—but these very values, which the offender must accept and for which he must develop a loyalty, are flouted and thereby weakened if due recognition is not given to the importance of retribution, whose function is to support values. Thus reformation and deterrence to be effective need retribution, which in turn is facilitated when they are effective.

The efficacy of the methods of punishment also is affected by the values of the culture in which they are used. It is clear, therefore, that a method of punishment which is suitable today may have been unsuitable in the past and may again become unsuitable in the future. In the United States, with its humanitarianism, increasing impersonality in social relationships, and growing belief in the powers of science, capital and corporal penalties have become unacceptable to many persons and have been almost entirely replaced with imprisonment, probation, and parole. And since in the program of handling offenders more emphasis is now placed on the understanding of the causes of crime, the redirection of the individual in the light of such understanding, and the modification of the conditions which produce criminality, some criminologists have recommended that this program be called treatment instead of punishment. In this way, it is urged, this increased emphasis will be clearly and publicly recognized, and the program will not be burdened with any undesirable implications which the term "punishment" may carry. However, the latter is so deeply rooted in general usage that it is not likely to be discarded, except perhaps by certain specialists and academicians in the fields of social science and social welfare.

But this question cannot be so easily put aside, for there are important implications here that need to be examined. Treatment is a process during which causes in the individual case are studied and the knowledge thus obtained is used to produce the desired effects. The extent to which the subject participates in this process depends upon the circumstances of the case and the techniques that are used. In producing the desired effects, the experience of pain may be deliberately utilized, but more often no such pain is sought, or if it is caused, it is merely incidental to action which is directed to other goals. Always, however, the emphasis is on the individual, his nature, his problems, and his interests. On the other hand, in the process of punishment the emphasis is on the group. The crime is considered to be a threat to the group, and the individual must suffer so as to protect the group and its moral code. However, just as punishment can not disregard the individual, whose reformation is one of its goals, so treatment can not ignore the group, to which the "treated" individual must be returned.

Furthermore, the two processes of treatment and punishment must operate in terms of values—the values of organized society, which if it is to survive, must establish and preserve its norms. Therefore, although both the interests of the individual and the group must be considered in the handling of offenders, the interests of the group are always paramount, and treatment and punishment must be administered within the limits imposed by the moral code, the values of which must be guarded by retribution.

Furthermore, "it must be recognized that it is highly dubious, even from a purely theoretical viewpoint, whether any interference with normal living can ever be completely nonpunitive."[26] Punishment and treatment are so integrated as to be inseparable. "Even the most kindly treatment imaginable—as Shaw once put it, confinement in the Ritz, with very solicitous attentions on the part of the jailer—has its punitive element; any normal person would oppose it."[27] In fact, "the notion that it is possible to administer medical and psychological treatment without at the same time applying punishment would disappear on any acquaintance with even the best asylums for mentally diseased offenders—confinement and close supervision are punitive regardless of the attitude of the attendants. Just as treatment is to some extent punitive, so punishment, if wisely administered, also rehabilitates."[28] Moreover, both the sensations of pain and pleasure can be utilized profitably during the process of rehabilitation. It is not, then, a question of whether there should be one or the other of these sensations, or whether there should be retribution, or reformation, or deterrence, or whether there should be treatment or punishment, but rather how both treatment *and* punishment can be most

[26] Hall, p. 473.
[27] *Ibid.*, p. 421.
[28] *Ibid.*, p. 535. See also Hervey Cleckley, *The Mask of Sanity* (St. Louis: C. V. Mosby Co., 1941), p. 285.

judiciously balanced to produce the best results in the control and modification of behavior. Retribution and deterrence meet a need that cannot
be ignored, despite the protestations of many well-meaning but naïve and
unrealistic writers. The term "punishment" indicates this frankly and
unequivocally, while the term "treatment" does it grudgingly if at all.
Indeed, in the hands of extreme determinists the term "treatment" appears
better fitted for a "planned" society controlled by "experts," who indoc-
trinate others to be subservient to centralized government and sit in judgment on those charged with being "socially dangerous," than for a society
in which free men rule through their chosen representatives and are atten-
tive to the dictates of their conscience, sensitive to their duties and responsibilities, and jealous of their rights. In other words, it is not only a question
of having both treatment and punishment operate in terms of values and
of supporting these values by retribution, but also of having these values
express the will of the people through the legislative channels of republi-
can government. If the responsibilities of citizenship are transferred to
the "experts," then the citizen will lose his legal rights to the "experts,"
who will not only punish the offender for being "wrong" but, unrestrained
by the checks that now protect the accused in the administration of justice, will also tell the citizen what is "right." But aside from these considerations, is it not farcical and misleading to speak of treatment to the
exclusion of punishment when our knowledge of human behavior is so
meager and the number of professionally trained workers in our correctional agencies and institutions is so pitifully inadequate?

Courts and correctional institutions can never be just therapeutic agencies. They must be also moral agencies in the sense that they must express,
protect, and strengthen the values of the organized society in which they
function. This is not to ignore the fact that values change and that considerable confusion regarding moral standards exists in the United States.
The point is that courts and correctional institutions cannot avoid their
responsibility as moral agencies. They must do what they can to reduce
this confusion. They must consider the interests of the offender and respect his rights, but they must also take their stand with the community
and insist that he learn to discharge his duties and assume his responsibilities as a member of society, thus giving encouragement and support
to law-abiding citizens and helping to maintain the public sense of justice.
To do otherwise would contribute to the growth of indifference and
cynicism regarding the duties and responsibilities of citizenship and to
an already alarming trend toward centralization of power in the hands
of a few, who, under the guise of science and treatment, often impose
their own values upon an increasingly disorganized people. Indeed, what
is now hailed as humanitarianism is frequently just public indifference
about the way in which delinquents and criminals are handled.

One must admit, however, that in our complex culture the deterrent and retributive effects are indirect and uncertain in many cases, while the return of almost all criminals to society is a real and indisputable fact. It is evident that reformation must be given an important place in our system of punishment; our society should do everything within its power to understand criminals and to create and foster in them such tendencies as make for constructive and useful lives. This is not only the most sensible and profitable way of dealing with our criminals, but also the most effective method of expanding the knowledge we already have regarding crime causation and crime prevention.

What has been said up to this point should not be interpreted to mean that the criminal should be coddled or pampered or kept in a "prison palace." We are not in any way confronted with the problem of having to choose between granting leniency or inflicting pain. As we have explained, the process of reformation inevitably involves suffering, and since liberty is highly prized in modern society, imprisonment may be an exceedingly painful experience. But the essential point here is that the process of reformation should be guided by a detailed study of what the prisoner is physically, mentally, and emotionally, as measured by the best available knowledge.

Moreover, a system of punishment in which reformation is considered to be important does not have to interfere in any way with aggressive law enforcement and effective criminal prosecution. Nor does it entail the elimination of any of the discomforts, inconvenience, and disgrace involved in the arrest, trial, and conviction of a criminal. Consequently, with such a system it is still possible to have the retribution and deterrence that society needs.

But far more important than an understanding of this is the recognition that punishment itself is only one element in the much larger system of social control that exists in society. In this larger system it is not the fear of legal penalties that keeps many persons from violating the law, but rather the desire to find love, respect, and security among relatives, friends, and business associates. This is an important form of social control, and it will always function regardless of what methods are used in dealing with criminals.

18
Methods of Punishment

VARIETY OF METHODS

Down through the ages, man's fertile imagination has devised a great variety of methods for the punishment of criminals. The most common ones have been death, physical torture, mutilation, branding, public humiliation, fines, forfeiture of property, banishment, transportation, and imprisonment; but each of these has had many forms.[1] Thus, death has been accomplished by flaying, crucifixion, beheading, hanging, impaling, drowning, and burning;[2] physical torture, by flogging, dismemberment, and starvation; public humiliation, by stocks, pillory, ducking stools, branks, and branding; and imprisonment, by confinement in dungeons, galleys, "hulks," jails, houses of correction, workhouses, and penitentiaries. Although this list is far from complete, it does indicate the wide range of forms that have been used. Few of these, however, have survived in modern society; and during the past few decades in Western civilization the principal methods of punishment have been death, whipping, transportation, fines, restitution, imprisonment, probation, and parole.

Professor Sutherland has classified the methods of punishment into the four major categories of financial loss, physical torture, social degradation (by which he referred to such penalties as confinement in the stocks and the pillory and branding), and removal from the group (in which he placed death as well as exile and imprisonment).[3] A moment's thought, however, will reveal the extent to which these categories overlap. For example, mutilation involves not only social degradation but also physical torture, and imprisonment means not only removal from the group but

[1] Walter C. Reckless, *Criminal Behavior* (New York: McGraw-Hill Book Co., Inc., 1940), pp. 265–67.

[2] During the history of the United States there is at least one case on record of burning at the stake. This occurred in South Carolina in 1825 (*Penal System Papers*, Library of the South Carolina Archives Commission, Columbia, S.C.).

[3] Edwin H. Sutherland, *Principles of Criminology* (Philadelphia: J. B. Lippincott Co., 1947), pp. 333–45.

also social degradation. But perhaps such overlapping must be the fate of any classification of the great variety of methods that have been employed to punish criminals.

MITIGATION OF PENALTIES

As we have already explained, Western civilization, with its humanitarianism, scientific progress, and impersonality of social relationships, has largely replaced capital and corporal penalties with imprisonment.[4] It is necessary now to call attention to several other factors that have contributed to this change. Thus, the democratization of society in many countries of the West has brought a greater appreciation of the individual and his freedom; and imprisonment, therefore, which involves the loss of man's highly prized freedom, has come to be regarded by him as sufficiently painful for even the most serious offenders. Then, too, industrialization has spectacularly demonstrated the value of labor and the folly of its waste. Since the penalties of death and mutilation destroy this value, sound public policy has supported their replacement with imprisonment, which makes possible the conservation of man's labor and its utilization for the service of the state. Finally, the stabilization of social life and the concentration of great units of population in urban centers have not only provided enough manpower to make the building of large prisons feasible, but also, with the accompanying decline in the infliction of capital and corporal punishments, necessitated the construction of such institutions to accommodate the increasing number of prisoners.

Yet, even before the emergence of imprisonment as the principal method of punishment, man created effective devices to mitigate the existing penalties. One of these was the right of sanctuary, which permitted an offender to find refuge in a certain city or building such as a church, where he might remain unpunished or have his penalties reduced. Gradually restricted and made inapplicable to such serious crimes as murder, rape, burglary, robbery, and arson, it eventually disappeared entirely. England abolished the right of sanctuary in 1623; but despite this, it persisted for many years thereafter in a few privileged places that defied the law of the realm.[5]

The benefit of clergy was another device used to protect the offender from full impact of the criminal law. The exemption of the clergy from secular jurisdiction was one of the privileges claimed by the Catholic Church, and during the Middle Ages its leaders acted to remove all members of the clergy from the jurisdiction of lay courts and to make them

---

[4] See Chapter 17.

[5] James F. Stephen, *A History of the Criminal Law of England* (London: Macmillan and Co., Ltd., 1883), Vol. I, pp. 491, 492.

subject to ecclesiastical courts only. In this the Church was successful, and the privilege became known as the *benefit of clergy*. Trial by an ecclesiastical court was a distinct privilege, as the Church did not use the death penalty and, in general, was more merciful. Originally only a few enjoyed the benefit of clergy in England, but gradually not only the clergy but also members of the laity who could read were entitled to its protection. However, they were permitted to claim this protection only once, and then when they did, unless they were peers or peeresses, they were burned on the left thumb. England abolished the benefit of clergy in 1827 for all except the nobility, and for them in 1841.[6]

Still another device used to reduce the severity of the criminal law was the pardon, which has been utilized for this purpose since ancient times. The authority to pardon is still vested in the chief executives of modern governments, and today its exercise is considered an essential part of the administration of criminal law.

CAPITAL PUNISHMENT

Meaning and Forms. Capital punishment is the infliction of the death penalty upon a person convicted of a serious crime. Just as men's ideas have differed regarding what crimes should be punishable with this penalty, so also have their ways of inflicting it. Indeed, it appears that men have exhausted their ingenuity in the destruction of the condemned criminal. They have hanged him, burned him, flayed him alive, boiled him in oil, thrown him to wild beasts, crucified him, drowned him, crushed him, impaled him, stoned him, strangled him, torn him apart, beheaded him, disemboweled him, and smothered him.

But mere killing has not always satisfied men's thirst for venegeance, and so sometimes, as a hideous prelude to death, they have added the most fiendish and excruciating torture. Thus, they have skinned the criminal alive and hung his body upon a sharp stake, where he remained, in agony and exposed to the hot rays of the sun and the vicious attacks of birds and insects, until death mercifully intervened. They have subjected him to slow death from insect bites. This was the terrible fate to which Mithridates, the Persian general, was condemned. He was encased in a box from which his head, hands, and feet protruded, forcibly fed with milk and honey, which was also smeared on his face, and then exposed to the sun. For seventeen days he lingered on in this horrible condition until he had been devoured alive by insects and vermin, "which swarmed about him and bred within him."[7]

[6] *Ibid.*, pp. 457–75.
[7] Frederick Howard Wines, *Punishment and Reformation* (New York: Thomas Y. Crowell Co., 1919), p. 70.

They have drawn and quartered the criminal, stretched him to his death on the rack, delivered him to the fatal embrace of the "iron maiden," broken him on the wheel, sawed him into pieces, and slowly crushed him to death beneath the weight of stones and iron. When the condemned was drawn and quartered, a horse was hitched to each of the man's legs and arms, and then he was pulled into four pieces by leading the horses in opposite directions. The rack was an engine of torture consisting of a large frame and having rollers at each end to which the limbs of the victim were fastened and between which he was stretched into eternity. The iron maiden was a hollow form shaped like a human being and made of iron or wood braced with iron strips. It was hinged to admit the victim who, as it was closed, was impaled on the spikes which studded its interior. Breaking on the wheel was accomplished by stretching the victim out on a frame resembling a wheel. His arms and legs were fastened to the frame and were broken by striking them with an iron bar. Then the broken and bloody limbs were tied across the middle of the victim, and he was whirled on the wheel, amid a scattering of gore, until life was driven from his body. A common method of cutting a man to pieces was to hang him up by his feet and then saw him in half vertically. In order to crush the condemned criminal to death, he was usually placed on a solid platform and weights were piled on his breast until he died beneath their pressure.[8]

Although men in modern society continue to inflict capital punishment they now use only a few of its forms, the most important among which are electrocution, hanging, asphyxiation, shooting, and beheading. Electrocution was first used at the Auburn State Prison in New York State on August 6, 1890.[9] It is recommended by many who argue that it provides a relatively painless method of execution, but this contention has been strongly disputed.[10] Here is a description of an electrocution given by the late Warden Lewis E. Lawes:

It takes but a matter of a minute for the executioner to apply one electrode to the calf of the right leg and another to the crown of the head, while three prison keepers fasten the straps pinioning the arms, legs and torso. The final strap adjusted, the executioner—who has now taken his place in the alcove—throws the switch which sends a killing current of man-made lightning hurtling through the prisoner's body.

As the switch is thrown into its socket there is a sputtering drone, and the body leaps as if to break the strong leather straps that hold it. Sometimes a thin grey wisp of smoke pushes itself out from under the helmet that holds

---

[8] Harry Elmer Barnes, *The Story of Punishment* (Boston: The Stratford Co., 1930), pp. 14, 15, 234; Wines, pp. 61–71.

[9] For a description of the first execution by electrocution, see the brochure, *Auburn State Prison*, published by the New York State Department of Correction (n.d.), p. 17.

[10] Barnes, pp. 243–45.

the head electrode, followed by the faint odour of burning flesh. The hands turn red, then white, and the cords of the neck stand out like steel bands. After what seems an age but is, in fact, only two minutes, during which time the initial voltage of 2,000 to 2,200 and amperage of 7 to 12 are lowered and reapplied at various intervals, the switch is pulled and the body sags back and relaxes, somewhat as a very tired man would do. As a rule, the switch is thrown only once, but sometimes a second shock is given if the attending doctors consider it advisable.[11]

Hanging has been the most widely used form of capital punishment, and it is still the one most frequently employed throughout the world today. In the past it was usually a public spectacle, and in its crudest form it merely involved the putting of a slip noose around the victim's neck, pulling him from the ground or platform, and leaving him to die of slow strangulation. During the early years of the modern period, the corpse was gibbeted, that is, it was hung in chains, and then, sometimes after being soaked in tar to preserve it from the elements, it was allowed to remain as a gruesome warning to evil-doers. At present, however, a hanging is relatively secret, and a drop or trap is used in order to break the neck of the victim and thus hasten his death. The condemned crim-inal is made to stand or sit upon a trap door in a platform which is about ten or twelve feet from the ground. Above his head is a crossbeam to which is attached a rope, and the noose formed in the lower end of this rope is put around his neck. A black cap is pulled down over his head, and, at a given signal, the trap door is released, dropping him through the opening with a jerk which is supposed to break his neck and cause instant death.

But to hang a man with the minimum of pain requires the exercise of considerable art. If the arrangement of the noose and the distance of the drop are not right, the neck may not be broken, in which case death is caused by slow strangulation, or the neck may be severely lacerated. Thus, in the hanging of one Patrick Harnet, the drop was too great and the head was virtually jerked from the body. As the victim dropped to a stand-still, a heavy gurgling sound was heard, and soon a torrent of blood poured out on the floor from the gash caused by the head's being pulled back on the shoulder.[12] It is because of such a possibility that hanging is being supplanted by electrocution and other forms of the death penalty that are more certain and supposedly less painful.

During the past few decades, asphyxiation in a lethal chamber has been adopted as a form of capital punishment by some states in the United States. The condemned person is placed in an air-tight chamber, and into

[11] From *Life and Death in Sing Sing*, by Lewis E. Lawes. Copyright 1928 by Doubleday and Company, Inc., pp. 170, 171.
[12] Barnes, p. 237.

this is sent a gas which causes painless and almost instantaneous death. It appears that this is the quickest and most humane of the various forms of the death penalty that are now being used. When a man is hanged, he may remain conscious for many minutes after the trap is released. When he is electrocuted, he may have to be given several shocks before he is dead. And when he is executed by shooting, he may not lose consciousness immediately even though his wounds are mortal. But when he is asphyxiated with lethal gas, he dies without pain and without delay, although he must still pass through the anguish of awaiting the execution.

Beheading has been one of the most generally employed forms of capital punishment and has been regarded as a relatively noble and enviable way of being sent to one's Maker. One of the earliest ways of effecting decapitation was by a two-handed and broad-bladed sword, which, when wielded swiftly and deftly, neatly dispatched the culprit. During medieval and early modern times, the block and broad axe were usually employed for beheading, and this procedure was revived in Nazi Germany, where much pomp accompanied the execution. However, the most elaborate device for beheading thus far invented is the well-known guillotine, named after Dr. Joseph Ignace Guillotin, a French physician and member of the French Revolutionary Assembly. It consists of a heavy steel blade held in position by grooves in an upright wooden frame. The blade, which is pulled to the top of the frame and then released, gains enough force in its descent to sever the head from the criminal's neck, the front of which rests in a curved depression in a block at the foot of the machine. Beheading by guillotine is still the form of capital punishment used in France.[13]

It is generally assumed that decapitation is painless, but Dr. Frederic Gaertner offers testimony to the contrary. He gives the following description of the behavior of a decapitated head, which was delivered into his custody after the execution:

Immediately after the head was severed and dropped into the basket, I took charge of it. The facial expression was that of great agony, for several minutes after decapitation. He would open his eyes, also his mouth, in the process of gaping, as if he wanted to speak to me, and I am positive he could see me for several seconds after the head was severed from the body. There is no doubt that the brain was still active. . . . His decapitated body, which was previously fastened by a strap upon a bench, was in continuous spasmodic and clonic convulsions, lasting from five to six minutes, also an indication of great suffering.[14]

Trends in Its Use. Several significant trends may be observed in the use of capital punishment during the past two centuries. One of these has

13 *Ibid.*, pp. 234–36; Wines, pp. 57–60.
14 Quoted by Barnes, pp. 235, 236.

been the tendency to abolish the death penalty. By 1962 this penalty had been virtually eliminated, either by law or tradition, in more than twenty countries. In the United States the trend to abolish capital punishment has never been very strong, although it has gathered some additional momentum during the past few years. Four states, two in the last century (Wisconsin in 1853 and Maine in 1887)[15] and two in this century (Minnesota in 1911 and Michigan in 1963) have completely abolished the death penalty and have not restored it.[16] When Alaska (in 1959) and Hawaii (in 1959) entered the Union, they had already removed the death penalty from their statutes. Thus by 1964 six states had completely abolished capital punishment, although two others (Rhode Island and North Dakota) prescribed it in only very exceptional cases.[17] Delaware, the first state to abolish capital punishment in about forty years, took this step in 1958 but reintroduced the death penalty in 1961.

A second trend can be found in the reduction of the number of capital crimes. England in the eighteenth century had more than two hundred capital crimes, but in 1962 she had only four major ones. In the United States all the states have a combined total of only eight major capital crimes,[18] no one state having all eight of these and most of them having one, two, three, or four.

A third trend has been the substitution of a permissive death penalty for the mandatory one. As a result, in almost every jurisdiction in the United States the jury or the court, or both, in all cases have the power of deciding whether the convicted person must be executed or whether he may be given a sentence less than death.

A fourth trend is reflected in the reduction of the number of executions. During the past few decades of this century this trend in the United States has varied from state to state and has fluctuated for the country

[15] Maine abolished the death penalty in 1876, reintroduced it, but in 1887 again abolished it.

[16] Michigan abolished capital punishment in 1846 for all crimes except treason and eliminated the death penalty for this offense on May 10, 1963—substituting life imprisonment for it. Some other states have abolished capital punishment but have later restored it. Among these have been Iowa, Kansas, Colorado, Washington, Oregon, South Dakota, Arizona, Missouri, and Delaware.

On November 3, 1964, just before this book went to press, the citizens of Oregon voted to abolish capital punishment in that state. Oregon, therefore, became the ninth state which either no longer imposes the death penalty or prescribes it in only very exceptional cases.

[17] North Dakota prescribes the death penalty for treason and for first-degree murder committed by a prisoner serving a life term for first-degree murder; Rhode Island, for murder by a prisoner serving a life sentence.

[18] These major capital crimes are treason, first-degree murder, kidnapping, rape, armed robbery, burglary, arson, and train wrecking. Recently the sale of narcotics has been made a capital crime in several jurisdictions, and some states have statutes on exceptional capital crimes such as attempts to kill the President of the United States.

as a whole.[19] Table 4 shows the number of executions in the United States, classified by race, for each year during the period 1930 to 1963, inclusive.

Table 4. Prisoners executed under civil authority in the United States, by race, 1930–63.

Year	Total	White	Negro	Other
1930	155	90	65	0
1931	153	77	72	4
1932	140	62	75	3
1933	160	77	81	2
1934	168	65	102	1
1935	199	119	77	3
1936	195	92	101	2
1937	147	69	74	4
1938	190	96	92	2
1939	159	80	77	2
1940	124	49	75	0
1941	123	59	63	1
1942	147	67	80	0
1943	131	54	74	3
1944	120	47	70	3
1945	117	41	75	1
1946	131	46	84	1
1947	153	42	111	0
1948	119	35	82	2
1949	119	50	67	2
1950	82	40	42	0
1951	105	57	47	1
1952	83	36	47	0
1953	62	30	31	1
1954	81	38	42	1
1955	76	44	32	0
1956	65	21	43	1
1957	65	34	31	0
1958	49	20	28	1
1959	49	16	33	0
1960	56	21	35	0
1961	42	20	22	0
1962	47	28	19	0
1963	21	13	8	0
Totals	3,833	1,735	2,057	41
Per cent	100.0	45.3	53.7	1.0

SOURCE: The figures for this table were drawn from Table 1 of *National Prisoner Statistics*, No. 34 (May, 1964), Federal Bureau of Prisons, Washington, D.C.

[19] In a number of states, the death penalty has been virtually abolished in practice. Thus during thirty-four years from 1930 to 1963, inclusive, there were 4 executions in Vermont, 1 in New Hampshire, 0 in Rhode Island, 0 in Michigan, 0 in North Dakota, 1 in South Dakota, 4 in Nebraska, 11 in Kansas, 12 in Delaware, 6 in Montana, 3 in Idaho, 6 in Wyoming, and 8 in New Mexico.

A fifth trend can be seen in the exclusion of the public from executions. Today in the various jurisdictions of this country, Canada, Great Britain, and many other countries, the number and type of witnesses attending executions are highly restricted by law and administrative regulations.

A sixth trend is manifested in the adoption of relatively swift and painless methods of execution. In the United States this has led to the gradual replacement of hanging with electrocution and lethal gas. Thus, in 1962, the District of Columbia and twenty-three states had adopted electrocution. Eleven other states had provided for execution by lethal gas, and in one (Utah) of the eight states[20] where hanging was still used, the convicted person was permitted to choose shooting instead of hanging.[21]

Arguments For and Against. The arguments advanced here should be considered against the background of the broader and more fundamental discussion of the philosophy of punishment presented in Chapter 17. The most important arguments for and against capital punishment may be summarized as follows:

1. THE ARGUMENT OF RETRIBUTION. One argument advanced in favor of capital punishment is that the criminal should die because he has committed a terrible crime, and that only his death will satisfy the public and keep it from taking the law into its own hands. Opponents of the death penalty, however, contend that the evidence does not support this argument. The tendency, they claim, has been to reduce the number of capital crimes and to make the method of execution as painless as possible. Indeed, in the United States only eighteen states prescribe the death penalty for so revolting a crime as rape; and only seven, for the dangerous crime of armed robbery.[22] Thus, the opponents conclude, the law does not reflect a strong demand for the death penalty even in serious crimes. Furthermore, studies do not show that there is a positive correlation between

[20] The eight states still using hanging were Delaware, Idaho, Iowa, Kansas, Montana, New Hampshire, Utah, and Washington. Although Rhode Island and North Dakota prescribe capital punishment for certain very exceptional offenses, these states have not used any method of execution for many years.

[21] Frank E. Hartung, "Trends in the Use of Capital Punishment," *The Annals of the American Academy of Political and Social Science,* CCLXXXIV (Nov., 1952), 8–19 (this entire issue of the *Annals* is devoted to articles on capital crimes and the death penalty); Sol Rubin, Henry Weihofen, George Edwards, Simon Rosenzweig, *The Law of Criminal Correction* (St. Paul, Minn.: West Publishing Co., 1963), pp. 315–41; *Capital Punishment* (New York: United Nations, Department of Economic and Social Affairs, 1962), pp. 5–25, 71–75; Leon Radzinowicz, *A History of English Criminal Law* (New York: The Macmillan Co., 1948), Vol. I, pp. 3–8; James A. McCafferty, "Major Trends in the Use of Capital Punishment," *Federal Probation,* XXV (Sept., 1961), 15–21.

[22] More states (forty-one) prescribe the death penalty for murder than for any other crime.

lynchings and the abolition of capital punishment.[23] In fact, lynchings no longer constitute a serious problem in the United States.

But, reply the advocates of capital punishment, retribution should not be made synonymous with revenge. The law dispenses retribution according to the gravity of the offense as measured by the moral code. Capital punishment thus upholds this code and by a spectacular exhibition helps to unify society against crime. The value of the life of one individual ranks lower in the moral code than other values—such as the security of the state, the sanctity of the home, and the life of the innocent victim—and may have to be sacrificed for the preservation of these values. The criminal law recognizes this possibility and justifies homicide in such cases as self-defense, the prevention of a felony, and the lawful arrest of a felon. Just as the individual has the right to defend his life against unlawful aggression, so the state has the right to defend itself against external enemies by waging war and against serious internal enemies by inflicting capital punishment. And, insist these advocates, the judge who orders an execution is no more guilty of playing God than the health officer who quarantines a town to keep its inhabitants from spreading deadly germs. What we need, then, is more, not fewer, executions.

But, retort the opponents of the death penalty, even if all this is conceded, capital punishment does not—in fact, cannot—effectively uphold the moral code and unify society. Some of the most serious crimes no longer carry the death penalty. Many offenders who are convicted of capital crimes are given some punishment other than the death penalty. Few executions take place each year. The general public is excluded from executions, and no special effort is made to give them publicity. And, furthermore, the impersonality of social relationships and the humanitarianism in our culture would interfere with any move to change this situation. The supporters of the death penalty, however, remain unconvinced. They believe that all this would change if the public were made to understand the seriousness of the problem of crime and the criminal law were more vigorously and efficiently enforced and administered.

2. THE ARGUMENT OF ECONOMY. Some who favor the death penalty argue that it is cheaper than the cost of maintaining a prisoner for life, or for a long period of time, at the taxpayers' expense. Opponents, however, contend that much of the weight of this argument disappears when it is carefully examined. A life-termer, if given the opportunity, can help to support himself, contribute to the maintenance of his dependents, and, if necessary, make payments to the victim of his crime or to the relatives

---

[23] See Raymond T. Bye, *Capital Punishment in the United States* (Philadelphia: The Committee on Philanthropic Labor of Philadelphia Yearly Meeting of Friends, 1919), p. 66.

of the victim. Furthermore, how far should the argument of economy be pressed? If it is valid in the case of those who are now condemned to die, may it not also be applied to all prisoners who are not self-supporting? Obviously, the possibility of such executions cannot be seriously considered. The humanitarian feelings of the American public would not tolerate it. Finally, one cannot ignore the fact that the state incurs considerable expenses in the conviction, sentencing, and execution of a prisoner who is fighting for his life.

3. THE ARGUMENT OF PROTECTION. A third argument for the death penalty is that it protects society from dangerous criminals by insuring that they neither commit other crimes nor spread their undesirable hereditary traits. This contention, assert opponents, can be met with strong counterarguments. The possibility of releasing dangerous prisoners into the community could be greatly reduced by improving the rehabilitation facilities of our correctional institutions and by strengthening our pardon and parole procedure.

Then, too, although many criminals who commit capital crimes have mental or physical defects, so have many prisoners who have been convicted of noncapital crimes. Besides, it is one thing to say this and quite another to say that such defects are the cause of criminal activities. Sometimes physical and mental defects do contribute to crime, but on the other hand, many persons who have them never come into conflict with the law at all. The fact is that crime is a very complex phenomenon and is produced in the individual by the interaction of many factors as he seeks adjustment with his environment. Further complicating this situation is the fact that, although heredity may cause a certain type of defect in one individual, environment may cause the same type of defect in another; and at the present time science in many cases cannot determine which caused the defect. Moreover, since many persons who are apparently normal may carry recessive defective genes and consequently may have defective children, it is clear that even if all persons who have hereditary physical and mental defects could be identified and were killed, the next generation would produce a whole new group of defective individuals.

Besides, in the United States today we are executing only a very small percentage of all persons who commit capital crimes. In 1962 the estimated number of murder and nonnegligent manslaughter cases totaled 8,404,[24] while the executions for all capital crimes amounted to only 47.[25] And such factors as wealth, education, and position rather than those

[24] Federal Bureau of Investigation, *Uniform Crime Reports, 1962*, p. 35.
[25] Federal Bureau of Prisons, *National Prisoner Statistics*, No. 32 (April, 1963), Table 1.

that make persons a threat to society may determine whether criminals are executed. There is always present, also, the possibility that an innocent man may be sent to his death.

4. THE ARGUMENT OF DETERRENCE. The most frequently advanced and widely accepted argument in favor of the death penalty is that the threat of its infliction deters people from committing offenses. In attacking this argument, opponents admit at the outset that human behavior can be influenced through fear, and that since man tends to fear death, it is possible to use capital punishment as a deterrent. But the real question, they explain, is whether individuals think of the death penalty *before* they act and whether they are thereby deterred from committing crimes. For an analysis of this question and other important considerations regarding the deterrent influence of punishment, regardless of the method used, the reader is referred to the discussion of the philosophy of punishment in Chapter 17. Here it is necessary only to call attention to a few additional points that opponents of capital punishment emphasize.

It is clear, they argue, that the way in which the death penalty is being administered in the United States is not fitted to secure the greatest deterrent influence for the death penalty. In addition to the uncertainty of detection and apprehension, long delays often occur in court procedures as each side, spurred on by the fact that a human life is at stake, furiously fights for victory. It is also true that when the penalty may be death, some juries are not inclined to convict, and some witnesses are not willing to testify. Furthermore, the death penalty is almost always permissive rather than mandatory. Moreover, only a very small percentage of all persons who commit capital crimes are executed, and when executions do take place, they are closed to the general public and made as swift and painless as possible. Finally, although the results of the best statistical studies are not entirely conclusive, they do indicate that capital punishment in the United States does not have any significant effect on the frequency of crimes punishable with death or the safety of law-enforcement officers. Similar studies conducted throughout Western civilization point to the same conclusion regarding other countries, insist the opponents.[26] They conclude their case by stating that the death penalty probably can never be made a deterrent, because "its very life seems to depend on its rarity and, therefore, on its ineffectiveness as a deterrent."[27]

Proponents of the death penalty, however, are undaunted. They not only stress the inconclusiveness of the existing statistics but also contend that capital punishment exerts a deterrent influence beyond that caused

[26] Karl F. Schuessler, "The Deterrent Influence of the Death Penalty," *The Annals of the American Academy of Political and Social Science,* CCLXXXIV (Nov., 1952), 54–62; George B. Vold, "Can the Death Penalty Prevent Crime?" *The Prison Journal,* XII (Oct., 1932), 4–9; Sutherland, pp. 563–66.

[27] Thorsten Sellin, "Common Sense and the Death Penalty," *The Prison Journal,* XII (Oct., 1932), 12.

by the threat of death. By labeling certain offenses as capital crimes, it helps to create attitudes in opposition to these crimes and in support of the moral code and the law. And, contend the proponents, this influence extends across the boundaries of the states that have the death penalty into the states that have abolished it, and thus the latter in their weakness actually benefit by the firm and wise stand taken by the former.

Conclusion. The movement against capital punishment in the United States has gained some strength during the past few years but, nevertheless, it has won few victories in the legislative bodies of this country. In general, the Congress and the great majority of the state legislatures want to keep the death penalty in the law for a few serious crimes, such as first-degree murder and treason, and in this position they appear to be supported by many, perhaps most, Americans.[28]

CORPORAL PUNISHMENT

Meaning and Forms. Corporal punishment means the infliction of physical pain upon a convicted criminal. During the medieval and early modern periods some form of corporal punishment less than death was usually employed in cases that did not involve capital crimes. Flogging, branding, mutilating, confinement in the stocks or the pillory, and "ducking" were among the most popular types of this punishment.[29]

Branding was often used to burn the first letter of his offense on the forehead, cheek, or hand of the criminal. This was a common form of the penalty in the American Colonies, where, as the severity of the criminal code was mitigated, branding was replaced in some cases by the wearing of badges indicating the crimes committed. So the wearing of the odious "scarlet letter" was part of the sentence imposed upon the adulteress. Closely associated with branding was the piercing of the tongue with a hot iron, which was sometimes prescribed for such crimes as perjury and

[28] Edwin M. Borchard, *Convicting the Innocent* (Garden City, N.Y.: Garden City Publishing Co., 1932); *Capital Punishment*, pp. 53–68; Richard M. Gerstein, "A Prosecutor Looks at Capital Punishment," *Journal of Criminal Law, Criminology, and Police Science*, LI (July–Aug., 1960), 252–56; Arthur Koestler, *Reflections on Hanging* (New York: The Macmillan Co., 1957); John Laurence Pritchard, *A History of Capital Punishment* (New York: Citadel Press, 1960); Rubin, Weihofen, Edwards, Rosenzweig, pp. 342–57; Thorsten Sellin, *The Death Penalty* (Philadelphia: The American Law Institute, 1959); Margaret Wilson, *The Crime of Punishment* (New York: Harcourt, Brace and Co., Inc., 1931), pp. 138–88; Marvin E. Wolfgang, *Patterns in Criminal Homicide* (Philadelphia: University of Pennsylvania, 1958).

[29] For a description of these punishments, reference may be made to William Andrews, *Old-Time Punishments* (Hull, England: W. Andrews and Co., 1890); George Ives, *A History of Penal Methods* (London, Eng.: Stanley Paul and Co., 1914); Harry Elmer Barnes, *The Story of Punishment* (Boston: The Stratford Co., 1930); and Alice M. Earle, *Curious Punishments of Bygone Days* (Chicago: S. Stone and Co., 1896).

blasphemy. Mutilation was another widespread form of punishment, and it frequently involved the removal of the offending member. Thus, thieves lost their hands; perjurers, their tongues; spies, their eyes; and sex criminals, their genitals. The cutting off of ears and hands persisted down into the eighteenth century. Such punishments as these, in which society strove to adapt the penalty to the particular crime committed, are sometimes called "poetic punishments." Even in cases where it was difficult to repay the offender in kind, our ancestors succeeded in contriving many chastisements that were associable equivalents. Thus, a baker who sold loaves which were short of weight was exhibited with the bread tied around his neck; and a fishmonger convicted of selling bad fish was paraded with a collar of stinking smelts slung over his shoulders.

Confinement in the stocks or pillory was the lot of many offenders, and to this indignity was often added that of being pelted with garbage, filth, and stones thrown by the jeering crowd that had come to witness the culprit's degradation. The stocks were a wooden frame in which the feet or the feet and hands of the offender were fastened. The pillory consisted of a frame of adjustable parts erected on a post and having holes in which the head and hands of the criminal were locked. It was not abolished in Delaware until 1905 and was last used there on February 11 of that year, when two men were confined in it for having committed felonies in New Castle County.[30] Sometimes the ears of the offender were nailed to the pillory and when he was released, they were either torn loose or cut off. Such was the fate of Negro Dick in Delaware. He was convicted of assault with intent to ravish, and on August 11, 1789, he was sentenced to pay the costs of the prosecution, stand four hours in the pillory with both ears nailed thereto, and finally, before being taken down from the pillory, have both ears cut off close to his head.[31]

The ducking stool was a device fixed on the end of a long pole. The offender was strapped in and then plunged into water. Usually employed for the punishment of common scolds, gossips, and disorderly women, it was sometimes replaced with the brank, which had the peculiar merit of silencing the offender during his punishment. The brank, or dame's bridle, was a contrivance which fitted over the head of the offender. It had a metal plate, occasionally sharpened or covered with spikes, which was put into the person's mouth so that it pressed against his tongue and effectively kept him quiet.

Flogging has been the most widely used form of corporal punishment and is the only one that has survived in Western civilization. Various instruments have been employed to administer floggings. Rods, whips,

[30] Robert G. Caldwell, *Red Hannah* (Philadelphia: University of Pennsylvania Press, 1947), p. 38.
[31] *Ibid.*, p. 11.

The Female Culprit

The Shortest Culprit

Sketch of the whipping post and pillory at Georgetown, Delaware, in 1876. (*Harper's Weekly*, November 18, 1876)

canes, straps, and the cat-o'-nine-tails, which consisted of knotted cords or thongs, usually nine, attached to a handle—all have been applied to the bare backs of criminals. Probably the most fiendishly cruel was the Russian knout; this was an instrument made of a number of dried and hardened thongs of rawhide interwoven with wires, which were often hooked and sharpened on the ends so that they would rip and tear the flesh. A severe flogging with the knout almost invariably produced death.[32]

The flogging of certain criminals is still legal in some European and Asiatic countries and in the state of Delaware in the United States.[33] However, England abolished corporal punishment in 1948; Canada terminated its use in 1957; and Maryland, which had prescribed it for wife-beating, removed it from its code in 1953. In Delaware, however, public whippings may be administered at the discretion of the court for twenty-five different crimes.[34] Among these are poisoning with intent to murder, maiming by lying in wait, assault with intent to ravish, wife-beating, robbery, assault to rob, burning of certain kinds, various forms of burglary, breaking and entering, larceny, knowingly receiving certain types of stolen property, embezzlement, counterfeiting, wilfully and feloniously showing false lights to cause a vessel to be wrecked, unlawfully obstructing railroad tracks so as to make them unsafe, perjury or subornation of perjury, and tampering with, altering, or destroying legislative bills or acts.[35]

During the period 1900 to 1942 inclusive in Delaware, 7,302 prisoners were convicted of crimes for which they might have been whipped. Of these, however, only 22.0 per cent were actually lashed, and although the percentage whipped was 70.4 in 1900, it declined to 6.7 per cent in 1942. Of the prisoners who received lashes, 68.1 per cent were Negro, 86.5 per cent had been convicted of either breaking and entering or larceny, and 48.3 per cent belonged to the age group twenty-six to fifty inclusive.[36]

Although the movement to abolish Delaware's whipping post has not achieved its objective, some progress has been made. In 1889 the whip-

---

[32] Barnes, *The Story of Punishment*, p. 58.

[33] The term "flogging" as used here refers to that which is inflicted as part of the sentence of the court, and it should be distinguished from that which is employed as a disciplinary measure in a prison, the latter still being permitted in some of the prisons of the United States.

[34] In 1959, the legislature of Delaware passed a bill making whipping mandatory for the crime of robbery; but Governor Boggs vetoed the bill, and the legislature did not override the veto.

[35] Caldwell, Appendix A, Table 1, pp. 119–21.

[36] *Ibid.*, pp. 57, 69, 70, 129. Although a much higher percentage of the Negroes than the whites among those who had been convicted of crimes punishable with whipping were whipped, the evidence did not show that the courts discriminated against the Negro in the use of the whipping post (*ibid.*, pp. 73, 74).

ping of women was abolished; in 1905 the pillory was eliminated; in 1925 the use of the "post" was placed entirely within the discretionary powers of the court; in 1941 petty larceny was removed from the list of crimes punishable with whipping. Thus, stripped of many of its dramatic aspects, the whipping post is only a shadow of its former self, and it has become, therefore, much more difficult to arouse public opinion against its use.[37] It is possible that the obstacles that block the movement to abolish Red Hannah,[38] Delaware's whipping post, may be overcome; but it now seems that the process of attrition, by which the use of the "post" has been reduced, will go on until corporal punishment, although still prescribed by law, will no longer be inflicted.

Arguments For and Against Whipping. The arguments presented in favor of whipping are that it is retributive, that it is economical, that it unifies public opinion against the criminal, that it reforms the offender, and that it deters others from committing crimes. Much of what was said in the discussion of the philosophy of punishment (Chapter 17) and the death penalty is relevant here, and in addition certain other considerations specifically applicable to whipping have been emphasized by opponents of the "post."

In Delaware, although the whippings are made public by law, opponents state that few persons attend the whippings and little is done to give them publicity. In fact, the opponents explain, the photographing of whippings has been illegal since 1935. Besides, the criminals are not severely whipped even though the law specifies that the lashes be well laid on the bare back. Certainly these facts do not lend support to the contention that whippings are retributive and conducive to solidifying public opinion against crime and criminals. Furthermore, it is difficult to understand why whipping is economical. Delaware's criminal code prescribes imprisonment for every crime for which whipping may be inflicted, although wife-beaters may be sentenced to pay a fine instead of being sent to prison. And the term of imprisonment is not shortened when a whipping is included in the sentence. Thus, the expense of maintaining prisoners in Delaware is not affected in any significant way by the use of the whipping post.

Moreover, continue the opponents, the facts do not substantiate the argument that the "post" reforms. Of 320 offenders whipped in New Castle County, Delaware, during the period 1920 and 1939 inclusive, 61.9 per cent were again convicted of some crime after their first whipping and before the end of 1942, and of those who were whipped at least twice

37 *Ibid.*, pp. 51, 61, 67, 68.
38 Many years ago the "post" in southern Delaware was painted red, and the Negroes there used to call it "Red Hannah." When a prisoner was whipped, they would say that he had "hugged Red Hannah."

in this group of 320 offenders, 65.1 per cent were again convicted of some crime after their second whipping and before the end of 1942. A large proportion of the subsequent crimes were serious crimes for which whipping might have been inflicted. On the other hand, of the 516 prisoners who were convicted in New Castle County, Delaware, during 1928, 1932, 1936, and 1940 of crimes for which they might have been whipped but were not, 52.3 per cent were again convicted of some crime before the end of 1944. Thus, it will be seen that the amount of recidivism was not only great among those who had been whipped, but also actually greater than it was among those who might have been whipped but were not.

The opponents of the whipping post contend that, in view of all that has been said up to this point, the argument of deterrence does not seem impressive. If the actual experience of a whipping is not effective in keeping those who are so punished from again committing some crime, then, insist the opponents, it is difficult to understand how the mere possibility of a whipping can exert a deterrent influence. The falsity of the claim that the "post" prevents crime in Delaware becomes even more apparent when it is realized that very few of the criminals who might be whipped are actually so punished. In 1941 only 5.9 per cent of such persons were whipped, in 1942 the percentage was only 6.7, and from 1953 to 1963, inclusive, no one was whipped.[39] Under such circumstances, if criminals think of the lash at all, they will certainly be inclined to take the slight risk of being sent to the "post."

Fortunately, conclude the opponents, two other studies have been made within recent years to determine the effectiveness of whipping as a punishment for criminals. In 1937 a committee was appointed to consider the question of corporal punishment in England, Wales, and Scotland. After a careful study, this committee decided that whipping had not been effective and recommended "the repeal of all existing powers to impose sentences of corporal punishment on persons convicted on indictment.[40] In 1956 a similar committee, after declaring that corporal punishment had failed in Canada, recommended that it be abolished in

---

[39] Letter dated December 13, 1963, from the Acting Director of Corrections of Delaware. In 1963 the supreme court of Delaware declared that public whipping did not violate the provisions of the state and federal constitutions that prohibit cruel and unusual punishments. The ruling came on an appeal of a man sentenced to twenty lashes for having violated the conditions of his probation (*Cannon v. The State of Delaware*, No. 30, 1963). This case, however, was remanded to the lower court for a new hearing.

[40] *Report of the Departmental Committee on Corporal Punishment,* presented by the Secretary for the Home Department to Parliament by Command of His Majesty, March, 1938 (Printed and Published by His Majesty's Stationery Office, London), p. 94.

that country.[41] Thus, on balance, it appears that the retention of whipping cannot be justified by the experience of Delaware, Great Britain, or Canada.

TRANSPORTATION

Transportation in the criminal law means the removal of the convict from his own country to another, usually, a penal colony, there to remain under some form of restraint for a prescribed period. It has been used in various ways by many countries, and although it is a product of modern times, its precursors in Western civilization can be found in some of the penal practices of the ancient world. In the Greco-Roman period, criminals were frequently sent away to mines or quarries, and many were put to sea as galley slaves, a practice which continued through the Middle Ages down into early modern times.

Portugal, Spain, Italy, Holland, and Denmark in Europe, and Chile, Ecuador, and Mexico in Latin America have employed transportation to a certain extent in dealing with some of their criminals, but it reached its greatest development in the hands of the English, French, and Russians. In England the first modern legislation authorizing transportation was enacted in 1597, but it is doubtful whether many criminals were punished by this method until after the first few decades of the seventeenth century had passed.[42] The obsolescence of the galley, the decline in the use of the death penalty, and the growth of crime due to widespread social changes had greatly increased the number of prisoners in England's already inadequate jails. The transportation of convicts to America not only provided the mother country with an acceptable method of reducing its jail population but also gave to the colonies a supply of much needed labor. England continued to send its convicts to the New World until the beginning of the American Revolution, and it is estimated that approximately 50,000 had been transported by that time.[43]

The elimination of America as a receptacle for convicts produced a new crisis in England's penal system. The jails were again overcrowded, and many prisoners were sent to the dreaded, unhealthful, dismal "hulks," or prison ships, anchored in the various rivers and ports of the British Isles. Finally, after some wild and fruitless proposals for the solution of the penal problem had been made by members of Parliament, the transportation of convicts to Australia began in 1787, and by 1867, when the practice was abandoned, an estimated 135,000 criminals had been sent

[41] *Corporal Punishment in Delaware* (Wilmington, Del.: The Prisoners' Aid Society of Delaware, 1961).
[42] Ives, pp. 107–23.
[43] Wilson, pp. 94–100.

to England's penal colonies on the other side of the world.[44] One of the most famous of these was located on Norfolk Island, about a thousand miles to the east of Australia, where Captain Maconochie in 1840 introduced a program of reform which proved to be an important step toward the establishment of the modern parole system.[45]

The annals of England's years of transportation are filled with ghastly tales of brutality, sordidness, desperation, and depravity. For example, here is a grisly excerpt from one told by a witness at the scene of a flogging in an Australian convict station:

I saw a man walk across the yard with the blood that had run from his lacerated flesh squashing out of his shoes at every step he took. A dog was licking the blood off the triangles, and the ants were carrying away great pieces of human flesh that the lash had scattered about the ground. . . . The scourger's feet had worn a deep hole in the ground by the violence with which he whirled himself round on it so as to strike the quivering and wealed back, out of which stuck the sinews, white, ragged, and swollen. The infliction was one hundred lashes at about half-minute time, so as to extend the punishment through nearly an hour. . . . They had a pair of scourgers who gave each other spell and spell about, and they were bespattered with blood like a couple of butchers.[46]

The strenuous opposition to transportation by the free settlers in Australia is cited as the chief reason for its abandonment by England, but important, too, were its great expense and its failure as a method of punishment.[47]

France has transported convicts to Africa and New Caledonia, far off in the South Pacific; but her most important penal colonies were in French Guiana on the northern coast of South America. Like the English, the French, after a history of dismal failure and appalling degradation, which began about the middle of the nineteenth century, have abandoned transportation as a method of punishment. The last of her penal colonies, located in Guiana and including the infamous Devil's Island, were abolished during World War II.[48] Soviet Russia, however, following the example set by the Tzars, has continued to exile convicts to Siberia, and apparently the millions who have been sent there since the revolution of 1917 have been subjected to treatment as brutal and degrading as any imposed by Imperial Russia.[49]

[44] Ives, pp. 123–63; Wines, pp. 168–77.
[45] See Chapter 28.
[46] Quoted by Ives, p. 152.
[47] *Ibid.*, pp. 163–70; Wilson, pp. 100–37.
[48] Wines, pp. 177–81. See also René Belbenoit, *Dry Guillotine* (New York: Dutton, 1937); and Mrs. Blair Miles, *Condemned to Devil's Island* (London: Jonathan Cape, 1928).
[49] Wines, pp. 181–86; George Kennan, *Siberia and the Exile System* (New York: The Century Co., 1891). See also Margarete Buber, *Under Two Dictators* (New York: Dodd, Mead and Co., Inc., 1951); and Elinor Lipper, *Eleven Years in Soviet Prison Camps* (Chicago: Henry Regnery Co., 1951).

In spite of this long record of failure, transportation still finds favor with some who argue: (1) that it provides an opportunity for the criminal to begin life anew away from the old environment and outside an institution; (2) that it makes possible normal family life, which cannot be allowed in a prison; and (3) that it permits a prisoner to support himself and his dependents. However, those who oppose transportation contend: (1) that it is difficult to find unoccupied lands which are suitable for penal colonies; (2) that free settlers will always object to having convicts near them and their families; (3) that it is impossible to build a normal community composed almost entirely of those who have already failed in society; (4) that it is highly questionable whether children should be reared in such an environment; (5) that the isolation of a penal colony hides it from the view of the public and thus tends to encourage brutal treatment and sadistic administrative practices; and (6) that it is doubtful whether a group of convicts, many of whom are certain to be unskilled and poorly educated, can become self-supporting. In view of the fact that probation, modern correctional institutions, and adequate parole and release procedures can do everything that transportation can do, and more effectively, it does not appear that there is any place for transportation in a modern correctional program.

Banishment is somewhat like transportation in that it compels a criminal to leave a city, place, or country for a specified period of time. However, banishment merely forbids the return of a person before the expiration of the sentence, while transportation involves the deprivation of liberty after the convict arrives at the place to which he is sent. Banishment has always been employed in some way by organized societies, and several forms of it are to be found in the United States today. Thus, aliens who commit crimes under certain circumstances may be deported, and offenders may sometimes be given the choice of leaving a town, county, or state within a stipulated number of hours or of being imprisoned. The latter is sometimes called "sunset parole," or "floating," since it is often used in handling tramps or "floaters," and often involves the unethical shifting of responsibility from one community to another.

FINES

A fine is a pecuniary penalty imposed upon a person convicted of a violation of the law. The imposition of financial penalties in the form of a fine or forfeiture of property has been a common method of punishment for a long time in Western civilization. Under the old English common law, a criminal might suffer not only the death penalty but also the total forfeiture of lands and goods, and today vehicles, machinery, and equipment used in violation of the law may be confiscated and sold at public auction.

At first, criminals were not fined by the court, but in some cases they were permitted to pay a certain sum as a substitute for the penalty imposed. This meant, in effect, that the offender made an end, *finem facere*, to his imprisonment; hence, the derivation of the term "fine." In the modern sense of the term, that is, an original penalty imposed by the court, fines were not used in England until the sixteenth century.

In the United States fines are by far the most common penalty imposed by our courts. They may be used as a supplement to imprisonment or as a substitute for it, and their amount is usually determined at the discretion of the judge, who fixes it between the limits set by the legislature. Excessive fines, however, are prohibited by the Constitution of the United States and the constitutions of the several states. If the prisoner cannot pay the fine, he may be imprisoned and compelled to serve a term which is considered equivalent to the amount of the fine; but in such cases an increasing number of courts are placing the offender on probation and permitting him to pay his fine in installments.

Those who favor fines argue: (1) that they are economical for they cost little to administer and do not require the maintenance of prisoners; (2) that they provide a source of revenue for the state, county, or city; (3) that they do not interfere with the occupation or the business of a person and so do not affect the financial support of his dependents; (4) that they do not stigmatize him, endanger his self-respect or self-initiative, or disrupt his family life as does imprisonment and therefore, do not create problems of readjustment in the community; (5) that they do not expose the individual to the corrupting influence of hardened criminals; (6) that they are flexible and can be easily adjusted to the nature of the offense and the character and the economic status of the person; (7) that they strike at a fundamental interest of an individual—his economic security—and consequently are an effective deterrent; (8) that they are the only penalties that are completely revocable in cases where mistakes are made; (9) that they can be utilized, in part at least, to compensate the victim of the crime for his loss; and (10) that they are one of the few methods that can be employed to punish legal persons such as corporations, which cannot be imprisoned or subjected to corporal punishment.

On the other hand, those who oppose fines state: (1) that in practice they tend to be adjusted to the offense regardless of the economic status of the person and, therefore, bear more heavily on the poor; (2) that often they must be paid by relatives or friends, who thus carry the burden, instead of by the offender; (3) that they are customarily used to punish habitual offenders, such as alcoholics, drug addicts, prostitutes, and pickpockets, upon whom they exert no reformative influence; (4) that they are not usually large enough to offset the economic gain of an illegal act, and so such offenders as gamblers, bootleggers, and prostitutes, upon whom they are often imposed, may regard them as one of the expenses of their lucrative business and may actually increase their activities to secure reimbursement; and (5) that they are easily manipulated for political and dishonest purposes, since they can be publicly imposed to create a good impression and later secretly remitted to friends, political supporters, and those willing to pay for such favors.[50]

These objections are serious, it is true, but they are directed primarily at the evils that have crept into the administration of fines rather than at their continued use. Fines have an important role to play in law enforcement, but they must be used with discrimination and understanding. They function best in the handling of cases of minor offenders who have been guilty of careless or selfish technical infractions of the law to which no serious moral stigma is attached, such as the less important violations of traffic and licensing regulations. They should be adjusted not only to the nature of the offense but also to the ability of the person to pay, so that they will not be treated lightly by the rich and will not be an inequitable burden to the poor. If the person cannot pay his fine, he should not be jailed, which is contrary to the original purpose of the fine and amounts to imprisonment for poverty, but should be placed on probation and permitted to pay it in installments. If he is the kind of person who cannot be trusted to do this, then he should not be fined at all, but should be dealt with in some other way. Furthermore, fines should not be used in dealing with habitual offenders, like prostitutes, drug addicts, and alcoholics. Case studies should be made of such persons to discover, if possible, the causes of their difficulties, and programs of correction should then be formulated in the light of the findings.[51]

RESTITUTION

Restitution is an act done by order of the criminal court and consists of the restoration of stolen property to its rightful owner, or the payment of a sum to the victim of the crime to compensate him for any loss that he has suffered, or both. This method of punishment may be used to supplement imprisonment or as a substitute for it and may be derived from all or part of a fine or imposed independently of any other penalty.

[50] Sutherland, pp. 572–76; Albert Morris, *Criminology* (New York: Longmans, Green and Co., Inc., 1934), pp. 297–99; Charles H. Miller, "The Place of the Fine in Modern Penology," *Proceedings of the American Prison Association, 1951*, pp. 208–15; Stephen, Vol. I, pp. 57, 84, 104, 122–124, 132; Rubin, Weihofen, Edwards, Rosenzweig, pp. 221–65.

[51] *Guides for Sentencing* (New York: National Probation and Parole Association, 1957), pp. 22, 23; *Model Penal Code, Proposed Official Draft* (Philadelphia: The American Law Institute, 1962), Section 702.

The victim of a crime may go to the civil courts in order to obtain compensation for any loss caused by the crime, but if he does this, he may find himself confronted with some serious obstacles. The expense of a civil suit may be more than he can afford, or the criminal may be insolvent or may have successfully concealed or disposed of the stolen property. Thus, the victim of the crime may find himself in the baffling position of having cooperated with the court to bring the criminal to justice and to protect the public, but at the same time of having no adequate remedy for his own loss. Knowing this, professional thieves seek to deal directly with the victim and offer to restore the property in return for the promise that charges will not be pressed. Since many victims are more interested in regaining their property than in supporting law enforcement, a considerable number of criminals undoubtedly avoid prosecution in this way. To rescue the victim from this predicament and to insure the punishment of more offenders, there is growing support for the wider use of restitution by the criminal court.

If the offender is solvent, his property should be attached when proceedings against him are begun so that he can be compelled to make restitution by order of the court. If the offender is insolvent and he is imprisoned, little can be done at present to compensate the victim for his loss since prisoners receive so little for their work in our correctional institutions. However, if a schedule of higher wages for prisoners were established—and this appears to be a much needed reform—then deductions could be made so that the victims might receive restitution in installments.[52]

It is in dealing with minor offenders, however, that the criminal court can best utilize restitution. If the offender cannot make restitution immediately, he should be placed on probation and permitted to compensate the victim on an installment plan. This not only helps the victim, prevents the offender from being unnecessarily subjected to the stigmatizing experience of a jail sentence, and avoids the necessity of maintaining a minor offender at public expense, but also exerts a greater influence on the offender for whom the loss of money undoubtedly has greater meaning than a brief stay in the local jail. Habitual offenders, however, should not be handled in this way, but should be disposed of in accordance with the findings of case investigations, although restitution may be included in the sentence imposed by the court.

PROBATION, IMPRISONMENT, AND PAROLE

Probation, imprisonment, and parole, which, with the exception of fines, are now much more frequently used than the other methods of

[52] Sutherland, pp. 576, 577.

punishment, will be discussed in detail later. When probation, imprisonment, and parole are seen as procedures during which nonpunitive techniques can be employed, they may be classified also as methods of treatment. However, it should be emphasized that *both* punishment and treatment must be given a place in modern penology; and in practice, they are inextricably interwoven at almost every stage in the handling of offenders. The broader term "correction" may be used to include within its meaning both treatment and punishment. It is sometimes said that the offender is sent to prison *as* punishment and not *for* punishment. Although this statement does emphasize the importance of treatment during the offender's institutionalization, it does not recognize the complex nature of correction, which involves, and must involve, *both* punishment and treatment during all its phases, including the entire periods of probation, imprisonment, and parole. As we explained in Chapter 17, the important question is: How can we most judiciously balance treatment and punishment in the correctional process?

19

Probation

NATURE OF PROBATION

Not every adjudged delinquent nor every convicted criminal is committed to an institution. Instead, many children and adults are handled according to a procedure known as probation—a term derived from the Latin *probare*, meaning to prove. As it is used in the field of criminology, probation may be defined as a procedure whereby the sentence of an offender is suspended while he is permitted to remain in the community, subject to the control of the court and under the supervision and guidance of a probation officer. The offender is given the opportunity to demonstrate that he can abide by the conditions imposed by the court and conduct himself as a law-abiding member of society. Thus, as the term's Latin etymology indicates, probation involves the testing of an offender and his proving that he is worthy of his freedom.

An analysis of the definition of probation which we have given here will reveal that its basic elements are (1) a suspension of sentence, (2) a period of trial for the offender in the community, (3) the offender's observance of the law and adherence to the conditions imposed by the court, and (4) the supervision of the offender by a probation officer. Some writers urge that the concept of probation be divorced entirely from that of the suspended sentence so that the constructive and rehabilitative aspects of probation will be emphasized. Although it is recognized that this side of probation must be clearly understood, and that some other phrase, such as "postponement of final judgment" instead of "suspension of sentence," might better describe the action of the court, it is also believed that it would be wholly unrealistic not to see probation as a substitute for commitment to an institution, to which the court must usually resort when probation fails. In other words, whether it is explicitly stated or not, commitment to an institution is always a possibility and is held in suspense in every case of probation. Furthermore, since this is true and since probation itself is a sentence, it would be more accurate to say that the commitment rather than the sentence is suspended in probation.[1]

The suspension of the sentence may involve either the suspension of the imposition of the sentence or the suspension of the execution of the sentence. In some states the imposition is suspended, in some, the execution, while in still others, either may be suspended. In cases where the imposition of the sentence is suspended and probation is revoked, the court is in a position to impose any sentence which it might have originally imposed; but in cases where a sentence has already been imposed and its execution suspended, the court in revoking probation merely puts into effect this sentence and thus as a rule cannot take into consideration the circumstances of the violation. In all cases, however, the individual whose probation is revoked must stand trial for any new crime which he has committed.

Many courts suspend the sentence of an offender and release him without supervision into the community. In such a case the understanding is that if the offender does not behave himself, he will be committed to an institution. There is a place for the use of the suspended sentence in cases where the supervision of the offender is not necessary. However, this practice should not be confused with probation, which cannot be said to exist unless some form of supervision is present. The reason for making this distinction can be understood when it is remembered that one of the purposes of probation is to provide the offender with regular and definite assistance in his efforts to achieve successful adjustment in the community.

ORIGIN AND DEVELOPMENT OF PROBATION

Nevertheless, it is true that probation was originally an outgrowth of the practice of suspending sentences. In fact, modern probation legislation in the United States is generally traced to these two sources: (1) the common law practice of suspending sentence for an indefinite time during good behavior, which it is alleged was based upon a smiilar practice

[1] A few states and the federal courts place some adults on probation without trial and conviction, and many juvenile courts use what they call "unofficial probation" in cases where they have not adjudged the child a delinquent. Whether this informal procedure is employed in the case of an adult or a juvenile, it is a serious violation of due process and should be abolished. In the name of "treatment," this practice not only disregards the rights of the individual but also may later hinder the state in its efforts to dispose of the case in some other way if probation fails. If a person is accused of crime or delinquency, he should be given the opportunity to defend himself in a judicial proceeding. If he is not so accused but needs help, then he should be referred to an agency that is better equipped than a court to render the required service.

of the English Courts; and (2) early American statutes which specifically authorized the courts to suspend either the imposition or execution of sentence. These in turn, it may be explained, had developed out of earlier devices,[2] such as the *benefit of clergy, judicial reprieve, provisional release on bail,* and *the release of an offender on his own recognizance* or "binding over for good behavior," which also had been designed to mitigate the severity of the criminal law.[3]

The suspension of sentences by the courts gave rise to the need of having some kind of security for the continued good behavior of the persons who were released. In some cases, this security was provided by having the offender furnish a financial guaranty for his good conduct during the suspension of his sentence, but more frequently some friend or reliable citizen would agree to be responsible for the offender and to assist him in his efforts to reform. Thus, as Fred E. Hynes has pointed out, the introduction of probation merely provided formal organization for the informal arrangements that were already in existence under suspended sentences.[4]

Credit for the introduction of probation in the United States must go to Massachusetts, for it was in that state that probation originated after a period of experimentation under private leadership. In it the first true probation law was enacted, and in it, too, the early experiments in the development of the probation system were conducted and evaluated. In short, as the Attorney General's Survey states, "probation in the United States has no early history apart from the development of the Massachusetts system."[5]

Among the early volunteers in Massachusetts who assisted offenders during the period of their suspended sentences was one who has become known as the "first probation officer." He was John Augustus, a prosperous shoemaker of Boston. By the time of his death in 1859 he had as-

[2] See *The Attorney General's Survey of Release Procedures,* "Probation" (Washington, D.C.: Government Printing Office, 1939), Vol. II, pp. 1–15; and Frank W. Grinnel, "The Common Law History of Probation," *Journal of Criminal Law and Criminology,* XXXII (May–June, 1941), 15–34; Sol Rubin, Henry Weihofen, George Edwards, Simon Rosenzweig, *The Law of Criminal Correction* (St. Paul, Minn.: West Publishing Co., 1963), pp. 152–61, 176–83; Arne R. Johnson, "Recent Developments in the Law of Probation," *Journal of Criminal Law, Criminology, and Police Science,* LIII (June, 1962), 194–206.

[3] Originally, *benefit of clergy* enabled members of the clergy to be tried by ecclesiastical courts instead of by lay courts. They were thus protected from the death penalty and other severe punishments of the criminal law. Later, not only the clergy, but also members of the laity who could read were entitled to claim *benefit of clergy.*

Judicial reprieve was a practice whereby the judge temporarily suspended the execution of a sentence and thus enabled the offender to apply for relief from the severity of the law.

[4] Fred E. Haynes, *Criminology* (New York: McGraw-Hill Book Co., Inc., 1935), p. 422.

[5] *Attorney General's Survey,* p. 16.

sumed responsibility for about two thousand such persons, including men, women, and children.[6]

In 1863 the Children's Aid Society of Boston was founded, and from the beginning it was active in the field of probation, exerting its efforts in this direction largely through the work of Rufus R. Cook and Miss L. P. Burnham.[7] Another important force in the development of probation in Massachusetts was the work of the State Visiting Agency of the Board of State Charities, which was established in 1869. By law, it was authorized to send its visiting agents into any court, except the superior court, whenever application was made for the commitment of a child to a state reformatory. As a representative of the state the agent was to protect the child as well as to promote the best interests of the community.[8]

In 1878, Massachusetts passed a law which authorized the mayor of Boston to appoint a probation officer for Suffolk County. This law, as Professor Haynes has emphasized, marks the official origin of probation as a legal system.[9] It was followed two years later by the passage of another law which permitted cities and towns throughout the state to appoint probation officers. Finally, in 1891, a law was enacted making it mandatory instead of permissive for the judges of all lower courts to make such appointments. State-wide probation in Massachusetts, therefore, dates from 1891. Seven years later the authority to appoint probation officers was extended to the state's superior courts so that probation might be used in dealing with more serious offenders.

Thus Massachusetts set an example in the field of probation which other states began to follow. As a result, in 1915 thirty-three states had adult probation in some form, and two years later only Wyoming had no provision for juvenile probation. The federal government, however, did not pass a probation law until 1925,[10] although federal judges placed offenders on probation before they were specifically authorized to do so

[6] *John Augustus—First Probation Officer* (New York: National Probation Association, 1939), pp. 4, 5; Charles L. Chute, "Probation Yesterday and Today," *Proceedings of the American Prison Association, 1941,* p. 168.

[7] N. S. Timasheff, *One Hundred Years of Probation* (New York: Fordham University Press; Pt. I, 1941; Pt. II, 1943), Pt. I, pp. 7–12; Donald W. Moreland, "John Augustus and His Successors," *Yearbook, 1941,* (New York: National Probation Association, 1941), pp. 1–22.

[8] Moreland, pp. 18–22.

[9] Haynes, pp. 422, 423.

[10] *Attorney General's Survey,* pp. 21–33. See also Charles H. Z. Meyer, "A Half Century of Federal Probation and Parole," *Journal of Criminal Law, Criminology, and Police Science,* XLII (Mar.–Apr., 1952), 707–28; Charles L. Chute, "The Campaign for Federal Probation," *Federal Probation,* XIV (June, 1950), 3–9; J. M. Master, "Legislative Background of the Federal Probation Act," *ibid.,* 9–16; Charles Lionel Chute and Marjorie Bell, *Crime, Courts, and Probation* (New York: The Macmillan Co., 1956), pp. 88–111.

by law.[11] By 1957 all states, the District of Columbia, and the federal courts had been provided with some sort of legislation authorizing the probation of both juveniles and adults. However, various restrictions are imposed upon the use of probation in the United States. Many states do not permit its use in case of serious offenses; some states make only first offenders eligible for probation; still others stipulate that only certain types of courts or courts in political subdivisions with populations of a specified size may exercise probationary powers.

Probation has also been adopted in England, on the Continent, and in some other parts of the world. It was introduced into English statute law in 1879. A few years later, in 1887, Parliament passed the Probation of First Offenders Act, but this act restricted probation to first offenders and did not authorize the appointment of probation officers. In 1907 England removed the limitation which restricted probation to first offenders and provided for salaried probation officers and then in 1925 provided for probation officers in all its courts. Today England and Wales apply probation to both juveniles and adults. Belgium, in 1888, authorized probation for adults, and three years later, France took similar action.[12]

Two trends in the development of probation in the United States should be noted here. One is that juvenile probation has received greater attention and support than adult probation. This has been due largely to the deeper public sympathy with juveniles, the stronger belief in the feasibility of their reformation, and the spread of the juvenile court movement. The lag in adult probation is most noticeable in municipal courts having jurisdiction over misdemeanor cases,[13] probably because the large volume of petty cases coming before these courts makes it impossible to give any single offender very much attention. And yet, since many of these cases involve first offenders and persons who are in acute need of counseling and guidance, an excellent opportunity for the prevention of crime and delinquency is being neglected. It appears, then, that this is an area of criminal prosecution where probation can be used most profitably.

[11] In 1916 in the so-called *Killits case,* the United States Supreme Court ruled that the federal courts had no power, in the absence of statute, to suspend a sentence indefinitely. See *Ex parte* United States, 242 U.S. 27 (1916). This decision served as a stimulus for the enactment of laws specifically authorizing the suspension of sentence and the use of probation.

[12] Fred R. Johnson, *Probation for Juveniles and Adults* (New York: Appleton-Century-Crofts, Inc., 1928), pp. 8–16; Irving W. Halpern, "Probation," *Encyclopedia of Criminology* (New York: The Philosophical Library, 1949), p. 389; N. S. Timasheff, Part I, pp. 1, 12–15, 25, 26, 31, 32, 66–77, 82–85. England also had its pioneers in probation. For example, Matthew Hill of Birmingham, England, pioneered in his country in 1841, the same year that John Augustus began his work in Boston, Massachusetts.

[13] Will C. Turnbladh, "Current Status of Probation," *Contemporary Correction,* ed. Paul W. Tappan (New York: McGraw-Hill Book Co., Inc., 1951), p. 395.

The other trend has been the uneven geographical development of probation. In general, rural areas have lagged behind urban areas, but many towns and cities also have failed to provide effective probation facilities. The sparsity of population in rural areas and the lack of financial resources in many communities have been important factors in this trend, but perhaps more important than these has been the failure to educate the public to an understanding of the advantages of probation. Although most states have the necessary basic legal provisions for probation, this does not mean that all courts or areas in these states have probation service. As a matter of fact, in 1951 it was estimated that courts which served approximately one-third of the population of the United States did not have any probation service and that the service furnished to another third of the population was inadequate because of the limitation of part-time and ex officio probation officers and excessive case loads.[14] Recognition of these trends has led criminologists to advocate greater participation of the state in the development of probation facilities so as to raise standards and to extend this service to all segments of the population in both rural and urban areas.

EXTENT OF PROBATION

No general statistics showing the extent to which adult probation is now used in the United States are available. The best source of information on this subject is the report entitled *Judicial Criminal Statistics,* formerly published by the Bureau of the Census but discontinued in 1947. Although it covers only the major offenses handled by courts of general jurisdiction in the District of Columbia and in those states which cooperated with the Bureau of the Census in the accumulation of the data, and although it does not distinguish between probation and the suspended sentence, nevertheless we can still get some idea of the extent to which probation is used by referring to the figures for the last year shown in this report. This was the year 1945, the figures for which covered 43,290 defendants who had been convicted and sentenced in twenty-four states and the District of Columbia during that year. Of these defendants, 31.6 per cent were placed on probation or were given suspended sentences. There was considerable variation among the states in the use of these methods of handling offenders. Rhode Island, with 64.6 per cent, used them the most, while Iowa, with 13.0 per cent, used them the least. Here are percentages for some of the other states listed

[14] *Ibid.,* p. 394. In 1962, William Sheridan, of the United States Children's Bureau, expressed the opinion that probably as many as half of the juvenile courts had no adequate local probation services (news release, Nov. 17, 1962, by the U.S. Department of Health, Education, and Welfare).

in the report: Massachusetts, 27.0 per cent; New York, 34.6 per cent; Wisconsin, 38.2 per cent; and California, 32.8 per cent.[15]

The federal courts placed 12,047 offenders on probation during the fiscal year ending June 30, 1963. This represented 40.4 per cent of the 29,803 offenders sentenced in the federal courts during this period.[16] The most inclusive figures that we have regarding juvenile probation are those published by the United States Children's Bureau for the year 1962. These figures show that the juvenile courts used probation in 22 per cent of all their cases (49 per cent of those that were handled officially) during that year.[17]

Thus all the available statistics regarding the extent to which probation is being used indicate that about one-quarter to one-half of all offenders convicted in our state and federal courts of general jurisdiction[18] are placed on probation or given a suspended sentence. The use of probation, however, varies greatly from county to county, and from district to district, ranging from little or none in some counties to a considerable amount in others.

ADVANTAGES OF PROBATION

Any analysis of the advantages of probation must begin with the recognition that (1) it is a substitute for commitment to a correctional institution, and that (2) nearly all persons who are committed to correctional institutions return to the community—most of them within a short time. In fact, about 95 per cent of adult prisoners return to the community, the great majority within two or three years. In cases where probation is used, it is not a substitute for permanent incarceration but, in all probability, a substitute for a short term in a correctional institution, where there is often little effort to rehabilitate the offender, and from which he is often discharged without guidance or assistance into an unfriendly community.

The interests of the public are paramount in the handling of every offender. Probation, therefore, is not a satisfactory substitute for com-

[15] Bureau of the Census, *Judicial Criminal Statistics, 1945* (Washington, D.C.: Government Printing Office, 1947), p. 5, Table 4.

[16] *Annual Report of the Director of the Administrative Office of the United States Courts, 1963* (Washington, D.C.: Government Printing Office, 1964), p. 243, Table D5.

[17] United States Children's Bureau, *Juvenile Court Statistics: 1962*, Statistical Series No. 73 (Washington, D.C.: Government Printing Office, 1964), p. 13, Table 6. The percentages on juvenile probation shown above are based on data taken from monthly reports received from 22 of the 30 courts serving the largest cities in the United States.

[18] Courts of general jurisdiction include what are usually called county and district courts but not magistrates, justices of the peace, or other members of the minor judiciary.

mitment to an institution unless the interests of the public are taken into consideration. This can be done most effectively when probation involves: (1) an adequate presentence investigation; (2) a careful decision by the court that there is a reasonable probability of the offender's making good on probation; and (3) a systematic supervision of the probationer by a qualified person who is not burdened with an excessive case load. Hence, it must be remembered that the advantages of probation are most fully realized when it has these three features.

With this as a background, we are now in a position to consider the advantages of probation. Important among these are the following:

1. The offender remains in the community where he can lead a normal life and learn to assume the responsibilities of a law-abiding member of society. Since his ultimate adjustment must be in the community and not in some institution, he is in the best situation in which to develop the qualities which he must have for this adjustment.

2. The probationer can support himself, discharge his obligations to his family, and make restitution or reparation to those who have suffered from his crime.

3. The offender is not exposed to a penal experience which may leave him embittered, stigmatized as a convict, further schooled in crime through association with other prisoners, and unfit to take up the life of a free man because of forced isolation from normal contacts and responsibilities.

4. The offender is not alone in his efforts to find successful adjustment in the community, but is under the supervision of a probation officer who guides and assists him. Acting as counselor, confidant, and friend, as well as a representative of the law, the probation officer is also in a position to discover and modify the conditions in the probationer's family and neighborhood that are producing crime and delinquency.

5. It costs the state much less to keep a man on probation than to maintain him in an institution. However, it must be admitted that probation and parole would cost more if they were administered in accordance with the highest standards, but this would be true also of institutions.

6. The offender is kept out of already overcrowded correctional institutions. Wisely administered, probation can help to maintain the populations of these institutions at a level where the individual needs of each prisoner can be given greater consideration.

OBJECTIONS TO PROBATION

Many of the objections that have been raised regarding probation actually have not been directed against it, but rather against procedures that only slightly resemble it. Sometimes offenders are released under

suspended sentences but without supervision, and this is called probation. Sometimes sentences are suspended and offenders are asked to
report periodically to the judge, to the sheriff, or to their clergymen, and
this is called probation. Often such procedures are deserving of criticism, but they are not probation, and their failures should not be cited
to discredit probation. This should be borne in mind as we consider the
following objections:

1. Probation pampers the offender, enabling him to avoid punishment. It thus fails to operate as a deterrent to crime and delinquency and
discourages citizens who are interested in maintaining law and order.
Probation, however, is not intended to be a form of leniency, and when
properly administered, it precludes the pampering of an offender. He is
selected for this kind of correction only after the court decides there is a
reasonable probability that he will adjust successfully in the community.
Besides, while under the supervision of a probation officer he must abide
by the conditions of the court, and because his sentence is suspended, he
may be committed to an institution if he fails in any way. So the probationer does not escape all pain. He must suffer all the inconvenience, embarrassment, and disgrace connected with his apprehension, trial, and
conviction; and throughout his probationary period he is subject to restrictions on his freedom, and there remains the possibility that he may
yet be committed to an institution. Consequently, the use of probation
does not mean that society's desire for the suffering of the offender is
ignored or that there is no possibility of exerting deterrence through this
method of correction. And since the alternative to probation is not permanent imprisonment, but, in all probability, a short term of confinement
from which there is often release without supervision, it can be seen that
probation may actually constitute a more rigorous method of correction
than its alternative, imprisonment. In short, probation involves a balancing of punishment and treatment in the individual case.

2. Probation provides an opportunity for those with influence to "fix"
a case and thus avoid commitment to an institution. This may happen,
but there is no evidence that it happens very often. As a matter of fact,
if the situation is such that the case can be "fixed," it is much more likely
that an easier and a less conspicuous method will be used. In any event,
the remedy for this is not the elimination of probation, but rather the
improvement of criminal procedure and the selection of more honest
court officials.

3. Probation does not protect the community, since the offender is
still at large and may repeat his crimes or delinquencies. Here, again,
the real nature of probation is overlooked. It involves investigation prior
to probation and supervision during probation, both of which operate to

prevent the exposure of the community to further law violations on the part of the offender.

4. Probation often permits the offender to return to the same family and community environment that contributed to his crime or delinquency. He is, therefore, exposed to the same influences all over again. This objection is disturbing, but like the other objections mentioned above, it does not meet the issue squarely. It is true that the probationer often returns to the same environment from which he came, but this does not have to happen, and he does not go alone; with him goes a probation officer who guides and advises him and who seeks to modify the situation in which the probationer must adjust successfully. If there is not this kind of supervision, the answer is to be found in an improvement of the probation system and not in its elimination. And, it may be added, the offender who is discharged from a correctional institution often returns to the same environment from which he came, and often there is no one there to guide or assist him as there is in the case of a probationer.

5. Probation is impracticable in many jurisdictions because of inadequate investigations, heavy case loads, and an insufficient number of trained personnel. These conditions, of course, make it impossible to have the proper selection and supervision of probationers, and so when they exist, it is highly questionable whether probation should be used. However, in view of the great advantages of probation, the solution here is not the abandonment of probation, but the elimination of the conditions which make its use difficult or impossible.

ADMINISTRATION OF PROBATION

We have already seen that the extent to which probation is used in the United States varies from place to place. We are now to learn that another of the characteristics of probation is the diversity of its administrative systems. Most juvenile probation departments are under the control of courts, and so, like them, are administered on a local, county, or district basis. However, three states, Connecticut, Rhode Island, and Utah, have state-wide juvenile court probation systems, and many other states authorize some state agency, such as a probation commission, a welfare department, or a department of correction to participate in some way in the probation of juveniles. This participation ranges all the way from the actual appointment and direction of juvenile probation officers and the supervision of probationers to the giving of advice, financial support, or statistical assistance to the various juvenile probation departments functioning in the state.

Many states have, or are authorized to have, some kind of statewide adult probation service. In some of these states adult probation and parole are administered by the same agency, while in others adult and juvenile probation have been similarly integrated. On the other hand, in some states adult probation is administered on a local or county basis, sometimes, however, with financial or other assistance from the state.

This diversity of the administrative systems of probation has caused some interesting questions to be raised. Is it better, for example, to have probation controlled by a court or by a nonjudicial agency? And can probation be more effectively administered on a local, county, or state basis?[19] Experts on the subject differ among themselves as to how these questions should be answered. Some have argued that probation can be better protected from politics when it is controlled by the courts. Others, however, have asserted that judges have neither the time nor the training to enable them to assume this responsibility and that furthermore the administration of probation on a state level makes it possible to give financial support to poor or rural counties and thus bring standards up to a higher and more uniform level. In reply to this, opponents of the state plan have insisted that only local or county administration can provide probation officers who are acceptable to the judges under whom they must serve, and who are familiar enough with local conditions to function successfully in the communities where they must work.

As a matter of fact, however, in practice there has been a tendency to blend both local and state administration and judicial and nonjudicial control. In the face of this it seems wise to conclude that there is no one system that is the best for every state and that the variety of conditions existing in the different states will continue to require the diversity of administrative systems. As Professors Barnes and Teeters have explained: "The system employed advantageously in one state may not be the best for another. Smaller states may well use the state control method. Larger states may find this system quite unsatisfactory."[20]

Nevertheless, if the control of probation is kept on a local or county level, then there should also be a state agency, such as a state probation commission, which can support the local or county facilities in an advisory, supplementary, and educational way. This agency, in the performance of its duties, should conduct educational campaigns for the extension and strengthening of probation facilities, develop standards for probation services, establish training courses for probation personnel, investigate the work of probation officers, collect, analyze, and periodically publish statistical information and other facts regarding probation work

[19] See Ralph Hall Ferris, "Building a State Probation Service," *Proceedings of the American Prison Association, 1941,* pp. 192–202.

[20] Harry Elmer Barnes and Negley K. Teeters, *New Horizons in Criminology* (Englewood Cliffs, N.J.: Prentice-Hall, Inc., 1959), p. 558. See also *Probation and Parole Directory, 1963* (New York: National Council on Crime and Delinquency, 1963).

in the state, and furnish special services—for example, psychiatric examinations—for localities and counties unable to provide such services for themselves. Such an agency might also administer interstate compacts regarding reciprocity in the supervision of probationers. These compacts are now in effect in all states. They make it possible for probationers to be transferred from one state to another and at the same time remain under supervision. Thus an offender who has been granted probation in New York may move to New Jersey and there be placed under the supervision of a New Jersey probation officer.

THE PROBATION OFFICER

The probation officer is the most important single element in the whole process of probation. His presence makes the difference between the suspended sentence and what we call probation, and when he is competent and not burdened with an excessive case load, his influence gives the fullest expression to the potentialities of probation. It is estimated that we have about thirteen thousand probation and parole officers at work throughout the country, when we actually need over forty thousand if we are to maintain reasonable case loads. Although there is a growing recognition of the importance of training for probation work, the persistence of county residence requirements, low salaries, and the insecurity of tenure have been serious obstacles to the development of professional standards.[21]

Furthermore, not all of the probation officers that we do have are employed full-time in probation work. Many of them have other duties to perform such as those of sheriff, clerk of the court, school attendance officer, and welfare worker. It is true, of course, that there is an unknown number of volunteer workers in the field of probation and the value of their services should not be underestimated. Nevertheless, the volunteer should never be considered a satisfactory substitute for the competent professional worker who is employed on a full-time basis in probation service.

Why is the probation officer so important? Examine his duties and you will find the answer. You will learn that he is charged with the great responsibility of making a presentence investigation of offenders who are being considered for probation. He must do this in order to secure information upon which the judge can base his decision in each case. Whether or not the judge's decision is wise will depend to a great extent upon

[21] Turnbladh, p. 395. For data on salaries, see *Salaries of Probation and Parole Officers and Juvenile Detention Staff in the United States, 1962–1963* (New York: National Council on Crime and Delinquency, 1963). These data show an increase in many salary scales, reflecting the relationship of salaries to obtaining and retaining qualified staff.

the thoroughness and skill with which the probation officer performs this duty. And it is one which requires much time and effort, involving frequent attendance at court, many interviews and conferences, much correspondence, the examination of numerous records, and the preparation of analytical reports for the court. But this is not all. He must also supervise probationers, and here his work to be effective must include patient counseling, time-consuming home visits, tactful interviews with employers and other interested parties, the discovery and use of other resources in the community, such as clinics and recreational facilities, in order to supplement his own efforts, and the keeping of detailed records. In the event of a serious violation of probation he must be prepared to assume the role of a policeman and to act promptly and fearlessly in the enforcement of the law.[22]

In addition to his work with the offender, the probation officer has other important duties. He should thoroughly know the community in which he works—its customs, traditions, and institutions—so that he can function harmoniously with its people and understand how and when to use its resources. He should cooperate with public officials and community leaders in preventing crime and delinquency. He should promote public understanding and support of probation in every way that he can. And as a public servant he should seek to build good public relations by doing a courteous, efficient, and economical job at all times.[23]

You can see how important the probation officer really is, and you can also understand why he must have certain qualifications if he is to perform his duties well. But just what qualifications should he have? He should, of course, have a good character and a balanced personality. And the National Council on Crime and Delinquency holds that the best preparation for the correctional field can be secured by graduation from a school of social work. Many correctional authorities, however, differ with this view. They claim that persons entering correctional work need a broad education in the social and behavioral sciences, knowledge of criminal law and procedure and the administration of justice, an understanding of the administration and operation of correctional and law-enforcement agencies and institutions, familiarity with the field of community organization and welfare services, and training and experience in interviewing, counseling, investigation, and case recording. But this kind of preparation cannot be secured today in either a school of social work

[22] Generally, a probation officer performs both investigation and supervision duties, but in a few large departments, he specializes in either one or the other.

[23] See Nino Lo Bello, "Probation and the Newspaper," *Federal Probation*, XVI (Mar., 1952), 36–39; John M. Zuck, "A Probation Department's Role in Delinquency Prevention," *Federal Probation*, XII (Dec., 1948), 16–19; and J. O. Reinemann, "Developing Community Understanding of Probation and Parole Work," *Journal of Criminal Law and Criminology*, XXXIII (May–June, 1942), 23–31.

or a graduate program in sociology and criminology.[24] In the opinion of the author, what is needed is an educational program designed especially for correctional workers.

In order to insure the selection of well-qualified persons, the National Council on Crime and Delinquency has recommended that probation and parole officers be appointed from eligible lists based on competitive merit examinations. However, this council recognizes that there are many devoted and successful officers who are qualified by self-education and assimilated experience. It emphasizes, therefore, that its standards and recommendations refer only to the training and qualifications of future appointees and should not be interpreted to mean that it favors the replacement of competent workers already employed in the field. That this view is a realistic one should be fully appreciated, for it seems doubtful whether any probation department, except some in our large cities, could at present meet the standards of the National Council on Crime and Delinquency.

Moreover, it must be realized that even the most fully qualified officers cannot do good work if their case loads are too heavy. In some situations fifty cases may be too many for an officer; in others, one hundred may not be excessive. One estimate states that in general about seventy-five cases would be satisfactory,[25] while the National Council on Crime and Delinquency recommends a case load of not more than fifty. Actually, however, many officers are burdened with two hundred or more cases at one time. Under such a handicap, how can even the best officer function effectively? Probation work must be personal in its character if the officer is to get close enough to the probationer to influence his behavior, and large case loads tend to reduce the service to formal and mechanical contacts. And the quality of service is further affected by the prevalence of low salaries, insecurity of tenure, and political appointments, all of which tend to keep many competent persons out of probation and parole

[24] For a discussion regarding the training of probation and parole officers, see Walter C. Reckless, "Training Probation and Parole Personnel," Focus, XXVII (March, 1948), 44–48; "Training Reconsidered" (comments on Reckless' article), Focus, XXVII (Nov., 1948), 180–82; Walter C. Reckless, "The Controversy about Training," Focus, XXVIII (Jan., 1949), 23–25; Clarence M. Leeds, "Probation Work Requires Special Training"; and Loren J. Hess, "A Graduate School and Court Cooperate in Training for Probation Work," both in Federal Probation, XV (June, 1951), 25–32; Peter P. Lejins, "Professional and Graduate Training in Corrections," Proceedings of the American Correctional Association, 1959, pp. 35–50; Standards for Selection of Probation and Parole Personnel (New York: National Probation and Parole Association, 1954); Lyle W. Shannon, "The Problem of Competence To Help," Federal Probation, XXV (Mar., 1961), 32–39. For a survey of college and university programs in corrections, see The United Prison Association of Massachusetts, "What's New in Education for Correctional Work?" Correctional Research, Bull. No. 13 (Nov., 1963).

[25] Barnes and Teeters, p. 560.

positions. The present state of affairs has moved Paul W. Tappan to observe, "It must be apparent that the wide dispersion of energies required by the organization of functions, combined with a lack of training in most probation departments, may cut to a merest pretense that individualization of diagnosis and treatment which is supposed to characterize modern probation."[26]

OPERATION OF PROBATION

The selection of an offender for probation can be effective only if it is based upon a thorough presentence investigation into his history and personality. Such an investigation, in order to provide an insight into the behavior of the offender, should cover such matters as the record of his crimes and delinquencies, his family history, his school and employment record, his economic status, his habits, associates, and affiliations, and his mental and physical condition.[27] The presentence investigation has a twofold purpose: first, to assist the judge in deciding whether the offender should be placed on probation; and second, to guide the probation officer in his supervision of the offender. Furthermore, if the offender fails on probation, a report on the presentence investigation should be forwarded to the institution to which he is committed.

A few states permit the defense to inspect the presentence investigation report, and federal judges may permit this at their discretion. The majority of probation authorities, however, favor the confidentiality of the report, emphasizing that the disclosure of its contents tends to dry up the sources of information. Even so, some writers claim that the right to disclosure acts as a check on the accuracy and fairness of the report. The American Law Institute, seeking a compromise on the question, has recommended that the factual contents and conclusions be disclosed to the defense but that the sources of information be kept confidential.[28]

[26] Paul W. Tappan, *Juvenile Delinquency* (New York: McGraw-Hill Book Co., Inc., 1949), p. 335. See also *Standards and Guides for Adult Probation* (New York: National Council on Crime and Delinquency, 1962), pp. 57, 58. The estimate on case loads made by the National Council on Crime and Delinquency is based on "work units," each supervision case being counted as one work unit, and each presentence investigation, as five. Since the maximum monthly load for a probation officer is placed at fifty work units, this may mean just fifty supervision cases or, for example, forty supervision cases and two completed presentence investigations.

[27] It is the general practice to provide a psychiatric examination for an adult offender who is being considered for probation only when he is thought to be abnormal. However, the tendency has been to use psychiatric service more extensively in the presentence investigation of juveniles.

[28] Rubin, Weihofen, Edwards, Rosenzweig, pp. 90–101. See also *Williams v. New York,* 337 U.S. 241 (1949); *Model Penal Code, Proposed Official Draft* (Philadelphia: The American Law Institute, May 4, 1962), Section 7.07 (5); *Standard Probation and Parole Act* (New York: National Probation and Parole Association, 1955), p. 10.

It is generally believed that probation should be used for those who offer the "greatest hopes of readjustment in terms of age, mental-emotional status, and attitudes toward society."[29] In effect, this means that probation should not be granted to the hardened in crime or to those who are not willing and eager to try it in preference to imprisonment. However, even if the court believes that the offender can adjust successfully on probation, it must also take into consideration the values and interests of the public. Obviously, it is unwise to outrage public opinion by granting probation to an offender who has been convicted of a shocking crime. To do so would be to flout the very values to which the probationer himself must learn to adjust and to subject probation to public condemnation and discredit. In fact, the legislatures in most of the states have imposed statutory limitations on the courts in order to prevent this very thing from taking place. The limitations take the form of denying probation to offenders who have been convicted of certain crimes or who have had previous criminal records. The crimes which usually preclude eligibility for probation are those which society most abhors, or with which law-abiding agencies have found it difficult to cope, and may be classified as follows: (1) crimes of violence, (2) crimes involving the use of a deadly weapon, (3) sexual crimes, (4) crimes against government, and (5) crimes carrying certain penalties, such as life imprisonment and capital punishment.

Even though consideration of public interests and values dictates the imposition of restrictions upon eligibility for probation, it is generally agreed that the court should have broad discretionary powers in the use of this method of punishment. Moreover, any restrictions that are imposed should be periodically examined and modified in the light of changing public opinion so that as much latitude as possible can be given to the discretion of the court. It must be emphasized, however, that this discretion should at all times be exercised on the basis of information secured by intensive presentence investigations and with the assurance that the probationer will be carefully supervised.

Attempts have been made to construct prediction tables which can be used as a guide in the selection of probationers and parolees.[30] These tables are based upon various factors, such as age of offender, offense committed, and marital status, which appear to be associated with either success or failure on probation and parole. As one would expect, the studies that have been made to construct prediction tables agree that offenders who have better previous records and better social backgrounds

[29] David Dressler, *Probation and Parole* (New York: Columbia University Press, 1951), p. 37. For a guide to the presentence report, see Paul W. Keve, *The Probation Officer Investigates* (Minneapolis: University of Minnesota Press, 1960).

[30] See Chapter 28 for further discussion of prediction tables.

do better on probation. Althought prediction tables may offer clues, they should never be used as a substitute for the careful study of the individual case, which must always be considered on the basis of its own merits.[31]

When probation is granted to an offender, he is expected to abide by certain conditions which are imposed by the court. These conditions have their source in the provisions of the law, the judgment of the court, and the rules and regulations of the probation department. They generally include such items as payment of fines, making restitution, observance of all laws, supporting dependents, notification to the court of any change in address, keeping good company, making reports as required, and the like. These conditions serve the purpose of not only protecting society and supporting its values, but also furnishing a basis for the rehabilitation of the probationer. For society, they provide specific standards by which to measure the behavior of the probationer and, if necessary, to sustain the charge that his probation should be revoked. For the probationer, they are danger signals beyond which he may get into trouble and signposts by which he can find his way back into acceptance among his fellow men.[32]

These conditions tend to give the probationer a feeling of security. He knows what is expected of him, and he has the assurance that compliance will bring its rewards in freedom. But more than this, they symbolize the authority of society, acceptance and respect for which is a prerequisite to the enjoyment of the rights of community life. However, these conditions are not just negative in their nature; they have a positive side too. They form a definite common ground upon which both the officer and the probationer can meet, and which can be used to deepen and develop their relationship.

But the conditions imposed by the court can be used effectively in probation only if they are realistic and formulated in such a way as to give latitude to the discretion of the probation officer. Not all conditions should be applied without discrimination in every case; and the limitations of many should be reduced as the probationer nears the successful conclusion of his probation. Certainly the infraction of a rule should not necessarily bring the revocation of probation, but it should always be judged in the light of the entire situation in which the probationer is seeking adjustment. In other words, these conditions should be used

[31] Dressler, p. 77.

[32] The use of a fine, restitution, or family support or a brief jail term prior to conditional release as a condition of probation has drawn the objection that this is punitive and therefore contrary to the philosophy of probation. However, this objection fails to recognize that an unpleasant experience may contribute to rehabilitation and that probation, like all correction, must always involve a combination of treatment and punishment. Nevertheless, it would be better to employ the term "parole" in referring to supervision in the community after a jail term.

constructively as correction tools in the promotion of the interests of society and the probationer.[33]

Various systems are used for assigning probationers to probation officers.[34] These may be classified into: (1) assignment by districts, which involves giving all probationers living in a certain geographical area to one probation officer; (2) assignment by characteristics of the probationer, such as sex, race, or religion; and (3) assignment by problems, which involves giving all probationers with a certain kind of problem to a probation officer who is a specialist in dealing with that kind of problem. Assignments by districts, sex, and race are those most commonly found, while assignment by problems, as one would expect, can be used only in the most elaborately organized departments.

The continuing relationship between the probation officer and the probationer is known as supervision. This should be neither mere policing, which is negative and repressive in nature, nor coddling, which is misguided sentimentality and indulgence. Instead, supervision should be conceived of as individualized correction in the community setting. This is a process in which social services and counseling are used to help the probationer to help himself toward an acceptable adjustment in the community, and it is supported and restricted by the authority of the law. It must begin with the establishment of a relationship of trust and understanding. This means that the probationer must be induced to believe that the officer is sympathetic and interested in him as a person, that he respects his feelings, and that he sincerely wants to help. But on the other hand, the probationer must also clearly understand that the officer expects him to respect the law, abide by the conditions imposed by the court, and assume definite responsibilities in the modification of his own behavior.

The development of the relationship between the officer and the probationer must revolve about the change in the attitudes of the probationer. Although we have considerable knowledge about attitudes, we do not have any neat, simple formula by which to change them. In this work with attitudes there is no substitute for the knowledge, skill, and good judgment of the probation officer as he deals with the interplay of influences in the life of the probationer. Supervision is a creative process which must emerge from the art of the probation officer.

There are, however, a few generally accepted principles to which the officer can look for guidance. Above all, he must be a leader, courageous and resourceful, conscious of his responsibility to the community, able and willing to take the initiative whenever the situation requires him to do so, and ready to use his authority and to act decisively in order to protect

[33] *Ibid.*, pp. 85–92, 119, 120.
[34] Edwin H. Sutherland, *Principles of Criminology* (Philadelphia: J. B. Lippincott Co., 1947), pp. 391, 392.

the interests of the public. But the term "leader" as used here should not be construed to mean that the probation officer should employ only the technique of leadership in the correctional process and merely issue orders and impose his will upon the probationer. Instead, it means that the probation officer must always be in command of the situation, and that he, and not the probationer, should be the one to decide what techniques are needed and how and when they should be used. In other words, the probation officer should always firmly maintain his position as director of the entire correctional process. Because in doing this he may have to subdue recalcitrant offenders, it should be clear that the officer must be skilled in the methods and techniques of law enforcement.

And obviously he must also be familiar with the techniques of probation and parole work. David Dressler has classified these as follows:

1. *Manipulative techniques,* which are used to modify the offender's environment so as to make him more comfortable, healthier, and happier. Job-finding, home-finding, betterment of community conditions—these would be included here.

2. *Executive techniques,* which are used to discover and put into service other resources in the community in order to supplement the efforts of the probation officer. Medical care, legal aid, educational and vocational guidance, social agency help, recreation—these would be covered here.

3. *Guidance, counseling, and leadership techniques,* which are used in dealing with the probationer himself to reduce his conflicts and modify his behavior patterns.[35]

The officer, furthermore, must realize that his own conduct speaks louder than his words. He must not be caught in a false position or in one inconsistent with the values he expects the probationer to accept. At all times he must, by his own conduct, set an example for the probationer to follow; and by his acts, even more than by his words, he must show that he wants to help the probationer.

In addition, the probation officer must recognize that all human behavior, including criminality and delinquency, is the product of the interaction of personality drives and environmental pressures. He must, therefore, work not only with the probationer but also with his environment. He must appreciate that attitudes are greatly affected by social contacts, and he must strive to modify and enlarge those of the probationer, bringing into play all the resources of the community—an interested employer, a loyal friend, a skillful counselor, a helpful clergyman, a "Big Brother," a "Big Sister," or a hobby club. He must know the probationer's home environment and act to make it a force for law-abiding behavior. Thus the

[35] Dressler, pp. 154–56.

probationer will secure intimate friends and relatives who are interested in him, who will stand by him, and who are more worth while than the old ones who led him into trouble. Personality touches personality in this interplay of subtle influences, and the probationer is immersed in relationships that tend to provoke socially acceptable responses.

All this does not mean that the probationer plays a passive role in the process of rehabilitation. On the contrary, his role must be increasingly dynamic as the relationship between him and the officer develops. Preaching, ordering, or threatening is not very effective in influencing the behavior of most people. The desire for change must be created in the probationer as he gains an insight into his own character and acquires a sense of responsibility for his own actions. As Frank T. Flynn has said, "The core of modern probation work lies in recognizing that the probationer must participate in the solution of his own problems."[36] He must actually wrestle with his own problems if he is to learn about them. He must test his own strength if he is to increase it. He must discover his own weakness if he is to correct it. He must learn to plan his own affairs if he is to assume responsibility for them.

Some writers have defined the process of supervision as case work in an authoritarian setting. But the fact that the probationer has not sought assistance voluntarily, is not free to withdraw from the relationship, and has a suspended sentence hanging over his head has troubled some students of case-work methods. They have wondered how it is possible in such a situation to establish the relationship of mutual confidence and respect which is necessary if the officer is to help the probationer. And so they have raised this question: Can case work be used in an authoritarian setting? The answer to this is that not only can case work, however defined, be so used, but it must be so used. All of life's relationships involve some degree of authority. It is simply an aspect of the responsibility which every member of society must assume as payment for the rights and benefits he would enjoy. It is present in parent-child, husband-wife, teacher-pupil, doctor-patient, employer-employee, and all other social relationships. It follows, then, that all case work is in an authoritarian setting. The authority of the child-welfare worker may not be so conspicuous, but it is there nevertheless, differing only in degree and not in kind. Clients in all case-work relationships must comply with certain rules, and they inevitably come to look upon the case worker as having the authority to enforce these rules.

It must be realized, therefore, that everyone, regardless of his position, must bow to certain limitations, which are the realities of every situation and which are expressed in the authority of organizations and their repre-

[36] Frank T. Flynn, "Probation and Individualized Justice," *Federal Probation,* XIV (June, 1950), 72.

sentatives. Laws, customs, morals, and ethics hedge us about on all sides. And all of us must learn to adjust to these limitations or be confronted with the possibility of more restrictive ones. The probation officer is but a representative of these realities; and his authority, a symbol of them. Actually, rehabilitation achieved through case work is the product of the interaction between worker and client as they *both* seek adjustment to authority.

Thus, authority does not need to be an obstacle to case work. Whether it is or not will depend upon the way it is used. In the hands of a clumsy, arbitrary, and unimaginative officer it will make the use of case-work methods impossible. In the hands of a competent officer it is an instrument that can be used constructively in getting the probationer to face reality and to come to grips with his own problems.[37]

Other writers, however, argue that the nature of supervision during probation is such that this process should not be called case work at all. The chief concern of supervision is the welfare and safety of the community and not the personality adjustment and happiness of the probationer, and it therefore aims primarily at keeping him from violating the law and the conditions imposed by the court. In order to accomplish this, the probation officer may have to control, direct, lead, command, and even threaten. In fact, he may have to strengthen the inhibitions, repressions, and feelings of guilt of the probationer. Furthermore, although the probation may be successful, the probationer may not be any happier or better satisfied than he was before, and some of his personal problems may be even greater. All this, these writers contend, is in sharp contrast to the true meaning of case work which emphasizes nondirective techniques and always strives to reduce the frustrations and tensions of the individual and to guide him to deeper insights and greater self-understanding and personality adjustment.[38] All this impels the author to conclude that it would be more realistic to see supervision as individualized correction in which punishment and treatment are balanced in the community setting.

During the period of supervision contacts between the probation officer and the probationer usually take place in the home of the probationer and in the office of the probation officer. The home visits permit the officer to become familiar with the home environment, to observe the probationer

[37] Dressler, pp. 121–26; Richard A. Chappell, "Case Work," *Contemporary Correction,* ed. Paul W. Tappan (New York: McGraw-Hill Book Co., Inc., 1951), pp. 384–94; Kenneth L. M. Pray, "The Principles of Social Casework as Applied to Probation and Parole," *Federal Probation,* IX (April–June, 1945), 14–18.

[38] Elliot Studt, "Casework in the Correctional Field," *Federal Probation,* XVIII (Sept., 1954), 19–26; Ben Meeker, "Probation Is Casework," *ibid.,* XII (June, 1948), 51–54; Marilyn A. Blake, "Probation Is Not Casework," *ibid.,* 54–57; Sanford Bates, "When Is Probation Not Probation?" *Federal Probation,* XXIV (Dec., 1960), 13–20; Lewis Diana, "What Is Probation?" *Journal of Criminal Law, Criminology, and Police Science,* LI (July–Aug., 1960), 189–208.

in the intimate relationships that are so influential in molding his character, and, if need be, to undertake reconstructive work with the whole family. Home visits also afford the members of the family an opportunity to participate in the correctional process and to feel that they have a responsibility in its promotion. Contacts in the office of the probation officer are established by requiring the probationer to report there at regular intervals. These contacts provide a privacy that cannot be secured in the home of the probationer, enable the officer to get better acquainted with the probationer, give the probationer training in responsibility and regularity, and tend to create in him a sense of participation in the correctional process.[39] But office contacts should never be considered a substitute for home visitation, which, it is generally agreed, is an indispensable part of the correctional process.

The supervision of probationers cannot be conducted satisfactorily without the creation and maintenance of case records and the preparation of regular and adequate reports. The results of presentence investigations should be carefully recorded and the case records kept up to date as the supervision of probationers develops. Included in these case records should be an analysis of the probationer's attitudes and problems, his family and neighborhood relationships, and his interests, inclinations, and activities. In addition, every probation department should make studies of its own activities, attempt to evaluate the effectiveness of its program, and periodically publish reports regarding the results of its work.[40]

Excessive case loads can seriously interfere with the keeping of adequate case records—indeed, with the entire probation program. One realistic approach to a solution of this problem has been the classification of cases into various groups on the basis of the time and effort which each case apparently will require. Supervision can then be allotted to these groups in accordance with their estimated requirements.[41]

Probation work can be strengthened also by the use of volunteer workers, who can render valuable service, especially in smaller towns and sparsely populated areas. But volunteers should serve under the direction of a professional supervisor and should never be used in order to avoid the appointment of professional probation officers. Particularly good results with volunteers have been secured through cooperation with Big Brother and Big Sister organizations and similar youth service agencies. Since volunteers are not law-enforcement officers and are not being paid to interest themselves in crime and delinquency, they may be more readily

[39] John Otto Reinemann, "Principles and Practices of Probation," *Federal Probation*, XIV (Dec., 1950), 28, 29; Sutherland, pp. 392–95.

[40] See John Otto Reinemann, "Research Activities in the Probation Department," *Proceedings of the American Prison Association, 1946*, pp. 39–48.

[41] Chappell, pp. 391, 392.

acepted as true friends by probationers, and their influence may thus be very effective in the correctional process. However, volunteers should be carefully selected because excessive sentimentality, morbid interest, and domineering attitudes can do far more harm than good in probation work. In addition to their services as volunteers, these men and women can also assist in promoting greater public understanding and support of probation and crime-prevention programs.[42]

How long should probation last? It is obvious that no categorical answer can be given to this question. The probationer's needs and potentialities vary from case to case, and since correction is a creative process, it cannot be neatly fitted to prearranged specifications. In recognition of this, the law usually gives the judge considerable latitude within which to use his discretion regarding the length of the probationary period, and most juvenile courts do not limit the time of probation in advance. However, the law usually makes the maximum probationary period for adults the same as the maximum prison sentence that may be imposed for the offense. In most states, the probationary period of the juvenile may legally last until his twenty-first birthday, even though the juvenile court originally could not exercise jurisdiction over him up to that age. Experienced officials generally believe that the period of probation should be from eighteen months to two years in length, and the *Juvenile Court Standards,* published by the United States Children's Bureau, recommends a general minimum probationary period of from six months to one year for juvenile delinquents.[43]

Implicit in the philosophy of probation is the assumption that an offender who does not have the capacity to adjust to the demands of community life within a reasonably short period of time should not be placed on probation. He probably belongs in an institution. Unnecessarily prolonged periods of probation can only tend to pile up case loads and to reduce the incentives of both the officer and the probationer to show definite progress in the correctional process.

The period of probation is terminated either by its revocation or by the discharge of the probationer. In cases where a definite time limit has been set, the probationer who has met all requirements is discharged when that time limit is reached. On the other hand, in cases where there is no time limit, the probation officer and the court decide when the probationer should be discharged. Probation may be revoked either because the probationer has violated a law or because, in the judgment of the probation officer and the court, he has failed to conform to the conditions of his

---

[42] James V. Bennett, "A Sponsorship Program for Adult Offenders," *Federal Probation,* XIII (Mar., 1949), 17–20.

[43] Richard A. Chappell, "Federal Probation Service: Its Growth and Progess," *Federal Probation,* XI (Oct.–Dec., 1947), 32.

probation.[44] Most states require that a probationer be given due notice
and a hearing before his probation is revoked, and considerations of fair
play dictate that this should be done so that the offender will have an
opportunity to defend himself before he is deprived of his conditional
freedom. In fact, this has become part of the regular juvenile court procedure and is the practice generally followed by courts in dealing with
adult probationers. When the courts revoke probation and commit the
offender to an institution, they usually do not give him any credit for the
time he has spent on probation.[45]

EVALUATION OF THE EFFECTIVENESS OF PROBATION

How effective has probation been in the rehabilitation of offenders?
The annual reports of probation departments throughout the United
States generally show that more than 70 per cent of their cases succeed on
probation.[46] Professor Sutherland has estimated the figure at about 75 per
cent.[47] The *Attorney General's Survey of Release Procedures,* published in
1939, reported an analysis of the cases of 19,256 offenders who had been
placed on probation. Of these, 61 per cent revealed no recorded violations
during the probation period, 18 per cent had new-offense violations, and
21 per cent showed violations of the conditions of probation. However, in
only 19 per cent of the total 19,256 cases was it necessary to revoke
probation.[48]

On the other hand, some studies of probation have not been so reassur-
ing. The Gluecks, in a study of juvenile delinquents, analyzed the careers
of 1,000 delinquent boys over a period of fifteen years and found that of
the 806 who had been on probation at some time during this period, 20.3
per cent always succeeded in making a satisfactory adjustment, 21.8 per
cent sometimes succeeded, and 57.9 per cent always failed.[49] Another
study by the Gluecks examined the careers of 500 male criminals, all of
whom had served terms in correctional institutions. Three hundred ninety
of these men had been on probation at some time during the fifteen
years covered by the study. According to the rigid standards used in this

[44] The use of the Nalline test by probation and parole agencies has proved helpful
in some cities in the detection of drug addiction. Nalline is antagonistic to opium and
its derivatives, and when it is injected into an addict, it will quickly produce withdrawal symptoms and other diagnostic signs.

[45] The *Standard Probation and Parole Act,* issued by the National Probation and
Parole Association in 1955, stipulates that the initial period of probation fixed by the
court should not exceed five years, and that the probationer should be given a hearing
whenever he is charged with any violation of the conditions of his release.

[46] Halpern, p. 393.

[47] Sutherland, p. 402.

[48] *Attorney General's Survey,* p. 337.

[49] Sheldon and Eleanor T. Glueck, *Juvenile Delinquents Grown Up* (New York:
The Commonwealth Fund, 1940), pp. 153, 161.

study, of those who had been on probation, only 2.4 per cent always behaved satisfactorily, 0.8 per cent succeeded at first and later failed, 4.0 per cent failed at first and later succeeded, 0.4 per cent were erratic as to behavior, and 92.4 per cent always failed.[50]

In a more encouraging study made by Lowell J. Carr in six counties in Michigan, 53.9 per cent of the 230 juvenile probationers who were investigated were classed as having made successful adjustment on probation, 26.1 per cent were regarded as doubtful, while 20 per cent were definitely classed as failures.[51]

Although these studies have raised some doubts about the way in which probation has been used, belief in its principles remains unshaken among criminologists. It is their contention that probation could be made much more effective if sufficient funds were provided to staff each department with an adequate number of competent persons and to administer its operation in accordance with modern standards.

Among those who strongly support probation is Austin H. MacCormick, Executive Director of the Osborne Association. In commenting upon its effectiveness in dealing with juveniles, he has written:

> Based on actual performances over a term of years, a good juvenile court and probation service, operating in a community with adequate social resources and utilizing them fully, can put as high as 90 per cent of its juvenile delinquents on probation the first time around and 50 to 75 per cent the second or third time around, and get as high as 75 to 80 per cent successes.[52]

The percentages of violation and revocation which are shown in the annual reports of probation departments seem to throw a favorable light on probation. But despite this, they require careful examination. In the first place, it must be realized that probation standards are not uniform throughout the United States. If the strict policies of revocation and intensive supervision which are employed in some probation departments prevailed everywhere, the percentages of violation and revocation in many departments would probably rise and the general averages for the country as a whole would thereby be increased. Furthermore, not all of the violations of probation are detected and recorded. Some escape the

---

[50] Sheldon and Eleanor T. Glueck, *Criminal Careers in Retrospect* (New York: The Commonwealth Fund, 1943), pp. 149, 151. In this study, as well as that cited in footnote 49, a probationer was judged as having failed if he was arrested while on probation, if he more than occasionally violated the conditions of his probation, if he was committed to an institution for violation of probation, or if it was known that he had committed an offense for which he might well have been arrested while on probation, but was not.

[51] Lowell Julliard Carr, *Delinquency Control* (rev. ed. New York: Harper & Bros., 1950), pp. 248, 249. See also Belle Boone Beard, *Juvenile Probation* (New York: American Book Co., 1934), pp. 147, 208, 209.

[52] Austin H. MacCormick, "The Community and the Correctional Process," *Focus*, XXVII (May, 1948), 88.

notice of even the best departments, and in other departments only the most flagrant violations are discovered. These percentages, therefore, tend to make probation appear more effective than it really is. Moreover, many probationers would "make good" without supervision—in fact, in practice many actually do—so their records can hardly be cited as proof of the value of probation.[53]

The measurement of the effectiveness of probation by means of the percentages of violation and revocation leaves an important question unanswered. Is probation more effective than some other method that might be used in dealing with offenders? Is it more effective, for example, than commitment to an institution or the mere suspension of sentence? It should be clear that the ultimate test of the effectiveness of probation must be made by such a comparison. Unless this is done, it may be contended that, even if probation has low percentages of violation and revocation, it is still less effective than other methods. However, such a comparison is difficult to make because in order for it to be valid the offenders who are being handled by the different methods must have about the same characteristics. But actually, this does not tend to happen. For example, the tendency is to place "good prospects" on probation and to send the "least promising" to institutions. If the post-release behavior of those who are committed to institutions is less law-abiding than that of those who are placed on probation, this may be subject to the interpretation that the former are more difficult to rehabilitate, rather than that the method used in dealing with them is less effective than probation. Nevertheless, some attempts have been made to compare the effectiveness of probation and institutionalization, although with inconclusive results, and more such studies are needed.[54]

Still another aspect of this problem of measuring the effectiveness of probation should be considered. The percentages of violation and revocation, which we have discussed above, refer only to the behavior of offenders during their period of probation. But how do probationers behave after their discharge from probation? In other words, does probation have a lasting effect on their behavior? As one can see, this question, too, must be taken into account in any discussion of the value of probation, and some studies have been made in an effort to answer it. Several of these studies, as reported by Professor Sutherland, "show that the number of failures is not greatly increased after the end of the probation period."[55] One of the more recent studies of this kind was made by Morris Caldwell. He studied the careers of 403 persons after their dis-

[53] Ralph W. England, Jr., "What Is Responsible for Satisfactory Probation and Post-Probation Outcome?" *Journal of Criminal Law, Criminology, and Police Science,* XLVII (Mar.–Apr., 1957), 667–76; Diana, 202–204.

[54] See Sutherland, p. 403.

[55] *Ibid.*, pp. 403, 404.

charge from probation and found that 337, or 83.6 per cent of them, committed no offenses during the post-release period, and that of the 66 who again became offenders, only 8 committed felonies.[56] In this study, the post-release period covered eleven years and seven months, and all cases had a minimum period of five and one-half years after discharge from probation. Ralph England made a similar study of 490 federal offenders who had been discharged from probation. He found that only 17.7 per cent of them were subsequently convicted of crimes during a period of six years or more, and only 27 per cent of their crimes were felonies.[57]

Although such studies as these furnish us with some valuable information about the careers of offenders after their final discharge, nevertheless, their adequacy as a measure of the effectiveness of probation must be questioned, because the continued success or ultimate failure of discharged persons results from such a complex interaction of factors in community life. For example, the discharged offender may continue to be law-abiding largely because of the influence of some new friend, experience, or opportunity, or he may eventually commit another crime largely because of a misfortune that would crush even the best of men. Perhaps he is better, or worse, for having had the correctional experience —but who can tell? But even so, to criticize probation solely on the basis that many discharged offenders eventually commit another crime appears to be unwarranted.

SOME STEPS TO IMPROVE PROBATION

Despite the fact that there is considerable difference of opinion regarding the effectiveness of probation, no well-informed person today would advocate its abolition. Instead, the principal question now is: What steps should be taken to improve probation services throughout the United States?[58] Some of the more important of these may be summarized as follows:

1. Every possible medium should be used to inform the public about the nature and advantages of probation. The "probation story" has not been adequately told, and most people know virtually nothing about it.

2. New legislation should be passed to give the courts greater discretionary powers in the use of probation, to strengthen the service with

[56] Morris Gilmore Caldwell, "Review of a New Type of Probation Study Made in Alabama," *Federal Probation*, XV (June, 1951), 3–11.

[57] Ralph W. England, "A Study of Postprobation Recidivism among Five Hundred Federal Offenders," *Federal Probation*, XIX (Sept., 1955), 10–16.

[58] See Chappell, "Case Work," *Contemporary Correction*, pp. 393, 394; Will C. Turnbladh, "Probation and the Administration of Justice," *Proceedings of the American Prison Association, 1950*, pp. 233–40; George W. Smyth, "The Destiny of Probation and Parole," *Proceedings of the American Prison Association, 1951*, pp. 141–52.

more adequate financial support, to establish minimum qualifications for probation officers, and to provide for their appointment on the basis of merit examinations.

3. The geographical area served by many probation departments in rural areas should be enlarged in order to provide them with greater financial support. This can be done in some cases by having a single probation department serve two or more counties.

4. In states where probation is not organized along state lines, a state agency, such as a probation commission, should be created to support the local or county facilities in an advisory, supplementary, and educational way. Under its supervision would be such matters as the collection and publication of probation statistics and the development of standards.

5. Judges should be induced to use probation in all cases where it is advisable to do so. In the past, the attitudes of some judges toward probation have been a formidable obstacle to its development.[59]

6. Facilities for the training of probation officers must be improved. Courses on probation should be offered in colleges and universities, and probation departments should establish in-service training programs or improve the ones they already have.

7. Probation departments must be staffed with an adequate number of competent persons, and higher standards of case-work performance should be developed.

8. Closer coordination should be created between correctional institutions and probation and parole facilities so that each can benefit from the experience, knowledge, and services of the other.

9. Probation departments should make greater use of community resources and services through the establishment of closer relations with such agencies and organizations as psychiatric clinics and hospitals, medical departments, welfare agencies, family societies, churches, and businessmen's clubs.

10. Additional research is needed in order to throw further light on the advantages and limitations of probation and to develop new techniques and methods.

Although probation has had an uneven development and in some jurisdictions has been subjected to excessive restrictions, nevertheless, it has definitely established itself as an effective method for dealing with certain types of offenders. In fact, in the opinion of many authorities it offers the greatest hope for the rehabilitation of the great majority of delinquents and criminals.

[59] See *Attorney General's Survey*, pp. 411–46.

20

History of Correctional Institutions

IMPRISONMENT AS A METHOD OF PUNISHMENT

"As soon as men had learned the way to build in stone, as in Egypt, or with bricks, as in Mesopotamia, when kings had many-towered fortresses, and the great barons, castles on the crags, there would be cells and dungeons in the citadels."[1] Thus wrote George Ives at the beginning of his history of penal methods.

It should be emphasized, however, that such prisons were only places of detention or temporary confinement for military captives, persons awaiting trial or execution, and for those unfortunates who had aroused the sovereign's ire.[2] Viewed as such, the prison, at least in some societies, probably goes back as far as the time of the practice of cannibalism when the chief course of the menu was fattened in the stockades. Many instances can be found in the history of ancient times of the incarceration of political and religious offenders. "Joseph was thrust into Potiphar's prison, Samson into that of the Philistines, and Jeremiah's dungeon, into which he was let down by ropes, is never to be forgotten."[3]

Prisons as places for the reception of ordinary criminals, as distinct from state or political offenders, did not exist until many centuries later. Moreover, imprisonment as a punishment in itself, to be deliberately inflicted in accordance with definite regulations, must be considered to be

[1] George Ives, *A History of Penal Methods* (London: Stanley Paul and Co., 1914), p. 1.

[2] Thorsten Sellin, "Penal Institutions," *Encyclopedia of the Social Sciences*, Vol. XII, p. 57.

[3] Frederick Howard Wines, *Punishment and Reformation* (New York: Thomas Y. Crowell Co., 1919), p. 108.

of relatively recent origin. In fact, this method of punishment did not reach its worst phase until the nineteenth century.[4]

It is impossible to fix the exact date of the general beginning of imprisonment as a punishment for crime. The only statement in this respect that can be made with accuracy is that punitive imprisonment was not used to any great extent until the middle of the sixteenth century in England and the beginning of the seventeenth century in Continental Europe. Not until the beginning of the nineteenth century did it succeed in displacing the capital and corporal penalties for serious crimes.[5] The eighteenth century may be considered as the period of transition from corporal punishment to imprisonment, although the process of change did not reach its greatest rate until the last quarter of that century.[6]

ORIGIN OF JAILS IN ENGLAND

In England, during the early Anglo-Saxon period, which began about the middle of the fifth century, there was no need for elaborate penal machinery. When the freemen were able, they atoned for their transgressions with fines; when they could not, they were enslaved, mutilated, outlawed, or put to death. Slaves were cruelly flogged or ruthlessly slaughtered since there were not even prisons for them. But as time passed the power of the central government gradually increased until about the tenth century, after the Danish troubles had ended; and in the eleventh century, under the Norman rule the king was strong enough to extend his power and protection.

In the twelfth century the old system of *bot* and *wer*,[7] which was designed to compensate the injured and keep the peace among the fierce and warlike race of freemen, began to give way to one under which the king exacted punishment and tribute, which he administered and collected through itinerant judges, sheriffs, and other officers. The heavy fines imposed on places and people became an important source of revenue to the crown and to the barons and the lords of manors to whom rights of jurisdiction were frequently delegated. The idea of damage done

[4] Ives, *loc. cit.*

[5] Thorsten Sellin, "Imprisonment," *Encyclopedia of the Social Sciences*, Vol. VII, p. 617; Max Grünhut, *Penal Reform* (London: Oxford University Press, 1948), 11–13.

[6] Harry Elmer Barnes, *The Evolution of Penology in Pennsylvania* (Indianapolis: Bobbs-Merrill Co., 1927), p. 54.

[7] In old English law, the *bot* was reparation or amends for any damage done. In Anglo-Saxon and Germanic law, the *wer*, or *wergild*, was the fixed price to be paid by the kindred of a manslayer to the kindred of the slain person as compensation to avoid the blood feud. A fixed scale of values was established varying from that of the churl to that of the king. Originally, its acceptance was optional, but later it was made compulsory.

to the individual was merged and lost in the greater trespass alleged to have been committed by the offender against the peace and the code of the king.

In order to keep prisoners in safe custody until the king's judges came to hold the next court, places of detention had to be provided. These became the common gaols of England, of which there were about two hundred during the years between the sixteenth and eighteenth centuries. Originally they were not used for punitive imprisonment, and so simple arrangements sufficed. Often the gaol was but a single room or two in a castle, or in a market house, or perhaps just a part of the gaoler's own dwelling.

Up to the middle of the twelfth century, some of the counties were without public gaols or prisoners' cages, and Henry II (reigned 1154–89) commanded their construction in 1166. Sometimes the prisoners had to wait for months or even years for their trials, and many who could not get bail died of want or disease. Meanwhile, the prisoners and their families were kept at their own expense. Those that had the means were well fed; those that did not might die of starvation. The prisoners who survived were finally tried, but even these still faced the possibility of horrible punishments if they were convicted. Traitors might be broken on the wheel, and the "common" criminal might be hanged or subjected to ghastly mutilations. Until Henry III (reigned 1216–72), the penalty for poaching in the king's forests was death or the loss of eyesight; and until Edward I (reigned 1272–1307), the punishment for rape might involve the loss of eyes and emasculation.

During the reign of Henry III the wrongdoer rarely went to prison, since the justices wanted to get his money rather than to keep him in custody. By the time of Edward I, we begin to arrive at sentences of imprisonment, but as a general rule they were only preparatory to fines, the prisons being used as "squeezers" to extort the money. No significant changes were made in the punishment of criminals during the sixteenth century. Under the Tudor sovereigns (1485–1603), the rack was ever creaking to wring out confessions, and the "common" criminals were treated with the utmost severity. In 1530 an act was passed which provided for the boiling alive of all poisoners. Burning was the penalty for heresy, treason, and several other offenses, and this was a legal penalty until 1790. The right hand might be taken off before hanging for aggravated murder, or the culprit might be hung in chains and left to perish. Some executions consisted of drawing and quartering, and ordinary hangings were numerous.[8]

[8] Ives, pp. 7–15.

ORIGIN OF THE HOUSE OF CORRECTION

About the year 1552 the authorities of London selected what had been a palace in St. Bridget's Well (later corrupted to Bridewell) for locking up, employing, and whipping beggars, prostitutes, and night-walkers of all sorts. Thus England obtained its first house of correction,[9] and the name of Bridewell came in time to be applied not only to this particular institution but to any institution of this kind. In 1597 plans were made for the construction of other houses of correction, and in 1609 orders were issued for the construction of one in every county.[10]

There has been a tendency for many to assume that the houses of correction were merely part of the machinery of the Elizabethan Poor Law, and indeed, they were closely connected with it; but it should be made clear that these bridewells were penal institutions. In them, punishment by imprisonment was given a new importance, and labor was introduced as a corrective discipline.[11] Misdemeanants, such as rogues, idlers, vagabonds, strumpets, and whores, formerly punished under the criminal law by other methods, were committed to these institutions and there compelled to work under strict discipline. Gradually the variety and number of offenses which made one liable to commitment to a bridewell increased, and the house of correction later merged with the jail in all except name.

On the other hand, the workhouse was originally founded as an institution in which employment was furnished to those able and willing to work; industrial training was given to the young, and it was not a penal institution but part of the poor-relief system. The house of correction, however, from the first was a part of the penal system and was utilized to protect the poor-relief funds against encroachments by those able but unwilling to work. In practice, however, the two institutions are hardly distinguishable during the larger part of their history in England and America, the original distinction having been lost sight of. The two terms, therefore, have been used interchangeably for a long time.

During the seventeenth century in England the gaolers remained all-powerful, sometimes friendly, often sullen and cruel, always extortionate. In order to obtain charity, prisoners hung collecting bags out of their

[9] Available evidence seems to indicate that these English houses of correction served as a model for the workhouses that later appeared on the continent (Austin Van der Slice, "Elizabethan Houses of Correction," *Journal of Criminal Law and Criminology,* XXVII [May–June, 1936], 45–67). For the history of the early houses of correction in Amsterdam, see Thorsten Sellin, *Pioneering in Penology* (Philadelphia: University of Pennsylvania Press, 1944).

[10] Ives, p. 15.

[11] Van der Slice, pp. 65, 66.

windows on Sunday mornings. Confirmatory evidence as to how prisoners fared in 1667 may be found in a statute of Charles II. This statute stated that sufficient provision had not yet been made for the relief and setting to work of poor and needy persons committed to the common gaol, who many times perished before their trial, and that the poor there, living idly and unemployed, became debauched and came forth instructed in the practice of thievery and lewdness.[12]

GAOLS OF THE EIGHTEENTH CENTURY

The gaols of the eighteenth century were very much like those that had existed in England for many years, but we know more about them because of the indefatigable labors of John Howard, that grim and conscientious Puritan who went where the ruling classes neither cared nor dared to venture. In the airless, gloomy rooms and dungeons through which he went there arose a dreadful stench which stuck to his notes and garments; and amidst the putrefaction of those places there lurked the dreaded typhus or gaol fever, which was spread mainly by the infesting vermin.

But if the ruling classes did not go to the gaols, its fever came to them, and the prisoners were not the only ones who died of its ravages. In 1522, at the court of Cambridge, many of the knights and gentlemen who were in attendance contracted it, and hundreds were infected and perished at Exeter in 1586 and at Taunton in 1730. In 1750 the Lord Mayor of London, some of the aldermen, two of the judges, the undersheriff, many lawyers, and a number of spectators died of gaol fever. Howard asserts that, from 1773 to 1774, more people succumbed to this disease than were executed throughout the kingdom. And, it should be added, the number of crimes defined as capital offenses by the law was truly enormous. From 1688 onward, such offenses in the law steadily increased until there were more than two hundred. The law, however, had overreached itself. Rough and often brutal as the people of that day were, they would not enforce many of the sanguinary penalties, and the death penalty was used in not more than twenty-five to thirty classes of offenses.

Nevertheless, the gallows load was heavy, and this, together with transportation, kept clearing the gaols, which were entirely inadequate to accommodate the criminal population of England. Many of the gaols were in poorly constructed buildings that were damp, drafty, and unheated. Some were so insecure that the inmates had to be placed in irons at night to guard against their escape. Unsanitary conditions prevailed. Water was scarce. Few gaols had any bathing facilities or infirmaries. Open sewers

[12] Ives, p. 16.

ran through the courtyards, adding their nauseating smells to the overpowering stench of the gaols.

The inmates were shamelessly abused and exploited, being completely the prey and property of warders, keepers, and assistant gaolers. Little provision was made for their meals, clothing, or bedding, and they were robbed for room, squeezed for food, and fleeced and pillaged by their fellow gaolbirds.[13] Many had only rags to cover their emaciated bodies and but filthy straw for beds at night. And in all these vile places there was no employment, no discipline, no segregation of inmates. The prisoners awaiting trial, the convict awaiting punishment, the hardened in crime, the tender in years, men, women, children, debtors, thieves, prostitutes—all were thrown together indiscriminately, sometimes locked up together in a single room.

Devoid of privacy and restrictions, its contaminated air heavy with the stench of unwashed bodies, human excrement, and the discharges of loathsome sores, the gaol bred the basest thoughts and the foulest deeds. The inmates made their own rules, and the weak and the innocent were exposed to the tyranny of the strong and the vicious. Prostitutes plied their trade with ease, often with the connivance and support of the gaolers, who thus sought to supplement their fees. Even virtuous women sold themselves to obtain food and clothing, and frequently the worst elements of the town used the gaol as they would a brothel. Thus, idleness, vice, perversion, profligacy, shameless exploitation, and ruthless cruelty were compounded in hotbeds of infection and cesspools of corruption. These were the common gaols of England.

AGITATION FOR PENAL REFORM

Forces were already operating, however, to produce a change in the treatment of criminals. The barbarism and evils of the old order in Europe had been effectively attacked in the writings of the French philosophers, such as Montesquieu, Voltaire, Diderot, Turgot, and Condorcet, and their English associates and contemporaries, like David Hume, Adam Smith, Thomas Paine, and Jeremy Bentham. The doctrine of these writers introduced rationalism into social and political philosophy and with it the unshakeable belief that a better social order could be had through the use of reason. They upheld man as the supreme achievement of God's creative ingenuity and emphasized his importance more than any previous thinkers save some of the Greeks and Romans and a few of the more radical humanists of the Renaissance. It was the convic-

---

[13] Ives, pp. 16–21; Leon Radzinowicz, *A History of English Criminal Law* (New York: The Macmillan Co., 1948), Vol. I, p. 140; Luke O. Pike, *History of Crime in England* (London: Smith, Elder and Co., 1873–76), Vol. II, pp. 110, 111, 619, 620.

tion of the rationalists that man should not have to wait for the life after death to find happiness; he was deserving of it in this life. With their insistence upon the importance of man as man, the advocates of rationalism did much to arouse greater interest in the improvement of social conditions by eliminating abuses and oppressions.[14]

It was inevitable, therefore, that the sanguinary penal codes and the cruel treatment of prisoners should be scrutinized and condemned in the light of the theories of rationalism. Among the most influential in this attack was the Frenchman Montesquieu (1689–1755), who vigorously criticized the French jurisprudence and recommended that punishments be made less severe and more nearly fitted to the crime.

The stream of humanitarian influence was widened and deepened by the confluence of other tributaries. In England Sir Samuel Romilly (1757–1818) and Sir William Blackstone (1723–80), the famous jurist, condemned the injustices of their country's criminal code. John Howard (1726–90) and Jeremy Bentham (1748–1832) extended the range of the humanitarian movement to include the welfare of jail inmates, and the Quakers urged a more moderate and charitable treatment of offenders.[15]

The work of John Howard,[16] the distinguished English prison reformer, was especially influential in the penal reform movement. In his travels of inspection between 1773 and 1790, he visited many continental institutions, including the house of correction for errant boys, founded by Pope Clement XI in 1703 as a part of the Papal Hospice of Saint Michael in Rome, and the Ghent Workhouse, to which prisoners were admitted in 1775.[17] These two institutions provided for the separation of various classes of inmates, the housing of the criminals in individual cells, and the employment of the prisoners at productive labor. Howard was deeply impressed by their construction and administration.[18] The house of cor-

[14] Harry Elmer Barnes, *The History of Western Civilization* (New York: Harcourt, Brace and Co., 1935), Vol. II, p. 226.

[15] Harry Elmer Barnes, *The Evolution of Penology in Pennsylvania* (Indianapolis: Bobbs-Merrill Co., 1927), pp. 76, 77; Harry Elmer Barnes and J. P. Shalloo, "Modern Theories of Criminology and Penology," *Contemporary Social Theory*, ed. Harry Elmer Barnes, Howard Becker and Frances B. Becker (New York: Appleton-Century-Crofts, Inc., 1940), p. 689; Blake McKelvey, *America Prisons* (Chicago: University of Chicago Press, 1936), pp. 1–5.

[16] John Howard became sheriff of Bedfordshire in 1773, and the evils he found in the gaols led him to devote the remainder of his life to penal reform. It was while he was on an inspection tour of gaols, which carried him to the distant shores of the Black Sea, that he died there in January, 1790, of the dreaded gaol fever.

[17] John Howard, *The State of the Prisons* (New York: E. P. Dutton and Co., Everyman's Library, 1929), pp. 94–96, 114–18; Thorsten Sellin, "The House of Correction for Boys in the Hospice of Saint Michael in Rome," *Journal of Criminal Law and Criminology*, XX (Feb., 1930), 533–53.

[18] For European antecedents of our penal systems, see Thorsten Sellin's articles: "Filippo Franci—A Precursor of Modern Penology," *Journal of Criminal Law and Criminology*, XVII (May, 1926), 104–12; "Dom Jean Mabillon—A Prison Reformer

rection of Saint Michael is said to have been the world's first cellular penitentiary; but it never became widely known even after Howard described it in his writings, and it seems to have had little influence upon later penal experiments.

In his writings, Howard vividly described the continental institutions that he had visited, as well as the gaols of England. His descriptions were free of emotional condemnation, but the blunt facts that he presented pounded their way into the minds of many of the leaders of England. Challenged by the sharp contrast between the wretched English prisons and the foreign institutions, such able men as Popham, Blackstone, Bentham, and Romilly joined Howard in his campaign for penal reform. In this they were strongly supported by the religious forces of the latter part of the eighteenth and the beginning of the nineteenth centuries, which implemented the philosophical ideals and helped to put them into practice in the legislative halls, courts, and penal institutions of the nation.

ORIGIN OF THE ENGLISH PRISON SYSTEM

While John Howard was patiently presenting the harsh and inexorable facts of England's gaols, the outbreak of the American Revolution closed the colonies to the transportation of convicts and compelled the country's leaders to grapple anew with the penal problem. The "hulks," or prison ships, provided them with an answer for the time being, but many soon came to think of institutions for punitive imprisonment as the ultimate solution. Sir William Blackstone and Sir William Eden drafted a bill for the erection of one or more national penitentiaries which were to put into effect John Howard's four principles of secure and sanitary structure, systematic inspection, abolition of fees, and reformatory regimen. In addition, the inmates were to be kept in solitary confinement at night but employed together under supervision during the day. The bill was passed in 1779 but never became operative, and it was superseded twenty years later by the celebrated contract with Jeremy Bentham for a monster "Panopticon"—a scheme which was in its turn to prove abortive.[19] The plans for the "Panopticon," or inspection-house, called for a huge tanklike structure, which was to be covered by a glass roof. The cells were to be arranged around a central apartment, from which the custodians could keep all cells under close scrutiny. The plans of Bentham, however, were doomed to failure, and the "Panopticon" was never built.

---

of the Seventeenth Century," *ibid.*, XVII (Feb., 1927), 581–602; "The House of Correction for Boys in the Hospice of Saint Michael in Rome," *ibid.*, XX (Feb., 1930), 533–53.

[19] Sidney and Beatrice Webb, *English Prisons Under Local Government* (New York: Longmans, Green and Co., Inc., 1922), pp. 38–40.

Eighteenth-century convict hulk at anchor in the dockyard at Portsmouth, England. These hulks were widely used in England during the last half of the eighteenth century for the confinement of convicted prisoners. (Courtesy of Federal Bureau of Prisons)

One of the consequences of Howard's revelations had been the erection of quite a number of gaols designed to provide cellular confinement in different parts of England. The reformation-by-solitude theory was then hailed on all sides as the Magna Charta of prison management, the idea being that if you made prisoners think, they would see the error of their ways.

To give effect to the new theories the construction of Millbank Penitentiary was begun about 1812. By 1821 this huge, gloomy, and many-towered prison, which looked like a thick-spoked wheel, had been erected. It contained three miles of corridors and hundreds of cells and is said to have cost nearly $2,500,000. The prisoners were well treated, although from the beginning the rule of separation and solitude was strictly enforced.

In 1832, William Crawford (1788–1847) was sent to the United States to examine and report upon the prisons there. He had been secretary to the London Prison Discipline Society and was afterward appointed an inspector of prisons by the government. Crawford was very much im-

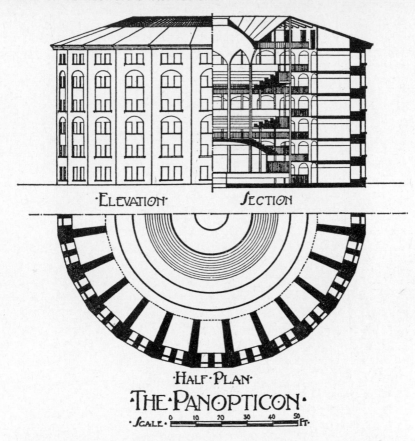

·ELEVATION· ·SECTION·

·HALF·PLAN·

·THE·PANOPTICON·

·SCALE· 0 10 20 30 40 50 ·FT·

Plan of the famous Panopticon Prison, devised by Jeremy Bentham, 1791. (Courtesy of Federal Bureau of Prisons)

pressed by the separate system which he found in effect at the Eastern Penitentiary in Pennsylvania; and after his return to England, Parliament in 1839 provided for the construction of a "model" prison at Pentonville, where the isolation theory was carried out under Crawford's personal supervision. The ruling notion was that the meeting of prisoners must be avoided under all circumstances. For two years, at the beginning, and later, for eighteen months, every man was kept in isolation. However, many inmates gave way under the stress of solitude, and the discipline had to be continually modified. Pentonville was completed in 1842, and within the next six years fifty-four new prisons were built on this "model" plan in England.

In order to assist in providing employment for the prisoners, Sir William Cubitt (1785–1861), an eminent engineer, devised the treadwheel in 1818. In its ordinary form it was something like a very wide mill wheel, such as is turned by water power, and contained twenty-four steps. Each prisoner held on to a wooden bar above his head, and kept on treading as the steps went around. The tasks set for the treadwheel, or treadmill as it was sometimes called, varied a great deal. At first prisoners had to ascend a number of steps, ranging from 5,000 to 14,000 feet, but in later times the regulation task was 8,640 feet for the day's work. Sometimes the wheel was employed in pumping or grinding; sometimes it accomplished nothing—just going around and around like a "damnation mill."

The crank, a still more "model" instrument for the cell theorist, dates from a later period, having been invented at Pentonville about 1846. Next to the cell itself, it soon became the chief "reforming engine" of the "model" system. The new machine might be compared to a churn in appearance. It consisted of a metal box, which could be raised to a convenient height by a support, and had a handle to be turned and a clock-like face upon one side to count the revolutions made. The requisite amount of resistance was secured by a metal band which could be tightened with varying force pressing inside upon the axle. The usual number of revolutions required was 14,400 a day at the rate of 1,800 an hour.

Following the example of Pentonville, other prisons adopted the crank, and although at first it was intended only for vagrants and short-sentence men, after 1848 it tended more and more to oust other labor altogether. The crank naturally lent itself to the persecution of prisoners, and in the Birmingham Jail in England it became a monstrous engine of torture.[20]

PENAL INSTITUTIONS IN COLONIAL AMERICA

The American Colonies inherited the Old World's sanguinary methods of punishment. Eventually, all of them put into effect in varying degrees the barbarous English code, which, in general, prescribed some form of corporal punishment less than death for crimes that were not classified as capital. Despite this, the colonial criminal laws were never so severe as those of the mother country, and even the notorious "Blue Laws" of Connecticut, adopted in 1642 and 1650, provided for only fourteen capital crimes. On September 25, 1676, Governor Andros by proclamation made the laws of the Duke of York applicable to the settlements along the Delaware, which he had taken from the Dutch. These laws had been first promulgated in March, 1664, at Hempstead, Long Island, and their criminal code is therefore usually called the Hempstead Code. This code

20 Ives, pp. 176–94.

classified eleven crimes as capital and prescribed milder penalties, especially various forms of corporal punishment, for other offenses.

However, in 1682, shortly after William Penn arrived in America, his "Great Law" was adopted, and its criminal code, therefore, superseded that of the Duke of York in what is now Pennsylvania and Delaware. The difference between the Quaker philosophy and practices and those of the other colonies and of England are clearly reflected in Penn's criminal code, which generally substituted imprisonment at hard labor for the death penalty and corporal punishment.[21] But as the influence of the Quakers waned in America, their humane criminal laws were gradually weakened by additional acts which tended to reintroduce corporal punishment for various offenses. Finally Pennsylvania and Delaware, in 1718–19, swept away the last vestiges of Penn's code.[22]

When the English settled in America they enacted laws providing for the construction of gaols and houses of correction, institutions which had been established by their ancestors many years before in the old country. The laws of the Quakers provided for another type of penal institution. Penn's "Great Law" adopted in 1682 and its additions in 1683 stipulated that all prisons should be workhouses for "felons, thieves, vagrants, and loose, abusive, and idle persons." It should be noted that the workhouse of the Quakers was to be used not only for the confinement of vagrants, loose and idle persons, and other misdemeanants (as was the typical English house of correction or workhouse), but also for the imprisonment and employment of felons. This workhouse was intended to be an important penal institution since the predominant modes of punishment under the Quaker criminal code were imprisonment at hard labor and the imposition of fines. However, apparently outside of Philadelphia this type of institution was primarily statutory rather than an actuality. Therefore, even in Penn's colony the gaol was the characteristic penal institution and was used for all kinds of criminals, debtors, and vagrants.[23]

Gaols and houses of correction were established in the colonies soon after the English arrived. At the beginning the gaols were used for the detention of persons awaiting trial, but as opposition to corporal punishment increased, they became also places of imprisonment for some convicted petty offenders, especially drunkards and vagrants. The house of correction began its life in the colonies as an institution for the punish-

[21] The criminal code of West Jersey, which was originally a Quaker colony, had been adopted in 1681, and its provisions were similar to those of Penn's code.

[22] *Charter to William Penn and Laws of the Province of Pennsylvania, 1682–1700*, ed. George, Nead, and McCamant (Harrisburg: L. S. Hart, State Printer, 1879), pp. 14, 15, Historical Notes, Appendix B, pp. 144, 192–220, 455–58.

[23] *Ibid.*, pp. 120, 121, 139, 140; Robert G. Caldwell, *The Penitentiary Movement in Delaware, 1776–1829* (Wilmington, Del.: Historical Society of Delaware, 1946), pp. 27–30, 55–57.

ment of convicted misdemeanants, but like its English prototype although it retained its name, it became no different from many of the gaols.

Prisoners of all classes were constantly exposed to the crafty venality and rapacity of their keepers. No serious classification or differentiation of inmates was even attempted, and all types of criminals of all ages mingled together in degrading idleness and vice. However, since in the great majority of cases the punishments inflicted on criminals were corporal, capital, or the imposition of fines, while as a rule debtors were placed out in service for the benefit of their creditors, usually the only prisoners who required attention were those awaiting trial between the sessions of the courts.[24]

EARLY AMERICAN PRISONS (1790–1830)

When the Revolutionary War came to a close, America had no penal institutions similar to the present state prisons, and the jails were sometimes worse, rarely better, than those in England at that time. However, the same philosophical, humanitarian, and religious forces that had operated to produce penal reform in England were active also in America and contributed in a significant way to the modification of the criminal codes and the movement for state prisons. America, in general, and Philadelphia, in particular, were well situated to feel the effect of these new forces. A large number of foreigners, especially Frenchmen, visited America during the Revolution and brought with them the stimulating ideas of their scholars and publicists. Famous Americans, in particular Benjamin Franklin, during the latter part of the colonial period had become increasingly aware of the humanitarian trends in Europe. It was through the writings of Howard and his associates that America gained a knowledge of the advanced ideas and ideals of the new penology, which stressed separate confinement in cells and labor for inmates as a means of reformation. This exchange of ideas strengthened the spirit of reform in the colonies, especially in Philadelphia, the center of American cultural and political life.

It is important to remember that Philadelphia had been the scene of a penal reform movement during the early days of Penn's colony. Although this movement gradually lost momentum and died in the reactionary code of 1718, the roots of the Quakers' humanitarian theories remained; in addition, many considered the English criminal jurisprudence a foreign product that had been forced upon the colonists by a despotic king. Thus Philadelphia was well prepared to assume its role of leader in penal reform in America.[25]

[24] Caldwell, *loc. cit.*
[25] Harry Elmer Barnes, *The Evolution of Penology in Pennsylvania*, pp. 74–79; McKelvey, p. 2.

Immediately after the Revolution the forces of reform, including such prominent persons as Benjamin Rush, Benjamin Franklin, William Bradford, and Caleb Lownes, began their attack upon the savage criminal codes of the colonial days. The Quakers again became leaders in penal reform, many of them becoming members of the Philadelphia Society for Alleviating the Miseries of Public Prisons,[26] the first president of which was Bishop White of the Protestant Episcopal Church. This society, fired by the zealous efforts of Friend Roberts Vaux and his son, Richard, became the most influential organization for penal reform in America.

Believing that the prevention of crime was the sole end of punishment, the Quakers contended that punishment that did not serve this end was not only unnecessary, but cruel and tyrannical. Penalties should be apportioned to the offense so that the criminal might not be plunged more deeply into evil ways. The prison should be a penitentiary, that is, a place where persons might reflect upon their crimes and become penitent, and thus it was to produce better men and women, not to make them more vicious and perverted.[27]

The reform of Pennsylvania's criminal code was begun with the adoption of the state constitution of 1776, which directed the substitution of imprisonment for the various types of corporal punishment; but the outbreak of war interrupted this progress, and it was not until April, 1794, that the criminal code was thoroughly revised. At that time the list of capital crimes was reduced to murder in the first degree, and imprisonment at hard labor was provided for the other serious offenses. This law, which was the first important American departure from the sanguinary criminal codes of earlier days, remained the basis of criminal procedure in Pennsylvania until 1860.[28]

The reform of the criminal code, which made imprisonment the principal method of punishment, necessitated the establishment of a prison system to take the place of the jails and workhouses, many of which could provide neither secure confinement nor employment for long-term prisoners. Thus, the desire for greater security and the hope of using prison labor were two important immediate motives for the creation of state prisons. By legislative acts from 1789 to 1794, the Walnut Street Jail in Philadelphia was converted into a state prison, and an addition was built

[26] This society was originally organized in 1776, under the name of the Philadelphia Society for Assisting Distressed Prisoners, and it is now called the Pennsylvania Prison Society. For a history of it, see Negley K. Teeters, *They Were in Prison* (Philadelphia: The John C. Winston Co., 1947).

[27] O. F. Lewis, *The Development of American Prisons and Prison Customs, 1776–1845* (Albany: The Prison Association of New York, 1922), pp. 14, 15.

[28] Harry Elmer Barnes, *The Story of Punishment* (Boston: The Stratford Co., 1930), pp. 104–11.

for the confinement of the worst type of prisoners in separate cells.[29] Included in these important laws was the Act of April, 1790, which is regarded as the beginning of the modern system of prison administration in America; it established the principle of solitary confinement upon which the Pennsylvania system and later the Auburn system of prison discipline were based, and it provided for remodeling the Walnut Street Jail in accord with this principle. In the operation of the jail, segregation was provided for the sexes, the vicious, the less dangerous, the debtors, and the witnesses. Convicts in solitary confinement were not allowed out of their cells either for work or recreation, although the other convicts worked together in shops during the day.

The Walnut Street Jail, originally built to serve as a detention jail, thus became the first American penitentiary. At present the terms "prison" and "penitentiary" are used synonymously, but they were not so used by the Quakers. For them the term "penitentiary" referred to a place where both crime and sin could be atoned for and penitence produced through solitary labor, meditation, and communion with God. It was this type of institution, then, and not a mere prison that the Quakers and their associates in Pennsylvania sought to create in the Walnut Street Jail.

For ten years the program at this institution apparently worked admirably, and it became the model for other states in the development of their penal systems. By the end of 1817, New York, New Jersey, Kentucky, Virginia, Massachusetts, Vermont, Maryland, New Hampshire, Ohio, and Georgia had established penitentiaries which drew their inspiration from and followed the plan and program of the Walnut Street Jail. Antedating all these institutions was Connecticut's famous underground prison, known as Newgate Prison, which was located in an abandoned copper mine at Simsbury. Although called the first state prison, it was a black hole of horrors and really belonged to the barbaric past. It was superseded in 1827 by the prison at Wethersfield.

It would be too simple to say that the methods introduced at the Walnut Street Jail were completely original, since attempts along the same line had been made in Europe and in the early days of Penn's colony. The significance of the events in Philadelphia in 1787 to 1790 is that "here was started again and continued without interruption what proved to be a permanent change in the official program of dealing with criminals, both in America and throughout the civilized world."

According to the First Report of the Prison Discipline Society of Boston published in 1826, there was then a total of about 3,500 prisoners in all the state penitentiaries in the United States, of which 60 per cent

---

[29] *Ibid.,* p. 129. For the story of the Walnut Street Jail, see Negley K. Teeters, *The Cradle of the Penitentiary* (Philadelphia: The Pennsylvania Prison Society, 1955).

The Walnut Street Jail, Philadelphia, Pennsylvania, 1790—the birthplace of the modern prison system and of the Pennsylvania system of solitary confinement. (Courtesy of Federal Bureau of Prisons)

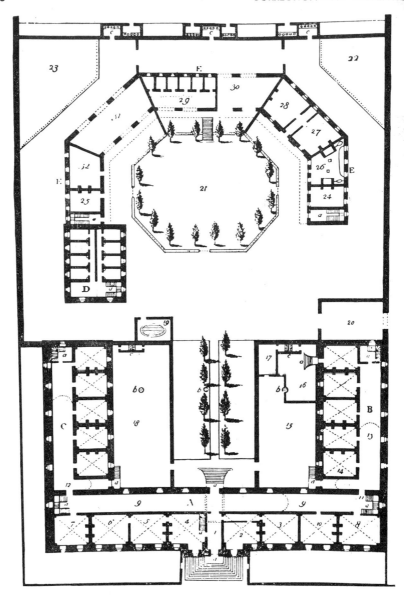

Ground plan of the Walnut Street Jail, Philadelphia, Pennsylvania, 1790. *D* in this plan indicates the block of sixteen cells (eight in the second story and eight in the third) erected in 1790 for the solitary confinement of the "more hardened offenders." This block of cells, which became known as the "Penitentiary"—the first of its kind in this country—laid the basis for the Pennsylvania system of solitary confinemest. (Courtesy of Federal Bureau of Prisons)

were in the penitentiaries of New York, Pennsylvania, and Massachusetts. Most of these prisoners were confined in institutions patterned after the Walnut Street Jail. In spite of promising beginnings in this institution, the attempt to carry out the new methods of punishment there proved an almost complete failure. The causes of this were widespread and produced similar failures in the other state prisons. Thus, the first period of penology in the United States saw the early American prison, with its simple housing, classification in "nightrooms" and its handicraft industries, go down to defeat because of the welter of politics, incompetent personnel, overcrowding, idleness, and inadequate financial support.[30]

THE AUBURN AND THE PENNSYLVANIA SYSTEMS (1830–70)

As early as 1817, the Philadelphia Society for Alleviating the Miseries of Public Prisons began to plan for a reorganization of the prisons of Pennsylvania. Their plan, which called for the solitary confinement of inmates without employment, was embodied in legislation enacted in 1818 and 1821 and provided for the construction of prisons at Pittsburgh and Philadelphia. The Western Penitentiary[31] at Pittsburgh, opened in 1826, had a circular arrangement of cells and was the first important American prison with complete individual housing for convicts. The Eastern Penitentiary[32] at Cherry Hill in Philadelphia, opened in 1829, was constructed in a radial form with seven blocks of outside cells[33] extending like the spokes of a wheel from a central rotunda. As measured by present standards these cells, never originally occupied by more than one inmate, were unusually large, being eleven feet nine inches long, seven feet six inches wide, and sixteen feet high. Each cell had two doors, one leading to the corridor and the other to an individual high-walled and unroofed exercise yard, eight by twenty feet in size. The inmate lived, slept, read his Bible and religious tracts, received moral instruction, and spent his entire day within his cell, except for the one hour each day when he was permitted to use the exercise yard. The Eastern Penitentiary became an architectural model for later prisons and was widely copied.

[30] *The Attorney General's Survey of Release Procedures,* "Prisons" (Leavenworth, Kan.: Federal Prison Industries, Inc., Press, 1940), Vol. V, pp. 1–14. For a description of the conditions in the early American prisons see Lewis, *op. cit.*

[31] The Western Penitentiary was designed by William Strickland, who was undoubtedly influenced by Jeremy Bentham's "Panopticon."

[32] The Eastern Penitentiary was designed by John Haviland. It is not known to what extent he secured his ideas from other structures, but his plan combined the radiating cell blocks of the Ghent Workhouse and the outside cells of the papal house of correction of Saint Michael in Rome.

[33] Outside cells are those that have direct access by doors or windows to the outside.

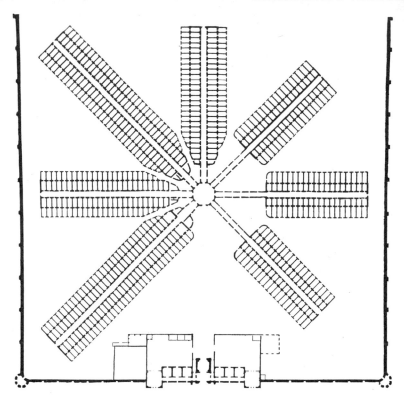

Ground plan of the Eastern Penitentiary at Cherry Hill in Philadelphia, Pennsylvania, 1829. This was the parent institution of the Pennsylvania system of prison design and architecture. Although it exerted
only a limited influence in the United States, it was extensively imi-
tated in Europe. (Courtesy of Federal Bureau of Prisons)

After witnessing the results of inmate unemployment at the Western
Penitentiary, Pennsylvania's legislators changed the law in 1829 and provided for solitary labor in the cells of the state's two prisons, which were
to be penitentiaries in the true sense of the word. The plan for solitary
confinement at all times, with employment for convicts at such trades as
weaving, tailoring, shoemaking, and carpentry in their own cells, became
the basis of the Pennsylvania, or separate, system of imprisonment.

By 1816, the situation at the Newgate Prison in New York had become
so intolerable that the state began the erection of a new prison at Auburn,
patterned after other early American prisons with a few solitary cells
and sizable night rooms for the accommodation of the bulk of the prisoners. As originally designed, the Auburn Prison had a square tower in the
center, in which was located the entrance to the institution, and two

rectangular wings containing the interior cell blocks, which extended to the left and right of the tower. The first individual cells in the prison were ridiculously small, being only seven feet long, three feet six inches wide, and seven feet high.

In 1821, inspired by the Pennsylvania system, an experiment was conducted with a group of prisoners who were placed in solitary confinement to test its effect upon them. After it had caused much sickness and insanity among the convicts, the experiment was abandoned in 1823 as a hopeless failure. However, the experiment was not a fair test of the Pennsylvania system, for it did not employ the perfected form of that system, which called for solitary confinement at hard labor in a large roomy cell and exercise in a small outside yard. Instead, during the experiment the prisoners were placed in solitary confinement in small inside cells where they had neither work nor adequate physical exercise.

Nevertheless, the Pennsylvania system was rejected, and a plan was adopted whereby all inmates were locked in *separate cells at night* but *worked together* in enforced silence in congregate workshops *during the day*. This system became known as the Auburn system. It so happened that the builder of the Auburn Prison, for reasons of economy, placed the cells back to back in tiers within a hollow building, the doors of the cells opening out upon galleries which were eight to ten feet from the outer wall. Thus emerged the interior cell block, which has become one of the unique characteristics of American prisons.

Although the Auburn system was an adaptation and a variant of the Pennsylvania system, the two systems came to be thought of as completely independent, and a vigorous competition developed between them. From 1825 until 1860 the partisans of the two systems waged a bitter controversy. The main conflict was between the Prison Discipline Society of Boston, which espoused the Auburn system, and the Philadelphia Society for Alleviating the Miseries of Public Prisons, which championed the Pennsylvania system. Both sides of the controversy were partisan and unscrupulous in their use of statistics, and they conducted their crusades with fierce and unrelenting zeal.

The supporters of the Pennsylvania system claimed (1) that it facilitated the control of prisoners, (2) that it permitted greater consideration of their individual needs, (3) that it prevented contamination through contact with other convicts, (4) that it provided opportunity for meditation and repentence, and (5) that it secured relative anonymity upon discharge. In reply the advocates of the Auburn system contended (1) that it was cheaper to introduce, (2) that it provided greater opportunities for vocational training, and (3) that it produced more revenue for the state.

Inside-cell block in old south wing of Auburn State Prison, New York. Parent corridor of Auburn–Sing Sing pattern. Note the narrow cells, which were characteristic of the first Auburn-type prisons. (Courtesy of Federal Bureau of Prisons)

Actually, both these systems had many weaknesses, and neither could measure up to the claims made for it by its exponents. Under the Pennsylvania system the construction of prisons was costly, the instruction of inmates was difficult, solitary vices developed, and the mental and physical condition of the prisoners deteriorated. Under the Auburn system the administration of prisons was difficult, prisoners were exploited for the sake of profits, and inmates were as subject to vice and as unfit for release as those under the rival system.

Nevertheless, the Auburn system eventually prevailed in America, and all the states except Pennsylvania adopted it. In all the institutions that used this system the architecture, the program, and often the very rules, regulations, and punishments were substantially the same. Always there were the dimly lighted, interior cells, the program of daily work, the Sunday religious service, the ugly uniforms, the monotonous diet, the "prison smell," the ever-changing, politically appointed personnel, and the petty rules and cruel punishments.

Finally, even Pennsylvania legally permitted the congregation of prisoners in the Western Penitentiary in 1869 and in the Eastern Penitentiary in 1913, but long before 1913, the latter institution had become in fact just another congregate prison. This triumph of the Auburn system was due largely to its economic advantages and the persistence and zeal of Louis Dwight of the Boston Prison Discipline Society. However, the Pennsylvania system favorably impressed many foreign investigators, and it was widely adopted in Europe. The controversy between these two systems gradually died out after 1860. An era had ended and a new one was about to begin. But in the meantime the population of the prisons had greatly increased, and in 1870 the Federal Census reports showed that 32,901 inmates were confined in the prisons of the United States.

The second period of American penology (1830 to 1870) witnessed the development and decline of two opposing systems of prison discipline. The fifty years which followed the opening of the Auburn Prison, though filled with great activity in prison development and administration, did not produce a single lasting contribution to penology. The program of noncommunication, the chief experiment of these years, has been generally abandoned in favor of more normal living conditions. The most that can be said for the second period of American penology is that despite all its crudities and stupidities it was better than a return to the capital and corporal punishments of the earlier years.[34]

[34] *Attorney General's Survey*, pp. 14–21; Barnes, pp. 125–44; Federal Bureau of Prisons, *Handbook of Correctional Institution Design and Construction* (Washington, D.C.: Federal Bureau of Prisons, 1949), pp. 26–32. For the story of the Pennsylvania system, see Negley K. Teeters and John D. Shearer, *The Prison at Philadelphia: Cherry Hill* (New York: Columbia University Press, 1957).

EARLY AMERICAN INSTITUTIONS FOR JUVENILE DELINQUENTS

While the controversy between the Pennsylvania and Auburn systems was waxing and waning, institutions for juvenile delinquents were being established and developed in the United States. The first juvenile reformatory was the New York House of Refuge, which was opened in January, 1825. Its establishment was the work of the Society for Reformation of Juvenile Delinquents,[35] which sought to protect children from vice, poverty, and neglect and to remove them from the degrading association with the hardened criminals in the county jails and state prison. Built on a site now forming part of the present Madison Square in New York City, it was at that time well uptown and away from the business of the city. Boston followed the example of New York and opened a House of Reformation in 1826, and Philadelphia founded its House of Refuge in 1828. These three were the only institutions for juvenile delinquents in the United States until 1845, when New Orleans erected a municipal boys' reformatory. All were founded by private reform societies, and private funds were used in their maintenance. It was not until 1847, when Massachusetts opened a reform school for boys at Westborough (now the Lyman School for Boys), that a state reformatory was established. It was the first strictly public institution for juvenile delinquents in the United States.

The intention of the founders of these early institutions was that they should be schools in which juveniles were to be instructed and reformed. In actual practice, however, they retained much of the atmosphere and methods of treatment found in penal institutions for adults. Their chief value was that they removed juveniles from association with hardened and adult criminals. But even this advantage was not enjoyed by many delinquents, since there were few separate institutions for children. Most juvenile delinquents, therefore, continued to be kept in jails and prisons, although some were cared for by private agencies.

One of the most important developments in American juvenile reformatories during the nineteenth century was the introduction of the cottage system, which had originated in Europe. This substituted a group of cottages, each under the direction of "cottage parents," for the old cell-block structure. It was first used in the United States at the institution for girls at Lancaster, Massachusetts, in 1855, and two years later it was put into effect at the state reform school for boys at Lancaster, Ohio. This system has won general approval because it makes possible more homelike surroundings and greater ease of classification of juveniles. It is now used

[35] The earlier name for this society was the Society for the Prevention of Pauperism. This name was changed to the one above in 1823. It received authority from the state to manage the school.

in most state institutions for juvenile delinquents in the United States.[36]

By 1865, in addition to the one that had been established in Massachusetts, state reformatories for juvenile delinquents were in operation in New York, Pennsylvania, Maine, Connecticut, Michigan, Ohio, New Hampshire, and New Jersey. And by 1900 there were sixty-five reformatories for juveniles in the United States, some of which were private and local public institutions.[37]

THE MARK SYSTEM OF MACONOCHIE

In 1840 Captain Alexander Maconochie, of the Royal Navy, was placed in charge of the English penal colony on Norfolk Island, which was about a thousand miles to the east of Australia. Before this, he had had experience in penal establishments and had written on convict management. The problem that confronted him at Norfolk Island was a tremendous one, for most of the convicts in the colony were hardened criminals who had been living under the most degrading conditions. In dealing with it, Maconochie introduced a mark system as his chief instrument for the establishment of good order and efficient administration on the island.

The fundamental principle of the mark system was the substitution of a specific task for the customary time sentence. Instead of requiring the convicts to serve a fixed term regardless of what they did or failed to do while in his charge, Maconochie gave them an opportunity to reduce their sentences. Upon arrival at the penal colony, each prisoner was debited with a number of marks proportional to the seriousness of his offense. These he had to redeem by deportment, labor, and study, and when he had cancelled all of his marks, he was eligible for conditional release or ticket-of-leave. By means of marks he also secured food, supplies, and special privileges, and by the forfeiture of them, he was punished for his misconduct. The purpose of the system was to give the prisoner an incentive to work and to improve himself through the development of initiative and responsibility. As Maconochie so aptly explained, "When a man keeps the key of his own prison, he is soon persuaded to fit it to the lock."

Although Maconochie was handicapped by the limited authority of his position, he did demonstrate the value of his system, and he was justified in saying, "I found Norfolk Island a hell, but left it an orderly and well-regulated community." Even so, his innovations received little support in Australia. They were, however, praised by the reformers in Great Britain, and in 1849 he was made governor of the Birmingham Jail in England.

[36] See Lewis, pp. 40, 160, 302, 303, 316; McKelvey, pp. 13–15, 37, 38.
[37] Paul W. Tappan, *Juvenile Delinquency* (New York: McGraw-Hill Book Co., Inc., 1949), p. 441.

There he installed and expanded his mark system, but after only two years he was charged with being too lenient and forced to resign.[38]

THE IRISH SYSTEM

By 1850, English prisons had come to be divided into two classes: (1) convict prisons, in which were confined offenders committed for the longer sentences known as "penal servitude"; and (2) local prisons, to which were committed those sentenced for shorter terms. At that time the convict prisons were under the direct control of the central government, while the local prisons were administered by the county justices of the peace and by municipal corporations; but later, in 1877, they too were put under the management of the central government. Those who were sentenced to long terms, that is, to "penal servitude," were required to go through three stages of punishment: (1) twelve months of solitary confinement; (2) work in association with other convicts, chiefly in outdoor labor on public works; and (3) conditional release for a period of remission earned by hard work and good conduct, which was always liable to revocation.

In 1854, Sir Walter Crofton became director of the Irish convict prisons, and during the next eight years, while he occupied that office, he established an administration that attracted the attention of penal authorities throughout the world. In the development of his program he utilized the mark system of Maconochie, and to the three stages of penal servitude listed above he added a fourth, which became known as the "intermediate prison." During this stage, which was never less than six months, prisoners lived in comparative freedom under the supervision of a few unarmed guards. They worked together and were housed in unlocked portable huts. The ruling principle was individualization of treatment, and the number of prisoners in a colony was not allowed to exceed one hundred. The purpose of the "intermediate prison" was to determine whether the prisoner had reformed and to train him for full freedom by the enjoyment of partial freedom as a preliminary step. Every prisoner had to pass the test of the "intermediate prison" before he could secure his ticket-of-leave. Thus, as its name indicates, this stage was between the stages of solitary confinement and labor in association on one hand, and the stage of conditional release on the other.

Promotion from stage to stage was dependent upon the accumulation of marks by the prisoner. In this way he was made to realize that his progress to liberty could be furthered only by the cultivation and application of qualities opposed to those which led to his conviction. How-

---

[38] Wines, pp. 192–95; Barnes, p. 145; Webb, pp. 164–79. See also the pamphlets by Alexander Maconochie, especially his "The Mark System of Prison Discipline."

ever, employment in the community had to be found for the prisoner before he was conditionally released, and during this stage he was also kept under supervision.

Crofton's great contribution to prison discipline was his intermediate prison at Lusk, which was fifteen miles from Dublin, Ireland. Of more than a thousand prisoners who passed through this institution, it is said that only two attempted to escape. Taking its name from the land in which it was developed, Crofton's program of penal administration became known as the Irish system, and it was by this name that it achieved fame in America.[39]

THE REFORMATORY SYSTEM IN AMERICA (1870–1900)

The idea of reformation had always been present to some extent in American penology, but overcrowding, politics, incompetence, and the drive to make prisons self-supporting had pushed it into the background. As a result, the work of reformation had been left largely to the chaplains and volunteers. However, as knowledge of the Irish system spread throughout the country, attention was attracted to the innovations of Crofton, and interest in the reformation of the prisoner was again aroused. Leading American penologists, such as Theodore W. Dwight and E. C. Wines of the New York Prison Association, F. B. Sanborn of Massachusetts, Z. R. Brockway, Superintendent of the Detroit House of Correction, and Gaylord Hubbell, Warden of Sing Sing, began to consider the possibility of introducing the Irish system into the prisons of this country. The New York Prison Association became the nucleus for an agitation for making reformation the primary object of penal institutions. As a result a national prison association was organized at Cincinnati in October, 1870; at that time, it adopted a declaration of principles which stressed the indeterminate sentence and the classification and reformation of prisoners.

This was the beginning of a new era. Overcrowding, which again became evident in the late sixties, called for the construction of additional institutions, and into these the new reformatory program, an adaptation of the Irish system, was introduced. These institutions became known as reformatories. They had a dual purpose: (1) to prevent the young offender from coming into contact with the older and more hardened criminals; and (2) to provide a definite program of rehabilitation for those who had not as yet become habituated to crime. The first of the

---

[39] Ives, pp. 201–6; Webb, pp. 180–231; Mary Carpenter, *Reformatory Prison Discipline as Developed by the Right Honorable Sir Walter Crofton in the Irish Convict Prisons* (London: Longman and Co., 1872); Stephen Hobhouse and A Fenner Brockway, *English Prisons Today* (London: Longmans, Green and Co., Inc., 1922), pp. 55, 214.

new institutions was the Elmira Reformatory in New York, which was opened in 1876; it became the model for all the others that followed. Zebulon Brockway was Elmira's first superintendent, and he remained in office until 1900. To this institution were committed youthful offenders between the ages of sixteen and thirty, who were serving their first prison term.

In structure Elmira was like the typical Auburn Prison, having interior cell blocks for solitary confinement at night and workshops for congregate employment during the day. In program the only difference between the reformatory and the prison was the greater emphasis on trade training and academic education. The operation of contract industries was to continue as in other New York prisons, although with the program of training as an excuse, the institution was relieved somewhat of the necessity to be self-supporting. However, in two outstanding features the reformatory was different from the typical prison of this era. These were: (1) sentences to the reformatory were indeterminate, and prisoners could be released on parole; and (2) all inmates in the reformatory were graded into three classes according to achievement and conduct. Prisoners on admission to the reformatory were placed in the second grade for the first six months and were demoted to the third grade for bad conduct or promoted to the first grade as they earned their "marks." Only those who were in the first grade were eligible for parole.

Within twenty-five years of the establishment of Elmira, reformatories were constructed in twelve other states. Enthusiasm for the reformatory program ran high, and predictions were made that it would sweep the country; but the movement had already passed its peak and was on the decline by 1910. A few more reformatories were opened, but on the whole the program did not outlive its own founders.

Britain had greatly influenced America in the rise of the reformatory movement. It was now America's turn to influence Britain. In 1897 Sir Evelyn Ruggles-Brise (1857–1935), director of the English prisons arrived in the United States to study the reformatory system. While here he visited Elmira and the Massachusetts Reformatory at Concord, and upon his return to England he opened a specialized institution at the small town of Borstal for male offenders between the ages of sixteen and twenty-one. Thus was begun the now famous Borstal System, which took its name from the small town in which its first institution was established. The system is based entirely on individualized treatment, both in the institution and during the period of aftercare.[40]

[40] See Evelyn Ruggles-Brise, *The English Prison System* (London: Macmillan and Co., Ltd., 1921), chap. viii; William Healy and Benedict S. Alper, *Criminal Youth and the Borstal System* (New York: The Commonwealth Fund, 1941); and Molly Mellanby and R. L. Bradley, "The English Borstal System after the War," *Federal Probation*, XII (Dec., 1948), 19–22.

It is not difficult to find the important factors that caused the failure of the reformatory system in the United States. They are the same ones that had caused failures in the past. Foremost among these was the persistent preoccupation with mere custody and security, which stifled all ingenuity and enterprise and dominated the construction and operation of the great majority of the reformatories. Elmira itself was established in a structure that originally had been built as a maximum-security prison for hardened adult criminals. Inadequate appropriations, incompetent personnel, politics, overcrowding, and repressive discipline helped to complete the picture of bitter disillusionment and failure. The reformatories soon became junior prisons in which education and trade training were largely nominal and the grading system degenerated into a mechanical routine.

During the period from 1870 to 1900, additional prisons were constructed in sixteen states. All of these were of the Auburn type and were not unusual in any way except that their cells were provided with plumbing, running water, and ventilating systems. Most of them introduced some kind of rudimentary educational program, including a prison library, but in general this affected only a small fraction of the institutional population. In the South, the War between the States had virtually eliminated the beginnings of the penitentiary system. While northern and western states were abandoning the lease and contract systems of prison labor in favor of the piece-price, state-account, and state-use systems, the border states continued to use the contract system, and the more southern states reverted to the leasing out of prisoners to private companies. By 1900, Louisiana and Mississippi had replaced their leases with prison farms and set the pace for other southern states, but it was not until the nineteen twenties that the lease and contract systems were entirely eliminated in the South.

Until the last decade of the nineteenth century, the federal government had no prisons of its own, and federal offenders were confined in state prisons; but in 1889 Congress passed an act authorizing the establishment of three penal institutions. Since no appropriations were made to implement this law, nothing was done to provide for the housing of prisoners until July 1, 1895, when the Department of Justice took over the military prison at Fort Leavenworth, Kansas. The following year Congress authorized the acquisition of 1,000 acres of the land adjoining Fort Leavenworth and the erection thereon of a penitentiary with a capacity of 1,200 prisoners. Work began in 1897, and thus the federal government moved to acquire its first prison. The second federal prison, located at Atlanta, Georgia, was formally occupied in 1902. These two institutions, together with the small territorial jail located on Puget Sound, which later became the McNeil Island Penitentiary, constituted the entire federal prison system until 1925.

In summary, it may be said that the reformatory period (1870–1900) made two lasting contributions to American penology. These were (1) the introduction of the indeterminate sentence and parole, and (2) the establishment of a positive reform program through education. Although the second failed, chiefly because of the inadequacy and incompetence of the prison personnel, it did modify the thinking and the recognized objectives of the Auburn type of institution and made discipline and routine more tolerable.[41]

THE INDUSTRIAL PRISON IN AMERICA (1900–1935)

During the period from 1904 to 1935, the population of state prisons increased nearly 140 per cent, and in 1935 there were 126,258 inmates in state prisons and reformatories. To meet this great increase old facilities were expanded and eleven new state prisons (ten of the Auburn type and one at Stateville, Illinois, patterned after Jeremy Bentham's Panopticon) were established.

The federal institutions, also, had been subjected to overwhelming population pressure; and Congress in 1925 authorized the construction of two reformatories, one for women at Alderson, West Virginia, and the other for men at Chillicothe, Ohio. A few years later, in 1930, Congress created the Federal Bureau of Prisons, and Sanford Bates became its first director. Before the period closed other units were added to the federal system. Important among these were: (1) the Northeastern Penitentiary at Lewisburg, Pennsylvania; (2) the Southwestern Reformatory at El Reno, Oklahoma; (3) the United States Penitentiary on McNeil Island, Washington; (4) the Medical Center for Federal Prisoners at Springfield, Missouri; and (5) the maximum-security prison on Alcatraz Island, California.

As the prisons adopted the reformatory philosophy, although very little of its practice, the reformatories became more and more like prisons. In fact, in some states, except for the ages of the inmates there was little or no difference between these two types of institutions; but in general the reformatories did maintain vocational and academic day schools for part of their population. The program in almost every prison during this period was custodial, punitive, and industrial. The adoption of cellular confinement had eliminated the plan of classification and moral instruc-

[41] Barnes, pp. 144–48; *Attorney General's Survey*, pp. 21–27; Sanford Bates, *Prisons and Beyond* (New York: The Macmillan Co., 1936), pp. 127, 128; Snell Putney and Gladys J. Putney, "Origins of the Reformatory," *Journal of Criminal Law, Criminology, and Police Science*, LIII (Dec., 1962), 437–45; *Handbook of American Prisons and Reformatories* (New York: The Osborne Association, Inc., 1942), p. 95.

Interior view of one of the Panopticon cell houses at the Stateville
prison, Illinois. (Courtesy of Federal Bureau of Prisons)

tion which had characterized the early American prison before 1830; and
noncommunication, which was the hope of the Auburn and Pennsylvania
systems, had vanished with the development of prison industries in congregate workshops. Thus, except for the changes in housing, imprisonment
for the majority of inmates during this period became what it had been
one hundred years before. Meanwhile, the decline in the enthusiasm for
the reformatory program and the necessity of keeping prisoners employed
to prevent trouble and to help pay expenses again made industry the
mainstay of the penitentiary system.

But the very prominence and effectiveness of prison industry fore-
shadowed the end of another period in American penology. Free industry
and organized labor, aroused by this development and aided by a series
of investigations which exposed the exploitation of inmate labor for the
benefit of private companies, maintained a strong campaign to eliminate
the sale of prison-made goods in competition with free products. Under
the pressure of public opinion and restrictive legislation, prisons were
forced to modify their industrial programs. Finally, in 1929 Congress
passed the Hawes-Cooper Act and in 1935, the Ashurst-Sumners Act.
These were chiefly "enabling acts" designed to encourage the states to

enact legislation restricting the sale of prison-made goods. Prison industry, therefore, might have survived despite them if the widespread unemployment of free labor, caused by the great depression of 1929 to 1933, had not goaded the majority of the states into action. By passing laws which restricted the sale of prison-made goods to governmental agencies and institutions, they virtually prohibited the disposition of these goods on the open market and thus sounded the death knell of industrial prisons.[42]

AN ERA OF EXPERIMENTATION (1935–   )

During the more than one hundred fifty years that comprise the history of American prisons before 1935, attempts were made to develop prisons as agencies of moral instruction, as educational institutions, and finally as great industrial centers, but in each instance the attempt failed. The fall of the industrial prison in America plunged many penal administrators into confusion and sent all in search of a new integrating principle of operation. This quest continues, and although it is not yet clear what form the prison of tomorrow will assume, some important developments have culminated during the years since 1935 which seem to indicate the trend.

These developments, which will receive more detailed treatment in succeeding chapters, may be summarized as follows:

1. The long radial cell blocks of the Eastern Penitentiary and the flanking rectangular cell houses of the Auburn design are no longer held in favor by realistic prison architects. During the earlier part of this period they preferred the telephone-pole construction for the maximum-security prison, and the telephone-pole construction, the open-campus plan, or the self-enclosed design for the medium-security and minimum-security institutions.

The telephone-pole construction is so named because it has a long covered central corridor that bisects the cell houses, and usually the service facilities and shops, at right angles. This arrangement has many advantages. It provides protected and easy access to all parts of the prison and facilitates lighting, heating, and ventilation. It originated in France in 1898 and was introduced into the United States not long after the beginning of the twentieth century. The Minnesota State Prison at Stillwater, which was opened for occupancy in 1914, was the first state prison in the United States to utilize some of the features of the telephone-pole design. Today this design forms the basis of some of the most modern prison structures in our country, including the federal penitentiaries at Lewisburg, Pennsylvania, and Terre Haute, Indiana, the United States

---

[42] *Attorney General's Survey*, pp. 27–34; Bates, pp. 128–48; James V. Bennett, "The Federal Prison System" *Contemporary Correction*, ed. Paul W. Tappan (New York: McGraw-Hill Book Co., Inc., 1951), pp. 63–74.

Army disciplinary barracks at Camp Cooke in California, and the Riker's Island city prison in New York City.

The open-campus plan, as the name indicates, calls for the grouping of dormitories and service facilities in a functional pattern, usually around a common well-sodded and landscaped courtyard. All the buildings, or some of them, may be surrounded by a woven-wire fence, topped with barbed wire—the so-called "cyclone fence." The federal correctional institution at Tallahassee, Florida, which was opened in 1938, is constructed according to this plan.

In the self-enclosed type of institution, the buildings are so arranged that they constitute the enclosing walls. Thus one or more enclosed yards are provided for the use of the inmates or for other purposes. The federal correctional institution, at Danbury, Connecticut, built between 1938 and 1940, is an example of this type of construction.[43]

However, recent experience with the telephone-pole and the self-enclosed types of construction has revealed that they tend to impose excessive rigidity on institutional design and operation. On the other hand, the open-campus plan not only permits a great deal of flexibility in the arrangement of buildings but also facilitates the introduction of modern correctional programs. The growing popularity of the open-campus plan is reflected in its use in a number of new minimum-security and medium-security institutions. Where the telephone-pole and self-enclosed designs are now being used, they are modified in order to reduce their weaknesses. Thus in the new federal penitentiary at Marion, Illinois, which was opened in 1963, the telephone-pole design is transformed into four short radiating corridors, the so-called "pinwheel plan," which provides definite zones for ordinary housing, special housing, work areas, and recreational-educational activities.

Another type of construction, the so-called "satellite plan," has recently been adopted to provide quick and cheap accommodations for rising prison populations. It has been especially favored in California, where it has been used in the Correctional Training Facility at Soledad, the men's colony at Los Padres, and the Youth Training School at Ontario. The satellite plan calls for the economical clustering of small specialized facilities around a parent institution, which supplies them with power, light, water, food storage, medical care, and other such services. Although each of the smaller facilities is intended to function as an independent rehabilitation unit, in many ways the entire collection of units operates as a

[43] Federal Bureau of Prisons, *Handbook of Correctional Institution Design and Construction* (Washington, D.C.: Federal Bureau of Prisons, 1949), pp. 60–107; *Handbook of American Prisons and Reformatories*, (New York: The Osborne Association, Inc., 1938), p. 129; Alfred Hopkins, *Prisons and Prison Building* (New York: Architectural Book Publishing Co., Inc., 1930).

single institution, thus making inevitable the undesirable intermingling of different types of offenders. The satellite plan has been described by the Federal Bureau of Prisons as an "unhappy development in prison architecture."

During the years from 1950 to 1960, the amount of institutional construction in the United States reached new heights, and correctional architecture appears to be entering another period of vitality. Although the developments have not been uniform, the trend now seems to be toward smaller, more flexible, and better-lighted facilities that can be more easily adapted to normal living and individualized correctional programs.[44]

2. In 1944, California passed a prison reorganization act which provides for a unique administrative setup. Its purpose is to provide a unified statewide organization of correctional activities under a state department of corrections. Included in this new organization are the administrator of corrections, the board of corrections, the board of trustees of the women's institution, the adult authority, which has wide discretion over the sentencing and parole of adult males, and the youth authority, which has similar jurisdiction over juveniles and young adults. It is still uncertain how much this departure in penal administration will affect other states, but its emphasis upon the importance of coordinating correctional functions has caused considerable discussion and exercised a stimulating influence throughout the country.

3. The classification of inmates is probably the most significant recent development in American prisons. This procedure has as its purpose the individualization of the correctional process based upon detailed educational, medical, psychiatric, psychological, and sociological examinations. It operates through such programs of rehabilitation as religious instruction, academic education, vocational training, recreation, and medical care. Classification received its first systematic development in New Jersey during the years immediately following World War I, and since then it has become a fundamental part of the prison systems of an increasing number of states and the federal government.

4. The diversification of institutions has become increasingly important in American penology. This is interrelated with the development of classification, since the latter cannot function adequately without diversification of not only institutional programs but also institutional facilities. The Federal Bureau of Prisons has contributed much of the leadership in this diversification and has constructed a variety of institutions, including

---

[44] Federal Bureau of Prisons, *Recent Prison Construction, 1950–1960* (Washington, D.C.: Federal Bureau of Prisons, 1960), pp. 1–6; Norman Johnston, "The Changing Face of Correctional Architecture," *The Prison Journal*, XLI (Spring, 1961), 14–20; Howard B. Gill, "Correctional Philosophy and Architecture," *Journal of Criminal Law, Criminology, and Police Science*, LIII (Sept., 1962), 312–22.

penitentiaries, reformatories, correctional institutions, prison camps, institutions for juveniles, a medical center, and a detention headquarters. In the federal system, the term "correctional institution" is used to refer to a medium-security or a minimum-security institution. Many penologists believe that the great promise of the future in prison work lies in the expansion of medium- and minimum-security construction and the reduction in the number of maximum-security prison plants.

The federal minimum-security institution, located at Seagoville, Texas, has attracted considerable attention. Originally built for female offenders, it was opened in 1940, leased during World War II to the Immigration and Naturalization Service, and returned to the Federal Bureau of Prisons in 1945. At that time it was converted into a minimum-security institution for male offenders, and it has become the outstanding demonstration in the federal system of the use of minimum custody facilities for inmates classified as "security risks." Seagoville is constructed on the open-campus plan and has a normal capacity of 417. Since its operation as an institution for male offenders, it has had a very low escape rate.

5. Group therapy has been introduced into some correctional institutions. This, like individual therapy, seeks to modify the inmate's attitudes, but it operates through the processes of association in groups. Used in the treatment of military prisoners during World War II, it has been recommended by some penologists, but it is still not certain what role it will play in the prison work of the future.

6. There has been an almost complete substitution of public systems of prison labor for the private ones. This tendency had appeared before the passage of the restrictive laws of 1929, 1935, and 1940, but they have virtually eliminated what remained of the private systems.

7. The federal prison system has attained full stature. It is now in a position not only to do pioneering work in many forms of correctional treatment but also to provide a constructive and stimulating leadership for the entire country.[45]

[45] *State and National Correctional Institutions* (New York: The American Prison Association, 1952). See also Walter M. Wallack, "Stone Walls Do a Prison Make," *Federal Probation*, XVI (Sept., 1952), 7–13; and Kenyon J. Scudder, *Prisoners are People* (Garden City, N.Y.: Doubleday and Co., Inc., 1952).

21

Correctional Institutions Today

TYPES OF CORRECTIONAL INSTITUTIONS

In the United States, the most common correctional institutions are prisons or penitentiaries, reformatories, farms, ranches, camps, jails, houses of correction, workhouses, and training or industrial schools. Prisons[1] or penitentiaries provide maximum or medium security for felons, usually for older felons. Reformatories are designed to give maximum or medium security for youthful felons, usually for those between the ages of sixteen and thirty. Prison farms, ranches, and road camps are used for felons of all ages, but usually for those who need only minimum security. Jails, workhouses, houses of correction, farms, and road camps are used for misdemeanants. Training or industrial schools, farms, and camps are operated for juvenile delinquents.

The correctional institutions for adults in the United States constitute a heterogeneous group of over 250 federal and state prisons, reformatories, farms, camps, and ranches,[2] and more than 3,500 federal, county, and municipal jails, houses of correction, workhouses, farms, and road camps for short-term offenders. State prisons or penitentiaries have been established in every state. Delaware, the last state to establish a state prison system, enacted legislation for this purpose in July, 1955. Some states, for example, California, Illinois, New York, and Pennsylvania, have more than one state prison or penitentiary. Many of the states have reformatories for men and most of them have completely separate or partially separate institutions for women, which are often called reformatories.

[1] The word "prison" is used also as a convenient over-all designation for adult correctional institutions above the level of the jail, house of correction, and workhouse.

[2] *Directory of State and Federal Correctional Institutions, 1963* (New York: The American Correctional Association, 1963).

Some states, however, still segregate their women in one section of the state prison for men.

The first separate institution for women in the United States, the Indiana women's prison, was opened in 1873, but only four more were established during the next forty years. Since 1913, however, the number of completely separate or partially separate institutions has increased more rapidly, and in 1963 there were thirty-one such institutions in the United States (twenty-nine in twenty-seven states, one in the District of Columbia, and one operated by the federal government). Of these thirty-one institutions, the women's reformatory of the District of Columbia, the federal reformatory for women, and twenty-eight institutions in twenty-six states are physically separate institutions. The failure to provide more adequate facilities for women prisoners in the United States is due partly to the fact that there are comparatively few of these prisoners and most of them are not serious offenders.[3]

The South, whose mild climate especially favors agriculture, has established extensive prison farms. Texas, Mississippi, Louisiana, and Florida have led in this development. The South also operates many road camps and employs convict labor throughout the year in the construction of highways. Both felons and misdemeanants are sentenced to these road camps.

There are now thirty-seven institutions in the federal prison system. These range all the way from maximum-security institutions, through the various medium-security and minimum-security institutions for men and women, to prison camps and prerelease guidance centers. Six of the federal institutions are penitentiaries, five are reformatories, five are institutions for juvenile and youth offenders, eight are correctional institutions (the name used in the federal system to designate medium-security and minimum-security institutions), five are prison camps, two are detention centers, one is a medical center, one is the federal jail in Alaska, and four are prerelease guidance centers. The super-security institution on Alcatraz Island, California, was abandoned in 1963, largely for reasons of economy. In addition to the foregoing institutions, which are operated by the Federal Bureau of Prisons, the federal government has two hospitals administered by the United States Public Health Service for the treatment of felons who are drug addicts and certain voluntary patients, one disciplinary barracks maintained by the Department of the Army, one naval disciplinary command maintained by the Department of the Navy, and one retraining group operated by the Department of the Air Force.

[3] *Manual of Correctional Standards* (New York: The American Correctional Association, 1959), pp. 464, 465; *Directory of State and Federal Correctional Institutions, 1963;* Henrietta Additon, "Women's Institutions," *Contemporary Correction,* ed. Paul W. Tappan (New York: McGraw-Hill Book Co., Inc., 1951), pp. 297–309.

Former federal super-security prison, Alcatraz Island, San Francisco Bay, California. Alcatraz, which earlier had been an army prison, was used until 1963 as an institution for intractable federal offenders. (Courtesy of Federal Bureau of Prisons)

Today the typical state prison in the United States is a walled fortress of stone and steel. Within are cell houses, administrative offices, schools, chapels, factories, workshops, a dining hall, an auditorium, a hospital, a recreation yard, and sometimes a gymnasium. Outside are the main administrative office, houses for the warden and his principal assistants and their families, and sometimes one or more prison farms. The normal capacity of the state prison may range from a few hundred to thousands. Many institutions have a capacity of 1,000 to 3,000; a few, 3,000 to 4,000; and one, the Michigan State Prison at Jackson, which is the largest prison in the United States, has a normal capacity of more than 5,000. Most of the state prisons are built along the lines of the original Auburn plan with interior cell blocks. The cells are small, the average being about five feet wide, eight feet long, and eight feet high. They are usually equipped with an iron bed, bedding, a locker, a small table, a chair, an electric light, a toilet, and a wash bowl.

The typical men's reformatory looks very much like a state prison. Although usually the reformatory is smaller, its facilities and equipment are the same as those of the prison. Women's prisons and reformatories, however, are quite different. In general, their buildings are attractive and well kept, having individual bedrooms and pleasant living and dining rooms. Some of the newer correctional institutions for women are built on the cottage plan. Even when women are confined in a section of the men's prison, their quarters are more attractive than those of other prisoners in the institution. Prison farms and camps have dormitories and farm buildings, often surrounded by a barbed wire fence. Road camps may have either permanent buildings or portable structures, and these, too, may be enclosed by a fence.

At the end of 1962 a total of 219,030 prisoners were confined in state and federal institutions for adult offenders in the United States. Of this total, 23,944 were in federal institutions and only 8,002, or 3.7 per cent, were women. During the year 1962 the total number of prisoners admitted into these institutions was 124,546, and the total number discharged was 126,352.[4] The total number of prisoners confined at the end of 1962 represented a drop of 0.6 per cent from the record high of 220,318 prisoners incarcerated at the close of 1961. This was the first time that the prison population had decreased since December 31, 1951. The largest prison population for any federal institution on December 31, 1961, was that of the United States Penitentiary at Atlanta, Georgia, which had 2,588 inmates. At the same time, four state institutions—one in each of the four states of California (5,481), Illinois (5,228), Michigan (4,505), and Ohio

---

[4] These figures do not include those prisoners who were transferred from one institution to another (Federal Bureau of Prisons, *National Prisoner Statistics*, No. 33 [Dec., 1963], pp. 1, 15, Table 1).

(4,427)—had prison populations of more than 4,000. These were the largest in the country.[5] Table 5 shows the recent trends in the rates of commitment to state and federal institutions for the period 1936 to 1961, inclusive.

Table 5. Number of prisoners in state and federal institutions and received from court, 1939–61, inclusive, per 100,000 of the estimated civilian population.

Year	Present at End of Year			Received from Court		
	All insti- tutions	Federal insti- tutions	State insti- tutions	All insti- tutions	Federal insti- tutions	State insti- tutions
1939	137.6	15.1	122.5	*	*	*
1940	131.9	14.6	117.3	55.5	11.5	44.0
1941	125.7	14.0	111.7	52.2	11.7	40.5
1942	114.8	12.7	102.2	44.9	10.5	34.5
1943	107.6	12.6	95.0	39.3	9.6	29.7
1944	104.5	14.3	90.2	39.6	11.1	28.5
1945	104.8	14.6	90.2	41.7	11.1	30.6
1946	101.2	12.7	88.5	44.3	10.8	33.5
1947	106.1	12.0	94.1	45.5	9.1	36.4
1948	107.4	11.2	96.2	43.9	8.6	35.4
1949	111.0	11.4	99.5	46.7	8.9	37.8
1950	110.6	11.4	99.2	46.3	9.5	36.8
1951	109.7	11.5	98.1	44.5	9.3	35.1
1952	109.7	11.7	97.9	46.2	10.0	36.3
1953	111.2	12.4	98.8	47.6	10.5	37.1
1954	115.0	12.6	102.4	50.9	10.5	40.4
1955	114.5	12.4	102.2	48.4	9.4	38.9
1956	114.7	12.2	102.5	47.2	8.1	39.0
1957	116.1	12.1	103.9	47.8	7.9	39.9
1958	120.0	12.6	107.4	51.8	8.1	43.7
1959	118.8	12.9	105.9	49.9	7.9	42.0
1960	119.8	13.0	106.7	49.8	7.7	42.1
1961	121.7	13.1	108.7	51.7	7.5	44.3

* Comparable data not available.

SOURCE: This table is based on data taken from the Federal Bureau of Prisons, *National Prisoner Statistics,* No. 30, August, 1962.

On April 1, 1960, according to the Federal Bureau of the Census, there were 45,695 persons (33,765 males and 11,930 females) in 454 correctional institutions (including forestry camps) for juvenile delinquents. Of these persons, 38,359 (29,681 males and 8,678 females) were in 358 public institutions and 7,336 (4,084 males and 3,252 females) in 96 private insti-

[5] Federal Bureau of Prisons, *National Prisoner Statistics,* No. 30 (Aug., 1962), Table 6. The Federal Bureau of Prisons did not publish the prison populations for the various correctional institutions for 1962.

tutions.[6] On the basis of its records, the United States Children's Bureau reported that on June 30, 1962, there were 230 public correctional institutions for juvenile delinquents in the United States, Puerto Rico, and the Virgin Islands, including 183 training schools (43 local, 139 state, and one federal) and 47 forestry camps, one of which was operated by the federal government. At that time there were approximately 39,000 children in these institutions, almost 87 per cent of whom were in those run by the states and 78 per cent of whom were boys.[7]

TRENDS IN CORRECTIONAL INSTITUTIONS

It is exceedingly difficult to generalize about American correctional institutions because they present such a diversity of characteristics. Some have changed but little over a period of many years and still resemble the prisons of the early nineteenth century. Some, however, have become the most progressive in the world and have adopted the most advanced practices and procedures. Between these two extremes there is distributed a great variety of institutions in all stages of development. But despite this, it is possible to identify the following important trends in the history of American correctional institutions:

1. They have become increasingly specialized. It will be recalled that originally all types of prisoners, regardless of age, sex, or physical or mental condition, were kept together in the same institution. Today, however, separate institutions have been established for males and females, felons and misdemeanants, adults, youthful offenders, and juveniles, the sane and the insane, the alcoholic and the drug addict, and for those who need maximum-, medium-, and minimum-security imprisonment.

A maximum-security institution is a walled institution in which the majority of the prisoners are housed in cells, employed within the walls, and so guarded and restricted as to reduce the danger of escape to the minimum. A medium-security institution is one with no wall, but perhaps surrounded with a wire fence of the industrial type. In it the majority of the prisoners are housed in outside cells or dormitories and employed outside as well as inside the enclosure, and less emphasis is placed on preventing escapes. A minimum-security institution is an open institution, usually a farm or camp. Its prisoners live in unlocked and unfenced buildings and work outdoors or in ordinary structures. While at work, the

[6] Federal Bureau of the Census, "Inmates of Institutions," *U. S. Census of Population: 1960* (Washington, D.C.: Government Printing Office, 1963), p. 11, Table 11; p. 13, Table 13.

[7] United States Children's Bureau, *Statistics on Public Institutions for Delinquent Children: 1962*, Statistical Series No. 70 (Washington, D.C.: Government Printing Office, 1963). This report does not include institutions or camps that were primarily for young adult offenders.

Maximum-security inside-cell block at Federal Reformatory, Chillicothe, Ohio. (Courtesy of Federal Bureau of Prisons)

inmates are under the supervision of overseers rather than under the surveillance of guards. In this type of institution there is a minimum emphasis on preventing escapes.[8] The tendency, however, is to provide all levels of security—maximum, medium, and minimum—in each institution, especially in the maximum-security type, although institutions continue to be classified on the basis of their major security characteristics.

2. Their administration has become increasingly centralized. Only a few states still retain local administrative boards for their state correctional institutions. This type of administration has been generally supplanted by some kind of central agency which exercises control over all state correctional institutions. In fact, the central agency in a few states has assumed some control over the local institutions for minor offenders, having the authority, for example, to inspect and rate them in accordance with approved standards.

3. Their programs have become more individualized. Some states through the classification of inmates now strive to adapt a person's correctional treatment to his individual needs and provide him with religious, educational, recreational, welfare, and employment programs that are designed to promote his rehabilitation. This is a far cry from the early American prison in which noncommunication and moral instruction were generally regarded as the most effective curative regimen.

4. Their living conditions have been improved. In general, correctional institutions are cleaner, better ventilated, and more satisfactorily lighted than ever before. Their inmates are given more adequate meals and medical care, are subjected to less rigid discipline, and are usually not branded with such marks of degradation as the shaving of the head, the lock-step, striped clothing, and the ball-and-chain.

5. Their social activities have been expanded. The solitary confinement of the Pennsylvania system has been generally abandoned except as punishment for the violation of institutional rules and regulations, and even the rule of silence, which was a feature of the Auburn system, is either not enforced at all or is used only at certain times, for example, during meal periods. Indeed, the whole movement in modern correctional administration is away from such restraints and toward the encouragement and development of contacts among inmates and between them and persons outside of the institution. To an increasing extent this movement has found expression in our correctional institutions through the introduction of athletic events, recreational programs, educational classes, and inmate councils.

6. The importance of personnel standards and training has been increasingly recognized. Although it is still true that the great majority of

[8] *Manual of Suggested Standards for a State Correctional System* (New York: The American Prison Association, 1946), p. 17.

those who are employed in our correctional institutions have had no formal training for their positions and that many of them are not qualified to discharge their duties, public opinion is nevertheless becoming increasingly aware of this problem, and many farsighted correctional administrators are urging the adoption of higher standards of employment and in-service training. The activities of the National Wardens' Association, the Federal Bureau of Prisons, and the American Correctional Association (formerly the American Prison Association) have contributed in a significant way to this trend.

OBSTACLES TO EFFECTIVE INSTITUTIONAL CORRECTION

Despite these trends, many serious obstacles stand in the way of effective institutional correction in the United States. That this is a problem which concerns every American is evidenced by the fact that most of the inmates of correctional institutions are released within a comparatively short period of time. In fact, it is estimated that 95 per cent of the inmates of our prisons and reformatories return to society, the great majority of them within two or three years. It must be clear, therefore, that society should do everything within its powers to make our correctional institutions effective agencies of rehabilitation. Only in this way can the community hope to benefit from the contributions of released prisoners rather than suffer from their crimes.

At present, the most important obstacles[9] to effective institutional correction are the following:

1. Many institutions are old and antiquated. Almost one-half of the state prisons now in use were constructed over seventy-five years ago, and many have been in operation for over one hundred years. Fewer than twenty-five of the state prisons have been built since 1920. Of the federal penitentiaries, only one—the institution at Marion, Illinois, which was opened in 1963—has been built since 1940, and two have been in use since around 1900. Fifteen of the state men's reformatories were established between 1876 and 1925, and fewer than ten since then. Three of the federal reformatories for men were opened between 1926 and 1934; one, in 1959; and the one federal reformatory for women, in 1927. Old institutions are difficult to maintain, and since they were built to serve the purpose of antiquated correctional policies, they are not readily adaptable to modern methods and programs. The situation is not so serious as it might be, however, because the federal government and some of the states, like California, Florida, North Carolina, Ohio, and Texas, have created addi-

---

[9] This discussion of obstacles refers primarily to institutions for adult male felons, but to a lesser degree, it applies also to all other correctional institutions.

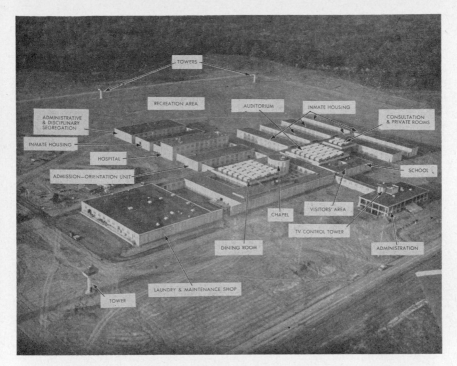

The new federal prison at Marion, Illinois, during its construction. Note the four short radiating corridors, the so-called "pinwheel plan," which provide definite zones for various types of housing and prison activities. (Courtesy of Federal Bureau of Prisons)

tional medium- and minimum-security facilities to help care for the rising prison population.

2. Many institutions are too large or overcrowded. Some suffer from both of these defects. There is a growing conviction among penologists that no correctional institution ought to have more than 1,200 inmates, and many feel that a population of only 500 or 600 would be closer to the ideal. Yet most of the state prisons for men in the United States had an average population of more than 1,000 during 1961, while about twenty had over 2,000, and four had more than 4,000. Small institutions make it possible for their administrators to know intimately not only the inmates but also the employees and to deal intelligently with each individual's problems. When an institution is both excessively large and overcrowded, all administrative problems are increased. Two, and sometimes three or four, inmates must share a cell built for one. All possibility of privacy vanishes, perversions flourish, idleness is rampant, mass methods prevail,

and programs of rehabilitation degenerate into procedures and regulations designed to maintain order and insure security.

3. In general, the living quarters are unnecessarily uncomfortable and unsuitable. Most of the men's prisons and reformatories are of the Auburn type and are equipped with interior cell blocks. The typical modern interior cell block is housed in an oblong building and is composed of four or five tiers of cells. In each tier, there is a double row of cells, arranged back to back and separated by a service corridor; across the front of each tier is a gallery which provides access to the cells and passageways for the patrolling guards. Although modern sanitary, ventilating, and lighting facilities have somewhat improved the interior cell blocks, they have not changed the essential surroundings of their inmates. If there are more prisoners than cells, two or more may occupy a cell too small for one, and sometimes they may be locked up in their small cubicles from 4:30 or 5:00 P.M. to 7:00 A.M. every day and all day Sunday, except for a few hours during religious services and meal periods.

Modern correctional administrators, who believe that the emphasis in institutions should be on rehabilitation, put much stress on making the institutional atmosphere as much like ordinary living as possible.[10] They feel that too much regimentation militates against successful adjustment after release and that a prisoner is better prepared to assume his responsibilities in the community if he has the self-respect that comes from having been treated like a grown man instead of a caged animal or an unruly child. Furthermore, they assert, only about 25 per cent of our prisoners need maximum-security confinement, and even these, they argue, should be given as much freedom as is commensurate with security.

4. The personnel in the great majority of our correctional institutions is inadequate. In general they are not qualified to assume their duties, and they receive little or no training while on the job. Although the number of professionally trained persons is increasing, there are still comparatively few psychiatrists, psychologists, sociologists, and social workers in the employ of these institutions. Moreover, the prospects of securing better personnel are not encouraging. In many states the salaries are low; the hours, long; the tenure, insecure. Often politics governs the appointment of guards or wardens or both, so that a continuity of policy is difficult to maintain and the development of a career service is almost impossible. In some prisons inmates with money or political influence

[10] Over thirty years ago Howard B. Gill, superintendent of the State Prison Colony at Norfolk, Massachusetts, from 1928 to 1934, made "normal living for inmates" an essential part of his administrative policy. In fact, he described his institution as "a supervised community within a wall." Criticism of his administration eventually resulted in his removal. See Carl R. Doering (ed.), *A Report on the Development of Penological Treatment at Norfolk Prison Colony in Massachusetts* (New York: Bureau of Social Hygiene, Inc., 1940).

have no trouble in obtaining special privileges. As a result of all this, the turnover of personnel in our correctional institutions is high, and the morale in many of them is low.

5. The segregation of inmates is not widely enforced. Most correctional officials pay at least lip service to the thesis that the hardened criminals, the mentally ill, and the homosexuals should be segregated from the general institutional population. However, in practice this is seldom done, and the presence of these groups tends to undermine any program of rehabilitation and contributes to unrest and disturbances.

6. Unemployment is a major problem in America's correctional institutions. At least half of the nation's prisoners are idle, and even those who are employed often do not have enough work to keep them busy. Maintenance details are likely to be overmanned, and other institutional work seldom involves a full working day.

7. Institutional discipline tends to become rigid. Rules accumulate to promote operational efficiency, to regulate relationships within the institution, to facilitate the supervision of inmates, and to prevent escapes and disturbances. Unless officials are on the alert to check the tendency toward rigidity, an institutional machine is created which becomes an end in itself. When this happens, some inmates mechanically obey and drift along in an apathetic and listless existence. Others rebel, are punished, and become hard, bitter, and cynical. Many thus acquire qualities that interfere with successful adjustment after release. Although brutality in the enforcement of rules has been weeded out of most institutions, it is still openly practiced in some places. Whipping as a method of discipline is allowed by law in a few states and is inflicted illegally in others.

8. Parole policies and practices are sometimes unfair or inefficient. For many inmates, parole is the one great hope. If the parole board does not give them due consideration, they become discouraged, resentful, and bitter. All that the institution has been able to accomplish in their rehabilitation may thus be destroyed.

9. Institutional life tends to be monotonous and oppressive. The typical day for the male inmate in many prisons and reformatories begins when he is awakened at about 6:30 A.M., sometimes by the ringing of a bell. He washes, dresses, makes his bed, arranges his cell in accordance with the rules, and then stands behind his cell door for the morning count. After this the cell doors are unlocked, and he steps out into the corridor, and marches under supervision to the mess hall, where at a given signal he sits down and, in many prisons, eats in enforced silence. Usually the prisoner has about twenty minutes for breakfast, after which at another signal he arises and marches from the mess hall.

When the weather permits, he has a short period of exercise after breakfast. Often this consists of marching in silence around the prison yard. After his exercise he marches to his place of employment, but even there he finds little relief from the monotonous routine. His work is seldom in line with his experience, aptitude, and plans for the future after his release. Usually he is not interested in it and finds little opportunity for self-expression in the performance of his duties. Rules govern every aspect of his work, and he may not leave it without permission.

At his noonday and evening meals he follows the same routine that regulated his movements during breakfast. After his evening meal he marches back to his cell, where he may be immediately locked up for the night or, as is the case in some prisons, he may be permitted to walk up and down in the cell block before he is again placed in his cell. In some prisons he may go to night classes, participate in band or orchestra practice, occasionally attend plays, lectures, or moving pictures, or lie in his cell and listen to his radio, usually to programs selected for him by the institution's radio control center. Lights go out in all cells at the same time, usually at nine o'clock, and he may not have his light out until then.

His weekend is often more monotonous than his working days. In many prisons he may devote Saturday afternoon to recreation or leisure, but even where he has this privilege he is often locked in his cell at half-past four or five on Saturday afternoon and does not come out again until seven o'clock Monday morning, except for an hour or two on Sunday for religious meetings and meals.

This, then, is the typical week for the male inmate in many prisons and reformatories, and it repeats itself week after week with little variation except for the privilege of receiving visitors several times a month on specified days and at specified hours. But here, too, the routine continues and strictly regulates all contacts with outsiders. It is this monotonous routine—this piling up of rules, signals, marching, and supervision day after day—that causes demoralization among many male inmates and fails to prepare them for a place in a competitive society, where initiative and ambition are essential to success.

The life of women confined in a section of a men's prison is often more monotonous and restricted than that of the men, because of the limited number of available occupations and recreations and the absence of any meaningful rehabilitation program. However, women incarcerated in their own prisons and reformatories are usually much more fortunate. In general, they have considerable opportunity for individual expression and their surroundings are attractive and homelike. Even so, all institutions for women have difficult problems, because they must accept offenders ranging in age from girls to senile women and presenting a wide range of sentences and offenses, personality traits, backgrounds, mentalities, needs, and potentialities, and most of these institutions have to struggle with the additional problem of a small and fluctuating population—all of which militates against the introduction of an effective treatment program.

10. Institutional budgets are inadequate. At every legislative session there is a struggle to secure sufficient funds to operate our correctional institutions. The public is not inclined to spend money on those who violate the law, and during these days of high taxes it is more reluctant than ever to do this. And yet, without adequate funds, even the best and most progressive administrator must reduce his efforts to provide modern programs for his institution and rely largely upon authority, force, and repression in the performance of his duties. Thus, inadequate budgets are the cause of many of the obstacles that stand in the way of effective institutional correction.

11. Correctional institutions have certain inherent limitations. It must be recognized that even if correctional institutions had adequate budgets and measured up to modern standards, their administration would still be confronted with limitations that spring from the very nature of the correctional institutions themselves. We can achieve a deeper understanding of these limitations if we see the prison as a community.

THE PRISON COMMUNITY

When a group of human beings is forcibly confined, rules for the regulation of their behavior must be established, and in every decision regarding them, explicitly or implicitly, there is the weight of institutional authority. The larger the group and the greater the required security, the more numerous and elaborate the rules must be. There is, then, the inevitability and reality of inmate rules.

In the enforcement of these rules, all persons who are involved fall naturally into two major groups: those who enforce the rules, the administrators, the custodial force, whose official position is emphasized by their uniforms, and the professional staff; and those against whom the rules are enforced, the inmates. Everyone belongs to one group or the other. He cannot belong to both.[11] Inevitably, therefore, a social distance exists between these two groups which can be neither ignored nor entirely bridged. In fact, those who enforce inmate rules must recognize this social distance or lose much of their effectiveness as custodians. For example, fraternization between guards and inmates endangers the formality and impersonality essential to the maintenance of authority.

However, those who enforce the rules do not present a completely united front. Not only do their personalities and backgrounds differ and thus affect their attitudes toward the inmates, but also their various occu-

---

[11] A possible exception to this exists where the undesirable practice of using inmates as guards is still followed.

pational pursuits relate them in different ways to the institutional rules. Even so, in the performance of their duties prison administrators and the custodial force tend to develop a set of common attitudes. As law-enforcement officers reflecting the view of the public, they are inclined to have attitudes of superiority, antagonism, resentment, and suspicion toward all prisoners. Although such attitudes give administrators, prison officers, and guards a sense of cohesiveness, fortify their belief in the importance of prison rules, and strengthen their morale, they also sharply define and tend to fix the social distance between them and their prisoners. To some extent, the members of the professional staff share in these attitudes, but special interest in the individual inmate and occupational concern with his rehabilitation often induce the professional worker to use considerable discretion in the application of rules and thus reduce the consistency of their enforcement. Furthermore, administrators, custodial officers, and professional workers alike are engaged in a competition for status in the hierarchy of the institution, and their drive for economic advantage and power may propel them into factional disputes and the turmoil of institutional politics. Cracks and openings thus split the wall of rule enforcement, and the inmates, eager to make their confinement as short and comfortable as possible, quickly exploit these weaknesses, frequently using guard against guard, professional worker against guard, professional worker against professional worker, or even the governor against the warden, in a shifting succession of schemes, strategems, plots, and tactical maneuvers.

The imprisoned, too, share a common experience, the experience of an enforced confinement. Out of this emerge certain influences that tend to draw the inmates together in a common cause against their keepers. The close physical proximity in which prisoners must live destroys virtually all privacy and presses them toward conformity, while their isolation limits the range of experience, magnifies every word and act, and thus intensifies the regulating influence of talk, gossip, and public opinion within the walls. Furthermore, a monotonous equalitarianism increases the psychological impact of prison life. Prisoners occupy similar cells, wear the same kind of clothing, eat the same food, do the same thing at the same time according to the same rules—day in and day out, year after year—and without having to compete for worldly goods or struggle for economic security. Life may hold little for prisoners, but what it does hold they share in common. And all this happens under the same authority, an authority which is direct, immediate, imperative, and inescapable. Everything that the prisoners have, every deprivation that they suffer is traceable to that authority. Food, clothing, rules, pleasures, indignities, abuse, pains, sorrows, cruelties—all appear to emanate from the same source. And for all this, the warden is the symbol. He gives and takes away, and about him revolve the affairs of prison life. The inmate body, therefore, has a definite object upon which to fasten its hopes and against which to direct its displeasures and hatreds.

Thus, there are strong influences within the institution that tend to unite the attitudes, beliefs, and habits of the inmates into a prison culture and to create a code by which they live. By this code they rate their fellows, giving great recognition and respect to those who have demonstrated skill and courage and achieved financial success in the commission of their crimes. By this code, also, they value highly physical strength and violence, predatory attitudes, and exploitative sex relations, give moral support to the individual in his struggles and contentions with prison officials, confer honor and prestige upon those who can effectively cope with the administration and its policies, and brand the informer as a "stool pigeon," a "rat," and a "snitch"—a cowardly betrayer of a common trust. To the extent that these influences affect the prisoner, he identifies himself with the inmate body and projects his feelings of hostility and hatred against the guards and prison officials, finding delight in the annoyance, outwitting, and embarrassment of his custodians. Sometimes opposition to the administration becomes so solidified that suppressed feelings erupt into mass protests and prison riots. From identification with his fellow prisoners, and sometimes with certain cliques, the inmate derives much courage and strength to bear his sorrows and troubles, satisfies his desire for friendship and recognition by winning their approval and admiration, and develops a rationale of his way of life. That this psychological support is often criminal in nature has a direct bearing on his self attitudes and his prospects of rehabilitation.

The prison culture is buttressed by a distinct argot, which provides not only a means of private communication but also a symbol of opposition to the administration and organized society. In terms of this argot, the "right guy," or "con," is one who manifests an aggressive disregard for administrative interests and conventional values. Inmate cliques tend to form about the "right guys" in opposition to the "square johns," or those inmates who align themselves with the authorities and the moral code of society. These cliques exercise their control informally through such pressures as gossip, laughter, ridicule, threats, and isolation, and their strength fluctuates as they vie with one another for power and adjust themselves to the changing policies of the administration. In this process, the inmate "politician" plays an important part, using his influence and skill to build and manipulate a system of favors and obligations by which he climbs to power in the prison world.

But it would be a mistake to assume that all the influences of prison life make for unity in the inmate body. On the contrary, there are some strong influences that counteract this. All kinds of people go to prison—

the poor, the rich, the old, the young, the first offender, the recidivist,— and the way in which they react to prison life and the extent to which they are affected by its influences will depend upon their personalities and the different backgrounds from which they have come. Many, it is true, have been reared in a world of conflict, passion, fear, hatred, and gang loyalty and steeped in the philosophy that life owes them a living and that "every man has his price"; and they quickly succumb to the influences that unite prisoners in a conflict with their keepers. But others have come from good homes, have had few difficulties with the police, and have strong law-abiding impulses and a desire to reform. They tend to obey the rules, cooperate with prison officials, and work for "good time" and early parole.

Furthermore, simply because an individual commits a crime does not mean that he respects or wants to be friendly with others who commit crimes. In fact, he may have only the greatest contempt and the deepest loathing for certain types of criminals, such as the rapist or other sex offenders. Besides, although prisoners are suspicious of prison administrators, they are also suspicious and jealous of one another. And while not competing for worldly goods, they do compete for favors from their guards and for consideration from the parole board, and often they advance their own interests even at the expense of their fellows. It appears, then, that the prison code operates most effectively in crises when the welfare of the inmate body as a whole is endangered, but it is very brittle in many ordinary situations. And just as the inmates exploit the weaknesses of their custodians, so the custodians take advantage of the disunity of the inmates in order to strengthen institutional authority, promote their own welfare, comfort, and job security, and facilitate the correctional process.

Moreover, in order to have effective enforcement of rules, there must be some cooperation on the part of those against whom they are applied, and so in the prison world, as in the world outside, accommodations tend to bridge the social distance between the groups involved as each side tests, maneuvers, and puts out "feelers" for a more satisfying and stable relationship. Sometimes planned adjustments are made; more often toleration, compromise, and practical arrangements emerge—almost unconsciously—from the give-and-take and improvisations of everyday living. Custodial officers are judged largely on the basis of their ability to maintain order and "to handle" their charges with a minimum of noise and trouble. Competent guards are fully aware of this, and they use their skill and imagination to build cooperative and "easy" relations with the inmates. In accomplishing this, they not only exercise authority wisely but also employ various indirect techniques, such as sympathetic understanding, persuasion, humor, and rewards in the form of recommendations for institutional privileges and jobs. Weak and incompetent guards, on the other hand, baffled by the responsibilities of their position and unable to cope with the situation, often make degrading concessions in order to curry favor with inmates but succeed only in incurring derision and contemptuous exploitation.

From this process of accommodation there develops much of the system of informal social control that penetrates and gives meaning to every relationship in the prison world and helps to lubricate the official and formal rules and regulations of the administration. In this system of informal controls, the inmate leaders, the prison elite, in their position of privilege and influence, exert a restraining and stabilizing influence, and the "prison-wise" know how to "operate" as they strive to avoid trouble and "do their time." Only when major dislocations in administrative policy shake the "prison-wise" loose from their position of relative comfort and security do they join the young and less experienced inmates in demanding reforms, and they may then become leading figures in any ensuing disturbances and riots.

But the prison world is not an isolated one,[12] and its culture reflects, and is functionally related to, that of the outside world, even though in the microcosm of the prison, subcultural contrasts may be heightened, and hostilities and rebellious feelings may be exacerbated. No prisoner is entirely criminal, and he continues to express his feelings and satisfy his desires in terms of many of the values that he learned as a member of organized society. Moreover, the prison now has more educational, religious, and recreational contacts with outside groups and organizations than ever before, and through its channels of communication it is constantly influenced by the social changes that are occurring in the society it serves. Besides, no inmate is just an inmate; no guard, just a guard; no professional worker, just a professional worker; no warden, only a warden. Each plays many, and often conflicting, roles. As husband, father, brother, or sweetheart, as craftsman, laborer, property owner, creditor, or debtor, as believer or heretic, as liberal or conservative, each struggles with his lot and grapples with the realities of his life. There are differences between "inside" and "outside"—and these must not be forgotten—but there are also many similarities—and these must be understood and appreciated or one's perspective of the prison will be greatly distorted.

All this points to one important conclusion: The correctional administrator must see the inmate as a member of a community which contains within itself the seeds of social cohesion, moral leadership, and a sense of right and wrong. The exercise of the administrator's art, therefore, involves the curbing of the influences that tend to align prisoners against

[12] Recognition that the prison world is not an isolated one reminds us again that the prison can never be just a therapeutic agency but must be also a moral agency. See Chapter 17, "The Philosophy of Punishment."

him in a common cause and the fostering of some of the influences that counteract such an alignment. As the sociologist would say, he must prevent the social relationships within the prison from hardening into an in-group–out-group pattern. To accomplish this, the correctional administrator must employ guards who can understand and apply the principles of the modern correctional program; he must maintain open channels of communication with his prisoners; he must create and nourish loyalties for law and order; he must convince the inmate that institutional authority is merely a reflection of the authority to be found anywhere and that it is simply an aspect of the responsibility which every member of society must assume as payment for the rights he would enjoy; he must dissolve the prisoner's resentment and enlist his cooperation and support in the process of rehabilitation. In short, the warden or superintendent must introduce the principles of modern correctional administration, with their emphasis upon the classification and rehabilitation of prisoners.

Although it is important to see the prisoner as a member of a community, it is also necessary to understand that he is living in an abnormal community. He is cut off from association with the opposite sex, family, relatives, and friends and deprived of their direct influences, all of which are essential elements in a normal life. Besides, he has only slight control over his daily life. He exercises little initiative and makes few independent decisions. He is fed, clothed, and housed, no matter what he does. Most of his fundamental wishes are denied, the yearnings of his deepest nature are blocked. Personality defenses erected against the harshness of prison life may leave him hardened, insensitive, and unsociable. Repressions and frustrations furnish fertile soil in which perversions and distortions of personality may flourish. These are not experiences which can be counted on to prepare the inmate to assume the responsibilities of free life or to face the stigma with which the public brands the ex-convict.[13]

These limitations, it is true, can be reduced. Rules can be made more reasonable and flexible. The social distance between institutional personnel and inmates can be shortened and adjusted to the individual needs of the inmate. Attitudes can be modified. Institutional programs and services can be individualized to a greater extent. But these limitations can never be entirely eliminated, for they are an inherent part of imprison-

---

[13] National Commission on Law Observance and Enforcement, *Report on Penal Institutions, Probation, and Parole,* Report No. 9 (Washington, D.C.: Government Printing Office, 1931), pp. 20–24, 215, 216. The process of assimilation by which inmates, with varying degrees of completeness, acquire the values and behavior patterns of the prison culture has been called "prisonization."

The analysis of the prison community presented above indicates the great complexity of that community. Unfortunately, some writers, seeking to subject its subtleties to quantitative analysis, have described it in sharply defined dichotomies and have then deceptively garbed their over-simplification in statistical raiment.

ment.[14] This suggests, then, the importance of using probation and parole wherever the interests and views of the public and the needs and the potentialities of the individual make it possible to do so.[15]

Even so, it should not be concluded that the limitations of imprisonment make the rehabilitation of the inmate impossible. On the contrary, some offenders respond better to institutionalization than they do to any other method of correction and are reformed through its influence. Moreover, the support of the moral code, the protection of the community, public opinion, the complexities of social relationships, and the inadequacies of our knowledge regarding human nature will probably always require the imprisonment of certain types of offenders. Nor should we disregard the fact that every method of correction, including probation and parole, has its own inherent limitations and its own degree of authoritarianism; indeed, that authority is implicit in every relationship in free life. Nevertheless, even when all this is taken into consideration, these two facts still remain: (1) the best place for most offenders to learn how to adjust to normal living and to assume the responsibilities of freedom is in the outside community itself; and (2) most offenders when placed under adequate supervision can find successful adjustment without institutionalization.

EVALUATION OF INSTITUTIONAL CORRECTION

In view of the many serious obstacles to institutional correction, it is not surprising that many prisoners, guards, prison officials, and criminologists claim that correctional institutions in the United States are a failure.

[14] For a sociological analysis of prison life, see Donald Clemmer, *The Prison Community* (Boston: The Christopher Publishing House, 1940); Donald R. Cressey (ed.), *The Prison: Studies in Institutional Organization and Change* (New York: Holt, Rinehart, and Winston, Inc., 1961); Richard H. McCleery, *Policy Change in Prison Management* (East Lansing, Mich.: Michigan State University, 1957); Lloyd E. Ohlin, *Sociology and the Field of Corrections* (New York: Russell Sage Foundation, 1956); Gresham M. Sykes, *The Society of Captives: A Study of a Maximum Security Prison* (Princeton, N. J.: Princeton University Press, 1958); *Theoretical Studies in Social Organization of the Prison* (New York: Social Science Research Council, 1960). For an inmate's view of the prison community, see Robert Neese, *Prison Exposures* (Philadelphia: Chilton Co., Publishers, 1959). See also Hans Reimer, "Socialization in the Prison Community," *Proceedings of the American Prison Association, 1937,* pp. 151–55; Norman S. Hayner and Ellis Ash, "The Prison as a Community," *American Sociological Review,* V (Aug., 1940), 577–83; S. Kirson Weinberg "Aspects of the Prison's Social Structure," *American Journal of Sociology,* XLVII (Mar., 1942), 717–26; Donald R. Taft, "The Group and Community Organization Approach to Prison Administration," *Proceedings of the American Prison Association, 1942,* pp. 275–84; F. E. Haynes, "The Sociological Study of the Prison Community," *Journal of Criminal Law and Criminology,* XXXIX (Nov.–Dec., 1948), 432–40; Clarence Schrag, "Leadership Among Prison Inmates," *American Sociological Review,* XIX (Feb., 1954), 37–43; Morris G. Caldwell, "Group Dynamics in the Prison Community," *Journal of Criminal Law, Criminology, and Police Science,* LXVI (Jan.–Feb., 1956), 648–57.

[15] Review the philosophy of punishment discussed in Chapter 17.

They admit that in general institutionalization provides a high degree of security against escapes,[16] but they also argue that it fails not only to rehabilitate offenders but also to deter others from violating the law. In order to substantiate their criticism they cite personal experiences, prison riots, and the available statistics of crime and criminals. It is estimated that 2,048,370 major crimes were committed in the United States during 1962, which may mean that this country has the highest crime rate in the world.[17] It is also said that between 40 and 70 per cent of the men in most of our prisons have been incarcerated before[18] and that at least 55 to 60 per cent of the prisoners leaving prisons today will return within five years.[19] In 1946, of the total number of all prisoners released from state and federal prisons and reformatories, 51.1 per cent were known to have had previous records of commitment.[20]

As a matter of fact, however, we lack objective criteria by which to measure the effectiveness of institutional correction. Certainly, there are so many variables involved that no one can determine the effect of institutionalization upon the rates of crime and recidivism in the United States. Moreover, by the time that many offenders enter our institutions their habits and attitudes are already so set that no existing techniques can change them. Then, too, the influence of even the most modern institution is only one of many that enter into the life of a released prisoner. His institutional correction may be the best that can be provided and very much worth while and yet be entirely counteracted by later experiences. However, the unpleasant fact remains that most of the prisoners who are discharged from our prisons and reformatories continue to commit crimes. It is evident, therefore, that additional research is urgently needed to determine how the effectiveness of institutional correction can be increased.[21]

[16] For the calender year 1952, less than 200 escapees from state prisons and reformatories remained unaccounted for at the end of the year. Between 1937 and 1954, upward of 300,000 men were committed to federal prisons, and out of those who had escaped or walked away from farms and camps, only 7 were unaccounted for by 1954 (James V. Bennett, "Evaluating a Prison," *The Annals of the American Academy of Political and Social Science*, CCXCIII [May, 1954], 11).

[17] Federal Bureau of Investigation, *Uniform Crime Reports, 1962*, pp. 1, 2.

[18] Marshall B. Clinard, "Prison Systems," *Encyclopedia of Criminology* (New York: The Philosophical Library, 1949), p. 373.

[19] Bennett, p. 10. Glaser has questioned the validity of the estimates which claim that a high percentage of released inmates are again committed to prison. See Daniel Glaser, *The Effectiveness of a Prison and Parole System* (Indianapolis: The Bobbs-Merrill Co., 1964), pp. 13–35.

[20] Federal Bureau of the Census, *Prisoners in State and Federal Prisons and Reformatories, 1946* (Washington, D.C.: Government Printing Office, 1948), p. 94, Table 59.

[21] George B. Vold, "Does the Prison Reform?" *The Annals of the American Academy of Political and Social Science*, CCXCIII (May, 1954), 42–50. See also George B. Vold, *Theoretical Criminology* (New York: Oxford University Press, 1958), pp. 291–304.

PRISON RIOTS

Although it is true that the situation confronting correctional institutions in the United States is exceedingly difficult, there is also no doubt that most of them are operating on a level far below modern standards. Nor can it be denied that prison riots have from time to time dramatically revealed serious weaknesses in our prison system. During 1929 and 1930, serious prison riots broke out in many institutions throughout the country. These reached a high point in April, 1930, when the Ohio State Penitentiary at Columbus became the scene of a fire in which more than 300 inmates were literally roasted alive. A series of investigations followed and produced some sweeping prison reforms, one of which was the reorganization of the federal prison system and the establishment of the Federal Bureau of Prisons.

The most serious prison riots in American history took place during 1952 and 1953.[22] Beginning in New Jersey, these riots swept across the country "like sparks blown from a bonfire" until they involved some 8,000 state convicts, or about 5 per cent of the total number of inmates in state prisons and reformatories. The most serious of these riots—in fact, the worst one in the history of the United States—took place in the Michigan State Prison, at Jackson, the largest walled prison in the world. There 176 inmates seized eleven hostages and barricaded themselves in a disciplinary cell block. The uprising spread throughout the prison, and hundreds of inmates, "armed with clubs, knives, and broken, jagged-edged bottles," wrecked the dining hall, set fire to the laundry, nearly destroyed the chapel, library, and gymnasium, and broke thousands of windows. Before order was restored one prisoner had been killed, ten others seriously injured, and property destroyed and damaged to the estimated amount of $2,500,000.[23]

What caused these riots? There have been many answers. Some have been simple, like spring fever, plain boredom, or a reflection of general unrest on the outside. But it is obvious that no simple answer will suffice. Authorities in the field of criminology who have attempted an analysis of the situation have cited such causes as overcrowding, idleness, inadequate personnel, lack of segregation of hardened and dangerous criminals, the monotony of prison life, unfair parole practices, low budgets, and the

22 Austin H. MacCormick lists 39 riots, strikes and other serious disturbances in prisons and reformatories for men in the United States during the period May, 1951 to December 31, 1953 (Austin H. MacCormick, "Behind the Prison Riots," *The Annals of the American Academy of Political and Social Science*, CCXCIII [May, 1954], 18).

23 "U. S. Prisons: How Well Do They Protect Us?" *Platform* (New York: Newsweek Club and Educational Bureaus, Sept., 1952), 2.

psychological reaction of inmates to the news of disturbances in other institutions.[24]

According to the Committee on Riots of the American Prison Association, the basic causes of prison riots may be listed as follows:

1. Inadequate financial support and official and public indifference.
2. Substandard personnel.
3. Enforced idleness.
4. Lack of professional leadership and professional programs.
5. Excessive size and overcrowding of institutions.
6. Political domination and motivation of management.
7. Unwise sentencing and parole practices.[25]

However, the fact that many prisons suffered from all these conditions and still did not have riots forces us to recognize the importance of seeing the prison as a community in which powerful social, cultural, and psychological forces are at work. Too little thought has been given to the pent-up feelings, the conflicts, tensions, and pressures, the bitterness and sense of grievance that constitute the mental and emotional state in which prisoners are ready to riot. All of this has its root in the community life of the prison and frequently is the product of many months of frustration and irritation. Usually the riot erupts when some incident, often trifling in itself, sets off the explosion of suppressed feelings, and the prison bursts into flames of fury and hysteria before anyone realizes what has happened.[26]

The prison riots of 1952 and 1953 were the most destructive in American history. Nevertheless, we may still gain something from these uprisings if we recognize them as acute symptoms of chronic weaknesses in our prisons and reformatories and take definite steps to reduce the obstacles to effective institutional correction.

[24] James V. Bennett, "Prisons in Turmoil," *Federal Probation*, XVI (Sept., 1952), 3–6; Report of the Special Committee to Study the Michigan Department of Corrections. *The Michigan Prison Riots* (Feb., 1953); "Why Convicts Riot," *U. S. News and World Report* (Dec. 19, 1952), 18–21; Donald Powell Wilson and Harry Elmer Barnes, "A Riot Is an Unnecessary Evil," *Life* (Nov. 24, 1952), 138–50.

[25] *Prison Riots and Disturbances* (New York: The American Prison Association, May, 1953), p. 7.

[26] National Commission on Law Observance and Enforcement, p. 35. See also Peg and Walter McGraw, *Assignment: Prison Riots* (New York: Henry Holt and Co., 1954); John Bartlow Martin, *Break Down the Walls* (New York: Ballantine Books, 1954), pp. 80–106.

22

Institutions for Detention and Short-Term Offenders

MEANING OF DETENTION

Some persons who come into contact with the machinery of the law are shortly thereafter released either because there is no legal basis for keeping them in custody or because some method has been used to secure their availability in the future. Others, however, are detained, and these include: (1) persons who are awaiting trial and who have not been released on bail or on their own recognizance; (2) important witnesses who might otherwise disappear; and (3) the insane, the feeble-minded, and others who are suffering from mental or physical conditions and who, although they are not charged with any offense, are being detained for their own protection until some other arrangements can be made for their care.

Detention, therefore, is not the punishment of a convicted offender or the adjudged delinquent, but rather the holding of a person for a comparatively short period of time in order to protect him or society or both. Those awaiting trial have yet to be proved guilty and, of course, those held in protective custody are not even charged with any violation of the law. It should be obvious, then, that persons held in detention are entitled to all the rights and privileges of the innocent; and they should be subjected only to such inconveniences, discomforts, and hardships as are necessary to achieve the purpose for which they are being held.

But there is more to the meaning of detention than this. Each year thousands of Americans undergo this experience, and for many, especially the young and the first offender, it may well prove to be a crucial one in the development of their attitudes toward law and law-enforcement officers. If these Americans receive the impression that public institutions are infested with vice and corruption, that fair play is impossible, and that justice is secured only by the favors and the influence of the rich and the privileged, their respect for the law and its agents may be seriously impaired or even destroyed. And if the young and the first offender are indiscriminately thrown into association with the hardened, the cynical, and the vicious, their education in vice and crime may be effectively fostered. Thus, detention has an important significance not only for the one who is held in custody but for society as well.

TYPES OF INSTITUTIONS

Institutions for detention and short-term offenders may be classified as follows: (1) the city lockup, which is operated under the control of the city police department, is usually located in the district police station, is almost exclusively used for very short periods of detention, and is seldom used for the purpose of punishment; (2) the municipal jail or small-town lockup, which is usually operated under the control of the police department or the town marshal and is used in much the same way as the city lockup except that misdemeanants, especially those who have failed to pay their fines, are more often kept in it for the purpose of punishment; (3) the county jail, which is usually operated under the control of the sheriff and is usually employed not only for the purposes of detention but also for the punishment of convicted offenders, almost always those who are serving sentences for misdemeanors; and (4) specialized places of detention for women and children.[1]

No one knows exactly how many institutions for detention and short-term offenders there are in the United States. However, we do know that there are about 3,100 county jails[2] and that about 1,750 municipalities with populations of more than 5,000 maintain city jails or lockups.[3] Any statement beyond this is mere guesswork since almost every township, regardless of size, has at least one so-called lockup or cell for the temporary detention of prisoners. A few years ago, Roy Casey estimated the total number of county, city, and town jails and lockups in the United States to be at least 10,000.[4] Whatever the actual number of these institu-

[1] Edwin H. Sutherland, *Principles of Criminology* (Philadelphia: J. B. Lippincott Co., 1947), pp. 263, 264.

[2] Although the great majority of institutions for misdemeanants are called jails, some are known by various other names, such as workhouse, house of correction, work farm, prison camp, and house of detention. In this chapter, however, unless otherwise indicated, the general term "jail" will be used to refer to all institutions for misdemeanants.

[3] *Manual of Correctional Standards* (New York: The American Correctional Association, 1959), p. 421.

[4] Roy Casey, "Catchall Jails," *The Annals of the American Academy of Political and Social Science*, CCXCIII (May, 1954), 28.

tions may be, it is certain that there are far more of them in the United States than the combined total of all the other institutions in our correctional systems.

POPULATION OF THE JAILS

Although most authorities believe that more than 500,000 persons[5]—some put the figure as high as nearly 2,000,000[6]—may pass through our jails each year, we have no up-to-date, accurate information on this or on how many persons are in them at any particular time. However, some light can be thrown on the question of how many are in our jails at any particular time by the fact that on April 1, 1960, a total of 119,671 persons were in our local jails and workhouses. Of this total, 6.5 per cent were females, 35.2 per cent were Negroes, 14.7 per cent were under twenty-one, and 63.4 per cent were twenty-one to forty-four years old.[7]

Nor do we have any recent adequate information on the composition of the population of the jails. For a general picture, we must rely on a census of county and city jails which was made a number of years ago.[8] According to this census, taken in 1933, of the 240,930 convicted prisoners who were received during the first six months of that year, 73 per cent were white, 22.8 per cent were Negro, 4.2 per cent were of other races, 6.8 per cent were female, 10.7 per cent were under twenty-one, 69.6 per cent were twenty-one to forty-four years old, 58.5 per cent were recidivists, 70 per cent had been sentenced for drunkenness and disorderly conduct, larceny (except auto theft), vagrancy, or violation of liquor laws, 31.4 per cent had been committed for nonpayment of fines, 94.8 per cent had been sentenced for less than one year, and about 70 per cent, for less than two months.

Despite the fact that we lack recent data that would provide an overall picture of the composition of the jail population, informed observers generally agree that this population constitutes a very heterogeneous group which, when compared with the general population, contains a disproportionate number of the colored races, the poor and the homeless, the emotionally unstable, the dull and the feeble-minded, the unskilled, the alcoholic, and the physically ill and handicapped.[9] Besides, as many

[5] Roberts J. Wright, "The Jail and Misdemeanant Institutions," *Contemporary Correction,* ed. Paul W. Tappan (New York: McGraw-Hill Book Co., Inc., 1951), p. 312.

[6] Casey, p. 29.

[7] Federal Bureau of the Census, "Inmates of Institutions," *U. S. Census of Population: 1960* (Washington, D.C.: Government Printing Office, 1963), p. 4, Table 4; p. 21, Table 25.

[8] Federal Bureau of the Census, *County and City Jails, 1933* (Washington, D.C.: Government Printing Office, 1935).

[9] See, for example, Louis N. Robinson, *Jails* (Philadelphia: The John C. Winston Co., 1944), chap. iv; Casey, pp. 28, 29.

have pointed out, the jail tends to be a catchall for a nondescript collection of prostitutes, pimps, panderers, perverts, vagrants, derelicts, drug addicts, dope peddlers, confidence men, gamblers, amnesia victims, traffic law violators, and bums.

STATE OF THE JAILS

About forty years ago Joseph F. Fishman, who was inspector of jails for the federal government, defined "jail" in terms which have become classic in the literature of criminology:

Jail: An unbelievably filthy institution in which are confined men and women serving sentences for misdemeanors and crimes, and men and women not under sentence who are simply awaiting trial. With few exceptions, having no segregation of the unconvicted from the convicted, the well from the diseased, the youngest and most impressionable from the most degraded and hardened. Usually swarming with bedbugs, roaches, lice, and other vermin; has an odor of disinfectant and filth which is appalling; supports in complete idleness thousands of able-bodied men and women, and generally affords ample time and opportunity to assure inmates a complete course in every kind of viciousness and crime. A melting pot in which the worst elements of the raw material in the criminal world are brought forth blended and turned out in absolute perfection.[10]

Although this definition may be too sweeping to be completely valid today, many who know American jails very well believe that much of it is still as appropriate as it was when originally formulated. Thus, the *Manual of Correctional Standards,* published by the American Correctional Association in 1959, states that "despite the steadily increasing number of exceptions, the average jail is characterized by poor administration, poor sanitation standards, idleness, little if any attention to screening and segregation of prisoners, poor food, low medical standards, and untrained, disinterested personnel."[11]

Some students of the jail problem, while condemning existing conditions, claim that there is a trend toward higher standards in our jails. Among these is Louis N. Robinson, who in 1944 wrote: "This trend is the only hopeful thing about the situation. The status quo is on the whole disgustingly bad and one which would make any candid observer admit that the democratic process of government often reflects only the selfish and ignorant desires of a community."[12] Roy Casey, also, sounds a note of hope when he says: "There is, however, rapidly developing in a large and

[10] Joseph F. Fishman, *Crucible of Crime* (New York: Cosmopolis Press, 1923), pp. 13, 14.

[11] *Manual of Correctional Standards,* p. 421. Se also Edgar M. Gerlach, "Treatment Prior to Trial," *Yearbook, 1946* (New York: National Probation Association, 1947), pp. 100–15.

[12] Robinson, p. 24.

Close-up view of a cell in the Forsyth County Jail, Winston-Salem, North Carolina. Note its clean and spacious interior. (Courtesy of Sheriff of Forsyth County)

influential segment of the American public an awareness that problems of health, of public welfare, of economy, of justice, and of community self-respect are involved and that there is need for better managed local jails."[13]

According to the *Manual of Correctional Standards,* quoted above, there is both evidence of "an increasing interest throughout the country in improving standards of jail management," and a "general agreement among correctional administrators on the desirable minimum jail standards."[14] Although there may be some difference of opinion regarding this, all observers agree that some towns, cities, and counties have made definite progress in the improvement of their jails.

In design and construction, American jails range all the way from antiquated, simple structures containing a few cells, built of bricks or stones, and erected many years ago, to the expensive "skyscraper or penthouse jail" recently constructed in some rich urban communities. Most jails,

[13] Casey, p. 29.
[14] *Manual of Correctional Standards,* p. 421.

however, are of "unnecessarily costly constructions and lack facilities for handling the highly diversified groups of inmates" committed to them, and even many of the expensive new jails are "monumental failures with respect to detentional, correctional, and remedial requirements" since "they have been designed according to ideals and standards inherited from the days when jails permanently housed dangerous malefactors."[15]

In their administration and operation, jails present as great a diversity as they do in their architecture, but most of them are alike in being under the control and direction of officials who are untrained to perform the very complex and important duties of administration with which they are charged. As it has been since the earliest times, the county jail remains, with but few exceptions, under the control of the sheriff, who often delegates this responsibility to a deputy sheriff or a jailer. Usually an elected officer and having many duties other than those involved in the management of the jail, the sheriff holds office for only a short period of time and often is not permitted to remain in his position for two successive terms. In effect this means that his ability to administer a jail is not considered to be an important qualification for his position, and in many cases by the time he has acquired the experience that enables him to administer the jail in an acceptable manner, he leaves office and is succeeded by another untrained person, who in turn must learn in the same costly and inefficient manner.

Furthermore, the office of sheriff is an important "patronage plum" in county politics and is much sought after not only for the financial opportunities that it affords but also for the prestige and influence that it brings in party affairs. It is not surprising, therefore, that the administration of the jail is often considered as something merely incidental to the revenue that the jail can produce through the operation of the fee system. When this system is used, sheriffs and deputies are paid on the basis of the number of persons received and maintained in the jails. Thus, the more persons received and maintained, the more money these officials are paid. Since often no accounting is made of the way the money is spent, there is a strong temptation to fill the jail and to reduce expenditures regardless of the legality of the methods used or the effect upon the welfare of the inmates. This system is deeply rooted in the traditions of our culture, and it is understandable why many sheriffs continue to use it to get as much money as possible out of their jobs. This, however, does not relieve it of

---

[15] *Handbook of Correctional Institution Design and Construction* (Washington, D.C.: Federal Bureau of Prisons, 1949), p. 168. For some examples of new jail construction, see Federal Bureau of Prisons, *Recent Prison Construction, 1950–1960* (Washington, D.C.: Federal Bureau of Prisons, 1960), pp. 59–91. In referring to these examples, James Bennett, Director of the Federal Bureau of Prisons, has stated that they show little regard for either the requirements of prisoners or the taxpayers (*ibid.*, p. 5).

its iniquitous character nor reduce its undermining influence in the administration of our jails. Fortunately, the extent of the fee system is gradually but steadily diminishing in the United States.

It can be seen from what has been said that the jail is an integral part of county politics, and its operation can be understood only when this fact is appreciated. As Roberts J. Wright has succinctly put it: "Jails mean *jobs*. Jails mean *income*. Jails mean *power*. Jails mean *influence*. Jails mean *patronage*. Jails mean *votes*."[16]

Even so, what has been said here should not be interpreted to mean that all sheriffs are indifferent to their duties as administrators of our jails. On the contrary, some have worked diligently and courageously to improve the management and condition of the institutions under their charge. These sheriffs are deserving of our recognition and praise, but unfortunately they are definitely in the minority.

Although the following excerpt from a jail inspector's report should not be considered as descriptive of the average jail, it does indicate the extent to which the administration of a jail can degenerate under the conditions prevailing in many counties in the United States:

When I arrived at the jail, the front door was open but no one was around. A stairway leading to the second floor was barred by a wooden door with a steel bar dropping into two slots. A small hammer would have shattered its panels. I finally located the jailer in the sheriff's office a block away, entertaining a few of the town loafers. We went back to the jail and I started an inspection. The number of things that can be done wrong in operating a jail is almost unbelievable.

All four prisoners were on the second floor with nothing but that flimsy wooden door between them and their freedom. None of them were locked in quarters. The steel bar could not be replaced from the inside, so the wooden door was left open as we went upstairs, the jailer wearing his keys on one hip and his revolver on the other. This left the jail wide open with four young "jack rabbits" ready to run. Why they didn't take the gun, I'll never know— they didn't need the keys. I suggested that the jailer lock them in a dormitory until the inspection was completed. He complied grudgingly.

Then, in quick succession, it was found that the jailer kept practically no records, made no counts, let arresting officers tell him that prisoners were "clean"; all officers entered prisoners' quarters with guns; visitors were turned into the jail for unsupervised visits; packages were not always inspected; the jailer often left the jail unattended for long hours at a time while the prisoners did just as they pleased. There was no cleaning program; all cells, floors, walls, beds, bedding, toilets, and bathtubs were dirty to filthy. The upstairs hallway was filled with extra cots, burned mattresses, blankets, bottles, jugs, and broken cleaning equipment, while the basement was a shambles of dangerous tools

[16] Roberts J. Wright, "The Jail and Misdemeanant Institutions." By permission from *Contemporary Correction*, ed. by Paul W. Tappan. Copyright, 1951, McGraw-Hill Book Co., Inc., p. 310.

(including an axe), barrels of disinfectant, broken cots, brooms, mops, et cetera.

No night supervision is attempted, which means that prisoners are practically without supervision at any time. The introduction of almost any kind of contraband is possible, and many other irregularities are almost a certainty. The jailer is not entirely to blame for all these conditions. He is totally inexperienced and has received no instructions from the sheriff. The sheriff showed no particular interest when the deficiencies were called to his attention. There seems little hope for any improvements under the present administration.[17]

Many of our jails, because of their construction or administration, or because of both, are insecure. Barnes and Teeters state, "It is estimated that some 3,000 persons escape or walk away from our county jails annually."[18]

Weakness in the structure of the jail was the major cause of an escape reported a few years ago in these words by the jailer:

The window bars are mounted with ½" x 3" cross-bars of steel held in place by only four inches of mortar joint and extending only one-half the thickness of a brick into the wall at each side of the window. The jail is old and the mortar had deteriorated to such an extent that the prisoner was able to kick the bars loose with his foot and escape through the window in broad daylight.[19]

Jails are often dirty and unsanitary and infested with vermin. Lighting and ventilation tend to be insufficient, and the cells of many are hot and stifling in the summer and cold and drafty in the winter. In a large number of jails bathing and toilet facilities are inadequate, poorly maintained, and seldom cleaned. Bed clothing and mattresses in many cases are rarely aired and washed. Kitchens are often dirty and alive with roaches, while the cooking utensils, dishes, and tableware in many jails are indifferently cared for or greasy and spotted with the dried food of past meals. Physical examinations are seldom given to incoming prisoners, and the well and the sick, the clean and the infected are thrown into close association in crowded quarters, the air of which is too often heavy with the mingled odors of disinfectants, cabbage, bean soup, and unclean bodies.

Conditions like the following, which were found a few years ago and reported by a federal jail inspector, are still typical of many jails:

On going up into the jail section on the top floor, I found conditions more revolting than in the basement. Here I found one white juvenile, sixteen years

[17] Quoted in Myrl E. Alexander, "Jottings on Jails and Jailers," *The Prison World*, XIII (July–Aug., 1951), 30.

[18] Harry Elmer Barnes and Negley K. Teeters, *New Horizons in Criminology* (New York: Prentice-Hall, Inc., 1959), p. 393.

[19] Quoted in Myrl E. Alexander, "Jottings on Jails and Jailers," *The Prison World*, XIII (Sept.–Oct., 1951), 31.

old, who had been sentenced to an institution until his majority for car theft, being held in solitary confinement, the boy had been held in this manner at that time for four days. The solitary cell is approximately 6′ x 8′, with a 7′ ceiling. The only opening for air is at the bottom of the solid steel door where the inmate's food is passed in. In the small corridor outside this cell the windows of the building were closed and the odors of human excretion here were overpowering and nauseating. I ordered the jailer to open these window immediately. This visit was early on Thursday afternoon and they kept this boy in this cell until the following Saturday morning. During this period of punishment the jail doctor had not visited the prisoner at any time. Two other white juveniles, fifteen and sixteen years of age, were found quartered under conditions very little less revolting. These latter boys were held in a cellblock of four two-bunk cells, and they were occupying adjoining cells. The natural light here was not totally excluded, but when the door to the block was closed the interior was darker than semi-darkness. The cells occupied by the two boys both had the wash basins stopped up and these bowls were filled with a thick, soupy, blackish liquid which gave off a terrible stench. The toilets in the cells were both working but were filthy. The next cell to the one occupied by these boys had formerly been occupied by some inmate who had vomited on the floor; this excretion had not been cleaned up but was dehydrating and giving off odors very offensive, if not injurious, to any human being. The air in this cellblock was terrible and the living conditions beyond description.[28]

In general, the meals served in our jails are inadequately balanced and poorly prepared. Usually cooked by an untrained person, they are often restricted in quantity and quality so that sheriffs who must rely on the fee system for their compensation can secure for themselves a large percentage of the funds allowed them for each inmate per day of imprisonment.

One of the worst features of our jails, however, is their tendency to throw together without any attempt at classification, except on the basis of sex and sometimes of age, a highly heterogeneous group of young and old, well and sick, sane and insane, innocent and vicious, naïve and cynical, unsophisticated and debauched, tender and hardened, and then condemn them to the degrading and demoralizing experience of long hours of idleness unrelieved by the rehabilitative influences of spiritual, educational, and recreational leadership. It is the unusual jail which provides a program of employment, and it is the highly exceptional one which boasts of any kind of supervised programs of education and recreation. In most jails the young, the naïve, and the uninitiated readily turn to the old, the hardened, and the vicious for knowledge, excitement, and entertainment and find in this association a deepening stream of depravity and corruption. It is no wonder, then, that jails have been called schools of vice and crime, for a more effective way of contaminating the young and the innocent could scarcely be imagined.

[20] Quoted in Wright, pp. 314, 316.

And besides, children are still kept in many of our jails. We have no nationwide statistics on this, but a few years ago the National Probation and Parole Association[21] estimated that between 50,000 and 100,000 children were being confined each year in our county jails.[22] Many authorities believe that the situation is still about the same. Furthermore, women who are confined in our jails are often harshly treated and exposed to the brutality and exploitation that are the natural products of many of these institutions.[23] Although some of the larger jails have quarters for women that are in units entirely separated from those for men and staffed by women, most jails merely segregate women in separate cells or rooms in the main building. In fact, in many of the small jails the two sexes are within speaking distance of each other and can easily engage in an exchange of obscenity and abuse. Rarely do any of the smaller institutions employ matrons. If the women inmates in them are to receive supervision and care by members of their own sex, these must come if at all from members of the sheriff's family. Even when matrons are provided, the type of work and the low salary usually attract the uneducated and untrained. It must be added, also, that since comparatively few women are confined in our jails and must, therefore, be specially handled, they tend to live an even more restricted and abnormal life than do the men.

Some sheriffs do not care what their prisoners do as long as they cause no disturbance or try to escape. Discipline, therefore, becomes lax, and the indifference or incompetence of jail officials, together with the necessity of maintaining some sort of order among the prisoners, creates a situation in which a form of inmate tribunal called a "kangaroo court" may appear. We are not certain how this term originated, but the practice to which it refers has existed for centuries and can be traced back to the early jails of England. Where it functions today, this "court" is generally under the control of a clique of the most aggressive and brutal inmates and presided over by their ringleader.[24] Usually operating with the knowledge and connivance of the sheriff, who is thus relieved of the responsibility of handling many of the internal problems of his institution, the "kangaroo court" enforces a set of rules dealing with the housekeeping of the jail and the personal habits and daily routine of the prisoners. When these rules are violated, the inmate is brought before the "court" and the penalty, commonly a fine or a beating, is imposed.

[21] The National Probation and Parole Association is now called the National Council on Crime and Delinquency.

[22] Austin H. MacCormick, "Children in Our Jails," *The Annals of the American Academy of Political and Social Science*, CCLXI (Jan., 1949), 151.

[23] Robinson, chap. xii.

[24] Nina Kinsella, "The County Jails," *Proceedings of the American Prison Association, 1935*, pp. 283–89.

Although this may appear to provide the prisoners with an excellent opportunity for regulating their affairs in a democratic manner, it actually results in a form of cruel despotism and exploitation involving the arbitrary infliction of unjust, often brutal, punishment, sometimes for the most trivial infraction of the rules, and the exposure of the weakest and most inoffensive to gross indignities and painful beatings by the most vicious and hardened, who themselves obey or disobey the rules as they please. In some cases prisoners have been seriously injured by the action of this "court," and within recent years a few have been killed. Severely condemned by all who are familiar with the situation in our jails, the "kangaroo court" has been almost completely eliminated,[25] but it still tends to appear, sometimes surreptitiously, wherever and whenever jail officials fail to assume the responsibility of introducing an adequate system of discipline into their institutions.

In addition to all the other undesirable features of our jails, there remains the fact that they are expensive to operate. Barnes and Teeters, in discussing this point, quote an estimate that puts the annual cost of our county jails at a total of more than $50,000,000. But this does not cover the entire cost, for thousands of dependents of jail inmates must be supported at the public expense.[26]

FEDERAL INSPECTION OF LOCAL JAILS

Since it is not feasible to maintain federal prisons or detention facilities near most federal courts, the government of the United States contracts with local jails for housing federal prisoners held to await court action or sentenced to extremely short terms. In order to determine whether local jails measure up to acceptable standards for the confinement of these prisoners, the Federal Bureau of Prisons subjects such places of detention to periodic inspections. During the fiscal year ended June 30, 1963, an average of 3,297 federal prisoners were detained in local jails and other non-federal institutions in the Continental United States.[27]

The county jails in which federal prisoners must be held continue to present serious problems of overcrowding and management. As a result of a beating given to a federal prisoner by his fellow prisoners in the county jail at Phoenix, Arizona, on September 21, 1961, all federal pris-

25 Casey, p. 34.

26 Barnes and Teeters, p. 393.

27 During the fiscal year ended June 30, 1963, federal inspectors visited about 700 jails in 49 states and the Territory of Guam, and the Federal Bureau of Prisons used 1,251 nonfederal institutions to house federal prisoners at one time or another. Federal jail inspectors no longer rate jails as "good," "fair," "poor," or "bad," but merely list them as "approved" or "disapproved" for housing federal prisoners (letter dated July 1, 1964, from the Federal Bureau of Prisons).

oners there were removed, and the Federal Bureau of Prisons finally found it necessary to build a detention center at the federal prison camp at Florence, Arizona.[28] Even so, in 1963, Chief Miller, of the Federal Jail Inspection Service, reported that progress was being made in the construction and remodeling of local jails and in the improvement of their dietary and treatment programs.[29]

In 1948 the Federal Bureau of Prisons, in an effort to promote the improvement of our jails, published a manual of jail management which contains the following set of standards for the operation of a jail:

1. A jail should be under the direct management and control of a person qualified by training and experience to supervise and control prisoners.

2. Jail officials should have a set of policies and regulations for the operation of the jail, for the employees and for the inmates.

3. The building should be structurally sound, secure, fire-resistant, properly heated, ventilated, and lighted.

4. All parts of the jail should be kept immaculately clean.

5. Kangaroo courts or similar inmate organizations should be prohibited.

6. Brutal treatment by employees or prisoners should be prohibited.

7. A competent physician should be available to take care of the medical needs of the prisoners and to give each prisoner a medical examination when admitted to the jail.

8. Juveniles should not be held in jails, but if committed should be definitely segregated and well supervised.

9. Prisoners with contagious diseases, hardened criminals, and the sexes should be segregated.

10. Women prisoners should be under the supervision of a matron at all times.

11. Prisoners should be fed three times each day.

12. Adequate bathing and toilet facilities should be available, and water, soap, towels, and toothbrushes should be supplied to prisoners.

13. Convicted prisoners should be kept employed.

14. There should be good reading material available.

15. The legal rights of prisoners should be protected and prisoners should be given every reasonable opportunity to confer with their attorneys, but the jail officials should prevent their prisoners from being fleeced or exploited by unscrupulous persons.

[28] Federal Bureau of Prisons, *Federal Prisons, 1962*, pp. 22, 23. The federal detention center at Florence, Arizona, was officially opened on March 15, 1963.

[29] R. A. Miller, "Jail Inspection Service, Federal Bureau of Prisons," *American Journal of Correction*, XXV (Nov.–Dec., 1963), 24–27.

16. Regular visiting by the family and friends of the prisoners should be permitted under reasonable conditions and under supervision.[30]

A PROGRAM FOR THE IMPROVEMENT OF JAILS

All persons who are familiar with the conditions in our jails seem to agree that a program for the improvement of these institutions should be designed to:

1. Educate the public regarding the conditions in the jails.
2. Keep as many people as possible out of the jails.
3. Reduce the period of confinement of the unsentenced inmate, for example, the witness and the person awaiting trial.
4. Establish a better system of handling sentenced inmates, who are almost always misdemeanants serving short sentences (one year or less).[31]

1. **Educate the Public.** It is difficult to arouse the public over the state of the jails. The great mass of jail inmates are poor, often homeless, and friendless. What happens to them, therefore, provokes little protest. Furthermore, jails are often located away from the main part of town; and so, out of sight, they tend to be out of the minds of the citizens, who in any case want to forget such unpleasant things as crime.

Nevertheless, if the jails are to be improved, the public must be kept informed about them and aroused to the point where it demands higher standards of operation. For this purpose every means should be employed, including regular jail visits by citizens' groups and organizations, grand jury investigations and reports, talks and lectures by jail officials and interested citizens, radio and television programs, and newspaper stories and articles.

2. **Keep People Out of Jail.** Too many people are sent to jail; many of them should be confined in some other type of institution. In order to

---

[30] Federal Bureau of Prisons, *Manual of Jail Management* (Apr., 1948), pp. 5, 6. This manual is now out of print and will not be reissued. Individual jailers, upon request, are given recommendations about their particular problems. In addition, a correspondence course, which is divided into ten lessons, is conducted by the Federal Bureau of Prisons for jailers and their assistants. See also "Jail Standards Approved by the National Jail Association," *Proceedings of the American Correctional Association, 1956*, pp. 100–109.

[31] For some general programs for the improvement of jails, see Roy K. Flannagan, "Report of the Committee on Jails," *Proceedings of the American Prison Association, 1937*, p. 320; Russell B. DeVine, *The American Jail: What It Is and What To Do About It* (New York: The American Prison Association, 1937), pp. 14–22; Robinson, pp. 273–91; The National Jail Association, "Basic Principles of a Jail Association," *The Prison World*, VII (July–Aug., 1945), 7, 14, 15; Wright, pp., 317–21; *A Manual of Correctional Standards*, pp. 96–117.

reduce the jail population, more towns, cities, and counties should take the following steps:

a. Reduce the number of arrests. All evidence indicates that a large percentage of the persons who are arrested are released without prosecution, or if prosecuted, are released without conviction. Some of this is due to the inefficiency of the courts, but some of it is the result of unnecessary arrests. Better training and more adequate supervision of police, combined with a policy of using summonses wherever possible, can do much to reduce such arrests.

b. Remove certain types of inmates from the jails. Such persons as the chronic alcoholic, the feeble-minded, the insane, the juvenile delinquent, the drug addict, and the aged should be confined in some other type of institution, if institutional care is necessary, and not in the jail. As Roberts Wright has emphasized: "The insane belong in hospitals for the mentally ill, *not* jails. The aged belong in rest homes, *not* jails. The children belong in foster homes or approved detention homes, or their own homes, *not* jails. The physically ill belong in hospitals, *not* jails."[32]

c. Make greater use of approved release procedures. Wherever it is possible to do so, persons should be released on bail or on their own recognizance. Bail should be made easier to obtain, and the bail-bond racket should be eliminated. In most cases, little is to be gained by keeping a person in jail while he is awaiting trial. And the friendless and the impoverished should not be subjected to the hardship of confinement in jail simply because they do not have the money or influence which opens the door to freedom for their more favored fellows.

d. Adopt the installment plan for the collection of fines. A large percentage of jail inmates are confined for nonpayment of their fines. If most of these offenders were permitted to pay their fines on the installment plan, they could still be punished by the payment of their fines, and at the same time they could also keep their jobs, support their families, and avoid the demoralizing effects of enforced idleness at the expense of the community, which is the usual lot of jail inmates.

e. Use the delayed sentence in selected cases. The delayed sentence, used in various areas, notably Wisconsin, permits the prisoner to live his normal life most of the time and confines him in jail only at night or on weekends. In this way, while punishing him, it does not disrupt his domestic and economic relationships.[33]

[32] Wright, p. 317.

[33] In Wisconsin the Huber law, which was enacted in 1913, provides that misdemeanants may be employed outside of the jail during working hours but must be confined during the rest of the time. This has been called the "work-release" or "day-parole" plan. For a study of this work-release plan, see *Wisconsin's Huber Law in Action* (Milwaukee: Wisconsin Service Association, 1958). At least twenty-four states formally provide for some form of work release, and in addition to this, judges and

f. Make greater use of probation. The extent to which this can be done will depend upon the improvement of probation facilities. When this method of punishment is properly employed, it not only reduces the jail population but also increases the possibility of rehabilitation.

3. **Reduce the Period of Confinement of the Unsentenced Inmate.** Every effort should be made to reduce the time spent in jail by witnesses and those awaiting trial. Bail, personal recognizance, and release into the custody of reliable persons should be more extensively used. In addition, if financial sureties cannot be secured for a witness within a reasonable time, the law should provide that a deposition be made of his testimony in the presence of the defendant and authorized for use in the trial if the witness is not available at that time. This would make it unnecessary to keep certain witnesses in jail. Specific steps should be taken also to expedite trials and to reduce the many delays that at present clog the channels of justice and force many jail inmates to wait long periods of time for necessary judicial action.

4. **Establish a Better System for Handling Sentenced Inmates.** The establishment of such a system involves the following:

a. The creation of regional institutions for smaller cities and counties whose resources and number of jail inmates are not sufficient to justify their own institutions. Wherever it is necessary to do so, present facilities or a smaller unit could be used pending transfer to the central facility.

b. The design and construction of jails that not only provide adequate security but also make possible the classification of inmates, the segregation of inmate types (the unsentenced from the sentenced, the male from the female, the hardened from the youthful, the sick from the well, and so on), and the introduction of a modern jail program, including medical care, religious instruction and services, employment, education, recreation, and adequate visiting arrangements. The kind of jail that is needed in a particular place will be determined by such variables as climate, location, the number and types of inmates, etc. Forestry camps and farms are more suitable than the typical local jail in many areas.

c. The removal of the administration and operation of jails from politics and the placing of them under the control of well-trained and competent personnel selected on the basis of their qualifications. The fee

---

sheriffs informally make use of it in the handling of various cases. Although usually work-release laws apply only to misdemeanants, some states, like California, Washington, North Carolina, and a few others, have extended their laws to include felons (Stanley E. Grupp, "Work Release—Statutory Patterns, Implementation and Problems," *The Prison Journal*, XLIV [Spring, 1964], 4–25). All the articles in this issue of the *Prison Journal* are devoted to the subject of work release. See also Stanley E. Grupp, "Work Release in the United States," *Journal of Criminal Law, Criminology, and Police Science*, LIV (Sept., 1963), 267–72.

system should be completely eliminated and all personnel should be given fair and adequate salaries.

d. The introduction of efficient jail management policies and modern inmate programs. Jails should be operated on the basis of modern business methods, maintained in good repair, and kept clean at all times. Meals should be well balanced and prepared and served under sanitary conditions. Classification of inmates and the segregation of various types must be provided for at the same time that custodial care is exercised to insure against escapes, and rehabilitative influences must be exerted through the operation of well-planned and carefully supervised programs of religion, education, employment, recreation, discipline, and visiting.

e. The adoption of the indeterminate sentence and parole procedures for sentenced jail inmates. The use of short sentences makes it extremely difficult for any program of rehabilitation to operate successfully; in general, it prevents jail authorities from keeping prisoners long enough to modify their behavior. Furthermore, most offenders treat short sentences rather lightly, and upon release many quickly return to their criminal habits. The adoption of the indeterminate sentence for misdemeanants would do much to change this and would provide an opportunity for a more effective program of rehabilitation in our jails. This program could then be further strengthened by the extension of parole procedures to sentenced jail inmates, many of whom are especially in need of supervision after their release into the community.

f. The inspection of jails by the state, which should have the authority to enforce standards and to order the closing of jails that do not meet established requirements of operation. Inspection service backed by law has proved effective in improving the conditions in jails wherever it has been introduced and is now well established in such states as California, New York, Wisconsin, Pennsylvania, and Virginia. The state inspection service should maintain a full set of records regarding the conditions in the jails and publish regular reports on these institutions. This will not only bring undesirable jail conditions under public scrutiny but also provide recognition for those cities, towns, and counties that receive high ratings for the operation of their jails.

The following recommendations, made by the National Jail Association in 1945, provide a concise summary of the principal features of the program for the improvement of the jail which we have just outlined above:

Take these out of your jail system:

Children	Fee system
The physically and mentally ill	Political debt-paying staff jobs
Inefficient management	Insecurity of personnel
Special privilege	Extravagance
Idleness	Unsanitary conditions
Cruel treatment	Kangaroo courts

Put these into your jail system:

Safe custody
Segregation and classification
Discipline
Cleanliness
Wholesome food
Medical service
Good management
Economy
Trained staff
Individual treatment of prisoners
Work and recreation

Nonpolitical control
Indeterminate sentence
Chaplain service
Adaptation of architecture to
　best use
Probation
Parole
Installment payment of fines
Greater use of bail and
　recognizance[34]

LOCKUPS

Although our discussion thus far has been largely devoted to jails, what we have said about the conditions in our jails and the steps needed for their improvement applies to a great extent to lockups. These institutions, which are generally under the control of city or town police departments, are primarily places of detention, although some are used for the punishment of minor offenders. They are much more numerous than jails and like them have received a great deal of severe criticism. When Dr. Hastings H. Hart investigated lockups in 1930 for the National Commission on Law Observance and Enforcement, he declared them to be a public nuisance and unfit to be used as places of detention.[35] Although no general survey of lockups has been made since that time, all evidence indicates that in general Dr. Hart's statement regarding them is still true.

A few years ago, a study of Chicago's lockups revealed the most shocking conditions, and on the basis of the findings it classified seven as "good," ten as "fair," and twenty-two as "poor."[36] However, a later study made of these same lockups in 1962 found that they had been greatly improved and were in clean condition and apparently efficiently administered.[37] A survey of municipal lockups throughout the state of New

[34] The National Jail Association, "Basic Principles of a Jail Association," *The Prison World*, VII (July–Aug., 1945), 7, 14, 15. See also Vernon Kilpatrick, "The Jails of California," *Proceedings of the American Prison Association, 1947*, pp. 53–57. For two recent manuals on the construction and administration of the jail, see Myrl E. Alexander, *Jail Administration* (Springfield, Ill.: Charles C. Thomas, Publisher, 1957); Roy Casey, *The Modern Jail: Design, Equipment, Operation* (Keene, Tex.: Continental Press, 1958).

[35] Hastings H. Hart, "Police Jails and Village Lockups," *Report on Penal Institutions, Probation, and Parole*, Report No. 9, National Commission on Law Observance and Enforcement (Washington, D.C.: Government Printing Office, 1931), p. 330.

[36] Eugene S. Zemans, *Held Without Bail* (Chicago: John Howard Association, 1949), pp. 42–44.

[37] For the findings and recommendations of this study, see Johnson Levering, Ruth Shonle Cavan, and Eugene S. Zemans, *Chicago Police Lockups* (Chicago: John Howard Association, 1963).

Jersey, which was conducted by the division of inspection of the department of institutions and agencies of that state in February, 1949, showed that even in New Jersey where much emphasis has been placed upon the improvement of jails and lockups, over one-third of the lockups were definitely unsatisfactory. Today New Jersey has a jail-inspection program and provides its chiefs of police with a set of suggestions to be used as a guide in promoting adequate standards for city jails and lockups.[38]

THE DETENTION OF JUVENILES

Juveniles who have come into contact with the law are usually permitted to remain in their own homes while their cases are before the court, but sometimes it is necessary to detain[39] juveniles in order (1) to protect the community because of the seriousness of their offenses or because they cannot be controlled by their parents or guardians; (2) to protect them, because otherwise they may be harmed by themselves or by others, or because they are in physical or moral danger in their own homes; or (3) to insure their availability for future action by the court, because this cannot be accomplished in any other way.[40] Since the available statistics are incomplete, we do not know exactly how many children are being detained each year in the United States, but it is estimated that the number may be as high as 300,000.[41]

The juvenile court laws of most states provide for the protective custody and care of children prior to the final disposition of the case by the court and usually prohibit the detention of anyone under sixteen years of age in jails and lockups; but since there are often no provisions for the enforcement of these laws, they are frequently violated.[42] At present, children who require detention are being kept in a variety of places,

[38] Walter C. Reckless, *The Crime Problem* (New York: Appleton-Century-Crofts, Inc., 1961), pp. 460, 461, 471–73.

[39] Some writers now make a distinction between detention and shelter care. According to this view, detention is the temporary care of alleged or adjudged delinquents who require secure custody in physically restricted facilities pending court disposition or transfer to another jurisdiction or agency. Shelter care, on the other hand, is the temporary care of children—usually those who are dependent or neglected—in physically unrestricting facilities, such as subsidized boarding houses; see *Standards and Guides for the Detention of Children and Youth* (New York: National Council on Crime and Delinquency, 1961), pp. 1–9; 33–43. See also Sherwood Norman, *Detention Practice: Significant Developments in the Detention of Children and Youth* (New York: National Probation and Parole Association, 1960).

[40] Sherwood Norman, "A Nationwide Survey of Juvenile Detention," *Proceedings of the American Prison Association, 1945,* pp. 244, 245; National Conference on Prevention and Control of Juvenile Delinquency, *Report on Juvenile Detention* (Washington, D.C.: Government Printing Office, 1947), pp. 18, 19.

[41] Katharine F. Lenroot, "The Juvenile Court Today," *Federal Probation,* XIII (Sept., 1949), 10.

[42] Alice Scott Nutt, "Juvenile and Domestic Relations Courts," *Social Work Year Book, 1949* (New York: Russell Sage Foundation, 1949), p. 274.

including lockups, jails, boarding houses, orphanages, hospitals, alms-houses, detention homes, and correctional institutions.

In view of what has been said about jails and lockups, it should be clear that they are not fit places in which to detain children. As a matter of fact, most of the other facilities that are being used for this purpose are far from satisfactory. This was clearly shown by Sherwood Norman, field consultant for the National Probation Association, who conducted a survey of the best detention facilities for children in the United States. In 1946 he reported that he had visited and intensively studied 43 facilities in 29 communities. He found that two-thirds of them were over-crowded, that even those which offered reasonably good physical care frequently did not provide the kind of life that was conducive to mental health, that none had a building which could be considered a model for the special demands of detention care, and that only four had an adequate program for children and a sound in-service training program for the staff.[43] In 1960, at the annual meeting of the American Society of Criminology, Sherwood Norman reported that with rare exceptions, conditions in juvenile detention facilities throughout the United States were depressingly inadequate. Staffs were poorly selected, paid, trained, and supervised; overcrowding made rehabilitative programs ineffective; inadequate classification and segregation converted some institutions into veritable "crime schools."

Some county detention homes are no better than jails, being catchalls where homeless and neglected children are indiscriminately mingled with the delinquent, the feeble-minded, and the mentally ill, and where in enforced idleness, they are introduced to all the degrading practices of vice and crime and exposed to brutal treatment and exploitation by other juveniles, sex perverts, and untrained employees. Others are used as places where children can be kept indefinitely, simply because judges, probation officers, and social workers do not know what else to do with them, or because those in authority have failed to provide for a satisfactory disposition of their cases.

All the available evidence on the subject indicates that the methods and facilities of juvenile detention are in need of great improvement.[44] Basic in any move to effect this improvement is the establishment of the following minimum standards of juvenile detention:

1. Every effort should be made to keep children out of jails and lockups. If for any reason it is necessary to detain children in a jail or lockup,

---

[43] Sherwood Norman, "Detention Facilities for Children," *Yearbook, 1946* (New York: National Probation Association, 1947), pp. 86–99. See also Sherwood Norman and Helen Norman, *Detention for the Juvenile Court: A Discussion of Principles and Practices* (New York: National Probation Association, 1946).

[44] Belle Boone Beard, "Detention: The Weakest Link," *Federal Probation*, XIII (June, 1949), 18, 19.

they should be segregated from adults, preferably in quarters designed especially for juveniles.

2. The number of children detained should be kept as low as possible. The child's relation with his home should be preserved whenever it is possible to do so.

3. The period of detention should be made as short as possible. Detention, no matter how ideal, can never be a substitute for normal life in the community.

4. Juveniles who are awaiting court hearing for alleged delinquency should be segregated from the dependent, the neglected, the homeless, the emotionally disturbed or mentally ill nondelinquent, the juvenile witness held in custody, etc., all of whom should not be held in detention facilities but should be cared for in other institutions or foster homes.

5. Detention facilities should not be used as "juvenile jails" or commitment institutions to which children are sentenced for punishment by the court. If a child is held in a detention home while he is awaiting transfer to a correctional institution, his stay in the detention home should be as brief as possible.

6. Children should be given a physical examination on admission to detention in order to prevent the spread of disease; they should then be classified and segregated by type of case. During the period of their confinement they should be provided with adequate medical, religious, educational, recreational, and counseling services.

7. Detention facilities should be made safe, healthful, and homelike, placed under the supervision of competent persons, subjected to state inspection service, and required to meet specified standards of operation.

8. The public should be educated to appreciate the importance of juvenile detention, and support for it should be cultivated through regular public relations work.

9. Detention service should be closely integrated with other services for children in the community so that all resources are made accessible for the care of the detained children.[45]

In discussing the various types of detention facilities, Sherwood Norman states that the average county wishing to abandon the use of the jail or jail-like detention has the following alternatives:

1. The specially constructed detention home which, in the opinion of Norman, "is the best solution because it combines secure custody, homelike appearance, varied indoor activity areas designed to secure constant

---

[45] Federal Security Agency, *Recommendations on Standards for Detention of Juveniles and Adults* (Washington, D.C.: Government Printing Office, 1945), pp. 7–13; Norman and Norman, *Detention for the Juvenile Court,* pp. 2, 3; Sherwood Norman, "New Goals for Juvenile Detention," *Federal Probation,* XIII (Dec., 1949), 29–35.

supervision, and other important features." He recognizes these three types of the specially constructed detention home:

a. The family-type home which is designed as a home for a man and wife and has facilities for up to eight children.
b. The single-unit home, which may or may not have a resident staff and is designed for from eight to sixteen children.
c. The two-unit or multi-unit home, which has separate living and sleeping quarters for two or more groups of children, each group not exceeding a maximum of fifteen.

2. The converted residence, which is a house owned or rented by the administering agency and remodeled for detention purposes.

3. Boarding homes for detention, which can be used for most children who need to be detained, provided skillful boarding parents can be found and given adequate financial support and supervision. However, when such homes are used, there are always some children who must be held elsewhere in a more secure detention facility.

4. The combination of detention with other facilities by providing rooms in a courthouse, county office building, hospital, county home, training school, or other institution. This may be better than using the jail, but it is not recommended except as a stopgap measure.[46]

Regardless of the kind of detention that is used, it must be well supported with a competent staff and an effective program. And what is more important, unnecessary detention should be avoided in all cases involving juveniles.[47]

---

[46] Sherwood Norman, "New Goals for Juvenile Detention," *Contemporary Correction*, ed. Paul W. Tappan (New York: McGraw-Hill Book Co., Inc., 1951), pp. 340–42. For a detailed discussion of the planning and construction of juvenile detention homes, see Federal Bureau of Prisons, *Handbook of Correctional Institution Design and Construction* (Washington, D.C.: Federal Bureau of Prisons, 1949), pp. 154–67. See also Sherwood Norman, *The Design and Construction of Detention Homes for the Juvenile Court* (New York: National Probation Association, 1947); *ibid., Standards and Guides for the Detention of Children and Youth*, pp. 105–44.

[47] Paul W. Tappan, *Juvenile Delinquency* (New York: McGraw-Hill Book Co., Inc., 1949), p. 414.

23

Prison Administration

ORGANIZATION

The kind of organization that a state correctional administration has significantly affects such matters as the appropriation of funds, the selection of personnel, the formulation of administrative policies, and thus the operation of the correctional system. An examination of the names of the state correctional administrations quickly reveals their variety and the absence of any standard type of organization. Every historical stage of refinement and development in correctional organization has a contemporary representative, but the trend toward centralization of authority and responsibility is distinct and unmistakable.[1] Even so, the variety of conditions existing in the different states will continue to require diversity of administrative organization, and for any given state the best form of organization is the one that most adequately serves the needs and interests of that state.

The typical form of organization up to the time of the War Between the States was the local board of trustees. However, the increasing number of institutions and the need of greater coordination gradually led to the creation of central state boards, which were usually known as "state boards of charities and corrections." Originally these state boards, the members of which were appointed by the governor, exercised only general supervisory authority and coexisted with the local boards of trustees, but soon they acquired additional functions and began to replace those on the local level. Among the first states to have such state boards were Massachusetts, New York, Pennsylvania, Ohio, and Illinois, each of which

---

[1] Richard A. McGee, "State Organization for Correctional Administration," *Contemporary Correction,* ed. Paul W. Tappan (New York: McGraw-Hill Book Co., Inc., 1951), pp. 75–90; Jason A. Aisner and Dane M. Shulman, "Correctional Department Administration," *The Prison World,* XIII (Mar.–Apr., 1951), 28, 29, and XIII (July–Aug., 1951), 24, 25.

organized one before 1879. State boards of control emerged as the third step in the increasing centralization of correctional administration. These boards, usually composed of paid, full-time members, had far more comprehensive responsibilities than previous boards. In some states the members were appointed by the governor; in others, they were elected. In accord with a legislative proposal made in 1868, Rhode Island established the first board of control. Wisconsin organized one in 1891, and was followed within a few years by Iowa and Minnesota as they took similar action.[2]

The departmental form of organization represents the most recent stage in the development of correctional organization in this country. It owes its origin to the desire for greater economy and efficiency in state government, and most states have now adopted it. However, the integration of administrative functions into a single department has not always produced a separate department of corrections. Sometimes, as, for example, in Illinois, New Jersey, Ohio, and Wisconsin, these functions have been gathered together under a division in a new department of institutions or welfare, but in some other states, like California, New York, Minnesota, and Michigan, a separate department of corrections under a single executive head has appeared.

Many states, however, still operate their correctional system under some kind of administrative board. In a few states, like Mississippi, this is a local board of trustees, the members of which serve on a part-time basis, sometimes without compensation. Although this kind of board may be conscientious and zealous in the assumption of its responsibilities, its efforts are likely to be handicapped by limitations of technical knowledge and infrequency of meetings.

In several states the correctional system is under an ex officio board, that is, one that is composed of high state elective officials, such as the governor, the comptroller, the state treasurer, and the attorney general. The chief argument in favor of this type of board is that it does not cost much to operate, but its effectiveness is likely to be limited by the fact that its members have so many other duties that they can give little time and thought to the management of correctional institutions.

Iowa and several other states still have a board of control, and it manages several types of institutions, including correctional institutions and hospitals. Although all these institutions have much in common, no single administrative board can possibly have all the technical knowledge that the modern operation of each requires. The board of control is primarily interested in the fiscal aspects of administration, but there is the very human tendency for its members to meddle in the management of

[2] Blake McKelvey, *American Prisons* (Chicago: University of Chicago Press, 1936), pp. 53–56, 126–29.

the institutions under their charge. This leads to the formation of cliques among subordinates, friction, intrigues, and conflicts.

Centralized prison boards or commissions, appointed by the governor, function in Idaho, Utah, and some other states. The law usually provides that both major parties be represented on these boards so as to protect prison administration from partisan politics. Critics of the centralized board or commission have claimed that its membership is frequently nonprofessional; its decisions, slow and based on compromise; its responsibility, diffused; and its operation, undermined by jealousies, suspicions, and internal conflicts.

Experienced administrators generally agree that plural executives, for example, boards and commissions, are unsatisfactory, and that it is desirable to have the correctional system under the direction of a single administrator. There is, however, a difference of opinion as to whether correctional administration should be lodged in an independent and separate state department or in a division of the state department of welfare.

In favor of the separate department of corrections its proponents argue that: (1) it emphasizes the importance of the correctional program and thus attracts superior administrative personnel; (2) it increases the chances of securing adequate funds for physical facilities and personnel; (3) it guards against the subordination of correctional work to such matters as health, welfare, and public assistance; and (4) it prevents the possibility of interference with the correctional system by noncorrectional administrative superiors.

Those who argue in favor of placing the correctional system in a division of the state department of welfare contend that: (1) it emphasizes the fact that the correctional system is an integral unit in the state's whole public welfare program; (2) it facilitates coordination of welfare, public health, and correctional services; (3) it tends to professionalize the correctional services and attract a higher grade of personnel to them; (4) it causes the correctional services to gain in public esteem since it links them with other services of great value and significance to the public; (5) it increases the chances that the correctional system will secure adequate appropriations and decreases the interdepartmental competition for funds; and (6) it is more practicable in sparsely populated states wherein there are only a few correctional institutions.

Although this clash of opinion continues, experienced administrators generally emphasize the desirability of having a separate department of corrections whenever the size of the correctional problem in the state warrants this. The American Correctional Association, while recognizing that the same kind of administrative organization cannot be justified for every state, recommends that the administration of the state correctional system be in a *separate state department,* called a *department of corrections,* and that the department be under a *single administrator.* Correctional administration is a highly specialized activity, requiring considerable training and extensive previous experience, and it should therefore never be submerged in a larger department.[3] However, some authorities in the correctional field believe that if a separate department of corrections is given authority over both juvenile and adult offenders, the independence of administration for juvenile institutions and services should be guaranteed by the creation of two divisions within the department, one for juveniles and one for adults.

There is some difference of opinion, also, as to whether the head of the correctional system should be appointed by a board of laymen or by the governor. The principal argument in favor of having a board select the director or commissioner is that this removes the appointment from partisan politics and protects the correctional system from political interference. This argument, however, is subject to serious criticism. Political considerations often dominate a board as much as an official. Personality clashes and an ineffectual chairman may prevent the appointment of a qualified executive. Besides, if the correctional executive has to operate through a board, instead of having direct access to the governor, he may find it much more difficult to get quick and clear decisions on urgent questions. And if the governor does not have direct contact with the correctional executive, he loses some of his authority over matters of policy for which the voters hold him responsible. Finally, neither appointment by a board nor any other procedural device can completely counteract the bad effects produced by the election of a weak or venal governor.[4] However, if the appointment of the correctional executive be made by a board, it has been suggested that this be done by a board of corrections composed of five to nine members and appointed by the governor for staggered terms sufficiently long to avoid a heavy turnover in any one governor's administration, that the board be a policy-making and not an administrative agency, and that the members of the board receive no salaries but be given a *per diem allowance.*[5]

A correctional system has usually been regarded as concerned only with institutions. Recently, however, the continuity of the correctional process from arrest to release has been greatly stressed. It is argued that since probation, institutional care, and parole are parts of the same process, all of these should be included in the administrative structure

---

[3] *Manual of Correctional Standards* (New York: The American Correctional Association, 1959), pp. 39–45.

[4] McGee, pp. 84, 85; *Manual of Correctional Standards,* pp. 42, 43.

[5] *Manual of Suggested Standards for a State Correctional System* (New York: The American Prison Association, 1946), pp. 9, 10.

of the state correctional system. Steps have already been taken to accomplish this in some states, for example, in Michigan and Wisconsin; but until now the idea has been carried further in California than in any other state. Its department of corrections operates under the direction of the administrator of the Youth and Adult Corrections Agency. Serving under him are the Board of Corrections, the Correctional Industries Commission; the Adult Authority, the Youth Authority, the Board of Trustees of the Institution for Women, and several other allied commissions. The Adult Authority, composed of seven members appointed by the governor, is an important feature of the California system. Its duties include the study of adult offenders committed by the courts to state institutions, the fixing of sentences between the limits imposed by the law, the granting of parole, the revocation of parole, and service as an advisory pardon board.[6]

PERSONNEL

The Director or Commissioner. Regardless of the form of organization that is adopted, the correctional system should be headed by a professionally qualified administrator with the title of commissioner or director. However, most authorities in the correctional field believe that this administrative head and perhaps his chief assistants should be exempt from civil service. They argue that the governor should be able to surround himself with policy-making assistants whose views are in harmony with his and with those of his party so that he will not face needless opposition in his efforts to put into effect the platform upon which he stood for election. Opponents of the civil service method of appointment also insist that it encourages the commissioner or director to remain in office far beyond his span of efficiency and effectiveness and makes the removal of a poor administrator exceedingly difficult.[7] The risk of not having the commissioner or director under civil service is that he may be dismissed with each new incoming governor. This problem can be met in part by having the statutory expiration date of the commissioner's or director's term in office so set as not to be coincidental with that of the governor. This prevents hasty dismissals during the confusion and turmoil attendant upon the coming into office of a new administration.

There is considerable opposition also to the inclusion of wardens and other institutional heads under civil service. Here the opposition argues that it is difficult to dispense with the services of incompetent or inefficient wardens or other institutional heads when they are protected by

---

[6] For further discussion of the California Adult Authority, see Chapter 28.

[7] *Manual of Correctional Standards*, pp. 43–45. For an analysis of the administration of a maximum-security prison, see Joseph E. Ragen and Charles Finston, *Inside the World's Toughest Prison* (Springfield, Ill.: Charles C. Thomas, Publisher, 1962).

Panopticon-shaped dining room, Illinois State Penitentiary, Stateville, Illinois. (Courtesy of Federal Bureau of Prisons)

tenure regulations of civil service. However, with the exception of wardens and other institutional heads, there is general agreement among prison authorities that all positions below the top administrative level should be under civil service and that all personnel for these positions should be selected and promoted on the basis of merit examinations and be required to meet high standards of character, personality, intelligence, education, and experience. All powers of appointment, within the limits of civil service laws and regulations, should be vested in the commissioner or director so that his authority will be commensurate with his responsibility, and the law should permit him to delegate these powers, or some portion of them, to subordinates.[8]

Warden or Superintendent. The executive officer in charge of each correctional institution is the warden or superintendent. He is assisted by one or more deputies, guards, foremen, stewards, shop and school instructors, chaplains, physicians, and to an increasing extent, by psychiatrists, psychologists, sociologists, and social workers. In addition, inmates are often employed as clerks and instructors, and, sometimes, as guards.

[8] *Manual of Correctional Standards,* pp. 51, 52.

The warden or superintendent is the general manager of the correctional institution, and he is responsible for its maintenance, operation, policies, regulations, and programs. He has been called the ruler of an autocracy, and there is no question that he exercises great power over the lives of many persons. Even though a state board or the head of the correctional system lays down certain fundamental policies, the warden or superintendent has wide latitude in which to carry on the daily administration of the institution. In fact, so much depends on his character and personality that there is much truth in the statement that a prison is but the shadow of its warden.

Yet with all his power, the warden or superintendent has tremendous responsibilities. He must hold prisoners in safe custody and prevent riots and escapes. He must operate his institution, often antiquated and overcrowded, at a minimum cost. He must find employment for a great mass of inexperienced, inefficient, and untrained inmates, many of whom are recalcitrant, sullen, and unruly. He must make his institution as self-supporting as possible and at the same time avoid competition with free labor and private industry. He must keep his institution from becoming a detriment to the party from which he received his appointment. He must periodically persuade legislators and the public to provide him with adequate appropriations to maintain and operate an institution for those who have harmed and perhaps outraged law-abiding citizens. And now, in response to increasing public demands and despite antiquated buildings, insufficient funds, and inadequate personnel, he must try to convert his charges, many of whom are embittered, hardened, and vindictive, into law-abiding and responsible citizens. Thus, he is expected to be an efficient custodian, a strict disciplinarian, an able administrator, an astute businessman, a wise humanitarian, a competent educator, a skillful reformer, an expert diplomat, and a shrewd politician.

A herculean task, you say? Indeed, it is—one requiring great courage, ingenuity, and diligence. That we have as many good institutions as we have is largely a tribute to the dedication of conscientious wardens and superintendents and their loyal assistants. In general, the American people, the great majority of whom are ignorant, uninterested, and apathetic regarding correctional problems, have better correctional institutions than they deserve.

Unfortunately, the office of warden or superintendent is not held in high esteem by the public. Some of the same stigma that is attached to the prisoner clings to his custodian. In the mind of the average citizen, the chief task of the warden or superintendent is to keep the inmate in safe custody, which to the uninitiated does not appear to require much intelligence, skill, or training. It is not surprising, then, that the salary is not nearly commensurate with the great responsibilities of the position

SILENT SYSTEM
DINING HALL FOOD SIGNALS & SIGNS

BREAD	WATER	STEW	SALT & PEPPER
COFFEE	VINEGAR	GRAVY	MILK
DRESSING	POTATOES	DESSERT	SMALL Amount
MEAT	SPAGHETTI	VEGETABLES	BEANS

"Silent system" formerly used in dining hall, Iowa State Penitentiary, Fort Madison, Iowa.

and that tenure is insecure. Special training for the office is thought to be unnecessary, and appointment to it is generally regarded as a suitable reward for loyalty to a political party. There are some signs that this highly undesirable situation is changing, but progress is slow. At present, few wardens and superintendents in the United States have had professional training. Nevertheless, authorities in the field agree that a warden or superintendent should be chosen on the basis of his qualifications and fitness for the office, that he should hold his position as long as his conduct and work are satisfactory, and that the salary of the office should be materially increased.

Deputy Warden or Deputy Superintendent. The deputy or associate warden or deputy superintendent is usually the chief security officer, having all the institution's guards under his command. He supervises the general routine, assigns inmates to their work, superintends the enforcement of the rules, and determines what discipline should be imposed when the rules are broken. He must be vigilant and firm but also prudent and fair and be able at times to overlook the infraction of rules if the net result is beneficial to the morale of the institution. He must be a man of penetrating insight, possessed of great courage and a deep understanding of the ways and habits of prisoners. Much of the success of any institution depends upon his knowledge, skill, and decisive action in critical situations. Usually he is appointed by the warden or superintendent and serves directly under him.

Guards. The guard, or, as he is sometimes called, the custodial or correctional officer, occupies a pivotal and strategic position in the prison. Upon his competence and loyalty, upon his resourcefulness and skill, depend both the safety of the prison and the spirit of the inmates. He is the first line of attack in case of escapes and the most immediate instrument for the proper handling of the prisoners. He must enforce the rules and regulations. He must be on the alert to detect signs of uprisings and to prevent the introduction of contraband into the prison and its circulation among the inmates. He must count the prisoners under his charge several times each day. He must patrol his gallery and periodically inspect the cells there. He must administer to the inmates' needs and make reports regarding their condition and behavior. During the day he must supervise the prisoners while they are at work and play and as they march from place to place. At night he must lock them in, see that the lights are out, and make certain that all is secure.

The guard's duties, then, are difficult and onerous, but what is more, they must be performed under the most unpleasant conditions. He is locked up in an unattractive institution with large numbers of hostile, restless, and sometimes desperate inmates. He must never relax his vigilance; but the prisoners watch him as he watches them. At all times he must appear alert, strong, self-confident, and competent. The possibilities of friction and conflict are always present. The pressure becomes greater than some guards can bear. Some meet their problems by becoming brutal and sadistic; some, by being "good fellows," which usually earns for them only the contempt of their prisoners.

Strict rules govern the guard's conduct and his relations with inmates. What he takes into and out of prison is carefully regulated. He must

Dining hall, Iowa State Penitentiary, Fort Madison, Iowa.

maintain a firm and impersonal attitude toward the prisoner, avoiding needless conversation with him. In fact, while in the institution, the guard himself is virtually a prisoner.[9]

Usually the guard is appointed by the warden, serves directly under the captain of his shift, and at the time of his appointment has had no training for his position. Often he has had little education, is subject to political influence, and is without security of tenure. In some institutions the hours are still long. Often the pay is low and the guard force under-manned.

The employment and retention of competent guards is one of the most serious problems confronting the warden. It is obvious that such things as higher wages, shorter hours, longer vacations, and an opportunity for promotion must be provided if our correctional system is to be improved. At the time of his appointment, a guard should be between the ages of twenty-five and thirty-five, at least a high school graduate, in sound physical condition, and possessed of good character and balanced personality. He should be under civil service, chosen on the basis of merit examinations, and given in-service training. He should have security of tenure, but only as long as his conduct and work are satisfactory. He should receive regular increments in salary, promotion on merit, retirement on pension, and adequate vacations and annual sick leave.[10]

Today, in some institutions, the guard is expected to be not only a custodial officer but also a counselor, engaged in improving the inmates' attitudes and behavior. He must study his charges, analyze their problems and personalities, and assist the psychiatrist, psychologist, and sociologist in the operation of the rehabilitation program. Since he is in continuous daily contact with prisoners, he is in an excellent position to do this work.[11] In fact, many observers believe that guards influence the lives of inmates more than do professional workers. However, it is difficult to secure persons who have all the qualities necessary to fit them for both custodial and counseling services. It is difficult, also, for a guard to maintain the kind of social relationship with a prisoner which is conducive to the best performance of both these services. For these reasons,

---

[9] National Commission on Law Observance and Enforcement, *Report on Penal Institutions, Probation, and Parole,* Report No. 9 (Washington, D.C.: Government Printing Office, 1931), pp. 40–47.

[10] *Manual of Suggested Standards for a State Correctional System,* pp. 19, 20; *In-Service Training Standards for Prison Custodial Officers* (New York: The American Prison Association, 1951), pp. 23, 24; A. A. Evans, "Correctional Institution Personnel—Amateurs or Professionals?" *The Annals of the American Academy of Political and Social Science,* CCXCIII (May, 1954), 70–78.

[11] Walter M. Wallack, *The Training of Prison Guards* (New York: Bureau of Publications, Teachers' College, Columbia University, 1938), pp. 59, 60, 223, 224; Jean S. Long, "The Functions of a Guard in Modern Penal and Correctional Institutions," *Proceedings of the American Prison Association,* 1938, pp. 139–48.

some prison authorities recommend that the custodial and counseling services be separated, and that a prison police force perform the custodial function and a group of guidance officers do social case work and perform other services in connection with the rehabilitation program.[12]

The success of correctional institutions is largely dependent upon the caliber of their personnel, who must be not only carefully selected but also properly trained. In recognition of this the federal government and a few states like New Jersey, New York, and California have instituted in-service training programs. Such programs are designed primarily for the guards, or custodial officers, the great majority of whom enter the service without having had prior instruction in correctional work. By in-service training is meant the formal instruction that is given to employees in correctional service, both at the beginning of their employment and during the entire period of their service.[13]

Relations Between the Custodial and Professional Staffs. The custodial staff, consisting of guards and their supervisory officers, and the professional staff, including physicians, chaplains, psychiatrists, psychologists, sociologists, social workers, dentists, and nurses, constitute the largest segment of personnel in a correctional institution.[14] In the larger institutions, each of these staffs may be under a deputy or associate warden or an assistant superintendent. Each must exist if institutionalization is to accomplish its purposes. Each exercises authority over the prisoner in its own way in order to carry out its specific objectives. Each must maintain a certain social distance by means of its own devices if it is to perform its services.

However, the conflict between these two staffs is one of the major administrative problems in the correctional field. Professional workers, while placing great emphasis on the individual and his treatment, tend to overlook the importance of punishment and the interests of the state, fail to adjust their services and techniques to the limitations of the correctional community, often underestimate the skills and intelligence of

[12] Walter C. Reckless, "Treatment Personnel in a Correctional Institution," *Proceedings of the American Prison Association, 1947*, pp. 77–81; Price Chenault, Treatment Techniques in Correctional Institutions," *ibid.*, pp. 63, 64; Milton Chernin, "Training for Correctional Work," *ibid.*, pp. 106–11. For a recommended curriculum for those interested in entering the field of corrections, see Alfred C. Schnur, "Pre-Service Training," *Journal of Criminal Law, Criminology, and Police Science*, L (May–June, 1959), 27–33. See also William F. Masimer, "The Correctional Officer as a Counselor," *Federal Probation*, XXIII (Mar., 1959), 32–36.

[13] For the nature and goals of in-service training, see *In-Service Training Standards for Prison Custodial Officers*, pp. 3, 4, 28.

[14] *Handbook on Classification in Correctional Institutions* (New York: The American Prison Association, 1947), pp. 49–52, 68, 69, 72, 73; Ralph A. Brancale, "Psychiatric and Psychological Services," *Contemporary Correction*, ed. Paul W. Tappan (New York: McGraw-Hill Book Co., Inc., 1951), pp. 191–204.

custodial officers, and in many instances approach their duties with an extreme deterministic theory of human behavior. On the other hand, custodial officers tend to stress punishment to the exclusion of treatment, often resist changes necessary for the operation of treatment programs, and frequently look with suspicion and hostility on both inmates and professional workers. Thus the roots of this conflict reach far into the life of the institution.[15]

Nevertheless, the interests of the public must be paramount, and the authority of the warden or superintendent, who is held responsible for what happens in his institution, must be supreme in his institution. There cannot be two centers of authority in a correctional institution, one for the custodial staff and one for the professional staff. Both must recognize the authority of the warden or superintendent. Professional employees, therefore, must operate within the limits essential to the maintenance of the security program and adapt their skills and techniques to the restrictions of the correctional community.

Even so, there is no reason why they cannot do their work effectively in an authoritarian setting such as that found in a correctional institution.[16] Indeed, their work must always be done in this kind of setting regardless of where they are. Some authority, defining and limiting individual action, is implicit in every social situation. Looked at in another way, authority is merely the total of responsibilities which an individual must assume if he is to exercise his rights. The institutional situation is not different in kind from any other social situation. Professional workers themselves, wherever they are, must accept authority. Such acceptance is essential to adjustment for everyone everywhere. Teaching respect for authority, therefore, is part of the rehabilitation process and helps to prepare the inmate to assume responsibilities which will confront him after his release. It is the manner in which authority is used, rather than its mere presence, that determines whether it interferes with the rehabilitation program.[17]

The professional worker may be placed in a difficult position when an inmate confides in him. If the worker reveals confidential information, he may destroy his reformative influence over that inmate. And yet the worker has an obligation which transcends any that he may owe to any

[15] Charles McKendrick, "Custody and Discipline," *Contemporary Correction*, ed. Paul W. Tappan (New York: McGraw-Hill Book Co., Inc., 1951), pp. 159, 160; George H. Weber, "Conflicts between Professional and non-Professional Personnel in Institutional Delinquency Treatment," *Journal of Criminal Law, Criminology, and Police Science*, XLVIII (May–June, 1957), 26–43.

[16] Kenneth L. M. Pray, "Case Work Paves the Way in Preparation for Freedom," *Proceedings of the American Prison Association, 1945*, pp. 132–38.

[17] For a discussion of rehabilitative work in the authoritarian setting of probation and parole, see Chapters 19 and 28.

particular inmate or to the inmate body. If the information indicates that the safety of others, the security of the institution, the effectiveness of the institution's program, or the interests of the public are endangered in any way, the worker must bring this fact immediately to the attention of the administration.

Violations of the institution's rules by professional workers cannot be tolerated any more than can similar violations by other employees. Above all, professional workers must never use their position to encourage disrespect of the authority of the custodial force or to promote friction between the custodial force and the inmate. If the professional worker believes that any inmate is not being fairly treated or that the rules are unnecessarily strict, he should bring this to the attention of his superior so that the warden or superintendent can be properly informed and not try to change the situation himself. If he feels that he cannot function within the necessary limitations of the correctional community, he should resign rather than try to undermine the policies of the institution or to foment discord within its walls.

Definite steps, however, can be taken to reduce the possibilities of conflict between the professional and custodial staffs. Each must come to understand and appreciate the objectives and techniques of the other and to recognize that both are making important contributions to the successful operation of the institution. To this end, each should be instructed regarding the work of the other. The custodial staff should receive continuous training leading toward the professionalization of their position and the improvement of their status in the hierarchy of the institution. Meetings and conferences should be held for the discussion of the problems common to both staffs and the exploration of ways and means of reducing friction. Grievances between the two should be thoroughly aired, and handled with frankness and a respect for the views and interests of all concerned. At all times, the unity of the correctional community should be strongly emphasized and clearly recognized in the formulation of policies and programs.

DISCIPLINE

Discipline in correctional institutions is commonly thought of as referring only to the process of preventing misconduct, disturbances, and escapes and of imposing punishment when they occur. In the broader and more realistic sense of the term, however, discipline means not only this but also the maintenance of proper standards and the reasonable regulation of everyday institutional life so that the institution will be an orderly, self-respecting community. For example, in the broader sense of the term, discipline is concerned with the establishment of orderly procedures in the mess hall so that the inmates can be fed with a minimum of confusion and friction. Moreover, discipline must be related to the rehabilitation program. It must look beyond the limits of the prisoner's term of confinement. It must not merely require the inmate to conform to the rules of the institution; it must also aim to inculcate standards that will contribute to his successful adjustment after release. In the accomplishment of this purpose the example of the members of the custodial and professional staffs is most important. Thus, if the warden wants his prisoners to believe a high standard of honesty is workable, he and his assistants must prevent petty graft by employees, theft of food, possession of contraband, the granting of special privileges to favored inmates, and the many other dishonest practices that tend to confirm the cynical attitude that most prisoners have toward law and law enforcement.

That discipline is best which disciplines least. Rules and regulations that cover every minute detail of a prisoner's daily activities are certain to produce infractions followed by punishments and more infractions in a vicious circle. The only sound basis of good discipline is good morale, which is the product of the entire institutional program. Discipline within an institution must have the moral support of the correctional community to be effective. To command this support, discipline must be firm but fair. It must be consistent and predictable, not vacillating and whimsical. Each inmate must receive what he deserves, and above all, officials must act impartially on the basis of a careful investigation of the facts of each case. This involves the full use of the services of the professional staff as well as those of the custodial staff.

The rules and regulations of a correctional institution, along with any necessary instructions, should be in printed form and each inmate should be supplied with a small pocket-size manual containing this information. The book should be informative and explanatory in tone rather than harsh and threatening. It should include information on institutional activities and procedures, educational opportunities, library facilities, religious services, parole and good conduct regulations, visiting and mail privileges, authorized punishments, and so on. It is neither wise nor necessary to have a long list of "thou-shalt-nots." On the contrary, there should be as few rules as possible, and the ones that are used should be stated in clear and simple language.

Today, most correctional institutions issue printed or typewritten rules and regulations for inmates. Some have attempted to revise the traditional rule book so as to make it more personal. For example, Warden John Burke, of the Wisconsin State Prison at Waupun, sends a series of seven letters to each inmate during his stay in quarantine. These take the place of the set of dry, formal rules that are usually issued in prisons. That

Warden Burke has used his imagination and insight is shown by the introduction of the first of these letters. This states:

Because you are new to us and we're new to you, this is the first of a series of "letters" which we want every newcomer to Waupun to read—and to remember.

We ask you to read them carefully because these letters are the only way we have to quickly and briefly tell you about our institution, about our rules and regulations, and about what we are going to try to do to make it possible for *you to help yourself* while you are here.

Waupun is a prison, but it is not simply a place to "do time." It has walls, to be sure, but nevertheless it is a place where you have a chance to make good.

You will be given a registry number, but the number will be used simply for purposes of record. Without a number you might find your mail, your clothes, etc., mixed up with someone else's by the same name. You have a name by which you should expect to be called and you will be addressed by it.

Now then: You have been sent here for a certain period of time; and our job is to keep you here; and if possible, to send you away a better man than when you came.

The employees here haven't had anything to do with your coming here. Many of them never will know why or how you came here—or how long your term is—unless for some reason they have to ask. They have nothing to do with, and know but little of, your case; and they can't shorten or lengthen your sentence. But they, the employees, are in charge of you while you are here. They have rules *they* must obey and it is necessary that you carry out the orders that those officials are obligated to enforce.

You are perhaps wondering, "How do they treat us here?" The answer is that we treat you like men.

Unless you show us otherwise, we will assume that you are a gentleman and we will act toward you as we want you to act toward us. If you cooperate and enter heartily into the program of this institution, you will get along well while you are here. It is our intention to help and try to show you the right course to take when you return home. *The rest is up to you.*[18]

Even more important than the manual for inmates is the one that should be issued to all staff members. This should contain a copy of the inmate's manual as well as all the other general and specific information that the employee needs in order to understand the aims and policies of the institution and his rights, duties, and responsibilities.

During the reception period, newly admitted inmates should be given systematic instruction in the programs and procedures of the institution, in their opportunities, privileges, and responsibilities, and in the detailed rules and regulations with which they need to be familiar. Furthermore, refresher instruction should be given thereafter as often as individuals and groups seem to require it, and new procedures or regulations should be carefully explained to all concerned.

[18] Wisconsin State Prison Warden's Bulletin, No. 59, p. 1.

The deputy warden or assistant superintendent ordinarily has the primary responsibility for the maintenance of discipline. Since discipline, in its broadest sense, is one of the most important factors in institutional life, this responsibility should not be delegated any farther down the administrative scale than is absolutely necessary. Every infraction of discipline important enough to necessitate action should be reported in writing and the inmate should be given a hearing before any punishment is administered. The hearing should be an orderly attempt to arrive at the truth, not a contest between the staff member and the inmate to establish guilt or innocence. As much of the inmate's case history as is pertinent should be taken into consideration, and not merely his criminal history and previous infractions. A written record should be made of the important aspects of every hearing.

There is a growing belief that it is better to have a three-member disciplinary committee or board conduct the hearings than a single official. Not only are several heads better than one in disciplinary matters, but also it is better to make punishment as impersonal as possible and to avoid having one official held responsible for all decisions in disciplinary problems. A disciplinary board also has a tendency to establish a basis for mutual understanding between the custodial and professional staffs. The composition of the disciplinary committee will differ according to the size and the personnel of the institution, but the person in charge of disciplinary matters in the institution, who is usually the deputy warden or assistant superintendent, should be a member of the committee and should preside at its meetings. It has also been suggested that the disciplinary board be a subcommittee of the classification committee. Since the classification committee is charged with the formulation of the inmates' programs of rehabilitation, this arrangement, it is claimed, would tend to keep the disciplinary action against an inmate consistent with the institution's efforts to rehabilitate him.[19] Among the generally approved penalties that the disciplinary board or official may impose are: a reprimand, the loss of some privilege (such as letter writing, visits from relatives and friends, and attendance at motion picture shows), confinement in the inmate's own cell, the loss of good time, a suspended sentence, and segregation in a solitary confinement cell with restriction of diet.

On the other hand, corporal punishment, for example, flogging, beating with fists or clubs, spraying with a stream of water under high pressure, and stringing up by the wrists, which used to be a common method of

[19] *Manual of Suggested Standards for a State Correctional System,* pp. 61–65; *Report on Penal Institutions, Probation, and Parole,* pp. 18–40; McKendrick, pp. 167–70; *The Attorney General's Survey of Release Procedures,* "Prisons" (Leavenworth, Kansas: Federal Prison Industries, Inc., Press, June, 1940), Vol. V, pp. 109–22; *Handbook on Classification in Correctional Institutions,* pp. 78, 79; *Manual of Correctional Standards,* pp. 231–57.

enforcing discipline in correctional institutions, should never be used under any circumstances. However, whipping is still legalized as a disciplinary measure in a few states, and it is used illegally and surreptitiously in others. Nor should rock piles be used for disciplinary purposes. The "making of little ones out of big ones" when it has no productive value is at the opposite pole from the operation of quarries and rock crushers to produce rock for roads, which is an excellent prison industry if properly operated. It is justifiable to assign some prisoners to especially hard and disagreeable work, such as the digging of ditches or the clearing of land, but the work should have definite productive value.[20] But regardless of the penalties imposed, the administration of discipline clearly reveals the falsity of the claim that an offender is sent to prison *as* punishment and not *for* punishment, because not only is imprisonment a continuous punishment but also conformity to its restrictions is enforced by additional punishments.

INMATE PARTICIPATION

The term "inmate participation" refers to the part that prisoners play in the general management of the correctional institution. More specifically, it means the share that they have in such matters as the making of rules and regulations, the formulation of programs, and the organization and administration of activities in the institution. In the movement to develop this aspect of institutional life the outstanding personality is Thomas Mott Osborne (1859–1926).[21] For fifteen years he was president of the board of trustees of the George Junior Republic, a school for delinquent boys at Freeville, New York, and became deeply impressed with its system of self-government. William R. George, who had founded the school in 1895, had organized it as a community in which the boys were citizens, having certain rights, duties, and responsibilities, very much like those a citizen would have in any normal community. As a result of his association with the George Junior Republic, Osborne conceived the idea of introducing the same kind of program into correctional institutions for adult offenders. He called his plan of self-government the Mutual Welfare League. It was based upon his belief that prisoners can be reformed only by training them in the duties and responsibilities of

[20] McKendrick, pp. 168, 169; *Manual of Suggested Standards for a State Correctional System*, pp. 65–71; *The Attorney General's Survey of Release Procedures*, pp. 122–30; *A Manual of Correctional Standards*, pp. 354–64.

[21] One of the forerunners of Osborne was Warden Hiram F. Hatch of the Michigan State Penitentiary at Jackson, who inaugurated a program of inmate self-government there in 1885. For a discussion of this, see Harold M. Helfman, "Antecedents of Thomas Mott Osborne's 'Mutual Welfare League' in Michigan," *Journal of Criminal Law and Criminology*, XL (Jan.–Feb., 1950), 597–600.

citizenship. With the cooperation of the governor of New York and the warden, Osborne initiated his program of self-government at Auburn Prison in 1914.

Under the Mutual Welfare League, the inmates elected a body of delegates who, through their officers and committees, and within limits set by the warden, made the rules of discipline for the institution, held hearings in cases involving the violation of rules, imposed penalties, and participated in the organization of such activities as education, recreation, and the operation of the commissary. The League gradually extended its influence as it gained the confidence of the warden. It undertook the supervision of the prisoners as they marched from place to place in the institution. Then the guards were removed from the shops and the prisoners were left under the supervision of their foremen. The Mutual Welfare League was successful at Auburn and attracted the attention of prison authorities throughout the country. Later in 1914, Osborne became warden at Sing Sing and there he introduced and further developed the Mutual Welfare League. At first he experienced little difficulty, but soon he was severely criticized, especially by his political opponents. In December, 1915, after he had been warden at Sing Sing for a little more than one year, Osborne was indicted for perjury and neglect of duty. The case against him was eventually dismissed, but nevertheless he shortly thereafter resigned.

In August, 1917, Osborne was commissioned as lieutenant commander and placed in charge of the Portsmouth Naval Prison in New Hampshire. He put the Mutual Welfare League into operation there and served as head of the prison until March, 1920. During the remainder of his life he devoted his time and efforts to prison reform. In 1922, as a part of this work, he organized the National Society for Penal Information, which was to help in developing an intelligent, sustained, and disinterested public opinion regarding prisons. After his death in 1926, the name of this society was changed to the Osborne Association as a memorial to him.

Much of the success which the Mutual Welfare League achieved in the three institutions where it functioned was due to Osborne's genius for personal relationships. He exerted a remarkable influence over prisoners and those who worked with him. After he left Sing Sing, the League deteriorated until little of it remained. However, it was somewhat revived under Warden Lawes, and many of the privileges instituted under it were retained.[22]

[22] For a more complete discussion of the work of Osborne, see Thomas Mott Osborne, *Society and Prisons* (New Haven, Conn.: Yale University Press, 1916); Thomas Mott Osborne, *Prisons and Common Sense* (Philadelphia: J. B. Lippincott Co., 1924); Frank Tannenbaum, *Osborne of Sing Sing* (Chapel Hill, N.C.: University of North Carolina Press, 1933); Rudolph W. Chamberlain, *There is no Truce* (New York: The Macmillan Co., 1935).

The work of Osborne inspired others to introduce similar inmate self-government systems into their institutions. One of the most extreme of these was that inaugurated in 1920 by Warden Mordecai Plummer at Delaware's New Castle County Workhouse, which was being used as the state prison. He instituted sweeping reforms, the most important and basic of which was the establishment of his system of inmate self-government, which he called the "honor system." Plummer had a deep and abiding faith in his fellow men, and the "honor system" was based on his own deeply religious, almost fanatical, convictions. The "honor system" found its most concrete expression in the establishment of an inmate guard system and the inmate "honor court." Warden Plummer believed that the most efficient prison guards were men who were themselves prisoners. Even the turnkeys were long-term inmates. In the shops the foreman was a prisoner, as were the "committeemen" who were responsible for good order. During Warden Plummer's administration, there was no formal set of rules and regulations such as that used by his predecessors. The "honor court," which heard cases involving inmates, by its decisions virtually determined the rules of the prison. A little more than two years after he had become warden, death ended the remarkable career of Mordecai Plummer. His successor, Warden Leach, courageously sought to carry on the program initiated by Plummer, but eventually forces beyond his control entirely swept away the "honor system."[23]

None of the systems of inmate self-government patterned after Osborne's Mutual Welfare League has survived. This, however, does not mean that their influence has died with them. In no small measure, they are responsible for the fact that inmate participation is now recognized as an essential part of modern correctional administration, that inmate councils now function in a number of correctional institutions, and that today many inmates share in the planning and administration of their educational, recreational, and athletic programs.[24]

Inmate participation can make many important contributions to the successful operation of a correctional institution. It provides a medium by which the institutional staff and the inmates can come to a better understanding of each other's interests and needs, and thus it tends to soften their attitudes of mutual antagonism and suspicion. It creates a channel through which the grievances of inmates can be aired, their feelings relieved, and their tensions reduced, and thus it acts as a safety valve by which the pressure toward disturbances and riots in the institu-

[23] Robert G. Caldwell, *The New Castle County Workhouse* (Newark, Del.: Delaware Notes, University of Delaware, 1940), pp. 93–180.
[24] *Manual of Correctional Standards*, pp. 408–12; J. E. Baker, "Inmate Self-Government," *Journal of Criminal Law, Criminology, and Police Science*, LV (Mar., 1964), 39–47.

tion is lowered. It affords an opportunity for the inmate to live in a more normal community and to develop qualities, such as initiative and a sense of responsibility, which will assist him in the process of adjustment after release. Through such contributions as these, inmate participation has established itself as an essential element in the administration of the modern correctional institution.

24

Prison Admission and Classification

ADMISSION ROUTINE

After an offender has been convicted and sentenced to imprisonment, a sheriff, a deputy sheriff, or some other local, state, or federal officer delivers him to a correctional institution. There, upon arrival and before admission, he is given an initial "shakedown," or examination for contraband, and is then subjected to the admission routine.

The admission routine in all prisons and reformatories consists of at least registration, identification, "dressing in," and a physical examination, although these do not necessarily occur in the order in which they are listed here. Registration usually takes place in the records office where the prisoner's commitment papers are delivered to the records clerk. The clerk examines them to make sure that they are correct, notes their delivery in the records, signs a receipt for the new prisoner, officially lists him as an inmate, gives him a number, and records some preliminary data regarding his characteristics, life, offense, and criminal history.

Identification involves taking the fingerprints and the photograph of the prisoner and making a record of his age, height, weight, body build, race, scars, birthmarks, physical peculiarities, the color of his eyes and hair, and other such items as his birthplace, nationality, occupation, religion, criminal history, and the names and addresses of his nearest relatives. When the prisoner is "dressed in," he is stripped, again examined for contraband, required to bathe, given a haircut, supplied with prison clothing, and furnished with such articles as a toothbrush, toothpaste, soap, comb, and towel. A record is made of his belongings, including his civilian clothing, money, jewelry, and other personal effects, and these are then either put into storage at the institution or sent to the prisoner's home.

The physical examination of the prisoner virtually completes the admission routine in many institutions, and the deputy warden then usually interviews the prisoner and assigns him to his place in the work program. However, in most prisons and reformatories the prisoner is kept in quarantine and apart from the main inmate body for a period ranging for a few days to six or seven weeks. During this period of quarantine the prisoner is given his physical examination and interviewed by the deputy warden, the chaplain, and perhaps by other prison officials. In an increasing number of institutions this period is also utilized for giving psychological and educational examinations to the prisoner, requiring him to fill in questionnaires, and compiling his case history. The federal government and some states, notably New York, New Jersey, Pennsylvania, Virginia, Illinois, Michigan, Wisconsin, and California, have gone beyond this and introduced what has come to be known as classification.

CLASSIFICATION

Meaning of Classification. Classification is a method by which diagnosis, the formulation of a program of correction, and the execution of the program are coordinated in the individual case. It is not, as its name seems to suggest, the mere placing of inmates in various categories. It is not, in itself, training and treatment, although it is the process through which these can be applied effectively in the individual case. It is not the segregation of like or similar groups of offenders in separate institutions, although the classification program is more efficient when there are separate and specialized facilities available for different types of offenders. Rather, it is the organization of personnel and procedures through which the rehabilitation facilities of the institution may be directed most effectively toward a solution of the problems presented by the individual inmate. The purposes of classification are accomplished: (1) by studying the individual inmate and analyzing his problems through the use of every available technique and procedure; (2) by formulating in a staff conference a program of custodial care, treatment, and training that is best suited to the inmate's particular needs, abilities, and potentialities; (3) by assuring that this program is put into operation; (4) by providing guidance for the inmate through interviews and counseling; (5) by observing the progress of the inmate, and by modifying or changing his program from time to time when this is necessary; and (6) by making recommendations with respect to the inmate's readiness for parole at the appropriate time.[1]

[1] *Handbook on Classification in Correctional Institutions* (New York: The American Prison Association, 1947), pp. 2, 3; *Manual of Suggested Standards for a State Correctional System* (New York: The American Prison Association, 1946), p. 21; *Manual of Correctional Standards* (New York: The American Prison Association, 1959), pp. 283–97.

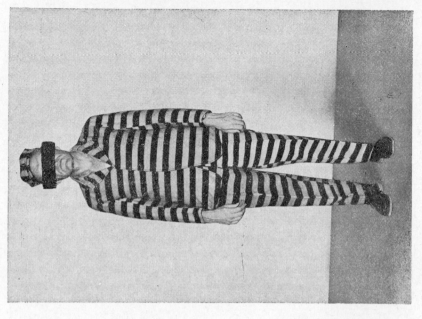

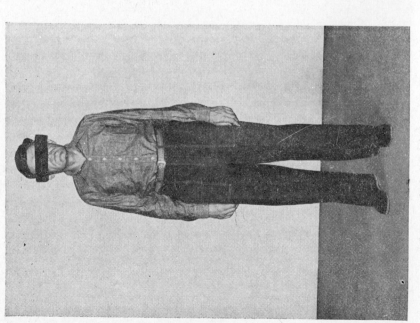

Prison clothing worn now (*left*) and previously (*right*) by inmates at the Iowa State Penitentiary, Fort Madison, Iowa.

Operation of Classification. The successful operation of a classification program is dependent upon the enthusiastic support and active leadership of the warden or superintendent. Harmonious relations, therefore, must be maintained between him and the members of the classification committee. It is most important that they recognize him as the responsible head of the institution and thus the one in charge of the classification program; he should fully understand the objectives of classification and appreciate what it can do for his institution.

Classification begins with the admission of the inmate to the institution. It includes the procedures of registration, identification, and "dressing-in," which have already been described. When these have been completed, the inmate is placed in quarantine, which means that he is segregated from the main inmate body. Wherever it is possible to do so, special quarantine facilities should be provided. These should have sufficient room for interviewing and examining the prisoners and have access to an outside recreation area. If special facilities are not provided, certain tiers, cell blocks, or wings should be set aside for the confinement of the new inmates.

The period of quarantine has three purposes. First, it segregates new prisoners from the general population long enough to ascertain whether or not they are suffering from any communicable diseases. Second, it gives the staff time to acquaint the inmate through an orientation program with the policies, regulations, and educational facilities of the institution. Third, it provides an opportunity for the members of the classification committee or their assistants to make a thorough study of the inmate by means of interviews, physical, psychiatric, and psychological examinations and tests, and an investigation of his social background and community relationships. To accomplish these purposes the period of quarantine should be not less than thirty days, and the desired minimum is nearer two months.

It can be seen, therefore, that the period of quarantine is one of great significance for the program of classification and correction. During this period the diagnostic procedures essential to the planning of the correctional program are placed in operation. During this period, also, the inmate forms attitudes which will affect his adjustment to the institution and his acceptance of the rehabilitation program.

The results of the interviews, examinations, tests, and investigation conducted during the period of quarantine are compiled and combined into an *admission summary* for presentation to the classification committee. The admission summary should contain basic information readily available for immediate reference, including such items as the inmate's name and aliases, birth date, legal address, criminal history, type of offense, sentence, social history, and the findings and recommendations of the educational department, the medical and psychiatric services, the psychologist, and the chaplain. Copies of the admission summary should be given to the members of the classification committee one or two days before its meeting so that they may have an opportunity to study the complete report before taking it up for consideration.

The classification committee should be composed of representatives of the various services and departments which deal with the inmate. Its size and composition varies in accordance with available personnel in the institution, but it should have at least five members so that it will be representative and large enough to give adequate consideration to all questions coming before it. On the other hand, it should not be so large as to be unwieldly and cumbersome. The essential point is that the committee should be representative of the institution's departments and services so that the diagnosis and recommended program will be as complete as possible. In the more adequately staffed institutions, the classification committee may be composed of (1) the warden or superintendent, (2) the deputy warden or assistant superintendent, (3) the supervisor of classification, (4) the social worker or sociologist, (5) the supervisor of education, (6) the vocational supervisor or counselor, (7) the chaplains, (8) the chief medical officer, (9) the psychiatrist, (10) the psychologist, and (11) the officer in charge of the admission or reception unit.

The warden or superintendent, or his deputy or assistant should serve as chairman of the committee so that the head of the institution may exercise his leadership and the recommendations of the committee may carry with them the authority of the administration. However, the chief function of the warden or superintendent in the classification program is to provide the supporting leadership essential to its success. He should take an active interest in the coordination of all parts of the program and in the continuous development and improvement of its facilities, personnel, and procedures. The supervisor of classification is responsible for scheduling the meetings, preparing the agenda, and making certain that the committee's recommendations are carried out.

When the classification committee meets, it discusses all the data contained in the admission summary of the new inmate and devises an integrated program aimed at correcting his deficiencies, developing his abilities, and preparing him for his release to the community. Included in this program should be recommendations regarding his custodial care, mental hygiene, medical treatment, work assignment, vocational training, education, recreation, and religious instruction. The committee must also decide what social service should be extended to the inmate's family and whether he should be transferred to another correctional institution which can better meet his needs and custody requirements.

The inmate should have an opportunity to share in the committee's planning for him. After his program has been tentatively formulated, he should be given an opportunity to discuss it with the committee. He will be more likely to cooperate in a program if he feels he has had a voice in its making. The interview with him should be so conducted as to put him at his ease and to impress him with the fact that the committee is sincerely interested in helping him to help himself. The discussion should center around an interpretation of the program, the reasons for the particular assignments given, and any future plans that the committee may wish to indicate to the prisoner. The program that is finally adopted becomes the official one for the individual and should not be subjected to major revisions without the approval of the committee.

It should not be assumed, however, that classification ends with diagnosis and program planning at the time of the inmate's admission. If a program of individualized correction is to be effective, study of the inmate must be a continuous process, and the program must be changed to eliminate its original inadequacies and to keep it consistent with the inmate's changing needs. To accomplish this, the inmate's behavior must be kept under observation, and records of all significant developments in his case must be maintained by the various departments in the institution. These records should be consolidated into progress reports, which in turn, should be forwarded to the classification committee and used as the basis for the *reclassification* of the inmate.

The fundamental principle of *reclassification* is that the case should be brought to the attention of the classification committee whenever any significant change should be made in the inmate's program. A member of the committee or an officer who has an inmate under his direct supervision may request the committee to consider the inmate for reclassification at any time. In addition to this individualized method of bringing cases up for reclassification, most institutions require that cases be reclassified at intervals according to a definite routine. For example, some institutions stipulate that reclassification occur at least once a year. Unless such a routine is in force, there is always the possibility that some inmates who need to have their cases reviewed will be overlooked. These are usually the inmates who try to abide by the regulations and make no requests, but who may become "institutionalized" unless encouraged and directed. The inmate may or may not be called before the committee during his reclassification. When he is not, he is informed later of the action of the committee by one of its members, usually the deputy warden or the supervisor of classification.

The continuity in planning and correction which is fundamental in classification should be extended into the parole process. This follows from the fact that the task of re-establishing the inmate in the community is the central purpose of the whole institutional program. Therefore, the parole board and the parole officer who is to supervise the released prisoner in the community should utilize the classification reports in making their decisions and plans.

Since the operation of the classification program requires the close coordination of the various parts of the institution, all information regarding each prisoner should be kept in one place and made readily accessible to those who have a legitimate reason for examining it. A central file with a folder for each prisoner should be maintained in each institution. The use of such a file will eliminate duplication of effort, waste motion, and working at cross-purposes, and will serve as a ready reference for anyone desiring a complete and current picture of the case. Inmate clerks, however, should not have access to confidential material on prisoners.

Although classification functions within the institution, it cannot achieve its greatest effectiveness unless it becomes a statewide program. Such a program is required so that there may be uniformity in quality of work, classification records and procedures, personnel standards, and the methods and policies of transferring inmates from one institution to another.[2] Within the institution, classification can function effectively only if it has the services of an adequate number of professionally trained workers and the active support of both the administration and the custodial staff. In some institutions where classification has been introduced, failure to secure these has deprived it of its vitality and left it a mere empty gesture, utterly devoid of meaning.

Types of Classification Systems. In the United States today there are three general types of classification systems. First, there is the *classification clinic system*. This system involves the operation of a diagnostic unit located within the institution. This unit is staffed with professional personnel, and its function is limited to the making of a diagnostic report with recommendations. The report is submitted to the administrative officials who may or may not act in accordance with its recommendations. Although excellent diagnostic work may be done under this system, there is no assurance that any action will be taken on the basis of the findings. The classification clinic system is being used in only a few states.

The second type of classification system is one in which both professional and administrative personnel of the institution sit on the classification committee and together make the recommendations for each inmate. The executive head of the institution or his authorized representative is the chairman of the classification committee. Its decisions, therefore, carry his official stamp of approval and are binding upon those who have the authority to translate them into action.

[2] Adapted from *Handbook on Classification in Correctional Institutions*, pp. 38–65.

This type, which has been called the *integrated classification system,* is the one commonly used in the United States. It is superior to the classification clinic system for several important reasons. First, the decisions of its committee are mandatory, not merely advisory. Second, the meetings of its committee provide an educational experience in which the administrative and professional staffs can come to an understanding and appreciation of the contributions that each can make to the total success of the institution.

The third and most recently developed type of classification system is the *reception center system.* Under this system all prisoners are committed to a central receiving institution or diagnostic center for study regarding their training, treatment, and custodial care. When this is completed in each case, the inmate is sent to an institution which, it is believed, can best meet his needs and custodial requirements. There the institution's classification committee assumes responsibility for continuing the work with the inmate.

This type of classification system places the major responsibility for collecting diagnostic information upon one agency and thus permits specialization of a high degree. It insures a more careful selection of the institution in which the prisoner is to be confined than either of the other two systems. It should be emphasized, however, that diagnosis and correction must not stop when the inmate leaves the reception center. There must be continued diagnosis and constant revision of the inmate's program. This means that each correctional institution must have professional personnel similar to that of the reception center, and that close coordination must be established between the reception center and all the correctional institutions in the state. The reception center, as a separate institution, because of its complex organization, expensive personnel, and high cost of operation, is feasible in only the more densely settled states that have large prison populations. Only a few states, notably New York, New Jersey, and California, have thus far introduced this type of classification system.[3]

Advantages of Classification. It should be clear from what has been said that classification provides the carefully regulated and sensibly developed procedures whereby the institution makes a definite contribution to the reorientation of the inmate. The inmate gains by acquiring a greater understanding and control of his own behavior and a revived faith in his future; and the community profits by receiving a released inmate who

[3] *Handbook on Classification in Correctional Institutions,* pp. 20, 21; Frank Loveland, "Classification in the Prison System," *Contemporary Correction,* ed. Paul W. Tappan (New York: McGraw-Hill Book Co., Inc., 1951), pp. 93, 94; Glenn Kendall, "Reception Centers," *ibid.,* pp. 107–23. See also Walter M. Wallack, "The Service Unit," *ibid.,* pp. 141–53.

has developed stronger law-abiding tendencies and a greater capacity to suport himself and his family. But classification also helps to make the job of the warden much easier. Through its operation, escape artists, agitators, potential leaders of unrest, and homosexuals can be identified and kept under adequate supervision and control; the abilities, interests, and ambitions of inmates can be given more consideration in employment assignments, and thus the productivity of inmates can be increased; inmate problems and tensions can be more quickly detected and more easily handled, and the possibility of disturbances and riots can thereby be reduced; custodial and professional staffs can be brought to a deeper understanding of how both are making important contributions to the successful operation of the institution, and thus serious cleavages and conflicts between them can be prevented; and information regarding the significant characteristics and trends of the institutional population can be secured and used in such a way as to avoid the wasteful expenditure of public funds in the construction and operation of maximum-security facilities for the confinement of inmates who might be safely supervised under medium-security or minimum-security conditions.[4]

TESTS AND MEASUREMENTS

In the field of criminology, tests and measurements are used in a great variety of agencies and institutions, including prevention agencies, police laboratories, guidance clinics, court clinics, and correctional institutions.[5] They help the criminologist to determine how well an individual performs in certain activities and under certain conditions, to discover areas of personality maladjustment, to provide a basis for counseling and treatment, to indicate the progress of therapy, and to predict future behavior and adjustment. It can be seen, therefore, that tests and measurements are a valuable tool in the classification and rehabilitation of prisoners.

Lee J. Cronbach has defined a test as a systematic procedure for comparing the behavior of two or more persons.[6] A measurement is a test which attempts to assign a number, on a scale of equal units, to each person for each characteristic. Although all measurements are tests, not all

[4] Robert G. Caldwell, "Classification: Key to Effective Institutional Correction," *American Journal of Correction*, XX (Mar.–Apr., 1958), 10, 26–28; *Handbook on Classification in Correctional Institutions*, pp. 5–10. In order to increase the effectiveness of classification, treatment teams, or classification subcommittees, have been created in several institutions in the federal prison system. See Daniel Glaser, *The Effectiveness of a Prison and Parole System* (Indianapolis: The Bobbs-Merrill Co., 1964), pp. 199–213.

[5] Samuel B. Kutash, "Mental Tests and Measurements in Criminology," *Encyclopedia of Criminology* (New York: The Philosophical Library, 1949), pp. 242–48.

[6] Lee J. Cronbach, *Essentials of Psychological Testing* (New York: Harper and Bros., 1949), p. 11.

tests are measurements. One way to study something is to measure it, but an equally helpful way is to describe it accurately. Thus, tests of personality often seek to describe a person rather than report his behavior in terms of numbers. At present we must use both measurement and description in the study of human behavior. Indeed, it is likely that some aspects of human behavior will never be subjected to measurement.[7]

There are many different kinds of tests designed for many different purposes. In the selection of a suitable test the validity, reliability, and norms must be considered. Validity is the extent to which a test measures what it is intended or purports to measure. Reliability is the extent to which a test yields the same result when repeated on the same individual. The term "norms" refers to the kind and size of the group upon which the test is standardized. Here the question is: Was the test constructed on the basis of a sufficiently large and representative sample of the kind of persons for whom the test is intended? If we want to test a group of urban adult criminals, we certainly should not use a test that has been standardized on a group of rural, second-grade school children.

Tests may be classified in many different ways, for example, according to form, purpose, and content. However, a very simple way of classifying them distinguishes between "tests seeking to measure the maximum performance of which the subject is capable and those seeking to determine his typical behavior."[8] A test of maximum performance is a test of ability. A test of typical performance is used to study habits and personality. The difference between these two types of tests is that in the test of maximum performance the subject knows what is considered good and strives to achieve it, while in the test of typical performance he does not have this knowledge.

Tests may be subdivided according to purpose. Thus, maximum performance tests may be referred to as mental tests, intelligence tests, aptitude tests, special ability tests, psychomotor tests, achievement tests, etc. Mental tests are tests of ability to perform mental tasks, while intelligence tests usually seek to measure the general over-all mental ability. Some writers prefer to restrict the term "test" to measures of ability and use various other words to refer to devices for determining typical performance. This is particularly true in the case of self-report devices, which consist of standardized questions for obtaining the subject's estimates of his own behavior. They are referred to by such names as "inventory," "questionnaire," "opinionaire," and "checklist." All of these are usually thought of as "personality tests" and may be subdivided into adjustment tests, attitude tests, interest tests, and so on.[9]

[7] *Ibid.*, p. 12.
[8] *Ibid.*, p. 13.
[9] *Ibid.*, pp. 14–17.

The classification of tests is a convenience, but as Professor Cronbach has pointed out, we must recognize that all such classifications are arbitrary. One of the striking current trends in testing is the breakdown of traditional dividing lines. Thus, intelligence tests are being used to study personality, and some of the newest personality tests give estimates of intelligence.[10]

Value of Tests. The use of tests tends to objectify and give explicit and definite form to facts about the offender which otherwise would be expressed in rather general and vague terms.[11] Furthermore, tests may reveal unsuspected areas of tension and conflict in the personality of the offender and thus make possible a more effective program of rehabilitation. They also exercise a check upon clinical concepts and judgments, help to counteract bias, and through standardized procedures give results which can be criticized and checked by another observer. They thus make possible cooperative endeavor in the continuous study and improvement of the techniques and methods of personality analysis.

On the other hand, tests cannot give us the complete answer. They can provide only an approximate measure of a particular individual at a certain time and in terms of a comparison with others. Besides, it is impossible to eliminate all subjective and intrusive influences.[12] The results of the test are likely to be affected by such factors as the attitudes, physical and mental conditions, and language difficulties of the subject, the lack of rapport between the subject and the examiner, disturbing conditions in the environment in which the test is given, and the bias of the examiner. This is especially true in the case of offenders, many of whom are bitter, resentful, suspicious, emotionally disturbed, hostile, recalcitrant, despondent, homesick, or generally uncooperative.

[10] *Ibid.,* p. 18.

[11] Some of the tests that have proved most useful in the study of delinquents and criminals are the Revised Stanford-Binet Intelligence Scale, the Wechsler-Bellevue Intelligence Scale, Kent's Emergency Tests, the Otis Self-Administering Tests of Mental Ability, the Arthur Point Scale of Performance Tests, the Babcock-Levy Revised Examination for the Measurement of Efficiency of Mental Functioning, the Minnesota Mechanical Assembly Test, the Strong Vocational Interest Inventory, the Bernreuter Personality Inventory, the Bell Adjustment Inventory, the Minnesota Multiphasic Personality Inventory, the Rorschach Psychodiagnostic Technique, and the Thematic Apperception Test (T.A.T.). For a description of these tests, see Saul Rosenzweig, *Psychodiagnosis* (New York: Grune and Stratton, Inc., 1949); Cronbach; Edward B. Greene, *Measurements of Human Behavior* (New York: The Odyssey Press, 1952); Harold H. Anderson and Gladys L. Anderson, *An Introduction to Projective Techniques* (New York: Prentice-Hall, Inc., 1951); Charles Hanley, "The Gauging of Criminal Predispositions," *Legal and Criminal Psychology,* ed. Hans Toch (New York: Holt, Rinehart and Winston, Inc., 1961), pp. 213–42.

[12] The great weakness of the self-report tests stems from their implicit assumption that the individual knows and is able and willing to tell the facts about himself when, as a matter of fact, much of personality is covert or unconscious.

Moreover, tests are primarily fact-finding rather than explanatory devices. They can only make the evidence clearer; they cannot make decisions for the clinician. Thus, a test may reveal that the subject deviates from the normal in certain qualities, but this is not the same as demonstrating why he deviates or that this deviation is, or will be, the cause of a certain type of behavior. The complexity of life still defies man's efforts to reduce it completely to a quantitative basis. In other words, tests give some facts, but these can be clothed with meaning and translated into a causal explanation only through the imagination and interpretation of the clinician. Here, again, the subjective element enters into the appraisal.

Tests also fail to provide us with a picture of the total personality. They give us an insight into this trait or that one, but they do not show how the various traits interact in the functioning of the personality or reveal the interplay of emotional relationships. They thus produce a fragmentation of the personality, the totality of which can be depicted only through the subjective approach and the creative efforts of the clinician. The projective techniques[13] were designed to overcome this limitation, but at present they are but crude instruments and still in the experimental stage of development. It is problematical whether the subjective element in these techniques can ever be greatly reduced.

Another limitation of the tests of typical performance, such as the personality tests, is that they deal with qualities that are changeable, and so their findings are of limited assistance in prediction. Indeed, the detection of a certain trait may result in the deliberate attempt to modify it in the treatment of the individual. Thus, in the rehabilitation of the offender, efforts are made to replace feelings of insecurity and inadequacy with those of security and self-confidence. Intelligence tests deal with much more stable concepts, and so the facts obtained through their use provide a sounder basis for prediction. But even the best of these cannot enable us to predict with great accuracy what a person will do in complex learning or vocational situations.

What, then, may we conclude regarding the value of tests? There can be no question that they are extremely valuable as aids in diagnosis. But they are only tools and should not be considered a substitute for the skill, insight, experience, and creative imagination of the experienced clinician.

[13] The projective techniques, such as the Rorschach Psychodiagnostic Technique (the ink-blot test) and the Thematic Apperception Test (T.A.T.), attempt to probe the inner content and organization of the personality "by eliciting spontaneous reactions to stimulus materials that are themselves ambiguous, equivocal, or in some other sense only partially structured" (Rosenzweig, pp. 108–10). For a general survey of the field of projective techniques, see Harold H. Anderson and Gladys L. Anderson, *An Introduction to Projective Techniques*.

At present, there is no method of firmly established validity which is capable of measuring or describing personality. Diagnosis, despite the enthusiastic claims of some testers, is not now, and probably never will be, a mere mechanical procedure. On the contrary, it appears that diagnosis will always remain a creative process in which professionally trained clinicians use tools, such as tests, to study their subjects and various concepts to interpret their findings.[14]

PSYCHOTHERAPY

According to a widely quoted definition, psychotherapy is "a form of treatment for problems of an emotional nature in which a trained person deliberately establishes a professional relationship with a patient with the object of removing, modifying, or retarding existing symptoms, of mediating disturbed patterns of behavior, and of promoting positive personality growth and development."[15] Wolberg divides psychotherapy into three types: (1) *supportive therapy*, which aims to strengthen defenses and restore adaptive equilibrium, and which includes such approaches as guidance, environmental manipulation, persuasion, suggestive hypnosis, drug therapy,[16] shock therapy, and inspirational group therapy; (2) *reeducational therapy*, which seeks to develop insights into the more conscious conflicts and produce a definite personality readjustment, and which includes such approaches as therapeutic counseling, casework therapy, and reeducative group therapy; and (3) *reconstructive therapy*, which strives to achieve insights into unconscious conflicts and effect extensive alterations of character structure, and which includes such approaches as psychoanalysis, hypnoanalysis,[17] and analytic group therapy.[18]

In practice, however, these distinctions tend to blur as the therapist calls upon all his resources in the treatment of a case. In fact, the therapist

[14] Carl R. Rogers, *The Clinical Treatment of the Problem Child* (New York: Houghton Mifflin Co., 1939), pp. 16–60; Kutash, pp. 243, 244; Cronbach, pp. 451–54; Rosenzweig, pp. 367–72; Anderson and Anderson, pp. 51–53; Greene, pp. 16, 153, 546, 665, 667, 689, 729, 730.

[15] Lewis R. Wolberg, The Technique of Psychotherapy (New York: Grune and Stratton, 1954), pp. 3–6.

[16] For the use of drugs in psychotherapy, see Leonard Uhr and James G. Miller (eds.), *Drugs and Behavior* (New York: John Wiley and Sons, Inc., 1960). The tranquilizing drugs are being used to an increasing extent in correctional institutions, where they have been effective in reducing the tensions and hostilities of inmates. See also Henry Brill, "Tranquilizing Drugs and Correctional Psychiatry," American Journal of Correction, XIX (Mar.–Apr., 1957), Part I, 29–31; *ibid.*, (May–June, 1957), Part II, 18, 19, 28, 29.

[17] Hypnosis is used in hypnoanalysis to accelerate the process of psychoanalysis.

[18] Wolbert, pp. 7–16.

should never be a slave to any particular type of therapy but should at all times remain in command of the situation, employing whatever kind of approach, skill, or technique that in his judgment will produce the best results.

Psychotherapy should also be distinguished from social case work and counseling. In the strict sense of the word, social case work is a process in which a trained worker renders one or more specific services to a client. Counseling is a form of interviewing in which the client is helped to understand himself more completely so that he may solve some problem or improve some relationship. In directive counseling, the counselor assumes the role of an authority, gives the client an evaluation of his problem, and defines his courses of action. In non-directive counseling, the counselor encourages the client to express his own feelings, explore his own thoughts, develop his own goals, and plan his own course of action. Sometimes in social case work and counseling the emphasis is on the external problem or social situation and not on the inner distress or illness. At other times, however, the emphasis is shifted from the external to the internal problems of the client, and when this happens, social casework and counseling become forms of psychotherapy.[19]

Any discussion of the use of psychotherapy in the correctional program must give consideration to these points:

1. Treatment must be administered according to the moral code, by which the offender is judged and for which he must develop loyalty and respect. His treatment, therefore, cannot be separated from his punishment; both must be present during the entire process of his correction. (See "The Philosophy of Punishment," Chapter 17.)

2. Even if an inmate is pronounced "rehabilitated," he may have to remain institutionalized so that the moral code will be upheld and deterrence exerted. A correctional institution can never be just a therapeutic agency. It must be also a moral agency.

3. The chief purpose of treatment is to prevent the inmate from again violating the law—not necessarily to effect his "adjustment"—and his feelings of guilt and frustration may actually be increased as the professional worker strives to accomplish this purpose.

4. The relationship in treatment is not permissive; the inmate must be induced to accept authority; his sense of responsibility must be strengthened; and he should not be told that he is just a victim of circumstances

[19] Wolberg, pp. 17–105; Robert L. Kahn and Charles F. Cannell, *The Dynamics of Interviewing* (New York: John Wiley and Sons, Inc., 1957), pp. 3–64; Roy E. Grinker, Helen McGregor, Kate Selan, Annette Klein, Janet Kohrman, *Psychiatric Social Work: A Transactional Case Book* (New York: Basic Books, Inc., 1961), pp. 3–27, 109–35; Max Rosenbaum and Milton Berger, *Group Psychotherapy and Group Function* (New York: Basic Books, Inc., 1963), pp. 1–41, 273–339.

or a "sick person"[20] but should be encouraged to believe that he can overcome his difficulties.

In other words, in a correctional institution psychotherapy must operate under conditions which many therapists believe to be inimical to its success. A realistic approach to correctional work, however, not only dictates the acceptance of these conditions, but also supports the belief that psychotherapy can function within their limitations. Even so, deep therapies have been used very infrequently in correctional institutions. Not only are they costly, dangerous,[21] and time-consuming, but also they require the services of skilled practitioners who are usually not available.[22] What has been used in many institutions is supportive therapy and directive counseling. But of what value are these? There is little specific information on this point, but apparently they drain off tensions and hostilities, make inmates more susceptible to institutional discipline, training, and education, and thus reduce disciplinary problems and increase the productivity of inmate labor. However, much research will have to be done before we can speak with any certainty regarding the effectiveness of psychotherapy in the correctional program.

Group Psychotherapy. Within recent years, the term "group psychotherapy" has been increasingly used in the literature on the rehabilitation of prisoners. Apparently, this term first emerged in recorded form in 1931, when Jacob L. Moreno suggested it in a report on "The Application of the Group Method to the Classification of Prisoners." He and J. H. Pratt of Boston are generally credited with having created the method which is now known by this name. As early as 1906 Pratt introduced "mass instruction" into the treatment of tuberculous patients and later extended this to psychoneurotics and other mentally disturbed cases. Moreno began his work with the method in Vienna in 1911 and developed it, both abroad and in this country, until his psychodrama and sociometry were officially

[20] The disease concept of crime is particularly objectionable, for it carries the false implications that the inmate can do little to help himself and that he must be "cured" by "experts" who know how to do this. This point of view not only grossly exaggerates our knowledge of criminal behavior but also undermines the individual's sense of responsibility and the community's code of morality. This, of course, is not to deny that some criminals are mentally or physically ill and that therefore they need special treatment.

[21] During deep therapy, the loss of a person's defenses, which cover the breaches in his personality and make life tolerable, may be a crushing experience, leaving him in a worse condition than he was before.

[22] On December 31, 1961, there were only 56 full-time and 60 part-time psychiatrists in all the correctional institutions for adults in the United States. In fact, on that date 23 states had no psychiatrists; 19, no psychologists; and 8 no social workers in their correctional institutions for adults (Federal Bureau of Prisons, "Personnel in State and Federal Institutions, 1961," *National Prisoner Statistics*, No. 31 [Mar., 1963], Tables 1, 2, 3, 4). See also Elmer H. Johnson, "The Present Level of Social Work in Prisons," *Crime and Delinquency*, IX (July, 1963), 290–96.

accepted by the profession of psychiatry. Group psychotherapy, or group therapy as it is often called, progressed slowly in this country until World War II when it was widely put into practice in the treatment of maladjusted soldiers and sailors. Today almost all state hospitals have some form of group psychotherapy, and a number of correctional institutions have made it a part of their programs of rehabilitation.[23] During 1959, a survey was conducted to ascertain the extent to which group therapy was being used in the correctional institutions in the United States.[24] This survey indicated that the use of group therapy was spreading in this country,[25] that 72 per cent of the federal institutions were employing it whereas only one-half of the state institutions were doing so, and that state reformatories and training schools were utilizing it to a greater extent than were the state prisons.

Various forms of group psychotherapy are being used, but each is basically an attempt to reorient and re-socialize persons through group interaction. Thus, its purpose is to employ the dynamics of the group as a therapeutic tool to produce a fundamental modification of the personality of each member of the group. No technique of group therapy has as yet been standardized, but an examination of the extensive literature in the field permits the identification of three basic approaches: the repressive-inspirational, the didactic, and the analytic. The repressive-inspirational approach, as represented by Alcoholics Anonymous, employs "the emotional appeal of the evangelistic revival meeting combined with the commercial techniques of salesmanship to urge the participant to control himself by suppressing asocial or worrisome thoughts or wishes and, at the same time, find an inspiration in life," for example, in one's religion, family, or work. The didactic approach, using the class method, is based on the assumption that "intellectual insight and verbal knowledge of psychodynamics constitute treatment." The analytic approach uses "free association and intuitive interpretation of material presented by group members and urges the loosening of repression and the conscious recognition and analysis of unconscious asocial wishes."[26]

The form of group therapy that is employed in an institution depends upon the professional background and training of those who administer it. In this way, the group therapy program may have a psychiatric, psycho-

[23] Joseph I. Meiers, *Origins and Development of Group Psychotherapy*, Psychodrama Monographs, No. 17 (New York: Beacon House, 1946), pp. 3–10.

[24] Lloyd W. McCorkle and Albert Elias, "Group Therapy in Correctional Institutions," *Federal Probation*, XXIV (June, 1960), 57–63.

[25] Of the 220 correctional institutions cooperating in this survey, 50 per cent reported that they were using group therapy whereas only 35 per cent of the facilities that replied to a questionnaire during a similar survey in 1950 were doing so. See Lloyd W. McCorkle, "Group Therapy in the Treatment of Offenders," *Federal Probation*, XVI (Dec., 1952), 22.

[26] McCorkle, 22; Wolberg, pp. 34, 35, 50–52, 85, 86.

logical, sociological, social case work, or counseling emphasis. The leader must have the ability to achieve insight into others and to bring together in a meaningful way the contributions of the group. At the time that the survey cited above was made, 43 per cent of the institutions were using the analytic type of group therapy, 29 per cent, the didactic approach, 10 per cent, the repressive-inspirational, and 18 per cent, a variety of other approaches.[27]

In the California correctional program, a distinction is made between group counseling and group therapy, the latter term being used to refer to a deeper form of treatment, provided by psychiatrists, psychologists, and other clinically trained personnel, for offenders who have serious personality difficulties. On the other hand, group counseling is done by such employees as correctional officers, vocational and academic teachers, job foremen, and parole agents. Group treatment, in its various forms, is now an important part of the correctional program in California. In 1963 over two-thirds of the more than 25,000 inmates in that state were included in some form of group treatment, approximately 12,000 of the inmates being in the group counseling program. The research that has been conducted thus far in California seems to suggest that group counseling can improve inmate attitudes, reduce disciplinary difficulties, improve work production, and contribute to staff development.[28]

The following have been presented as some of the basic considerations that should be taken into account in guided group interaction:

1. The inmates who are to participate in the program should be selected on the basis of their ability to work together and to contribute to the maintenance of the group.

2. The leader and the inmates should be suited to each other.

3. The inmates should be of the same age, education level, and intelligence.

4. Voluntary participation is a desirable objective.

5. The group should not have more than twenty members.

6. Each group should meet at regular intervals and at specified times.

7. The continuity of group membership is important, since a high rate of turnover makes it difficult to develop common bonds of understanding and sympathy.[29]

[27] McCorkle and Elias, 60. In 1959, Alcoholics Anonymous programs were operating in 58 per cent of the correctional institutions for adults in the United States (ibid., 62).

[28] Robert M. Harrison, "An Overview of Group Counseling in the California Department of Corrections," Proceedings of the American Correctional Association, 1963, pp. 361–70. See also Norman Fenton, An Introduction to Group Counseling in State Correctional Service (New York: The American Correctional Association, 1958); Mabel A. Elliott, "Group Therapy in Dealing with Juvenile and Adult Offenders," Federal Probation, XXVII (Sept., 1963), 48–54.

[29] McCorkle, pp. 26, 27.

Here are some of the arguments that have been advanced by those who favor the use of group psychotherapy in correctional institutions:

1. It makes the institution's personnel and inmates aware of one another as personalities rather than as "screws," "punks," "cons," "finks," "hipsters," "squares," or "jerks."

2. It reduces tensions in prisoners and thus makes them both more amenable to rules and regulations and more susceptible to the influence of the rehabilitation program.

3. It gives the inmate greater insight into his own behavior and that of others.

4. It provides the inmate with a sense of security which arises from the sharing of common experiences and the feeling that others are interested in him.

5. It makes the inmate aware that others have problems like his and that his lot is much like theirs. It thus rekindles hope and restores self-confidence, which is essential in the process of rehabilitation.

6. It opens channels of communication between the "world of inmates" and the "world of administrators" and thus increases mutual understanding and respect.

7. It provides meaningful social experiences for many inmates and thus helps to prepare them for successful adjustment after release.

Although these advantages have been claimed for group psychotherapy, even its most enthusiastic advocates admit that there are a number of problems connected with its administration. Important among these are:

1. The group therapy program may become a focal point of inmate unrest, discontent, and conflict. Since it tends to release suppressed hostilities, these may overflow into other relationships and result in the violation of rules and regulations. To guard against this the administration must clearly and firmly define the limitations within which the therapy group must operate and insist that it not interfere in any way with the necessary restrictions of the security program. The inmates must differentiate between their role in the therapy sessions and other roles in the institution and understand that mere membership in the therapy group does not give them a special status in the institution. Here, as elsewhere, rehabilitation must take place within an authoritarian setting. Indeed, as we have already learned, the acceptance of authority is an essential part of the preparation for release.

2. It may be exploited by inmate leaders to gain power and control over the inmate body. The solid core of loyal followers in the therapy group may be the spearhead of such a movement; and the confidential information divulged in the therapy sessions, an effective weapon to intimidate stragglers and force them into line. This may lead to clashes between opposing inmate groups, institution "politics" involving even

members of the staff, and a general undermining of the institution's program. To prevent this, the administration must carefully select the personnel in charge of the group therapy program and the inmates who participate in it, clearly explain its purpose, and closely observe its procedure, progress, and results.

3. It may cause friction between the professional staff and the custodial staff and widen the gap that tends to exist between them. To meet this problem the warden must actively support the group therapy program and set up channels for the clearance of any grievances regarding it. All aspects of the group therapy program should be explained and discussed at regular staff conferences attended by both professional and custodial officers, and a similar procedure should be followed at the meetings of the inmate council.

4. It may be relied upon as a panacea and a cheap and easy solution of all the problems of rehabilitation. To avoid this, the administration must understand that group psychotherapy can never be more than one element in the total program of rehabilitation, and that not all inmates can be reached through it. The use of the group process cannot supplant, but must supplement, the "one-to-one" service of the case worker. In fact, successful utilization of the group process involves an analysis of the significant factors revealed by clinical study and the individual case history.

In addition to these problems, some basic and critical questions command our attention. What kind of leadership and procedure produces the most successful group therapy program? Will group therapy function equally as well in all kinds of correctional institutions and with all types of inmates? And then there is this one which is probably the most crucial of all: What effect does group therapy have upon the discharged person when he returns to free life and is subjected to the disorganizing influences of society? These and similar questions remain unanswered, and light can be thrown upon them only through further research.[30]

[30] F. Lovell Bixby and Lloyd W. McCorkle, "Applying the Principles of Group Therapy in Correctional Institutions," *Federal Probation*, XIV (Mar., 1950), 36–40; Hugh P. O'Brien, "The Use of Group Methods in Correctional Treatment," *Proceedings of the American Prison Association, 1950,* pp. 263–68; Joseph Abrahams and Lloyd W. McCorkle, "Group Psychotherapy of Military Offenders," *American Journal of Sociology*, LI (Mar., 1946), 455–64; Marshall B. Clinard, "The Group Approach to Social Reintegration," *American Sociological Review*, XIV (Apr., 1949), 257–62; S. R. Slavson, "Group Psychotherapy in Delinquency Prevention," *Journal of Educational Sociology*, XXIV (Sept., 1950), 45–51; F. Lovell Bixby and Lloyd W. McCorkle, "Guided Group Interaction in Correctional Work," *American Sociological Review*, XVI (Aug., 1951), 455–61; Hans A. Illing, "The Prisoner in His Group," *International Journal of Group Psychotherapy*, I (Sept., 1951), 264–77; Gisela Konopka, "The Group Worker's Role in an Institution for Juvenile Delinquents," *Federal Probation*, XV (June, 1951), 15–23; Eric K. Clarke, "Group Therapy in Rehabilitation," *Federal Probation*, XVI (Dec., 1952), 28–32.

25

Prison Programs

In a larger sense, anything that happens to a person while he is in prison affects the possibility of his rehabilitation and therefore may be thought of as falling within the scope of correction. This is a sobering thought when we realize the kind of conditions and influences that exist in many prisons. Indeed, it is this very fact which helps to explain the frequent failure of an institution to exert a rehabilitative influence. In a more restricted sense, however, correction refers to those methods, techniques, and programs which are specifically designed to produce certain desirable results in the lives of inmates.[1]

In order to be most effective in the correction of inmates, prison programs should have the following essential characteristics:

1. They should be designed and administered in such a way as to place as much emphasis as possible on rehabilitation.

2. They should be integral parts of the institution's over-all program and should be coordinated with it.

3. They should be planned in accordance with the capacities, interests, and needs of the institution's population.

4. They should be broad and varied so that as much attention as possible can be given to the individual needs and potentialities of inmates.

5. They should be so operated that assignments to them are made by the classification committee, on which each of the programs should be represented.

6. They should be under the supervision of trained directors, assisted by an adequate number of well-qualified workers, and supported by sufficient funds which are regularly included in the institutional budget.

7. They should be provided with adequate facilities, equipment, and supplies, which should be used to the maximum throughout the day.

---

[1] The discussion in this chapter is devoted entirely to correctional programs and should be read with reference to the material on methods, techniques, and programs presented in Chapters 23 and 24.

8. They should be explained and discussed in staff meetings, administrative bulletins, and inmate publications so that their significance and accomplishments will be understood by the public, the custodial and professional staffs, and the inmate body.[2]

THE MEDICAL PROGRAM

The past few decades have brought a notable growth in the understanding of the importance of medical services in correctional institutions. Contributing to this has been the development of the physical and social sciences, which have produced a deeper insight into the nature of the human organism, greater knowledge regarding its behavior and diseases, and better techniques and methods for its protection and treatment. Furthermore, progress in engineering and building construction has made possible brighter, more cheerful, better ventilated, cleaner, and more sanitary correctional institutions, and the increase in humanitarianism has softened the public's attitude toward the convict.

Although still somewhat fearful of pampering prisoners by providing too much medical service, the public in general now accepts the principle that when the state takes away a person's liberty, it must assume the responsibility for his health. Most citizens also appreciate the fact that the inmate's chances of making good on release are increased if he is not handicapped by poor health or disabilities, but instead has the sense of well-being that comes from good health.[3]

The problem with which the prison medical program deals has its roots in the kind of persons committed to prison, the conditions peculiar to prison life, and the limitation of resources available for the treatment of patients. The penal institution is full of the abnormal, the subnormal, the maladjusted, and the socially undesirable, who are subjected to all the complicated forces of prison life. Many institutions are antiquated, overcrowded, and inadequately financed. Inmates are often housed in poorly ventilated and insufficiently lighted cells, fed on a monotonous diet, provided with little employment, allowed only a restricted amount of exercise, and given no opportunity for self-expression. All are deprived of normal social contacts, family relationships, and association with the opposite sex. These are conditions that would wilt even the hardiest men and women.

[2] Although the programs described in this chapter are primarily for male adult prisoners, the principles involved are applicable also to female and juvenile offenders.
[3] *Manual of Suggested Standards for a State Correctional Ssystem* (New York: The American Prison Association, 1946), p. 23; Fred E. Haynes, *The American Prison System* (New York: McGraw-Hill Book Co., Inc., 1939), pp. 262–64; Justin K. Fuller, "Medical Services," *Contemporary Correction*, ed. Paul W. Tappan (New York: McGraw-Hill Book Co., Inc., 1951), pp. 172–74.

Interview of inmate in hospital, Men's Reformatory, Anamosa, Iowa.

What resources are available for the formation of a modern medical program in our prisons? On December 31, 1961, there were 194 full-time and 449 part-time physicians and surgeons and 143 full-time and 150 part-time dentists in all the correctional institutions for adults in the United States. However, 15 states provided only part-time medical service, and one state had none; 16 states provided only part-time dental service, and 4 had none.[4] The minimum medical service offered in most prisons is the daily "sick line," which is an important feature of the whole prison medical program. It gives the sick inmate an opportunity to receive medical examination and treatment and the doctor an opportunity to meet and know his patients, to diagnose their ills, to detect the symptoms of communicable diseases, to adopt measures to prevent the spread of such diseases, to anticipate the rise of serious disciplinary problems, and to exert a rehabilitative influence through the intimate relationship that exists between physician and patient. However, the sick line also affords the neurotic and the malingerer an opportunity to complain of imaginary ills, avoid duties and responsibilities, and exchange prison fare and cell

[4] Federal Bureau of Prisons, "Personnel in State and Federal Institutions, 1961," *National Prisoner Statistics*, No. 31 (Mar., 1963), Tables 1, 2, 3, 4. Alaska was not included in this survey. For an earlier survey, see *The Attorney General's Survey of Release Procedures*, "Prisons" (Leavenworth, Kansas: Federal Prison Industries, Inc., Press, 1940), Vol. V, pp. 159–75.

accommodations for the special diet and the comparative luxury of the hospital. The most effective way of dealing with such patients is through the regular medical procedure, where the physician can exercise his own judgment and imagination in handling these chronic complainers.

Medical care in American prisons varies from a service equivalent to first aid to one providing complete medical and surgical practice. On the whole it is humane, and in many instances it is better than that given to the average person on the outside. In most prisons, it meets the day-to-day needs of the prison population but without much effort to go beyond this. Only in a few prisons is the attempt made to relate medical care to criminality or to use the results of medical research to further the understanding of criminal behavior.

Progressive correctional officials take the position that the medical services of a prison should prevent and correct as well as treat, and that they should cover the fields of both physical and mental health. If they are to accomplish this, however, the correctional system itself should have a variety of well-equipped and well-staffed facilities or have easy access

Dormitory, prison farm, Iowa State Penitentiary, Fort Madison, Iowa.

to them. When the correctional system has a medical center, each institution need have only enough hospital and clinical facilities to make diagnoses, to care for ordinary illnesses and injuries, to hold sick line, to administer venereal and other treatment of the type not requiring transfer to the medical center, and to segregate contagious or infectious cases pending their ultimate disposition. When there is no medical center, each institution must have facilities for all types of medical service, including surgery, unless arrangements can be made with a nearby hospital to care for surgical cases, patients requiring X rays, and others needing special types of treatment.[5]

THE RELIGIOUS PROGRAM

Religion has always exerted an important influence in American prisons. The early chaplains were the prison's first teachers, librarians, counselors, and social workers. They clearly recognized the reformative value of individualized treatment and tirelessly labored to carry the light of God's word into the darkness of the inmate's life. Clergymen and prominent members of religious sects have been leaders in every important penal reform movement in the United States. The work of the Quakers in Penn's colony left a permanent mark upon America's criminal laws and penology. Both the Pennsylvania system and the Auburn system owed much of their vigor to the zeal of religious groups who made the Bible an essential element in their reform programs. It was a minister, the Reverend Louis Dwight, whose conscience was so shocked by the appalling abuses in the prisons of his time that he devoted years of his life to penal reform and became the great, indefatigable champion of the Auburn system.

Everywhere, churches and religious organizations have participated in the movement to create separate facilities and institutions for juvenile and female offenders and to establish probation and parole procedures. Virtually every prisoners' aid society in the country originated in the imagination, ardor, and courage of religious workers. And who was it that played such a dominant role in the organization of the National Prison Association, which is now the American Correctional Association and the greatest force for penal reform in the entire world? It was Dr. Enoch Cobb Wines, a former minister and a man fired with religious zeal. In 1870 he became the first president of this association, helped to formulate its Declaration of Principles, which is still a beacon light for penal reform in America, and assisted in initiating the reformatory movement.

[5] *Manual of Suggested Standards for a State Correctional System*, pp. 23–26; *Manual of Correctional Standards* (New York: The American Correctional Association, 1959), pp. 258–69; The United Prison Association of Massachusetts, "What's New in Medical Services in Correctional Institutions?" *Correctional Research*, Bull. No. 12 (Nov., 1962); Federal Bureau of Prisons, "Correctional Medicine," *Progress Report*, XI (Jan.–Mar., 1963).

Protestant chapel, Iowa State Penitentiary, Fort Madison, Iowa.

Down through the years religious men and women have worked sincerely, quietly, and unobtrusively to carry new hope and courage to prisoners, to comfort them and their families in their despair, illness and privation, and to restore their faith in God and their fellow men. No one can measure the deep significance of this work. But neither can anyone deny that prisons are better places because religious men and women have worked in them, or that many prisoners have found the way to a better life because religion has given them a guiding light. In fact, today correctional authorities put great emphasis upon the importance of religion and consider it an essential element in the life of the prison community.[6]

We do not know how effective the existing religious programs are, although they have been favorably and unfavorably evaluated in general terms by inmates, wardens, and chaplains. They have been praised by wardens as anchors of law and order, by chaplains as a powerful force for righteousness, by inmates as a cushion against despair and a source of inspiration. On the other hand, they have been condemned by wardens as useless and a cause of trouble and dissension, by chaplains as dull, stereotyped, and unrealistic, and by inmates as insincere, empty, silly, stale, and platitudinous. The fact is that the programs vary greatly from institution to institution and represent both the best and the worst in the

[6] "Declaration of Principles, Revised and Approved," Principle XVII, *Proceedings of the American Correctional Association, 1960,* p. 487. See also *Manual of Correctional Standards,* pp. 366, 367.

field of religion.[7] However, not even the most severe critics advocate the elimination of religious programs. What everyone wants is their general improvement.

It is generally agreed that every institution should have at least one chaplain, but if the needs of the prison population warrant it, an institution should have resident chaplains for each of the major faiths. Provision should be made for religious worship and individual counseling, and every inmate should be given the opportunity to attend the religious services and receive the religious teachings of his own choice. If there are so few representatives of any one faith that it is not feasible to employ a chaplain for that group, arrangements should be made with a neighboring community to provide them with religious leadership.

All chaplains, both part-time and full-time, should be selected in accordance with the highest standards and given adequate compensation. The chaplain's duties should be confined to religious activities. These include conducting religious services, doing pastoral and counseling work, providing religious education and directed reading, interviewing inmates and their relatives, contacting inmates' families, maintaining relationships with outside religious organizations, participating as a religious representative in the classification program, and sitting on various institutional boards and committees. This is enough to keep the chaplain busy without requiring him to assume such responsibilities as the censorship of inmate mail or the supervision of institutional tours for visitors. In institutions where there are no other staff members who can take care of such matters as social case work or the administration of the library, and the chaplain is requested to assume these duties, then arrangements should be made for him to receive training to fit him for the additional work.

In addition to having all the qualifications that make him a worthy representative of his denomination and a competent religious leader, he must also understand the ways and problems of the criminal, the policies and methods of law enforcement, and the customs and practices of prison life. He must be the kind of man who can command respect and convey the idea of righteousness and right living more effectively through his own life, character, and conduct than through words, rites, and ceremonies.

It is desirable to have a separate chapel for each of the three major faiths, but if this is not possible and it is necessary to use an auditorium as a chapel for all faiths, then every effort should be made to give it as much religious atmosphere as possible. The chapel should be equipped

[7] *The Attorney General's Survey*, pp. 176–84; Francis J. Miller, "The Inmate's Attitude Toward Religion and the Chaplain," *Proceedings of the American Prison Association, 1938*, pp. 431–35; Carl R. Dueill, "The Religious Authorities in Rehabilitation," *ibid., 1947*, pp. 189–92; A. C. Price, "Religion in the Cure and Prevention of Crime," *ibid., 1947*, pp. 193–97.

with an organ or at least with a piano of good quality. Each chaplain should have an adequate office and a room in which he can interview inmates with complete privacy.[8]

THE RECREATIONAL PROGRAM

Today, the recreational program has a very important place in the life of every well-managed prison. Experienced administrators appreciate its value and point to it as a vital part of the rehabilitative process, as an effective disciplinary control measure, as a positive factor in the mental and physical health of inmates, as a wholesome outlet for energies that might otherwise find expression in destructive thoughts and behavior, and as an excellent means of teaching cooperation and teamwork. In placing such a high value on recreation, these administrators have the increasing support of the public. More people than ever before accept the idea that correctional institutions must try to rehabilitate prisoners, and that this is more easily accomplished when prisoners are mentally and physically healthy. Therefore, anything like recreation which contributes to this tends to attract public favor.

This attitude toward recreation on the part of both administrators and the public is quite different from that which existed only a few decades ago when widespread protests were hurled against the introduction of baseball, radio, movies, and other forms of recreation for prisoners on the ground that it amounted to "pampering the inmates" and "converting the prison into a country club."[9] It is, however, quite in keeping with a tendency that began many years ago during the latter part of the nineteenth century when the Auburn system, with its rule of silence, broke down and wardens tended to grant more and more privileges like "freedom of the yard," lectures, musicals, and theatricals. Such departures from the strict rule of silence culminated during the second decade of the twentieth cen-

[8] *Manual of Suggested Standards for a State Correctional System*, pp. 53–55; Frederick C. Kuether, "Religion and the Chaplain," *Contemporary Correction*, pp. 254–65; Francis A. Shearer, "The Chaplain in Contact with the Families of Prisoners and the Parole System," *Proceedings of the American Prison Association, 1944*, pp. 175–77; James V. Bennett, "The Role of the Modern Prison Chaplain," *ibid., 1937*, pp. 379–88; E. S. Belden, "The Ideal Chaplain and His Qualifications," *ibid., 1938*, pp. 436–41; Dallas F. Gladson, "The Chaplain's Concern about the Inmate and His Program," *ibid., 1950*, pp. 284–89; C. E. Krumbholz, "Message from the President of the National Chaplain's Association," *ibid., 1944*, pp. 170–72; The United Prison Association of Massachusetts, "What's New in the Work of the Church and the Chaplain in Correctional Institutions?" *Correctional Research*, Bull. No. 11 (Nov., 1961); Federal Bureau of Prisons, "The Prison Chaplain," *Progress Report*, XI (Apr.–June, 1963); George F. McKinney, "The Work of a Chaplain in a Correctional Institution," *American Journal of Correction*, XXII (Nov.–Dec., 1960), 10–12.

[9] *Manual of Suggested Standards for a State Correctional System*, p. 57.

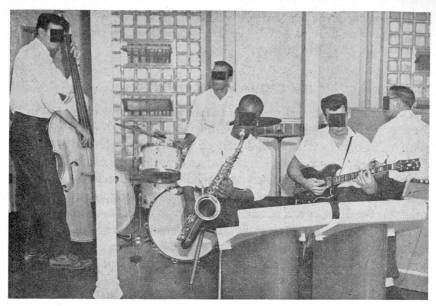

Small instrumental group, Music Department, Men's Reformatory, Anamosa, Iowa.

tury in a recreational movement that swept the last vestiges of the old Auburn techniques out of the prisons.[10]

There are, however, some prisons where recreation is still kept on a minimum basis. This regrettable situation can usually be traced to the officials' lack of interest or lack of ingenuity in utilizing existing resources. In institutions of this type, recreation often consists of a twenty-minute walk around the yard and motion picture shows on Sundays and holidays.[11] Failure to develop recreation beyond this point tends to be reflected in low morale, general unrest, and occasional disturbances.[12]

[10] Blake McKelvey, *American Prisons* (Chicago: University of Chicago Press, 1936), pp. 41, 162, 163, 229, 230.

[11] We do not have any clear picture of existing prison recreational programs. *The Attorney General's Survey,* unfortunately, contains no information regarding them, and the Wickersham *Report on Penal Institutions, Probation, and Parole,* published in 1931, has only a brief note on the subject. Barnes and Teeters, however, have furnished us with the digests of two surveys on prison recreation which were conducted by graduate students. See Harry Elmer Barnes and Negley K. Teeters, *New Horizons in Criminology* (New York: Prentice Hall, Inc., 1951), pp. 685–87. For a survey of recreational programs in federal correctional institutions, see Federal Bureau of Prisons, "Recreation in Correctional Institutions—A Survey," *The Progress Report,* IX (Jan.–Mar., 1961), 6–8.

[12] For the recreational program recommended by the American Correctional Association, see *Manual of Correctional Standards,* pp. 335–48. See also Darwin E. Clay, "Physical Education and Recreation in Correctional Treatment," *Proceedings of the American Prison Association, 1946,* pp. 139–44.

Athletic field, Iowa State Penitentiary, Fort Madison, Iowa.

THE EDUCATIONAL PROGRAM

Prison education is no panacea. In fact, as it functions in most institutions today, it probably does little to change the attitudes of prisoners. Besides, it is true that many crimes are committed by well-educated persons. Nevertheless, progressive prison administrators believe in education, desire to improve it, and would not want to run their institutions without it.

Their views on education are easily understandable. Education, when given the opportunity, can contribute in an important way to the rehabilitation of the prisoner. It can strengthen his self-respect, give him a deeper insight into his own behavior and that of others, help him to understand his country's history and its current problems, introduce him to fine literature, the loftiest thoughts of man, and the great works of art and music, teach him how to control himself and get along with others, provide him with skills and techniques so that he can earn an honest living for himself and his dependents, and revive his hope and his faith in the future. It appears, then, that the chances of a criminal's turning from crime can be increased if he receives some education while he is in prison. Furthermore, prison education can reduce disciplinary problems, show prisoners why they should cooperate with prison authorities, build up the inmate's morale, train him to work in the institution, and increase his productivity while he is there. However, even the most enthusiastic supporters of prison education will admit that it has not often been given the opportunity to accomplish these things. In many institutions, its progress has been seriously obstructed by inadequate funds, personnel, facilities, books, and supplies.

Certainly, education is needed in prison if it is needed anywhere. Most prisoners come from the underprivileged classes. Surveys indicate that about 10 to 30 per cent have less than a fifth-grade education and that about three-fifths of them are unskilled or semiskilled. Many have coarse tastes, crude manners, and deep feelings of frustration and insecurity. Moreover, the majority are young, and almost all are returned to society.

In short, the prison population constitutes a great challenge to the educator. And it is one that he cannot disregard, for, in the words of Austin H. MacCormick, "if we believe in the beneficial effect of education on man in general, we must believe in it for this particular group, which differs less than the layman thinks from the ordinary run of humanity."[13]

In America the first prison teachers were clergymen, who provided inmates with Bibles and religious tracts, gave them religious instruction, and sought their conversion. However, even before the Revolutionary

[13] Austin H. MacCormick, *The Education of Adult Prisoners* (New York: The National Society of Penal Information, 1931), p. 3.

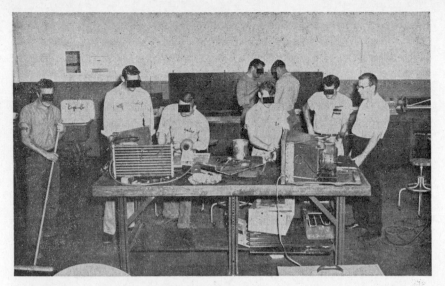

Vocational training class in session, Men's Reformatory, Anamosa, Iowa.

War, lay persons belonging to the Society of Friends initiated regular visitation of prisoners in Philadelphia. They, too, distributed Bibles and tracts and visited with the prisoners in their cells. During the early part of the nineteenth century the growing faith in public education had its influence on correctional institutions. School classes had been a feature of juvenile institutions from their beginning in 1825 and were started in the Boston house of correction in 1841; but it was not until 1847, when the New York legislature provided for the appointment of two instructors for cach of the state's prisons, that academic education was effectively introduced into major penal institutions.[14]

Other states followed the lead of New York, but prison education received its greatest impetus from the reformatory movement, whose hallmark was the establishment of New York's Elmira Reformatory in 1876. This movement placed great emphasis on education and vocational training, but as the years passed, although prisons were influenced by it, reformatories tended to become more and more like prisons.

During 1927 and 1928, Austin MacCormick conducted a survey of the education of adult prisoners in the United States. On this basis, he concluded that there was "not a single complete and well-rounded educational program, adequately financed and staffed" in the prisons and

[14] McKelvey, pp. 12, 41, 42; O. F. Lewis, *The Development of American Prisons and Prison Customs, 1776–1845* (Albany: The Prison Association of New York, 1922), pp. 51, 341.

Academic class in session, Men's Reformatory, Anamosa, Iowa.

reformatories of the country.[15] Prison education, however, has made considerable progress during the past two decades. In this recent development, New York and the federal government have played leading roles and have exerted an influence throughout the country. They have expanded their prison educational programs until today these offer worth-while opportunities for virtually all inmates who desire and need more education. Notable among the other prison systems that have recently made important gains in the development of their educational programs are those of California, Illinois, Michigan, Minnesota, New Jersey, and Wisconsin.[16] However, in most state prisons academic instruction for the inmate is still limited to the elementary grades, usually for not more than five or ten hours each week, and the development of a sound educational program is obstructed by inadequate staff and facilities and interfering industrial and maintenance activities.[17]

[15] MacCormick, pp. 38–40; Haynes, pp. 279, 280.

[16] Price Chenault, "Education," *Contemporary Correction*, pp. 224–26; Austin H. MacCormick, "Present Status of Penal Education," *Proceedings of the American Prison Association, 1937*, pp. 189–91. See also Allen Cook, "A Correctional Education Program Designed to Do the Job—What Does It Involve? From the Standpoint of an Institutional Administrator," *Proceedings of the American Prison Association, 1948*, p. 110–14.

[17] For an earlier survey of educational programs in correctional institutions, see *Attorney General's Survey*, pp. 232–83. For the educational program recommended by the American Correctional Association, see *Manual of Correctional Standards*, pp.

PROGRAM OF INMATE RELATIONSHIPS WITH OUTSIDERS

Inmate relationships with outsiders are developed and maintained through such means as radio, television, newspapers, motion pictures, magazines, books, letters, and visits. Such relationships are important, for they provide an opportunity for the release of feelings of loneliness and anxiety, the expression of affection toward loved ones, the restoration of normal feelings of social living, the establishment of closer cooperation between the staff of the institution and outsiders interested in the inmate's welfare, and the modification of the inmate's values and attitudes. Thus they can reduce disciplinary problems, contribute to the mental and physical health of prisoners, strengthen their morale, and promote their rehabilitation.

The institution, therefore, should foster the development and maintenance of desirable inmate relationships with outsiders by the provision of adequate facilities and procedures. It should make special efforts to create attractive visiting rooms, require pleasant and courteous behavior of personnel toward the inmates and their visitors or correspondents, and insure reasonable and considerate enforcement of custodial regulations regarding mail and visiting. However, this does not mean that the necessary security regulations should be relaxed in any way.

Arrangements should be made for case workers to participate in the handling of correspondence and the supervision of visiting since many clues of value for the individual treatment of inmates can be secured in this way. When neither letters nor visits are received by inmates, this condition should be studied and, if possible, remedied by administrative action. The participation of inmates in games, athletic events, and other group activities with outsiders should be encouraged. The potentialities of the different kinds of inmate furloughs should be carefully and objectively examined. Through the use of furloughs, the inmate can be kept in touch with the realities of ordinary community life and protected against institutionalization. For example, a realistic prerelease trial of an inmate in community living can be made through a carefully planned

---

316–34. For recommendations regarding the prison library, see *ibid.*, pp. 349–65; Mary Rudd Cochran, "The Library in a Correctional Institution—Its Contents," *American Journal of Correction*, XXIII (July–Aug., 1961), 14–17; Marion H. Vedder, "Guidelines for Planning a Model Library in a Correctional Institution—Physical Aspects," *ibid.*, XXIII (May–June, 1961), 4–8; Committee on Institution Libraries of the American Correctional Association, "Objectives and Standards for Libraries in Correctional Institutions," *ibid.*, XXIV (July–Aug., 1962), 26–30; Marion H. Vedder, "Report of the Committee on Institution Libraries," *Proceedings of the American Correctional Association, 1963*, pp. 236–40; *Library Manual for Correctional Institutions* (New York: The American Prison Association, 1950). See also Federal Bureau of Prisons, "Correctional Education—A Philosophy and a Program," *The Progress Report*, VII (July–Sept., 1959), 14–17.

furlough. At other times, the furlough can be used to permit the inmate to visit an ill relative or attend a funeral.[18]

Some writers have recommended the introduction of conjugal visitations in prison on the grounds that they would reduce sexual tensions, curb homosexuality and other perversions, promote rehabilitation, and preserve family ties.[19] Prison administrators, however, are overwhelmingly opposed to these visitations, contending that the public would strongly object to them, that homosexuals and other sex deviates would be the ones least likely to benefit by them, and that the children resulting from them would become additional problems for both the inmates involved and the state. Even so, consideration should be given to the possibility of granting home furloughs, as part of the preparation for release, to carefully selected married inmates nearing the end of their sentences.

THE LABOR PROGRAM

Prison labor, which for many years was the backbone of the American penal system, today constitutes its major problem. Despite the desperate efforts of many resourceful wardens, about half of the inmates in America's state prisons and reformatories are either entirely unemployed or occupied in some unproductive, makeshift work. And yet everybody recognizes the importance of keeping prisoners employed.

The reasons for this unanimity are not hard to find. Idleness in correctional institutions involves a great and needless waste of the taxpayers' money. It means that prisoners, who are supported at public expense, are neither engaged in productive work nor given an opportunity to learn a trade which will help them to become self-supporting after release. It insidiously undermines the morale of inmates and staff and increases unrest and disciplinary problems. It generates a feeling of apathy and eventually of contempt and cynicism toward all efforts at rehabilitation. It greatly reduces the chances that prisoners will lead useful, law-abiding lives upon

[18] Handbook on the Inmate's Relationships with Persons from Outside the Adult Correctional Institution (New York: The American Prison Association, 1953), pp. 9–14; Manual of Correctional Standards, pp. 402–17.

[19] Apparently in the United States only one prison, the Mississippi State Penitentiary at Parchman, officially permits conjugal visitations. However, some jails have been known to allow unofficial conjugal visitations. See Columbus B. Hopper, "The Conjugal Visit at Mississippi State Penitentiary," Journal of Criminal Law, Criminology, and Police Science, LIII (Sept., 1962), 340–43. A survey of twenty-eight countries revealed that with the exception of Mexico they did not favor conjugal visits within the Prison (Ruth Shonle Cavan and Eugene S. Zemans, "Marital Relationships of Prisoners in Twenty-eight Countries," Journal of Criminal Law, Criminology, and Police Science, XLIX [July–Aug., 1958], 133–39). See also Eugene Zemans and Ruth Shonle Cavan, "Marital Relationships of Prisoners," ibid. (May–June, 1958), 50–57; David A. Ward and Gene G. Kassebaum, "Lesbian Liaisons," Trans-Action, I (Jan., 1964), 28–32.

their return to the community. The total effect of such idleness is to increase the present and future costs of crime.

Why then are so many prisoners unemployed? The answer to this can be found in the ignorance and indifference of the public on the one hand and the pressure of organized groups on the other. The average person assumes that a criminal who is sentenced to prison will be put to work. He does not understand that even though the sentence carries the words "imprisonment at hard labor" the prisoner may spend most of his period of confinement in demoralizing idleness. If this fact is brought to the attention of the average person, he is inclined to receive it with cold indifference, to indicate that a criminal deserves whatever he gets, and to support legislation and administrative regulations designed to restrict the employment of prisoners, because he feels that this must be done to protect private enterprise and free labor. It is not surprising, therefore, that organized labor and business groups have been able to impose rigid limitations on the use of prison labor.[20]

Nevertheless, prison labor has survived and, as the foregoing suggests, now has these objectives:

1. Reduction of the cost involved in the maintenance of correctional institutions.
2. Exercise of rehabilitative influence on prisoners through employment in useful work.
3. Improvement of the physical and mental health of prisoners.
4. Vocational training of prisoners.
5. Improvement of the morale of inmates.
6. Reduction of disciplinary problems.[21]

Prison labor was originally intended to be punitive. It was imposed upon the offender as a penalty to be suffered by him in addition to his imprisonment. Thus, he worked on the treadmill, turned the crank, or engaged in the shot-drill, that is, carried a cannon ball back and forth in a long hall. Usually this expenditure of energy was entirely unproductive, but sometimes the crank or the treadmill was geared to pumps or other useful devices. For over a century, however, prison labor has been used primarily as a means of reducing the cost of the prison system and of providing industrial training for the inmates.

In the American Colonies, prisoners were often employed in the local houses of correction or workhouses, or bound out in service to farmers, craftsmen, or businessmen. In Pennsylvania, where the Quakers were influential, imprisonment at hard labor was prescribed for almost all the

20 *Manual of Suggested Standards for a State Correctional System*, p. 27.
21 See Louis N. Robinson, *Should Prisoners Work?* (Philadelphia: The John C. Winston Co., 1931).

serious crimes. The early nineteenth century brought the conflict between the Pennsylvania system, with its solitary confinement and handicrafts, and the Auburn system, with its congregate workshops. When the latter triumphed, it set the stage for the appearance of the modern prison labor problem in the United States. The success of the Auburn system was due primarily to the fact that prisoners could be more profitably employed in its congregate shops than in the solitary confinement of the Pennsylvania system. At first the states themselves operated the prison industries, but before long they began to place them under the more efficient management of private enterprise.[22] Out of this historical background in the United States there emerged six systems of prison labor, aside from agriculture—three private (the lease, the contract, and the piece-price) and three public (the public works and ways, the state-account, and the state-use).

In the public labor system, the state retains control of (1) the maintenance and discipline of the prisoners, (2) the employment of the prisoners, and (3) the sale of the products. In the private systems, however, private interests control at least one of these. Thus, in the *lease system* a private individual or company has control of all three; in the *contract system,* control of the employment of the prisoners and the sale of the products; and in the *piece-price system,* control of only the sale of the products.

The three public systems differ among themselves in the extent of the market open to each. The *state-account system* has an unrestricted market. The *state-use system* has a market restricted to the public institutions and agencies of the state in which the products are made. The *public works and ways system* is restricted to the public buildings and roads of the state having jurisdiction over the prisoners involved.[23]

The lease system represents the extreme form of private control over prison labor. In this system, the prisoners are turned over to a lessee who agrees to house, clothe, feed, and guard them and to pay to the state a stipulated amount of money for each prisoner received. In return, he has the right to work the prisoners and to keep the products of their labor. The lease system has existed since the early years of the United States, but it had its greatest development in the South after the War Between the States. There, hostilities had disrupted the prison systems and, lacking money to reorganize them, the states leased their prisoners to private parties who usually employed them on plantations or in lumber and tur-

---

[22] See Blake McKelvey, *American Prisons* (Chicago: University of Chicago Press, 1936), and O. F. Lewis, *The Development of American Prisons and Prison Customs, 1776–1845* (Albany: The Prison Association of New York, 1922).

[23] Federal Bureau of Labor Statistics, *Convict Labor in 1923,* Bulletin No. 372 (Washington, D.C.: Government Printing Office, 1925), pp. 3, 4.

pentine camps. From the very beginning, protests were directed against the lease system. The states could not adequately supervise its operation. Tales of the ruthless exploitation and cruel treatment of prisoners aroused public indignation. Investigations uncovered shocking conditions of graft, corruption, and cruelty and eventually forced the lease system out of all state penal institutions. It still lingers on, however, in some jails where it is used to provide employment for minor offenders.

Under the contract system, a private individual or company contracts with the institution for the labor of the prisoners at a stipulated amount per prisoner per day. The state assumes no risk since the contractor furnishes the raw materials, the foremen and inspectors, and the tools and machinery. In return, the institution supplies the prison labor, houses, feeds, clothes, guards, and disciplines the prisoners, and sometimes supervises their work.

The contract system, also, dates back to an early period in American history. It was actually in use in Massachusetts in 1807, but its growth was not notable until after 1820, when the development of business and industry in the United States began to create an effective demand for prison labor. In the prison the merchant and the industrialist found a reservoir of cheap labor; the state, a source of easy revenue; and the public, a means of securing low-priced articles. It is no wonder, then, that the contract system from the 1820's on, for a period of about fifty years, became the principal method of employing prisoners.

The contract system, like the lease system, is open to serious abuses. Prisoners in many institutions were ruthlessly exploited to provide profits for the contractor and revenue for the state. Working conditions were often bad. Prisoners were punished if their work did not satisfy the contractor. Some wardens and state officials profited dishonestly through corrupt arrangements with contractors. A strong public opinion was organized against the contract system, and as a result it has disappeared from American penal institutions.

The piece-price system is almost the same as the contract system. The only difference between the two is that in the piece-price system the contractor, instead of paying a stipulated amount per prisoner per day, agrees to furnish the raw material and to pay a specified price per piece for the finished product. Usually the contractor also supplies the machinery and tools. Thus, the piece-price system gives the state complete control over the prisoners and their employment. It also removes the contractor from direct contact with the prisoners and reduces the possibility of his using their labor entirely for his own selfish interests. However, there is still the chance for collusion between the contractor and the prison authorities. The piece-price system had its greatest development between 1880 and 1900, when the contract system was being severely criticized. Although it does not as readily lend itself to some of the abuses which undermined the contract system, it did not escape the effects of the agitation aroused against the latter, and it, too, has disappeared.

In the public works and ways system, prison labor is used in the construction and repair of public buildings, roads, parks, bridges, and in the work of flood control, reforestation, clearing land, preventing soil erosion, etc. Unlike the other two public systems, it does not involve the application of prison labor to the production of consumption goods.

The public works and ways system was used in America during the seventeenth and eighteenth centuries, but it was virtually abandoned until late in the nineteenth century when the demand for good roads caused its revival. It has been widely used in the South, where for years chain gangs in stripes and under guard were a common sight along the highways. Within recent years, however, conditions in the road camps in the South have greatly improved, and a new and promising period of development for the public works and ways system is beginning there. For many years, California has had penal work camps and used her prisoners in soil conservation and reforestation projects. The federal government also employs many of its prisoners in work camps in various parts of the country. Furthermore, many states, like Massachusetts, Pennsylvania, and Georgia, have profitably employed prison labor in the construction of new prisons and thus saved the taxpayers large sums of money.

In the state-account system, or, as it is often called, the public account system, the institution conducts the business enterprise and sells the product on the open market in competition with the goods produced by free labor. The state thus assumes all the risks and exercises complete control over the entire business. The state-account system was used generally in the early state prisons from about 1800 to 1825. It declined because of the lack of capital, equipment, and transportation facilities, the small demand for prison-made goods, and the introduction of machinery in private industry. It was largely replaced by the contract system, but it had a revival during the eighties when the contract system came under the fire of an aroused public opinion.

Under the state-account system, the manufacture of binding twine and farm machinery achieved great success in Minnesota. It enabled the Minnesota state prison to become one of the few self-supporting penal institutions in the United States, producing a revolving fund of about $4,000,000 for productive purposes in that institution. Nevertheless, in Minnesota, where it achieved its greatest success, and generally throughout the country, it is being abandoned in favor of the state-use system, which provides greater opportunities for vocational training and offers less competition for private enterprise and free labor.

Under the state-use system, the state carries on the business of production, houses, feeds, clothes, guards, directs, and supervises the prisoners, and markets the products to public institutions and agencies within its own borders.[24] The purpose of thus restricting the market is to avoid direct competition with private enterprise and free labor while utilizing prison labor for the benefit of the public.

The state-use system came into prominence during the last two decades of the nineteenth century, when it was adopted as one of the principal substitutes for the contract system. By 1899 twenty-four states had authorized its use. However, as the various states have introduced the state-use system as the chief means of using prison labor, they have found great difficulty in developing enough business under it to keep their prisoners employed. After having developed this system over a period of forty years, the New York state prison industries in 1936 showed a total annual production of only $2,087,000. This was sufficient for the employment of about 2,000 prisoners, working at one-fifth the efficiency of free workmen. The average population of New York's state prisons for that year was 14,390. If 25 per cent or 3,597 prisoners are allowed for maintenance work, this meant that 8,793 prisoners, or over 60 per cent of the total prison population, were idle. This situation has been typical of all states which have restricted the sale of prison products to state use.

The *Attorney General's Survey*, published in 1940, reported that under the state-use system the states had found it practicable to develop forty different prison industries, exclusive of farming, mining, construction, and road work. It classified these industries into seven major groups: textiles, garments, metal, wood, stone and cement, food products, and miscellaneous, including the manufacture of brooms, brushes, mops, mattresses, soap, and printing. At the time of this survey, twenty-two states and the District of Columbia relied exclusively on the state-use system, twenty-two states combined it with sales on the open market under the state-account system, and four states maintained both the state-use and the contract systems.[25]

[24] The term "state use" has been defined in different ways. According to its narrowest definition, the market for goods produced under the state-use system is limited to public institutions and agencies operated by a state, but does not include, as it does in the definition given above, public agencies and institutions run by a state's counties or municipalities. In the broadest definition of the term "state use," the market includes all federal, state, county, and municipal institutions, regardless of political boundaries. However, it seems that the term "states use" better describes this type of market and it is so employed in this text.

[25] *The Attorney General's Survey of Release Procedures*, "Prisons," Vol. V, pp. 185–225, 301, 302; National Commission on Law Observance and Enforcement, *Report on Penal Institutions, Probation, and Parole*, Report No. 9 (Washington, D.C.: Government Printing Office, 1931), pp. 80–110, 253–68; Edwin H. Sutherland, *Principles of Criminology* (Philadelphia: J. B. Lippincott Co., 1947), pp. 463–68.

For many years, criminologists have been advocating the extension of the state-use system into a states-use system. This plan involves the expansion of the market of each state to include the public agencies and institutions of other states and the federal government. As yet satisfactory arrangements for putting the states-use plan into effect have not been worked out on a large-scale basis, but steps in this direction have been taken. As a result, a number of states now exchange prison-made goods with each other under the provisions of federal statutes, which make exceptions to the limitations on interstate shipments of prison-made goods when they are to be used in public agencies and institutions. Leading industrial authorities believe that the pooling of the industrial resources and products of all the country's prisons, which is envisioned in the states-use plan, is not only legally possible but entirely feasible. It would be especially helpful for the smaller states whose requirements for manufactured goods do not permit the economical operation of a diversity of prison workshops.[26]

Each of the six systems just discussed has its strong and weak points. None is free from criticism, and none serves the ends demanded of an ideal system. The ultimate decision as to which system is preferable, therefore, depends upon a number of factors. Most important among these are (1) its effect on the health and well-being of the prisoner, (2) its influence upon his training and possible reform, (3) its bearing on the financial returns to the state, (4) its susceptibility to efficient administration, and (5) its competition with free labor and industry.

When measured in terms of these five factors, the private systems have been more detrimental to the health and well-being of the prisoner, have provided less training and exerted less reformative influence, and have competed more with free labor and industry. They have been open to such serious abuses as the ruthless exploitation of the prisoner, the domination of prison industries by dishonest businessmen and venal politicians, and the formation of corrupt practices for the securing of graft and the distribution of special favors. However, the private systems have been superior in providing steady employment for virtually all able-bodied prisoners, in bringing large financial returns to the state, and in being easier to administer.

The greatest weakness of the public system, and especially of the state-use system, has been the inability to cope with the problem of increasing idleness in the nation's prisons. This has been caused partly by the restrictions imposed upon the public systems in response to pressure exerted by free labor and private industry and partly by the superiority in salesmanship and production of free enterprise. The state-use system, on the

[26] *Manual of Suggested Standards for a State Correctional System,* p. 32.

other hand, because of the diversity of its production, clearly excels all others, both private and public, in offering opportunities for the expression of individual interests and abilities. Besides, since its products are not disposed of on the open market, the state-use system does not compete directly with private industry. In other words, it does not influence prices through the bargaining processes but rather through the quantity of goods produced. While this probably makes little difference in the long run, it has been sufficient in its immediate effects to attract the support of labor unions and business groups.

It is obvious that the relative merits and defects of the different systems cannot be accurately evaluated. Nevertheless, since more than 95 per cent of all adult inmates return to society after a comparatively short period of incarceration, it is equally obvious that their health, well-being, reformation, and training must be regarded as of primary importance. Many authorities, believing that such matters cannot be given due consideration under the private systems, have rejected these systems as undesirable and have turned to the public ones for a solution to the problem of prison labor.[27] However, much of this controversy over the relative merits and defects of the public and private systems is now largely academic. Whatever conclusions may be drawn from the history of prison labor in the United States, the fact is that restrictive legislation has virtually eliminated the private systems.

Prison industries enjoyed their greatest expansion during the last half of the nineteenth century and the early years of the twentieth. Then, under the pressure of both those who were sincerely interested in the welfare of prisoners and those who merely wanted to get rid of competition from prison-made goods, prison industries slowly but surely declined. Year after year legislators in response to the demands of many labor and business groups joined in the attack, and many states enacted legislation to curb the use of convict labor. Eventually this restrictive tendency culminated in the passage of three federal statutes in 1929 (the Hawes-Cooper Act), 1935 (the Ashurst-Sumners Act), and 1940.[28] As a result of these acts, prison-made goods, except for certain specified items, were completely excluded from interstate commerce. Although these acts have prepared the way for the development of the state-use system throughout the country and have stimulated the expansion of educational and recreational activities to fill the gaps left in the labor program, nevertheless, for the time being at least, they have caused an unprecedented idleness in

[27] National Commission on Law Observance and Enforcement, pp. 80–108; Sutherland, pp. 468–77; Fred E. Haynes, *Criminology* (New York: McGraw-Hill Book Co., Inc., 1935), pp. 361–65.

[28] The constitutionality of these acts has been upheld. See Kentucky Whip and Collar Company v. Illinois Central Railroad Company, 299 U.S. 334 (1937); Whitfield v. Ohio, 297 U.S. 431 (1936).

American prisons. Even so, the federal government and some states, like New York, Virginia, and California, have met this challenge by establishing adequately financed and well-planned programs of prison labor and vocational training.[29] For example, in 1963, Federal Prison Industries, Inc., whose assets amounted to $4,000,000 when it was organized in 1934, was operating 52 factories and shops and selling an annual total of goods and services valued at $40,000,000 to other government agencies. It was employing 6,000 inmates, or about one-fourth the total federal prison population, on a full-time basis, paying them an average of $35 a month, and financing the vocational training of 12,000 prisoners. Despite these expenditures, the corporation was earning a reasonable profit, and between World War II and 1963, it had paid a total of $47,000,000 in dividends into the Treasury of the United States.[30]

The keynote of the modern prison labor program must be diversification. This not only provides an opportunity for meeting the individual needs of prisoners but also prevents intense competition with any one type of private industry. Even though it would be better to include a limited state-account and a strictly controlled contract system in the labor program in order to insure adequate employment, prison officials have at their disposal little more than the state-use system, including agriculture, the public works and ways system, and the maintenance work involved in the operation of their institutions. Under the circumstances, the best solution for the prison labor problem is a combination of these types of employment, supported by legislation requiring all state, county, and municipal agencies and institutions to buy prison-made products that meet specified standards. To be successful, however, productive enterprises in prisons must be organized, staffed, equipped, and operated in accordance with the highest standards so that prison-made products can pass the strictest tests of private industry and released inmates can take their places on a modern production line.

The labor and educational programs must be skillfully correlated if due consideration is to be given to the vocational training and rehabilita-

---

[29] *Manual of Suggested Standards for a State Correctional System*, pp. 27, 28; National Commission on Law Observance and Enforcement, pp. 264–67; William H. Burke, "A Travesty of Justice," *Proceedings of the American Prison Association, 1946*, pp. 185–88; Richard F. Jones, Jr., "Prison Labor in the United States, 1940," *Monthly Labor Review*, LIII (Sept., 1941), 582, 587; Frank T. Flynn, "The Federal Government and the Prison-Labor Problem in the States," *The Social Service Review*, XXIV (Mar., 1950), 19–40, and (June, 1950), 213–36; Sanford Bates, *Prisons and Beyond* (New York: The Macmillan Co., 1936), pp. 100–10.

[30] A. A. Evans, "A Prison System Comes to Maturity," *American Journal of Correction*, XXV (Jan.–Feb., 1963), p. 8. For further reading on the federal correctional programs, see *The Federal Prison System—1964*, Hearing Before the Subcommittee on National Penitentiaries of the Committee on the Judiciary, United States Senate, Jan. 22, 1964 (Washington, D.C.: Government Printing Office, 1964).

tion of the inmate, and job assignments should be made on the basis of the recommendations of the classification committee. Furthermore, recognition must be given to the fact that prisoners will not work with maximum drive and efficiency without a wage or some other incentive like extra "good time," or a combination of these. Sound theory undoubtedly dictates that a prisoner be paid a wage comparable to that paid free labor, that a fair charge for his maintenance be deducted from his wages, and that he be required to support his family from the balance. Many difficulties, however, prevent the application of this theory. The payment of standard wages would not only increase the cost of operating correctional institutions—although this would be offset to some extent by the reduction of welfare payments to the dependents of inmates—but would also face the charge that prisoners were "being paid to go to prison." Furthermore, it is difficult to determine how much a prisoner should be charged for his maintenance. For example, should he be charged with a certain percentage of the salaries of personnel, the interest on bonded indebtedness for the construction of buildings, and the cost of his transportation to and from prison, or should he bear only the cost of his "room and board"? For these and other reasons, this type of wage is not being paid anywhere in the United States, although it is in a few European countries. The usual practice in this country is to pay as high wages as the productive enterprises can support and legislative and other authorities will permit. This means that where wages are being paid to inmates, they tend to be somewhere between five and fifty cents a day.

Competition with free labor and private industry has attracted more attention and provoked more criticism than any other aspect of the prison labor problem. In the examination of this aspect of the problem, it must be admitted at the very beginning that every system of prison labor produces such competition. The only way to eliminate all competition is to eliminate all prison labor, but this would not be tolerated by public opinion. Obviously, a more intelligent public understanding of the problem is needed. All must see the prison labor problem as a public one and not one of any particular person or group, for every taxpayer is greatly affected by the way it is handled. The movement to educate the public regarding this will eventually bring results, but much of the leadership here must continue to come from within the correctional field, for the employment of prisoners still encounters considerable opposition.[31]

[31] *Manual of Correctional Standards*, pp. 375–91. Frank T. Flynn, "Employment and Labor," *Contemporary Correction*, ed. Paul W. Tappan (New York: McGraw-Hill Book Co., Inc., 1951), pp. 245–50; The United Prison Association of Massachusetts, "What's New in Prison Industries?" *Correctional Research*, Bull. No. 6 (April, 1955); Charles F. Hanna, "Correctional Industries—Production versus Rehabilitation," *Proceedings of the American Correctional Association, 1963*, pp. 213–18.

26

Prison Shocks

By Tom Runyon[1]

I wish you would write about some of your most important prison experiences and your reaction to them," Dr. Robert G. Caldwell, author of this book, told me.

Knowing that picking the "most important" experiences of more than sixteen prison years might require an objectivity beyond me, I agreed to try. But I probably see a different prison picture than Dr. Caldwell, and I must try to fulfill his requirements in my own way. Like all guilty criminals, probably, prison experience started for me before ever I saw the inside of penitentiary walls. Possibly it started with my first crime, for the possibility of imprisonment had at least to be considered. Certainly it started with my arrest, and like other convicts, what I became after the first cell door key "thwocked" a kind of period to my life was partly the result of pre-prison experience. Before that I was a considerably different person.

I may or may not be a typical convict (whatever that is, if there is any such thing). My lifer's number, received in March, 1937, is a receipt for a second-degree murder conviction, for a crime committed while fleeing from a bank robbery, and receiving it marked the end of a five-year crime career. My first nickel was stolen—from a banker, with a pistol—

---

[1] Consultant for The Presidio, inmate magazine for the Iowa State Penitentiary, Fort Madison, Iowa, and author of *In For Life* (New York: W. W. Norton and Co., Inc., 1953). On April 10, 1957, Tom Runyon died of a heart attack while still an inmate in the Iowa State Penitentiary.

Note by the author of the text: No one but a prisoner can adequately describe the experiences of imprisonment. And yet, a text in criminology should certainly contain some information on this subject. I therefore asked Tom Runyon, a life-termer in the Iowa State Penitentiary, at Fort Madison, Iowa, to relate some of his reactions to life in prison. Although his account is that of only one prisoner and is naturally colored by his personality, he has told his story so well that no interpretation appears necessary.

in the spring of 1932 when the Depression rolled over me. I was nearly twenty-seven when I chose robbery instead of charity, and before that I had been a hard-working, largely intolerant, honest man, which is a long-winded way of explaining that where crime and punishment are concerned I have carried the rail and ridden it too. I thought little of crime and criminals except when some friend or neighbor was plundered, or when some particularly revolting crime flared into headlines. When that happened I wanted someone punished, plenty and in a hurry. In a vague kind of way I felt sorry for convicts when I drove past a prison, but that was about the only time I thought of them. Then the law of averages caught up with me and my viewpoint was forcibly changed. So in the course of years I've been the farmer driver and the toad beneath his harrow; the swimmer, and the floundering, terrified drowner; the miller, and the crushed and distorted product of his grinding. That's my background. With it as a springboard I'll try to meet Dr. Caldwell's requirements.

I think of my most important experiences as a series of shocks, and the first came with my arrest. Just like every gun-using ex-bandit I've talked to, I had formed a mental picture of the way officers would try to arrest me. They would come at me from such-and-such direction at a given time under certain conditions, and I would be ready for them. Instead they caught me so by surprise I wasn't even wearing a gun, and the sudden feeling of helplessness and aloneness was almost stupefying. Like a boxer staggered by the first punch, it left me off balance for the blows that followed during a week of being moved from jail to jail, of almost incessant questioning at all hours, of frantic squirming and parrying, first to get free entirely and then merely to dodge the hangman's noose. Shock piled on shock had me punch drunk long before I faced the judge.

Humiliation contributed to that condition. Being led around in handcuffs, on a long chain, surrounded by heavily armed officers like a dangerous wild beast, was a nightmare fully as bad as those other dreams of being caught nude in a crowd. After one of those police exhibitions it was a relief to be locked in a cell away from prying, fearful eyes of people who would crowd up behind the officers for a look at me. People facing my gun in holdups had never seemed as fearful as they did when I was shackled and utterly helpless, and the fear in their eyes hurt me more than their gloating. Take all dignity away from a man and something less than a man is left. Some part of me seemed to shrivel during that week of being treated like a side-show freak—a part that has left me with a certain amount of alien-feeling ever since.

Part of the shock came from unlearning so many things I had always known were so. My being innocent until proved guilty was just a big joke to everyone but me. That a prosecutor should meticulously protect my rights while endeavoring to prove my guilt never seemed to occur to anyone but me. A judge was several cuts above ordinary men, above and beyond petty malice and hatred, objectively interested in seeing that justice was done? I didn't find it so. For a thief I was an amazingly gullible character before my arrest, but it didn't take long to learn a few more facts of life after handcuffs were snicked onto my wrists. Very soon I learned I was up against a team—police and prosecution and court— that worked with devastating effectiveness, single-mindedly determined to destroy me. Out of that week's experience I got the impression that the team was just as ruthless, just as ready to use any expedient, as any criminal. While I cringed under the weight of hatred and fear and humiliation I was beginning to feel the "Law" was just as bad as I had ever been. With that belief I lost respect for everything about the Law except its power. From beat-walking cop to supreme court justice, I sneered at them all. Where I had been antisocial in deed, while paradoxically being social-minded, by the time the first prison cell door was slammed in my face I had a rather solid antisocial foundation under me. I was too dazed to realize the fact, but it was there just the same.

Being run over by a ten-ton truck while sleepwalking, I imagine, would be somewhat similar to receiving a life sentence in prison. You know you've been steam-rollered by something, but you can't fully understand what has hit you. Just as the truck would loom above in the darkness, huge and indistinct and terrifyingly out of perspective, so does his sentence tower over the new lifer's mind. He simply can't grasp what has happened to him, for trying to understand a life sentence is a lifetime task. The words "for the rest of your natural life" falling from the lips of a judge carry a typical dazing shock, for all new lifers seem to react much the same. It was that way for me, during the first week, and afterward trying to understand the "differentness" of my new world was something like smothering in wet sawdust. After the first few weeks I was sure I understood how a fish felt when it was suddenly yanked from the saneness of its world to flop and gasp on the alien river bank.

The prison's walls and bars and guards and clubs were much as I had expected. They were in every book I had read about prisons. But no amount of reading could prepare me for the atmosphere of hatred and fear I encountered. No normal man could imagine the foreign, angle-minded, suspicious prison way-of-thinking. It wasn't too hard to understand that suffering men might think and behave irrationally, for I wasn't thinking very straight myself, as I sometimes realized. But prison officials and their custodial force seemed perfect strangers to logic. The paranoid conditions established by officials seemed to have backfired, with their own minds being as subtly twisted and warped as those of their inmates.

In a maximum-security prison it made sense that gun towers on the thirty-foot walls were manned twenty-four hours a day, but it didn't seem sensible to constantly bedevil the men penned inside those walls. The loss of freedom was terrible enough punishment, certainly, without officials adding little sadistic frills of their own. Official self-interest alone should dictate considerate treatment of inmates, it seemed to me, for the better men were treated the better they would behave. But security-minded officials didn't see it that way. Uninterested in mollycoddling their charges by trying to teach or lead them, they drove us through months and years and decades with never a thought for any aftereffects of such treatment that might bring men back to prison after new and worse crimes. Thinking with their fists instead of their brains, they saw to it that the pressure closed in on us from the walls in an ever-tightening grip that dictated every move and tainted every thought. They even put it in writing.

Each cell contained a Rule Book listing nearly a hundred infractions ranging from attempts to escape and knifing another prisoner to "crookedness"; from "hair not combed" and grimacing to "laughing and fooling" and "dilatoriness." I never heard of one of the usually uneducated guards writing "dilatoriness" on a report, but they wore their pencils down to stubs "writing up" convicts for practically everything else. Punishment followed practically every report, often resulting in a stay in the "Hole"—solitary confinement in tiny cells often icy cold or frying hot, with one slice of bread each twenty-four hours and water if an unsympathetic guard cared to bring it, for periods ranging from three days to more than twenty. Afterward, for the balance of thirty days, the punished man would be in second grade, which meant no smoking, no mail, no light bulb or reading matter in his cell, no time on the yard, among other curtailment of privileges.

In one sense, certainly, my life sentence was the ultimate in social security. For the rest of my life I would be fed, after a fashion, and I could depend on being very carefully sheltered. It was a service guaranteed by my contract with Iowa and registered in many different files under the number printed on my shirt and trousers and cap. But there was utter insecurity, too. As long as a spark of life remained in my body that body would be locked up—beyond that fact there wasn't a second when I could be sure of anything.

There was no way I could get through a day without breaking one or a dozen of those rules, so when the cell door slammed shut at night I could only consider myself lucky I hadn't wound up in the Hole. Aggravated and tormented by petty things as we were, it was dangerously easy for a man to lose his temper and compound a trivial rule violation into a long stay in the Hole for "insolence." Individual guards added to our confusion and frustration by the way they enforced the rules. Each had his pet rules; break one and out came the pencil and away we went on report. And then chances were, even if the offense amounted to nothing, the Deputy Warden would feel he had to support his guards and punish us somehow. We were innocent? It would be safer to say we were guilty. What were we to say when the Deputy swiveled around from his desk and growled: "You mean to say that guard is a liar?" We *might* have proof of innocence, and we *might* beat the rap, but if we did we could be sure the guard and his friends would be laying for us, and it wouldn't take them long to get us dead to rights.

It was a shock to learn I had no rights at all. Over and over again that fact was dinned into us. Every single thing that made life bearable was a privilege. It was a privilege, not a right, to eat a meal or sleep or look at the sun or receive a letter, and that galling knowledge was with me every waking moment.

Trying to understand the innate suspicion of officials was difficult, for it went far beyond any question of security. Each request, no matter how trivial, was pawed over for some hidden meaning; taken apart in an effort to find the gimmick; dog-eyed from every angle except the obvious. A request for a clean shirt—other than the one we received each week after our Saturday morning bath—was met with nearly as much suspicion as a request to borrow a ladder. "How did it get dirty? It's torn? How did you tear it? Fighting, maybe? Skylarking? Don't you have enough work to keep you busy? You wait until Saturday, that's the time to get clean clothes around here."

By practically never following the dictates of common sense officials used a kind of logic of their own, for no logical convict could get a good start at outsmarting them, and in their devious hunting for hidden meanings and possibilities they were consistent. I was qualified for work in the hospital or on the paint gang, so, following their system, I was put to work in the tailor shop. Had I been a tailor or a mechanic I would have found myself in the kitchen or pushing a wheelbarrow. In the years to come, if I really wanted a certain job, I would never let them know, because no square pegs ended in square holes if they could help it.

It was difficult, learning that it was necessary to shoot an angle to get anything from a needle and thread and button to a pair of shoes—that it was much easier to steal the latter. It was difficult, making myself understand that I was to be frustrated in every possible way as a matter of policy—that my nerves were to be kept rubbed just as raw as possible by constant petty aggravations—and that I was to be kept guessing at all costs. "You don't need to think," officials told us, in effect. "We'll do the thinking for you!" Like porcupine quills the many-barbed irritations and humiliations worked deep and festered, and we struck back in any way we could.

Guard Smith was small, but noisy, worse than a feist dog worrying a bull, and just about as dangerous. He dearly loved to chew out some luckless convict for almost any violation but wrote few official reports. Too, he seemed to pick his men. On at least three occasions he caught me smoking in the tailor shop toilet, which was a sure Hole offense, and neither wrote me up nor said a word. But I nearly hated him for the way he humiliated other men, so I had little sympathy to spare when he got his comeuppance in the tailor shop one morning.

I was bent over a coat lapel, sewing away, my mind half a thousand miles away from the prison, out in the world where the sun would be shining brighter and life could be lived again, when the noise began. It was a deep, "mooing" kind of sound that came from everywhere and nowhere. I looked up and around but couldn't see what was causing it. But Smith knew. He was standing in the middle of the shop, almost dancing with rage. He knew practically every man in the shop was booing him (a traditional convict way of showing hatred for guard or official) but he couldn't actually point to a single guilty man. He was receiving the traditional salute of angry convicts—angry enough to risk showing their displeasure but not yet ready to start throwing things— and he didn't like it a bit. In fact he was just about ready to blow his top! But after imitating a whirling dervish with the hot foot for a few seconds, he stormed out of the shop like a pint-sized tornado, vowing to "burn every sonofabitch in the shop!" We convicts laughed and congratulated each other and agreed we ought to do it more often. Me too, even if I hadn't made a sound. Like the others, I felt good for hours.

Being constantly and painfully aware of my outcast status, I at first assumed other convicts would be as hurt and angry as myself; that we would stand shoulder to shoulder in a kind of brotherhood, facing a hostile world in officialdom and those luckier people beyond the walls. What I found should have shocked me so deeply I should have stopped assuming anything for the rest of my life. Instead of standing together and turning on their tormentors, convicts turned on each other, using about as much reason as a wounded, maddened snake that turns and bites itself. Knife fights were common and fist fights were a dime a dozen and worse than either was the vicious, irresponsible slander.

Within thirty days after starting to work in the tailor shop every man there had been denounced to me at least once by fellow convicts. "Don't have anything to do with so-and-son, Runyon," someone would sidle up and warn. "He'll go to the man on you the first chance he gets." Or it would be: "Don't rap to that character. He's a punk." Or, "Lay off that fellow. He's a fairy; he's as queer as a fruitcake."

The malice and envy and hatred I had seen outside was a pale imitation of the bighouse variety, and it ate at me every minute I was out of the cell. There was scorn, too—for some reason eight out of ten men seemed bound and determined to scorn *somebody*, for *something*. "Yeah, he may have scored for a few bucks, but look at the time that Hoosier drew! They oughta take them rape fiends out and string 'em all up! Well, I may be here for a sex offense, but thank God I'm not a thief!" It was an atmosphere guaranteed to make a man fear for his sanity, and I questioned mine more than once.

It wasn't hard to see that imprisonment brought out the very worst in men, causing them to conceal any better qualities they might have lest others see them as weakness. And my very first working mate showed me what years of prison could do to a man.

He had served twenty-seven years of his life sentence and was the most malevolent man I ever met. He was the only man I ever heard curse his own mother, and I believe he would have murdered any human if given a reasonably safe opportunity. Day after day, bit after bit, his hatred for all mankind poured forth until I learned that hatred could be as contagious as fear and shunned him when I could. Perhaps he had reason to hate. He claimed he was in Illinois when an Iowan was killed, but his family and friends had abandoned him. He showed me what long years of frustration and bitterness and lack of hope could do to a man. From him I sensed a little of how thoroughly the walls and years were going to shut out my world.

One morning the Deputy sent for him, and he returned wearing a dazed expression. Unexpectedly his life sentence had been commuted, making him eligible for parole, and he had to start thinking about getting a job. In 1937 he thought of work in 1910 terms. "You know," he told me, "I'm gonna try to get a job driving team on a brewery truck. That's fine work, and good pay. And they're the prettiest horses you ever saw." He didn't hate animals; it was only humans he hated. He had other ideas, all of them 1910 ideas. He tried to understand when I explained about changed conditions, but the world he saw was the world he had left. What a shock traffic-filled, horseless streets must have been to him! But as his time grew short he seemed to lose most of his bitterness—as most convicts do—and I never heard of him again after he left on parole. I didn't think much about him either—from the first few months I learned that prison acquaintances are like shipboard acquaintances for the most part, for the man who went out was soon forgotten.

"Satan," probably the first authentic "rape fiend" I knew, taught me more, both about myself and what time can do to a man. There was a

time-fogged story about a little girl, and a tin can, and. . . . Anyway,
Satan had served thirty-three years of a life sentence for rape, and to
earn that nickname in prison his crime must have been a blood-curdling
affair. But somehow I didn't recoil from Satan as I thought I should.
The slender, white-haired oldster had served more time than anyone else
in the prison and he just didn't look like the monster he must have been
once. The prison photographer, he played in the orchestra and started
wild rumors as a hobby. He was behind 80 per cent of the rumors that
swept through the prison like fire through a dry slough. Satan enjoyed
tipping me off when he started one, just to see what I would think of the
insane changes the story would receive during a week's circulation. It
was good training; it would keep me from putting too much blind faith
in the fabulous prison "grape vine" in the years to come.

I didn't exactly lose sleep over Satan, but my reaction to him made
me do considerable wondering. Then as now I had a special kind of ab-
horrence for the unnatural criminals who attacked children. But I couldn't
seem to loathe Satan as I should—every time I started to do so I would
think of his snowy white hair and his obvious harmlessness and the
thirty-three years he had served. Somehow they seemed to make up, in
a way, for any awful thing he had done. But if I couldn't react as I
thought I should toward the friendly oldster with the dry and caustic
wit, it was easier to react as expected to other things in my new world.

Henry and I worked together after I managed to get transferred away
from the old lifer and his corroding bitterness. We made coats for "our"
going-out suits. And as we sat on our table and sewed and talked away
hours that eventually stretched into years I began learning just how universal was the convict hatred for the "Police," for the "Law."

Warm-hearted, generous, loyal Henry was as good-natured as any man
I ever knew; yet his hatred for the Law was almost as great if not nearly
as loud as the old lifer's, and his quieter, more reasoning hatred impressed me greatly. I didn't exactly like the Law myself, but I was a
veritable "cop lover" compared to many convicts, and I learned a lot
from Henry.

Presumably no convict was born with a dislike for policemen, but
some, like Henry, learned it almost in the cradle. His was a family where
at least one member was forever getting out of or getting into jail, or
expecting momentary arrest. But the hatred was almost an instinct with
all prisoners, if not learned by bitter experience then by the experience
of other convicts—generations of others—who never forgot and never
failed to pass on real or fancied wrongs received from the police. A man,
even a bull-headed independent thinker like myself, could not possibly
remain long in prison without being influenced by that hatred. James
Agee, in the documentary film "The Quiet One," might well have been

speaking for convicts when he said: ". . . the generations of those maimed in childhood, each making the next in its own image, create upon the darkness, like mirrors locked face to face, an infinite corridor of despair."

Henry was one of those maimed in childhood, and there were many like him, and if a newcomer didn't already have reason to hate the police he would soon learn to do so. It didn't take me long to start bristling a little when I heard the hated word.

The word "police" covers a lot of conversational territory in prison. It means the man who walks a beat or rides around on his big fat kiester in a squad car or saps-up some suspects in the "back room." It means the playful chief of detectives in a midwestern city who liked to knock off an arrested man's hat and then, when the unsuspecting man bent over to retrieve it, kick him in the face or neck; there was a fellow coat maker there in the tailor shop who had a permanently injured throat from that detective's foot. "Policeman" also means sheriff or marshal or night watch- man. Anyone on the other side of the law from us could receive the label if they acted in an officious manner, even a plain but nosy citizen. They might be called "screws" or "fuzz" or "bell hops" if they were prison guards; if regular policemen it might be "coppers" or "harness bulls" or "town clowns" or perhaps a hundred others, mostly unprintable.

There were exceptions, however. The fellows in the tailor shop could recall several dead-square officers who were thoroughly respected and in some cases halfway liked by thieves. Sheriffs who were strict but fair and humane with criminals were rather common—no doubt it would have astounded many to hear themselves stoutly defended when a quorum of convicts were busily engaged in "cutting up" cops in general. (Years later I would even hear of a chief of detectives in Cedar Rapids, Iowa, who would work as hard to prove a man's innocence as he would to prove his guilt, and I would laugh scornfully at the very idea until too many thieves swore to it as a fact.) Even an occasional prison guard, absolutely fair and understanding, would receive Henry's highest praise: "He's no part of a policeman!"

Like most hurt and angry men, we didn't think things out in a cold and logical way. We *felt* them out. At the time there was a "hate the criminal, damn the convict, praise the policeman" cycle in full swing. Newspapers, magazines, radio, moving pictures—they all pictured us as something less than human. We suffered and cringed under that cycle as if it had been a wheel from Juggernaut, and returned hate for hate, with possibly a little profane interest. Ground into the sociological and psychological mud as we were, we had to look to each other—getting little satisfaction thereby—for reassurance that we were men at all. For what it did to confused and desperate men in the "thirties" society is still paying, for its hatred crushed many of them beyond redemption. But even then, instinctively knowing we had to find relief from hate and grief, we played endless little jokes on each other and hunted for laughs a little desperately. At times we carried on like a bunch of kids in a katzenjammer reform school, and only we knew the irony of our little battle cry—"I don't want justice; I want out!"

Because I thought it was right—or because it was the only recourse I could see—I tried to follow the hate-the-Law course consistently, and before long it was almost instinctive. But many of the loudest boosters of that course were inconsistent. If they stopped to think about it most prisoners, or at least most thieves, would protect a fellow convict from the guards if they could. With instinct it was something else again. Many fights took place just outside the dining room doors, just as men broke ranks to spread out on the yard after a meal. And as sure as two convicts started slugging or slicing it out they would instantly be surrounded by a solid ring of spectators that was guaranteed to attract the attention of every guard in sight. Then, when a guard came running, that ring would let him through instead of blocking him long enough for the fighters to escape in the crowd. When I saw a fight start I walked away without staring, partly because I didn't want to see it but mostly because I considered it dead wrong to attract attention to them. Many other prisoners did the same. But that ring, composed almost solidly of those who paid the loudest lip service to the hate-the-cops slogan, formed every time. It was the same trait that caused many supposedly "solid" convicts to loud-talk someone in the presence of a known stool pigeon—as far as I could see they might as well have taken their information directly to the guards. After about so much observation I decided the real antisocial showed up best in prison; that here he showed he was incapable of adjusting in any society; that the misanthropes and security-simple officials were almost equally responsible for almost unbearable prison conditions.

It would take me a long time to learn that most prisoners were quiet and essentially decent men who asked only to be allowed to do their own time. But at first I could hear only the noisy ones—the agitating, trouble-making minority—and during that time I began to grow a shell of reticence and suspicion that, like most long-time prisoners, I'll probably go on wearing despite efforts to discard it.

Trying to pin-point the far-back time when the mental kink that made it possible to turn criminal later on was received is a great indoor sport with convicts, and I was no exception. The cell—my seven and a half foot by five and a half foot niche in the filing cabinet life of prison—turned out to be the best part of prison, because there I could find the nearest approach to privacy, but I didn't always find peace there. "Antisocial" was a new word to me—a much-used new word in my new world—but it didn't take me long to apply it to myself when I began to notice how little in common I seemed to have with the fellows around me and remember it had been the same outside. There was more than a little shock connected with that soul-searching.

What kind of fellow was I, anyway? Why was it I liked practically none of the amusements most people seemed to like? There hadn't been time for me to think about stuff like that before, I suppose. At least, I never had worried about it before. But with concrete horizons squeezing me into shoulder-brushing closeness with so many others, and little else to do with time but think, I began trying to figure myself out.

Take baseball. Most men, inside or out, seemed crazy about it. Here in prison, they stood around in the blazing sun listening while the blaring radio loudspeaker broadcast some far-off game. They bet on the games and argued about them and fought over them. Me? I considered it all a noisy nuisance. But there had been a day when I liked it. That was before the broncho threw me into a pile of rocks and smashed my elbow so badly that throwing anything hurt like blazes for years. Before that I had pitched for kid pick-up teams and considered baseball a very sensible game indeed. What was the score with me? Was I sour-graping because I couldn't play for sour apples myself?

Was it the same with football? There had been no opportunity to play that as a boy, and I would have been much too small anyway, but was my indifference to it caused by inability to play it, and to win at it? How about the dancing that I had considered "sissy stuff" until nearly twenty; that had caused me only misery after I realized how important it was to girls and learned after a fashion? Here inside the walls where the only dancing was that of some time-happy Negro doing a tap dance while a friend played a mouth organ, I took time to consider that life-long bugaboo, self-consciousness. What the hell? Did I really believe I was so important everyone was intensely interested in every single thing I did?

Why did I have to be questioning things all the time? Why couldn't I be like most people and accept what "everyone knows" as fact? Did I have to pry and ponder everything, including myself? Certainly the "belongers" were happier than I was. The two hundred fellows crowding the card tables were getting away from the joint for hours at a time, weren't they? And I was doing time the hard way every single minute I was awake, wasn't I? In here I couldn't hunt or fish or play golf or do anything else single-o, so why couldn't I be like the others and make the best of things? It was a thin cry in a personal wilderness, and I received no answer. Outside, I realized, I had disliked crowds intensely—pool halls and bowling alleys and such had always repelled me—and had found pleasure only in very small gatherings or else by myself. That crowd-fear might be part of my trouble, but there was more, as I realized when one of our Big Days rolled around.

It was on the Fourth of July, 1937, that the State of Iowa tried to jam the "Star Spangled Banner" down my throat and make me like it. To please a friend I was in the crowded grandstand to watch the prison baseball team play an outside team before a crowd of outsiders and insiders. When the teams lined up at attention and a convict went out to the flag pole with a flag in his hands I paid no attention. I was not at all startled when the band started playing the National Anthem. Automatically I stood at attention and removed my cap. And then I received something of a shock when a guard came plowing through the crowd right below me.

"Get that cap off," he bawled. "What are you tryin' to do, make the Hole? Get it off!" And a wooden-faced convict fifteen feet away was slowly removing his cap. When I looked around a dozen more were doing the same, slowly, reluctantly, angrily. The guard left just as a bunch of boos became audible.

All my life I had stood at attention to honor the flag, saluting or uncovering, depending on whether I was in uniform (I had served in the Navy) or out of it. It was something I did without thought, like breathing. Like most citizens I had a deep, unspoken love for my country and there was no hardship in showing respect for its flag. So my first reaction there in the grandstand was resentment toward those who had not removed their caps. But it was quickly followed with a deeper resentment toward those responsible for gloating over us by playing that anthem inside prison walls.

There was a vast difference, I suddenly realized, between standing on a street outside and in a prison grandstand. Now my country had disowned me. It was no longer "my" flag that whipped in the breeze up there above me. I stood there among the hundreds who had sneeringly or indifferently or reverently removed their caps—and the alien-feeling was almost overpowering.

There was a big celebration in downtown Fort Madison that night, and through the open cell house windows we could hear the fireworks almost as clearly as the lucky ones who saw them, and it was an odd feeling to realize the celebrators neither knew nor cared about an anonymous lifer who lay on his sweat-soaked bed and yearned to share the fun with them. I knew it was morbid and even trite to think sad thoughts about being buried alive, but I couldn't help comparing my position to someone in the town's cemetery. Mine was worse, really—those under the ground could not be tortured by hearing life go on about them. So I batted my hard pillow through another sleepless, imagination-filled night of self-pity, growing farther away from the outside world by the minute.

A nagging fear of eventual insanity sent me prowling through the library catalog for books on psychology and sociology and philosophy. My less than seventh-grade education put much of their contents over my head, and I found no "answers," but learning I was not necessarily prowling the outskirts of normality when I wanted to be alone did help. It helped to learn I was not necessarily—although I had deeper and deeper suspicions I was getting that way antisocial because of no interest in group activities. When I "celebrated" my thirty-second birthday in September I was finding it very hard to be a philosopher and worrying a lot about the kind of philosophy I might be forming.

"There, you sonsofbitches! That's one year you'll never make me do again!" That was my New Year's celebration as I ripped 1937 off the calendar on my table and hung up 1938. "You may make me do a gang of others just like it, but I'll never do that one again!"

Perhaps I should have been grateful for the occasion's simplicity. There was no reason for "starting over" resolutions; no point in giving up anything or resolving to do this or that. The State would do my resolving from now on. Bitter and frustrated and fearful, without a grey hair in my head, at thirty-two I was feeling and thinking like an angry old man. At times, unconsciously, I think I was accepting the fact that my life was over and done with. I went to bed at nine o'clock on New Year's Eve.

Three hours later I came bouncing out of a dream, thinking the cell house was falling down. Tin cups were being raked back and forth across the cell bars. Blown-up paper bags were being exploded with reports like so many shotguns. Seizing an excuse to make a racket and annoy the screws, convicts were yelling "Happy New Year!" as loudly as they could. Over, under, and through the racket I could hear factory whistles in Fort Madison welcoming 1938.

"To hell with it!" I growled, and yanking the covers over my head I rooted my way back into oblivion.

Moral calluses formed by a brutal environment were never more evident than in convict reaction to capital punishment. Instead of the horror and fury I had expected, most prisoners appeared indifferent to the gruesome business. When they hanged two youngsters at the same time shortly after I entered prison, I lost considerable sleep while I cursed Iowa for being what I considered far more deliberately murderous than the two young killers.

"But what are you excited about?" an old-timer wanted to know when I said some of what I felt. "It's not your neck." On the morning the two youngsters "went" I was the only one on our nine-man table who did not eat breakfast. "You'll get over it," I was told. "There's nothing you can do about it, so why worry."

Instead of staging a demonstration, like those I had read about and seen on the screen, those who had been here during a few executions paid little attention. In fact I heard men growl loudly on the morning of an execution not because some convict was about to die but because the slamming cell doors, heralding the condemned man's last walk a little before sunrise, disturbed their sleep. The attitude of prisoners must have surprised officials, too. Each time a man was executed we were kept in our cells until it was all over. Then, with the guard force doubled in the dining room, we would be fed a kind of holiday breakfast. Afterward, most convict criticism I heard was about the people who besieged the warden for permission to witness executions—their avid curiosity enraged the most cynical of prisoners.

Years later I would be startled to realize the old-timers were right—a man *can* reach the point where, realizing he is helpless to do anything about it, he can practically ignore the commotion when a fellow convict's life is snapped away at the end of a rope.

There were other shocks, sometimes sharp, sometimes dull, each hammering away at me in its own way, causing me to wallow in self-pity or silently rage at the whole world or feel so hemmed-in I had the almost overpowering urge to literally ram my head against the bars like a frantic animal.

Even loneliness was a shock, for there was more to it than being caged away from family and former friends and all the little things embodied by the word "outside." As a thief I consorted with thieves, but as a "Depression Bandit" I didn't qualify as a real thief—I had stolen because I couldn't get work, not because I preferred to steal as a way of life. Despite the fact I had taken more money and raised more hell than most of the thieves, I just didn't fit in. With no reform school background—without even a Skid Row or pool room background—I found so little in common with my daily associates that I was staying more and more by myself two years after I came here when another shock hit me.

Despite their having known nothing about my bandit activities my family—mother and sister and wife and baby son—were standing by loyally and had partially convinced me there was hope for freedom after I had served ten years. Because I didn't want to face life without them I put thoughts of escape away and settled down, picking writing as a hobby and making real progress toward selling fiction. In fact I was getting along far better than a new lifer had any reason to expect when the federal government took me to Minnesota and gave me another life sentence, for robbing a bank, to be served if and when Iowa released me. Of course that additional sentence wiped out any hope. It stopped the writing, for I couldn't concentrate on anything but my troubles. It even wrecked my dreams, for instead of comforting me with reunions with my family they became filled with escape and violence. Bitterness worked on me until "get away" and "get even" filled my mind. When a half dozen planned escapes went wrong because some prisoner or ex-prisoner failed to do his part I began losing confidence in practically everyone. Possibly I thought like a lone wolf, too, for I grew more suspicious and wary by the week.

Looking back, prison life has been a kind of emotional roller coaster, with few climbs and many drops. One climb started when, thanks to a little writing ability and shooting a few angles, I was made associate editor of the monthly inmate magazine, the *Presidio*. Working without a guard watching me all the time—working to help fellow convicts instead of doing slave labor for the State—was an almost unbelievable break. With work to do that would occupy my mind instead of just my hands —work that had some purpose to it—I shook off a great deal of emotional tension and jumped at the chance to work long and hard, developing an interest in the troubles of my fellows and a white-hot desire to help them that proved I was not the misanthrope I had thought myself.

When the war started I even developed a little personal hope once more. It seemed logical to assume authorities would use convicts in the fighting, and my training as a navy pharmacist's mate should make me more valuable in the service than in prison. So I began dreaming of a chance to vindicate myself. Even if I got killed it would be a break, the way I saw it—then that small son would be able to say his dad had died in the war instead of in a prison cell. With a great many other convicts feeling much as I did, I wrote reams of copy urging that we be used.

But others didn't see it the same way. Despite an almost desperate need for men in industry, the Iowa Parole Board was releasing no more men than it had during Depression years. Apparently it was uninterested in the opportunity to rehabilitate men. And the government barred convicts from the armed services who had much more than petty larceny on their records. I kept trying, but I was growing more cynical by the day when I fell into another dizzy drop on that roller coaster.

Within two days, in the summer of 1942 after I served five years, I received a letter saying my wife wanted a divorce and a telegram saying my mother had died. Neither blow was unexpected—I had urged a divorce for years, and Mother's health had been very poor—but despite crossing both bridges many times in imagination I was a little numb for a week. I was still savagely fighting grief and despair by trying to work both night and day a year later when an escape route offered itself.

Oddly, I didn't really want to escape, and that fact worried me out of considerable sleep. Was I getting old, learning to like prison? Was the slight lessening of discipline that went with my job softening me up? Warden Glenn C. Haynes had died. Percy A. Lainson had replaced him and already the prison was becoming more liveable. But if I was reluctant to spend the rest of what might be a very short life with a hand always near a pistol, I was more averse to dying in prison. Then I tangled with the Parole Board, and any reluctance to "foul up the count" vanished.

After watching Parole Board members behave like so many punishment-minded policemen for years, wrecking lives and making criminals and doing anything but serve their taxpayer bosses as I thought they should, I voiced some of my more printable opinions in the *Presidio*. In a gentlemanly kind of way I took the Board apart. In critical but courteous fashion I took its hide and nailed it above the office door. When newspapers reprinted the article, the Board—always hypersensitive to any criticism—reacted like a scalded cat, and before I could say "rehabilitation" it had the all-powerful Board of Control on my neck.

Today there is an entirely different Board of Control (or this would not be written) which maintains an "open door" policy toward newspapers and outsiders in general and encourages the *Presidio*. The present Board is concerned about convicts, too, but in those days the Board hated any kind of publicity and wanted nothing but maximum security for prisoners. So, with it looking for an excuse to yank me off the magazine (no one ever denied that I told only the truth about the Parole Board) I knew it was only a matter of time before I found myself back in one of the shops, forbidden the use of any writing instrument more lethal than a lead pencil, and waited no longer.

One afternoon, six and a half years after I came here, I hid out in a tool house in the athletic field, and that night I escaped. In the next four days I learned just how much prison had hurt me. I wasn't only soft physically, I was soft morally. There was no satisfaction in having escaped. Robbing people, always a distasteful business, was more repugnant than ever. And I found myself in a world almost as alien as prison had once been, for the war had changed conditions unbelievably. I took a farmer's shotgun and car and went on my way as though it had been 1937, except now I had practically no purpose except to keep going until I was stopped. There was no longer any hate to drive me. Somewhere I had lost all desire to get even. Unable to relax and sleep I was soon in pitiful shape; yet I went bullheadedly on without even considering getting a job or giving myself up. Lonelier and more confused than ever, five nights after I burrowed under an electric fence at the prison, punch drunk from lack of sleep, my little adventure ended with what newspapers called a "gun battle" with police. I couldn't even hate them, and when I first missed with the shotgun and then couldn't get another shot at them I chose surrender to deliberate suicide.

Back in prison I spent ten months in "Solid Lockup," a section of isolated solitary confinement cells in a cell house basement where constant reading under twenty-five watt lights so wrecked my distance vision I had to wear glasses. There in the basement, free of agitation and bitterness and self-pity alike, I did relatively easy time. But, no doubt because of vanity, I came out determined to escape again, and felt confident I could do so.

One month later, running a saw in the furniture factory and hating every minute of it, I stumbled and brought the palm of my left hand down squarely on the spinning blade. When I got out of the hospital a month later the little finger was gone, and the remaining three fingers would be stiff and partially numb for the rest of my life. Now, in addition to the glasses, the police had a permanently maimed hand for ready identification. In pain, and losing confidence, I brooded and worried and became more bitter by the day.

Escape became an obsession as the months passed. I thought of little else. More and more I began to have periods of black depression that took me very close to suicide at times; times that would leave me sweating with fear of insanity for hours afterward. I was very close indeed to becoming "stir bugs," and although I realized it fully, at times, I could think of nothing to do about it. At times I caught myself wearing what I called the "old lifer look"—the unseeing, preoccupied stare that seemed to stiffen the faces of so many long termers in the crowded prison yard. Growing more and more suspicious of practically everyone, I was like a squirrel in a cage, hunting endlessly and for the most part aimlessly for a way out of prison. By the fall of 1947, with a little more than ten years served on my sentence, I was a mental mess. It was then that my sister, who had stood by unfalteringly from the day of my arrest, begged and bullied me into doing leatherwork as a hobby, and in some way I could never fully understand started me on the road to growing up.

That hobby gripped me. My subconscious mind seemed to grab at it as a drowning man might grab at a log. I talked hobby and thought hobby and worked at it each night until the lights went out. I had mostly "dummied up" on others, but now I had something to talk about and found my circle of acquaintances growing wider every day—it was a kind of miracle when I had time to look back over a mental shoulder at the way I had been thinking. I still intended to escape—there was no other way out of prison for me—but for the time being escape was less important than the leather which gave me a sense of creating something and, as important at least, a certain amount of pride because I was making a few dollars with it. And, compared with the new, pleased light in my sister's eyes when she came to visit me, escape was of very little importance indeed. It was a good shock, the new feeling I had, and I was rather securely under its influence when I began getting a series of other good ones.

In the fall of 1948 Warden Lainson, concerned over the number of men returning to prison and wanting to send prisoners out better men than when they came, if possible, began feeling his way toward a rehabilitation program. When he invited cooperation from Iowa State University faculty members it was quickly forthcoming. Thanks to one of them, Dr. Fred E. Haynes of the sociology department, I found myself one of four inmates sitting in on a series of conferences designed to find the prison's worst points and suggest possible ways to improve them. At that time I was listed as just about the poorest security risk in the prison, with a reputation for outspoken criticism of prison affairs, so it was a little shocking to receive an "off the record" invitation to say what I thought.

Very possibly some of the clear-thinking, well-meaning professors and graduate students who sat in on those talks from time to time realized what a treat it was for me to listen to them. Possibly with other-dimensional eyes they saw me as the long-dry sponge I felt like as I soaked up the logical ideas of men who did not think prison-style. And they may have realized that being listened to courteously and attentively when I made suggestions brought me still farther out of the defensive, duck-before-you're-hit shell that had all but covered me less than a year before.

Perhaps the change in my attitude was more apparent than I realized, for when editor Lloyd Eddy invited me back to the *Presidio* as co-editor he had Warden Lainson's approval. After the escape I never would have asked for the assignment. Getting it without asking was a startlingly good experience even if I did no longer expect the very worst from any prison official. So, thawing out more by the week, and with considerably more insight than before, again I began hammering away at prison problems, trying to promote better understanding between outsiders and insiders because I saw that as essential if prisons were ever to serve a constructive purpose. What I wrote was often reprinted in the newspapers and in other prison magazines, and each bit of encouragement had its snowballing effect.

When Eddy and I sold first one article and then another to *The Saturday Evening Post*, garnering dollars and prestige and some confidence, I began to believe it was possible for a man to accomplish something even inside prison walls if he would try hard enough. So I tried even harder, and as the time passed faster and faster I gained friends outside the walls, sometimes friends so busy and important I could hardly imagine their finding time to be interested in a convict lifer. I still had the alien-feeling, still dreaded meeting outsiders, still felt a pleasant shock when they treated me just like anyone else, but the feeling was nothing like it had been.

Where strict discipline and suspicion and frustration and hopelessness had made me think of nothing else, now I seldom thought of escape. Thanks to the federal authorities I had no least practical hope for eventual freedom, but I seldom worried about it. The prison was growing more liveable by the day, with an almost unbelievable lack of nervous tension. Now there were fewer fist fights than there were knife fights in the old days, and disciplinary reports of all kinds had fallen off to an amazing degree. Old-time officials and prisoners alike found it hard to believe—men fresh from other prisons found the atmosphere here astounding—and each ascribed it to changes in the other.

"I think it's the result of changes on both sides," I told Deputy Warden John E. Bennett. "But the change started at the top, as it must. First you relaxed discipline a little, then we cons eased up a little, and. . . ." The changes were all too small to point to one as having any specific effect, but they had an accumulative effect that allowed men to relax, that gave them time to think rather than merely hate.

For me 1952 was a busy, event-filled year, probably the most eventful year of my life and certainly so busy I had little time to sit back and think about it. First came an invitation from an old, established publishing company to write my autobiography—with permission to sleep beside my desk and work as late as I pleased, I worked almost day and night. Then a story on a fellow lifer who was free—partly because of the original story I wrote for the *Presidio*—after being forgotten for forty years sold to *Colliers* for what seemed to me an amazing price. With unbelieving eyes I read an invitation to write a "This I Believe" for Edward R. Murrow, and later an acceptance of my effort with the news it would be broadcast nationally. And then in the fall came my biggest and best shock.

My son, four months old when I entered prison, at my request had been allowed to believe I was dead, for I didn't want his childhood haunted by the knowledge of a convict father. Now he was sixteen, in his third year of high school, a crack athlete and good scholar and a splendid boy in every way. But my self-confidence was much too shaky to risk letting my sister tell him about me when she wanted to—what if he was horrified to learn about me; what if he hated me; what if he had nothing but contempt for a lifer father? What if the news would interfere with his school and social life?

Then he yanked the matter out of my hands. When he found a *Presidio* at my sister's house and opened it to one of my articles, he demanded an explanation and she gave him the facts. Two weeks after his immediate letter he was here to see me, and instead of acting ashamed or horrified he seemed almost proud of me, and mighty glad to find a live father even if he was in prison. So was I. In a daze for days afterward I sat and thought of my good luck. At night I slept like a log. At mealtime I ate like an undersized horse. And without the old spurs of frustration and anger and worry, all I could do was sit and look wordlessly at the typewriter. Good treatment and good luck had combined to throw me.

The book, titled *In For Life*, was published in late October of 1953, the butt-end of another busy year, and even after I had spent advance royalties and read reviews and absorbed compliments it still didn't seem possible that I could have written the book. Prison had knocked practically all confidence out of me and I had a hunch that effect would last. The book was a long and practical step forward in my running battle to make people understand more about prison life. It was a source of deep satisfaction to me when the letters I received cut right across social lines, coming from farm wives and ex-convicts, newspaper editors and columnists, librarians and college professors, prison officials and even policemen as they did. But it also so distracted me I could hardly write anything else, and I was still in a writing slump when I finished serving my seventeenth year behind the walls.

This time, as on each of the sixteen anniversaries before it, I did a kind of summing up. As usual, it didn't seem possible I had served that much time; it seemed like no more than six or seven years. As usual, I had the old sickening feeling of having thrown my life away. But now for the second time in a row I could feel there were a few items to go on the credit side of my personal ledger. Merely being the father of that clean-cut, intelligent son was a big item; it meant that my life was far from being completely wasted. A pleasing number of letters and newspaper reprints and verbal comments assured me I had made at least some progress in furthering understanding of prisoner and prison problems and promoting interest in them. It was comforting to know that I had tried hard for years to help my fellow convicts. I could well be proud of having made a young host of personal friends beyond the walls —friends that included best-selling novelists, former prisoners, lawyers and editors and reporters—men and women who believed in me and wanted to help me. More important, I could recognize changes for the better in myself—changes others had professed to see before but were hidden from me—and every now and then I could sense that I was growing up.

Have those seventeen years taught me anything that might be of value to penologists or criminologists or whatever? I believe so. Each time I was hurt—frustrated, deprived of hope, regimented, humiliated, punished —I became worse, either deliberately or unconsciously. Each time I was helped—given some small hope or purpose, treated as an individual, given even a small reason to be grateful to authorities—I became, and behaved, better. Each time needless discipline has been relaxed, each time they have been allowed to relax and to respect themselves, I've seen men in this prison become better prisoners and better risks as ex-convicts. Each time I've seen men really trusted—not partly trusted, as on the prison farms or other places with guards near—I've seen them try to deserve that trust.

Today I am trusted, inside the walls, to a large extent despite the fact that for over ten years I was the only man to escape from inside the walls after Warden Lainson took charge. He simply accepted my voluntary promise not to escape, and that fact makes it impossible for me to let him down. If it wasn't for the federal detainer that has been kept on me relentlessly for nearly fifteen years I'm reasonably certain I would as quickly be trusted outside the walls, and that belief alone makes me a better prisoner. More important, I have friends and relatives out there beyond the walls who believe in me. Allowed to come closer to emotional maturity as I have been, now I cannot let them down.

I believe my experiences and reactions to them have in many ways been the same as those of other convicts—that I reacted much as any citizen suddenly thrown into an utterly unnatural environment might have. Today, treated like a man, I feel compelled to act like a man.

27

Release from Prison[1]

TYPES OF RELEASE

Every time that a released prisoner steps out of the shadows of a prison gate society is confronted with the problem of providing him with the opportunity to lead a law-abiding life. And since less than 5 per cent of those who are sent to prison die there, this is a problem which is implicit in the commitment of virtually every offender. The kind of opportunity which the released prisoner receives is affected by how and under what circumstances he leaves prison. Therefore, even if there were no other reason, this makes it important for us to examine the ways in which prisoners may be released.

An offender is committed to prison in only one way, that is, by order of the court, but his release from prison may be accomplished by a number of different methods. These may be divided into two major types: methods of unconditional release and methods of conditional release. Those of unconditional release include expiration of sentence, pardon, and commutation, while those of conditional release include parole, conditional pardon, and other forms of release to which conditions are attached.[2]

Table 6 shows the number of prisoners released by each of these methods from state and federal institutions in the United States during 1962.[3] Examine this table and you will see that, of the more than 106,000 prisoners who were released during 1962, more than one-third (39,356) received unconditional releases, that is, were discharged absolutely.

[1] "Release" here refers to release from state and federal correctional institutions for adults, but not to release from city and local jails.

[2] Leaves of absence, or temporary releases, also, are granted to prisoners for such reasons as death of a relative or need of medical care, but these are not included here as a type of release.

[3] Federal Bureau of Prisons, *National Prisoner Statistics*, No. 33 (Dec., 1963), Table 1.

Table 6. Number of prisoners released from state and federal institutions, by type of release, in the United States during 1962.

Type of release	Number		Per cent
Conditional		66,787	62.9
Parole	59,335		55.9
Conditional pardon	9		.0
Other conditional release	7,443		7.0
Unconditional		39,356	37.1
Expiration of sentence	35,455		33.4
Pardon	12		.0
Commutation	3,889		3.7
Totals		106,143	100.0

Prisoners released at the expiration of their sentences, numbering 35,455, constituted the great majority of those who were released unconditionally. On the other hand, parolees, with a total of 59,335, made up the bulk of those who were released conditionally.

Two legal devices, "good-time" laws and indeterminate sentence laws, although not in themselves methods of release, are so closely related to them that they must be carefully considered in a discussion of this kind. Since they make possible the reduction of the period spent in prison and determine the time of release, it is appropriate for us to turn our attention to them first.

"GOOD-TIME" LAWS

A "good-time" law is a statute which provides for the reduction of the sentences of prisoners whose conduct is satisfactory while they are in prison.[4] The term "good-time," of course, refers to the time that is deducted from the prisoner's sentence as a reward for his good behavior. Statutes of this kind are in force today in almost all states of the United States. New York in 1817 was the first state to pass a "good-time" law. It provided that first-term prisoners serving sentences of five years or less could shorten their sentences by one-fourth for good behavior, but apparently this law was not used. Connecticut, following the lead of New York, enacted a "good-time" law in 1821, and during the next few decades other states, including Tennessee, Louisiana, Alabama, Georgia, Ohio, Massachusetts, Michigan, and Maine, fell into line. In the mean-

[4] *The Attorney General's Survey of Release Procedures*, "Parole" (Washington, D.C.: Government Printing Office, 1939), Vol. IV, p. 493; Sol Rubin, Henry Weihofen, George Edwards, Simon Rosenzweig, *The Law of Criminal Correction* (St. Paul, Minn.: West Publishing Co., 1963), pp. 307–14.

time, Maconochie, in 1842, had put the idea into use in dealing with convicts in Australia, and Marsangy, in 1846, had advocated its introduction in France. After the War between the States rising enthusiasm for the famous Irish system, which stressed the principle of reducing sentences for good behavior, gave added impetus to the movement for "good-time" laws in the United States; and by 1900 forty-three states and the federal government had passed such legislation.[5]

Under the "good-time" laws of some states the prisoner, as soon as he enters prison, is immediately credited with full deduction for good behavior, and this is reduced only as he violates the institution's rules. In other states, credit for good behavior is not given until it is earned. In all states, however, the purpose of "good-time" laws is to enable prison authorities to use their judgment in reducing sentences for good behavior in accordance with a schedule of deductions set up by the legislature. The extent to which a prisoner may reduce his sentence varies greatly from state to state, but the following schedule, which is in use in some states, illustrates the way in which allowances are made for good behavior:[6]

First year	1 month's deduction
Second year	2 months' deduction
Third year	3 months' deduction
Fourth year	4 months' deduction
Fifth year	5 months' deduction
Sixth and each succeeding year	6 months' deduction

Advocates of "good-time" laws argue that they are necessary to mitigate the severity of criminal laws, to provide prisoners with an inducement for behaving and improving themselves, to encourage greater production in prison industries, and to furnish authorities with an instrument for disciplinary action. The principal argument against these laws is that they tend to become mechanical, allowing credits to be given and forfeitures to be imposed automatically and often in an arbitrary manner. Thus, little regard may be given to the personality of the individual prisoner, who actually may be more criminally inclined when he is released than he was when he was committed to the institution. It is also claimed that the hardened and "prison-wise" convict, without being rehabilitated in any way, cleverly complies with all the rules in order to secure an early release, while the youthful offender, in prison for the first time and frequently a good prospect for reformation, may recklessly violate the rules in order to gain prestige among his fellow prisoners.[7]

[5] *Attorney General's Survey*, "Parole," pp., 495–97.
[6] *Ibid.*, pp. 494, 495, 499–501.
[7] *Ibid.*, pp. 510, 511; Leonard Logan, "Release Procedures," *Encyclopedia of Criminology* (New York: The Philosophical Library, 1949), pp. 419, 420.

After an analysis of the "good-time" laws in the United States, the *Attorney General's Survey*, in 1939, concluded that these laws could probably be eliminated if there were flexible parole laws, well-administered parole boards, and modern prison systems, but that until all these do exist, it is probably better to retain the "good-time" laws. On the other hand, many penal authorities believe that such laws serve a purpose beyond that served by the parole system. In support of their position, they point to the fact that prisoners naturally prefer an arrangement whereby they can compute exactly how much "good time" they can earn by proper conduct. Such an arrangement, they claim, gives prisoners a sense of security, reduces their tension, and makes them more tractable. Moreover, advocates of this point of view contend that the mechanical operation of "good-time" laws can be prevented by increasing the efficiency of their administration and by bringing them into closer relationship with individual guidance programs.

Undoubtedly, prisoners should not be forced into a system in which all certainty regarding the reduction of sentence is lost and release on parole depends entirely on capricious and unpredictable action by a board of parole. As the *Attorney General's Survey* emphasizes, "if parole is to take the place of good time, it must be so administered that the prison routine offers certain fairly well-defined opportunities for self-improvement leading with reasonable certainty to parole." In any event, it does not seem possible that the conditions envisaged by the *Attorney General's Survey* as prerequisites for the elimination of "good-time" laws will exist for many years to come.[8]

THE INDETERMINATE SENTENCE

A completely indeterminate sentence is one which has no specific time limits and is so called because the length of imprisonment is not fixed, or determined, in advance. Its advocates argue that no judge is in a position to know at the end of a trial just how long a prisoner should be confined in a penal institution, and that only after a study has been made of an inmate during his imprisonment is it possible to ascertain whether he is sufficiently rehabilitated to be returned to society.

There are no criminal laws in the United States under which completely indeterminate sentences can be imposed, but many states do have statutes which provide for maximum terms or for maximum and minimum terms and thus permit an administrative board, such as a parole board, to determine the exact time of release of a prisoner within the time limits fixed by the court or the legislature. It has become customary to refer to these

[8] *Attorney General's Survey*, "Parole," p. 511.

sentences as indeterminate, although since they do have specific time limits, it would be more exact to call them indefinite.[9]

Regardless of what they are called, they can be contrasted with definite sentences. In these sentences the exact time of release, instead of being set by an administrative board, is determined either by the legislature, which provides a definite sentence for the crime, or by the court, which is authorized by the legislature to impose a definite sentence within the limits specified by the legislature. Thus the law may specify that the penalty be from five to ten years for a certain crime, and the judge may then impose a definite sentence within these limits, for example, one for six years.

When indeterminate sentence laws were first enacted, judges were permitted to set the minimum limit of such a sentence anywhere below the maximum limit fixed by the legislature. As a result, some judges reduced these laws to an absurdity by using them to impose what amounted to definite sentences. Thus, a judge would sentence a prisoner under a law which provided for a ten-year maximum limit to a prison term of from nine years and six months to ten years. However, many states have taken action to prevent this abuse by specifying that the court may not make the minimum more than a certain percentage of the maximum term.

Although the indeterminate sentence was used by the Church as early as the Inquisition, it is largely an American contribution to penology. During the first part of the eighteenth century, commitments to some American workhouses were for an indeterminate period, but it was not until after the War between the States, when the Irish system, which included an indeterminate sentence, became well known in the United States, that a definite movement developed in this country to have the indeterminate sentence used in the commitment of criminals to state prisons. At first this movement met with serious opposition, and even though Michigan in 1869 became the first state to pass what is now known as an indeterminate sentence law, by 1900 only eleven states had adopted some form of indeterminate sentence. After the turn of the century, however, the movement gained momentum, and by 1922 the indeterminate sentence had spread to thirty-seven states.[10] In 1963 thirty-five states, the federal government, and the District of Columbia had indeterminate sentence laws applicable to at least some adult offenders.[11]

Nevertheless, it must be understood that not all prisoners in the states that have enacted indeterminate sentence laws are committed under this

[9] Since the term "indeterminate sentence" is universally applied in this country to a sentence having maximum and minimum time limits, it will be so used in this text.

[10] *Attorney General's Survey*, "Parole," pp. 14–22; Logan pp. 423, 424.

[11] Rubin, Weihofen, Edwards, Rosenzweig, pp. 134, 135. A few states have adopted the indeterminate sentence law and then abandoned it.

type of sentence. Usually it is not used in cases of misdemeanors or in those of the most serious felonies, but restrictions on its use vary from state to state. Arsonists, train-robbers, embezzlers of public funds, sexual perverts, kidnappers, and habitual offenders are among those who have been barred from receiving indeterminate sentences in various states. During 1946, according to the Bureau of the Census, 30,904 prisoners with definite sentences and 25,528 prisoners with indeterminate sentences were received from the courts by state and federal prisons and reformatories. At the end of 1961 about fifty-five per cent of all the prisoners in these institutions were serving indeterminate sentences.[12]

Considerable controversy has arisen over whether indeterminate sentences should have minimum and maximum time limits. The question is: Why not have completely indeterminate sentences and let an administrative board, such as a parole board, exercise unrestricted authority in determining the time of each prisoner's release?[13]

The principal argument in favor of the minimum limit is that it prevents a sentimental or corrupt board from releasing a prisoner too soon and insures that he will be punished at least to the extent of the minimum limit. In reply to this, it has been asserted that persons may be ready for release before they have served the minimum terms of their sentences; that prisoners have not been carelessly or dishonestly released in states that have abolished the minimum limit; and that furthermore, if the members of the board are vested with the authority to decide whether a criminal should be imprisoned for a number of years, then certainly they can be entrusted with the power to determine whether he should be held for three, or six, or nine months.

This reply, however, is not conclusive. Just because authority has not been abused in the few states that have abolished the minimum limit does not mean that it will never be abused. Moreover, it does not necessarily follow that because an administrative board is entrusted with grave responsibilities, it should also be given unrestricted authority. The interests and welfare of the inmate must be considered, but so must those of the public. Besides, it is always unwise to permit any administrative machinery to operate without legal checks on its authority, especially when the administrative machinery is as inadequate as that in our existing institutional and parole systems. The weight of the evidence is still in favor of keeping the minimum time limit. The hardship it imposes upon

[12] United States Bureau of the Census, *Prisoners in State and Federal Prisons and Reformatories, 1946* (Washington, D.C.: Government Printing Office, 1948), p. 37, Table 24; Federal Bureau of Prisons, *National Prisoner Statistics,* No. 30 (Aug., 1962), 2.

[13] See Edwin H. Sutherland, *Principles of Criminology* (Philadelphia: J. B. Lippincott Co., 1947), pp. 518–20, for a presentation of the case against maximum and minimum time limits in indeterminate sentences.

the few individuals who may be imprisoned too long is more than offset
by the protection it gives to the interests of the public.

The principal argument in favor of the maximum limit is that it prevents a board from abusing its authority or from making serious mistakes,
and thus unjustly condemning prisoners to life imprisonment or to unnecessarily long terms. However, those who oppose the retention of the
maximum limit argue that it permits prisoners to go free who obviously
are going to commit more crimes; that even though the members of a
board may err, so do courts and legislators; and that furthermore, since
a board has the opportunity to examine studies made of the prisoner during his confinement, it is in a better position to know the facts of an individual case, and, therefore, less likely than courts or legislators to make
costly mistakes.

But again the reply is not conclusive. The charge that the exercise of
unrestricted authority opens the door to the abuse of such authority has
not been met. Nor does it help to say that this is unlikely if the members
of the board are honest and competent. The tendency to abuse power
has always been a characteristic of those who wield it, whether they have
been called judges, psychologists, psychiatrists, or sociologists. In the
face of this, it is better to retain the maximum time limit and thus impose
checks upon the exercise of authority even if it be at the cost of releasing
some prisoners who, in all probability, will again commit crimes.[14]

In addition, it should be emphasized that the role of public opinion
and the moral code must be taken into consideration in any discussion of
this problem. If the public is suspicious of efforts to eliminate maximum
and minimum time limits and wants to retain them so as to be protected
against the possible abuse of power, then, of course, its wishes must be
respected. Furthermore, the minimum and maximum time limits of the
sentence must be far enough apart to permit the qualities of the prisoner
to be taken into consideration and yet not so far apart that they are not
proportioned to the gravity of the offense as measured by the moral code,
which must be supported by the system of punishment. That the problem
is a complex one is recognized by even so strong an opponent of time
limits as Professor Sutherland, who has admitted: "It would not be desirable, however, to remove these limits if everything else were to be left
just as at present. The administrative board must be able to do much
more efficient work than at present before it should be trusted with
authority of this nature."[15]

A compromise between the advocates and opponents of time limits
might be effected by having the court fix minimum and maximum terms

[14] For a discussion of the principle of legality, see Chapter 2.
[15] Sutherland, p. 520.

within the limits prescribed by statute and permitting the parole board, at its discretion, to petition the court to modify one or both of these terms when the facts in any particular case indicate that such action is advisable. In this way the sentence might be adjusted to the needs of the individual without exposing society to the possibility of inefficiency or arbitrary action on the part of an administrative board. Although this arrangement would place an additional burden upon the courts, it is worthy of consideration, for it comes to grips with the problem of balancing the interests of society and those of the individual prisoner.

In addition to the controversy over the time limits of the indeterminate sentence, there has also been one regarding the indeterminate sentence itself. The principal criticisms that have been directed against this type of sentence, together with the replies to them, may be summarized as follows:

1. The indeterminate sentence, while emphasizing the reformation of the prisoner, neglects the factors of retribution and deterrence. The balancing of these objectives of punishment has been analyzed in Chapter 17, and the student is again referred to that discussion. Here, it is sufficient to say that the board, like the court and the legislature, can take all the objectives of punishment into consideration, and that, therefore, in an indeterminate sentence none of these objectives has to be neglected. Furthermore, the evidence indicates that the actual amount of time spent in prison by criminals has increased where the indeterminate sentence has been used.[16] Thus, it appears that if the deterrent effect of imprisonment is increased by longer sentences, then the indeterminate sentence has actually strengthened, rather than weakened, the deterrent influence of imprisonment. The same, of course, can be said regarding the satisfaction of the public's desire for retribution.

The danger in the indeterminate sentence seems to be not the neglect of the factors of deterrence and retribution, but the possibility that it will not be coordinated with an effective program of rehabilitation and parole. If such coordination is not effected, then the indeterminate sentence tends to obstruct rather than promote the reformation of the criminal by keeping him confined for an excessively long term of imprisonment during which little is done in a positive way to modify his behavior.[17]

2. There is no satisfactory method by which a parole board can determine whether a prisoner is sufficiently reformed to be released. It must be admitted that no one can guarantee that a released prisoner will never

[16] See, for example, Sol Rubin, "The Indeterminate Sentence—Success or Failure?" *Focus,* XXVIII (Mar., 1949), 47–52; and Alexander Holtzoff, "The Indeterminate Sentence: Its Social and Legal Implications," *Federal Probation,* V (Jan.–Mar., 1941), 3–7.

[17] Rubin, pp. 47–52.

commit another crime. All that anyone can do is to use the best available knowledge as a basis for concluding that the released prisoner will probably become a law-abiding member of society. But this is a problem that confronts not only the administrative board but also the court and the legislature, and certainly the board, which has access to the accumulated studies of inmates made during their imprisonment, is in a better position to secure adequate information for a wise decision regarding the release of the prisoner. Furthermore, nothing should tend to improve our methods of measuring reformation more rapidly than the use of the knowledge and techniques that we already have to supply boards with the information that they need to render their decisions.

3. The indeterminate sentence leads to the persecution of prisoners and makes them servile and dependent. Brutal, hostile guards can prevent prisoners from being released by submitting unfair reports regarding them, and inmates tend to curry favor with their guards instead of applying themselves to a program of self-improvement. But this may happen under a system of definite sentences, too, and the answer in any case is better guards, better methods of supervision and discipline, and better prison administration.

4. The indeterminate sentence creates attitudes of suspicion, distrust, uncertainty, and insecurity in the prisoner. Under a system of indeterminate sentences, prisoners who have committed the same kind of offense do not necessarily serve the same length of time in prison; inmates suspect that graft and favoritism let some out sooner than others. This breeds distrust and undermines the relationships among prisoners, guards, and prison officials. Furthermore, since no one knows exactly when he will be released, prisoners are filled with anxiety and uncertainty, and their sense of insecurity makes them restless and intractable and affects their mental health.

It must be admitted that this is a serious problem and that there is no complete solution for it. But it must also be recognized that it is a problem which exists even when prisoners are serving definite sentences, for its roots are in the coercion and compulsion which are implicit in every penal situation. The same honest, fair, understanding, and firm policies and programs which make for successful prison administration in general will also tend to reduce and hold in check the problem of prisoners' attitudes. It must likewise be added that this problem would be intensified if the indeterminate sentence had no maximum time limit upon which the prisoner could count for his ultimate release.

5. The indeterminate sentence is open to certain constitutional objections. The most important of these has been that the use of an indeterminate sentence, with power in a board to fix the time of release, constitutes an impairment of the judicial power vested by the state and federal

constitutions in the courts. Other important objections have been that it is a delegation of legislative power to give an administrative board the authority to determine the time of detention, that it is an infringement on the pardoning power of the governor to allow any other agency to grant paroles, that it renders the punishment so uncertain that it falls within the constitutional prohibition of cruel and unusual punishments, and that it is an interference with the right of trial by jury.[18]

While such objections have prevailed in a few cases, they have generally been held to be not well founded, and the constitutionality of both parole and the indeterminate sentence has been clearly established. However, it must be emphasized that this statement does not apply to a completely indeterminate sentence. No state has a statute providing for such a sentence, and its constitutionality, therefore, need not be examined here. What has been declared constitutional is the indeterminate sentence with time limits. As the *Attorney General's Survey* has stated, it is possible that a completely indeterminate sentence would be declared invalid. And in this connection, it must be remembered that "it was only by holding the indeterminate sentence to be in legal effect a sentence for the maximum term that the courts preserved it from the objection of uncertainty and indefiniteness."[19]

The criticisms that have been directed against the indeterminate sentence have indicated its weaknesses and the need for its improvement. They have not proved that it should be abolished. No one can ascertain in advance how long a prisoner should be held. The best way to determine this is to observe him during the period of his incarceration. This is the thesis of the indeterminate sentence, and it remains unshaken despite adverse criticism. When combined with an effective program of rehabilitation and parole, the indeterminate sentence provides the best arrangement yet devised for balancing the interests of society and those of the individual in the process of sentencing the prisoner.

The indeterminate sentence may be used in combination with a "good-time" law. This combination may be made in three different ways. The "good-time" law may be applied to reduce the maximum limit; it may also be used in such a way as to affect only the minimum limit; or it may operate to modify both the maximum and minimum limits and thus hasten not only the time when the prisoner becomes entitled to absolute release but also the time when he becomes eligible for parole.[20]

The complicated sentencing system of the United States has been criticized on the grounds that, in general, the prison sentences imposed and the terms served are too long, and that in any particular offense they vary

[18] *Attorney General's Survey,* "Parole," pp. 21, 22.
[19] *Ibid.,* p. 22.
[20] *Ibid.,* pp. 493, 494.

too much not only from state to state but also within any one state. In order to improve this situation, the American Law Institute has proposed in its Model Penal Code that felonies be classified on the basis of their seriousness (as measured by the moral standards of society) into three degrees and that an indeterminate sentence be provided for each of these degrees. The minimum terms would be set by the court within the limits stipulated by law but the maximum terms would be fixed by statute.[21] In certain cases, however, the court might impose the death penalty for murder, and in certain other cases sentence persistent and dangerous offenders to "extended terms" of imprisonment.

The National Council on Crime and Delinquency has advanced much more extreme proposals for changing the sentencing laws of the United States. Its Model Sentencing Act entirely discards the moral standards as a basis for criminal penalties, gives scant recognition to deterrence, and relies largely on the rehabilitative influences of probation, suspended sentences, fines, and short prison terms, although it provides long periods of incarceration for "dangerous offenders," from whom the public is to be "protected" by the "experts." This revolutionary act assumes that we have much more knowledge of crime causation and far more ability to reform criminals than we actually have, greatly increases the influence of psychiatry and social work in the administration of justice, substitutes their value judgments for the moral standards of the community, reduces the control that the people can exert over their courts, and casts aside protective devices that have long guarded the accused and the public from the abuse of authority. The objectionable features of this act far outweigh any benefits that might be derived from it.[22]

PARDON

A pardon is an act of clemency, usually by the chief executive of a state, which exempts the individual to whom it is granted from the punishment imposed upon him by the court. It is used not only to rectify errors in justice and to restore innocent persons to freedom but also to

[21] See in particular Articles 6 and 7 of the *Model Penal Code, Proposed Official Draft* (Philadelphia: The American Law Institute, May 4, 1962). According to this code, felons would be punished as follows:

Degree of felony	Minimum term (set by court)	Maximum term (fixed by law)
1	1 to 10 years	Life
2	1 to 3 years	10 years
3	1 to 2 years	5 years

[22] See *Crime and Delinquency*, IX (Oct., 1963). This entire issue is devoted to an analysis of the "Model Sentencing Act," which was prepared by the Advisory Council of Judges of the National Council on Crime and Delinquency.

extend mercy to those who seem to have had sufficient punishment. However, it does not always return all of the civil rights that a convicted person has lost.

A pardon may be either absolute or conditional. One that is absolute frees the person without any restrictions whatsoever. One that is conditional, however, becomes operative or void, as the case may be, when the person performs a certain act which is required or forbidden in the stipulations included in the pardon. For example, a conditional pardon may require the person to whom it is granted to leave the country; if he fails to do so, his pardon becomes void, and he may be returned to prison.

A pardon should be distinguished from a commutation, an amnesty, and a reprieve—other acts by which the chief executive of a state can modify a penalty. A commutation is the substitution of a milder penalty for the one originally imposed; and thus while a pardon terminates punishment and results in the release of a prisoner, a commutation merely reduces punishment and may, or may not, involve the release of a prisoner. An offender who has served five years of a ten-year sentence may be released by having his sentence commuted to five years, but on the other hand, a commutation may simply mean that a death penalty has been reduced to life imprisonment. Furthermore, unlike a pardon, a commutation can neither obliterate guilt nor restore civil rights.

An amnesty is a pardon granted to a group of criminals, usually to those who have committed political offenses, and is given without reference to any particular one of them. Its purpose is to assist in the restoration of general order, clemency under the circumstances being considered more expedient than punishment. Thus, a government that has successfully suppressed a rebellion may grant an amnesty to many who were involved in the uprising. An amnesty has the same general effect as a pardon and releases the members of the group from prison. Although, like a pardon, amnesty has an ancient origin, it has been seldom used in the United States.[23] A reprieve, or respite, unlike a pardon and an amnesty, does not remove the penalty but merely postpones the execution of a sentence, usually one calling for the imposition of the death penalty; and its use permits further consideration of the case before punishment is finally inflicted.

The practice of granting pardons existed among the ancient Hebrews, Greeks, and Romans; and before the settlement of America, criminals were being pardoned in Germany, France, England, and other European countries. When the early colonists came to the New World, they brought the practice with them, and it is now deeply embedded in the culture of the United States. In the American Colonies the executive usually had

---

[23] Logan, p. 422.

the authority to grant pardons, but after the Revolution most of the states imposed restrictions on this authority or entirely removed it from the office of the governor. With the development of the political structure of the country, however, the pardoning power of the governor was generally increased, although within recent years pardon boards have been created in many states.

These pardon boards may be classified into four principal groups. First, there are boards which function in an advisory capacity. Usually applications for pardon must first be brought before these boards, but their recommendations may be disregarded by the governor, who may take any action which he deems proper. Second, there are boards whose favorable recommendations must be secured before the governor may grant a pardon. Third, there are boards that are vested with the pardoning power and of which the governor is a member and has one vote. In some states that have this type of board, the governor must cast an affirmative vote before a pardon can be granted. Fourth, in a few states there are boards, of which the governor is not a member, that have the exclusive power to grant pardons. In addition to these limitations, other restrictions on the exercise of the pardoning power exist in the law. In more than half of the states the governor may not grant pardons in cases of treason and in more than forty states he is not permitted to do so in cases of impeachment. The President of the United States has the authority to pardon those who are convicted of violations of federal laws except in cases of impeachment.[24]

The procedure to secure a pardon should be simple so that the prisoner can understand it and present his case without the aid of a lawyer if he so desires, and yet it should be thorough enough to make possible a decision based upon a careful investigation of the case. Hearings should be public so that all interested parties are properly represented and their welfare fully considered, but the board should confine its attention to matters that are relevant to the question of granting clemency.[25]

Pardons have been severely criticized. It has been claimed, for example, that they are loopholes in the legal system through which politically influential criminals can escape, that they break down respect for law because they give criminals a chance to avoid punishment, that governors have neither the time nor information to exercise the pardoning power wisely, and that it is unreasonable to subject the chief executives to the tremendous pressure exerted by prisoners and their relatives and friends, who constantly petition for acts of clemency. But such criticisms are not fundamental, and they can be deprived of their force by the creation of

[24] *The Attorney General's Survey of Release Procedures*, "Pardon" (Washington, D.C.: Government Printing Office, 1939), Vol. III, pp. 1–53, 94–122; Logan, pp. 420, 421; Rubin, Weihofen, Edwards, Rosenzweig, pp. 592–610.

[25] Logan, p. 421.

responsible pardon boards to work with the chief executives in the grant- ing of clemency and by the careful investigation of all cases. In fact, crim- inologists generally agree that the power to pardon should not be abolished since even under the best conditions mistakes are made, power is abused, and justice miscarries; but they also recommend that its use be greatly restricted and reserved for only those cases in which justice can be obtained in no other way.

Thus, many of them believe in eliminating that type of pardon which is granted for the sole purpose of restoring the civil rights of an offender after his release from prison. This could be accomplished without a par- don by having the released prisoner's civil rights restored after he has passed certain tests, for example, at the end of a certain period of suc- cess while on parole, or at the end of a certain period dating from the termination of his sentence during which he has not again violated the law. Certainly, if he can meet such conditions, it should be safe to permit him once more to exercise his rights as a citizen. Indeed, the restoration of these rights may actually help him to become a responsible member of society.

PAROLE

Parole is a procedure whereby an offender who has served a part of his sentence in a correctional institution is conditionally released into the community. There he remains under the control and supervision of the institution, or some other agency approved by the state, during the period of his parole and must abide by certain conditions until finally discharged from parole or face the possibility of being returned to the institution.

Parole must be distinguished from probation. Parole is a form of re- lease granted after an offender has served part of his sentence in a cor- rectional institution, while probation is granted without requiring any incarceration. Parole is granted by an administrative board or an execu- tive, whereas probation is almost always granted by a court. In the case of parole the offender must serve the first part of his sentence in an insti- tution, but he is released during the latter part of the sentence and re- mains at liberty as long as he abides by the conditions of his parole. On the other hand, in the case of probation, the person is not committed to an institution but instead remains at liberty as long as he observes the conditions imposed by the court. The term "bench parole," which is still used in some states, is nothing more than a suspension of sentence, often without supervision, and is therefore not parole at all but a form of pro- bation. The use of the word in this sense is improper and misleading and should be discontinued.[26]

[26] *Attorney General's Survey,* "Parole," p. 1.

Pardon, too, is different from parole. Pardon is an act of clemency usually granted by the chief executive of a state, while parole does not involve forgiveness and is an administrative device which is intended to assist the offender in readjusting himself to normal life in the community. While pardon removes the penalty, parole merely modifies it. Pardoned prisoners are free and usually in possession of all of their civil rights; but this is not true of parolees, whose sentences are still in force and who may be arrested and again incarcerated without a trial if they violate the conditions of their parole.[27]

Release on parole should not be based on any concept of clemency or be regarded as leniency, even though the prisoner is released before the expiration of his sentence. Its chief purpose is to bridge the gap between the closely ordered life within an institution and the freedom of normal life in the community.[28] It thus assumes that the period of confinement is only part of the correctional process and should be supplemented by a period of guidance and supervision in the community, and that the time immediately after release is a most crucial one in the adjustment of the offender. Parole, therefore, is not just a way of releasing prisoners. It is an integral part of the entire correctional program, and in it, as in all other aspects of this program, the interests of both society and the offender must be taken into consideration.

In the United States parole, the indeterminate sentence, and a "good-time" law usually operate together, but there is no reason why each cannot exist alone or in combination with one of the other two. In fact, even though all states now have parole laws, a prisoner serving either a definite or an indeterminate sentence may be released with or without parole. Furthermore, the expanded use of parole and conditional release has greatly reduced the practical difference between definite and indeterminate sentences.[29]

RELEASE AT EXPIRATION OF SENTENCE

At present more than one-third of the prisoners discharged from our state and federal correction institutions for adults are being unconditionally released without supervision. Having completed their sentences, they have passed beyond society's power to imprison them again for the crimes for which they were convicted. In general they have served longer sentences, are more hardened in crime, and will have greater difficulty in achieving successful adjustment in the community than those released on parole. So it can be understood why prisoners who can not qualify for pa-

27 *Ibid.*, pp. 2, 3.
28 *Ibid.*, pp. 3, 4.
29 For a discussion of the principles and problems of parole, see Chapter 28.

role should nevertheless be given some other form of conditional release before the expiration of their sentences and spend the last part of their terms under supervision in the community. In several jurisdictions prisoners who earn early release by good-time credits are kept under supervision and subject to certain conditions until the expiration of the maximum sentence imposed. If they violate the conditions of their release, they forfeit the remaining period of earned good time and are again institutionalized.[30]

Regardless of the way in which he is released, no prisoner should be discharged without some definite preparation for meeting the immediate problems that will confront him upon his return to the community Unfortunately, today few prisons go beyond merely giving a physical examination, an outfit of clothing, a small amount of money, and some transportation to prisoners released at the expiration of their sentences. The ideal would be to have a prerelease program for these offenders similar to that now provided for prospective parolees in many institutions. In their case, however, the program would have to be more restricted in scope, because included among these offenders are many hardened criminals. Despite this, in such a program all these prisoners should at least be put into the best possible health, given individual and group counseling, supplied with adequate shoes and clothing and sufficient money to cover their initial expenses upon release, and brought into relationship with such community agencies and institutions as churches, labor unions, welfare organizations, and prisoners' aid societies, to which they can later turn for assistance and guidance. For a selected group of those who are released at the termination of their sentences, a prerelease program should provide increased freedom and privileges within the institution, and after their release, suitable living quarters, employment, and sponsors, who will supply friendly advice and assistance in the community. Such provisions as these appear to be all the more desirable when it is realized that a prisoner may be required to serve his entire sentence not because his qualities render him unfit for release on parole, but because the nature of his offense makes him ineligible for parole, or because of the inefficiency or unfairness of the parole board. Furthermore, in all cases efforts should be made to dissuade the police from hounding released prisoners and thus perhaps driving them back into the criminal associations which were an important cause of their trouble in the first place. Naturally, this does not mean that correctional authorities should not cooperate in every reasonable way with the police in the apprehension of suspected criminals.

---

[30] This form of conditional release has been called "mandatory release," because release becomes mandatory when the accumulated time for good behavior and work credits, which is deducted from the sentence, makes it legally mandatory to release the prisoner.

RESTORATION OF CIVIL RIGHTS

In almost every state in the United States a person convicted of certain crimes loses one or more, and sometimes all, of his civil rights.[31] Usually, this happens when he is convicted of any felony or infamous crime, but some states provide for it only when certain felonies have been committed, while still other states do so not only in felony cases but also where certain misdemeanors are involved. At common law the infamous crimes were treason, felony, and all offenses based upon falsification, such as perjury, forgery, and cheating. According to federal law, however, a crime is infamous if it is punishable by imprisonment in a penitentiary or by any imprisonment accompanied by hard labor. Many states follow the common law in their definition of infamous crimes, but in some states the rule is that infamy may be determined either by the nature of the crime, as in common law, or by the nature of the punishment which may be inflicted, as in federal cases.

Among the important civil rights that have been taken away from convicted criminals are (1) the right to vote, (2) the right to hold public office, (3) the right to appear as a witness or to serve as a juror, (4) the right to make a contract, and (5) the right to practice certain professions, such as law or medicine. In addition, in most states conviction of certain crimes is a ground for divorce. But it must be emphasized that the loss of civil rights is usually restricted to the state in which the offender is convicted and that such loss does not necessarily involve the loss of citizenship.

Most of the civil rights that accompany citizenship are derived from state constitutions or laws, and it is these that are usually taken away. In only a few instances is the offender deprived of any civil rights which he received from the federal constitution or laws. This, however, happens, when a person is convicted of treason, bribery of a federal judicial official, accepting a bribe while a federal judicial officer, or receiving unlawful compensation while a member of Congress. In these cases conviction results in disqualification to hold any office of honor, trust, or profit under the United States. Furthermore, a person who is convicted of treason or of desertion from the armed forces in time of war and dishonorably discharged from the service loses his citizenship. An alien who is convicted

[31] Alexander Holtzoff, "Civil Rights of Criminals," *Encyclopedia of Criminology* (New York: The Philosophical Library, 1949), pp. 55–58; Negley K. Teeters, "The Loss of Civil Rights of the Convicted Felon and Their Reinstatement," *Prison Journal,* XXV (July, 1945), 77–87; Daniel M. Lyons, "Forfeiture of Civil Rights by Reason of Conviction of Crime," *Proceedings of the American Prison Association, 1944,* pp. 165–69; Rubin, Weihofen, Edwards, Rosenzweig, pp. 611–44.

of a crime involving moral turpitude may be denied naturalization, or under some circumstances may be subject to deportation.[32]

Various writers have questioned the wisdom of depriving criminals of their civil rights. Others have argued that we could greatly liberalize this practice with very little threat to the public and the moral code and at the same time help the offender to maintain a legitimate measure of self-respect and thus contribute to his rehabilitation. They are, for example, in favor of letting the prisoner keep his rights to sue and to receive and convey real and personal property.[33]

There is great variation in the procedures by which released prisoners can regain their civil rights, and even when a pardon is the proper procedure, which is the case in the majority of states, the method of securing a pardon varies from comparative simplicity to great complexity. Since it is important to facilitate the process by which the conditionally released prisoner is made to feel that he is a member of the law-abiding group in society, the civil rights of the probationer or parolee should be restored by the court or the parole board, as the case may be, as soon as he has shown a sincere desire to become a responsible member of the community.[34] Each state should also establish a simple, definite procedure by which prisoners who are unconditionally released at the termination of their sentences can regain their civil rights after a certain period of satisfactory adjustment in the community. In all cases, however, the released prisoner must understand that the interests of the community are paramount, that civil rights are not something to be taken for granted, and that they cannot be enjoyed without the performance of civic duties.

Regardless of whether or not he loses any of his civil rights, the social status of a person found guilty of a crime suffers from the effects of his conviction. Even after the passage of many years, his application for a position or a license may be denied, and if he is convicted of another crime, his previous conviction may be counted against him in the imposition of his sentence. In order to assist convicted persons who later demonstrate that they can live respectable lives in the community, a few states have procedures for annulling or expunging convictions and the National

[32] Holtzoff, p. 57.

[33] See, for example, Paul W. Tappan, "The Legal Rights of Prisoners," *The Annals of the American Academy of Political and Social Science,* CCXLIII (May, 1954), 99–111.

[34] *The Standard Probation and Parole Act,* published by the National Probation and Parole Association in 1955, provides that probationers and persons released on suspended sentences shall not lose their civil rights, and that parolees shall have their civil rights restored when they are discharged from parole (Art. IV, Sec. 12, and Art. VI, Sec. 27).

Council on Crime and Delinquency has recommended the adoption of an act designed to accomplish this purpose.[35]

USE OF COMMUNITY RESOURCES

Just as the prisoner should be prepared to return to the community,[36] so the community should be prepared to receive the prisoner. Naturally, this involves the coordination of the functions of the correctional system with those of agencies and institutions in the community and is made possible only by the systematic utilization of the latter's religious, educational, welfare, and economic resources.[37]

An important area in which correctional workers may cooperate with community agencies is the financial situation of the released prisoner and his family. Here both private and public agencies can give direct relief. In order to assist in meeting this and other problems of parolees, the parole agency during the prerelease program should be furnished with a statement of social services already received by the inmate and his family or the actual correspondence between the correctional institution and the social agencies. Where the need for assistance still exists, the parole officer should visit the office of the local welfare department or other social agency in order to provide adequate money and services until the released prisoner is able to assume responsibility for the welfare of his family. Whenever possible, steps should be taken to put into effect the recommendations that have been made for the social welfare of released prisoners so as to insure their actual participation in activities that are planned for them. For example, when it is believed that a man should join Alcoholics Anonymous, arrangements should be made for him to receive an invitation to attend a meeting of this organization.[38]

The creation of a sponsorship for the paroled prisoner has proved to be an effective method of helping him to handle his problems. In fact,

[35] See National Council on Crime and Delinquency, "Annulment of a Conviction of Crime: A Model Act," *Crime and Delinquency*, VIII (April, 1962), 97–102. According to this act, the court where the person was convicted may order the annulment of the conviction when the person is discharged from the control of the court, from imprisonment or parole, or at any time thereafter if in its opinion the order would assist in rehabilitation and be consistent with public welfare.

[36] See, for example, Frank Loveland, "Financial and Material Aspects of Release Planning," and W. Jerry Head, "Job Finding for Prisoners," *Federal Probation*, XVI (Mar., 1952), 17–25; The United Prison Association of Massachusetts, "What's New in the Employment of Ex-Prisoners?" *Correctional Research*, Bull. No. 9 (Nov., 1959).

[37] *Handbook on Pre-release Preparation in Correctional Institutions* (New York: The American Prison Association, 1950), pp. 62–73.

[38] *Ibid.*, pp. 62–66.

before parolees are permitted to leave the institutions of the Federal Bureau of Prisons and of some state correctional systems, they must have a sponsor, or "first friend," approved by the correctional authorities. The sponsor, usually someone known to the inmate and approved by him, promises to give him close personal attention and to help him in whatever way he can. Thus, it can be seen that the sponsor occupies a strategic position in the protection of society and the rehabilitation of the released prisoner, and it is for this reason that he must be carefully selected. Not only must he be a person of integrity who is willing to assume responsibility for the welfare of the released prisoner, but also he must have such qualities that make possible easy rapport between them. His wisdom, sympathy, and understanding may easily make the difference between the continued freedom of the released offender and his return to prison.[39]

From the very beginning of our country's history prisoners' aid societies have played an important role in helping released prisoners. The earliest of these societies was the Philadelphia Society for Assisting Distressed Prisoners, which was organized in 1776. Reorganized in 1787 as the Philadelphia Society for Alleviating the Miseries of Public Prisons, it is now known as the Pennsylvania Prison Society. In its early days it gave assistance to prisoners discharged from the Walnut Street Jail, but its principal function was to improve prison conditions. Its model prison was the Eastern Penitentiary in Pennsylvania—the original institution for the system of solitary confinement. As a part of this system prison visiting was carried on regularly by members of the Philadelphia society.

Other important prisoners' aid organizations are the Prison Association of New York, the Women's Prison Association of New York, the John Howard Association in Illinois, the United Prison Association of Massachusetts, the Society for the Friendless, the Salvation Army, the Volunteers of America, and the Osborne Association. However, organizations of this kind are largely confined to the cities and more populous areas, and many of them are handicapped in their work by being understaffed and underfinanced. These organizations help the prisoner and his family both before and after his release. They give counsel and guidance, provide food, clothing, and shelter, locate employment, and promote the community's understanding of the released prisoner's problems.[40]

---

[39] *Ibid.*, pp. 67–69.

[40] *Ibid.*, pp. 69–73; A. G. Fraser, "What Is the Responsibility of a Prisoners' Aid Society in Job Placement, Sponsorship and Community Readjustment?" *Proceedings of the American Prison Association, 1941*, pp. 459–63; John F. McMahon, "The Work of the Volunteers of America in the Field of Correction," *American Journal of Correction*, XXV (May–June, 1963), 24–29.

Within recent years so-called half-way houses have been established in the United States. Some of these are operated as public agencies; others are supported by private or religious organizations. However, all of them are designed to provide a residential program for discharged inmates and parolees in order to assist them in bridging the gap between institutional confinement and the free life of the community.[41]

[41] Kenneth S. Carpenter, "Halfway Houses for Delinquent Youth," *Children*, X (Nov.–Dec., 1963), 224–29; Robert G. Crosswhite and Maurice A. Breslin, Jr. "Bridging the Gap from Confinement to Freedom," *Federal Probation*, XXIII (June, 1959), 46–52; Harry A. Manley and Melvin B. Sherman, "Summary of the Half-Way House in the Correctional Process," *Proceedings of the American Correctional Association, 1963*, pp. 311–15. For an appraisal of a private project devoted to the communal rehabilitation of narcotic addicts in California, see David Sternberg, "Synanon House– Correction," *Journal of Criminal Law, Criminology, and Police Science*, LIV (Dec., 1963), 447–55.

28

Parole

ORIGIN AND DEVELOPMENT

Parole did not originate in America, although today its greatest development is to be found in this country. Probably the first man to use the word "parole" in the sense of conditional release was Dr. S. G. Howe, of Boston, who, in a letter written to the Prison Association of New York in 1846, said, "I believe there are many prisoners who might be so trained as to be left upon their parole during the last period of their imprisonment with safety." "Parole" is French for "word" and is used here in the sense of "word of honor," *parole d'honneur*. Thus, the implication was that the prisoner would give his word (or word of honor) that he would abide by the terms of his conditional release. However, it appears that the choice of the word was not a fortunate one since most people distrust a "word of honor" given by a released prisoner, and it is not surprising that the French prefer the term "conditional liberation" to the one we have borrowed from them.[1]

In penal philosophy, parole is an organic part of the reformatory idea and an expression of the general trend in nineteenth century criminology in which much emphasis was placed upon reformation. But even so, parole had forerunners far back in the history of Europe. One of these was the conditional pardon granted in England to criminals who were transported during the seventeenth and eighteenth centuries to the American Colonies, where they worked as indentured servants subject to certain conditions. Violation of these conditions resulted in the nullification of their pardon. Other forerunners appeared on the Continent, where the efforts of Montesinos, a Spaniard, and Obermaier, a German, two prison administrators of the nineteenth century, contributed in an important way to the development of parole.

[1] *The Attorney General's Survey of Release Procedures,* "Parole" (Washington, D.C.: Government Printing Office, 1939), Vol. IV, pp. 4, 5.

However, chief credit for the parole system is due to Alexander Maconochie, who in 1840 began to use a ticket-of-leave, or conditional release, system at the English penal colony on Norfolk Island, about a thousand miles to the east of Australia, and to Sir Walter Crofton, who further developed the idea in the Irish prisons during the period 1854 to 1862. The Irish prison system, organized under the leadership of Crofton attracted the attention of American prison reformers, and in 1869 the resulting agitation led to the passage of the act which created the Elmira Reformatory in New York. This famous institution was opened in 1876, and for the first time in this country parole was used in a manner comparable to present-day parole administration. The year 1876, therefore, may be said to mark the beginning of parole in America.

Nevertheless, it must be explained that precursors of parole had existed in America as early as Colonial times. The first of these was the system of indenture for juvenile delinquents. By this system young prisoners were released without supervision, placed in the employ of private citizens to whom they were legally bound, and permitted to earn their final discharge from their employers. Later, a state visiting agent was appointed to supervise and protect these juveniles. A parallel development was the giving of aid to discharged prisoners by such philanthropic societies as the Philadelphia Society for Assisting Distressed Prisoners. Eventually, in 1846, Massachusetts appointed an agent to assist released prisoners, but this did not involve either release prior to the expiration of sentence or custody after release. Following this other states appointed similar agents, and their work contributed to the movement for parole legislation in the United States.

Despite these early American steps toward parole, the experiments of Maconochie and Crofton were more closely related to its modern development, and its real beginnings may be said to have been in Europe and Australia. After its introduction at Elmira, parole spread rapidly in the United States, and by 1910 thirty-two states and the federal government had adopted a parole system. Today, parole is being used in some way by all the states and the federal government.[2]

EXTENT OF PAROLE

During 1962 state and federal institutions released 106,143 prisoners. Of these, 55.9 per cent were released on parole. During this same year, of

[2] *Ibid.,* pp. 4–20, 126, 127; George G. Killinger, "Parole and Other Release Procedures," *Contemporary Correction,* ed. Paul W. Tappan (New York: McGraw-Hill Book Co., Inc., 1951), pp. 361, 362; G. I. Giardini, "Parole," *Encyclopedia of Criminology* (New York: The Philosophical Library, 1949), pp. 285, 286; Charles L. Newman, *Sourcebook on Probation, Parole, and Pardons* (Springfield, Ill.: Charles C. Thomas, Publisher, 1964), pp. 3–24.

their released prisoners, state institutions paroled 59.6 per cent and federal institutions paroled 33.2 per cent. The extent to which parole is used varies from state to state and from region to region, being influenced by such factors as population, geographical area, natural resources, political history, and social and economic conditions. During 1962, New Hampshire, with 98.1 per cent, had the highest percentage of its prisoners released on parole, and South Carolina, with 8.0 per cent, the lowest. For the same period the percentages of released prisoners placed on parole in the various regions of the United States were: 73.8 per cent for the northeastern states; 69.8 per cent for the north central states; 37.0 per cent for the southern states; and 80.8 per cent for the western states.[3]

ADVANTAGES OF PAROLE

The advantages of parole are similar to the advantages of probation, which we have already discussed,[4] and the most important ones may be summarized as follows:

1. Parole provides a transitional period between the regimentation of institutional life and the freedom of normal life in the community. During this time a parole officer guides and supervises the conditionally released offender and thus not only provides him with assistance in his efforts to become a law-abiding member of society but also helps to protect the community from the criminal inclinations which the released offender may still have. Furthermore, if the parolee violates the conditions of his parole, he may be immediately returned to a correctional institution without first receiving a trial, but in cases where the parolee has committed a new crime, he must later stand trial for it.

The importance of this advantage can be fully appreciated only if it is remembered that an offender who is not paroled is usually unconditionally released. This means that he has no official guidance during the critical early period of his freedom; and if he commits another crime, society is always put to the trouble and expense involved in his apprehension and conviction before it can again send him to an institution. Thus, society is much better protected when prisoners are paroled than when they are unconditionally released.

2. Parole permits an administrative agency to decide when an offender should be released. The theory of parole is based upon the assumption that such an agency, which has an opportunity to study the offender during his institutionalization, is in a better position than the sentencing judge to decide the exact time of release in each case. It is true that many

---

[3] Federal Bureau of Prisons, *National Prisoner Statistics,* No. 33 (Dec., 1963), Tables 1, 6.

[4] See Chapter 19.

offenders are ultimately discharged at the termination of their sentences regardless of the action of the parole agency; but even in these cases it would be better to have a period of conditional release, during which the individual's activities could be restricted by supervisory methods, than to have no transitional period whatsoever after release.[5]

3. Parole reduces the period of institutionalization. Since many correctional institutions still do little to rehabilitate offenders and may actually provide opportunities for further training in crime, parole may be a very great advantage in many cases. Besides, there is the tendency for even the best institutions, with their rules, regulations, and routine, to deprive inmates of their initiative and self-confidence, qualities which they must have if they are to adjust successfully in the outside world. The longer an offender remains in an institution, the greater this tendency becomes. Parole can prevent the loss of such qualities or can help to restore them in cases where they have been lost.

4. Parole makes it possible to release an offender at the time when he is mentally and emotionally ready to return to the community. Prison authorities and guards recognize that there is always such a time in every inmate's life, and that if he is not released when it arrives, the possibility of his committing another crime after release may be increased.

5. The parole officer can exert an influence for the prevention of delinquency and crime. Since he must become intimately acquainted with the parolee's family and neighborhood, he is in a position to detect and reduce the causes of these problems.

6. Parolees have the opportunity to support themselves and their dependents, thus relieving the state of this responsibility, and to make restitution to the victims of their crimes.

7. It costs less to keep an offender on parole than to maintain him in a correctional institution. While economy should not be the primary consideration in granting parole, it certainly cannot be disregarded when all other circumstances indicate that he should be so handled.

OBJECTIONS TO PAROLE

The opponents of parole argue that it permits politically influential offenders to reduce their sentences and thus avoid the full impact of their punishment, that it opens the door to the peddling of favors to those who can buy their freedom, that it lets naïve and maudlin "do-gooders" pamper and coddle criminals, that it frustrates and disillusions the public, who

[5] On October 9, 1933, the American Parole Association adopted a declaration of principles in which it stated that all offenders leaving correctional institutions should be released on parole. See *Journal of Criminal Law and Criminology*, XXIV (Nov.–Dec., 1933), 788–93.

want to see offenders receive the punishment that they deserve, that it shatters respect for the law and decreases the deterrent effect of punishment, and that it liberates dangerous criminals and exposes the community to their violence and murderous acts. But these objections are not fatal, and they can be stripped of whatever weight they may have by the appointment of competent, honest, and responsible parole boards, and by the careful selection and adequate supervision of parolees. When this is done, the welfare of both the individual and society can be considered and balanced to the best interests of all concerned.

ADMINISTRATION OF PAROLE

The administration of parole differs from state to state in the United States, but since we have such a variety of social conditions and customs, it appears that much diversity of administration is required to meet the present needs of the country. The administration of parole involves two major functions. The first is a semijudicial one and has to do with the granting and revoking of paroles. The second is entirely administrative in nature and has to do with the supervision and guidance of parolees. Since these two functions are so closely related, it is desirable that they be performed by the same agency, and this is the arrangement that prevails in most states.

In general, there are three types of agencies administering parole in the United States. They are governors, institutional boards, and central boards. At the time of the *Attorney General's Survey of Release Procedures,* the results of which were published in 1939, the governors had the sole power to grant parole in sixteen states. In most of these states the governor was assisted by an advisor or an advisory board. Today some states still give the governors the power to grant parole, although he exercises this power with the assistance of some kind of board. The institutional boards that function in various states are partly or entirely composed of members of institutional staffs.

All evidence points to the fact that central boards, composed of full-time members, are the best type of administrative agency in the field of parole. An agency of this type can devote all of its time to parole work, establish uniform standards and practices throughout a state, and handle all cases in all institutions in the same way without being unduly influenced by problems of institutional administration. It can be more adequately protected from political pressure than the governor, and it is less inclined than an institutional board to employ parole as a mere reward for good behavior in the maintenance of prison discipline or as a method to relieve congestion in an overcrowded institution.[6] The trend during the

[6] *Attorney General's Survey,* pp. 45–47, 75.

past few decades has been toward the creation of central boards, and this type of agency has been adopted by most states, although in some of these there are also institutional boards.[7]

However, it is a debatable question whether a central parole board should be located in a state department, for example, in a correctional or welfare department, or whether it should be an independent agency which is not part of any department. The major argument in favor of having an independent agency is that it insures freedom of the board from political or other improper influences and from interference by other agencies. But those who would place the parole board in some department insist that the best guarantee for the independence of the board lies not in its location, but in the appointment of personnel who have the integrity and courage to do their work without fear or favor, and that unless the board is part of a state department, the necessary coordination between institutional correction and parole work cannot be effected. There is general agreement, however, that regardless of where the parole board is located, close contact must be maintained between it and the correctional institutions, and that use must be made of the experience and knowledge of institutional officials in the selection and supervision of parolees.

Parole boards are usually appointed by the governor. They should be large enough to insure thorough deliberation and yet small enough to expedite administrative activity.[8] Most central boards have three members, and it is not advisable to have fewer than this number. In the selection of parole board members, the chief objective of legislators has been to prevent the domination of the board by any one political party. Although this is desirable, it is also important to have well-qualified parole officials, a matter which unfortunately has not been given adequate statutory recognition in many states. It is generally agreed that a parole board should be composed of full-time members who are appointed by the governor for long terms, paid adequate salaries, qualified for their positions by character, personality, education, training, and experience, and supported by sufficient clerical and field personnel.[9] Thus far, however, such boards have been established in only a few states, and they cannot be justified in some of the smaller ones that have very few

[7] *Probation and Parole Directory* (New York: National Council on Crime and Delinquency, 1963).

[8] Killinger, p. 370.

[9] The *Standard Probation and Parole Act,* published by the National Probation and Parole Association in 1955, provides that the board of parole should be composed of three full-time members appointed by the governor for staggered terms of six years, and that the members should not be removed except for disability, inefficiency, neglect of duty or malfeasance in office (Art. II, Sec. 3). See also *Parole in Principle and Practice: A Manual and Report* (New York: National Probation and Parole Association, 1957), pp. 75–78.

prisoners and parolees. In the latter case a feasible plan is to appoint a full-time parole commissioner and to provide assistance for him by having a part-time parole board composed of qualified citizens who are paid for their services at a *per diem* rate. In some states the same administrative agency grants both pardons and paroles. This is often justified in the interests of economy, and there is nothing inherently wrong in this arrangement; but the two procedures should not be confused. Acts of executive clemency should be limited to cases where an injustice must be corrected or a hardship relieved.[10]

In many states and in the federal system, the supervision of parolees and probationers is combined under the same administrative agency. This practice is a debatable one and has been criticized on the ground that probation officers should be acceptable to the court and subject to its authority since they must work so closely with it. Its advocates, however, argue that it has proved practicable and desirable where it has been introduced, that the supervisory duties in both probation and parole are about the same, and that it promotes efficiency by permitting better distribution of supervisory officers throughout the state.[11] Some of those who advocate this combination believe that since children and adults require different kinds of care, juvenile probationers and parolees should not be placed under the same agency that has jurisdiction over adults.[12] Still others contend that the selection of probationers and parolees as well as their supervision should be placed under the authority of a single state agency, but the preponderance of opinion is opposed to this and in favor of letting the authority to select probationers remain with the courts.

CALIFORNIA ADULT AUTHORITY

In 1944 California reorganized her prison system and established an Adult Authority composed of three members appointed by the governor.[13]

The primary responsibility of this agency was the administration of parole, but it was also given other broad powers so that it might help to coordinate the various steps in the process of rehabilitation from the time

[10] *Attorney General's Survey*, pp. 52–54; Sol Rubin, Henry Weihofen, George Edwards, Simon Rosenzweig, *The Law of Criminal Correction* (St. Paul, Minn.: West Publishing Co., 1963), pp. 593, 594.

[11] *Attorney General's Survey*, pp. 65, 66; Robert M. Hill, "State Administration of Adult Probation and Parole," *Yearbook, 1942* (New York: National Probation Association, 1942), pp. 237–50.

[12] David Dressler, *Probation and Parole* (New York: Columbia University Press, 1951), pp. 12–15.

[13] California Adult Authority, *Laws Relating to the Adult Authority Based on the California Penal Code* (Sacramento, Calif.: Department of Corrections, 1952); California Department of Corrections, *Biennial Report, Period Ending December 1, 1952*, p. 9.

of commitment, through institutional correction and community supervision, to final discharge from custody.[14] Critics of this plan, however, claimed that this attempted coordination was being secured at the cost of excessive centralization of authority and responsibility and that if adequate and competent personnel were provided, coordination could be achieved without the loss of an independent board of parole.

Time soon revealed that the Adult Authority had been given an excessive burden to bear. For example, during the two-year period from October 1, 1950, to September 30, 1952, "cases heard" increased 15.9 per cent and "approved institutional transfers" increased 37.3 per cent over the previous two-year period.[15] In order to enable the Adult Authority to carry its growing case load, its membership was increased from three to five and eventually to its present total of seven, and a staff of "hearing representatives" was assigned to the agency to assist it in the study of cases and the interviewing of prisoners. Furthermore, its administrative functions which overlapped with those of the department of corrections were eliminated so that the Adult Authority is now only a paroling agency, although it also acts as an advisory pardon board.[16]

In California, the criminal court merely imposes the sentence as prescribed by law on felons but does not fix their exact term of imprisonment. If the court places the prisoner on probation, suspends his sentence, or grants him a new trial, it retains control over him; but if it sentences an adult male to imprisonment for a felony, he comes under the jurisdiction of the Adult Authority.[17] After he has been in prison for at least six months, during which time he is examined, tested, and studied by a diagnostic clinic called a "guidance center," his case is reviewed by the Adult Authority and his term of imprisonment is then fixed. The Adult Authority may determine or redetermine the length of the sentence as often as it considers this necessary, both for the welfare of the individual and the protection of society. However, it cannot extend the time to be served beyond the maximum or reduce it below the minimum prescribed by the law.[18]

[14] California Adult Authority, *Principles, Policies, and Program* (Sacramento, Calif.: Department of Corrections, 1952), p. 4; Walter A. Gordon, "California Adult Authority," *Proceedings of the American Prison Association, 1947*, p. 215.

[15] California Department of Corrections, *Biennial Report, 1952*, p. 12. The student is referred to the discussion of the Youth Authority, which faces problems similar to those that have troubled the Adult Authority. See Chapter 16.

[16] *The Youth and Adult Corrections Agency* (Sacramento: California State Printing Office, no date).

[17] In California, the Youth Authority grants parole to juveniles and youthful offenders, and the Board of Trustees of the California Institution for Women performs the same function for female adult offenders.

[18] California Adult Authority, *Schedule of Felonies and Punishments* (Sacramento, Calif.: Department of Corrections, 1951).

In determining the length of the sentence, the Adult Authority takes into consideration the following factors:

1. The nature of the crime.
2. The deterrent effect of punishment.
3. The equalization of punishment to prevent wide variations in the penalties inflicted upon offenders who are convicted of the same crime committed under similar circumstances.
4. Previous criminal record.
5. Prison behavior and attitude.
6. The protection of society.[19]

THE PAROLE STAFF

The effectiveness of a parole agency is largely dependent upon the competence of its parole staff. This staff should include at least a chief parole officer, sufficient parole officers to carry on the work of investigation and supervision of parolees without excessive case loads,[20] and an adequate clerical force. In some of the larger parole systems one group of parole officers makes the investigations while another group conducts the supervision. However, it is preferable for the parole officer to do both the investigation and the supervision so that two officers will not have to become acquainted with the same parolee. The case load that a parole officer can carry depends on such factors as the degree of supervision required, geographical spread in the load, available transportation facilities, and extent to which visits must be made outside of working hours; but it is generally believed that an officer engaged in supervision should not carry more than fifty cases at one time and that this maximum case load should be reduced by at least three cases for every pre-parole or parole investigation that the officer makes per month.[21]

Members of the parole staff should be appointed from lists of eligibles established by competitive examinations and should have security of tenure as long as their performance of duty and conduct are satisfactory. They should be expected to meet as high professional and technical standards as possible, and if the parole officers lack previous training and experience in the parole field, they should be given an intensive course of training when they enter the service. It is also desirable that they receive further training during their service, including periodical refresher courses. At present some states are not financially able to recruit

[19] California Adult Authority, *Principles, Policies, and Program*, pp. 8, 9.

[20] The duties of a parole officer are very much like those of a probation officer, and so the student should now review the examination of the latter's duties that was presented in Chapter 19.

[21] *Manual of Correctional Standards* (New York: The American Correctional Association, 1959), pp. 541, 542.

a parole staff on a high level of education and professional training, but every state can maintain high standards of general intelligence, conscientiousness, integrity, sincerity, capacity for hard work, and personality. As public appreciation and support of good parole work increases, a state can gradually raise its educational and training standards for parole officers. However, no state can persist in keeping salaries of parole workers on a low level and expect to maintain a satisfactory parole system. Salaries must be high enough to attract and hold qualified workers in competition with the fields of education, social work, and law enforcement, and regular promotions and salary increases should be provided for on a merit basis.[22]

In most states today there are not enough parole officers. Besides, in general, salaries are too low, case loads are too heavy, and the selection of parole officers is too frequently made on a political basis without consideration of their qualifications. This means that much of the supervision in parole work is perfunctory or grossly inadequate. And although religious or private organizations (like the Catholic church, the Salvation Army, Jewish welfare agencies, and prisoners' aid societies) and private citizens, serving in the capacity of sponsors or volunteers, do render invaluable service in assisting and guiding parolees, their work should never be considered a satisfactory substitute for that of a professional, full-time parole officer. It cannot be repeated too often that qualified personnel are absolutely essential if good parole work is to be done.

SELECTION OF PAROLEES

In the selection of parolees the parole agency must operate within the limitations of the criminal code and of the sentence imposed in each case. The codes of most states include various statutory restrictions. Among these are provisions that make persons ineligible for parole if they are convicted of certain crimes, such as treason, murder, or rape, of if they are habitual offenders. In addition, usually a prisoner is eligible for parole only after he has served a specified portion of his definite or indeterminate sentence. The law should give broad discretionary powers to the parole agency and should impose upon it only such restrictions as are necessary to protect the rights of the prisoner and the parolee on the one hand, and the moral code and the welfare of society on the other.[23]

Every offender should be considered automatically for parole when he becomes eligible, although this does not mean that he should be granted parole at that time. In most states prisoners who are eligible for con-

[22] *Ibid.*, pp. 538–41.
[23] For a discussion of statutory limitations on the release of prisoners, see also Chapters 19 and 27.

sideration make application for a hearing or interview before the parole board. In their applications they set forth the reasons why they believe parole should be granted to them and outline tentative plans for future residence and employment. Both the institution and the board of parole, with its parole officers and other members of its staff, should participate in the preparation of the case for the parole hearing. This preparation should involve the investigation of the inmate and his background and the compilation of all the important information regarding him, including a basic history, a survey of available social, medical, psychiatric, and psychological findings, an analysis of the reports and records of his institutional conduct, and a summary of recommendations.[24] Wise parole authorities will always take into consideration the advice and recommendations of prison officials, who are in a position to observe closely the offender's behavior over a period of time. Parole agencies, unfortunately, often disregard this important source of information.

The thoroughness with which the investigation of the inmate is made will determine the effectiveness of the parole hearing, and members of the board should carefully study all the facts that are thereby made available before the hearing of the case begins. Yet, despite the importance of these prerequisites of good parole work, they are still lacking in many states. The hearing itself should be conducted in an atmosphere of objectivity, thoughtful consideration, and sympathetic understanding. The prisoner should always appear before the board during the hearing, and every effort should be made to put him at his ease; but levity and aimless conversation should be avoided. Much can be done to reduce the tensions and insecurity of the inmate by explaining the nature of parole to him and by clarifying what it does, and does not, require of the parolee. Although a personal interview may be misleading, it does provide the board with an opportunity to come face to face with the inmate, to examine and observe him, to gain additional insights into his personality, and to consider with him certain aspects of the case that need further exploration. When it appears that the interview has accomplished its purpose, it should be brought to a clear-cut and decisive conclusion and not permitted to drag on to the discomfort and embarrassment of both the inmate and members of the board.

The hearing should not be conducted as a retrial of the case, and the procedure should not be legalistic. It may be necessary for attorneys,

[24] Killinger, pp. 372, 373; Leonard Logan, "Release Procedures," *Encyclopedia of Criminology* (New York: The Philosophical Library, 1949), pp. 426, 427; *Parole in Principle and Practice: A Manual and Report,* pp. 79–89; *Manual of Correctional Standards,* pp. 544, 545. The parole hearing should be differentiated from the initial interview. The latter should be held within the first twelve months after the admission of the inmate to the institution and is designed to acquaint him with the board and its procedures.

relatives, and witnesses to participate, but their presence should be restricted to those cases where it is necessary to insure a just decision. The general public and the press should be excluded, although complete, permanent records should be kept of parole hearings and made available for legitimate public inspection, and the inmate should be given the right to petition for a judicial review of the board's decision in his case. In this manner may be avoided the opposite dangers of excessive secrecy and undue publicity, either of which may threaten the welfare of both the inmate and the public.[25]

In its selection of parolees the board must decide whether the applicant for parole is mentally, emotionally, and physically ready to return to the community and take up life there without endangering the welfare of the public and violating its feelings, and whether he can measure up to the requirements of parole and benefit by the opportunities it affords. And here, as in the case of probation, the public will not long countenance the release of persons that in its opinion should be kept imprisoned even though the board may consider them good risks for parole.[26]

The procedure used in the selection of parolees is often superficial and almost meaningless. The parole agency may merely review the record of the crime for which the prisoner was convicted and his conduct record while in prison, and on the basis of this arrive at a decision without even interviewing the inmate. Many parole agencies have such heavy loads that they can give only a few minutes to each case. Emotional appeals by relatives and friends, the legalistic and special pleading of attorneys, and the presence of the public and the press are too often permitted to destroy the objectivity so important in parole administration.

Studies indicate that inmates are more likely to be successful on parole if they are persons (1) of mature years or past adolescence, (2) who began their criminal careers fairly late in life, (3) who are married rather than single, divorced, or separated, (4) who have had little or no previous criminal history, (5) who have been well behaved during their incarceration, and (6) who have good work habits and capabilities.[27] In arriving at its decision the board should take this evidence into consideration, but its final action in any particular case should come only after a careful weighing and balancing of the positive and negative factors revealed by an objective and intensive investigation of that case.

However, prisoners are sometimes also required to fulfill certain specific conditions before they are paroled, even though they can qualify for parole in every other way. Thus, some states will not parole a prisoner

---

[25] Wilbur LaRoe, *Parole with Honor* (Princeton, N.J.: Princeton University Press, 1939), pp. 110–21; Killinger, p. 374; *Attorney General's Survey*, pp. 163–73.
[26] Dressler, p. 51.
[27] *Ibid.*, p. 76. See also *Attorney General's Survey*, pp. 488–92.

who has a detainer filed against him, but will compel him to serve the maximum term of his sentence. A detainer is a warrant filed by a competent officer against a person already in custody, authorizing the institution to hold him after the completion of his present term of imprisonment and thus insure his availability for the authority which has issued the detainer. States that refuse to parole for this reason take the position that a prisoner is not likely to succeed on parole if he must submit to another trial or enter another prison. However, most states will not delay a person's parole because there is a detainer against him, but will "parole in custody," that is, they will parole him and then turn him over to the custody of the authority that has issued the detainer. Institutions invariably recognize such a warrant and notify the authority which has filed it of the impending release of the prisoner. They do this not only out of courtesy to the other jurisdiction but also for the practical reason that they want their own detainers to be recognized.[28]

It is obvious that detainers constitute a serious problem for both the prisoner who appears ready to return to normal living in the community and for the institution that has sought to rehabilitate him. Further imprisonment may undo whatever the institution has been able to accomplish and actually unfit him for eventual release. And the situation is greatly aggravated by the irresponsible practice of filing detainers against prisoners because of the mere possibility that they may be the ones who are wanted. Since the official who files such detainers knows that the prisoners will be held until they are called for, he often does nothing to investigate the validity of the charges or to initiate action on them. Consequently this kind of detainer may remain on a man's prison record for a long time even though he is entirely innocent, interfering with his rehabilitation and eventually preventing his parole.

Various methods might be used to solve this problem.[29] For example, when a person is charged with crimes by several prosecuting officials within one state, all the charges should be consolidated and satisfied by a single prosecution. The problem is more difficult when a person is alleged to have committed crimes in different states. In this case he might be turned over to the jurisdiction in which he is charged with the most serious crime for which his conviction seems possible, with the understanding that if he is convicted therein, the other states will not thereafter file detainers against him. Then, if he is convicted, the judge might order a thorough presentence investigation of the case and after consultation with authorities in the other states might impose a penalty which is

---

[28] Garrett Heyns, "Detainers," *Encyclopedia of Criminology* (New York: The Philosophical Library, 1949), pp. 127–29.

[29] For a discussion of the problem of detainers, see the collection of articles in *Federal Probation*, IX (July–Sept., 1945), 3–18.

considered as adequate as the state's criminal code will permit in the punishment of a person convicted of the crime in question. If the prisoner is not convicted in the first jurisdiction, he might then be turned over to the one in which he is alleged to have committed his next most serious crime, and so on until he is convicted of some crime or acquitted of all the charges against him. An agreement for a solution of this kind might be contained in an interstate compact such as that which states have entered into with respect to the reciprocity in the supervision of proba-tioners and parolees. This compact might also include a provision that states should not require the return of a parole violator who has been serving a term of imprisonment in another state and is again eligible for parole, but should accept the recommendations of the authorities there and agree to a concurrent parole of the prisoner. In order to implement such compacts, the Interstate Commission on the Control of Crime might establish a service for the study of cases having interstate aspects, and its recommendations for an over-all disposition of these cases might then be used by judges to assist them in rendering their decisions. Although the question of how the problem of detainers should be solved is a controversial one—and the solution offered here does not pretend to cover all situations—it is generally agreed that some solution should be effected. No state should require a man to serve his maximum term simply because he has a detainer against him, and laws which make this mandatory should be repealed.[30]

Another specific condition which may be imposed as a prerequisite to parole is employment for the prisoner when he is released. Most states require such employment as a condition for parole, although some of these states make exceptions in certain cases. The securing of employ-ment for prisoners who are eligible for parole is one of the most difficult problems confronting parole authorities. If a prisoner is paroled without a job, the possibility of his relapsing into crime is considerably increased. On the other hand, where employment is made a rigid condition for parole, prisoners frequently resort to fictitious employment in order to qualify for parole, many prospective parolees have to be kept in prison for lack of jobs, employers may exploit parolees who are forced to accept any sort of job in order to be paroled, and parole officers must spend much of their time in finding work for parolees, some of whom might benefit psychologically if they secured their own jobs. There is no doubt that parole authorities should thoroughly investigate employment possi-bilities for all parolees and guard against fictitious employment and the exploitation of parolees. But it is also certain that they should not adhere

[30] Heyns, p. 129; *Parole in Principle and Practice: A Manual and Report*, pp. 113, 114. For an analysis of some of the legal aspects of detainers, see Rubin, Weihofen, Edwards, Rosenzweig, pp. 419–26.

rigidly to employment as a parole condition in all cases. As in many other phases of parole work, the answer to the question of employment must be found to a great extent in individualization of correction, rather than in rigid regulations that operate mechanically regardless of the circumstances in the case.[31]

The decision regarding parole should be made by the majority of the board or of a quorum of its membership. If the board decides to parole the prisoner, then the date of his release should be set within a reasonable length of time after the hearing so that the corrosive effects of prolonged waiting will not undermine his morale. If, however, the board does not parole him, then it should reconsider his case at least once a year thereafter until it does take such action.[32]

PAROLE PREDICTION

For many years various prediction tables have been constructed in an effort to provide parole agencies with a reliable guide in the selection of parolees. These tables are based upon an analysis of the different factors, such as the nature of the offense, the age of the offender, marital status, etc., which appear to be associated with either success or failure on parole. The assumption is that the chances of success on parole can be calculated on the basis of the extent to which the factors that have been associated with such success in the past are found to exist in any given case. One of the leading pioneers in this development was Professor E. W. Burgess, who in 1928 published the first study presenting a prediction table for the selection of parolees. Since then considerable refinement has been made in such tables, but as yet they have been put to use in only a few states.[33]

Parole prediction tables have been criticized on a number of different points. Important among these are the following:

1. It is not at all certain that the tables have used the most significant factors that have been associated with success and failure on parole. Perhaps all that they have done is to identify the most obvious factors and have missed the subtle but much more fundamental ones. The elusive factors, like attitudes, have not been successfully captured and

[31] *Attorney General's Survey*, pp. 179–82, 185, 186.

[32] *Model Penal Code, Proposed Official Draft* (Philadelphia: The American Law Institute, May 4, 1962), Sections 305.6–305.10.

[33] Elio D. Monachesi, "Prediction of Criminal Behavior," *Encyclopedia of Criminology* (New York: The Philosophical Library, 1949), pp. 324–30; Andrew A. Bruce, Ernest W. Burgess, Albert J. Harno, and John Landesco, "A Study of the Indeterminate Sentence and Parole in the State of Illinois," *Journal of Criminal Law and Criminology*, XIX, No. 1, Part 2 (May, 1928), 5–306; Lloyd E. Ohlin, *Selection for Parole* (New York: Russell Sage Foundation, 1951).

appraised. Besides, each factor does not operate alone, but in interaction with others in a pattern of causation which is different in each case. The existing tables, despite efforts to overcome this weakness, do not reflect the subtle, dynamic character of the parole process.

2. The records upon which the tables are based are inadequate and incomplete. Sometimes this makes it difficult to determine whether a given factor exists in a man's background. Furthermore, not all violations are detected, and therefore factors may receive false weights on the prediction scale. Thus, if 55 per cent of the men with factor A are known to have violated parole when actually 75 per cent of them violated parole, factor A is not correctly represented in the scale. Besides, the records show only the gross behavior of parolees. A man may successfully serve his term of parole and yet be a personal failure and even a social menace. So critics have questioned the validity of the concepts "success" and "failure" that are used in the tables.

3. The tables do not provide a satisfactory standard for selecting parolees. No factor bears a 100 per cent correlation with outcome on parole. On the basis of the tables no one can say that simply because an inmate possesses factor A, B, or C he will inevitably fail on parole. One can only say that there is a certain possibility that a particular prisoner will fail on parole. But where should the parole agency draw the line? Should it grant parole to all who have fifty chances out of a hundred to succeed, or only to those who have better than eighty chances out of a hundred to succeed?

And what about those whose chances on parole are not good? Should they be kept in prison until they have served the maximum term, even though this may actually lessen the possibility of their adjusting successfully after release? The tables can give no answer to these questions.

4. A prediction table reflects the parole conditions which existed for a sample of parolees in a particular place at a certain time. Since, say critics, the prerelease program, supervision, economic factors, and other parole conditions continuously change, routine readjustment of prediction tables is necessary if they are to retain their alleged usefulness.

5. Prediction tables do not give sufficient consideration to the seriousness of the offense and the reaction of the community to it. The parole board, however, must consider not only the readiness of the prisoner for parole but also the effect of his release on others and the moral code. Some prisoners, therefore, should not be paroled even though they receive high scores on the prediction table.

6. It is a generally accepted fact that every prisoner reaches a point in his sentence when he is a better parole risk than at any other time. If he is kept beyond this point, his chances for success on parole are likely to decrease. But parole prediction tables do not tell us when to parole,

but only attempt to reveal what the chances of success or failure are after a prisoner has been released.

7. Although prediction tables may rate the past and the present with some degree of accuracy, they do not evaluate the immediate future. Indeed, they cannot. Who can tell what the reaction of the prisoner will be to the fact of parole? How can we evaluate the influence of this parole officer as contrasted with that one? Or of this job instead of that one? Or of this friend instead of that one? Or of this boarding house instead of that one? Intangibles such as these defy our most valiant efforts to reduce man's experiences to a quantitative basis.[34]

Undoubtedly these weaknesses have contributed to the reluctance of parole agencies to use prediction tables, but perhaps more important has been the distaste of the average official for statistics of any kind. When the tables have been sufficiently refined they may provide an important instrument for parole agencies, but even if they are perfected, it does not appear that they can ever replace a detailed investigation of each case. The most hardened criminal may have "gotten it out of his system" and become ready for parole despite his past record, and a young inmate may simply not be old enough to have a "bad record," even though he is a poor parole risk.

In short, each case is unique, and each individual must be studied as an individual. Prediction tables may furnish clues, but there is no reason to believe that they will ever be efficient tools of selection if used alone. In fact, one may ask whether tables of any kind are necessary if carefully prepared case studies are made available, and whether prediction tables might not give parole agencies a false sense of security, discouraging the use of case studies and causing officials to lose sight of the prisoner as a living and changing personality.

PRERELEASE PROGRAM

Although the preparation of a prisoner for release should begin as soon as possible after his conviction, this preparation should be intensified and brought to a head in a prerelease program. This involves work not only with the prospective parolee but also with the community so that it will be prepared to receive him when he is released. The parole agency may require that the plan for the prerelease program of an inmate be completed before the hearing, or it may grant parole on the condition that a satisfactory plan be completed before his release. All aspects of the plan should be directed toward bridging the gap between the institu-

[34] For a symposium on parole prediction tables, see *Crime and Delinquency*, VIII (July, 1962), 215–38. This entire issue is devoted to articles on parole prediction tables. See also Norman S. Hayner, "Why Do Parole Boards Lag in the Use of Prediction Scores?" *The Pacific Sociological Review*, I (Fall, 1958), 73–76.

tion and the community so that the forces of both are joined together in contributing to the normal adjustment of the parolee after his release.[35]

During this program the inmate should be put into the best possible health. He must be supplied with adequate shoes and clothing and sufficient money to cover his initial expenses. Desirable housing and a wholesome family situation should be awaiting him in the community, and usually suitable employment for which he is qualified must be secured. Sometimes it is advisable to enlist the services of a responsible private citizen to act as a sponsor (parole adviser),[36] although the supervisory services of a volunteer should never be considered a satisfactory substitute for those of a competent parole officer; and an effort should be made to encourage a few of the parolee's friends to lend him a helping hand when the "going gets rough" after his release. Since correction during parole is but an extension of institutional correction, the inmate's programs of education, recreation, religion, and vocational training should be continued, when this is deemed necessary, after his release.[37]

Psychological problems are the greatest ones that confront persons who are leaving correctional institutions. Inmates must be prepared to accept the difficulties of adjustment in society, to assume the responsibilities of law-abiding behavior, and to take the initiative in carving out for themselves acceptable positions in the community. They must be encouraged to think of themselves as law-abiding persons and as supporters of law-enforcement agencies. Individual and group counseling can be especially helpful in solving these problems. Prerelease courses have also proved valuable in many prisons. These are designed to answer the questions of inmates leaving prison, to help them meet the practical problems of life in the community, and thereby to reduce their fears, worries, and anxieties. These courses should also include instruction regarding the meaning of parole, the reasons for parole supervision, relationships with parole officers, the rules and regulations that must be observed while on parole, etc. Parole officers may participate in these courses. This gives them an excellent opportunity to establish good rapport with their prospective parolees.[38]

In addition to the prerelease procedures already mentioned, other provisions are sometimes made to pave the way for the inmate's transition to life in the community. Among these are more freedom within the institution, increased mail and visiting privileges, the opportunity to wear

---

[35] *Handbook on Pre-release Preparation in Correctional Institutions* (New York: The American Prison Association, 1950), pp. 11–28; Reed Cozart, "Release Preparation of the Prisoner," *Federal Probation*, XVI (Mar., 1952), 13–16.

[36] Edwin B. Cunningham, "The Role of the Parole Adviser," *Federal Probation*, XV (Dec., 1951), 43–46.

[37] *Handbook on Pre-release Preparation in Correctional Institutions*, pp. 33–42.

[38] *Ibid.*, pp. 29–32, 43–51.

the kind of clothing and shoes that the inmate will have when he is released, and permission to work during the day in homes, stores, factories, or on farms in the vicinity of the institution and to return to the institution at night. In some correctional systems the preparation for release takes place in facilities especially designed for this purpose. These may be honor cell blocks within the institution, or minimum custodial facilities, separation centers, and honor camps outside its walls.[39]

Alert institutional and parole staffs should also cooperate in utilizing all the available resources in the community in order to provide the parolee with additional opportunities for assistance, guidance, and development after his release. Important among these resources are employment offices, welfare agencies, recreation centers, churches, libraries, adult education facilities, labor unions, and prisoners' aid societies.[40]

CONDITIONS OF PAROLE

Various conditions, sometimes specified by law and sometimes by administrative agencies, are imposed upon all parolees at the time of release, and these serve as minimum standards of good conduct for the guidance of the parolee. Violation of any of these conditions renders the parolee liable to reimprisonment without a court hearing. The conditions vary from state to state, but the ones most commonly imposed require that the parolee abstain from the use of intoxicants, submit written or personal reports at stated intervals, not violate any law, not associate with other parolees or ex-convicts, not change his address or employment without permission, and not own or operate an automobile, marry, or leave the state unless he has the consent of the parole authorities.[41]

In general such conditions are intended to protect society and to assist the parolee. Discriminating enforcement of them by understanding parole officers need not constitute unnecessary hardship. However, the mere enforcement of conditions should not be considered adequate supervision. Such supervision must be aimed ultimately at inducing the parolee to become a law-abiding citizen, and to accomplish this a close relationship between the officer and the parolee is necessary. But this is possible only if the rules governing the parolee are flexible and elastic enough to permit the exercise of discretion in each case.[42]

[39] *Ibid.*, pp. 57–61.

[40] See also Chapter 27; for some job-finding techniques for the parolee, see Arthur F. Lykke, *Parolees and Payrolls* (Springfield, Ill.: Charles C. Thomas, Publisher, 1957).

[41] *Attorney General's Survey*, pp. 212, 213; *Model Penal Code, Proposed Official Draft*, Section 305.13.

[42] Since the principles which should govern the application of the conditions of parole are the same as those which we have already discussed with respect to probation, the student is referred to this discussion in Chapter 19.

SUPERVISION OF PAROLEES

The supervision of parolees is designed to protect society, whose interests are always paramount in the handling of all offenders, and to assist and guide the parolee. While the conditions of parole must be enforced, a positive approach to the problems of supervision can largely obviate the necessity for repressive methods and disciplinary measures. For the parolee the period of supervision should be one of readjustment from prison life to a normal law-abiding existence. It is the parole officer's duty to establish a personal and confidential relationship with the parolee, and on the basis of this, to develop a definite program of correction. For this he will need to discover and utilize all the resources of the family and the community. But at the same time the parole officer must make it quite clear that he expects the parolee to abide by all the conditions of his parole and to assume definite responsibilities in the solution of his own problems. Besides, if the circumstances of the case demand it, he must be ready to use his authority as a law-enforcement officer and act swiftly and courageously to protect the interests of the community. Thus, here, as in the field of probation, supervision is individualized correction in the community setting.[43]

In order to enforce the conditions of parole and to carry out its objectives, the parole officer must maintain close contact with the parolee, the members of his family, and the community in which he lives. This entire pattern of relationships should be developed so that it becomes a constructive force in the life of the parolee. However, as the process of parole progresses satisfactorily, supervision can be gradually relaxed by requiring less frequent reports and visits on the part of the parolee and by reducing the restrictions imposed in such things as types of employment, travel, and the operation of vehicles.[44]

Formerly out-of-state parole, where it was permitted, meant no supervision. But now interstate compacts, which are in effect in all states, make it possible for parolees to be transferred from one state to another and at the same time remain under supervision. Out-of-state parole is frequently advisable so as to permit the parolee to join his family, to secure suitable employment, or to avoid the undesirable influence of former associates in crime.

[43] The fundamental principles of supervision are the same in both probation and parole work. For a more complete discussion of them, see Chapter 19. See also G. I. Giardini, *The Parole Process* (Springfield, Ill.: Charles C. Thomas, Publisher, 1959), pp. 240–345.

[44] *Attorney General's Survey*, pp. 234, 235, 530, 531.

TERMINATION OF PAROLE

The period of parole, which cannot extend beyond the maximum limit of the sentence, may be terminated either by the discharge of the parolee or by the revocation of parole. In some states the time of discharge is specified by statute. In others, the maximum parole period is provided for by law, but the parole authorities have the power to grant final discharge before the maximum period elapses. In a third group of states authority is given to the parole agency to use its discretion in determining the length of the parole period in each case. It should be clear that the rehabilitation of convicted criminals is not a matter of a fixed period of time, and that the effectiveness of parole may be seriously impaired where excessive legal restrictions prevent the supervising authority from retaining custody of the parolee until such time as his attitudes, habits, and condition are, at the very least, improved. Yet, in many jurisdictions statutory limitations and administrative regulations so curtail the duration of the parole period that no effective work can be done before the parolee is eligible for final discharge. If parole is to exert the influence that it should, the supervising authorities must be empowered to exercise wide discretion in modifying or extending the period of parole supervision according to the needs of the individual case. Obviously, parole should not be terminated until it is reasonably certain that the parolee has made a proper adjustment to society.

In general, final discharge from parole has the same effect as the expiration of sentence, and consequently, when it is granted, the offender cannot again be imprisoned on the sentence from which he has been paroled. An important question raised by the final discharge of the parolee is its effect upon his legal status. Civil rights, which are lost in most states when persons are convicted of certain crimes, are restored automatically in some states when parole is granted. However, in others they are restored only when the person is discharged from parole, while in still another group of states they can be regained, if at all, only by a pardon from the governor. Since environmental conditions should be made as nearly normal as possible for the discharged parolee in order to facilitate his adjustment, his civil rights should be restored to him not later than the time of his final discharge from parole.[45]

Parole may be revoked either because the parolee has violated a law or in the judgment of the parole agency has failed to abide by the conditions of his parole. In practice parole agencies usually permit some technical violations without revoking parole, but when they do revoke parole, the offender may be returned to an institution without a court trial, for

[45] *Ibid.*, pp. 303, 304, 536, 537.

in such matters the decision of the parole agency is final. However, in cases where the parolee has committed a new crime, he must later stand trial for it. When it is decided that a person has violated his parole, a warrant for his arrest is issued and served if he can be located. Although parole authorities are not, as a rule, required to hold hearings on the question of parole violation, they usually do so, and this is considered good practice since it affords an opportunity for all the facts concerning the alleged violation to be presented and for any mistake or bias on the part of the parole officer to be corrected. No uniform procedure is followed by the states in their treatment of parole violators, but in most of them some penalty in addition to mere re-incarceration is imposed. Thus, the offender may be declared ineligible for another parole and required to serve the unexpired portion of a definite sentence or the maximum term of an indeterminate sentence, as the case may be. Furthermore, he may be deprived of the privilege of earning "good time." Good practice dictates that each case be handled on the basis of the individual's needs rather than automatically in accordance with certain legal specifications.[46]

EVALUATION OF THE EFFECTIVENESS OF PAROLE

But these questions persist: How effective is parole as a rehabilitative process? What do the records tell us about the results of parole work? The annual reports of parole departments throughout the United States indicate that an average of about 20 to 30 per cent fail on parole. These reports customarily state the violation rate as the ratio between paroles granted during the year and paroles violated during the same year. The adequacy of this method of computing parole violations has been questioned, since a large number of persons remain on parole for many years. The *Attorney General's Survey of Release Procedures* reported an analysis of the case histories of 90,664 adult male felons whose parole began and terminated within the period of January 1, 1928, to December 31, 1935. This analysis showed that less than 28 per cent violated their paroles.[47]

Other studies of parole have shown higher rates of violation. The Gluecks in an analysis of the careers of 474 male offenders paroled from the Massachusetts reformatory found that 55.3 per cent were officially known to have violated their paroles.[48] A study by Professor E. W. Burgess in Illinois indicated that 40 per cent violated their parole and

[46] *Ibid.*, pp. 533–36. For the recommendations of the American Law Institute regarding parole violators, see *Model Penal Code, Proposed Official Draft*, Sections 6.10, 305.15, 305.16, 305.17. See also Rubin, Weihofen, Edwards, Rosenzweig, pp. 558–66.
[47] *Attorney General's Survey*, pp. 311, 312, 541.
[48] Sheldon and Eleanor T. Glueck, *500 Criminal Careers* (New York: Alfred A. Knopf, Inc., 1930), pp. 167–69.

were returned to prison,[49] while an analysis of the records of parolees in Pennsylvania revealed that 31.9 per cent of them failed on parole,[50] and an investigation of released offenders in New York showed that 35 per cent violated their parole.[51] A more recent study by Austin MacCormick showed that about 35 per cent of a group of parolees in New York State failed on parole.[52]

Although such studies as these make it appear that the reports of parole departments give too optimistic a picture of parole, they have also revealed the difficulty of securing an accurate evaluation of its effectiveness in the United States. As in the field of probation, the investigator here is confronted with the fact that standards and practices are not uniform throughout the country. Parole laws, eligibility for parole, the selection of parolees, the efficacy of supervision, the criteria used in judging parole failure—all these differ from state to state. Furthermore, here too not all violations are detected and recorded, and so one does not have all the facts by which to judge the effectiveness of parole. And again, as in the case of probation, one may question whether the rate of violation by itself is an adequate measure of effectiveness. Is it not necessary to go beyond this and ask: Is parole more or less effective than the unconditional and unsupervised release of prisoners at the termination of their sentences? But in order for this comparison to be valid, the offenders who are being handled by the two methods must have about the same characteristics. Otherwise variations in the postrelease behavior may be attributed to differences in the personalities of the offenders rather than to differences in the efficacy of correction. In practice, however, offenders who are handled by these two methods do not tend to have the same characteristics. Thus, the tendency is to keep in prison until the termination of their sentences only those who are judged least likely to succeed after release. Therefore, it is exceedingly difficult, if not impossible, to put parole to this further test.

The use of the parole violation rate as a criterion for measuring the effectiveness of parole has been further criticized on the ground that it refers only to the period of parole and does not reflect the activity of the offender after his release from parole. Numerous studies have been con-

---

[49] See *Illinois Inquiry Commission Report,* "The Prison System in Illinois" (Springfield, 1937), p. 617.

[50] Leon T. Stern, "Twenty-one Years of Parole," *Prison World,* IX (Sept.–Oct., 1947), 22.

[51] David Dressler, "Parole Results," *Proceedings of the American Prison Association,* 1941, pp. 422, 423.

[52] Austin H. MacCormick, "Correctional Treatment of the Criminal," at Boulder, Colorado, Crime Conference, 1949. See proceedings, entitled "Crimes of Violence" (Boulder, 1950), p. 69. Cited by Harry Elmer Barnes and Negley K. Teeters, *New Horizons in Criminology* (New York: Prentice-Hall, Inc., 1951), p. 795.

ducted to discover what happens to persons after their discharge from parole. One of the most intensive of these was made by the Gluecks. In their study of a group of male offenders released from the Massachusetts reformatory, they found that almost 80 per cent of the 422 men who were involved committed offenses during the five-year period following the expiration of their parole.[53]

As we explained in our discussion of probation, the studies of the postrelease behavior of offenders do throw additional light on their careers, but the great complexity of the influences operating in the lives of human beings makes it inadvisable to use such studies as the sole basis for evaluating parole. Certainly no competent student of the problem would argue for the abolition of parole. Almost without exception criticism has been directed toward its modification and improvement rather than its elimination. As long as we release offenders from our institutions, we shall be confronted with the question of how this should be done. Common sense and hard experience indicate that eventually every offender who is released from an institution should be released conditionally. In the light of the facts the present practice of paroling the "most promising" and of unconditionally releasing the "bad risks" without supervision appears to be indefensible.

ESSENTIAL ELEMENTS OF A GOOD PAROLE SYSTEM

Since many of the aspects of parole in the United States have been critically examined in this chapter, it is now in order to summarize the essential elements of what is considered to be an adequate parole system. According to the American Correctional Association (formerly the American Prison Association), these include the following:

1. Complete freedom from improper control or influence, either political or otherwise.

2. Sufficient flexibility in the laws governing sentences and parole to permit the parole of an offender at the time when his release under supervision is in the best interests of society.

3. A parole board composed of members qualified by intelligence, training, and experience to weigh the complex problems of human behavior involved in parole decisions and having the patience and integrity required to render wise and just decisions.

4. A staff of supervisory and administrative personnel, parole officers, and clerks adequate in numbers to care for the case load of the parole system, composed of persons selected in accordance with high standards

[53] Glueck, p. 184. See also their *After-Conduct of Discharged Offenders* (London: Macmillan and Co., Ltd., 1945), pp. 31–41.

of ability, character, training, and experience, and appointed on a career-service basis.

5. An administrative structure within the framework of the state government that enables the parole system, without sacrifice of proper independence, to function in complete coordination with other departments and services, especially with the probation services, correctional institutions, and departments of health, mental hygiene, welfare, and public safety.

6. A parole procedure which makes provision for the orientation of the prisoner toward parole, the preparation of all pertinent data on each case for the parole board, the holding of a parole hearing based upon such data, the formulation of a satisfactory parole plan, and the release of the parolee under adequate supervision.

7. Operation within the correctional institution of a program which aims at utilizing the period of confinement for preparing the inmate physically, vocationally, mentally, and spiritually for his return to society, and which exerts intensive effort at the close of the term toward effecting his release under optimum conditions as far as he, his dependents, and the community are concerned.

8. A proper public attitude toward the parolee, so that he is given fair and helpful treatment in his efforts to make good, especially in matters of employment and social integration.[54]

It is evident that much improvement must be made in most of the parole systems of the United States if they are to measure up to these standards. But this is equally clear: Parole has definitely established itself as an indispensable part of our correctional system. The road ahead involves the betterment of personnel, the refinement of selective techniques, the accumulation of more adequate information upon which parole agencies can base their decisions, the strengthening of supervisory practices, the increase in coordination between parole and other parts of the correctional program, and the education of the public to appreciate the great contributions that an efficient parole system can make toward the control and prevention of crime in modern society.

[54] *Manual of Correctional Standards,* pp. 533, 534.

29

Prevention

The person who commits a crime must be apprehended, tried, convicted, sentenced, and punished. But after all this has been done, we are still confronted with this question: How can we reduce the number of persons who must be handled by society in this way? In other words, how can we prevent crime and delinquency?

The importance of prevention can hardly be exaggerated, for the cost of crime and delinquency in the United States is enormous. Although we do not have sufficient data to arrive at an accurate computation of the annual economic cost of crime and delinquency, estimates range all the way from the approximate total of $900,000,000 offered in 1931 by the National Commission on Law Observance and Enforcement, to the approximate total of $20,000,000,000 presented in 1954 by J. Edgar Hoover, Director of the Federal Bureau of Investigation. But these estimates do not include such items as the misery, shame, degradation, family disorganization, and loss of productivity that result from crime and delinquency. Such costs cannot be evaluated in terms of dollars and cents. They are, however, far more important than the economic cost involved.

All sorts of ideas have been advanced as remedies for crime and delinquency. At one extreme, these ideas lose themselves in a jungle of particularistic suggestions. We are warned against corner lounging, truancy, malnutrition, inadequate recreation, divorce, poverty, police corruption, unemployment, lack of religious training, indecent movies, comic books, alcohol, narcotics, focal infections, and so on and on. Although each of these may contribute in its own way to crime and delinquency, no one of them can be considered as *the* cause. At the other extreme, the schemes to end crime and delinquency fly off into the "wide blue yonder" and disappear into the mists of visionary dreams calling for a planned reorganization of our entire society. But we are not given any blueprint as to how this is to be accomplished; nor are we told what we should do about crime and delinquency while we are waiting for the planned utopia to become a reality.

It is because of the confusion growing out of the multiplicity of proposals to end crime and delinquency that we should bear in mind the following considerations in our approach to a discussion of their prevention:

1. Crime and delinquency are symptoms of social and personality disorganization. We must, therefore, look beyond the acts of crime and delinquency, attempt to discover underlying causes, and center our attack upon them.

2. Crime and delinquency are social problems as well as individual problems. We must, therefore, organize our attack against them not only in terms of the individual, who is unique and so needs individualized correction, but also in terms of his social relationships with others.

3. As social problems, crime and delinquency are the products of many causes, are interrelated with all other social problems, and are relative to time and place. Being products of many causes, they must be met with a complex attack that utilizes the resources of all fields of human knowledge and understanding. Being interrelated with all other social problems, they must be subjected to a many-sided attack that strikes at them directly through remedial measures designed specifically for them as well as indirectly through various measures aimed at the reduction of broken homes, unemployment, mental disorders, and other social problems. Being relative to time and place, they must be exposed to a dynamic attack that can be adjusted to fit changing conditions and the peculiarities of different communities and states.

4. A major source of criminal behavior is to be found in the early development of human beings, and it is easier to rehabilitate plastic young offenders than hardened criminals. Much of the attack upon crime and delinquency, therefore, must deal with children and adolescents. It must go beyond keeping criminals from repeating their crimes and emphasize keeping persons from becoming criminals.

5. Crime and delinquency have been with us for a long time, and there is no indication that we shall ever be completely rid of them. The attack upon these problems, therefore, must be a continuing one, calculated to reduce them and keep them under control.

6. It is obvious that no attack upon crime and delinquency can succeed without the support of the public in whose behalf it is launched. It must be buttressed, therefore, by an educational program that keeps the people informed regarding the nature and extent of crime and delin-

quency and encourages them to participate in every possible way in the efforts that are directed against these problems.[1]

A complete discussion of prevention programs would cover a very large area of human relationships, since any program that reduces other social problems, such as prostitution, divorce, and unemployment, tends to reduce crime and delinquency. It is obvious that we cannot present such a discussion here, but we shall examine some of the most important programs that are contributing directly to the prevention of crime and delinquency.

THE HOME

The home has well been called "the cradle of human personality," for in it the child forms fundamental attitudes and habits that endure throughout his life. In fact, the kind of conscience that a child develops depends largely upon the kind of parents that he has. They are the persons who give the child the love, attention, guidance, security, moral standards, a sense of responsibility, and all the other things that he needs. If they are kind, loving, honest, sincere, firm, and stable, he comes to regard people as friendly, understanding, dependable, loyal, and worthy of his respect and admiration. If, however, they are cold, despairing, rejecting, neglectful, irresponsible, or cruel, he learns to distrust, to dislike, or even to hate people. Children are the mirrors of the family life about them, and they persistently reflect what they learn in it. Thus the home can be a potent force for either good or evil, for either law-abiding behavior or for crime and delinquency. Given a good home, the child tends to become a good citizen.[2] Without a solid foundation of good homes, other agencies of social control can accomplish little.

According to the report on home responsibility of the National Conference on Prevention and Control of Juvenile Delinquency, a home is a good home for a child if the following conditions are present:

1. The child is loved and wanted and knows it.

2. He is helped to grow up by not having *too much* or *too little* done for him.

[1] See Edwin J. Lukas, "Crime Prevention: Who Prevents What?" *Federal Probation*, XII (April–June, 1948), 19–23; Lowell Juilliard Carr, "Organization for Delinquency Control," *The Annals of the American Academy of Political and Social Science*, CCLXI (Jan., 1949), 69, 70; Albert Morris, "Wanted: A Core of Basic Knowledge for the Prevention and Control of Crime," *Federal Probation*, XI (Jan.–Mar., 1947), 20–22; Harrison Allen Dobbs, "Getting at the Fundamentals of Preventing Crime and Delinquency," *Federal Probation*, XIII (Apr.–June, 1949), 3–9; Negley K. Teeters, "Fundamentals of Crime Prevention," *Federal Probation*, X (Apr.–June, 1946), 30, 31.

[2] The findings of the Gluecks indicate that if the family life of a child is adequate, the chances of his becoming a delinquent are only three in one hundred. See Sheldon and Eleanor T. Glueck, *Unraveling Juvenile Delinquency* (New York: The Commonwealth Fund, 1950), pp. 257–71. For an evaluation of the Gluecks' study, see "Symposium on the Gluecks' Latest Research, *Federal Probation*, XV (Mar., 1951), 52–58.

3. He has some time and some space of his own.

4. He is a part of the family, has fun with the family, and belongs.

5. His early mistakes and "badness" are understood as a normal part of growing up, and he is corrected without being hurt, shamed, or confused.

6. His growing skills—walking, talking, reading, making things—are enjoyed and respected.

7. He plans with the family and is given real ways to help and feel needed throughout childhood.

8. He has freedom that fits his age and needs, and he has responsibilities that fit his age, abilities, and freedom.

9. He can say what he feels and talks things out without being afraid or ashamed. He can learn through mistakes as well as successes, and his parents appreciate his successes rather than dwell upon his failures.

10. As he grows older he knows his parents are doing the best they can, and they know the same amout him.

11. He feels his parents care as much about him as they do about his brothers and sisters.

12. The family sticks together and the members help one another.

13. He is moderately and consistently disciplined from infancy, has limits set for his behavior, and is helped to take increasing responsibility for his own actions.

14. He has something to believe in and work for because his parents have lived their ideals and religious faith.[3]

In the opinion of this report, "good homes are much more common than people realize." Most parents love their children and want to do the best that they can for them. Nevertheless, at times even the best parents can profit by advice and services from outside agencies. In any event, our concern for human values should be organized into doing the things which make it possible for more families to meet their needs and assume their responsibilities. To this end, marriage and divorce laws should be improved and more efficiently administered, and programs designed to strengthen the home should be expanded and made available to more people. Among these programs are: (1) education in marriage and child rearing; (2) premarital counseling; (3) adult education; (4) family counseling; (5) family social work; (6) child guidance; (7) nursery schools and play groups for preschool children; (8) workshops in child development and family life education for local professional workers, teachers, doctors, home demonstration agents, social workers, nurses,

---

[3] National Conference on Prevention and Control of Juvenile Delinquency, *Report on Home Responsibility* (Washington, D.C.: Government Printing Office, 1947), pp. 5–18.

etc.; and (9) cooperative institutes and conferences on various phases of family life given on local, state, and national levels.

THE SCHOOL

The school is in a strategic position to prevent crime and delinquency. In fact, only the home is in better position to do this. The school exercises its authority over every child who is of school age. It receives him when he is young, observes, supervises, and teaches him for many hours each week during some of his most impressionable years, has an excellent opportunity to influence his attitudes and behavior, has the support of public opinion and the law in its work, and enjoys the confidence and trust of almost all parents. Thus it can well serve as the spearhead in an over-all attack against crime and delinquency.

In this attack the school has a fourfold responsibility.[4] *First,* it should plan an adequate school program that fits the needs of all children and results in their wholesome growth and development. To accomplish this, it should: (a) devote its energies to the *study of the individual pupil;* (b) make a *continuous study* of every child, using all the available scientific means and devices for analyzing individual differences; (c) take these *individual differences* into consideration and attempt to provide each child with the kind and the amount of education he needs; (d) *hold failures among pupils to a minimum* (although not at the price of indiscriminate promotion) so as to prevent the feelings of insecurity and rejection which can contribute directly to maladjustments; and (e) set up its aims and objectives in terms of *desired changes in behavior* so that the pupil will develop into a well-integrated and useful citizen.

Second, the school should identify those children who show signs of being susceptible to delinquent patterns of behavior and take proper preventive or remedial measures to insure better adjustments. All members of the staff should be alert to the telltale signs of potential or beginning delinquency. The teacher should not be expected to be a psychiatrist, psychologist, or case worker, but he should be trained to recognize the symptoms of personality problems. In their classes teachers should be sensitive to the needs of the children who are surrounded with such frustrating situations as economic need, broken homes, inadequate family relationships, limited academic abilities, conflicting cultures, and family mobility. They should be particularly observant of children who play truant, lie, cheat, destroy property, belong to destructive gangs, or appear sullen, seclusive, or unhappy. The number of these children is

---

[4] National Conference on Prevention and Control of Juvenile Delinquency, *Report on School and Teacher Responsibilities* (Washington, D.C.: Government Printing Office, 1947), pp. 3–8.

large. It has been estimated that 12 per cent of the children in our schools are in urgent need of expert professional help from psychologists and psychiatrists.[5] Professor William C. Kvaraceus is of the opinion that if a school staff is alerted to the telltale signs of potential delinquency, it can be expected "to pick out at least 75 per cent of the boys and girls who will face the juvenile judge in the courts of tomorrow."[6] However, if the school is to do a systematic job of identifying potential delinquency, it must have a carefully planned program of teacher selection and teacher education financed to provide adequate salaries.

Many schools now provide a variety of specialized guidance and clinical services for the assistance of children with unusual adjustment problems. In 1953 it was said that at least 60 per cent of all public school pupils had access to specialists in certain phases of pupil personnel work.[7] Among these specialists are counselors, attendance workers, visiting teachers, and psychologists. In the larger school systems the various specialized programs for dealing with maladjusted pupils are often organized as units of "pupil personnel" services.[8] Such a unit has been established at Passaic, New Jersey. It is called the Passaic Children's Bureau and operates under the administration of an assistant superintendent of schools. The staff of this bureau includes attendance officers, a social worker, psychologists, specialists in reading problems, and four police officers. The administration is responsible, also, for the guidance program, and a staff of counselors serves all secondary and several elementary schools.[9]

An unusual feature of this plan is that it coordinates in the school agency many community services for maladjusted and delinquent youth. Other school systems have coordinated the functions of the visiting teacher, the social worker, and the guidance clinic, but the Passaic plan goes beyond this and includes the activities of juvenile police. The police officers assigned to the schools work together with the school's guidance personnel in effecting solutions for the problems of delinquent children, and

[5] Eli M. Bower, "How Can Schools Recognize Early Symptoms of Maladjustment in Children and Youth?" *Federal Probation*, XVI (June, 1952), 4.

[6] William C. Kvaraceus, "The Role of the School in a Delinquency Prevention and Control Program," *Federal Probation*, XI (July–Sept., 1947), 12. The Gluecks and others have attempted to use various scales to identify potential delinquents among school children, but as yet these efforts have not been very helpful. See Chapters 9 and 28 for general criticisms of prediction tables. See also Hermann Mannheim and Leslie T. Wilkins, *Prediction Methods in Relation to Borstal Training* (London: Her Majesty's Stationery Office, 1955); William C. Kvaraceus and Walter B. Miller, *Delinquent Behavior: Culture and the Individual* (Washington, D.C.: National Education Association of the United States, 1959), pp. 122–41.

[7] Arthur S. Hill, Leonard M. Miller, and Hazel F. Gabbard, "Schools Face the Delinquency Problem," *The Bulletin* (a publication of the National Association of Secondary-School Principals), XXXVII (Dec., 1953), 188.

[8] *Ibid.*, 194.

[9] *Ibid.*, 194, 195.

only the most urgent cases requiring immediate court action come into contact with legal agencies.[10]

A number of larger school districts have attempted to meet the challenge of maladjustment and delinquency by providing special schools and classes. In 1947–48 more than 15,000 truants and children with behavior problems were enrolled in special classes staffed by approximately 700 public day-school teachers. This development includes "special schools devoted entirely to the rehabilitation of delinquent and maladjusted youth, special adjustment classes located in elementary and secondary schools, public school units located in hospitals for emotionally disturbed children, and similar programs in juvenile detention homes."[11] New York City maintains several schools for maladjusted pupils in special centers serving many neighborhood elementary schools, and in institutions, detention homes, and psychiatric hospitals.[12]

Although the school can do many things to prevent or eliminate behavior problems through its own program, it should also look to other agencies and resources within the community for assistance in this work. "Early identification followed by corrective treatment of the potential delinquent and referral to other agencies as needed is the unique contribution of the school" in a program of crime and delinquency prevention.[13]

Third, the school should work closely with parents and neighborhood leaders to assist them in better understanding of the individual child and to help them remove neighborhood influences that are inimical to child welfare. In doing this, the school should not attempt to take the place of the home and all the character-building and welfare agencies in the community, but rather it should seek to strengthen and reinforce them. When it discovers that children are being subjected to harmful influences, it should call this to the attention of the proper authorities and then join with other agencies in providing more interesting and attractive substitutive activities in which children can engage.

One way in which the school can work with parents and neighborhood leaders is by putting its resources to better use through extended school programs. Some communities keep their school buildings open during the

[10] See William C. Kvaraceus, *Juvenile Delinquency and the School* (New York: World Book Co., 1945); George C. Boone, "The Passaic Children's Bureau," *Crime and Delinquency,* VII (July, 1961), 231–36. This entire issue of *Crime and Delinquency* is devoted to the school and delinquency.

[11] Hill, Miller, and Gabbard, p. 196; Edward H. Stullken, "The Schools and the Delinquency Problem," *Journal of Criminal Law, Criminology, and Police Science,* XLIII (Jan.–Feb., 1953), 570–72.

[12] Hill, Miller, and Gabbard, pp. 197, 198. See also William C. Kvaraceus and William E. Ulrich, *Delinquent Behavior: Principles and Practices* (Washington, D.C.: National Education Association of the United States, 1959), pp. 174–220.

[13] National Conference on Prevention and Control of Juvenile Delinquency, *Report on School and Teacher Responsibilities,* p. 6.

afternoons, evenings, Saturdays, and summer months for the use of pupils and their parents. In addition, some departments of education and local boards have established programs to provide enriched living for youth in their leisure time. Included in these programs are such activities as camping, organized recreation, music, dramatics, homemaking, and arts and crafts.

In 1952 Georgia set up an extended school program on a state-wide basis in large and small, rural and urban communities. It is designed to supplement the regular school services and operates over a four- to six-week period during vacation months. Where facilities permit, day and overnight camping is included, and some school buildings are used as centers for a wide range of creative activities. Young people have found in the centers a place to see their friends and a recreational outlet for their energies, which are directed along constructive and wholesome channels. All groups and agencies concerned with children and young people are cooperating in making this program a success.

At the end of its first year, Georgia's extended school program was operating in eighty-four school systems throughout the state, and 81,000 children and adults were enrolled. About 75 per cent of the participants were in the age range of six to thirteen years, a period of life when children are active and likely to get into trouble if they are unsupervised. A staff of 1,385 teachers was employed as leaders, and an additional 1,568 persons were serving as volunteers.[14]

Even after the child is going to school, his home and family relationships continue to operate as the most important factors in his life. Consequently, if the school is to deal effectively with him, it must know and understand his home and establish and maintain the closest possible working relationship with his parents. In the smaller community the teacher must bear the responsibility of bridging the gap between school life and family life and maintaining a working relationship between the home and the school. However, in the larger towns and cities professionally trained workers, such as counselors, visiting teachers,[15] or school social workers may be employed to do this work. The relationship between the home and the school should be further strengthened through a carefully planned program of parent education in child development and family relations under the direction of a person who is fully qualified for such an assignment. In addition to this, there should be frequent conferences between

---

[14] Hill, Miller, and Gabbard, pp. 215–17. See also Adele Franklin, "The All-Day Neighborhood Schools," *Crime and Delinquency*, VII (July, 1961), 255–62.

[15] See Harry J. Baker, "The Visiting Teacher Program and Delinquency Prevention," *Federal Probation*, XI (Jan.–Mar., 1947), 30–34; Rachel D. Cox, "The School Counselor's Contribution to the Prevention of Delinquency," *Federal Probation*, XIV (Mar., 1950), 23–28.

the school staff and parents, utilization of the special abilities of certain parents in the planning and development of the school's program, and the organization and operation of parent-teacher groups under the guidance of professional leadership. All these activities will help to combine the home and the school into a single effective force for the wholesome growth and development of the child and thus help to prevent undesirable behavior.

And the "moral climate" in which these activities take place is important. In our society the increasing emphasis on material possessions, the permissive attitudes of parents, and the everlasting evasion of effective discipline in the home and the school are contributing to the "get-away-with-it" philosophy of youth. Parents and teachers might well direct more attention to moral conduct and show less concern for the "flowering of personality" theory of child development. Children need and want the sense of security that comes from being so loved that they are told what to do. A definition of responsibility and a consistent application of penalties in both the home and the school would help children to accept the authority to which they must adjust in community life.

Fourth, The school should cooperate with all other community agencies and organizations, such as churches, child guidance clinics, family societies, welfare agencies, visiting nurses' associations, and labor unions, in a coordinated plan to meet the needs of the child in the most effective and constructive way. Only if this is done can the community and the nation expect to effect a substantial reduction in crime and delinquency.[16]

THE CHURCH[17]

Religion, with its emphasis on life's highest spiritual values, the worth and dignity of the individual, and respect for the person and property of others, generates powerful forces in opposition to crime and delinquency. Here we are concerned with the specific steps that the church can take to prevent these problems. Some of these steps can be outlined as follows:[18]

1. The church should cooperate closely with the police, probation officers, judges, social welfare workers, school officials, mental hygiene

[16] National Conference on Prevention and Control of Juvenile Delinquency, *Report on School and Teacher Responsibilities,* p. 8; Kvaraceus and Ulrich, pp. 244–339. Although "school dropouts" often get into trouble, not all of them are potential delinquents. See Daniel Schreiber, "Juvenile Delinquency and the School Dropout Problem," *Federal Probation,* XXVII (Sept., 1963), 15–19.

[17] The term "church" is used here in a broad sense to refer to all religious sects.

[18] Adapted from National Conference on Prevention and Control of Juvenile Delinquency, *Report on Church Responsibilities* (Washington, D.C.: Government Printing Office, 1947), pp. 15–19. See also Robert and Muriel Webb, "How Churches Can Help in the Prevention and Treatment of Juvenile Delinquency," *Federal Probation,* XXI (Dec., 1957), 22–25.

clinics, correctional institutions, and other agencies dealing with problem children, delinquents or criminals.

2. It should provide official representatives to serve as qualified counselors in courts, probation and parole departments, and other agencies dealing with delinquents or criminals.

3. It should present a united front in attacking the forces that are detrimental to family life and general morality and in promoting proper law enforcement, adequate regulation of commercial recreation, and the development of better recreational facilities.

4. It should cooperate with neighborhood organizations and citizen groups in handling common community problems, including the prevention of crime and delinquency. In doing this it can furnish effective leadership as well as buildings, facilities, and volunteer workers.

5. It should strive to give religion a more dignified and influential position in the programs of correctional institutions.

6. It should point the way to the development of more effective correctional programs by utilizing in its own correctional institutions and agencies the best that science and human experience have to offer.

7. It should be constantly engaged in finding ways and means of putting its religious teachings into practice.

8. It should offer educational programs designed to prepare people for marriage and family life and to assist parents in the handling of their family problems.

9. It should direct its attention to the types of understanding and skills needed in the organization of lay services for underprivileged youth.

10. It should encourage young people to participate in the formation of their own programs so that they will have a sense of responsibility in making them a success.

11. It should seek to stimulate interest in the prevention of crime and delinquency in small towns and rural communities.

12. It should endeavor to secure the cooperation of the press, radio, television, motion pictures, and other mass media in making the public conscious of the importance of crime and delinquency prevention.

An example of how the church can cooperate with other agencies in a prevention program is provided by the referral plan of the Youth Services Board of Philadelphia. Through this plan the names of all boys who are taken into custody by the police, or who are referred to the association as complaint cases by schools, agencies, and individuals, are referred once a month to boys' clubs, community councils, churches, and other organizations throughout the city. A representative of the organization, to which a case is referred, visits the boy to determine the nature of the problem and to use whatever resources are available in the community to help in his adjustment. The purpose of the referral plan is to make certain that no boy in the city of Philadelphia who shows signs of becoming a problem will be without help from some agency in the community.[19]

ORGANIZED RECREATION

Organized recreation has been advanced as an important preventive of crime and delinquency. Under the heading of organized recreation are usually included such agencies as camps, playgrounds, scout and ranger organizations, clubs, and settlement houses. These agencies promote the teaching of outdoor and athletic skills, games, arts and crafts, and otherwise offer leisure-time services and entertainment. Those who favor organized recreation as a preventive of crime and delinquency argue that persons who are engaged in wholesome leisure-time activities will not at the same time commit acts of crime or delinquency and will have their interests and energies directed into law-abiding activities.

Most programs of organized recreation utilize the group-work method, although some provide case-work services. Group work is a way of helping individuals in groups and the "group-as-a-whole" with problems which interfere with personal growth and corporate action. The group worker usually reaches individuals through the medium of the group, and he affects the group interaction in such a way that the individuals receive help from one another, from the group worker, and from the approval or disapproval of the group-as-a-whole. The group thus becomes a source of strength to the members who achieve adjustment through the processes of interaction. Within the group the social worker encourages socially acceptable attitudes and behavior. In situations outside group meetings he helps the individual through personal interviews.

Case work, which emphasizes the individual rather than the group, is a way of helping a person to help himself. It is based upon the recognition that the power for solving a problem lies largely with the individual, who must be challenged to assume increasing responsibility in the handling of his own affairs. To this end the social worker must establish a relationship of trust and confidence with his client and let him act independently in so far as his situation and the agency's responsibility permit.[20]

The boys' club is the typical illustration of the group-work method of supervising the leisure time of children. Frederic Thrasher has made

[19] J. Francis Finnegan, "The Work of the Crime Prevention Units of Philadelphia," *Proceedings of the American Prison Association, 1949,* p. 265; Evelyn Trommer, "Citizen Participation in the Philadelphia Youth Services Board Program," *Proceedings of the American Correctional Association, 1956,* pp. 37–42; "Philadelphia Youth Services Board," *American Journal of Correction,* XX (Jan.–Feb., 1958), 20, 21, 29.

[20] National Conference on Prevention and Control of Juvenile Delinquency, *Report on Case Work—Group Work* (Washington, D.C.: Government Printing Office, 1947), pp. 13–15, 22, 23.

what has been described as "the most careful and intensive study of the effect of a boys' club on delinquency."[21] He analyzed the operation of the Boys' Club of New York City during its initial four years from 1927 to 1931,[22] and the results of his study had a chastening effect upon those who were making exaggerated claims regarding the role of the boys' club as an agency of prevention. Not only did the study show that the members of the club were more delinquent than other boys in the community who were not members, but it also revealed that boys were more delinquent while active members than before or after the period of their membership. Although it is true that the study covered only the four initial years of the club's existence and that the club drew largely on the underprivileged classes for its membership, the fact remains that for the period under study the club was not an effective agency of prevention. Despite this study Thrasher feels that the boys' club is one of the most important and essential elements in any crime and delinquency prevention program. This feeling seems to be borne out by a study of a boys' club in Louisville, Kentucky, where it was found that the delinquency rates decreased steadily over an eight-year period in the area where the club operated but increased during the same period in two other areas which had no youth-serving agencies. However, the study acknowledges that some influences other than that of the boys' club might have affected the delinquency rates in its area.[23] Be that as it may, the available evidence does indicate that the boys' club is in a field where it has an opportunity to work with delinquents. For example, Healy and Bronner found that delinquents are generally more interested, skillful, and active in games and sports and more attracted to clubs than nondelinquents.[24]

A few years ago, the Chicago Recreation Commission made a study of five selected communities in the Chicago area in order to discover the relationship between recreation and juvenile delinquency.[25] The commission found that a higher percentage of nondelinquents than delinquents participated in supervised recreation, that when delinquents took part in supervised recreation they preferred competitive sports and activities such as those in the game room where there was little supervision, and

[21] Edwin H. Sutherland, *Principles of Criminology* (Philadelphia: J. B. Lippincott Co., 1947), p. 619.

[22] Frederic M. Thrasher, "The Boys' Club and Juvenile Delinquency," *American Journal of Sociology*, XLII (July, 1936), 66–80.

[23] Roscoe C. Brown, Jr., and Dan W. Dodson, "The Effectiveness of a Boys' Club in Reducing Delinquency," *The Annals of the American Academy of Political and Social Science*, CCCXXII (Mar., 1959), 47–52. This entire issue of the *Annals* is devoted to articles on the prevention of juvenile delinquency.

[24] William Healy and Augusta F. Bronner, *New Light on Delinquency and Its Treatment* (New Haven: Yale University Press, 1936), pp. 71, 72.

[25] See Ethel Shanas and Catherine E. Dunning, *Recreation and Delinquency* (Chicago: Chicago Recreation Commission, 1942), pp. 236–44.

that participation in supervised recreation reduced juvenile delinquency. On the basis of their study the commission recommended that more supervised recreation should be provided in all the neighborhoods of Chicago, especially where the delinquency rate was higher than the average for the city as a whole, that recreational agencies should make an effort to reach and hold boys of fourteen years and over, that recreation programs should be designed to attract and influence delinquents and energetic adolescents, that "unofficial" delinquents should be given individualized treatment, and that the home and all community agencies should be organized into a coordinated attack against delinquency.

A study made in Philadelphia by the crime-prevention association of that city disclosed that recreation programs resulted in a reduction of minor offenses or misdemeanors, or what is called "hell-raising" activities, but did not meet with any success in reducing the number of serious offenses. However, this association was confident that "recreation if used properly does have therapeutic value in the adjustment of behavior cases."[26] Nor was a study of the effect of group-work agencies on delinquency in Cincinnati any more conclusive. Although the rate of delinquency among the clientele of the group-work agencies there was not so high as that of the city as a whole, the claim could not be made that the group-work program was the preventive agent.[27]

Since it has become apparent that some young people cannot be reached through conventional recreational activities, efforts have been made in some cities, for example, in Boston, New York, and Chicago, to influence the members of gangs by a process of "boring from within." This consists of establishing contact with the gangs in their own "hangouts," winning the acceptance of the boys or girls, and then slowly redirecting their activities along more conventional lines. As yet, however, little success can be claimed for these efforts, and more studies of this type of approach are needed.[28]

There can be no doubt that organized recreation can play an important part in the prevention of crime and delinquency. The "absorption of the energies of youth in harmless or constructive pursuits not only takes up much of the time that might otherwise be put to vicious and antisocial

[26] Finnegan, p. 266.

[27] Ellery F. Reed, "How Effective Are Group-Work Agencies in Preventing Delinquency?" *Focus,* XXVIII (Nov., 1949), 170–76.

[28] For some of the studies that have used this approach, see Paul L. Crawford, James R. Dumpson, and Daniel I. Malamud, *Working with Teen-Age Gangs* (New York: Welfare Council of New York City, 1950); Walter B. Miller, "Preventive Work with Street-Corner Groups: Boston Delinquency Project," *The Annals of the American Academy of Political and Social Science,* CCCXXII (Mar., 1959), 97–106; John M. Gandy, "Preventive Work with Street-Corner Groups: Hyde Park Youth Project, Chicago," *ibid.,* 107–16.

uses, but is an entering wedge to winning the confidence of youth and exerting an influence for good in other than recreational activities.[29] But to operate as an agency of prevention, organized recreation must be sufficiently attractive to provide a substitute for the excitement of delinquency, skillfully planned to meet the needs of the individual, adequately staffed with professionally trained personnel, well supported with guidance facilities and individualized supervision and treatment, and closely coordinated with other community agencies in a general attack on crime and delinquency. Above all, it should not be considered a panacea for these problems, but rather regarded as one of the important elements in the broader program of prevention.[30]

COUNSELING AND GUIDANCE

The child guidance clinic, which is part of the general mental hygiene movement, is an agency where the problems of young people may be thoroughly studied by psychiatrists and psychologists in order to discover the causes of maladjustment. Sometimes child guidance clinics function mainly for diagnostic purposes in connection with juvenile courts and other organizations offering treatment, but sometimes they also provide various forms of treatment designed to correct delinquent tendencies. The child guidance movement began shortly after the turn of the century, and today there are approximately 500 full time and part-time clinics for children in the United States. The first child guidance clinic was operated exclusively for delinquents. It was established in Chicago in 1909 under the directorship of Dr. William Healy, who later took charge of the Judge Baker Foundation in Boston.[31]

Various studies made of child guidance clinics indicate that their methods have been effective in dealing with some children. For example, one study made in Berkeley, California, revealed that problem children who were treated in school clinics during a two-year period improved, whereas some maladjusted children who were not so treated showed little improvement.[32] Another study, conducted by Healy and Bronner, showed that 70 per cent of the juvenile delinquency cases handled by a guidance

[29] Sheldon and Eleanor T. Glueck, *Preventing Crime* (New York: McGraw-Hill Book Co., Inc., 1936), p. 20.

[30] National Conference on Prevention and Control of Juvenile Delinquency, *Report on Recreation for Youth* (Washington, D.C.: Government Printing Office, 1947), p. 3.

[31] National Conference on Prevention and Control of Juvenile Delinquency, *Report on Mental Health and Child Guidance Clinics* (Washington, D.C.: Government Printing Office, 1947), pp. 2, 3.

[32] Nathaniel Cantor, "Organized Efforts in Crime Prevention," *The Annals of the American Academy of Political and Social Science*, CCXVII (Sept., 1941), 158.

clinic responded satisfactorily to treatment.[33] Writing on the subject of crime prevention in 1941, Professor Nathaniel Cantor stated: "The evaluation of the work done by the child guidance clinics throughout the country seems to show that approximately one-third of all cases make satisfactory adjustment."[34] However, since other factors, such as the influence of parents, continue to operate in the lives of the children who are so treated, the guidance clinic cannot claim all the credit for the success which is achieved. Nevertheless, in 1954 the United States Children's Bureau concluded that although child guidance clinics could do little for those who had been subjected to very harmful environmental influences or who were suffering from extreme personality disorders, they could help most of the other delinquents that they were accepting for treatment.[35]

In 1935 the late Dr. Richard Cabot established a ten-year research project in delinquency prevention in Cambridge, Massachusetts. This project, which is known as the Cambridge-Somerville Youth Study, involved the treatment of some 325 boys by counselors, who used whatever skills they were capable of applying. The "essence of the relationship between the boy and his counselor was personal intimacy and friendship." An important feature of this study was the careful selection of a control group which received no help at all from the counselors.

The conclusions of the Cambridge-Somerville Youth Study may be summarized as follows:

1. The special work of the counselors was no more effective than the usual forces in the community in preventing delinquency.

2. The evidence seems to point to the fact that although the first stages of delinquency were not wholly averted when treatment was begun at the 8-11 year level, the later and more serious stages were to some degree averted.

3. An examination of the records and interviews shows that in many cases, even in the lives of many of the delinquent boys, emotional conflicts were alleviated, practical problems were dealt with successfully and boys were given greater confidence to face life's problems.[36]

In a later appraisal of this study, the McCords, on the basis of a comparison between twelve "treated" and twelve "untreated" boys—which

[33] William Healy and Augusta F. Bronner, *Treatment and What Happened Afterward* (Boston: The Judge Baker Guidance Center, 1939), pp. 42, 43.

[34] Cantor, p. 158.

[35] Helen L. Witmer and Edith Tufts, *The Effectiveness of Delinquency Prevention Programs*, U.S. Children's Bureau Publication No. 350 (Washington, D.C.: Government Printing Office, 1954), p. 40.

[36] Edwin Powers, "An Experiment in Prevention of Delinquency," *The Annals of the American Academy of Political and Social Science*, CCLXI (Jan., 1949), 77–88. See also Edwin Powers and Helen Witmer, *An Experiment in the Prevention of Delinquency:* The Cambridge-Somerville Youth Study (New York: Columbia University Press, 1951).

they admit was an inadequate sample—concluded that "intimate, long-term, 'supportive' counseling may prevent crime." Nevertheless, in their opinion, judged by the "standard of 'official' criminal behavior," the Cambridge-Somerville Youth Study was "largely a failure."[37]

Another recent study made of a training school program at Highfields, New Jersey, which emphasized counseling and guided group interaction, revealed that the rate of recidivism was lower for its former inmates (37 per cent) than for the youths released from Annandale (53 per cent), a traditional public training school located in the same state.[38] Although these findings seem to indicate that the brief and intensive treatment program at Highfields was more successful in the rehabilitation of juvenile delinquents, any such conclusion does not stand up under careful scrutiny, since the youths sent there were not only better prospects for rehabilitation but also more leniently treated after release than those committed to Annandale. In defense of the Highfields program, however, its supporters have argued that it was at least as effective as the one at Annandale, and this, within a much shorter period of time and at a much lower cost.

COORDINATING COUNCILS

A coordinating council is "an organization composed of representatives of governmental departments, private social agencies, civic organizations, religious and educational institutions, and other groups and services, as well as interested citizens, to promote cooperation among them, to integrate their efforts and functions, to study conditions and resources, to inform the public regarding conditions, and to secure democratic action in meeting local needs."[39] The first coordinating council was organized in Berkeley, California, in 1919 through the efforts of Dr. Virgil Dickson, who later became the superintendent of schools of Berkeley, and August Vollmer, the city's chief of police.[40] The idea of the coordinating council spread throughout California and to a number of other states, and by 1940 "it is probable that there were more than 700 coordinating councils in the United States."[41]

---

[37] Joan and William McCord, "A Follow-up Report on the Cambridge-Somerville Youth Study," The Annals of the American Academy of Political and Social Science, CCCXXII (Mar., 1959), 89–96.

[38] See H. Ashley Weeks, Youthful Offenders at Highfields (Ann Arbor: University of Michigan Press, 1958).

[39] Dictionary of Sociology (New York: The Philosophical Library, 1944), p. 69.

[40] Kenneth S. Beam, Coordinating Councils in California (California Department of Education, Bulletin No. 11 [Sept. 1, 1938]), pp. 7–10; Kenyon J. Scudder, in Preventing Crime, pp. 25–28.

[41] Lowell Juilliard Carr, Delinquency Control (New York: Harper & Bros., 1941), p. 331.

As the coordinating council movement spread, it adapted itself to the peculiar conditions in different localities and therefore assumed various forms. However, Kenneth S. Beam, reporting in 1937 after a study of coordinating councils in ninety-two cities located in thirty states, found that they had the following distinctive characteristics:

1. They were organized on a community basis in towns and small cities and on a neighborhood basis in large cities.

2. They were composed of public officials and representatives of private welfare agencies and civic organizations.

3. They emphasized the importance of citizen or lay participation.

4. They did not function as agencies, but in a coordinating or counseling capacity.

5. They were interested in the prevention of delinquency, sometimes making this their principal objective.[42]

According to the National Conference on Prevention and Control of Juvenile Delinquency, which was held in 1946, the following general principles of organizing and operating coordinating councils have emerged:

1. Their function should be community organization rather than the direct operation of services.

2. Their membership should be drawn from as broad a citizen base as possible, including representatives of local civic, social, religious, labor, professional, consumer, and business groups.

3. They should be composed of both professional workers and lay citizens.

4. Their organizational pattern should be kept flexible and simple.

5. They should be autonomous bodies, free to determine their own program and to initiate their own action.

6. In a given city they should be related to each other and to a broad welfare planning through an over-all community welfare council.

7. Their staffs should be composed of trained and experienced community organizers.

8. In order to attack realistically the problem of juvenile delinquency their program should be concerned with the total field of welfare and not confined to one interest like recreation.[43]

The coordinating council is not a panacea for crime and delinquency, but when properly organized, wisely directed, enthusiastically supported by public officials, and adequately staffed with paid personnel, it has

[42] Kenneth S. Beam, "Community Coordination," in Report of a National Survey of Coordinating and Neighborhood Councils, *Coping with Crime, Yearbook of the National Probation Association, 1937* (New York: National Probation Association, 1937), pp. 47, 48.

[43] National Conference on Prevention and Control of Juvenile Delinquency, *Report on Community Coordination* (Washington, D.C.: Government Printing Office, 1947), pp. 15–17.

accomplished worth-while things. It has promoted community organization, integrated welfare activities, prevented duplication of services,
directed a concerted attack against crime and delinquency, encouraged
lay citizens and groups to participate in welfare programs, and helped to
educate the public regarding community problems. However, when it has
been forced upon local leaders, directed by amateur volunteers, extended
over too large a population base, and exposed to unresolved community
conflicts, it has failed. Like the other programs to which we have already
referred, the coordinating council must be considered as only one element
in the much larger program of prevention.[44]

COORDINATED COMMUNITY PROGRAMS

The essence of the coordinated community program appears to be
"the recognition of the interrelationship of the various elements in community life, their reformulation according to some desirable standard of
communal soundness, the strengthening of constructive elements and the
weakening or removal of others, and the guidance of the community's
growth, under appropriate leadership, toward the realization of wholesome values in the lives of the community and its denizens."[45] Among
other things, it includes the education of the public in the aims and
methods of a cooperative effort to reduce crime and delinquency, and
the liberal use of citizens' groups, civic organizations, and individuals in
the planning and operation of the prevention program. It thus emphasizes
the principle that the local community should play the leading part in the
reduction of its own problems.

A coordinated community program that has attracted wide attention is
the Chicago Area Project. This project, which began in 1932 as an outgrowth of the well-known "delinquency area" studies of Clifford Shaw
and his colleagues, continued to grow until in 1948 it included fourteen
local neighborhood units operating in ten areas of high delinquency in
Chicago. It is based upon the belief that the reduction of crime and delinquency depends upon the extent to which the people themselves understand and want a program of community betterment and are willing to
support it and call it their own. Its primary and distinctive emphasis,
therefore, is upon the development of the greatest possible participation
on the part of the residents of the neighborhood in the planning and
operation of *their own* program for the welfare of *their own* children
under the direction of *their own* leaders. The program thus tends to reflect
the basic needs, interests, and sentiments of the people themselves

[44] Carr, p. 343.
[45] Glueck, pp. 13, 14.

PREVENTION 717

although it does receive financial support from the outside and guidance from professionally trained workers, who, however, seek to remain in the background. In developing the work in each area, the local committee of residents is encouraged to secure the cooperation of churches, schools, recreation centers, labor unions, industries, and other resources in an effort to create a coordinated attack upon neighborhood problems.[46] As yet little objective evidence is available regarding the effectiveness of the Chicago Area Project, and even those who have been associated with it disagree as to its accomplishments. Professor Sutherland, in attempting to make an evaluation, states that "perhaps the best that can be said in appraisal of these Area Projects is that they are consistent with an important theory of criminal behavior and with the ideals of democracy."[47] More recently, Kobrin has expressed the opinion that the project has probably reduced delinquency in the areas where it has operated, although this reduction cannot be precisely measured, and Sorrentino, while admitting that the project cannot definitely claim credit for the prevention of delinquency, does insist that it has "encouraged wider participation in democratic social action programs."[48] However, this project may be faced with increasing difficulties since the composition of the population in its area is rapidly changing and the new residents may not be so responsive to its principles nor so inclined to organize and direct their own programs as were their predecessors.[49]

Another well-known coordinated community program is that established through the work of the Industrial Areas Foundation. Like the Chicago Area Project, it encourages the community to participate in the organization and operation of its own program and represents a reaction against the mere "coordination" of professional agencies which are superimposed upon the community. Unlike the Chicago Area Project, its primary objec-

[46] Clifford R. Shaw and Henry D. McKay, *Juvenile Delinquency and Urban Areas* (Chicago: University of Chicago Press, 1942), pp. 442–46; American Prison Association, *Report of the Committee on Crime Prevention* (New York: The American Prison Association, 1942), pp. 8, 9; Clifford R. Shaw and Jesse A. Jacobs, *The Chicago Area Project: An Experimental Community Program for Prevention of Delinquency in Chicago* (Chicago, Ill.: Institute of Juvenile Research [Mimeographed]). Cited by Walter C. Reckless, *The Crime Problem* (New York: Appleton-Century-Crofts, Inc., 1950), pp. 517, 518.

[47] Sutherland, p. 618.

[48] Solomon Kobrin, "The Chicago Area Project—A 25-Year Assessment," *The Annals of the American Academy of Political and Social Science*, CCCXXII (Mar., 1959), 19–29; Anthony Sorrentino, "The Chicago Area Project after 25 Years," *Federal Probation*, XXIII (June, 1959), 40–45.

[49] Anthony Sorrentino, *The Story of the Chicago Area Project*, mimeographed (Chicago: The Chicago Area Project, April, 1962). The program of the Chicago Area Project is now conducted in collaboration with the state of Illinois, which through its Youth Commission furnishes most of the personnel.

tive is not the prevention of crime and delinquency but rather the development of a "democratically minded people" who are informed about all aspects of their community life and organized to promote their own welfare. The work of the Industrial Areas Foundation was initiated in 1939 under the leadership of Saul Alinsky, and its best-known enterprise is the Back of the Yards' Neighborhood Council, which is located in the area near the stockyards in Chicago. Alinsky has described this council as "an experimental demonstration of a community organizational procedure predicated upon a functional conception of the character of a community and its problems." It has operated a successful program and has effected not only a tangible improvement in the way of life of the local residents but also the development of an unusual sympathy and understanding between organizations which previously had been in opposition and conflict.[50] Although, as Alinsky emphasizes, it is important to have the people themselves participate in the organization and operation of their own program and to recognize the fundamental relationship of all social problems, it is also necessary to have professional leadership and guidance and to center the attack on specific problems. All these elements must be present in any successful program of crime and delinquency prevention.

CONCENTRATED ATTACK ON MULTI-PROBLEM FAMILIES[51]

During 1957 the New York City Youth Board, the city's official agency for the prevention and control of juvenile delinquency, learned through its research facilities that 75 per cent of New York City's delinquency had its source in an estimated twenty thousand multi-problem families, which constituted less than one per cent of all the families in that city.[52] On the basis of these findings, a citywide register of multi-problem families was established so as to reduce duplication of effort and the possibility of neglect and to create a coordinated service plan for each of the families thus identified. A technique called "aggressive casework," which is so called because it searches for the client instead of waiting for him to apply for help, is used to provide intensive treatment for these families. With some modifications, the same technique is being used in Chicago and St. Paul in a similar approach to the delinquency problems of those cities.

[50] American Prison Association, *Report of the Committee on Crime Prevention*, pp. 9, 10; Saul D. Alinsky, *Reveille for Radicals* (Chicago: University of Chicago Press, 1946), pp. 77–86.

[51] Within recent years a number of states and cities have established a variety of publicly financed programs for the prevention of crime and delinquency. Limitations of space, however, permit only the mention of the attack on multi-problem families, which has attracted considerable attention.

[52] Ralph W. Whelan, *Annual Report to the Mayor by the Executive Director, 1957* (New York: New York City Youth Board, Jan. 10, 1958).

Although it has been said that the concentrated attack on multi-problem families has been effective, thus far little evidence has been advanced to substantiate this claim.[53]

CITIZENS' CRIME COMMISSIONS

The first citizens' crime commission was formed in Chicago in 1919. It was composed of persons representative of the city's best citizenship and was instructed to study the subject of crime suppression and prevention, to secure the preparation of necessary legislation, and to function thereafter as "a body charged with the duty of securing the proper administration of such laws as may be enacted by the officials charged with such administration."[54] Within the next few years a number of commissions like this were created in some of the country's larger cities, and in 1927 twenty-six of them were represented at a conference held in Washington, D. C., at the instance of the National Crime Commission. However, most of these organizations, including the National Crime Commission, ceased to function after a relatively short period of time, and it was not until the Kefauver Committee in 1951 recommended the formation of citizens' crime commissions that great interest regarding them was again aroused. Since then numerous citizens' organizations have been established in large cities throughout the country.[55]

According to Virgil W. Peterson, operating director of the Chicago Crime Commission, many, if not most, of the citizens' crime commissions have been formed because of "intolerable local conditions arising out of widespread lawlessness, official laxity or inefficiency, and corruption."[56] At present their functions vary from city to city. A few concentrate on statistical studies of local conditions, some direct most of their efforts toward an improvement of law-enforcement agencies, while others concern themselves primarily with the problem of organized crime.[57]

The Chicago Crime Commission has a membership of about 150 men, prominent in business, industry, and the professions, and it operates on an annual budget of approximately $150,000. It has a staff of about twenty-five full-time employees, including observers in the criminal courts, investigators, and those engaged in office administration and clerical or

[53] Charles J. Birt, "Family-Centered Project of St. Paul," *Social Work,* I (Oct., 1956), 41–47; Sophia M. Robison, "Why Juvenile Delinquency Preventive Programs Are Ineffective," *Federal Probation,* XXV (Dec., 1961), 34–41.

[54] Virgil W. Peterson, "Citizens' Crime Commissions," *Federal Probation,* XVII (Mar., 1953), 9.

[55] *Ibid.,* 9–12; U.S. Senate Special Committee to Investigate Organized Crime in Interstate Commerce, *Third Interim Report* (Washington, D.C.: Government Printing Office, 1951), pp. 26, 27.

[56] Peterson, 12.

[57] *Ibid.*

secretarial work. It advises complaining witnesses in criminal cases and protects them against intimidation and attempts at bribery. It assigns observers to criminal courts and issues public reports regarding abuses found there and the types of sentences imposed. For many years it has played an important part in securing the enactment of a number of important laws[58] as well as the improvement of the administration of criminal justice. It conducts investigations, and "armed with incontrovertible facts," it is in a "position to compel lax, inefficient, and unwilling officials to perform their duty." It makes special studies and on the basis of its findings publishes recommendations for the improvement of law-enforcement agencies. It has also issued manuals on the law of arrest, search, and seizure, and on criminal law and procedure.[59]

The effectiveness of a citizens' crime commission rests largely upon its financial independence, which enables it, without fear or favor, to publish accurate facts concerning crime conditions and law enforcement, and upon the adequacy and competency of its staff, which provides it with such facts. It cannot work miracles or provide a cure-all for crime and delinquency. "Nevertheless, in view of the complex and impersonal character of big city government, a citizens' crime commission affords virtually the sole source of accurate information regarding crime conditions and the efficiency of responsible authorities."[60]

THE POLICE

A police agency that vigorously and efficiently enforces the law operates as a definite deterrent to the commission of crime and delinquency and, therefore, contributes in a significant way to the prevention of these problems.[61] But should the police go beyond this and set up a special program for the prevention of crime and delinquency? According to the National Conference on Prevention and Control of Juvenile Delinquency, the police should take this action for the following reasons:

1. They have the most clearly defined legal authority to do so.

2. They have the best local and national records on offenders and their methods and the nature, extent, fluctuation, and trend of crime and delinquency.

[58] For example, the citizens' crime commission secured the passage of an effective bail bond law and, with the aid of the Chicago Motor Club, of a uniform motor vehicle theft law.

[59] Peterson, 12–15. See also Virgil W. Peterson, *A Report on Chicago Crime for 1962* (Chicago: Chicago Crime Commission, June 28, 1963).

[60] Peterson, "Citizens' Crime Commissions," 15. See also Virgil W. Peterson, "How to Form a Citizens' Crime Commission," *Journal of Criminal Law, Criminology, and Police Science*, XLVI (Nov.–Dec., 1955), 485–99.

[61] See Chapter 13 for a discussion of the work of the police and the ways in which it can be improved.

3. They are the best equipped to detect and identify offenders and most of the conditions contributing to crime and delinquency.

4. Although undermanned, they have more manpower than any other agency interested in these problems and are on duty twenty-four hours every day.

5. Often they are the first to learn about law violations and usually have the first contact with offenders.

6. Police agencies have methods of coordinating their activities on a nation-wide basis through such channels as those provided by the International Association of Chiefs of Police and the Federal Bureau of Investigation.[62]

Although police officials differ among themselves regarding the extent to which they should participate in the prevention of crime and delinquency, they generally agree that they could contribute more in this field if the following obstacles were removed:

1. Inadequate salaries and working conditions for police personnel.

2. Inadequate personnel in police agencies.

3. Insufficient respect for law and law-enforcement officers.

4. Failure to seek police opinions concerning proposed legislation affecting law enforcement, crime prevention, and the handling of juveniles.

5. Inefficient administration of parole and probation systems.

6. Laws which prevent the apprehension and restraint of juveniles and youths when the safety of the community is involved.

7. The unavailability of juvenile court records to police.

8. The failure of the community to provide places of detention for juveniles.

9. The prohibition against taking fingerprints of juveniles.[63]

A police prevention program should be based upon the recognition that police agencies must give first consideration to support of the law and the protection of society and secondary consideration to the needs and privileges of the individual. Such a program should include at least the following elements:

1. The patrol and inspection of liquor establishments, dance halls, poolrooms, bowling alleys, swimming pools, skating rinks, parks, play-

[62] National Conference on Prevention and Control of Juvenile Delinquency, *Report on Role of Police* (Washington: Government Printing Office, 1947), pp. 7–9. See also O. W. Wilson, *Police Administration* (New York: McGraw-Hill Book Co., Inc., 1963), pp. 327–29.

[63] National Conference on Prevention and Control of Juvenile Delinquency, *Report on Role of Police*, pp. 15–17; Wilson, pp. 329–31. In general, Professor Wilson, an authority on police administration is not in favor of fingerprinting juveniles. He states, "As a general rule youthful offenders should not be fingerprinted by the police because the experience may have an unfortunate effect on the child and usually any advantage gained is not sufficiently great to justify this risk" (Wilson, p. 336).

grounds, vacant lots, and other places where youth may congregate and become subject to unwholesome influences. The primary purposes of patrol and inspection activities are: (a) to eradicate unwholesome influences, to lessen the opportunity for misconduct by the presence of the police, to enforce regulations, and to apprehend persons contributing to the delinquency of juveniles; (b) to discover persons in need of correction; (c) to assist in the supervision of problem children being dealt with by the police; and (d) to discover the need of prevention activities.[64]

2. The investigation of situations to ascertain the facts that are essential to detection and correction of criminals and delinquents.

3. The participation of the police in the broader community program of crime and delinquency prevention. Some authorities on police problems believe that the police should do more than this and actually assume a position of leadership in the development and operation of community councils.[65]

Many of the larger police departments have organized a juvenile division which handles such cases as offenses against the family (including desertion, abandonment, nonsupport, neglect and abuse of children, and contributing to the delinquency of a minor), sex offenses, possession or sale of obscene literature or pictures, and crimes involving juveniles. Policewomen are often assigned to the cases of women and children. The staff of the juvenile division participates in community activities directed toward the prevention of delinquency and cooperates in community surveys and studies.[66]

Rural police units are usually limited to one or two men. This means that the rural officer handles all types of police work and has little or no staff, inadequate crime detection equipment, and relatively meager detention facilities. Furthermore, the independent and self-sufficient mode of life of most rural people prevents the peace officer from getting very close to family problems. Nevertheless, the rural police officer's effectiveness in dealing with juvenile delinquents and predelinquents may be strengthened by the creation of a community council or similar coordinating device which assumes responsibility in planning and developing ways by which needed services for young people can be provided. In

[64] Wilson, pp. 338–40.

[65] *Ibid.*, pp. 340–42, 347–52.

[66] *Ibid.*, pp. 331–38, 342–47; V. A. Leonard, *Police Organization and Management* (Brooklyn: The Foundation Press, Inc., 1964), pp. 250–54; John P. Kenney and Dan G. Pursuit, *Police Work with Juveniles* (Springfield, Ill.: Charles C. Thomas, Publisher, 1959), pp. 27–48, 331–50; Richard A. Myren and Lynn D. Swanson, *Police Work with Children*, United States Children's Bureau Publication No. 399 (Washington, D.C.: Government Printing Office, 1962), pp. 1–19. For an examination of the curfew question, see "Curfew Ordinances and the Control of Nocturnal Juvenile Crime," *University of Pennsylvania Law Review*, CVII (Nov., 1958), 66–101; John E. Winters, *Crime and Kids* (Springfield, Ill.: Charles C Thomas, Publisher, 1959), pp. 27–34.

addition, farm organizations, schools, churches, parent-teachers associations, and service clubs can be used for the marshaling of public-opinion in support of the improvement of rural police agencies.[67]

New York City has one of the most elaborately organized police programs for the prevention of crime and delinquency in the United States. The following units play an important part in the operation of this program:

1. The Juvenile Aid Bureau (JAB), the origin of which dates back to 1930. Reorganized in 1959 and now part of the Youth Division of the police department, it is "responsible for planning and instituting measures designed to prevent delinquency and to provide adequate social treatment for delinquents and wayward minors." The work of JAB is directed toward these objectives: (a) the modification of the behavior of delinquents coming to its attention; (b) the discovery and removal of community conditions which contribute to delinquency; (c) the creation of constructive forces for the prevention of crime; and (d) the creation of a more favorable attitude on the part of youth toward law and law-enforcement agencies, and the development of public support for an effective program designed to deal with incipient crime.

2. The Police Athletic League (PAL), which was organized in 1932. This agency was created to provide recreational facilities for those young people whose cases appear to require such remedial measures. It seeks to instill good character, a sense of responsibility, and the development of a friendly relationship between youth and police officers. During 1946 over a quarter of a million boys and girls participated in activities sponsored by the Police Athletic League, which is supported by private contributions, benefit performances, and the annual dues of over 100,000 associate members.[68]

3. Precinct Coordinating Councils, which were set up in 1943. Established in each of New York City's eighty-one patrol precincts, these councils bring together representatives of private and public agencies interested in youth and welfare work. They are designed not to render service but to coordinate and promote the work of existing agencies and to educate the public to an awareness of their responsibility to youth.[69]

[67] National Conference on Prevention and Control of Juvenile Delinquency, *Report on Role of Police*, pp. 9–11.

[68] Opinion is divided regarding the desirability of having the police operate recreation programs. The manual prepared by an advisory police committee and issued by the Federal Security Agency in 1944 recommends that the actual conduct and operation of such programs should be in the hands of experienced recreation supervisors— not members of the police force. See *Techniques of Law Enforcement in the Treatment of Juveniles and the Prevention of Juvenile Delinquency* (Washington, D.C.: Government Printing Office, 1944), p. 38.

[69] James B. Nolan, "The Crime Prevention Work of New York City's Police," *Federal Probation*, XI (Apr.–June, 1947), 18–21.

COURTS AND CORRECTIONAL AGENCIES AND INSTITUTIONS

To the extent that courts, probation officers, correctional institutions, and parole agencies operate effectively to rehabilitate juvenile and adult offenders and deter others from becoming delinquents and criminals, they function as agencies of prevention. Suggestions for making them more effective in this respect have already been presented in preceding chapters and will not be repeated here, but the student is urged to bear them in mind so that he will have before him the complete picture of crime and delinquency prevention.

PUBLIC SUPPORT

One fact clearly emerges from the foregoing discussion. It is this: No one program alone can deal effectively with crime and delinquency. The home, the school, the church, the welfare agency, the clinic, the police, the court, the probation department, the correctional institution, the parole agency, and all the other agencies and institutions that are interested in crime and delinquency must work together as a team through coordinating councils or through some similar coordinating device in a concerted attack on these problems. But the teamwork cannot be complete without public support. This support must be given in the form of interest in community affairs, participation in community programs, law observance, insistence on wholesome community conditions and abundant opportunity for young people, respect for law enforcement and effective court procedures, demand for an adequate number of well-qualified police officers, judges, probation officers, welfare workers, institutional employees, and parole officers, and a willingness to pay for programs that can deal effectively with social problems.

The best way for citizens to learn about their government is to participate in its affairs. The surest way for them to develop a sense of responsibility regarding its effectiveness is to put time and energy into the solution of its problems. Citizens can, and should, serve without compensation on boards, commissions, committees, and councils to guide the policies of agencies and institutions and to organize and direct appropriate social action. In the capacity of volunteers they can, and should, serve as club leaders or advisors for groups of boys and girls; as instructors in special skills, such as dramatics, crafts, music, dancing, sports and games, nature lore, playground activities; as discussion leaders or project advisors on special subjects, such as home-making, sex education, public affairs, and vocations; as sponsors for probationers and parolees; as members and directors of prisoners' aid societies; and as leaders and workers in all the other community programs and activities which are in such great need of citizen participation.[70]

Only in this way can citizens come to appreciate that they have a responsibility, as well as a right, to participate in community activities. Only in this way can community programs receive the public support which they must have if they are to be effective instruments for the prevention of crime and delinquency. In fact, only in this way can citizens preserve their rights, because if they do not assume the responsibility of deciding what is right and what is wrong, then somebody else—some government official or so-called expert—will do this for them and tell them what they must and must not do. We have no magic formula for the elimination of crime and delinquency, but in our long struggle with them we have discovered that teamwork by volunteer and professional workers, when given adequate public support, can do much to keep these problems under control.[71]

[70] National Conference on Prevention and Control of Juvenile Delinquency, *Report on Citizen Participation* (Washington, D.C.: Government Printing Office, 1947), pp. 2, 3, 11–13.

[71] See John M. Martin, "Three Approaches to Delinquency Prevention: A Critique," *Crime and Delinquency*, VII (Jan., 1961), 16–24; J. Edgar Hoover, "The Challenges of Crime Control," *Federal Probation*, XX (June, 1956), 10–14; Robison, 41; The United Prison Association of Massachusetts, "What's New in Citizen Participation in Correctional Programs?" *Correctional Research*, Bull. No. 10 (Aug., 1960).

Selected Bibliography

The list of books and articles shown below represents a minimum selected bibliography. It is divided into the same four parts as the Contents. For additional references, the student should examine the footnotes in the text. The following textbooks and readings, which are not included in the bibliography, also should be consulted on the various aspects of the subject:

BARNES, HARRY ELMER, and TEETERS, NEGLEY K. *New Horizons in Criminology*, 3d ed. Englewood Cliffs, N.J.: Prentice-Hall, Inc., 1959.

BLOCH, HERBERT A., and GEIS, GILBERT. *Man, Crime, and Society*. New York: Random House, Inc., 1962.

BRANHAM, VERNON C., and KUTASH, SAMUEL B. *Encyclopedia of Criminology*. New York: The Philosophical Library, Inc., 1949.

CAVAN, RUTH SHONLE. *Criminology*, 3d ed. New York: Thomas Y. Crowell Co., 1962.

ELLIOTT, MABEL A. *Crime in Modern Society*. New York: Harper and Bros., 1952.

GILLIN, JOHN LEWIS. *Criminology and Penology*, 3d ed. New York: Appleton-Century-Crofts, Inc., 1945.

HAYNES, FRED E. *Criminology*, 2d ed. New York: McGraw-Hill Book Co., Inc., 1935.

HURWITZ, STEPHAN. *Criminology*. London: George Allen and Unwin, 1952.

JOHNSON, ELMER HUBERT. *Crime, Correction, and Society*. Homewood, Ill.: The Dorsey Press, 1964.

JOHNSTON, NORMAN, SAVITZ, LEONARD, and WOLFGANG, MARVIN E. (eds.). *The Sociology of Punishment and Correction*. New York: John Wiley and Sons, Inc., 1962.

KORN, RICHARD R., and McCORKLE, LLOYD W. *Criminology and Penology*. New York: Henry Holt and Co., Inc., 1959.

MORRIS, ALBERT. Criminology. New York: Longmans, Green and Co., Ltd., 1934.

RECKLESS, WALTER C. *The Crime Problem*, 3d ed. New York: Appleton-Century-Crofts, Inc., 1961.

SUTHERLAND, EDWIN H., and CRESSEY, DONALD R. *Principles of Criminology*, 6th ed. Philadelphia: J. B. Lippincott Co., 1960.

TAFT, DONALD R. *Criminology*, rev. ed. New York: The Macmillan Co., 1950.

TANNENBAUM, FRANK. *Crime and the Community*. Boston: Ginn and Co., 1938.

TAPPAN, PAUL W. *Crime, Justice, and Correction*. New York: McGraw-Hill Book Co., Inc., 1960.

VEDDER, CLYDE B., KOENIG, SAMUEL, and CLARK, ROBERT E. (eds.). *Criminology: A Book of Readings*. New York: The Dryden Press, Inc., 1953.

WOLFGANG, MARVIN E., SAVITZ, LEONARD, and JOHNSTON, NORMAN (eds.). *The Sociology of Crime and Delinquency*. New York: John Wiley and Sons, Inc., 1962.

WOOD, ARTHUR E., and WAITE, JOHN B. *Crime and Its Treatment*. New York: American Book Co., 1941.

PART I: THE PROBLEM

Alcoholics Anonymous: The Story of How Many Thousands of Men and Women Have Recovered from Alcoholism. New York: Works Publishing, Inc., 1946.

AMERICAN BAR ASSOCIATION COMMISSION ON ORGANIZED CRIME. *Organized Crime and Law Enforcement*. New York: The Grosby Press. Vol. I, 1952; Vol. II, 1953.

AUSUBEL, DAVID P. *Drug Addiction: Physiological, Psychological, and Sociological Aspects*. New York: Random House, Inc., 1958.

BACON, SHELDON D. "Alcohol and Complex Society," *Alcohol, Science, and Society*. New Haven: Journal of Studies on Alcohol, Inc., 1945, 179–200.

BANAY, RALPH S. "Alcoholism and Crime," *Quarterly Journal of Studies on Alcohol*, Vol. 2, No. 4 (March, 1942), 686–716.

BEATTIE, RONALD H. *Manual of Criminal Statistics*. New York: The American Prison Association, 1950.

BODENHEIMER, EDGAR. *Jurisprudence*. Cambridge: Harvard University Press, 1962.

BONGER, W. A. *Race and Crime*. Translated by Margaret M. Horduk. New York: Columbia University Press, 1943.

BROMBERG, WALTER, and RODGERS, TERRY C. "Marihuana and Aggressive Crime," *American Journal of Psychiatry*, Vol. 102, No. 6 (May, 1946), 825–827.

CALDWELL, ROBERT G. "A Reexamination of the Concept of White-Collar Crime," *Federal Probation*, Vol. 22, No. 1 (March, 1958), 30–36.

CHAFETZ, MORRIS E., and DEMONE, HAROLD W., JR. *Alcoholism and Society*. New York: Oxford University Press, 1962.

CLINARD, MARSHALL B. "Criminological Theories of Violations of Wartime Regulations," *American Sociological Review*, Vol. 11, No. 3 (June, 1946), 258–270.

———. *The Black Market*. New York: Rinehart and Co., 1952.

———. *Sociology of Deviant Behavior*. New York: Holt, Rinehart and Winston, Inc., 1963.

CONWELL, CHIC. *The Professional Thief*. Annotated and Interpreted by Edwin H. Sutherland. Chicago: University of Chicago Press, 1937.

CRESSEY, DONALD R. *Other People's Money*. Glencoe, Ill.: The Free Press, 1953.

DAVIS, F. J., FOSTER, H. H., JR., JEFFREY, C. R., and DAVIS, E. E. *Society and the Law*. New York: The Free Press of Glencoe, 1962.

DAVIS, KINGSLEY. "The Sociology of Prostitution," *American Sociological Review*, Vol. 2, No. 5 (October, 1937), 744–755.

DE RIVER, J. PAUL. *The Sexual Criminal*. Springfield, Ill.: Charles C. Thomas, Publisher, 1956.

EAST, W. NORWOOD. "Physical Factors and Criminal Behavior," *Journal of Clinical Psychopathology*, Vol. 8, No. 1 (July, 1946), 7–36.

ELDRIDGE, WILLIAM BUTLER. *Narcotics and the Law: A Critique of the American Experiment in Narcotic Drug Control*. New York: New York University Press, 1962.

FEDERAL BUREAU OF INVESTIGATION, UNITED STATES DEPARTMENT OF JUSTICE. *Uniform Crime Reports for the United States and Its Possessions*. Washington, D.C.: Government Printing Office.

FEDERAL BUREAU OF PRISONS, UNITED STATES DEPARTMENT OF JUSTICE. *Annual Reports on Federal Prisons*. Leavenworth, Kan.: United States Penitentiary.

————. *National Prisoner Statistics*.

GIBBONS, DON C., and GARRITY, DONALD L. "Definition and Analysis of Certain Criminal Types," *Journal of Criminal Law, Criminology, and Police Science*, Vol. 53, No. 1 (March, 1962), 27–35.

GRAY, JOHN CHIPMAN. *The Nature and Sources of the Law*. New York: The Macmillan Co., 1921.

HAGGARD, H. W., and JELLINEK, E. M. *Alcohol Explored*. New York: Doubleday and Co., Inc., 1942.

HALL, JEROME. *General Principles of Criminal Law*. Indianapolis: The Bobbs-Merrill Co., Inc., 1960.

HARTUNG, FRANK E. "White-Collar Offenses in the Wholesale Meat Industry in Detroit," *American Journal of Sociology*, Vol. 56, No. 1 (July, 1950), 25–34.

————. "White-Collar Crime: Its Significance for Theory and Practice," *Federal Probation*, Vol. 17, No. 2 (June, 1953), 31–36.

HOEBEL, E. ADAMSON. *The Law of Primitive Man*. Cambridge: Harvard University Press, 1954.

JELLINEK, E. M. *The Disease Concept of Alcoholism*. New Haven: Hillhouse Press, 1960.

KOLB, LAWRENCE. *Drug Addiction*. Springfield, Ill.: Charles C. Thomas, Publisher, 1962.

LAPIERE, RICHARD T. *A Theory of Social Control*. New York: McGraw-Hill Book Co., Inc., 1954.

LESSA, WILLIAM A. "An Appraisal of Constitutional Typologies," No. 62, Memoirs Series, American Anthropological Association, *American Anthropologist*, Vol. 45, No. 4, Part 2 (October, 1943), 5–96.

LINDESMITH, ALFRED R. *Opiate Addiction*. Bloomington, Ind.: Principia Press, Inc., 1947.

LINDESMITH, ALFRED R., and DUNHAM, H. WARREN. "Some Principles of Criminal Typology," *Social Forces*, Vol. 19, No. 3 (March, 1941), 307–314.

LLEWELLYN, KARL N. *Jurisprudence*. Chicago: The University of Chicago Press, 1962.

MALINOWSKI, BRONISLAW. *Crime and Custom in Savage Society*. New York: Harcourt, Brace and Co., Inc., 1926.

MAURER, DAVID W., and VOGEL, VICTOR H. *Narcotics and Narcotic Addiction*. Springfield, Ill.: Charles C. Thomas, Publisher, 1962.

MERTON, ROBERT K. *Social Theory and Social Structure.* Glencoe, Ill.: The
  Free Press, 1957.
MILLER, JUSTIN. *Handbook of Criminal Law.* St. Paul, Minn.: West Publishing
  Co., 1934.
MOWRER, HARRIET R. "A Psychocultural Analysis of the Alcoholic," *American
  Sociological Review,* Vol. 5, No. 4 (August, 1940), 546–557.
NATIONAL COMMISSION ON LAW OBSERVANCE AND ENFORCEMENT. *Report on
  the Cost of Crime,* Report No. 12. Washington, D.C.: Government Printing
  Office, 1931.
PERKINS, ROLLINS M. *Criminal Law.* Brooklyn, N.Y.: The Foundation Press,
  Inc., 1957.
PERLMAN, I. RICHARD. "The Meaning of Juvenile Delinquency Statistics," *Fed-
  eral Probation,* Vol. 13, No. 3 (September, 1949), 63–67.
PESCOR, M. J. "The Problem of Narcotic Drug Addiction," *Journal of Criminal
  Law, Criminology, and Police Science,* Vol. 43, No. 4 (November–December,
  1952), 471–481.
PETERSON, VIRGIL W. *Barbarians in Our Midst.* Boston: Little, Brown and Co.,
  1952.
PITTMAN, DAVID J., and SNYDER, CHARLES R. (eds.). *Society, Culture, and
  Drinking Patterns.* New York: John Wiley and Sons, Inc., 1962.
POSPISIL, LEOPOLD. *Kapauku Papuans and Their Law.* New Haven: Yale Uni-
  versity Publications in Anthropology, No. 54, 1958.
POUND, ROSCOE. *An Introduction to the Philosophy of Law.* New Haven: Yale
  University Press, 1954.
RADZINOWICZ, LEON. *A History of English Criminal Law.* New York: The
  Macmillan Co. Vol. I, 1948; Vol. II, 1957; Vol. III, 1957.
RECKLESS, WALTER C. "A Sociologist Looks at Prostitution," *Federal Probation,*
  Vol. 7, No. 2 (April–June, 1943), 12–16.
ROSS, EDWARD A. *Social Control.* New York: The Macmillan Co., 1916.
SCHUESSLER, KARL F., and CRESSEY, DONALD R. "Personality Characteristics
  of Criminals," *American Journal of Sociology,* Vol. 55, No. 5 (March, 1950),
  476–484.
SCHUR, EDWIN M. *Narcotic Addiction in Britain and America.* Bloomington:
  Indiana University Press, 1962.
SCHWARTZ, EDWARD E. "Statistics on Juvenile Delinquency in the United
  States," *The Annals of the American Academy of Political and Social Science,*
  Vol. 261 (January, 1949), 9–20.
SEAGLE, WILLIAM. *The History of Law.* New York: Tudor Publishing Co.,
  1946.
SELLIN, THORSTEN. "The Basis of a Crime Index," *Journal of Criminal Law and
  Criminology,* Vol. 22, No. 3 (September, 1931), 335–356.
———. *Research Memorandum on Crime in the Depression.* New York: Social
  Science Research Council, Bulletin 27, 1937. Chap. 4, "The Index Question."
———. "The Uniform Criminal Statistics Act," *Journal of Criminal Law and
  Criminology,* Vol. 40, No. 6 (March–April, 1950), 679–700.
———. "The Significance of Records of Crime," *The Law Quarterly Review,*
  Vol. 67 (October, 1951), 489–504.
SHAW, CLIFFORD R. *The Jack Roller: A Delinquent Boy's Own Story.* Chicago:
  University of Chicago Press, 1930.
SHAW, CLIFFORD R., MCKAY, HENRY D., and HANSON, HAROLD B. *Brothers in
  Crime.* Chicago: University of Chicago Press, 1938.

SHAW, CLIFFORD R. and MOORE, M. E. *The Natural History of a Delinquent Career*. Chicago: University of Chicago Press. 1931.

STEPHEN, JAMES F. *A History of the Criminal Law of England*. London: Macmillan and Co., Ltd., 1883.

SUTHERLAND, EDWIN II. "White-Collar Criminality," *American Sociological Review*, Vol. 5, No. 1 (February, 1940), 1–12.

———. "Crime and Business," *The Annals of the American Academy of Political and Social Science*, Vol. 217 (September, 1941), 112–118.

———. "Is 'White-Collar Crime' Crime?" *American Sociological Review*, Vol. 10, No. 2 (April, 1945), 132–139.

———. *White Collar Crime*. New York: The Dryden Press, Inc., 1949.

TAPPAN, PAUL W. "Who Is the Criminal?" *American Sociological Review*, Vol. 12, No. 1 (February, 1947), 96–102.

———. "Crime and the Criminal," *Federal Probation*, Vol. 11, No. 3 (July–September, 1947), 41–44.

TYLER, GUS (ed.). "Combatting Organized Crime," *The Annals of the American Academy of Political and Social Science*, Vol. 347 (May, 1963).

UNITED STATES BUREAU OF THE CENSUS. *Annual Reports on Judicial Criminal Statistics*, 1932–45. Washington, D.C.: Government Printing Office, 1934–47.

———. *Annual Reports on Prisoners in State and Federal Prisons and Reformatories*, 1926–46. Washington, D.C.: Government Printing Office, 1929–48.

UNITED STATES CHILDREN'S BUREAU. *Juvenile Court Statistics*. Washington, D.C.: Government Printing Office.

———. *Report to the Congress on Juvenile Delinquency*. Washington, D.C.: Government Printing Office, 1960.

UNITED STATES SENATE, SELECT COMMITTEE ON IMPROPER ACTIVITIES IN THE LABOR OR MANAGEMENT FIELD. *Final Report*. Washington, D.C.: Government Printing Office, 1960.

UNITED STATES SENATE, SPECIAL COMMITTEE TO INVESTIGATE ORGANIZED CRIME IN INTERSTATE COMMERCE. *Interim and Final Reports*. Washington, D.C.: Government Printing Office, 1951.

WOOD, ARTHUR LEWIS. "Minority-Group Criminality and Cultural Integration," *Journal of Criminal Law and Criminology*, Vol. 37, No. 6 (March–April, 1947), 498–510.

PART II: CAUSATION

ABRAHAMSEN, DAVID. *The Psychology of Crime*. New York: Columbia University Press, 1960.

ALEXANDER, FRANZ, and HEALY, WILLIAM. *Roots of Crime*. New York: Alfred A. Knopf, Inc., 1935.

ALEXANDER, FRANZ, and STAUB, HUGO. *The Criminal, the Judge, and the Public*. Glencoe, Ill.: The Free Press, 1956.

ASCHAFFENBURG, GUSTAV. *Crime and Its Repression*. Translated by A. Albrecht. Boston: Little, Brown and Co., 1913.

BARNES, HARRY ELMER, and SHALLOO, J. P. "Modern Theories of Criminology and Penology," *Contemporary Social Theory*. New York: Appleton-Century-Crofts, Inc., 1940. Chap. 20.

BERNALDO DE QUIROS, C. *Modern Theories of Criminality*. Translated by Alfonso de Salvio. Boston: Little, Brown and Co., 1911.

BLOCH, HERBERT A., and NIEDERHOFFER, ARTHUR. *The Gang: A Study in Adolescent Behavior*. New York: The Philosophical Library, Inc., 1958.

BLUMER, HERBERT, and HAUSER, PHILIP M. *Movies, Delinquency, and Crime*. New York: The Macmillan Co., 1933.

BONGER, W. A. *Criminality and Economic Conditions*. Translated by H. P. Horton. Boston: Little, Brown and Co., 1916.

BROMBERG, W., and THOMPSON, C. B. "The Relation of Psychosis, Mental Defect, and Personality Types to Crime," *Journal of Criminal Law and Criminology*, Vol. 28, No. 1 (May–June, 1937), 70–89.

CLINARD, MARSHALL B. "The Process of Urbanization and Criminal Behavior," *American Journal of Sociology*, Vol. 48, No. 2 (September, 1942), 202–213.

———. "Rural Criminal Offenders," *American Journal of Sociology*, Vol. 50, No. 1 (July, 1944), 38–45.

———. "Sociologists and American Criminology," *Journal of Criminal Law and Criminology*, Vol. 41, No. 5 (January–February, 1951), 549–577.

CLOWARD, RICHARD A., and OHLIN, LLOYD E. *Delinquency and Opportunity: A Theory of Delinquent Gangs*. Glencoe, Ill.: The Free Press, 1960.

COHEN, ALBERT E. *Delinquent Boys*. Glencoe, Ill.: The Free Press, 1955.

COHEN, ALBERT, LINDESMITH, ALFRED, and SCHUESSLER, KARL (eds.). *The Sutherland Papers*. Bloomington: Indiana University Press, 1956.

CRESSEY, DONALD R. "Application and Verification of the Differential Association Theory," *Journal of Criminal Law, Criminology, and Police Science*, Vol. 43, No. 1 (May–June, 1952), 43–52.

DURKHEIM, ÉMILE. *Suicide: A Study in Sociology*. Translated by John A. Spaulding and George Simpson. Glencoe, Ill.: The Free Press, 1951.

ESTABROOK, ARTHUR H. *The Jukes in 1915*. Washington, D.C.: The Carnegie Institution of Washington, Publication 240, 1916.

FERRERO, GINA LOMBROSO. *Criminal Man*. New York: C. P. Putnam's Sons, 1911.

FERRI, ENRICO. *Criminal Sociology*. Translated by Joseph I. Kelly and John Lisle. Boston: Little, Brown and Co., 1917.

FINK, ARTHUR. *Causes of Crime*. Philadelphia: University of Pennsylvania Press, 1938.

GARAFALO, RAFFAELE. *Criminology*. Translated by Robert W. Millar. Boston: Little, Brown and Co., 1914.

GITTLER, JOSEPH B. (ed.). *Review of Sociology: Analysis of a Decade*. New York: John Wiley and Sons, Inc., 1957. Chap. 14.

GLUECK, SHELDON, and GLUECK, ELEANOR T. *500 Criminal Careers*. New York: Alfred A. Knopf, Inc., 1930.

———. *One Thousand Juvenile Delinquents*. Cambridge: Harvard University Press, 1934.

———. *Five Hundred Delinquent Women*. New York: Alfred A. Knopf, Inc., 1934.

———. *Later Criminal Careers*. New York: The Commonwealth Fund, 1937.

———. *Unraveling Juvenile Delinquency*. New York: The Commonwealth Fund, 1950.

———. *Physique and Delinquency*. New York: Harper and Bros., 1956.

GODDARD, HENRY H. *The Kallikak Family*. New York: The Macmillan Co., 1912.

———. *Human Efficiency and Levels of Intelligence*. Princeton: Princeton University Press, 1920.

GORING, CHARLES. *The English Convict*, abridged ed. London: His Majesty's Stationery Office, 1919.

HALL, CALVIN C., and LINDZEY, GARDNER. *Theories of Personality*. New York: John Wiley and Sons, Inc., 1957.

HEALY, WILLIAM. *The Individual Delinquent*. Boston: Little, Brown and Co., 1915.

HEALY, WILLIAM, and BRONNER, AUGUSTA F. *Delinquents and Criminals*. New York: The Macmillan Co., 1926.

———. *New Light on Delinquency and Its Treatment*. New Haven: Yale University Press, 1936.

HILGARD, ERNEST R. *Theories of Learning*. New York: Appleton-Century-Crofts, Inc., 1956.

HOOTON, EARNEST A. *Crime and the Man*. Cambridge: Harvard University Press, 1939.

JONASSEN, CHRISTEN T. "A Re-Evaluation and Critique of the Logic and Some Methods of Shaw and McKay," *American Sociological Review*, Vol. 14, No. 5 (October, 1949), 608–617.

KARPMAN, BENJAMIN. *Case Studies in the Psychopathology of Crime*. New York: The Mental Science Publishing Co., 1939.

KVARACEUS, WILLIAM C., and MILLER, WALTER B. *Delinquent Behavior: Culture and the Individual*. Washington, D.C.: National Education Association of the United States, 1959.

LINDESMITH, ALFRED, and LEVIN, YALE. "The Lombrosian Myth in Criminology." *American Journal of Sociology*, Vol. 42, No. 5 (March, 1937), 653–671.

LINDNER, ROBERT M. *Rebel Without Cause*. New York: Grune and Stratton, Inc., 1944.

———. *Stone Walls and Men*. New York: Odyssey Press, 1946.

LOMBROSO, CESARE. *Crime, Its Causes and Remedies*. Boston: Little, Brown, and Co., 1911.

MANNHEIM, HERMANN. *Pioneers in Criminology*. Chicago: Quadrangle Books, Inc., 1960.

MERTON, R. K., BROOM, L., and COTTRELL, L. S., JR. (eds.). *Sociology Today: Problems and Prospects*. New York: Basic Books, Inc., 1959. Chap. 23.

MORRIS, TERENCE. *The Criminal Area: A Study in Social Ecology*. London: Routledge and Kegan Paul, Ltd., 1958.

MUNROE, RUTH L. *Schools of Psychoanalytic Thought*. New York: The Dryden Press, Inc., 1955.

NATIONAL COMMISSION ON LAW OBSERVANCE AND ENFORCEMENT. *Report on the Causes of Crime*, Report No. 13. Washington, D.C.: Government Printing Office, 1931. Vols. 1, 2.

NYE, F. IVAN. *Family Relationships and Delinquent Behavior*. New York: John Wiley and Sons, Inc., 1958.

PARMELEE, MAURICE. *The Principles of Anthropology and Sociology in Their Relations to Criminal Procedure*. New York: The Macmillan Co., 1911.

PARSONS, TALCOTT. *Essays in Sociological Theory*. Glencoe, Ill.: The Free Press, 1954.

———. *The Social System*. Glencoe, Ill.: The Free Press, 1951.

PHILLIPSON, COLEMAN. *Three Criminal Law Reformers*. New York: E. P. Dutton and Co., Inc., 1923.

POLLAK, OTTO. *The Criminality of Women*. Philadelphia: University of Pennsylvania Press, 1950.

RADZINOWICZ, L., and TURNER, J. W. C. (eds.). *Mental Abnormality and Crime*. English Studies in Criminal Science, Vol. II. London: Macmillan and Co., Ltd., 1949.

RECKLESS, WALTER C. *The Etiology of Delinquent and Criminal Behavior*. New York: Social Science Research Council, Bulletin 50, 1943.

ROBISON, SOPHIA M. *Can Delinquency Be Measured?* New York: Columbia University Press, 1936.

SALEILLES, RAYMOND. *The Individualization of Punishment*. Boston: Little, Brown and Co., 1911.

SCHLAPP, MAX G., and SMITH, EDWARD H. *The New Criminology*. New York: Boni and Liveright, 1928.

SELLIN, THORSTEN. *Research Memorandum on Crime in the Depression*. New York: Social Science Research Council, Bulletin 27, 1937.

———. *Culture Conflict and Crime*. New York: Social Science Research Council, Bulletin 41, 1938.

———. (ed.). "Juvenile Delinquency," *The Annals of the American Academy of Political and Social Science*, Vol. 261 (January, 1949).

———. "The Sociological Study of Criminality," *Journal of Criminal Law and Criminology*, Vol. 41, No. 4 (November–December, 1950), 406–422.

SHALLOO, JEREMIAH P. (ed.). "Crime in the United States," *The Annals of the American Academy of Political and Social Science*, Vol. 217 (September, 1941).

SHAW, CLIFFORD R., and McKAY, HENRY D. *Juvenile Delinquency and Urban Areas*. Chicago: University of Chicago Press, 1942.

SHELDON, WILLIAM H., HARTL, EMIL M., and McDERMOTT, EUGENE. *Varieties of Delinquent Youth*. New York: Harper and Bros., 1949.

SHULMAN, HARRY MANUEL. "Intelligence and Delinquency," *Journal of Criminal Law and Criminology*, Vol. 41, No. 6 (March–April, 1951), 763–781.

SNODGRASSE, RICHARD M. "Crime and the Constitution Human: A Survey," *Journal of Criminal Law, Criminology and Police Science*. Vol. 42, No. 1 (May–June, 1951), 18–52.

TARDE, GABRIEL. *Penal Philosophy*. Translated by R. Howell. Boston: Little, Brown and Co., 1912.

THOMAS, WILLIAM I. *The Unadjusted Girl*. Boston: Little, Brown and Co., 1923.

THRASHER, FREDERIC M. *The Gang*. Chicago: University of Chicago Press, 1927.

VOLD, GEORGE B. *Theoretical Criminology*. New York: Oxford University Press, 1958.

WHYTE, WILLIAM F. *Street Corner Society*. Chicago: University of Chicago Press, 1943.

WOLFGANG, MARVIN E. *Patterns in Criminal Homicide*. Philadelphia: University of Pennsylvania, 1958.

PART III: CRIME AND JUSTICE

ADVISORY COUNCIL OF JUDGES OF THE NATIONAL PROBATION AND PAROLE ASSO-CIATION. *Guides for Sentencing*. New York: National Probation and Parole Association, 1957.

AMERICAN LAW INSTITUTE. *Model Penal Code, Proposed Official Draft*. Philadelphia: The American Law Institute, 1962.

————. *Youth Correction Authority Act*. Philadelphia: The American Law Institute, 1940.

BECK, BERTRAM M. *Five States: A Study of the Youth Authority Program As Promulgated by the American Law Institute*. Philadelphia: The American Law Institute, 1951.

BELDEN, EVELINA. *Courts in the United States Hearing Children's Cases*, United States Children's Bureau Publication No. 65. Washington, D.C.: Government Printing Office, 1920.

CALDWELL, ROBERT G. "The Juvenile Court: Its Development and Some Major Problems," *Journal of Criminal Law, Criminology, and Police Science*, Vol. 51, No. 5 (January–February, 1961), 493–511.

CALLAGY, MARTIN V. "Legal Aid in Criminal Cases," *Journal of Criminal Law, Criminology, and Police Science*, Vol. 42, No. 5 (January–February, 1952), 589–624.

CLARKE, HELEN I. *Social Legislation*. New York: Appleton-Century-Crofts, Inc., 1957.

COSULICH, GILBERT. *Juvenile Court Laws in the United States*. New York: National Probation Association, 1939.

DAX, HUBERT E., and TIBBS, BROOKE. *Arrest, Search and Seizure*. Milwaukee, Wisconsin: Hammersmith-Kortmeyer Co., 1950.

ELLINGSTON, JOHN R. *Protecting Our Children from Criminal Careers*. New York: Prentice-Hall, Inc., 1948.

FOSDICK, RAYMOND B. *American Police Systems*. New York: The Century Co., 1920.

FRANK, JEROME. *Courts on Trial*. Princeton: Princeton University Press, 1949.

GOLDSTEIN, IRVING. *Trial Technique*. Chicago: Callaghan and Co., Inc., 1935.

GREEN, EDWARD. *Judicial Attitudes in Sentencing*. London: Macmillan and Co., Ltd., 1961.

GURVITCH, GEORGES. *Sociology of Law*. New York: Philosophical Library & Alliance Book Corporation, 1942.

GUTTMACHER, MANFRED S., and WEIHOFEN, HENRY. *Psychiatry and the Law*. New York: W. W. Norton and Co., Inc., 1952.

HALL, JEROME. *Cases and Readings on Criminal Law and Procedure*. Indianapolis: The Bobbs-Merrill Co., Inc., 1949.

————. *Studies in Jurisprudence and Criminal Theory*. New York: Oceana Publications, Inc., 1958.

HARNO, ALBERT J. "Some Significant Developments in Criminal Law and Procedure in the Last Century," *Journal of Criminal Law, Criminology and Police Science*, Vol. 42, No. 4 (November–December, 1951), 427–467.

HOLTON, KARL. "California Youth Authority: Eight Years of Action," *Journal of Criminal Law and Criminology*, Vol. 41, No. 1 (May–June, 1950), 1–23.

HOOVER, J. EDGAR. *Persons in Hiding*. Boston: Little, Brown and Co., 1938.

Hyde, Laurance M. "The Missouri Plan for Selection and Tenure of Judges," *Journal of Criminal Law and Criminology*, Vol. 39, No. 3 (September–October, 1948), 277–287.

Inbau, Fred E. *Self-Incrimination*. Springfield, Ill.: Charles C. Thomas, Publisher, 1950.

Inbau, Fred E., and Reid, John E. *Lie Detection and Criminal Investigation*. Baltimore: The Williams and Wilkins Co., 1953.

———. *Criminal Interrogation and Confession*. Baltimore: The Williams and Wilkins Co., 1962.

Institute for Training in Municipal Administraton. *Municipal Police Administration*. Ann Arbor, Mich.: Lithoprinted by Cushing-Mallory, Inc., 1961.

Kaplan, Benjamin, and Hall, Livingston (eds.). "Judicial Administration and the Common Man," *The Annals of the American Academy of Political and Social Science*, Vol. 287 (May, 1953).

La Piere, Richard. *The Freudian Ethic*. New York: Duell, Sloan, and Pearce, Inc., 1959.

Lenroot, Katharine F. "The Juvenile Court Today," *Federal Probation*, Vol. 13, No. 3 (September, 1949), 9–15.

Leonard, V. A. *Police Organization and Management*. Brooklyn: The Foundation Press, Inc., 1964.

Lou, Herbert H. *Juvenile Courts in the United States*. Chapel Hill: University of North Carolina Press, 1927.

Ludwig, Frederick J. *Youth and the Law*. Brooklyn: The Foundation Press, Inc., 1955.

McCormick, Charles T. *Handbook of the Law of Evidence*. St. Paul, Minn.: West Publishing Co., 1954.

McEnnis, L. J., Jr. "The Background and Development of the Traffic Institute of Northwestern University," *Journal of Criminal Law, Criminology, and Police Science*, Vol. 42, No. 5 (January–February, 1952), 663–673.

MacNamara, Donal E. J. "American Police Administration at Mid-Century," *Public Administration Review*, Vol. 10, No. 3 (Summer, 1950), 181–189.

Michael, J., and Adler, M. J. *Crime, Law, and Social Science*. New York: Harcourt, Brace and Co., Inc., 1933.

Millspaugh, Arthur C. *Crime Control by the National Government*. Washington, D.C.: The Brookings Institution, 1937.

Moreland, Roy. *Modern Criminal Procedure*. Indianapolis: The Bobbs-Merrill Co., Inc., 1959.

National Commission on Law Observance and Enforcement. *Report on Prosecution*, Report No. 4. Washington, D.C.: Government Printing Office, 1931.

———. *Report on Criminal Procedure*, Report No. 8. Washington, D.C.: Government Printing Office, 1931.

———. *Report on Lawlessness in Law Enforcement*, Report No. 11. Washington, D.C.: Government Printing Office, 1931.

———. *Report on Police*, Report No. 14. Washington, D.C.: Government Printing Office, 1931.

National Probation and Parole Association. *Standard Family Court Act*. New York: National Probation and Parole Association, 1959.

———. *Standard Juvenile Court Act*, 6th ed. New York: National Probation and Parole Association, 1959.

O'HARA, CHARLES E. *Fundamentals of Criminal Investigation.* Springfield, Ill.: Charles C. Thomas, Publisher, 1956.

O'HARA, CHARLES E., and OSTERBURG, JAMES W. *An Introduction to Criminalistics.* New York: The Macmillan Co., 1952.

ORFIELD, LESTER BERNHARDT. *Criminal Procedure from Arrest to Appeal.* New York: New York University Press, 1947.

PERKINS, ROLLIN M. *Elements of Police Science.* Chicago: The Foundation Press, Inc., 1942.

PHILLIPS, ORIE L. "The Federal Youth Corrections Act," *Federal Probation,* Vol. 15, No. 1 (March, 1951), 3–11.

POUND, ROSCOE. *Criminal Justice in America.* New York: Henry Holt and Co., Inc., 1930.

———. "The Rise of Socialized Criminal Justice," *Yearbook, 1942.* New York: National Probation Association, 1942. Pp. 1–22.

———. "The Juvenile Court and the Law," *Yearbook, 1944.* New York: National Probation Association, 1945. Pp. 1–22.

Poverty and the Administration of Federal Criminal Justice. Report of the Attorney General's Committee on Poverty and the Administration of Criminal Justice. Submitted on February 25, 1963.

PUTTKAMMER, ERNST W. *Administration of Criminal Law.* Chicago: University of Chicago Press, 1953.

RUBIN, SOL. "Changing Youth Correction Authority Concepts," *Focus,* Vol. 29, No. 3 (May, 1950), 77–82.

———. "Protecting the Child in the Juvenile Court," *Journal of Criminal Law, Criminology, and Police Science,* Vol. 43, No. 4 (November–December, 1952), 425–440.

RUBIN, SOL, WEIHOFEN, HENRY, EDWARDS, GEORGE, ROSENZWEIG, SIMON. *The Law of Criminal Correction.* St. Paul, Minn.: West Publishing Co., 1963.

SCHWARTZ, LOUIS B. (ed.). "Crime and the American Penal System," *The Annals of the American Academy of Political and Social Science,* Vol. 339 (January, 1962).

SHALLOO, JEREMIAH P. *Private Police: With Special Reference to Pennsylvania.* Philadelphia: The American Academy of Political and Social Science, 1933. Monograph No. 1.

SMITH, BRUCE. *Rural Crime Control.* New York: Institute of Public Administration, Columbia University, 1933.

——— (ed.). "New Goals in Police Management," *The Annals of the American Academy of Political and Social Science,* Vol. 291 (January, 1954).

———. *Police Systems in the United States.* New York: Harper and Bros., 1960.

SNYDER, LE MOYNE. *Homicide Investigation.* Springfield, Ill.: Charles C. Thomas, Publisher, 1959.

SÖDERMAN, HARRY, and O'CONNELL, JOHN J. *Modern Criminal Investigation.* Revised by Charles E. O'Hara. New York: Funk and Wagnalls Co., Inc., 1962.

SOWLE, CLAUDE R. (ed.). *Police Power and Individual Freedom.* Chicago: Aldine Publishing Co., 1962.

SUSSMAN, FREDERICK B. *Law of Juvenile Delinquency.* New York: Oceana Publications, 1959.

SZASZ, THOMAS. *The Myth of Mental Illness.* New York: Hoeber-Harper, Inc., 1961.

TAPPAN, PAUL W. *Comparative Survey of Juvenile Delinquency,* Part I, North America. New York: United Nations Department of Economics and Social Affairs, 1958.

TIMASHEFF, N. S. *An Introduction to the Sociology of Law.* Cambridge: Harvard University Committee on Research in the Social Sciences, 1939.

VARON, JOSEPH A. *Searches, Seizures, and Immunities.* Indianapolis: The Bobbs-Merrill Co., Inc., 1961.

VOLLMER, AUGUST, and PARKER, ALFRED E. *Crime and the State Police.* Berkeley: University of California Press, 1935.

WAITE, JOHN BARKER. *Criminal Law in Action.* New York: Scars Publishing Co., Inc., 1934.

WEIHOFEN, HENRY. *Mental Disorder as a Criminal Defense.* Buffalo, N.Y.: Dennis and Co., Inc., 1954.

WHITEHEAD, DON. *The F. B. I. Story.* New York: Random House, Inc., 1956.

WILLIAMS, JACK KENNY. *Vogues in Villainy.* Columbia, S.C.: University of South Carolina Press, 1959.

WILSON, O. W. *Police Administration.* New York: McGraw-Hill Book Co., Inc., 1963.

PART IV: CORRECTION AND PREVENTION

ALEXANDER, MYRL E. *Jail Administration.* Springfield, Ill.: Charles C. Thomas, Publisher, 1957.

ALINSKY, SAUL D. *Reveille for Radicals.* Chicago: University of Chicago Press, 1946.

AMERICAN CORRECTIONAL ASSOCIATION. *Manual of Correctional Standards.* New York: American Correctional Association, 1959.

AMERICAN PRISON ASSOCIATION. *Report of the Committee on Crime Prevention.* New York: American Prison Association, 1942.

————. *Manual of Suggested Standards for a State Correctional System.* New York: American Prison Association, 1946.

————. *Handbook on Classification in Correctional Institutions.* New York: American Prison Association, 1947.

————. *Handbook on Pre-release Preparation in Correctional Institutions.* New York: American Prison Association, 1950.

————. *Library Manual for Correctional Institutions.* New York: American Prison Association, 1950.

————. *In-Service Training Standards for Prison Custodial Officers.* New York: American Prison Association, 1951.

————. *Handbook on the Inmate's Relationships with Persons from Outside the Adult Correctional Institution.* New York: American Prison Association, 1953.

————. *Prison Riots and Disturbances.* New York: American Prison Association, May, 1953.

Attorney General's Survey of Release Procedures. Washington, D.C.: Government Printing Office, 1939. Vol. II, "Probation."

Attorney General's Survey of Release Procedures. Washington, D.C.: Government Printing Office, 1939. Vol. III, "Pardon."

Attorney General's Survey of Release Procedures. Washington, D.C.: Government Printing Office, 1939. Vol. IV, "Parole."

Attorney General's Survey of Release Procedures. Leavenworth, Kansas: Federal Prison Industries, Inc., Press, 1940. Vol. V, "Prisons."

BARNES, HARRY ELMER. *The Evolution of Penology in Pennsylvania.* Indianapolis: The Bobbs-Merrill Co., 1927.
———. *The Story of Punishment.* Boston: The Stratford Co., 1930.
BATES, SANFORD. *Prisons and Beyond.* New York: The Macmillan Co., 1936.
BEAM, KENNETH S. "Community Coordination," Report of a National Survey of Coordinating and Neighborhood Councils, *Coping with Crime, Yearbook of the National Probation Association.* New York: National Probation Association, 1937.
BIXBY, F. LOVELL, and McCORKLE, LLOYD W. "Applying the Principles of Group Therapy in Correctional Institutions," *"Federal Probation,* Vol. 14, No. 1 (March, 1950), 36–40.
———. "Guided Group Interaction in Correctional Work," *American Sociological Review,* Vol. 16, No. 4 (August, 1951), 455–461.
CALDWELL, MORRIS GILMORE. "Review of a New Type of Probation Study Made in Alabama," *Federal Probation,* Vol. 15, No. 2 (June, 1951), 3–11.
CALDWELL, ROBERT G. *Red Hannah.* Philadelphia: University of Pennsylvania Press, 1947.
CASEY, ROY. *The Modern Jail: Design, Equipment, Operation.* Keene, Tex.: Continental Press, 1958.
Charter to William Penn and Laws of the Province of Pennsylvania, 1682–1700. Edited by George, Nead, and McCamant; Harrisburg: L. S. Hart, State Printer, 1879.
CLEMMER, DONALD. *The Prison Community.* Boston: The Christopher Publishing House, 1940.
COHEN, MORRIS RAPHAEL. *Reason and Law.* Glencoe, Ill.: The Free Press, 1950.
CRESSEY, DONALD R. (ed.). *The Prison: Studies in Institutional Organization and Change.* New York: Holt, Rinehart, and Winston, Inc., 1961.
DRESSLER, DAVID. *Probation and Parole.* New York: Columbia University Press, 1951.
FEDERAL BUREAU OF PRISONS. *Manual of Jail Management.* Washington, D.C.: April, 1948.
———. *Handbook of Correctional Institution Design and Construction.* Washington, D.C.: Federal Bureau of Prisons, 1949.
———. *Recent Prison Construction, 1950–1960.* Washington, D.C.: Federal Bureau of Prisons, 1960.
FISHMAN, JOSEPH F. *Crucibles of Crime.* New York: Cosmopolis Press, 1923.
GIARDINI, G. I. *The Parole Process.* Springfield, Ill.: Charles C. Thomas, Publisher, 1959.
GLUECK, SHELDON, and GLUECK, ELEANOR T. *Preventing Crime.* New York: McGraw-Hill Book Co., Inc., 1936.
———. *Juvenile Delinquents Grown Up.* New York: The Commonwealth Fund, 1940.
———. *Criminal Careers in Retrospect,* New York: The Commonwealth Fund, 1943.
———. *After-Conduct of Discharged Offenders.* London: Macmillan and Co., Ltd., 1945.
HALL, JEROME. *Theft, Law, and Society,* 2d ed. Indianapolis: The Bobbs-Merrill Co., 1952.
HAYNES, FRED E. *The American Prison System.* New York: McGraw-Hill Book Co., Inc., 1939.

HEALY, WILLIAM, and ALPER, BENEDICT S. *Criminal Youth and the Borstal System.* New York: The Commonwealth Fund, 1941.

HEALY, WILLIAM, and BRONNER, AUGUSTA F. *Treatment and What Happened Afterward.* Boston: The Judge Baker Guidance Center, 1939.

HILL, ARTHUR S., MILLER, LEONARD M., and GABBARD, HAZEL F. "Schools Face the Delinquency Problem," *The Bulletin* (A Publication of the National Association of Secondary-School Principals), Vol. 37, No. 198 (December, 1953), 181–221.

HOBHOUSE, STEPHEN, and BROCKWAY, A. FENNER. *English Prisons Today.* London: Longmans, Green and Co., Ltd., 1922.

HOWARD, JOHN. *The State of the Prisons.* New York: E. P. Dutton and Co., Inc., Everyman's Library, 1929.

IVES, GEORGE. *A History of Penal Methods.* London: Stanley Paul and Co., Ltd., 1914.

KENNEY, JOHN P., and PURSUIT, DAN G. *Police Work with Juveniles.* Springfield, Ill.: Charles C. Thomas, Publisher, 1959.

KVARACEUS, WILLIAM C. *Juvenile Delinquency and the School.* Yonkers, N.Y.: World Book Co., 1945.

KVARACEUS, WILLIAM C., and ULRICH, WILLIAM E. *Delinquent Behavior: Principles and Practices.* Washington, D.C.: National Education Association of the United States, 1959.

LaROE, WILBUR. *Parole with Honor.* Princeton: Princeton University Press, 1939.

LAWES, LEWIS E. *Life and Death in Sing Sing.* New York: Doubleday, Doran and Co., Inc., 1928.

LEVERING, JOHNSON, CAVAN, RUTH SHONLE, and ZEMANS, EUGENE S. *Chicago Police Lockups.* Chicago: John Howard Association, 1963.

LEWIS, O. F. *The Development of American Prisons and Prison Customs, 1776–1845.* Albany: The Prison Association of New York, 1922.

McCLEERY, RICHARD H. *Policy Change in Prison Management.* East Lansing, Mich.: Michigan State University, 1957.

McCORKLE, LLOYD W. "Group Therapy in the Treatment of Offenders," *Federal Probation,* Vol. 16, No. 4 (December, 1952), 22–27.

McCORKLE, LLOYD W., and ELIAS, ALBERT. "Group Therapy in Correctional Institutions," *Federal Probation,* Vol. 24, No. 2 (June, 1960), 57–63.

MacCORMICK, AUSTIN H. *The Education of Adult Prisoners.* New York: The National Society of Penal Information, 1931.

McKELVEY, BLAKE. *American Prisons.* Chicago: University of Chicago Press, 1936.

MEIERS, JOSEPH I. *Origins and Development of Group Psychotherapy,* Psychodrama Monographs, No. 17. New York: Beacon House, 1946.

MEYER, CHARLES H. Z. "A Half Century of Probation and Parole," *Journal of Criminal Law, Criminology, and Police Science,* Vol. 42, No. 6 (March–April, 1952), 707–728.

NATIONAL COMMISSION ON LAW OBSERVANCE AND ENFORCEMENT. *Report on Penal Institutions, Probation, and Parole,* Report No. 9. Washington, D.C.: Government Printing Office, 1931.

NATIONAL CONFERENCE ON PREVENTION AND CONTROL OF JUVENILE DELINQUENCY. *Reports.* Washington, D.C.: Government Printing Office, 1947.

NATIONAL COUNCIL ON CRIME AND DELINQUENCY. *Standards and Guides for the Detention of Children and Youth.* New York: National Council on Crime and Delinquency, 1961.

————. *Standards and Guides for Adult Probation.* New York: National Council on Crime and Delinquency, 1962.

NATIONAL PROBATION ASSOCIATION. *John Augustus—First Probation Officer.* New York: National Probation Association, 1939.

NATIONAL PROBATION AND PAROLE ASSOCIATION. *Standard Probation and Parole Act.* New York: National Probation and Parole Association, 1955.

NORMAN, SHERWOOD. *The Design and Construction of Detention Homes for the Juvenile Court.* New York: National Probation Association, 1947.

————. *Detention Practice: Significant Developments in the Detention of Children and Youth.* New York: National Probation and Parole Association, 1960.

NORMAN, SHERWOOD, and HELEN. *Detention for the Juvenile Court: A Discussion of Principles and Practices.* New York: National Probation Association, 1946.

OHLIN, LLOYD E. *Selection for Parole.* New York: Russell Sage Foundation, 1951.

OPPENHEIMER, H. *The Rationale of Punishment.* London: University of London Press, 1913.

PETERSON, VIRGIL W. "Citizens' Crime Commissions," *Federal Probation,* Vol. 17, No. 1 (March, 1953), 9–15.

PIGEON, HELEN D. *Probation and Parole in Theory and Practice.* New York: National Probation Association, 1942.

PIKE, LUKE O. *History of Crime in England.* London: Smith, Elder and Co., 1873–76.

RECTOR, FRANK L. *Health and Medical Service in American Prisons and Reformatories.* New York: The National Society of Penal Information, Inc. (Osborne Association), 1929.

ROBINSON, LOUIS N. *Jails, Care and Treatment of Misdemeanant Prisoners in the United States.* Philadelphia: The John C. Winston Co., 1944.

RUGGLES-BRISE, EVELYN. *The English Prison System.* London: Macmillan and Co., Ltd., 1921.

RUNYON, TOM. *In For Life.* New York: W. W. Norton and Co., Inc., 1953.

RUSCHE, GEORG, and KIRCHHEIMER, OTTO. *Punishment and the Social Structure.* New York: Columbia University Press, 1939.

SELLIN, THORSTEN. *Pioneering in Penology.* Philadelphia: University of Pennsylvania Press, 1944.

———— (ed.). "Murder and the Penalty of Death," *The Annals of the American Academy of Political and Social Science,* Vol. 284 (November, 1952).

————, (ed.). "Prisons in Transformation," *The Annals of the American Academy of Political and Social Science,* Vol. 293 (May, 1954).

SHANAS, ETHEL, and DUNNING, CATHERINE E. *Recreation and Delinquency.* Chicago: Chicago Recreation Commission, 1942.

SOCIAL SCIENCE RESEARCH COUNCIL. *Theoretical Studies in Social Organization of the Prison.* New York: Social Science Research Council, 1960.

SYKES, GRESHAM M. *The Society of Captives: A Study of a Maximum Security Prison.* Princeton, N.J.: Princeton University Press, 1958.

TAPPAN, PAUL W. (ed.). *Contemporary Correction.* New York: McGraw-Hill Book Co., Inc., 1951.

TEETERS, NEGLEY K. *They Were in Prison.* Philadelphia: The John C. Winston Co., 1937.

————. *The Cradle of the Penitentiary.* Philadelphia: The Pennsylvania Prison Society, 1955.

TEETERS, NEGLEY K., and SHEARER, JOHN D. *The Prison at Philadelphia: Cherry Hill.* New York: Columbia University Press, 1957.

TIMASHEFF, N. S. *One Hundred Years of Probation.* New York: Fordham University Press, Part I, 1941, Part II, 1943.

WEBB, SIDNEY, and WEBB, BEATRICE. *English Prisons Under Local Government.* New York: Longmans, Green and Co., Ltd., 1922.

WILSON, MARGARET. *The Crime of Punishment.* New York: Harcourt, Brace and Co., Inc., 1931.

WINES, FREDERICK HOWARD. *Punishment and Reformation.* New York: Thomas Y. Crowell Co., 1919.

ZEMANS, EUGENE S. *Held Without Bail, Physical Aspects of the Police Lock-ups of the City of Chicago, 1947–48.* Chicago: John Howard Association, 1949.

Name Index

Subject Index